POSTCARDS FROM

ⓕFrommer's®

Costa Rica 2002

D0769958

Mischievous squirrel monkeys live in and around Manuel Antonio National Park (see chapter 7) and the Osa Peninsula (see chapter 8). © Norman Owen Tomalin/Bruce Coleman, Inc.

With thermal pools, lush gardens, waterfalls, a swim-up bar, a restaurant, and spa services, Tabacón Hot Springs Resort, at the base of Arenal Volcano, is a playground for adults. See chapter 6.
© Robert Winslow/Vesti Collection, Inc.

Coffee and sugar cane thrive in the rich volcanic soil of the Central Valley. You can visit a coffee farm as a side trip from San José. See chapter 4. © Nicholas DeVore III/Bruce Coleman, Inc.

Costa Rica boasts an astounding diversity of tropical plant life. Here, the brilliant blooms of the heliconia marginata appear to unfold like origami birds. © Margarette Mead/Image Bank.

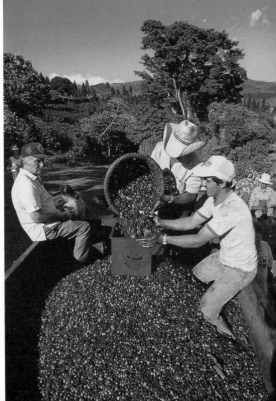

Coffee is one of Costa Rica's most important crops, and coffee farms dot the fertile Central Valley. See chapter 4. © J-C Carton/Bruce Coleman, Inc.

The Monteverde Cloud Forest Preserve is lush and largely untouched, with thousands of exotic ferns, orchids, and bromeliads, plus 400 varieties of birds and 100 species of mammals. Its well-organized infrastructure helps guarantee a rewarding experience for first-time eco-adventurers. See chapter 6. © Drew Thate/Bruce Coleman, Inc.

White-faced capuchin monkeys abound in Manuel Antonio National Park. See chapter 7.
© Wolfgang Kaehler.

Throughout the country, sunbathing iguanas are a common sight. © Russell Mittermeier/Bruce Coleman, Inc.

Green turtles nest and hatch in Tortuguero National Park. This just-hatched youngster is ready to plunge into the surf. See chapter 9. © Kevin Schafer/Tony Stone Images.

A tiny red-eyed tree frog. © *James Carmichael/Image Bank.*

A tropical land crab. © *Margarette Mead/Image Bank.*

Although the cone is often socked in by fog, Arenal Volcano experiences nearly constant rumblings and eruptions. See chapter 6. © *Macduff Everton/Image Bank.*

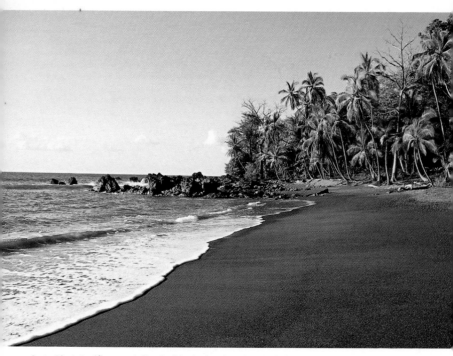

Costa Rica's Pacific coast is lined with glorious beaches, including this uncrowded stretch of sand in Corcovado National Park. See chapter 8. © *Dave G. Houser Photography.*

Here's what the critics say about Frommer's:

"Amazingly easy to use. Very portable, very complete."

—*Booklist*

"The only mainstream guide to list specific prices. The Walter Cronkite of guidebooks—with all that implies."

—*Travel & Leisure*

"Complete, concise, and filled with useful information."

—*New York Daily News*

"Hotel information is close to encyclopedic."

—*Des Moines Sunday Register*

Costa Rica

2002

by Eliot Greenspan

Hungry Minds™

Best-Selling Books • Digital Downloads • e-Books • Answer Networks •
e-Newsletters • Branded Web Sites • e-Learning

New York, NY • Cleveland, OH • Indianapolis, IN

About the Author

Eliot Greenspan is a poet, journalist, and travel writer who took his backpack and typewriter the length of Mesoamerica before settling in Costa Rica in 1992. Since then he has worked steadily for the *Tico Times* and other local media, and continued his travels in the region. He is also the author of *Frommer's Costa Rica and Belize from $35 a Day,* as well as the chapter on Venezuela in *Frommer's South America.*

Published by:

Hungry Minds, Inc.

909 Third Avenue
New York, NY 10022

ISBN: 0-7645-6459-5
ISSN: 1077-890X

Edited by Dog-Eared Pages
Production Editor: Tammy Ahrens
Photo Editor: Richard Fox
Design by Michele Laseau
Cartographer: Roberta Stockwell
Production by Hungry Minds Indianapolis Production Services

Special Sales

For general information on Hungry Minds' products and services please contact our Customer Care department; within the U.S. at 800-762-2974, outside the U.S. at 317-572-3993 or fax 317-572-4002. For sales inquiries and reseller information, including discounts, bulk sales, customized editions, and premium sales, please contact our Customer Care department at 800-434-3422.

Manufactured in the United States of America

5   4   3   2   1

Contents

8 The Southern Zone   283

9 The Caribbean Coast   310

Appendix A: Costa Rica in Depth   343

Appendix B: Glossary of Spanish Terms & Phrases   354

Index   357

List of Maps

Acknowledgments

I'd like to thank Ana Domb for too many things to list here, but most of all for putting up with me as the deadline approached and taking over some of the fact-checking responsibilities this year. I'd also like to thank my parents, Marilyn and Warren Greenspan, who showed unwavering love, support, and encouragement (well, one out of three ain't bad) as I pursued words and world-wandering over a more stable and lucrative career. Jody and Ted Ejnes (my sister and brother-in-law) deserve a mention; they risked life and limb (literally) leading to two important tips that may help you save yours. Thanks to Lisa Renaud and John Rosenthal for their editorial diligence. Finally, I'm eternally grateful to Anne Becher and Joe Richey, who were instrumental in getting me this gig—*muchas gracias.*

An Invitation to the Reader

In researching this book, we discovered many wonderful places—hotels, restaurants, shops, and more. We're sure you'll find others. Please tell us about them, so we can share the information with your fellow travelers in upcoming editions. If you were disappointed with a recommendation, we'd love to know that, too. Please write to:

Frommer's Costa Rica 2002
Hungry Minds, Inc. • 909 Third Avenue • New York, NY 10022

An Additional Note

Please be advised that travel information is subject to change at any time—and this is especially true of prices. We therefore suggest that you write or call ahead for confirmation when making your travel plans. The authors, editors, and publisher cannot be held responsible for the experiences of readers while traveling. Your safety is important to us, however, so we encourage you to stay alert and be aware of your surroundings. Keep a close eye on cameras, purses, and wallets, all favorite targets of thieves and pickpockets.

New! Frommer's Star Ratings & Icons

Every hotel, restaurant, and attraction listing in this guide has been ranked for quality, value, service, amenities, and special features using a star-rating scale. In country, state, and regional guides, we also rate towns and regions to help you narrow down your choices and budget your time accordingly. Hotels and restaurants in the Very Expensive and Expensive categories are rated on a scale of one (highly recommended) to three stars (exceptional). Those in the Moderate and Inexpensive categories rate from zero (recommended) to two stars (very highly recommended). Attractions, towns, and regions are rated according to the following scale: zero stars (recommended), one star (highly recommended), two stars (very highly recommended), and three stars (must-see).

In addition to the rating system, we also use seven icons to highlight insider information, useful tips, special bargains, hidden gems, memorable experiences, kid-friendly venues, places to avoid, and other useful information:

Finds	*Fun Fact*	*Kids*	*Moments*	*Overrated*	*Tips*	*Value*

The following abbreviations are used for credit cards:

AE	American Express	DISC	Discover	V	Visa
DC	Diners Club	MC	MasterCard		

FROMMERS.COM

Now that you have the guidebook to a great trip, visit our website at **www.frommers. com** for travel information on nearly 2,000 destinations. With features updated regularly, we give you instant access to the most current trip-planning information available. At Frommers.com, you'll also find the best prices on air fares, accommodations, and car rentals—and you can even book travel online through our travel booking partners. At Frommers.com you'll also find the following:

- Daily Newsletter highlighting the best travel deals
- Hot Spot of the Month/Vacation Sweepstakes & Travel Photo Contest
- More than 200 Travel Message Boards
- Outspoken Newsletters and Feature Articles on travel bargains, vacation ideas, tips and resources, and more!

What's New in Costa Rica

Costa Rica has been enjoying a boom for the past couple of years, and changes, both big and small, are nearly constant. The biggest projects (including a final completion of the airport renovation and expansion in San José and a couple of new golf courses and a lavish Four Seasons resort in Guanacaste) are still, mostly, works in progress. Others are up and running, and described in the pages of this book. Here are some of the highlights:

PLANNING YOUR TRIP

The first phase of the long-awaited remodeling and expansion of San José's **Juan Santamaria International Airport** is complete. Arriving passengers are now greeted with a modern and spacious new terminal. The baggage claim and customs areas are a huge improvement over the former setup, although lines at the immigration counter can still be long and slow during peak hours. Gone are the steep flight of steps and uncomfortable luggage conveyor belt travelers once had to negotiate after clearing customs. Most major rental-car agencies now have desks inside the terminal, directly in front of the customs area exit. Departing passengers, however, must still use the cramped and crowded old terminal. Moreover, despite the major remodeling, chaos and confusion still greet arriving passengers the second they step out of the terminal. As of this writing, it's not clear when, or even if, the new terminal will open fully.

SAN JOSÉ

Costa Rica has never been known for its cuisine; San José has the only really interesting and varied dining scene in the country. With the increase in international tourism and the need to please a more sophisticated palate, local chefs have begun to create a "nouvelle Costa Rican cuisine," updating time-worn recipes and using traditional ingredients in creative ways.

Among the latest restaurants to open in San José is **Le Bilboquet,** located downtown at the corner of Avenida 11 and Calle 3, in front of the Hotel Britannia (© **506/221-2302**); it's creating quite a stir with its creative nouvelle French cooking served up in a lively bistro environment. On the east side of town, **Shiraz** has closed its doors for good; while just across the street, **Balalaika,** 75 meters east of the Fuente de la Hispanidad, San Pedro (© **506/280-0002**), is a massive new complex housing two restaurants, two bars, and a pastry shop in about eight separate environments. Over on the west side, in the suburb of Escazú, the **Rincón de la Calle Real,** located on a small side street across from the U.S. Ambassador's residence on the Old Road to Santa Ana (© **506/ 289-5112**), is a new cafe and restaurant serving creative continental cuisine in a 200-year-old building.

The **Museo de Jade Marco Fidel Tristan** (Jade Museum), Avenida 7 between Calles 9 and 9B, 11th floor (© **506/287-6034**), has been closed for more than a year. A portion of the collection has been put on loan to the **Museo Nacional** (National Museum), Calle 1, between Avenida Central and Avenida 2 (© **506/257-1433**). No date has been set for the reopening of the Jade Museum, but work should be completed in mid- to late 2001.

Over in Heredia, there's the new **INBio Park,** 400 meters north and 250 meters west of the Shell station in Santo Domingo de Heredia (© **506/ 244-4730**), a large-scale natural-history project with some indoor exhibits, plus a network of trails running through living examples of several different Costa Rican ecosystems.

See chapter 4 for complete coverage of San José.

GUANACASTE & THE NICOYA PENINSULA

Work has begun on a deluxe **Four Seasons** resort, but that's not the only new opening in this region, which continues to boom as one of Costa Rica's most popular destinations.

The new **Hotel Borinquen** (© **506/ 666-0363;** borinque@racsa.co.cr) brings a bit of luxury to the **Rincón de la Vieja** area. This collection of bungalows and rooms enjoys a quiet mountain setting, with hot springs, pools, and mud baths on the grounds. Guests enjoy a modest range of spa facilities and treatments. You can also get tons of TLC and spa treatments at the new **Fusion Natural Spa** (© **506/ 670-0250**) in the beach town of **Playa Ocotal.**

In **Tamarindo,** locals and visitors alike are raving about the fresh seafood and creative international cuisine at **Pachanga** (no phone), located across the street from Hotel Pasatiempo.

The beach town of **Malpais** is one of the newest hot spots on the Guanacaste coast; a couple of new places have opened there, and more are on the way. The **Blue Jay Lodge** (© **506/**

640-0089; www.bluejaylodgecostarica. com) has rustic but comfortable bungalows in a wonderful forested setting. Sometime during the 2002 high season, look for the opening of **Sueño del Sur,** the new, luxurious sister property of Tamarindo's Sueño del Mar (© **506/653-0284**).

See chapter 5 for all the latest on this rapidly developing region.

THE NORTHERN ZONE

On August 23, 2000, the Arenal Volcano had an abnormally violent series of eruptions and pyroclastic flows that claimed the life of one Costa Rican tour guide and one American tourist, and severely burned another tourist (all three were hiking in an area generally considered too close for safety). Several hotels were temporarily shut down, and hundreds of tourists were evacuated. Three days later, a Sansa commuter flight crashed into the volcano, killing all eight people aboard. The volcano has since returned to its normal pattern of activity, and all of the hotels, restaurants, and attractions in the area are open for business. As of this writing, Sansa has still not restored its service to Arenal, but flights may have resumed by the time you travel.

Among the region's new developments is a new canopy tour run by the folks at the **Original Canopy Tour Company** (© **506/257-5149;** www. canopytour.com); this new operation is located right on the grounds of the **Tabacón Hot Springs Resort,** which is located on the main road between Arenal and La Fortuna (© **506/256- 1500;** www.tabacon.com). There are also 40 new deluxe rooms at the resort to meet the growing demand at this hot spot.

Centro Neotropico Sarapiquís (© **506/761-1004;** www.sarapiquis. org) is a new hotel complex in **La Virgin de Sarapiquí.** In addition to the

24 rooms housed in three immense thatch-roofed structures, the hotel has a series of suspension bridges and trails through the rain forest, a small natural-history museum, botanical gardens, and a pre-Colombian burial site under excavation.

If you're driving around Lake Arenal, be sure to stop in at **Willy's Caballo Negro,** near Nuevo Arenal (about 3km out of town on the road to Tilarán; ✆ **506/694-4515**), which serves wonderful German and European cuisine and has a nice little gift shop. Another nice stop on this route is **Toad Hall,** located 9km outside of Nuevo Arenal toward La Fortuna (✆ **506/381-3662; www.toadhall-gallery.com**), which has a very well-stocked gift shop and art gallery and serves great sandwiches, salads, baked goods, and fruit and coffee drinks.

Full details on the Northern Zone can be found in chapter 6.

CENTRAL PACIFIC

In Jacó, two mainstay beach hotels, the **Hotel Copacabana** (✆ **506/643-1005**; www.copacabanahotel.com) and **Hotel Club del Mar** (✆ and fax **506/643-3194**), have received major renovations and additions. The Club del Mar has been made over almost entirely and will be, by far, the nicest option in Jacó.

There have been a few changes in Quepos and Manuel Antonio. The Hotel Sí Como No has opened a second outlet of its **Regaleme Gift Shop** in downtown Quepos. **La Mansion Inn** (✆ **506/777-3489;** www.lamansioninn.com) is a new high-end boutique hotel located on the road to El Parador. And the folks at El Gran Escape have opened a popular new bar called **Epicentro** (no phone; next door to El Gran Escape, on the side road away from the water). There's lively music on the stereo, dartboards on the wall, and a couple of TVs showing international sporting events.

See chapter 7 for complete coverage of this area.

THE CARIBBEAN COAST

After numerous name and cuisine changes, the little open-air restaurant located just off of Cabinas Salsa Brava has settled down as simply **Salsa Brava,** located on the left-hand side of the main road heading south of Puerto Viejo, just after El Bambu (✆ **506/750-0241**). It serves up excellent fresh-grilled seafood and meats, as well as other Spanish and Mediterranean specialties.

See chapter 9 for full details on this region.

1

The Best of Costa Rica

For years, Costa Rica was the well-kept secret of a few biologists, backpackers, and beachcombers, but that's all changed. Today, the country is a major international vacation and adventure-travel destination, and tourism has become the nation's number-one source of income. Despite the boom in vacationers, Costa Rica remains a place rich in natural wonders and biodiversity, and far from the madding crowds. Here, you can still find unsullied beaches that stretch for miles, small lodgings that haven't attracted hordes of tourists, jungle rivers for rafting and kayaking, and spectacular cloud and rain forests with ample opportunities for bird watching and hiking. Perhaps the biggest sea change in recent years has been the opening of a handful of large luxury resorts (even the Four Seasons chain has begun to develop a new super-luxury resort in the northern province of Guanacaste).

This is my sixth year putting this book together, and the "best of" experiences keep racking up. Some of my personal highlights include watching the sun rise on the first day of a new year from the top of the Irazú Volcano, camping alone on a deserted beach in Guanacaste, battling a feisty snook in the Golfo Dulce, soaking in some newly discovered hot springs alongside a jungle river as a sun bittern majestically stalked its dinner, conducting a half-hour-long photo session with a remarkably calm eyelash viper, swimming in a pristine pool formed by a jungle waterfall, finding myself in the midst of a school of hammerhead sharks in the waters off Cocos Island, swooping from treetop platform to treetop platform on a canopy tour, seeing both the Pacific Ocean and Caribbean Sea at the same time from the summit of Mount Chirripó, and finally learning how to surf.

In this chapter, I've selected the very best of what this unique country has to offer. I'll show you where to find all of my favorite things in Costa Rica, as well as some personal bests of your own. Most of these places and experiences are covered in greater detail elsewhere in the book; this chapter is merely meant to give you an overview of the highlights so you can start planning your own adventure.

1 The Best of Natural Costa Rica

- **Rincón de la Vieja National Park** (northeast of Liberia, in Guanacaste): This is an area of rugged beauty and high volcanic activity. The Rincón de la Vieja Volcano rises to 6,159 feet, but the thermal activity is spread out along its flanks, where numerous geysers, vents, and fumaroles let off its heat and steam. This is a great place to hire a guide and a horse for a day of rugged exploration. There are waterfalls and mud baths, hot springs and cool jungle swimming holes. You'll pass through pastureland, scrub savanna, and moist secondary forest; the bird watching is excellent. See chapter 5.

- **Arenal Volcano/Tabacón Hot Springs** (near La Fortuna, northwest of San José): When the skies are clear and the lava is flowing, **Arenal Volcano** provides a thrilling light show accompanied by an earthshaking rumble that defies description. You can even see the show while soaking in a natural hot spring and having a drink at the swim-up bar at **Tabacón Hot Springs Resort** (© **506/256-1500;** www. tabacon.com). If the rushing torrent of volcano-heated spring water isn't therapeutic enough, you can get a massage here at an incredibly inexpensive price. See chapter 6.

- **The Río Sarapiquí Region** (north of San José between Guanacaste in the west and the Caribbean coast in the east): This is a prime place for an ecolodge experience. Protected tropical forests climb from the Caribbean coastal lowlands up into the central mountain, affording you a glimpse of a plethora of life zones and ecosystems. **Braulio Carrillo National Park** borders several other private reserves here, and there's a variety of ecolodges to suit any budget. See chapter 6.

- **Monteverde Biological Cloud Forest Preserve** (in the mountains northwest of San José): There's something both eerie and majestic about walking around in the early morning mist with the sound of bird calls all around and the towering trees hung heavy in broad bromeliads, flowering orchids, and hanging moss and vines. The preserve itself has a well-maintained network of trails, and the community is truly involved in conservation. Not only that, but in and around Monteverde and Santa Elena

you'll find a whole slew of related activities and attractions, including canopy tours that allow you to swing from treetop to treetop while hanging from a skinny cable. See chapter 6.

- **Manuel Antonio** (near Quepos on the central Pacific coast): There's a reason this place is so popular and renowned: monkeys! The national park here is full of them, even the endangered squirrel monkeys. But there's plenty to see and do outside the park as well. The road leading into Manuel Antonio provides numerous lookouts that consistently produce postcard-perfect snapshots of steep jungle hills meeting the sea. Uninhabited islands lie just off the coast, and the beaches here are perfect crescents of soft, white sand. See chapter 7.

- **Osa Peninsula** (in southern Costa Rica): This is Costa Rica's most remote and biologically rich region. **Corcovado National Park,** the largest remaining patch of virgin lowland tropical rain forest in Central America, takes up much of the Osa Peninsula. Jaguars, crocodiles, and scarlet macaws all call this place home. Whether you stay in a luxury nature lodge in Drake Bay or outside of Puerto Jiménez, or camp in the park itself, you will be surrounded by some of the lushest and most intense jungle this country has to offer. See chapter 8.

- **Tortuguero Village & Jungle Canals** (on the Caribbean coast, north of Limón): Tortuguero Village is a small collection of rustic wooden shacks on a narrow spit of land between the Caribbean Sea and a dense maze of jungle canals. It's been called Costa Rica's Venice, but it actually has more in common with the South American

The Best of Costa Rica

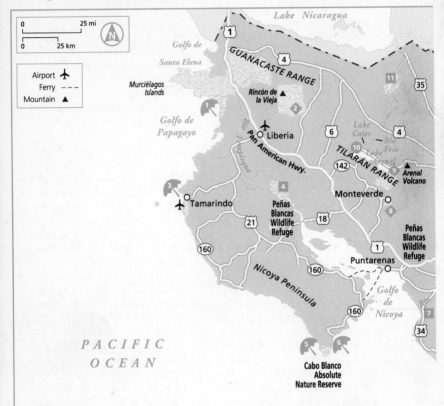

THE BEST OF NATURAL COSTA RICA
Arenal Volcano/Tabacón Hot Springs **9**
Braulio Carrillo National Park **13**
Manuel Antonio **21**
Monteverde Cloud Forest Preserve **8**
Osa Peninsula **24**
Rincón de la Vieja National Park **2**
The Rió Sarapiquí Region **14**
Tortuguero Village and Jungle Canals **16**

THE BEST BEACHES
Malpais **5**
Manuel Antonio **21**
Playa Montezuma **6**
Playa Tamarindo **3**
Punta Uva & Manzanillo **18**
Punta Uvita **22**
Santa Rosa National Park **1**

THE BEST ACTIVE VACATIONS
Diving off Isla del Coco **2727**
Hiking Mount Chirripó **23**
Kayaking in Golfo Dulce **25**
Mountain Biking Around Lake Arenal **10**
Surfing Pavones **26**
Windsurfing Lake Arenal **10**
Rafting the Upper Reventazon River **15**

THE BEST BIRD WATCHING
Aviarios del Caribe **17**
Caño Negro Wildlife Refuge **11**
Carara Biological Reserve **7**
Cerro de la Muerte **20**
La Selva Biological Station **12**
Palo Verde National Park **4**
Parque del Este **19**

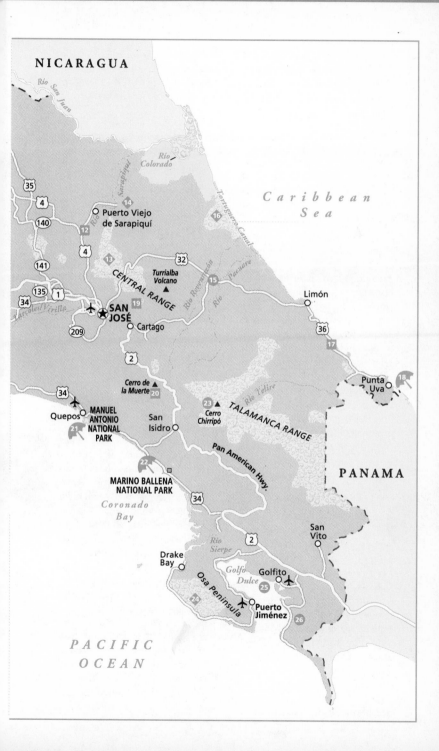

NICARAGUA

Río San Juan

Río Colorado

Río Sarapiquí

35

4

140

○ Puerto Viejo de Sarapiquí

12

4

13

141

CENTRAL RANGE

Turrialba Volcano ▲

32

14

16

Río Tortuguero Canal

C a r i b b e a n   S e a

135

1

34

Tárcoles/Virilla

✈ SAN JOSÉ

209

2

19

○ Cartago

15

Río Reventazón

Río Pacuare

Limón ○

36

17

Cerro de la Muerte ▲

20

34

✈

MANUEL ANTONIO NATIONAL PARK

Quepos ○

21

San Isidro ○

23 ▲
Cerro Chirripó

TALAMANCA RANGE

Río Telire

Punta Uva ○

18

PANAMA

22

MARINO BALLENA NATIONAL PARK

Coronado Bay

2

34

Pan American Hwy.

San Vito ○

Río Sierpe

Drake Bay ○

Golfo Dulce

Golfito ○ ✈

25

26

Osa Peninsula

24

✈ Puerto Jiménez

P A C I F I C   O C E A N

Amazon. You can fly into the small airstrip, but it's better to take one of the slow boats that ply the river and canal route. On the way you'll see a wide variety of herons and other water birds, three types of monkeys, three-toed sloths, and huge American crocodiles. If you come between June and October, you may be treated to the awe-inspiring spectacle of a green turtle nesting—the small stretch of Tortuguero beach is the last remaining major nesting site of this endangered animal. See chapter 9.

2 The Best Beaches

With more than 750 combined miles of shoreline on its Pacific and Caribbean coasts, Costa Rica offers beachgoers an embarrassment of riches.

- **Playa Tamarindo:** On the verge of becoming a little too overdeveloped, crowded, and chaotic, Tamarindo is still hanging onto its place on this list. Tamarindo has ample lodgings to suit every budget and excellent restaurants at almost every turn. The beach here is long and broad, with sections calm enough for swimmers and others just right for surfers. Located about midway along the beaches of Guanacaste province, Tamarindo makes a good base for exploring other nearby stretches of sand. There are plenty of surfers here, as well as one of the liveliest nightlife scenes on this coast. See chapter 5.
- **The Beaches Around Playa Sámara:** Playa Sámara itself is nice enough, but if you venture just slightly farther afield, you'll find some of the nicest and least developed beaches along the entire Guanacaste coast. **Playa Carillo** is a long, almost always deserted crescent of palm-backed white sand located just south of Sámara, while **Playa Barrigona** and **Playa Buena Vista** are two hidden gems, tucked down a couple of dirt roads to the north. See chapter 5.
- **Playa Montezuma:** This tiny beach town at the southern tip of the Nicoya Peninsula has weathered fame and infamy and yet retains a funky sense of individuality. European backpackers, vegetarian yoga enthusiasts, and UFO seekers choose Montezuma's beach over any other in Costa Rica. The waterfalls are what set it apart from the competition, but the beach stretches for miles, with plenty of isolated spots to plop down your towel or mat. Nearby are the Cabo Blanco and Curu wildlife preserves. See chapter 5.
- **Malpais:** If you're looking to visit Costa Rica's newest hot spot before the throngs discover it, head out to Malpais. Here, you'll find miles of nearly deserted beaches, great surf, and just a smattering of lodges, surf camps, and simple cabinas. If Malpais is too crowded for you, head farther on down the road to Santa Teresa, Playa Hermosa, and Manzanillo. See chapter 5.
- **Santa Rosa National Park:** If you really want to get away from it all, the beaches here in the northwest corner of Costa Rica are a good bet. You'll have to four-wheel-drive or hike 8 miles (13km) from the central ranger station to reach the beach. And once you get there, you'll find only the most basic of camping facilities: outhouse latrines and cold-water showers. But you will probably have the place almost to yourself. In fact, the only time it gets crowded is in

October, when thousands of olive Ridley sea turtles nest in one of their yearly *arribadas* (arrivals). See chapter 5.

- **Manuel Antonio:** The first beach destination to become popular in Costa Rica, it still retains its charms despite burgeoning crowds and mushrooming hotels. The beaches inside the park are idyllic, and the views from the hills approaching the park are enchanting. This is one of the few remaining habitats for the endangered squirrel monkey. Rooms with views tend to be a bit expensive, but many a satisfied guest will tell you they're worth it. See chapter 7.

- **Punta Uva & Manzanillo:** Below Puerto Viejo, the beaches of Costa Rica's Atlantic coast take on true Caribbean splendor, with turquoise waters, coral reefs, and palm-lined stretches of nearly deserted white-sand beach. Punta Uva and Manzanillo are the two most sparkling gems of this coastline. Tall coconut palms line the shore, providing shady respite for those who like to spend a full day on the sand, and the water is usually quite calm and good for swimming. See chapter 9.

3 The Best Adventures

- **Swinging Through the Treetops on a Canopy Tour:** This unique adventure is becoming quite the rage. In most cases, after a strenuous climb using ascenders, you strap on a harness and zip from treetop to treetop while dangling from a cable. There are canopy tours all around Costa Rica. **The Original Canopy Tours** (𝒞 and fax **506/257-5149;** www.canopytour.com) runs dependable operations in several locations. See chapter 3.

- **Mountain-Biking the Back Roads of Costa Rica:** The lack of infrastructure and paved roads that most folks bemoan is a huge boon for mountain-bikers. There are endless back roads and cattle paths to explore. Tours of differing lengths and all difficulty levels are available. Contact **BiCosta Rica** (𝒞 **506/446-7585;** www.yellowweb.co.cr/bicostarica.htm) or **Coast to Coast Adventures** (𝒞 **506/280-6055;** www.ctocadventures.com). See chapter 3.

- **Diving off the Shores of Isla del Coco** (off Guanacaste in the Pacific): Legendary among treasure seekers, pirate buffs, and scuba divers, this small island is consistently rated one of the 10 best dive sites in the world. A protected national park, Isla del Coco is surrounded by clear Pacific waters, and its reefs are teeming with life (divers regularly encounter large schools of hammerhead sharks, curious manta rays, and docile whale sharks). Since the island is so remote and has no overnight facilities for visitors, the most popular way to visit is on 10-day excursions on a liveaboard boat, where guests live, eat, and sleep onboard—with nights spent anchored in the harbor. See chapters 3 and 7.

- **Battling a Billfish off the Pacific Coast:** Billfish are plentiful all along Costa Rica's Pacific coast, and boats operate from Playa del Coco to Playa Zancudo. Costa Rican anglers hold world records for both blue marlin and Pacific sailfish. Go to Quepos (just outside Manuel Antonio) for the best après-fish scene, or head down to Drake Bay if you want some isolation. **Costa Rica Outdoors** (© **800/308-3394** in the U.S., or 506/282-6743; www.costaricaoutdoors.com) can help you find a good charter skipper or specialized fishing lodge. See chapters 3, 5, and 8.

- **Rafting the Upper Reventazón River** (near Turrialba): The Class V "Guayabo" section of this popular river is serious white water. Only experienced and gutsy river runners need apply. If you're not quite up to that, try a 2-day Pacuare River trip, which passes through primary and secondary forests and a beautiful steep gorge that, sadly, may be dammed soon. Get there quick! **Aventuras Naturales** (© **800/514-0411** in the U.S., or 506/225-3939 in Costa Rica; www.toenjoynature.com) or **Ríos Tropicales** (© **506/233-6455;** www.riostropicales.com) can arrange either of the above tours. See chapters 3 and 4.

- **Surfing & Four-Wheeling Guanacaste Province:** This northwestern province has dozens of respectable beach and reef breaks, from Witch's Rock at Playa Naranjo near the Nicaraguan border to Playa Nosara more than 62 miles (100km) away. In addition to these two prime spots, try a turn at Playa Grande, Punta Langosta, and Playas Negra, Avellanas, and Junquillal. Or, find your own secret spot. Rent a four-by-four with a roof rack, pile on the boards, and explore. See chapter 5.

- **Windsurfing Lake Arenal:** With steady gale-force winds and stunning scenery, the northern end of Lake Arenal (see above) has become a major international windsurfing hot spot. If you're an avid boardsailor, be sure to check in with Norm at **Rock River Lodge** (© and fax **506/695-**

5644; www.rokriverlodge.com). See chapter 6.

- **Hiking Mount Chirripó** (near San Isidro de El General on the central Pacific coast): The highest mountain in Costa Rica, Mount Chirripó is one of the few places in the world where (on a clear day) you can see both the Atlantic and the Pacific oceans at the same time. Hiking to Chirripó's 12,412-foot summit will take you through a number of distinct bioregions, ranging from lowland pastures and a cloud forest to a high-altitude *páramo,* a tundralike landscape with stunted trees and morning frosts. See chapter 7.

- **Kayaking Around the Golfo Dulce:** Slipping through the waters of the Golfo Dulce by kayak gets you intimately in touch with the raw beauty of this underdeveloped region. Spend several days poking around in mangrove swamps, fishing in estuaries, and watching dolphins frolic in the bay. **Escondido Trex** (© **506/735-5210;** www.escondidotrex.com) provides multiday custom kayaking trips out of Puerto Jiménez on the Osa Peninsula. See chapter 8.

- **Surfing Pavones** (on the south Pacific coast): Just 8 miles (13km) from the Panamanian border at the southern reaches of Costa Rica's Pacific coast, Pavones is reputed to have one of the longest rideable waves in the world. When this left-point break is working, surfers enjoy rides of almost a mile in length. Much more can be said about this experience, but if you're a surfer, you've heard it all before. Contact **Casa Siempre Domingo** (© **506/775-0131;** www.casadomingo.com), the most comfortable hotel in town, for current wave reports and other local information. See chapter 8.

4 The Best Day Hikes & Nature Walks

- **Lankester Botanical Gardens:** If you want a really pleasant but not overly challenging day hike, consider a walk among the hundreds of distinct species of flora on display here. Lankester Gardens (© **506/552-3247** or 506/552-3151) is just 17 miles (27.4km) from San José and makes a wonderful day's expedition. The trails meander from areas of well-tended open garden to shady natural forest. See chapter 4.

- **Rincón de la Vieja National Park:** This park has a number of wonderful trails through a variety of ecosystems and natural wonders. My favorite hike is down to the Blue Lake and Cangrejo Falls. It's 3.2 miles (5.1km) each way, and you'll want to spend some time at the base of this amazing lake, so plan on spending at least 5 hours on the outing, and bring along lunch and plenty of water. You can also hike up to two craters and a crater lake here, and there's the Las Pailas loop for those seeking a less strenuous hike. This remote volcanic national park is located about an hour north of Liberia (it's only 15½ miles/25km, but the road is quite rough), or about 5 hours from San José. See chapter 5.

- **La Selva Biological Station:** This combination research facility and rustic nature lodge has an extensive and well-marked network of trails. You'll have to reserve in advance (© **506/766-6565**) and take the guided tour if you aren't a guest at the lodge. But the hikes are led by very informed naturalists, so you might not mind the company. The Biological Station is located north-northeast on the Caribbean slope of Costa Rica's central mountain range. It'll take you about 1½ hours to drive from San José via the Guápiles Highway. See chapter 6.

- **Arenal National Park & Environs:** There's great hiking all around this area. The national park itself has several excellent trails that visit a variety of different eco-systems, including rain forest, secondary forest, savanna, and, my favorite, old lava flows. Most of them are on the relatively flat flanks of the volcano, so there's not too much climbing involved. There's also great hiking on the trails at the Arenal Observatory Lodge, and the trail down to the base of the La Fortuna Waterfall is a fun scramble. It's about a 3½-hour drive from San José to La Fortuna and Arenal National Park. See chapter 6.

- **Monteverde Biological Cloud Forest Preserve:** In morning rush of high season, when groups and tours line up to enter the preserve, you'd think the sign said CROWD FOREST. Still, the guides here are some of the most professional and knowledgeable in the country. Take a tour in the morning to familiarize yourself with the forest, then spend the late morning or afternoon (your entrance ticket is good for the whole day) exploring the preserve. Once you get off the main thoroughfares, Monteverde reveals its rich mysteries with stunning regularity. Walk through the gray mist and look up at the dense tangle of epiphytes and vines. The only noises you'll hear are the rustlings of birds or monkeys and the occasional distant rumble of Arenal Volcano. The trails are well marked and regularly tended. It's about 3½ hours by bus or car to

Monteverde from San José. See chapter 6.

- **Corcovado National Park:** This large swath of dense lowland rain forest is home to Costa Rica's second-largest population of scarlet macaws. The park has a well-designed network of trails, ranger stations, and camping facilities. Most of the lodges in Drake Bay and Puerto Jiménez offer day hikes through the park, but if you really want to experience it, you should hike in and stay at one or more of the campgrounds. This is strenuous hiking, and you will have to pack in some gear and food, but the reward is some of Costa Rica's most spectacular and unspoiled scenery. Because strict limits are placed on the number of visitors allowed into the park, you'll always be far from the madding crowd. See chapter 8.

- **Cahuita National Park:** The trails here are flat, well-maintained paths through thick lowland forest. Most of the way they parallel the beach, which is usually no more than 90 meters (100 yd.) away, so you can hike out on the trail and back along the beach, or vice versa. White-faced and howler monkeys are quite common here, as are brightly colored land crabs. See chapter 9.

5 The Best Bird Watching

- **Observing Oropendula & Blue-Crowned Motmot at Parque del Este:** A boon for city bird watchers, this San José park rambles through a collection of lawns, planted gardens, and harvested forest, but it also includes second-growth scrub and dense woodland. Oropendula and blue-crowned motmot are common species here. Take the San Ramón/Parque del Este bus from Calle 9 between Avenida Central and Avenida 2. See chapter 4.

- **Spotting Hundreds of Marsh & Stream Birds Along the Río Tempisque Basin:** Hike around the Palo Verde Biological Station, or take a boat trip down the Bebedero River with **TAM Tours** (© **506/668-1059;** www.tamtravel.com) or **Safaris Corobici** (© **506/669-1091;** www.nicoya.com). This area is an important breeding ground for gallinules, jacanas, and limpkins, as well as a common habitat for numerous heron and kingfisher species. Palo Verde is about a 3½-hour drive from San José. See chapter 5.

- **Looking for More Than 300 Species of Birds in La Selva Biological Station:** With an excellent trail system through a variety of habitats, from dense primary rain forest to open pasturelands and cacao plantations, this is one of the finest places for bird watching in Costa Rica. With such a variety of habitats, the number of species spotted runs to well over 300. Contact the **Organization for Tropical Studies** (© **506/240-6696;** www.ots.ac.cr) or see chapter 6.

- **Sizing Up a Jabiru Stork at Wildlife Refuge:** Caño Negro Lake and the Río Frío that feeds it are incredibly rich in wildlife and a major nesting and gathering site for aquatic bird species. These massive birds are getting less and less common in Costa Rica, but this is still one of the best places to see one. **Tilajari Hotel Resort** (© **506/469-9091;** www.tilajari.com) makes a good base for exploring this region. The Caño Negro Refuge is way up north near the Nicaraguan border. The most popular entry point is by boat from Los Chiles, which is about 4 hours from San José. See chapter 6.

- **Catching a Scarlet Macaw in Flight Over Carara Biological Reserve:** Home to Costa Rica's largest population of scarlet macaws, Carara Biological Reserve is a special place for devoted bird watchers and recent converts. Macaws are noisy and colorful birds that spend their days in the park but choose to roost in the evenings near the coast. They arrive like clockwork every morning and then head for the coastal mangroves around dusk. These daily migrations give birders a great chance to see these magnificent birds in flight. The reserve is located about 2 hours from San José along the central Pacific coast. See chapter 7.

- **Looking for a Resplendent Quetzal in the Cerro de la Muerte:** Don't let the name (Hill of Death) scare you away from the opportunity to see this spectacular bird, revered by the ancient Aztecs and Mayas. Serious bird watchers won't want to leave Costa Rica without crossing this bird off their life lists, and neophytes may be hooked for life after seeing one of these iridescent green wonders fly overhead, flashing its brilliant red breast and trailing 2-foot-long tail feathers. **Savegre Lodge** (☎ and fax **506/771-1732**) can almost guarantee a sighting. The Cerro de la Muerte is a high mountain pass located along the way to San Isidro de El General about 1½ hours from San José. See chapter 7.

- **Taking Advantage of the Caribbean's Best Birding at Aviarios del Caribe:** In just a few short years, Aviarios del Caribe (☎ **506/382-1335**) has established itself as the prime bird-watching resort on the Caribbean. If it flies along this coast, chances are good you'll spot it here; more than 310 species of birds have been spotted so far. Located on the Caribbean coast, Aviarios del Caribe is about a 3-hour drive from San José. See chapter 9.

- **Spotting Hundreds of Species at Wilson Botanical Gardens:** With more than 7,000 species of tropical plants and flowers, the well-tended trails and grounds of this beautiful research facility are fabulous for bird watching. Hummingbirds and tanagers are particularly plentiful, but the bounty doesn't end there—more than 330 different species of birds have been recorded here. Wilson Gardens is located about an hour outside of the town of Golfito. See chapter 9.

6 The Best Destinations for Families

- **San José:** If you're overnighting in San José, you'll probably want to be outside of the rough-and-tumble downtown area. The best place for all of you to experience Costa Rica's capital city (and still get a decent night's sleep) is the **Meliá Cariari Conference Center and Golf Resort** (☎ **800/227-4274** in the U.S. and Canada, or 506/239-0022 in Costa Rica; www. solmelia.com). With facilities that include several large pools, an 18 hole golf course, 11 tennis courts, and a game room (not to mention baby-sitting service), there's something here for everyone. If you're traveling with teens, they'll feel right at home at the new Mall Cariari, which has a multiplex theater, indoor skating rink, and, of course, a food court.

Located just 15 minutes from downtown, it's well situated for exploring all of the city's sights and attractions. See chapter 4.

- **Playa Hermosa:** The protected waters of this Pacific beach make it a family favorite. However, just because the waters are calm doesn't mean it's boring here. Check in at **Aqua Sport** (© **506/672-0050**), where you can rent sea kayaks, sailboards, paddleboats, beach umbrellas, and bicycles. See chapter 5.

- **Playa Tamarindo:** This lively surf town has a bit of something for everything. This is a great spot for teens to learn how to surf or boogie-board, and there are a host of tours and activities to please the entire family. **Hotel Capitan Suizo** (© **506/653-0353;** www.capitansuizo.com) has an excellent location on a calm section of beach, spacious rooms, and a great pool for kids and adults alike. See chapter 5.

- **Monteverde:** Located about 100 miles (160km) northwest of San José, this area not only boasts the country's most famous cloud forest, but it also sports a wide variety of related attractions and activities. After hiking through the preserve, you should be able to keep most kids happy and occupied riding horses, squirming at

the local serpentarium, or visiting the butterfly farm and humming-bird gallery. See chapter 6.

- **Playa de Jacó:** On the central Pacific coast, this is Costa Rica's liveliest and most developed beach town. The streets are lined with souvenir shops, ice-cream stands, and inexpensive eateries; there's even a miniature-golf course. This is a good place for a family to rent a few mopeds for an afternoon cruise. Older children can rent a boogie board, though everyone should be careful with the rough surf here. The **Club del Mar Condominiums and Resort** (© and fax **506/643-3194**) is situated at the calm southern end of the beach. The hotel has a large, free-form pool and some shady grounds and is accommodating to families traveling with small children. See chapter 7.

- **Manuel Antonio:** Manuel Antonio has a little bit of everything: miles of gorgeous beaches, tons of wildlife (with almost guaranteed monkey sightings), and plenty of active tour options. There's a load of lodging options, but **Hotel Sí Como No** (© **506/777-0777;** www.sicomono.com), with its large suites, two pools, water slide, and nightly movies, is probably your best bet. See chapter 7.

7 The Best Luxury Hotels & Resorts

"Luxury" is a relative term in Costa Rica. To date, no hotel I've found hits truly five-star standards across the board. Magnificent settings abound, but service and food can sometimes fall short. Several new major resorts and a couple of fabulous boutique hotels have done their darndest to meet the needs of upscale travelers. And the future looks good with the Four Seasons chain nearing

completion of a large resort in the northern province of Guanacaste.

- **Marriott Hotel and Resort** (San Antonio de Belén, San José area; © **800/228-9290** in the U.S. and Canada or 506/298-0844 in Costa Rica; www.marriott.com): Of all the contenders in the upscale urban market, the Marriott seems to be doing the best job. Maybe that's just because it's the newest, but everything is in great shape, the service is bend-over-backward, the restaurants are excellent, and there are all the facilities and amenities you could want. See chapter 4.

- **Meliá Playa Conchal** (on the northern Pacific coast; ✆ **888/336-3542** in the U.S. or 506/654-4123 in Costa Rica; www.solmelia.com): If you're looking for a large and luxurious resort with all the trappings, including an 18-hole Robert Trent Jones golf course, this place fits the bill. As a bonus, it's located on one of the nicest beaches in Costa Rica, the seashell-strewn wonder of Playa Conchal. See chapter 5.
- **Hotel Punta Islita** (on the Pacific coast in central Guanacaste; ✆ **800/525-4800** in the U.S. or 506/231-6122 in Costa Rica; www.hotelpuntaislita.com): This is a great getaway. Perched on a high, flat bluff overlooking the Pacific Ocean, Punta Islita is popular with honeymooners, and rightly so. The rooms are large and comfortable, the food is excellent, and the setting is stunning. If you venture beyond your room and the hotel's inviting hillside pool, there's a long, almost-always-deserted beach for you to explore, as well as a wealth of activities for the more adventurous. See chapter 5.
- **Hotel Sí Como No** (Manuel Antonio; ✆ **506/777-0777**; www.sicomono.com): Although there are fancier and more posh places in Costa Rica, the large modern suites and villas, spectacular views, attentive service, and first-rate facilities here earn this small resort a spot on this list. See chapter 7.
- **Villa Caletas** (north of Jacó; ✆ **506/637-0606**; www.hotelvillacaletas.com): Spread out over a steep hillside, high above the Pacific Ocean, these individual villas have a Mediterranean feel. The Greek Doric amphitheater follows the same motif. Carved into the steep hillside, the theater frequently features evening concerts of jazz or classical music. The "infinity pool" here was one of the first in Costa Rica and is still the most interesting. Sitting in a lounge chair at the pool's edge, you'll swear it joins the sea beyond. See chapter 7.
- **Los Sueños Marriott Beach & Golf Resort** (Playa Herradura; ✆ **800/228-9290** in the U.S., 506/298-0000 or 506/630-9000 in Costa Rica; www.marriotthotels.com): With large, luxurious rooms, an 18-hole golf course, tons of facilities and amenities, and a large maze of a pool built to resemble the canals of Venice, this is one of the finest luxury resorts in Costa Rica. The only real downside here is the decidedly mediocre beach. See chapter 7.

8 The Best Moderately Priced Hotels

- **Hotel Le Bergerac** (San José; ✆ **506/234-7850**; www.bergerac.com): This classy little hotel has been pleasing diplomats, dignitaries, and other discerning travelers for years. Ask for one of the garden rooms, or get the old master bedroom with its small private balcony. See chapter 4.
- **Hotel Grano de Oro** (San José; ✆ **506/255-3322**; www.hotelgranodeoro.com): San José boasts dozens of old homes that have been converted into hotels, but few offer the luxurious accommodations or professional service that can be found at the Grano de Oro. Throughout all the guest

rooms, you'll find attractive hardwood furniture, including old-fashioned wardrobes in some rooms. When it comes time to relax, you can soak in a hot tub or have a drink in the rooftop lounge while taking in the commanding view of San José. See chapter 4.

- **Villa del Sueño** (Playa Hermosa; ✆ and fax **506/672-0026;** www.villadelsueno.com): It's not right on the beach (you'll have to walk about 100 yards or so), but everything else about this place is right on the money, including clean, comfortable rooms, a nice refreshing pool, and an excellent restaurant. You can't do better in Playa Hermosa. See chapter 5.

- **El Sano Banano** (Playa Montezuma; ✆ and fax **506/642-0068;** www.elbanano.com): Isolated, private cabins with outdoor showers set amid lush grounds a stone's throw from the Pacific Ocean all add up to my idea of a tropical paradise. See chapter 5.

- **El Sapo Dorado** (Monteverde; ✆ **506/645-5010;** www.cool.cr/usr/sapodorado): Spacious wooden cabins with fireplaces and private porches are spread across an open hillside planted with fruit trees and tropical flowers. The hotel has an excellent restaurant and is a great place to enjoy some of the best sunsets in town. See chapter 6.

- **Cariblue Bungalows** (Playa Cocles; ✆ **506/750-0035,** or ✆ and fax 506/750-0057. www.cariblue.com): Try to get one of the private wooden bungalows here. If you do, you might be so happy and comfortable you won't want to leave. Just a 100 yards or so away, however, are the warm waves of the Caribbean Sea. See chapter 9.

9 The Best Ecolodges & Wilderness Resorts

The term "ecotourism" is fast becoming ubiquitous within the travel industry, particularly in Costa Rica. Ecolodge options in Costa Rica range from tent camps with no electricity, cold-water showers, and communal buffet-style meals to some of the most luxurious accommodations in the country. Generally, outstanding ecolodges and wilderness resorts are set apart by an ongoing commitment (financial or otherwise) to minimizing their effect on surrounding ecosystems and to supporting residents of local communities. They should also be able to provide naturalist guides and plentiful information. All of the following do.

- **Arenal Observatory Lodge** (near La Fortuna; ✆ **506/290-7011;** www.arenal-observatory.co.cr): Originally a research facility, this lodge has upgraded quite a bit over the years and now features comfortable rooms with impressive views of the Arenal Volcano. There are also excellent trails to nearby lava flows and a nice waterfall. Toucans frequent the trees near the lodge, and howler monkeys provide the wake-up calls. See chapter 6.

- **La Selva Biological Station** (south of Puerto Viejo; ✆ **506/240-6696;** www.ots.ac.cr): Sure, this place is geared more toward researchers than tourists, but that (along with the surrounding rain forest and extensive trail system) is what makes this one of the best ecotourism spots in the country. See chapter 6.

- **La Paloma Lodge** (Drake Bay; ✆ **506/239-2801;** www.lapalomalodge.com): If your idea of the perfect nature lodge is one where your front porch provides some prime-time viewing of flora and fauna, this place is for you. If you decide to leave the comfort of your porch, the Osa Peninsula's lowland rain forests are just outside your door. See chapter 8.

- **Bosque del Cabo Wilder-ness Lodge** (Osa Peninsula; ℂ and fax **506/735-5206;** www.bosquedelcabo.com): Large and comfortable private cabins perched on the edge of a cliff overlooking the Pacific Ocean and surrounded by lush rain forest make this one of my favorite spots in the country. There's plenty to do and there are always great guides here. See chapter 8.

- **Lapa Ríos** (Osa Peninsula; ℂ **506/735-5130;** www.laparios.com): Situated at the southern tip of the Osa Peninsula, this is the most luxurious ecolodge in Costa Rica. The 14 bungalow rooms all have spectacular views and are set into a lush forest. A lot of care went into the design and construction of this hotel. A host of tours is available for guests, and the guides are usually local

residents who are intimately familiar with the environment. See chapter 8.

- **Corcovado Lodge Tent Camp** (Playa Carate; ℂ **506/257-0766;** www.costaricaexpeditions.com): Located right on the border of Corcovado National Park, these accommodations are in spacious individual tents set within walking distance of the crashing surf. The whole operation is run by the very dependable and experienced Costa Rica Expeditions. See chapter 8.

- **Selva Bananito Lodge** (in the Talamanca Mountains south of Limón; ℂ and fax **506/253-8118;** www.selvabananito.com): This is one of the few lodges providing direct access to the southern Caribbean lowland rain forests. There's no electricity here, but that doesn't mean it's not plush. Hike along a riverbed, ride horses through the rain forest, climb 100 feet up a ceiba tree, or rappel down a jungle waterfall. There's fabulous bird watching here, and the Caribbean beaches are nearby. See chapter 9.

10 The Best Bed-and-Breakfasts & Small Inns

- **Finca Rosa Blanca Country Inn** (Santa Bárbara de Heredia; ℂ **506/269-9392;** www.fincarosablanca.com): If the cookie-cutter rooms of international resorts leave you cold, then perhaps the unique rooms of this unusual inn will be more your style. Square corners seem to have been prohibited here in favor of turrets and curving walls of glass, arched windows, and a semicircular built-in couch. It's set into the lush hillsides just 20 minutes from San José. See chapter 4.

- **Vista del Valle Plantation Inn** (near Grecia; ℂ **506/450-0900;**

www.vistadelvalle.com): This is a great choice for those who want something close to the airport but have no need for San José. The separate cabins are influenced by traditional Japanese architecture, with lots of polished woodwork and plenty of light. The gardens are also meticulously tended, and the chef is excellent. There's a nice tile pool and Jacuzzi that look out over a deep river canyon. See chapter 4.

- **Sueño del Mar** (Playa Tamarindo; ℂ and fax **506/653-0284;** suenodem@racsa.co.cr): You may think you're dreaming here. The rooms feature African dolls on the windowsills, Kokopeli candle-holders, and open-air showers with sculpted angelfish, hand-painted tiles, and lush tropical plants. The fabrics are from Bali and Guatemala. Somehow, all this works well together. Add in the requisite hammocks under shade trees right on the beach and a new small pool, and you really have something. The breakfasts here are earning local renown; yours comes with the price of your room. See chapter 5.

- **Arco Iris Lodge** (Monte-verde; ℰ **506/645-5067**; www. arcoirislodge.com): This small lodge is right in Santa Elena, and it's by far the best deal in the Monteverde area. The owners are extremely knowledgeable and helpful. See chapter 6.
- **Los Cocos** (Playa Zancudo; ℰ and fax **506/776-0012**; www.

loscocos.com): If you've ever dreamed about chucking it all and setting up shop in a simple house right on the beach, you should come here and give it a trial run first. See chapter 8.

- **Shawandha Lodge** (Playa Chiq-uita; ℰ **506/750-0018**; www. shawandha-lodge.com): Spacious, individual bungalows set amid flowering gardens and thick jungle make this the most comfortable lodge on the Caribbean coast. Artistic touches abound. See chapter 9.
- **Casa Verde** (Puerto Viejo; ℰ **506/750-0015**; cabinascasaverde@ hotmail.com): This is my favorite budget lodging along the Caribbean coast. The rooms are clean and airy and have comfort-able beds with mosquito nets. The owner is friendly and is always doing some work in the gardens or around the grounds. See chapter 9.

11 The Best Restaurants

- **Barbecue Los Anonos** (Escazú; ℰ **506/228-0180**): After thriving for more than 40 years, this place can rightfully be called an institu-tion. They serve aged Angus beef here, and there is a host of chicken, pork, and fish options as well. See chapter 4.
- **Le Bilboquet** (San José; ℰ **506/221-2302**): It may be too soon to tell, but this could quickly become one of the premier restaurants in San José. Le Bilboquet serves up refined nouveau French cuisine with world fusion flourishes in a relaxed, yet lively, bistro environ-ment. See chapter 4.
- **Tin Jo** (San José; ℰ **506/221-7605**): In a city with hun-dreds of Chinese restaurants, this place stands head-and-shoulders above the competition. In addi-tion to an extensive selection of Szechuan and Cantonese classics,

there are Japanese, Thai, Indian, and Malaysian dishes on the menu. Tin Jo has the most adven-turous Asian cuisine in Costa Rica. See chapter 4.
- **Playa de los Artistas** (Mon-tezuma; no phone): This place is the perfect blend of refined cui-sine and beachside funkiness. There are only a few tables here, so make sure you get here early. Fresh grilled seafood is served in oversized ceramic bowls and on large wooden slabs lined with banana leaves. See chapter 5.
- **El Gran Escape** (Quepos; ℰ **506/777-0395**): The prices are right, the portions are generous, and the fish is always fresh and expertly prepared. What more could you ask for from a seafood restaurant in a popular port town? See chapter 7.

- **El Nuevo Latino** (Playa Herradura; © **506/630-9000**): Located inside the Los Sueños Marriott resort, this place serves creative and modern takes on local and regional dishes. The service is a form of relaxed, resort formal, and the setting is stunning. See chapter 7.
- **Restaurant Edith** (Cahuita; © **506/755-0248**): Miss Edith cooks up some of the best and most authentic Caribbean cuisine. Service is slow, but you can spend your time chatting with other

hungry travelers at the large communal tables packed into this humble open-air affair. See chapter 9.
- **Amimodo** (Puerto Viejo; © **506/750-0257**): I'm not sure that a tiny surfer town on the remote Caribbean coast deserves such fine Italian food, but it's got it. The gnocchi here are delicate. If you don't want to lose sight of the fact that you're at the beach, have a fresh fillet of fish or the home-made ravioli stuffed with lobster. See chapter 9.

12 The Best Views

- **The Summit of Irazú Volcano** (near San José): On a very clear day you can see both the Pacific Ocean and the Caribbean Sea from this vantage point. Even if visibility is low and this experience eludes you, you will have a view of the volcano's spectacular landscape, the Meseta Central, and the Orosi Valley. See chapter 4.
- **El Mirador Ehecatl** (© **506/679-9104**): This humble little restaurant holds a commanding view of Bahía Salinas. It's not necessarily worth the drive from San José, and the food is basic, at best. But if you're anywhere near La Cruz, this is a must stop for sunset. See chapter 5.
- **Iguanazul Hotel** (Playa Junquillal; © and fax **506/658-8123**; www.iguanazul.com): Located on a high bluff above Playa Junquillal, this hotel has a wonderful view of the Pacific and the windswept coastline in either direction. It gets best around sunset, and better yet if you can commandeer one of the hammocks set in a little palapa on the hillside itself. See chapter 5.
- **Tabacón Resort** (near Arenal Volcano; © **506/256-1500**; www.tabacon.com): It seems so close, you'll swear you can reach out and

touch the volcano. Unlike on Irazú Volcano (see above), when *this* volcano rumbles and spews, you may have the urge to run for cover. Most rooms here have spectacular views from sheltered private patios or balconies. See chapter 6.
- **La Mariposa** (Quepos; © **506/777-0355**; www.lamariposa.com): This place has arguably the best view in Manuel Antonio, and that's saying a lot. Come for breakfast or a sunset drink, because unfortunately I've had bad luck with dinner here. See chapter 7.
- **The Outdoor Restaurant at Villa Caletas** (Playa Hermosa de Jacó; © **506/637-0606**): You'll have a view over the Golfo de Nicoya and the Pacific Ocean beyond. Sunsets here are legendary, but it's beautiful during the day as well. See chapter 7.
- **The Summit of Mount Chirripó** (near San Isidro): What more can one say: At 12,412 feet, this is the highest spot in Costa Rica. On a clear day you can see both the Pacific Ocean and Caribbean Sea from here. Even if it isn't clear, you can catch some pretty amazing views and scenery. See chapter 7.

13 The Best After-Dark Fun

- **El Cuartel de la Boca del Monte** (San José; © 506/221-0327): This is where San José's young, restless, and beautiful congregate. From Wednesday through Saturday the place is jam-packed. Originally a gay and bohemian hangout, it is now decidedly yuppie. There's frequently live music here. See chapter 4.

- **La Esmeralda** (San José; © 506/221-0530): This restaurant serves as a meeting place and central dispatch center for scores of local mariachi bands, some of which even print the restaurant's pay-phone number on their business cards. Hire your own combo for a song or two, or just enjoy the cacophony as the bands battle it out through the night. See chapter 4.

- **San Pedro** (San José): This is San José's university district, and at night its streets are filled with students strolling among a variety of bars and cafes. If you'd like to join them, keep in mind that **La Villa** (© 506/225-9612) caters to artists and bohemians; **Mosaikos** (© 506/280-9541) is popular with young Tico rockers; **Omar Khayyam** (© 506/253-8455) is a great place to grab an outdoor table and watch the crowds walk by; and **Pizza Caccio** (© 506/224-3261) seems to attract a good share of the U.S. students studying here. All of the spots listed above are located in a 3-block stretch that begins 200 meters east of the San Pedro Church and heads north. If you head straight 500 meters east from the church, you'll come to **Jazz Café** (© 506/253-8933), which as its name indicates often features live jazz. See chapter 4.

- **Mar y Sombra** (Manuel Antonio; © 506/777-0510): Located on the beach a couple of hundred yards from the national park entrance, this is the most happening spot in the Manuel Antonio area. There's a large, open-air dance floor and plenty of tables set in the sand. If the dancing gets too intense, you can always cool your feet in the ocean. See chapter 7.

- **San Clemente Bar & Grill** (Dominical; © 506/787-0055): This is a quintessential surfers' joint, but whether you hang 10 or not, this is where you'll want to hang out in Dominical at night. The fresh seafood and Tex-Mex specialties are hearty, tasty, and inexpensive. And there are pool, Ping-Pong, and foosball tables, as well as televised sporting events and surf videos. See chapter 7.

- **Johnny's Place** (Puerto Viejo; no phone): Picture yourself sipping a cold beer at a candlelit table set in the sand with the Caribbean lapping at your feet. Could you ask for more? If so, a few steps away there's a steamy dance floor that lets loose to loud reggae. See chapter 9.

14 The Most Useful Websites for Costa Rica

- **The Tico Times** (www.ticotimes. net): A selection from the English-language *Tico Times* makes it easy for norteamericanos (and other English speakers) to see what's happening in Costa Rica. It prints the top story from its weekly print edition, as well as news briefs, a business article, regional news, a fishing column, and travel reviews.

- **Costa Rica Supersite: Visitor Center (www.incostarica.net):** This is an extensive English-language tourism site from *La Nación,* Costa Rica's leading newspaper. It includes basics such as hotels (online booking is available) and rental cars, as well as attractions by region. The "Adventure" section includes pages on rock climbing, diving, surfing, mountain-biking, paragliding, and more. Small images are woven into the site, and the descriptions usually include e-mail addresses to enable you to easily contact outfitters. The site's search feature can help you narrow your search.
- **Yellow Web Costa Rica (www. yellowweb.co.cr):** This is the best all-around commercial information site and online guide to Costa Rica that I've found. Information is organized into helpful categories, and the listing of useful links is quite extensive.
- **Latin America Network Information Center** (LANIC; **http:// info.lanic.utexas.edu/la/ca/cr/):** Hosted by the University of Texas Latin American Studies Department, this site houses a vast collection of diverse information about Costa Rica. There are helpful links to a wide range of tourism and general-information sites.
- **Spanish-Language Schools in Costa Rica (www.westnet.com/ costarica/education.html):** This site lists about two dozen schools, with links to each of the schools' own websites. If you're thinking about studying Spanish in Costa Rica, this is a good place to start researching your options.
- ***La Nación* Digital (www.nacion. co.cr):** If you can read Spanish, this is a worthwhile site to browse. The entire content of the country's paper of record is placed online daily, and there's also an extensive searchable archive. It does maintain a small summary of major news items in English, although this section tends to run about a week behind the current events.

2

Planning Your Trip to Costa Rica

Costa Rica is one of the fastest-growing tourist destinations in the Americas, and as the number of visitors increases, so does the need for pre-trip planning. When is the best time to go to Costa Rica? The cheapest time? Should you rent a car (or will you need four-wheel drive) and what will it cost? Where should you go in Costa Rica? What are the hotels like? How much should you budget for your trip? These are just a few of the important questions that this chapter will answer so you can be prepared when you arrive in Costa Rica.

1 The Regions in Brief

Costa Rica rightfully should be called "Costas Ricas," since it has two coasts, one on the Pacific Ocean and one on the Caribbean Sea. These two coasts are as different from each other as are the Atlantic and Pacific coasts of North America.

Costa Rica's Pacific coast, which can be divided into three distinct regions (Guanacaste and the Nicoya Peninsula; the central coast; and the southern coast), is characterized by a rugged, though mostly accessible, coastline, where mountains often meet the sea. There are some spectacular stretches of coastline, and most of the country's top beaches are here. This coast varies from the dry, sunny climate of the northwest to the hot, humid rain forests of the south.

The **Caribbean coast** can be divided into two roughly equal stretches, one of which is accessible only by boat or small plane. The remote northeast coastline is a vast flat plain laced with rivers and covered with rain forest. Farther south, along the stretch of coast accessible by car, there are uncrowded beaches and even a bit of coral reef.

Bordered by Nicaragua in the north and Panama in the southeast, Costa Rica (19,530 square miles) is only slightly larger than Vermont and New Hampshire combined. Much of the country is mountainous, with three major ranges running northwest to southeast. Among these mountains are several volcanic peaks, some of which are still active. Between the mountain ranges are fertile valleys, the largest and most populated of which is the Central Valley. With the exception of the dry Guanacaste region, much of Costa Rica's coastal area is hot and humid and covered with dense rain forests.

SAN JOSÉ & THE CENTRAL VALLEY The Central Valley is characterized by rolling green hills that rise to heights between 3,000 and 4,000 feet above sea level. The climate here is mild and springlike year-round. It's Costa Rica's primary agricultural region, with coffee farms making up the majority of landholdings. The rich volcanic soil of this region makes it ideal for farming. The country's earliest settlements were in this area, and

The Regions in Brief

today the Central Valley (which includes San José) is densely populated, with decent roads, and dotted with small towns. Surrounding the Central Valley are high mountains, among which are four volcanic peaks. Two of these, **Poás** and **Irazú,** are still active and have caused extensive damage during cycles of activity in the past 2 centuries. Many of the mountainous regions to the north and to the south of the capital of San José have been declared national parks (Tapantí, Juan Castro, and Braulio Carrillo) to protect their virgin rain forests against logging.

GUANACASTE & THE NICOYA PENINSULA The northwestern corner of the country near the Nicaraguan border is the site of many of Costa Rica's sunniest and most popular **beaches.** Because many Americans have chosen to build beach houses and retirement homes here, Guanacaste in particular is experiencing quite a bit of new development. Don't expect a glut of Cancún-style high-rise hotels, but condos, luxury resorts, and golf courses are springing up like mushrooms. That's not to say you'll be towel-to-towel with thousands of strangers. On the contrary; you can still find long stretches of deserted sands. But maybe not for long. When the new international airport in Liberia is up and running for real, it will be possible to get here from North America without so much as a stopover in San José.

With about 65 inches of rain a year, this region is by far the driest in the country and has been likened to west Texas. Guanacaste province sits at the border of Nicaragua and is named after the shady trees that still shelter the herds of cattle that roam the dusty savanna here. In addition to cattle ranches, Guanacaste boasts semiactive volcanoes, several lakes, and one of the last remnants of tropical dry forest left

in Central America (dry forest once stretched all the way from Costa Rica up to the Mexican state of Chiapas).

THE NORTHERN ZONE This region lies to the north of San José and includes rain forests, cloud forests, hot springs, the country's two most active volcanoes (**Arenal** and **Rincón de la Vieja**), **Braulio Carrillo National Park,** and numerous remote lodges. Because this is one of the few regions of Costa Rica without any beaches, it primarily attracts people interested in nature and active sports. **Lake Arenal** boasts some of the best windsurfing in the world, as well as several good mountain-biking trails along its shores. The **Monteverde Cloud Forest,** perhaps Costa Rica's most internationally recognized attraction, is another top draw in this region.

THE CENTRAL PACIFIC COAST Because it's the most easily accessible coastline in Costa Rica, the central Pacific coast boasts the greatest number of beach resorts and hotels. **Playa de Jacó** is the most popular destination here, a beach within a few hours' drive of San José that attracts a large number of Canadian and German charter groups and plenty of Tico tourists on weekends. **Manuel Antonio,** the name of a popular coastal national park as well as the resort area that surrounds it, caters to people seeking a bit more tranquillity and beauty. At the same time, this region is also home to the highest peak in Costa Rica—**Mount Chirripó**—where frost is common.

THE SOUTHERN ZONE This hot, humid region is one of Costa Rica's most remote and undeveloped regions. It is characterized by dense rain forests and rugged coastlines. Much of the area is protected in **Corcovado** and **La Amistad** national parks. There is a wealth of wonderful nature lodges spread around the shores of the **Golfo Dulce** and along the **Osa Peninsula.** There's a lot of solitude to be found here, due in no small part to the fact that it's hard to get here and hard to get around. But if you like your ecotourism challenging, you'll find it to your liking.

THE CARIBBEAN COAST   Most of the Caribbean coast is a wide, steamy lowland laced with rivers and blanketed with rain forests and banana plantations. The culture here is predominantly black, with many residents speaking English or Caribbean patois. The northern section of this coast is accessible only by boat or small plane and is the site of **Tortuguero National Park,** which is known for its nesting sea turtles and riverboat trips. The towns of **Cahuita, Puerto Viejo,** and **Manzanillo,** on the southern half of the Caribbean coast, are increasingly popular destinations. The coastline here boasts many beautiful beaches and, as yet, few large hotels. However, this area can be rainy, especially between December and April.

2 Visitor Information

In the United States or Canada, you can get a basic packet of information on Costa Rica by contacting the **Costa Rican Tourist Board** (ICT, or Instituto Costarricense de Turismo) at © **800/343-6332.** Much of the same information is available at its website, **www.tourism-costarica.com**. (British, Irish, Australian, and New Zealand travelers will have to rely primarily on this website, as the ICT does not have offices or a toll-free number in these countries.)

In addition to this official site, you'll be able to find a wealth of web-based information on Costa Rica with a few clicks of your mouse. See "The Most Useful Websites for Costa Rica," on p. 20 in chapter 1 for some helpful suggestions about where to begin your online search.

3 Entry Requirements & Customs

ENTRY REQUIREMENTS
Citizens of the United States, Canada, Great Britain, and most European nations may visit Costa Rica for a maximum of 90 days. No visa is necessary, but you must have a valid passport. (U.S. citizens can enter with just a valid photo ID and a copy of their birth certificate, but I still recommend bringing a passport.) Citizens of Australia and New Zealand can enter the country without a visa and stay for 30 days. Citizens of the Republic of Ireland need a visa, a valid passport, and a round-trip ticket in order to enter.

If you overstay your visa or entry stamp, you will have to pay around $45 for an exit visa and a nominal fee for each extra month you've stayed. If you need to get an exit visa, a travel agent in San José can usually get one for you for a small fee and save you the hassle of dealing with Immigration. If you want to stay longer than the validity of your entry stamp or visa, the easiest thing to do is cross the border into Panama or Nicaragua for 72 hours and then re-enter Costa Rica on a new entry stamp or visa. However, be careful. Periodically, the Costa Rican government has cracked down on "perpetual tourists," and if it notices a continued pattern of exits and entries designed simply to support an extended stay, it may deny you re-entry.

If you need a visa or have other questions about Costa Rica, you can contact any of the following Costa Rican embassies: in the **United States,**

Lost Documents

If you lose your passport or need special assistance after you've arrived in Costa Rica, contact your embassy; locations are listed in "Fast Facts: Costa Rica," on p. 52 in this chapter. Most embassies can replace your passport and help you get an exit visa in about 24 hours.

If your embassy won't get your exit visa for you, see a local travel agent or **OTEC Viajes,** Edificio Ferencz, 2nd floor, Calle 3 between Avenidas 1 and 3, almost 3 blocks north of the National Theater (© **506/256-0633**). If you try to deal with Immigration yourself, you will face long lines, long waits, and endless frustration. Local travel agents and agencies regularly deal with Immigration and will charge you about $10 to $15 for the service (sometimes free if you ticket with them).

2112 S St. NW, Washington, DC 20008 (© **202/234-2945**); in **Canada,** 135 York St., Suite 208, Ottawa, Ontario K1N 5T4 (© **613/562-2855**); in **Great Britain,** 14 Lancaster Gate, London, England W2 3LH (© **71-706-8844**). There are no Costa Rican embassies in Australia or New Zealand.

In the United States, Costa Rica also maintains consulates in New York (© **212/509-3066**), Atlanta (© **770/951-7025**), New Orleans (© **504/887-8131**), Chicago (© **312/263-2772**), Denver (© **303/696-8211**), Houston (© **713/266-0484**), Los Angeles (© **213/380-6031**), San Francisco (© **510/790-0785**), and Miami (© **305/871-7485**).

CUSTOMS
WHAT YOU CAN BRING TO COSTA RICA

Visitors entering Costa Rica are entitled to bring in 500 grams of tobacco, 3 liters of liquor, and US$400 in merchandise. Cameras, computers, and electronic equipment for personal use are also permitted. Customs officials in Costa Rica rarely check tourists' luggage.

WHAT YOU CAN BRING HOME

Rules governing what you can bring back duty-free vary from country to country, and generally are posted on the Web.

Returning U.S. citizens who have been away for 48 hours or more are allowed to bring back, once every 30 days, $400 worth of merchandise duty-free. You'll be charged a flat rate of 10% duty on the next $1,000 worth of purchases. Be sure to have your receipts handy. On gifts, the duty-free limit is $100. You cannot bring fresh foodstuffs into the United States; canned foods, however, are allowed. You can also bring coffee home with you. For more information, contact the **U.S. Customs Service,** 1301 Constitution Ave. (P.O. Box 7407), Washington, DC 20044 (© **202/927-6724**), and request the free pamphlet *Know Before You Go.* It's also available on the Web at **www.customs.gov/travel/kbygo.htm.**

Canadians should check the booklet *I Declare,* which you can download or order from Revenue Canada (© **613/993-0534;** www.ccra-adrc.gc.ca). **British** citizens should contact HM Customs & Excise (© **020-7202-4227;** www.hmce.gov.uk). **Australians** can contact the Australian Customs Service (© **1-300/363-263** within Australia, 61-2/6275-6666 from outside Australia; www.customs.gov.au/). **New Zealand** citizens should contact New Zealand Customs (© **09/359-6655;** www.customs.govt.nz/).

4 Money

CASH & CURRENCY

The unit of currency in Costa Rica is the **colón.** In early 2001, there were approximately 320 colones to the American dollar, but because the colón has been in a constant state of devaluation, you can expect this rate to change. Because of this devaluation and accompanying inflation, *this book lists prices in U.S. dollars only.* To check the very latest exchange rates before you leave home, point your browser to **www.xe.com/ucc/full. shtml**.

The colón is divided into 100 **centimos.** There are currently two types of coins in circulation. The older and larger nickel-alloy coins come in denominations of 10, 25, and 50 centimos and 1, 2, 5, 10, and 20 colones; however, because of their evaporating value, you will rarely see or have to handle centimos. In 1997, the government introduced new gold-hued 5-, 10-, 25-, 50-, and 100-colón coins. They are smaller and heavier than the older coins, and they will slowly phase out the other currency.

There are paper notes in denominations of 50, 100, 500, 1,000, 2,000, 5,000, and 10,000 colones. You might also encounter a special-issue 5-colón bill that is a popular gift and souvenir. It is valid currency, although it sells for much more than its face value. You may hear people refer to a *rojo* or *tucan,* which are slang terms for the 1,000- and 5,000-colón bills, respectively. One-hundred colón denominations are called *tejas,* so *cinco tejas* would be 500 colones. The 2,000 and 10,000 bills are relatively new, and I've yet to encounter a slang equivalent for them.

In recent years, forged bills have become increasingly common. When **receiving change** in colones, it's a good idea to check the larger-denomination bills, which should have protective bands or hidden images that appear when held up to the light.

EXCHANGING MONEY

You can change money at all state-owned banks. However, the service at these banks is slow and tedious. This simple transaction can often take more than an hour and cause unnecessary confusion and anxiety. I don't recommend it.

Fortunately, you don't have to rely on the state's banks. In late 1996, Costa Rica passed a law opening up the state's banking system. Accordingly, private banks have been opening up around San José and in some of the larger provincial towns and cities. So far, these private banks are kicking the state banks' butts, providing fast service at reasonable commissions, with small or no lines.

Hotels will often exchange money and cash traveler's checks as well; there usually isn't much of a line, but they may shave a few colones off the exchange rate.

Be very careful about exchanging money on the streets; it's extremely risky. In addition to forged bills and short counts, street money-changers frequently work in teams that can leave you holding neither colones nor dollars.

ATMS

While ATMs are still mostly found at bank offices and major shopping centers in and around San José, they're beginning to pop up at major tourist destinations around the country. Think of your ATM card as a backup measure, since machines are not nearly as readily available or dependable in Costa Rica as you might expect, and you may encounter compatibility problems. So it's always a good idea to carry some cash with you.

ATMs are linked to a national network that most likely includes your bank at home. **Cirrus** (© **800/ 424-7787;** www.mastercard.com/ atm) and **PLUS** (© **800/843-7587;**

The Colón, the U.S. Dollar & the British Pound

Colones	U.S.$	U.K.£	Colones	U.S.$	U.K.£
5	.016	0.01	1,000	3.13	2.13
10	.03	0.02	5,000	15.63	10.62
25	.08	0.054	10,000	31.25	21.25
50	.156	0.106	25,000	83.33	56.66
75	.23	0.156	50,000	156.25	106.25
100	.313	0.21	75,000	234.38	159.12
200	.625	0.43	100,000	312.50	212.16
300	.94	0.63	200,000	625.00	425.00
400	1.25	0.85	300,000	937.50	637.50
500	1.56	1.06	500,000	1,562.50	1,062.50
750	2.34	1.59	1,000,000	3,125.00	2,125.00

www.visa.com) are the two most popular networks. Before traveling to Costa Rica, ask for a list of ATMs. Be sure to check the daily withdrawal limit before you depart, and ask whether you need a new personal ID number.

Finally, be aware that each time you withdraw cash, your bank will slap you with a fee of between $3 and $5 (check how much your bank charges before leaving home). Instead of taking out small denominations again and again, and worrying about whether you'll be able to find an ATM in the next small town, it makes sense to take out larger amounts more infrequently.

CREDIT CARDS

Credit cards are invaluable when traveling, and they are becoming widely accepted in Costa Rica (primarily American Express, MasterCard, and Visa). They are a safe way to carry money and provide a convenient record of all your expenses.

Since credit-card purchases are dependent upon phone verifications, some hotels and restaurants in more remote destinations do not accept them. Moreover, many add on a 5% to 10% surcharge for credit-card payments. Always check in advance if you're heading to a more remote corner of Costa Rica. Also note that many U.S. banks (including Citibank) are beginning to charge an additional 2% surcharge for transactions in a foreign currency; ask your credit-card company about its policy before you leave home.

Almost every credit-card company has an emergency toll-free number that you can call if your wallet or purse is stolen. However, in Costa Rica, since it's difficult to dial direct to toll-free numbers in the United States, these numbers aren't too helpful. **Credomatic** (© **506/257-0155** main office, or 506/257-4744 to report lost or stolen cards 24 hours) is the local representative of most major credit cards: American Express, MasterCard, and Visa. It has an office in San José across from the Banco de San José on Calle Central between Avenidas 3 and 5. It's open Monday through Friday from 8am to 7pm, and Saturday from 9am to 1pm. This office also serves as a traditional **American Express Travel Services** office, issuing traveler's checks and providing other standard services. You can call the number above to report all lost or stolen cards. To report a lost or stolen American Express card from inside Costa Rica, you can also call © **0-800-012-3211.** To report a lost or stolen **Diners Club** card from inside Costa Rica, call © **506/257-1766,** or call collect © **001-303-799-1504.** Once you contact your bank or issuing company, it may be able to wire you a cash advance off your credit card immediately; and in many places, it can deliver an emergency credit card in a day or two. Odds are that if your wallet is gone, the police won't be able to recover it for you. But your credit-card company or insurer may require a police-report number, so you may want to call the police anyway (after you cancel your credit cards).

TRAVELER'S CHECKS

With so many more ATMs popping up in every corner of the globe, traveler's checks seem less necessary these days. But if you prefer the security they offer, and don't mind showing identification every time you want to cash one, traveler's checks might still be for you.

You can get traveler's checks at almost any bank for a service charge of 1% to 4%. **American Express** traveler's checks can be ordered over the phone by calling © **800/ 221-7282** or 800/721-9768, or you can purchase checks online at **www. americanexpress.com**. AmEx gold or platinum cardholders can avoid paying the fee by ordering over the telephone; platinum cardholders can also purchase checks in person at AmEx Travel Service locations with no fee. American Automobile Association members can obtain checks with no fee at most AAA offices.

To report lost or stolen American Express traveler's checks within Costa Rica, call © **0-800-011-0080.**

5 When to Go

Costa Rica's high season for tourism runs from late November to late April, which coincides almost perfectly with the chill of winter in the United States, Canada, and Great Britain. The high season is also the dry season. If you want some unadulterated time on a tropical beach and a little less rain during your rain-forest experience, this is the time to come. During this period (and especially around the Christmas holidays), the tourism industry operates at full tilt—prices are higher, attractions are more crowded, and reservations need to be made in advance.

In recent years, local tourism operators have begun calling the tropical rainy season (May through mid-November) the "green season." The adjective is appropriate. At this time of year, even brown and barren Guanacaste province becomes lush and verdant. I personally love traveling around Costa Rica during the rainy season (but then again, I'm not trying to flee winter in Chicago). It's easy to find or at least negotiate reduced rates, there are far fewer fellow travelers, and the rain is often limited to a few hours each afternoon (although you can occasionally get socked in for a week at a time). One other drawback: Some of the country's rugged roads become downright impassable without four-wheel drive during the rainy season.

CLIMATE

Costa Rica is a tropical country and has distinct wet and dry seasons. However, some regions are rainy all year and others are very dry and sunny for most of the year. Temperatures vary primarily with elevation, not with season: On the coasts it's hot all year, while up in the mountains it can be cool at night any time of year. At the highest elevations (10,000–12,000 ft.), frost is common.

Average Daytime Temperatures & Rainfall in San José

	Jan	Feb	Mar	Apr	May	June	July	Aug	Sept	Oct	Nov	Dec
Temp. (°F)	66	66	69	71	71	71	70	70	71	69	68	67
Temp. (°C)	19	19	20.5	21.5	21.5	21.5	21	21	21.5	20.5	20	19.5
Days of rain	1	0	1	4	17	20	18	19	20	22	14	4

Generally speaking, the **rainy season** (or "green season") is from May to mid-November. Costa Ricans call this wet time of year their winter. The **dry season,** considered summer by Costa Ricans, is from mid-November through April. In Guanacaste, the dry northwestern province, the dry season lasts several weeks longer than in other places. Even in the rainy season, days often start sunny, with rain falling in the afternoon and evening. On the Caribbean coast, especially south of Limón, you can count on rain year-round, although this area gets less rain in September and October than the rest of the country.

In general, the best time of year to visit weatherwise is in December and January, when everything is still green from the rains, but the sky is clear.

HOLIDAYS

Because Costa Rica is a Roman Catholic country, most of its holidays are church-related. The biggies are Christmas, New Year's, and Easter, which are all celebrated for several days. Keep in mind that Holy Week (Easter Week) is the biggest holiday time in Costa Rica, and many families head for the beach (this is the last holiday before school starts). Also, there is no public transportation on Holy Thursday or Good Friday. Government offices and banks are closed on official holidays, transportation services are reduced, and stores and markets may also close.

Official holidays in Costa Rica include **January 1** (New Year's Day), **March 19** (St. Joseph's Day), Thursday and Friday of Holy Week, **April 11** (Juan Santamaría's Day), **May 1** (Labor Day), **June 29** (Saints Peter and Paul's Day), **July 25** (annexation of the province of Guanacaste), **August 2** (Virgin of Los Angeles's Day), **August 15** (Mother's Day), **September 15** (Independence Day), **October 12** (Discovery of America/Día de la Raza), **December 8** (Immaculate Conception of the Virgin Mary), **December 24 and 25** (Christmas), and **December 31** (New Year's Eve).

COSTA RICA CALENDAR OF EVENTS

Some of the events listed here might be considered more of a *happening* than an event—there's not, for instance, a Virgin of Los Angeles PR Committee that readily dispenses information. If I haven't listed a contact number, your best bet is to call the **Costa Rican Tourist Board (ICT)** at ☎ 800/343-6332 in the United States, or ☎ 506/223-1733 or ☎ 192 in Costa Rica.

January

Copa del Café (Coffee Cup), San José. An international event on the junior tennis tour. Matches are held at the Costa Rica Country Club (☎ 506/228-9333). First week in January.

Fiestas of Palmares, Palmares. Perhaps the largest and best organized of the traditional *fiestas.* Bullfights, a horseback parade (*tope*), and a wide range of concerts, carnival rides, and food booths. First 2 weeks in January.

Fiestas of Santa Cruz, Santa Cruz, Guanacaste. A religious celebration honoring the Black Christ of Esquipulas (a famous Guatemalan statue), featuring folk dancing, marimba music, and bullfights. Mid-January.

February

Fiesta of the Diablitos, Rey Curré village near San Isidro de El General. Boruca Indians wearing wooden devil and bull masks perform dances representative of the Spanish conquest of Central America; there are fireworks displays and an Indian handcrafts market. Date varies.

March

Día del Boyero (Oxcart Drivers' Day), San Antonio de Escazú. Colorfully painted oxcarts parade through this suburb of San José, and local priests bless the oxen. Second Sunday.

National Orchid Show, San José. Orchid growers the world over gather to show their wares, trade tales and secrets, and admire the hundreds of species on display. Exact location and date change from year to year.

April

Holy Week (week before Easter). Religious processions are held in cities and towns throughout the country. Dates vary from year to year (between late March and early April).

Juan Santamaría Day, Alajuela. Costa Rica's national hero is honored with parades, concerts, and dances. April 11.

May

Carrera de San Juan. The country's biggest marathon runs through the mountains, from the outskirts of Cartago to the outskirts of San José. May 17.

July

Fiesta of the Virgin of the Sea, Puntarenas. A regatta of colorfully decorated boats carrying a statue of Puntarenas's patron saint marks this festival. A similar event is held at Playa de Coco. Saturday closest to July 16.

Annexation of Guanacaste Day, Liberia. Tico-style bullfights, folk dancing, horseback parades, rodeos, concerts, and other events celebrate the day when this region became part of Costa Rica. July 25.

August

Fiesta of the Virgin of Los Angeles, Cartago. This is the annual pilgrimage day of the patron saint of Costa Rica. Many people walk from San José 15 miles to the basilica in Cartago. August 2.

Día de San Ramón, San Ramón. More than two dozen statues of saints from various towns are brought to San Ramón, where they are paraded through the streets. August 31.

September

Costa Rica's Independence Day. Celebrated all over the country. Most distinctive are the nighttime parades of children. September 15.

International Beach Clean-Up Day. A good excuse to chip in and help clean up the beleaguered shoreline of your favorite beach. Third Saturday in September.

October

Fiesta del Maíz, Upala. A celebration of corn with local beauty queens wearing outfits made from corn plants. October 12.

Limón Carnival/Día de la Raza, Limón. A smaller version of Mardi Gras, complete with floats and dancing in the streets, commemorates Columbus's discovery of Costa Rica. Week of October 12.

November

All Soul's Day/Día de los Muertos, celebrated countrywide. Although not as elaborate or ritualized as in Mexico, most Costa

Ricans take some time this day to remember the dead with flowers and trips to the cemeteries. November 2.

December

Día de la Polvora, San Antonio de Belen and Jesus Maria de San Mateo. Fireworks displays to honor Our Lady of the Immaculate Conception. December 8.

Fiesta de los Negritos, Boruca. Boruca Indians celebrate the feast day of their patron saint, the Virgin of the Immaculate Conception, with costumed dances and traditional music. December 8.

Fiesta de la Yeguita, Nicoya. A statue of the Virgin of Guadalupe is paraded through the streets accompanied by traditional music and dancing. December 12.

Las Posadas. A countrywide celebration during which children and carolers go door-to-door seeking lodging in a reenactment of Joseph and Mary's search for a place to stay. Begins December 15.

El Tope and Carnival. San José. The streets of downtown belong to horses and their riders in a proud recognition of the country's important agricultural heritage. The next day those same streets are taken over by carnival floats, marching bands, and street dancers. December 26 and 27.

Festejos Populares, San José. Bullfights and a pretty respectable bunch of carnival rides, games of chance, and fast-food stands are set up at the fairgrounds in Zapote. Last week of December.

6 Health & Insurance

STAYING HEALTHY

Staying healthy on a trip to Costa Rica is predominantly a matter of being a little cautious about what you eat and drink, and using common sense. Know your physical limits and don't overexert yourself in the ocean, on hikes, or in athletic activities. Respect the tropical sun and protect yourself from it. I recommend buying and drinking bottled water or soft drinks, but the water in San José and in most of the heavily visited spots is safe to drink. The sections below deal with specific health concerns in Costa Rica.

The **U.S. Centers for Disease Control and Prevention** (© 877/ 394-8747; www.cdc.gov) provides up-to-date information on necessary vaccines and health hazards by region or country.

TROPICAL DISEASES Your chance of contracting any serious tropical disease in Costa Rica is slim, especially if you stick to the beaches or traditional spots for visitors. However, malaria,

dengue fever, and leptospirosis all exist in Costa Rica, so it's a good idea to know what they are.

Malaria is found in the lowlands on both coasts and in the northern zone. Although it's rarely found in urban areas, it's still a problem in remote wooded regions and along the Atlantic coast. Malaria prophylaxes are available, but several have side effects, and others are of questionable effectiveness. Consult your doctor as to what is currently considered the best preventive treatment for malaria. Be sure to ask whether a recommended drug will cause you to be hypersensitive to the sun—it would be a shame to come down here for the beaches and then have to hide under an umbrella the whole time. Because malaria-carrying mosquitoes usually come out at night, you should do as much as possible to avoid being bitten after dark. If you are in a malarial area, wear long pants and long sleeves, use insect repellent, and either sleep under a mosquito net or burn mosquito coils (similar to incense but with a pesticide).

Of greater concern may be **dengue fever,** which has had periodic outbreaks in Latin America since 1993. Dengue fever is similar to malaria and is spread by an aggressive daytime mosquito. This mosquito seems to be most common in lowland urban areas, and Liberia and Limón have been the worst-hit cities in Costa Rica. Dengue is also known as "bone-break fever," because it is usually accompanied by severe body aches. The first infection with dengue fever will make you very sick but should cause no serious damage. However, a second infection with a different strain of the dengue virus can lead to internal hemorrhaging and may be life-threatening.

Many people are convinced that taking B-complex vitamins daily will help prevent mosquitoes from biting you. I don't think the American Medical Association has endorsed this idea yet, but I've run across it in enough places to think there may be something to it.

One final tropical fever I think you should know about (because I got it myself) is **leptospirosis.** There are more than 200 strains of leptospirs, which are animal-borne bacteria transmitted to humans via contact with drinking, swimming, or bathing water. This bacterial infection is easily treated with antibiotics; however, it can quickly cause very high fever and chills, and should be treated promptly.

If you develop a high fever accompanied by severe body aches, nausea, diarrhea, or vomiting during or shortly after a visit to Costa Rica, consult a physician as soon as possible.

Costa Rica has been relatively free from the cholera epidemic that has spread through much of Latin America in recent years. This is largely due to an extensive public-awareness campaign that has promoted good hygiene and increased sanitation. Your chances of contracting cholera while you're here are very slight.

AMOEBAS, PARASITES, DIARRHEA & OTHER INTESTINAL WOES Even though the water in San José and most popular destinations is generally safe, and even though you've been careful to buy bottled water, order *frescos en leche* (i.e., fruit shakes made with milk, rather than water), and drink your soft drink warm (without ice cubes—which are made from water, after all), you still may encounter some intestinal difficulties. Most of this is just due to tender northern stomachs coming into contact with slightly more aggressive Latin-American intestinal flora. In extreme cases of diarrhea or intestinal discomfort, it's worth taking a stool sample to a lab for analysis. The results will usually pinpoint the amoebic or parasitic culprit, which can then be readily treated with available over-the-counter medicines.

Except in the most established and hygienic of restaurants, it's also advisable to avoid *ceviche*, a raw seafood salad, especially if it has any shellfish in it. It could be home to any number of bacterial critters.

TROPICAL SUN Limit your exposure to the sun, especially during the first few days of your trip and, thereafter, from 11am to 2pm. Use a sunscreen with a high protection factor and apply it liberally. Remember that children need more protection than adults do.

RIPTIDES Many of Costa Rica's beaches have riptides, strong currents that can drag swimmers out to sea. A riptide occurs when water that has been dumped on the shore by strong waves forms a channel back out to open water. These channels have strong currents. If you get caught in a riptide, you can't escape the current by swimming toward shore; it's like trying to swim upstream in a river. To break free of the current, swim parallel to shore and use the energy of the waves to help you get back to the beach.

BEES & SNAKES   Although Costa Rica has Africanized bees (the notorious "killer bees" of fact and fable) and several species of venomous snakes, your chances of being bitten are minimal, especially if you refrain from sticking your hands into hives or under rocks in the forest. If you know that you're allergic to beestings, consult your doctor before traveling.

Snake sightings, much less snakebites, are very rare. Moreover, the majority of snakes in Costa Rica are nonpoisonous. If you do encounter a snake, stay calm, don't make any sudden movements, and do not try to handle it. As recommended above, avoid sticking your hand under rocks, branches, and fallen trees.

WHAT TO DO IF YOU GET SICK AWAY FROM HOME

If you worry about getting sick away from home, you may want to consider **medical travel insurance** (see below). In most cases, however, your existing health plan will provide all the coverage you need. Be sure to carry your identification card in your wallet.

If you suffer from a chronic illness, consult your doctor before your departure. For conditions like epilepsy, diabetes, or heart problems, wear a **Medic Alert Identification Tag** (℗ **888/633-4298;** www. medicalert.org), which will immediately alert doctors to your condition and give them access to your records through Medic Alert's 24-hour hot line. Membership is $35, plus a $20 annual fee.

Pack prescription medications in your carry-on luggage. Bring enough to last the duration of your trip, since certain scripts may be difficult to refill in Costa Rica. If there's a medication you can't live without, bring along a copy of your prescription in case you lose your pills. If you wear contact lenses, pack an extra pair in case you lose one.

The **International Association for Medical Assistance to Travelers** (IAMAT; ℗ **416/652-0137;** www. sentex.net/~iamat) offers its members tips on travel and health concerns in countries around the world and lists many local English-speaking doctors.

When you're in Costa Rica, any local consulate can provide a list of area doctors who speak English. The local English-language newspaper, the *Tico Times,* is another good resource. I've listed the best hospitals in San José in the "Fast Facts" in chapter 4, which have the most modern facilities in the country. Most state-run hospitals and walk-in clinics around the country have emergency rooms that can treat most conditions, although I highly recommend the private hospitals in San José if your condition is not life-threatening and can wait for treatment until you reach one of them.

INSURANCE

Most travelers' needs are met by their existing insurance policies (your homeowners' insurance should cover lost or stolen luggage, for example), but if you have any concerns, contact your insurance company before you leave home and ask them to detail what they'll cover. (Some HMOs may not cover you outside the country, and Medicare only covers U.S. citizens traveling in Mexico and Canada.) If you do decide you need additional specific travel coverage, most travel agents can sell you any number of insurance packages tailored to fit your specific needs. But check your existing policies first, and don't buy more than you need.

Among the companies offering specialized travel insurance policies are **Access America** (☎ **800/284-8300;** www.accessamerica.com), **Travel Guard International** (☎ **800/826-1300;** www.travelguard.com), and, for students, **STA Travel** (☎ **800/777-0112;** www.statravel.com). Among their policies are medical plans covering emergency evacuation, in case you need to be transported home for urgent care.

Trip-cancellation insurance may be a good idea if you've paid a large portion of your vacation expenses up front, say, by purchasing a package tour. Coverage should cost approximately 6% to 8% of the total value of your vacation, so a $3,000 trip could be insured for around $210.

7 Tips for Travelers with Special Needs

FOR TRAVELERS WITH DISABILITIES

Although Costa Rica does have a law mandating Equality of Opportunities for People with Disabilities, and facilities are beginning to be adapted, in general, there are relatively few handicapped-accessible buildings. In San José, sidewalks are crowded and uneven. Few hotels offer wheelchair-accessible accommodations, and there are no public buses thus equipped. In short, it's difficult for a person with disabilities to get around in Costa Rica.

However, there are two local agencies that specialize in tours for travelers with disabilities and restricted ability. **Vaya Con Silla de Ruedas** (☎ and fax **506/454-2810,** or 506/391-5045; www.gowithwheelchairs.com) has a ramp- and elevator-equipped van and knowledgeable bilingual guides. It charges very reasonable prices and can provide anything from simple airport transfers to complete multiday tours.

Kosta Roda Foundation (☎ and fax **506/771-7482;** chabote@racsa.co.cr) is a nonprofit organization dedicated to helping the Costa Rican tourist industry remove barriers (architectural and societal). It can provide assistance and information for travelers with disabilities.

Moss Rehab ResourceNet (www.mossresourcenet.org) is a great source for information, tips, and resources relating to accessible travel. You'll find links to a number of travel agents who specialize in planning trips for disabled travelers here and through **Access-Able Travel Source** (www.access-able.com), another excellent online source.

You may also want to join a tour catering to travelers with disabilities. One of the best operators is **Flying Wheels Travel** (☎ **800/535-6790;** www.flyingwheels.com), offering various escorted tours and cruises, with an emphasis on sports, as well as private tours in minivans with lifts. Other reputable operators are **Accessible Journeys** (☎ **800/TINGLES** or 610/521-0339; www.disabilitytravel.com), for slow walkers and wheelchair travelers; **The Guided Tour** (☎ **215/782-1370**); and **Directions Unlimited** (☎ **800/533-5343**).

FOR GAY & LESBIAN TRAVELERS

Costa Rica is a Catholic, conservative, macho country where public displays of same-sex affection are rare and considered somewhat shocking. In 1998, the archbishop of San José publicly denounced homosexuality. There followed two prominent protests in the tourist destinations of Manuel Antonio and Playa Hermosa, Guanacaste, that resulted in some inconvenience for the organizers and participants of openly gay and lesbian group tours. However, gay and lesbian tourism to

Costa Rica is quite robust, and gay and lesbian travelers are generally treated with respect and should not experience any harassment.

For a general overview of the current situation, news of any special events or meetings, and up-to-date information, gay and lesbian travelers should check in with the folks at **Uno@Diez**, in the Faisa Building on Calle 1, between Avenidas 9 and 11 in downtown San José (C **506/258-4561**; www.1en10.com), a coffeehouse, gallery, and Internet cafe.

If you're doing your research on the Web, check out **http://hometown. aol.com/GayCRica** ☞. You might also browse **www.gaycostarica.com** or **www.costaricagay.com**, although both sites are mostly in Spanish.

Two travel agencies that specialize in gay and lesbian travel are **Gay Adventure Tours, Inc.** (C **888/206-6523**; www.gayadventuretours.com) and **Maguines Travel** (C and fax **506/283-4510**; manfredg@racsa.co.cr).

If you want help planning your trip, the **International Gay & Lesbian Travel Association** (IGLTA; C **800/448-8550** or 954/776-2626; www.iglta.org), can link you up with the appropriate gay-friendly service organization or tour specialist. With around 1,200 members, it offers quarterly newsletters, marketing mailings, and a membership directory that's updated quarterly. Members are kept informed of gay and gay-friendly hoteliers, tour operators, and airline and cruise-line representatives.

General U.S. gay and lesbian travel agencies include **Family Abroad** (C **800/999-5500** or 212/459-1800); and **Above and Beyond Tours** (C **800/397-2681**). In the United Kingdom, try **Alternative Holidays** (C **020/7701-7040**; info@ alternativeholidays.com).

FOR SENIORS

Don't be shy about asking for discounts, but always carry some kind of identification, such as a driver's license, that shows your date of birth, especially if you've kept your youthful glow.

Be sure to mention the fact that you're a senior citizen when you first make your travel reservations, since many airlines and hotels offer senior discounts. In most cities, people over the age of 60 qualify for reduced admission to theaters, museums, and other attractions, and discounted fares on public transportation.

Members of the **American Association of Retired Persons** (AARP; C **800/424-3410**; www.aarp.org) get discounts on hotels (including chains that are represented in Costa Rica), airfares, and car rentals. **SAGA International Holidays** (C **800/343-0273**) offers inclusive tours and cruises for those 50 and older. SAGA also sponsors the more substantial "**Road Scholar Tours**" (C **800/621-2151**), which are fun-loving but with an educational bent.

If you want something more than the average vacation or guided tour, try **Elderhostel** (C **877/426-8056**; www.elderhostel.org), which offers educational travel for senior citizens. On these escorted tours, the days are packed with seminars, lectures, and field trips, and the sightseeing is all led by academic experts. The courses are ungraded, involve no homework, and often focus on the liberal arts. They're not luxury vacations, but are fun and fulfilling. Elderhostel runs regular educational trips to Costa Rica for those age 55 and over (and a spouse or companion of any age). Most tours last about 3 weeks, and many include airfare, accommodations in student dormitories or modest inns, meals, and tuition.

Due to its temperate climate, stable government, low cost of living, and friendly *pensionado* program, Costa Rica is popular with retirees from North America. There are excellent medical facilities in San José and plenty of community organizations to help retirees feel at home. If you would like to learn more about applying for residency and retiring in Costa Rica, contact the **Association of Residents of Costa Rica** in San José (✆ **506/233-8068;** www.casacanada. net/arcr.html).

FOR FAMILIES

Hotels in Costa Rica often give discounts for children under 12 years old, and children under 3 or 4 years old are usually allowed to stay for free. Discounts for children and the cutoff ages vary according to hotel, but in general, don't assume that your kids can stay in your room for free.

Many hotels, villas, and cabinas come equipped with kitchenettes or full kitchen facilities. These can be a real money-saver for those traveling with children, and I've listed many of these accommodations in the destination chapters that follow.

Hotels offering regular, dependable baby-sitting service are few and far between. If you will need baby-sitting, make sure your hotel offers it, and be sure to ask whether the baby-sitters are bilingual. In many cases they are not. This is usually not a problem with infants and toddlers, but it can cause problems with older children.

FOR STUDENTS

Costa Rica is the only country in Central America with a network of hostels affiliated with the International Youth Hostel Federation. Ask at the **Toruma Youth Hostel,** Avenida Central between Calles 29 and 31, San José (✆ **506/234-8186,** or ✆ and fax **506/224-4085;** www.hostelling-costarica.com), for information on hotels around the country that give discounts to youth and affiliated travelers, with participating hotels in sites that include Monteverde, La Fortuna, Lake Arenal, San Isidro, Jacó Beach, Liberia, Cahuita, Puerto Viejo, Golfito, Quepos, Playa Junquillal, Puerto Jiménez, and Rincón de la Vieja National Park.

In San José, there are now two student travel agencies: **OTEC** (✆ **506/ 256-0633;** www.otec.co.cr) is located at Edificio Ferencz, 2nd floor, Calle 3 between Avenidas 1 and 3, 275 meters north of the National Theater; **Sin Límites** (✆ **506/280-5182;** www. ucitworld.com) is located on Calle 35 and Avenida Central, 200 meters east of the Kentucky Fried Chicken in Los Yoses. If you already have an International Student Identity Card, you can use it to get discounts on airfares, hostels, national and international tours and excursions, car rentals, and store purchases. If you don't have one, stop by either the OTEC or Sin Límites office with proof of student status, two passport photos, and a passport or other identification that shows you are under 35 years old; for about $10, you can get an ID card.

In terms of pretrip planning, the best resource for students is the

A Note for Female Travelers

For lack of better phrasing, Costa Rica is a typically "macho" Latin-American nation. Single women can expect a nearly constant stream of catcalls, hisses, whistles, and car horns, especially in San José. The best advice is to ignore the unwanted attention, rather than try to come up with a witty or antagonistic rejoinder. Women should also be careful walking alone at night, both in San José and in other more remote destinations. I definitely don't recommend hitchhiking.

Council on International Educational Exchange (CIEE; www.ciee. org). You can get an ID card here, and the travel branch, **Council Travel Service** (© **800/226-8624;** www. counciltravel.com), is the biggest student travel agency operation in the world. It can get you discounts on plane tickets, hotels, tours, and the like. From CIEE you can obtain the student traveler's best friend, the $18 International Student Identity Card (ISIC). It's the only officially acceptable form of student identification, good for cut rates on accommodations, plane tickets, and other discounts. It also provides you with basic health and life insurance and a 24-hour help line. If you're no longer a student but are still under 26, you can get a GO 25 card from the same people, which will get you the insurance and some of the discounts (but not student admission prices to museums).

In Canada, **Travel CUTS,** based in Toronto (© **800/667-2887** or 416/614-2887; www.travelcuts.com), offers similar services. **USIT Campus,** 52 Grosvenor Gardens, London (© **020/7730-3402;** www.usitcampus. co.uk), opposite Victoria Station, is Britain's leading specialist in student and youth travel.

8 Getting There

BY PLANE

It takes between 3 and 7 hours to fly to Costa Rica from most U.S. cities, and as Costa Rica becomes more and more popular with North American travelers, more flights are available into San José's **Juan Santamaría International Airport.** Costa Rica keeps threatening to open a new international airport in Liberia, gateway to the beaches of the Guanacaste region and the Nicoya Peninsula, but at press time it still wasn't able to handle international flights.

THE MAJOR AIRLINES

There is a host of airlines flying into Costa Rica. Be warned that the smaller Latin-American carriers tend to make several stops (sometimes unscheduled) en route to San José, thus increasing flying time. In fact, Aviateca, Lacsa, and Taca are actually operating under a single parent company, and they practice code-sharing, so the flight you book on one of these airlines may in fact fly under another name.

The following airlines currently serve Costa Rica from the United States, using the gateway cities listed. **American Airlines** (© **800/433-7300;** www.aa.com) has daily flights from Miami and Dallas/Fort Worth.

Continental (© **800/525-0280** or 800/231-0856; www.continental. com) offers flights daily from Houston and Newark International. **Delta** (© **800/221-1212;** www.delta.com) offers flights from Atlanta. **Mexicana** (© **800/531-7921;** www.mexicana. com) offers flights from Montréal, Toronto, Chicago, Los Angeles, New York, Denver, Miami, Dallas/Fort Worth, San Antonio, San Jose (Calif.), and San Francisco. **Grupo Taca** (© **800/535-8780;** www. grupotaca.com) is a conglomeration of the Central American airlines, Aviateca, Taca, and Lacsa. Flights and connections travel to and from Los Angeles, San Francisco, Houston, New Orleans, New York, Miami, and Washington. **United Airlines** (© **800/241-6522;** www.ual.com) has daily flights from Los Angeles and Washington, with one stop either in Mexico or Guatemala.

From Europe, you can take any major carrier to a hub city such as Miami or New York and then make connections to Costa Rica. Alternately, **Iberia** (www.iberia.com) from Spain, **Condor Airways** (www. condor.de) from Germany, and **Martin Air** (www.martinair.com)

from Holland have established routes to San José, stopping in Miami.

FLY FOR LESS: TIPS FOR GETTING THE BEST AIRFARES

- **Take advantage of APEX fares.** Advance-purchase booking is often the key to getting the lowest fare. You generally must be willing to make your plans and buy your tickets as far ahead as possible. Be sure you understand cancellation and refund policies before you buy.

- **Watch for sales.** You'll almost never see them during the Christmas holidays, or in the depths of winter, when everyone wants to escape to the tropics, but at other times you can get great deals. If you already hold a ticket when a sale breaks, it may even pay to exchange it, which usually incurs a $50 to $75 charge. Note, however, that the lowest-priced fares are often nonrefundable, require advance purchase of 1 to 3 weeks and a certain length of stay, and carry penalties for changing dates of travel. So, when you're quoted a fare, make sure you know exactly what the restrictions are before you commit.

- If your schedule is flexible, ask if you can secure a cheaper fare by **staying an extra day** or by **flying midweek.** (Many airlines won't volunteer this information, so ask lots of questions.)

- **Consolidators,** also known as bucket shops, are a good place to find low fares, often below even the airlines' discounted rates. Basically, they're just big travel agents that get discounts for buying in bulk and pass some of the savings on to you. Before you pay, however, ask for a confirmation number from the consolidator and then call the airline itself to confirm your seat. Be prepared to book your ticket with a different consolidator—there are many to choose from—if the airline can't confirm your reservation. Also be aware that consolidator tickets are usually nonrefundable or come with stiff cancellation penalties.

We've gotten great deals on many occasions from **Cheap Tickets** (© **800/377-1000;** www.cheaptickets.com). **Council Travel** (© **800/226-8624;** www.counciltravel.com) and **STA Travel** (© **800/781-4040;** www.sta.travel.com) cater especially to young travelers, but their bargain-basement prices are available to people of all ages. Other reliable consolidators include **Lowestfare.com** (©**888/278-8830;** www.lowestfare.com); **1-800-AIRFARE** (www.1800airfare.com); **Cheap Seats** (© **800/451-7200;** www.cheapseatstravel.com); and **1-800-FLY-CHEAP** (www.flycheap.com).

- Search the **Internet** for cheap fares—though it's still best to take the time to do comparison-shopping by checking more than one site and calling the airlines yourself to see if you're really getting a bargain. A few of the better-respected virtual travel agents are **Travelocity** (www.travelocity.com), **Expedia** (www.expedia.com), and **Yahoo! Travel** (http://travel.yahoo.com).

BY BUS

Bus service runs regularly from both Panama City, Panama, and Managua, Nicaragua. If at all possible, it's worth the splurge for a deluxe or express bus. In terms of travel time and convenience, it's always better to get a direct bus, rather than one that stops along the way—and you've got a better chance of getting a working bathroom in a direct/express or deluxe bus. Some even have television sets showing video movies.

From Panamá City, it's a 20-hour, 558-mile (900km) trip. The one-way fare is around $18. **Panaline** has a daily bus leaving Panama City at noon, while **Tica Bus** has a daily bus leaving Panama City at 9am. Call Panaline (© **506/255-1205**) or Tica Bus Company (© **506/221-8954**) for further information.

From Managua, it's 11 hours and 279 miles (450km) to San José. Tica Bus leaves Managua daily at 6 and 7:30am; the one-way fare is around $10. Panaline has a bus leaving Managua daily at 2pm. None of these bus companies will reserve a seat by telephone, so buy your ticket in advance—several days in advance if you plan to travel on weekends or holidays.

Whenever traveling by bus through Central America, try to keep a watchful eye on your belongings, especially at rest and border stops, whether they're in an overhead bin or stored below decks in a luggage compartment.

BY CAR

It's possible to travel to Costa Rica by car, but it can be difficult, especially for U.S. citizens. After leaving Mexico, the Interamerican Highway (also known as the Pan American Highway) passes through Guatemala, El Salvador, Honduras, and Nicaragua before reaching Costa Rica. All of these countries can be problematic for travelers for a variety of reasons, including internal violence, crime, and visa formalities. If you do decide to undertake this adventure, take the **Gulf coast route** from the border crossing at Brownsville, Texas, as it involves traveling the fewest miles through Mexico. Those planning to travel this route should look through *Driving the Pan-Am Highway to Mexico and Central America* by Audrey and Raymond Pritchard, available from **Costa Rica Books** (© **800/365-2342**

in the U.S., or © and fax 506/232-5613 in Costa Rica).

CAR DOCUMENTS   You will need a current driver's license, as well as your vehicle's registration and the original title (no photocopies), in order to enter the country.

CENTRAL AMERICAN AUTO INSURANCE   Contact **Sanborn's Insurance Company,** 2009 S. 10th St., McAllen, TX 78505 (© **800/ 222-0158** or 956/686-3601; www. sanbornsinsurance.com),   located about 1½ hours from Brownsville, Texas; agents are at various border towns in the United States. These folks have been servicing this niche for over 50 years. They can supply you with trip insurance for Mexico and Central America (you won't be able to buy insurance after you've left the United States), driving tips, and an itinerary.

CAR SAFETY   Along the way, it's advisable not to drive at night because of the danger of being robbed by bandits. Also, drink only bottled beverages along the way, to avoid any unpleasant microbes that might be lurking in the local tap water.

BY CRUISE SHIP

More than 200 cruise ships stop each year in Costa Rica, calling at Limón on the Caribbean coast, and at Puerto Caldera and Puntarenas on the Pacific coast. Cruise lines that offer stops in Costa Rica include **Cunard** (© **800/7-CUNARD;** www.cunard. com), **Holand America** (© **877/ 724-5425;** www.hollandamerica.com), **Princess** (© **800/421-0522;** www.princesscruises.com), **Royal Caribbean** (© **800/398-9819;** www. rccl.com), and **Radisson Seven Seas Cruises** (© **800/285-1835;** www. rssc.com).

It might pay off to book through a travel agency that specializes in cruises; these companies stay on top of the latest specials and promotions. Try one of the following: **Cruises, Inc.** (© 800/854-0500 or 314/463-9695), the **Cruise Company** (© 800/289-5505 or 402/339-6800), or **Cruises American Express** (© 800/849-2301 or 704/556-8311).

PACKAGE TOURS

This book contains all the information and resources you need to design and book a wonderful trip, tailored to your particular interests and budget. Moreover, package tours are still a budding industry in Costa Rica, and do not offer the kinds of amazing bargains as those to Cancún or the Caribbean. In fact, many come with hidden charges and costs, so shop carefully. Still, some folks feel most comfortable when buying a complete package. What you lose in adventure, you may gain in time and money saved when you book accommodations, and maybe even food and entertainment, along with your flight.

Without question, your best bet is to go with a Costa Rica specialist; many of these companies emphasize adventure travel or ecotourism, and can put together a complete custom itinerary for you. For a complete listing of tour companies servicing Costa Rica, see chapter 3, section 1, "Organized Adventure Trips."

The airlines themselves are another good source of packages to Costa Rica. Your options include **American Airlines FlyAway Vacations** (© 800/321-2121; www.aavacations.com), **Delta Dream Vacations** (© 800/872-7786; www.deltavacations.com), and **Continental Airlines Vacations** (© 800/634-5555; www.coolvacations.com).

One of the biggest packagers in the Northeast, **Liberty Travel** (© 888/271-1584; www.libertytravel.com) boasts a full-page ad in many Sunday papers. You won't get much in the way of service, but you will get a good deal.

Before you book your package through a tour company, remember that with a few phone calls and e-mails, you can often organize the same thing on your own without having to pay the sometimes-hefty service fee.

9 Getting Around

BY PLANE

Flying is one of the best ways to get around Costa Rica. Because the country is quite small, flights are short and not too expensive. The domestic airlines of Costa Rica are **Sansa** (© 506/221-9414; www.flysansa.com), which offers a free shuttle bus from its downtown office to the airport, and **Travelair** ☆ (© 506/220-3054; www.travelair-costarica.com).

I personally highly recommend Travelair over Sansa. Sansa has an unfriendly and unwieldy reservation system, it frequently overbooks flights, and it has been known to change schedules with little notice. The one thing Sansa has going for it is that it flies out of the main airport, so it is

possible, albeit risky, to make same-day connections with international flights. Flight times are generally between 20 minutes and a little over an hour. Sansa operates from San José's Juan Santamaría International Airport, while Travelair operates from **Tobís Bolaños International Airport** in Pavas, 4 miles (6.4km) from San José. The ride from downtown to Pavas takes about 10 minutes, and a metered taxi fare should cost $6 to $8. The ride from the airport to downtown is a different story—most taxis refuse to use their meter, and the standard fee is set at double the metered rate, around $10 to $12.

In the high season (late November to late April), be sure to book

> ### Tips   What Travel Agents Don't Tell You
>
> You don't have to spend the night in San José. Some travel agents will encourage you to do this so that they can stick you with unnecessary and outrageous airport transfer fees—twice. But don't listen to them. If your flight arrives in San José early in the day, you should consider heading straight to your first destination. It's easy to catch a domestic flight to Liberia or Tamarindo from the San José airport. You'll have to carry your bags the 250 yards or so between the international and domestic termi- nals (or take a cab), and you'll also have to use the less reliable carrier Sansa, rather than Travelair, for your domestic flight (Travelair flights leave from an entirely different airport). But if this doesn't cause you any grief, you can leave the United States early in the morning and be loung- ing on the beach before sunset (and in some cases, by lunchtime).
>
> You can also drive to your first destination if you arrive early enough. However, if the thought of doing a 4-hour drive immediately after your 5-hour flight seems exhausting, my best advice is head to a hotel like Vista del Valle Plantation Inn, which is 20 minutes from the airport toward Guanacaste, Monteverde, and Arenal. You'll cut lots of time off your drive the next day. You can either grab your rental car at the airport or have it dropped off at your hotel.

reservations well in advance. For Sansa flights, you don't have to call Costa Rica to make reservations—you can book flights through **Grupo Taca** (© **800/535-8780;** www.grupotaca. com). But *be careful:* I've heard horror stories of ticket vouchers issued in the United States not being accepted in Costa Rica; always reconfirm once you arrive. You can book flights on Travelair via the Web or e-mail. If you plan to return to San José, buy a round-trip ticket—it's always nice to have a confirmed seat, and with Trav- elair you'll save a little money.

BY BUS

This is by far the most economical way to get around Costa Rica. Buses are inexpensive and relatively well maintained, and they go nearly every- where. There are three types: **Local buses** are the cheapest and slowest; they stop frequently and are generally a bit dilapidated. **Express buses** run between San José and most beach towns and major cities; they some- times operate only on weekends and holidays. A few **luxury buses** and

minibuses drive to destinations fre- quented by foreign travelers. For details on how to get to various desti- nations from San José, see the "Get- ting There" sections of the regional chapters that follow.

BY CAR

Renting a car in Costa Rica is no idle proposition. The roads are riddled with potholes, most rural intersections are unmarked, and for some reason, sitting behind the wheel of a car seems to turn peaceful Ticos into homicidal maniacs. But unless you want to see the country from the window of a bus (inconvenient) or pay exorbitant amounts for private transfers (expen- sive), renting a car is still your best option for independent exploring. Four-wheel-drives are particularly use- ful in the rainy season (May to mid- November) and for navigating the bumpy, poorly paved roads year- round.

Be forewarned, however: Although rental cars no longer bear special license plates, they are still readily identifiable to thieves and frequently targeted. (Nothing is ever safe in a car in Costa Rica, although parking in guarded parking lots helps.) Transit police also seem to target tourists. Never pay money directly to a police officer who stops you for any traffic violation.

Before driving off with a rental car, be sure that you inspect the exterior and point out to the rental-company representative every tiny scratch, dent, tear, or any other damage. It's a common practice with many Costa Rican car-rental companies to claim that you owe payment for minor dings and dents the company finds when you return the car. Also, if you get into an accident, be sure the rental company doesn't try to bill you for a higher amount than the deductible on your rental contract.

These caveats aren't meant to scare you off from driving in Costa Rica. Thousands of tourists rent cars here every year, and the large majority of them encounter no problems. Just keep your wits about you.

Note: It's sometimes cheaper to reserve a car in your home country, rather than book when you arrive in Costa Rica. If you know you'll be

renting a car, it's always wise to reserve it well in advance for the high season, as the rental fleet still can't match demand.

Among the agencies operating in Costa Rica are: **Alamo Rent A Car** (© **506/441-1260** at the airport, or 506/233-7733 in downtown San José; www.alamocostarica.com); **Avis Rent A Car** (© **800/331-1212** in the U.S., 506/442-1321 at the airport, or 506/293-2222 in downtown San José; www.avis.com); **Budget Rent A Car** (© **800/527-0700** in the U.S., 506/441-4444 at the airport, or 506/223-3284 in downtown San José; www.budget.co.cr); **Hertz Rent A Car** (© **800/654-3131** in the U.S., 506/441-0097 at the airport, or 506/221-1818 in downtown San José; www.hertz.com); **National Car Rental** (© **800/328-4567** in the U.S., 506/441-6533 at the airport, or 506/290-8787 in downtown San José; www.natcar.com); **Payless Rent A Car** (© **800/582-7432** in the U.S., 506/441-9366 at the airport, or 506/257-0026 in downtown San José; www.paylesscr.com); and **Thrifty Car Rental** (© **800/367-2277** in the U.S., 506/442-8585 at the airport, or

---

Tips Car-Rental Tips

While it's preferable to use the coverage provided by your home auto-insurance policy or credit card, check carefully to see if the coverage really holds in Costa Rica. Many policies exclude four-wheel-drive vehicles and off-road driving—much of Costa Rica can in fact be considered off-road. While it's possible at some car-rental agencies to waive the insurance charges, you will have to pay all damages before leaving the country if you're in an accident. If you do take the insurance, you can expect a deductible of between $500 and $1,250. At some agencies, you can buy additional insurance to lower the deductible. To rent a car in Costa Rica, you must be at least 21 years old and have a valid driver's license and a major credit card in your name. See the "Getting Around" section of chapter 4 for details on renting a car in San José. You can also rent cars in Quepos, Jacó, Liberia, Playa Conchal, Tamarindo, La Fortuna, and Limón.

506/257-3434 in downtown San José). For more listings of Costa Rican car-rental agencies, see "By Car" under "Getting Around," in chapter 4.

GASOLINE Gasoline is sold as "regular" and "super"; both are unleaded. "Super" is just higher octane. Diesel is available at almost every gas station as well. Most rental cars run on "super," but always ask your rental agent what type of gas your car takes. When going off to remote places, try to leave with a full tank of gas since gas stations can be hard to find. If you need to gas up in a small town, you can sometimes get gasoline from enterprising families who sell it by the liter from their houses. Look for hand-lettered signs that say gasolina. As of press time, a liter of "super" cost 215 colones, or roughly $2.50 per gallon.

ROAD CONDITIONS The awful road conditions in San José and throughout the country are legendary, and deservedly so. Despite constant promises to fix the problem, the hot sun, hard rain, and rampant corruption have continued to outpace any progress made toward improving the condition. Even paved roads are often badly potholed, so stay alert. Road conditions get especially tricky during the rainy season, when heavy rains and runoff can destroy a stretch of pavement in the blink of an eye.

Route numbers are rarely used on road signs in Costa Rica, though there are frequent signs listing the number of kilometers to various towns or cities. In recent years, the Transportation Ministry began placing helpful markers at major intersections and turnoffs, but your best bets for on-road directions are still billboards and advertisements for hotels located at your destination.

RENTER'S INSURANCE If you already hold **your own car-insurance policy** at home, you are most likely covered in the United States for loss of or damage to a rental car, and liability in case of injury to any other party involved in an accident. But coverage doesn't always extend outside the United States, however. Be sure to find out whether you'll be covered in Costa Rica, whether your policy extends to all persons who will be driving the rental car, how much liability is covered in case an outside party is injured in an accident, and whether the *type* of vehicle you are renting is included under your contract. (Rental trucks, sport-utility vehicles, and four-wheel-drive vehicles may not be covered.)

Most **major credit cards** provide some degree of coverage as well—provided they were used to pay for the rental. Again, terms vary widely, so be sure to call your credit-card company directly before you rent. Usually, if you are **uninsured or driving abroad,** your credit card provides primary coverage as long as you decline the rental agency's insurance. This means that the credit card will cover damage or theft of a rental car for the full cost of the vehicle. If you already have insurance, your credit card will provide secondary coverage—which basically covers your deductible. *Credit cards will not cover liability* or the cost of injury to an outside party and/or damage to an outside party's vehicle. If you do not hold an insurance policy, you may seriously want to consider purchasing additional liability insurance from your rental company. Be sure to check the terms, however: Some rental agencies cover liability only if the renter is not at fault; even then, the rental company's obligation varies from state to state.

Bear in mind that each credit-card company has its own peculiarities, so it's important to call your own credit-card company for details before relying on this coverage.

The basic insurance coverage offered by most car-rental companies, known as the **Loss/Damage Waiver**

(LDW) or **Collision Damage Waiver (CDW),** can cost as much as $20 per day. It usually covers the full value of the vehicle with no deductible if an outside party causes an accident or other damage to the rental car. Liability coverage varies according to the company policy. If you are at fault in an accident, however, you will be covered for the full replacement value of the car but not for liability. Most rental companies will require a police report in order to process any claims you file, but your private insurer will not be notified of the accident.

MAPS Car-rental agencies and the ICT information centers (see "Visitor Information" at the beginning of this chapter) at the airport and in downtown San José have adequate road maps. Other sources in San José are **Seventh Street Books,** Calle 7 between Avenidas Central and 1 (☎ **506/256-8251**); **Libreria Lehmann,** Avenida Central between Calles 1 and 3 (☎ **506/223-1212**); and **Librería Universal,** Avenida Central between Calles Central and 1 (☎ **506/222-2222**).

DRIVING RULES A current foreign driver's license is valid for the first 3 months you are in Costa Rica. Seat belts are required for the driver and front-seat passengers. Motorcyclists must wear a helmet. Highway police use radar, so keep to the speed limit (usually between 60 and 90kmph/37 and 56 m.p.h.) if you don't want to get pulled over. Maybe it just seems this way, but the police seem to target rental cars. Never give the police any money. Speeding tickets can be charged to your credit card for up to a year after you leave the country if they are not paid before departure.

BREAKDOWNS Be warned that emergency services, both vehicular and medical, are extremely limited once you leave San José, and their availability is directly related to the remoteness of your location at the time of breakdown. You'll find service stations spread over the entire length of the Interamerican Highway, and most of these have tow trucks and mechanics. The major towns of Puntarenas, Liberia, Quepos, San Isidro, Palmar, and Golfito all have hospitals, and most other moderately sized cities and tourist destinations have some sort of clinic or health-services provider.

If you're involved in an accident, you should contact the **National Insurance Institute (INS)** at ☎ **800/ 800-8000.** You should probably also call the **Transit Police** (☎ **506/222-9330** or 506/222-9245); if they have a unit close by, they'll send one. An official transit-police report will greatly facilitate any insurance claim. If you can't get help from any of these, try to get written statements from any witnesses. Finally, you can also call ☎ **911,** and they should be able to redirect your call to the appropriate agency.

If the police do show up, you've got a 50/50 chance of finding them helpful or downright antagonistic. Many officers are unsympathetic to the problems of what they perceive to be rich tourists running around in fancy cars with lots of expensive toys and trinkets. Success and happy endings run about equal with horror stories.

If you don't speak Spanish, expect added difficulty in any emergency or stressful situation. Don't expect that rural (or urban) police officers, hospital personnel, service-station personnel, or mechanics will speak English.

Lastly, a little tip: If your car breaks down and you're unable to get well off the road, check to see whether there are reflecting triangles in the trunk. If there are, place them as a warning for approaching traffic, arranged in a wedge that starts at the shoulder about 100 feet back and nudges gradually toward your car. If your car has no triangles, try to create a similar warning marker using a pile of leaves or branches.

BY FERRY

There are four different ferries operating across the Gulf of Nicoya. Three are car ferries: one across the Río Tempisque, one from Puntarenas to Playa Naranjo, and one from Puntarenas to Paquera; and one is a passenger ferry that runs from Puntarenas to Paquera.

HITCHHIKING

Although buses serve most towns in Costa Rica, service can be infrequent in the remote regions, and so local people often hitchhike to get to their destination sooner. If you're driving a car, people will frequently ask you for a ride. In rural areas, a hitchhiker carrying a machete is not necessarily a great danger, but use your judgment. Hitchhiking is not recommended on major roadways or in urban areas. In rural areas it's usually pretty safe. However, women should be extremely cautious about hitchhiking anywhere in Costa Rica. If you choose to hitchhike, keep in mind that if a bus doesn't go to your destination, there probably aren't too many cars going there, either. Good luck.

SUGGESTED ITINERARIES

If You Have 1 Week

Day 1 Visit the museums and the National Theater in San José.

Day 2 Make an excursion to the Orosi Valley, Lankester Gardens, and Irazú Volcano.

Days 3 & 4 Travel to Monteverde (or another cloud-forest region) and spend a day exploring the cloud forest.

Days 5 & 6 Head to one of the many Pacific coast beaches. I'd recommend Manuel Antonio for its accessibility and range of accommodations and activities.

Day 7 Return to San José.

If You Have 2 Weeks

Day 1 Visit the museums and the National Theater in San José.

Days 2 & 3 Make an excursion to the Orosi Valley, Lankester Gardens, and Irazú Volcano one day and go river-rafting on the other day.

Days 4 & 5 Travel to Lake Arenal to see the eruptions of Arenal Volcano, soak in some hot springs, and maybe go to Caño Negro National Wildlife Refuge.

Days 6 & 7 Travel to Monteverde (or another cloud-forest region) and explore the cloud forest.

Day 8 Explore Rincón de la Vieja or Santa Rosa National Park.

Days 9, 10, 11 & 12 Spend these days relaxing on a beach in Guanacaste, or perhaps explore a more remote location on the Osa Peninsula or along the Caribbean coast.

Days 13 & 14 Fly to Tortuguero National Park and spend a night there, returning the next day by boat and bus.

10 Spanish-Language Programs

As more and more people travel to Costa Rica with the intention of learning Spanish, the number of options continues to increase. You can find courses of varying lengths and degrees of intensiveness, and many that include cultural activities and day excursions. Many of these schools have reciprocal relationships with U.S. universities, so in some cases you can even arrange for college credit. Most Spanish schools can also arrange for homestays with a middle-class Tico family for a total-immersion experience. Classes are often small, or even one-on-one, and can last anywhere from 2 to 8 hours a day. Listed below are some of the larger and more established Spanish-language schools, with approximate costs. Most are located in

San José, but there are also schools in Heredia, Monteverde, Manuel Antonio, Playa Flamingo, and Tamarindo (I'd certainly rather spend 2 weeks or a month in one of these spots than in San José). Contact the schools for the most current price information.

Centro Cultural Costarricense Norteamericano, A.P. 1489-1000, San José, Costa Rica (✆ **506/ 207-7500;** www.cccncr.com), is an extension of the U.S. embassy and government programs in Costa Rica. Its facilities are the most extensive of any language school in the country. A 2-week intensive course with 4 hours of instruction per day costs $500. Homestays are also available for $175 per week.

Centro Lingüístico Conversa (★, A.P. 17-1007, Centro Colón, San José, Costa Rica (✆ **800/354-5036** in the U.S. and Canada, or 506/221-7649 in Costa Rica; www.conversa.net), has classes in both San José and Santa Ana (a suburb of the capital city). A 2-week course here with 4 hours of classes each day, including room and board with a Costa Rican family, costs between $850 and $1,400 for one person, depending on which campus you choose and the level of luxury you're looking for.

Centro Panamericano de Idiomas (CPI) (★, A.P. 151-3007, San Joaquín de Flores, Heredia, Costa Rica (✆ **888/682-0054** in the U.S., or ✆ and fax 506/265-6866 or 506/ 265-6213 in Costa Rica; www. cpi-edu.com). This school has three campuses: one in the quiet suburban town of Heredia, another in Monteverde, and a new facility in Playa Flamingo. A 4-week program, with 4 hours of classes per day and a homestay, costs $1,260.

CPH Language and Cross-Cultural School, A.P. 25-6150, Santa Ana, Costa Rica (✆ **888/233-1638** in the U.S., or ✆ and fax 506/282-9920 in Costa Rica; www.spanishincostarica. com), is located in the quiet western suburb of Santa Ana. A 2-week course with 4 hours of class per day, plus homestay, costs $765.

Costa Rican Language Academy, A.P. 336-2070, San José, Costa Rica (✆ **800/854-6057** in the U.S., or 506/233-8914; www.learn-spanish. com), has intensive programs with classes only on Monday through Thursday, to give students a chance to make longer weekend excursions. They also integrate Latin dance and Costa Rican cooking classes into the program. A 2-week class with 4 hours of class per day, plus homestay, costs $550–$625.

Costa Rica Spanish Institute (COSI), A.P. 1366-2050, San Pedro, Costa Rica (✆ **800/771-5184** in the U.S. or 506/253-9272 in Costa Rica; www.cosi.co.cr), offers small classes in the San Pedro neighborhood of San José, as well as a program at the Pacific beach of Manuel Antonio. The cost is $315 per week with a homestay in San José; at the beach it's $370, with room and board extra.

Forester Instituto Internacional (★, A.P. 6945-1000, San José, Costa Rica (✆ **506/225-3155,** or 506/ 225-0135; www.fores.com), is located 75 meters (82 yd.) south of the Automercado in the Los Yoses district of San José. I've received glowing reports from satisfied customers here. The cost of a 4-week language course with a homestay and excursions is approximately $1,360.

Institute for Central American Development Studies (ICADS) (★★, A.P. 3-2070, Sabanilla, San José, Costa Rica (Dept. 826, P.O. Box 025216, Miami, FL 33102-5216, in the U.S.; ✆ **506/225-0508;** www.icadscr.com). In addition to having one of the best and most extensive field-work and volunteer programs in Costa Rica, this institution runs quality Spanish-language immersion programs. A 4-week course with homestay costs $1,600. **Instituto Británico** 🏷️, A.P. 8184-1000, San José, Costa Rica (📞 **506/225-0256** or 506/234-9054; www.institutobritanico.co.cr). This venerable institution has installations in the Los Yoses neighborhood of San José. A bit more attention seems to be paid to teacher training and selection here than at other institutions around town. A 2-week course with 4 hours of classes per day and homestay costs $600.

Instituto Interamericano de Idiomas (Intensa), Calle 33 between Avenidas 1 and 3 (A.P. 8110-1000), San José, Costa Rica (📞 **506/224-6353;** www.intensa.com), offers 2- to 4-week programs. A 4-week, 4-hour-per-day program with a homestay costs $1,150 to $1,420.

La Escuela Idiomas D'Amore 🏷️, A.P. 67, Quepos, Costa Rica (📞 and fax **262/367-8598** in the U.S. or 📞 and fax 506/777-1143 in Costa Rica; www.escueladamore.com), is situated in the lush surroundings of Manuel Antonio National Park. A 2-week conversational Spanish course, including a homestay and two meals daily, costs $980. Fifteen percent of your tuition is donated to the World Wildlife Fund. This is a much nicer environment than San José for learning Spanish (for most everything else too, in fact).

Wayra Instituto de Español (📞 and fax **506/653-0359;** www.spanish-wayra.co.cr). This place is located in the beach town of Tamarindo. A week of classes, 4 hours per day, will run you $200. With a homestay, the cost is $320 to $350.

11 Tips on Accommodations

Tourism insiders had been predicting it for years: Despite the ever-increasing number of visitors, tough times and fierce competition have hit Costa Rican hoteliers. When the Costa Rican tourist boom began in the late 1980s, hotels began popping up like mushrooms after a few days of rain. In recent years, the country's first true mega-resorts have opened, and several more are under construction and near completion. There is a hotel glut, and this is good news for travelers and bargain-hunters. A weeding-out period has begun, and hotels that want to survive are being forced to reduce their rates and provide better service.

Glut notwithstanding, there are still few hotels or resorts here offering the sort of luxury you'll find in Hawaii or the Caribbean. Sure, there are hotels that meet international standards, but Costa Rica is not yet a luxury-resort destination (luckily, prices have remained a whole lot cheaper than

those in the Caribbean and Hawaii, too—Costa Rica's hotels are still a bargain by comparison). One item you're likely to want to bring with you is a beach towel. Your hotel might not provide one at all, and even if it does, it might be awfully thin.

Throughout this book, I've separated hotel listings into several broad categories: **Very Expensive,** $150 and up; **Expensive,** $100 to $150; **Moderate,** $50 to $100; and **Inexpensive,** under $50 double. *Rates given in this book do not include the 16.3% room taxes.* These taxes will add considerably to the cost of your room. Also note that with rooms at the beach that cost under $25, you usually don't get hot water.

HOTEL OPTIONS

Upscale travelers are finally starting to get their due in Costa Rica. It's taken time, but spurred on by the example and standards of several international

> **Tips Hotel Tip**
>
> If you are booking directly with your hotel (either by phone/fax or e-mail), remember that most hotels are accustomed to paying as much as 20% in commission to agents and wholesalers. It never hurts to ask if it will pass some of that on to you. Don't be afraid to bargain.

chains, service and amenities have been improving across the board, and particularly in the upscale market. The Marriott Los Sueños and Meliá Playa Conchal resorts are still the only large beach resorts able to please the demanding luxury traveler, but the soon-to-be-completed Four Seasons resort should up the ante. There are also several wonderful high-end boutique hotels, both in San José and the central valley, and around the country. The country's strong suit is its **moderately priced hotels.** In the $50-to-$100 price range, you'll find comfortable, and sometimes outstanding, accommodations almost anywhere in the country. However, room size and quality vary quite a bit within this price range, so don't expect the kind of uniformity you find in the United States.

If you're even more budget- or bohemian-minded, there are quite a few good deals for less than $50 per double room. But beware: Budget-oriented lodgings often feature shared bathrooms, and either cold-water showers or showers heated by electrical heat-coil units mounted at the shower head. These are affectionately known as "suicide showers." If you find your hotel has one, do not try to adjust it while the water is running. Unless specifically noted, all the rooms I've listed in this guide have a private bathroom.

Bed-and-breakfasts have also been proliferating. Though the majority of these are in the San José area, you will now find B&Bs (often gringo-owned and -operated) throughout the country. Another welcome hotel trend in the San José area is the renovation and conversion of old homes into small hotels. Most of these hotels are in the Barrio Amón district of downtown San José, which means you'll sometimes have to put up with noise and exhaust fumes, but these establishments have more character than any other hotels in the country. You'll find similar hotels in the **Paseo Colón** and **Los Yoses** districts.

Costa Rica has been riding the ecotourism wave, and there are now small nature-oriented **ecolodges** throughout the country. These lodges offer opportunities to see wildlife (including sloths, monkeys, and hundreds of species of birds) and learn about tropical forests. They range from Spartan facilities catering primarily to scientific researchers to luxury accommodations that are among the finest in the country. Keep in mind that though the nightly room rates at these lodges are often quite moderate, the price of a visit starts to climb when you throw in transportation (often on chartered planes), guided excursions, and meals. Also, just because your travel agent can book a reservation at most of these lodges doesn't mean they're not remote. Make sure to find out how you will be getting to and from your ecolodge and just what tours and services are included in your stay. Then think long and hard about whether you really want to put up with hot, humid weather (cool and wet in the cloud forests), biting insects, rugged transportation, and strenuous hikes to see wildlife.

A couple of uniquely Costa Rican accommodation types you may encounter are the *apartotel* and the *cabina.* An apartotel is just what it sounds like: an apartment hotel, where you'll get a full kitchen and one or two bedrooms, along with daily maid service. Cabinas are Costa Rica's version of cheap vacation lodging. They're very inexpensive and very basic—often just cinder-block buildings divided into small rooms. Occasionally you'll find a cabina where the units are actually cabins, but these are a rarity. Cabinas often have clothes-washing sinks or *pilas,* and some come with kitchenettes, since they cater primarily to Tico families on vacation.

12 Tips on Dining

Simply put, Costa Rican cuisine is less than memorable. San José remains the unquestioned gastronomic capital of the country, and here you can find the cuisines of the world served with formal service at moderate prices. At the most expensive restaurant in San José, you'll have to drink a lot of wine to spend more than $40 per person on dinner. It gets even cheaper outside the city. There are several excellent French and Italian restaurants around the San José area, as well as Peruvian, Japanese, Swiss, and Spanish establishments.

Costa Rica is a major producer and exporter of beef, and consequently, San José has plenty of steakhouses. Unfortunately, quantity doesn't mean quality. Unless you go to one of the better restaurants or steakhouses, you will probably be served rather tough steaks, cut rather thin.

One recent development is worth noting, and it is slowly making my opening caveat untrue: With the increase in international tourism and the need to please a more sophisticated palate, local chefs have begun to create a "nouvelle Costa Rican cuisine," updating time-worn recipes and using traditional ingredients in creative ways. Unlike most visitors to Costa Rica, however, this phenomenon hasn't traveled far outside of downtown San José.

Outside of the capital, your options get very limited, and quickly. In fact, many beach resorts are so remote that you have no choice but to eat in the hotel's dining room. Even on the more accessible beaches, the only choices aside from the hotel dining rooms are cheap local places or overpriced tourist traps serving indifferent meals. At remote jungle lodges, the food is usually served buffet or family style and can range from bland to inspired, depending on who's doing the cooking at the moment, and turnover is high.

If you're looking for cheap eats, you'll find them in little restaurants known as *sodas,* which are the equivalent of diners in the United States. At a soda you'll have lots of choices: rice and beans with steak, rice and beans with fish, rice and beans with chicken, or, for vegetarians, rice and beans. You get the picture. Rice and beans are standard Tico fare, and are served at all three meals a day. Also, though there is plenty of seafood available throughout the country, at sodas it's all too often served fried.

Costa Ricans love to eat, and they love to have a view when they eat. Almost anywhere you go in the country, if there's a view, there will be a restaurant taking advantage of it. These restaurants are often called *miradores.* If you are driving around the country, don't miss an opportunity to dine with a view at some little roadside restaurant. The food may not be fantastic, but the scenery will be.

I have separated restaurant listings throughout this book into three price categories based on the average cost per person of a meal, including tax and service charge. The categories are **Expensive,** more than $20; **Moderate,** $10 to $20; and **Inexpensive,** less than $10. (Note, however, that individual items in the listings— entrees, for instance—do not include the sales or service taxes.) Keep in mind that there is an additional 13% sales tax, as well as a 10% service charge. Ticos rarely tip, but that doesn't mean you shouldn't. If the service was particularly good and attentive, you should probably leave a little extra.

13 Tips on Shopping

FOOD FADS   Buy coffee. Even if you're not a coffee drinker, you're bound to know someone who is, and coffee is the best buy in Costa Rica. **Café Britt** is the most common brand, sold in hotels and souvenir shops all over the country. Sold in light, dark, and espresso roasts, this is the best widely available brand.

There are several quite good boutique brands and blends available. If you're in **Manuel Antonio,** pick up your coffee at Cafe Milagro (see chapter 7), and if you're in **Monteverde,** you can get some excellent fresh-roasted beans at CASEM (see chapter 6).

Just be sure you're buying whole beans (*grano entero*) and not ground (*molido*). Packaged Costa Rican grinds are much finer than U.S. grinds and often have sugar mixed right in with the coffee.

Costa Rica also produces its own coffee liqueur (**Café Rica**) and a creme liqueur, both of which are quite inexpensive. These are best purchased in a liquor store or a grocery store. In fact, grocery stores are where I do my best gift shopping.

If you'd like to add a little spice to your life, **Tipica Tropical Sauce** produces a line of spicy salsas made from mango, pineapple, passion fruit, and tamarind. A small bottle costs around 75¢ and makes a great gift. **Salsa Lizano,** a flavorful green sauce used the same way we use steak sauce in the United States, is another condiment worth bringing home with you.

HANDCRAFTS   Costa Rica is not known for its handcrafts, though it does have a town, **Sarchí,** that's filled with handcraft shops. Sarchí is best known as the home of the colorfully painted Costa Rican oxcart, reproductions of which are manufactured in various scaled-down sizes. These make excellent gifts. (Larger oxcarts can be easily disassembled and shipped to your home.) There's also a lot of furniture made here.

So scant are the country's hand craft offerings that most tourist shops sell Guatemalan clothing, Panamanian appliquéed textiles, El Salvadoran painted wood souvenirs, and Nicaraguan rocking chairs.

The small town of **Guaitíl,** in central Guanacaste, is famous for its pottery. You can find examples of this low-fired simple ceramic work in many gift shops.

There's quite a bit of Costa Rican wood carving, but it is, for the most part, either tourist-souvenir wooden bowls, napkin holders, and the like, or elegant and expensive art pieces. One exception is the work of **Barry Biensanz,** whose excellent hardwood creations are sold at better gift shops around the country.

COSTA RICAN SPECIALTIES   A few other items worth keeping an eye out for include **reproductions of pre-Columbian gold jewelry and carved-stone figurines.** The former are available either in solid gold, silver, or gold-plated. The latter, though interesting, are extremely heavy.

On the streets of San José you'll see a lot of **hammocks** for sale. I personally find the Costa Rican hammocks a little crude and unstable. The same vendors usually have single-person hanging chairs, which are strung similarly to the full-size hammocks and are a better bet.

Finally, one new item you'll see at gift shops around the country is **Cuban cigars.** Although these are illegal to bring into the United States, they are perfectly legal and readily available in Costa Rica.

FAST FACTS: Costa Rica

Business Hours Banks are usually open Monday through Friday from 9am to 3pm, though many have begun to offer extended hours. Offices are open Monday through Friday from 8am to 5pm (many close for an hour at lunch). Stores are generally open Monday through Saturday from 9am to 6pm (many close for an hour at lunch). Stores in modern malls generally stay open until 8 or 9pm and don't close for lunch. Most bars are open until 1 or 2am.

Cameras/Film Most types of film are available, as are developing services. However, prices are higher than in the United States, so bring plenty of film with you and wait until you get home for processing.

Climate See section 5, "When to Go," earlier in this chapter.

Currency See section 4, "Money," earlier in this chapter.

Documents Required See section 3, "Entry Requirements & Customs," earlier in this chapter.

Driving Rules See section 9, "Getting Around," earlier in this chapter.

Drug Laws Drug laws in Costa Rica are strict, so stay away from marijuana and cocaine. Many prescription drugs are sold over the counter here, but often the names are different from those in the United States and Europe. It's always best to have a prescription from a doctor.

Electricity The standard in Costa Rica is the same as in the United States: 110 volts AC (60 cycles). However, three-pronged outlets can be scarce, so it's helpful to bring along an adapter.

Embassies/Consulates The following embassies and consulates are located in San José: **United States Embassy,** in front of Centro Commercial, on the road to Pavas (© **506/220-3939**); **Canadian Consulate,** Oficentro Ejecutivo La Sabana, Edificio 5 (© **506/296-4149**); **British Embassy,** Paseo Colón between Calles 38 and 40 (© **506/258-2025**). There are no Australian or New Zealand embassies in San José.

Emergencies In case of an emergency, dial © **911** (which should have an English-speaking operator); for an ambulance, call © **128**; to report a fire, call © **118**; if 911 doesn't work, you can contact the police at © **506/222-1365** or 506/221-5337 and hopefully they can find someone who speaks English.

Holidays See section 5, "When to Go," earlier in this chapter.

Information See section 2, "Visitor Information," earlier in this chapter, and see the regional chapters that follow for local information offices.

Internet Access Staying connected on the road is getting easier. Internet cafes have popped up at most major tourist destinations. Many hotels allow guests to send and receive e-mail. It's best to set up a free Web-based mail account with someone like Hotmail, Yahoo!, Netscape, etc., before you leave for Costa Rica, since you are most likely to have only Web (and not POP) access. Rates run between $1 and $4 per hour.

Language Spanish is the official language of Costa Rica. *Berlitz Latin-American Spanish Phrasebook and Dictionary* (Berlitz Guides, 1992) is probably the best phrase book to bring with you. However, in most tourist areas, you'd be surprised by how well Costa Ricans speak English.

Laundry Laundromats are few and far between in Costa Rica—more common are hotel laundry services, which can sometimes be expensive. For listings of Laundromats, see individual city and town sections.

Liquor Laws Alcoholic beverages are sold every day of the week throughout the year, with the exception of the 2 days before Easter and the 2 days before and after a presidential election. The legal drinking age is 18, though it's almost never enforced.

Mail Mail to the United States usually takes a little over a week to reach its destination. At press time, it cost 70 colones (23¢) to mail a letter to the United States; 90 colones (30¢) to Europe; 55 colones (18¢) for a postcard. Given the Costa Rican postal service's track record, I recommend paying an extra 165 colones (55¢) to have anything of any value certified.

A post office is called a *correo* in Spanish. You can get stamps at the post office and at some gift shops in large hotels.

If you're sending mail *to* Costa Rica, it generally takes between 10 and 14 days to reach San José, although it can take as much as a month to get to the more remote corners of the country. Plan ahead. Also, note that many hotels and ecolodges have mailing addresses in the United States. Always use these addresses when writing from North America or Europe. Never send cash, checks, or valuables through the Costa Rican mail system.

Maps The **Costa Rican Tourist Board** (ICT; see section 2 of this chapter) can usually provide you with good maps of both Costa Rica and San José. See "By Car" under section 9, "Getting Around," for names of bookstores that sell good maps.

Newspapers/Magazines There are six Spanish-language dailies in Costa Rica and one English-language weekly, the *Tico Times.* In addition, you can get *Time, Newsweek,* and several U.S. newspapers at some hotel gift shops and a few of the bookstores in San José. If you understand Spanish, *La Nación* is the paper of record. Its "Viva" section lists what's going on in the world of music, theater, dance, and more.

Police In most cases, dial ℂ **911** for the police, and you should be able to get someone who speaks English on the line. Other numbers for the **Judicial Police** are ℂ **506/222-1365** and 506/221-5337. The numbers for the **Traffic Police (Policia de Transito)** are ℂ **506/222-9330** and 506/222-9245.

Radio/TV There are about 10 local TV channels; cable and satellite TV from the United States are also common. There are scores of radio stations on the AM and FM dials. 107.5 FM is my favorite English-language station, with a wide range of musical programming, as well as news and some talk shows.

Rest Rooms These are known as *sanitarios, servicios sanitarios,* or *baños.* They are marked *damas* (women) and *hombres* or *caballeros* (men). Public rest rooms are hard to come by. You will almost never find a public rest room in a city park or downtown area. There are usually public rest rooms at most national-park entrances, and much less frequently inside the national park (there are usually plenty of trees and bushes). In the towns and cities it gets much trickier. One must count on the generosity of some hotel or restaurant. Same goes for most beaches. However, most restaurants, and to a lesser degree hotels, will let you use their facilities, especially if you buy a soft drink or something. Bus and gas stations often have rest rooms, but many of these are pretty grim.

Safety Though most of Costa Rica is safe, crime has become much more common in recent years. San José is known for its pickpockets, so never carry a wallet in your back pocket. A woman should keep a tight grip on her purse (keep it tucked under your arm). Thieves also target gold chains, cameras and video cameras, prominent jewelry, and nice sunglasses. Be sure not to leave valuables in your hotel room. Don't park a car on the street in Costa Rica, especially in San José; there are plenty of public parking lots around the city.

Rental cars generally stick out, and they are easily spotted by thieves, who know that such cars are likely to be full of expensive camera equipment, money, and other valuables. Don't ever leave anything of value in a car parked on the street, not even for a moment.

Public intercity buses are also frequent targets of stealthy thieves. Never check your bags into the hold of a bus if you can avoid it. If this can't be avoided, keep your eye on what leaves the hold. If you put your bags in an overhead rack, be sure you can see the bags at all times. Try not to fall asleep.

See also section 6 of this chapter, "Health & Insurance."

Taxes All hotels charge 16.3% tax. Restaurants charge 13% tax and also add on a 10% service charge, for a total of 23% more on your bill. There is an airport departure tax of $17.

The **departure tax** is actually a separate little piece of paper that you must fill out (name, passport number, etc.) and that has a few official governmental stamps on the back. The tax/piece of paper is turned in to Immigration after check-in, as you enter the gate area. You must pay this tax prior to departure. You can buy the stamps and little piece of paper at several desks inside the airport, and at some of the individual airline check-in counters. You can also buy them at most travel agencies in San José. I no longer recommend purchasing them from the independent agents roaming around passenger drop-off points at the airport. Although it's generally safe, there have been instances where they have sold already-canceled stamps, which were then not accepted inside the airport, and the unwitting traveler has had to pay the tax twice.

Taxis Taxis are common and inexpensive in San José but harder to find and more expensive in rural areas. In San José, taxis are supposed to charge metered fares. Outside of the city and on longer rides, be sure to agree on a price beforehand. For more information on taxis in San José, see "Getting Around" in chapter 4.

Telegrams/Wiring Money **Western Union** (© 800/777-7777 in Costa Rica, or 506/283-6336) has numerous offices around San José and in several major towns and cities around the country. It offers a secure and rapid, although pricey, money-wire service, as well as telegram service. A $100 wire will cost around $15, and a $1,000 wire will cost around $50. **Radiográfica** (© **506/287-0087**), at Calle 1 and Avenida 5 in San José, also has telegram service.

Telephones/Faxes Costa Rica has an excellent phone system, with a dial tone similar to that heard in the United States. All phone numbers in Costa Rica have seven digits. For information, dial © **113**.

A pay phone costs around 10 colones (3¢) per minute. Pay phones will either take a calling card, or 5-, 10-, or 20-colón coins. Calling cards are becoming more and more prominent, and you can purchase them in a host of gift shops and pharmacies. However, there are several competing calling-card companies and certain cards work only with certain phones. Others work with complicated touch-tone dialing sequences. Moreover, pay phones are generally hard to find and frequently unreliable. It is often best to call from your hotel, although you will likely be charged around 100–200 colones per call.

For making international calling-card and collect calls, you can reach an **AT&T** operator by dialing © **0-800-011-4114, MCI** by dialing © **0-800-012-2222, Sprint** by dialing © **0-800-013-0123, Canada Bell** by dialing © **0-800-015-1161, British Telecom** by dialing © **0-800-044-1044,** and a **Costa Rican international operator** by dialing © **116** (pay phones may sometimes require a coin deposit).

The Costa Rican telephone system allows direct international dialing, but it's expensive. To get an international line, dial 00 followed by the country code (1 for the U.S.) and number.

You can make international phone calls, as well as send faxes, from the **ICE office,** Avenida 2 between Calles 1 and 3, in San José (© **506/255-0444**). The office is open daily from 7am to 10pm. Faxes cost around $2 per page to the United States. (Many hotels will also offer the same service for a fee.) **Radiográfica** (© **506/287-0087**), at Calle 1 and Avenida 5 in San José, also has fax service.

To call Costa Rica from the United States, dial the international access code, 011, followed by the country code 506, then the local number.

Time Costa Rica is on central standard time (same as Chicago and St. Louis), 6 hours behind Greenwich mean time. Costa Rica does not use daylight saving time, so the time difference is an additional hour from April through October.

Tipping Tipping is not necessary in restaurants, where a 10% service charge is always added to your bill (along with a 13% tax). If service was particularly good, you can leave a little at your own discretion, but it's not mandatory. Porters and bellhops get around 75¢ per bag. You don't need to tip a taxi driver unless the service has been superior—a tip is not usually expected.

Useful Telephone Numbers For directory assistance, call © **113**; for international directory assistance, call © **124**; for the exact time, call © **112**.

Visas See section 3, "Entry Requirements & Customs," earlier in this chapter.

Water Though the water in San José is generally safe to drink, water quality varies outside of the city. Because many travelers have tender digestive tracts, I recommend playing it safe and sticking to bottled drinks as much as possible and avoiding ice.

3

The Active Vacation Planner

Although it's possible to come to Costa Rica and stay clean and dry, most visitors want to spend some time getting their hair wet, their feet muddy, and their adrenaline pumping. To many, tropical rain forests and cloud forests are the stuff of myth and legend. Partly because evolution is a slow process, and partly because much of the country's natural landscape is protected in national parks and biore- serves, Costa Rica's primary forests, which are open to adventurous travel- ers, are still in much the same state as when early explorers such as Colum- bus found them. And that's not even mentioning the array of lovely tropical beaches.

There are myriad approaches to planning an active vacation in Costa Rica. This chapter lays out your options, from tour operators who run multi-activity package tours that often include stays at ecolodges, to the best places in Costa Rica to pursue active endeavors (with listings of tour opera- tors, guides, and outfitters that spe- cialize in each), to an overview of the country's national parks and biore- serves, with suggestions on how to plan an independent itinerary. I've also listed some educational and vol- unteer travel options for those of you with a little more time on your hands and a desire to actively assist Costa Rica in the maintenance and preserva- tion of its natural wonders.

1 Organized Adventure Trips

Since many travelers have limited time and resources, organized ecotourism or adventure-travel packages, whether arranged by tour operators in the United States or Costa Rica, are a popular way of combining several activities. Bird watching, horseback riding, rafting, and hiking can be teamed with, say, visits to Monteverde Biological Cloud Forest Preserve and Manuel Antonio National Park.

Traveling with a group has several advantages over traveling independently: Your accommodations and transportation are arranged, and most (if not all) of your meals are included in the cost of a package. If your tour operator has a rea- sonable amount of experience and a decent track record, you should proceed to each of your destinations quickly without the snags and long delays that those traveling on their own can occasionally face. You'll also have the opportunity to meet like-minded souls who are interested in nature and active sports. Of course, you'll pay more for the convenience of having all your arrangements handled in advance.

In the best cases, group size is kept small (between 10 and 20 people), and tours are escorted by knowledgeable guides who are either naturalists or biolo- gists. Be sure to ask about difficulty levels when you're choosing a tour. While most companies offer "soft-adventure" packages that those in moderately good, but not phenomenal, shape can handle, others focus on more hard-core activities geared toward only seasoned athletes or adventure travelers.

U.S.-BASED ADVENTURE-TOUR OPERATORS

These agencies and operators specialize in well-organized and coordinated tours that cover your entire stay. Many travelers prefer to have everything arranged and confirmed before arriving in Costa Rica, and this is a good idea for first-timers and during the high season. Be warned: Most of these operators are not cheap, with 10-day tours generally costing in the neighborhood of $2,500 per person, not including airfare to Costa Rica.

Abercrombie & Kent ⊛/⊛ (© 800/323-7308; www.abercrombiekent.com) is a premier luxury-tour company that offers upscale trips around the globe, and has added several tours of Costa Rica to its menu. One interesting option offered by this outfitter is the 10-day family vacation that hits San José, Arenal, Monteverde, and Manuel Antonio. In addition to a naturalist guide, the trip carries a children's activity coordinator and offers baby-sitting at all of the hotels visited. The cost is $2,995 per adult (children slightly less).

Costa Rica Connections (© 800/345-7422 or 805/543-8823; www.crconnect.com) specializes in natural-history tours of major national parks. There is a complete range of independent packages and scheduled group departures for fishing, ecotourism, kayaking/rafting, and dive trips, plus a special family-oriented package.

Costa Rica Experts ⊛ (© 800/827-9046 or 773/935-1009; www.crexperts.com) offers a large menu of a la carte and scheduled departures, as well as day trips and adventure packages.

International Expeditions ⊛ (© 800/633-4734 or 205/428-1700; www.ietravel.com) specializes in independent programs and 10-day natural-history group tours.

Journeys International (© 800/255-8735 or 734/665-4407; www.journeys-intl.com) offers small-group natural-history tours guided by Costa Rican naturalists. Eight-day, 10-day, and multiweek itineraries are available.

Mountain Travel–Sobek (© 888/687-6235 or 510/527-8100; www.mtsobek.com) offers natural-history tours with naturalist guides. Ten-day itineraries can include visits to Corcovado and Tortuguero National Parks, Monteverde, and Arenal Volcano; activities include jungle walks, boat rides, snorkeling, and swimming. You'll spend your nights in nature lodges or out camping, with the exception of the first and last nights of each itinerary, which are spent in hotels in San José.

Overseas Adventure Travel (© 800/493-6824; www.oattravel.com) offers good-value natural-history and "soft-adventure" itineraries, with optional add-on excursions. Tours are limited to 16 people and are guided by naturalists. All accommodations are in small hotels, lodges, or tent camps. Their "Real Affordable Costa Rica" 12-day package lives up to its name at $1,800 per person, including round-trip airfare from Miami.

Wilderness Travel (© 800/368-2794 or 510/558-2488; www.wildernesstravel.com) specializes in 14-day natural-history and bird-watching group tours. The cost of the trip goes down as the size of the group goes up (minimum 6 people, maximum 15). Tours include visits to Corcovado and Tortuguero National Parks, Monteverde, Arenal Volcano, and Caño Negro National Wildlife Refuge, among other destinations.

In addition to these companies, many environmental organizations, including the **Sierra Club** (© 415/977-5630; www.sierraclub.org), the **Nature Conservancy** (© 800/628-6860; www.tnc.org), the **Smithsonian Institute** (© 202/357-2700; www.si.edu), and the **National Audubon Society** (© 800/274-4201 or 212/979-3066; www.audubon.org), periodically offer organized trips to Costa Rica.

COSTA RICAN TOUR AGENCIES

Since many U.S.-based companies subcontract portions of their tours to established Costa Rican companies, some travelers like to set up their tours directly with these companies, thereby cutting out the middleman. While that means these packages are often less expensive than those offered by U.S. companies, it doesn't mean they are cheap. You're still paying for the convenience of having all your arrangements handled for you.

There are scores of agencies in San José that offer a plethora of adventure options. These agencies can arrange everything from white-water rafting to sightseeing at one of the nearby volcanoes or a visit to a butterfly farm. While it's generally quite easy to arrange a day trip at the last minute, other tours are offered only when there are enough interested people or on set dates. It pays to contact a few of the companies before you leave the United States and find out what they might be doing when you arrive.

Costa Rica Expeditions ✴✴ (© 506/257-0766 or 506/222-0333; www.costaricaexpeditions.com) offers everything from 10-day tours covering the whole country, to 3-day/2-night and 2-day/1-night tours of Monteverde Biological Cloud Forest Preserve, Tortuguero National Park, and Corcovado National Park, where they run their own lodges. It also offers 1- to 2-day whitewater rafting trips and other excursions. All excursions include transportation, meals, and lodging. Its tours are some of the most expensive in the country, but it is the most consistently reliable outfitter as well (and its customer service is excellent). If you want to go out on your own, Costa Rica Expeditions can supply you with just transportation from place to place.

Costa Rica Sun Tours ✴ (© 506/296-7757; www.crsuntours.com) specializes in multiday tours that include stays at small country lodges for travelers interested in experiencing nature. Destinations include Arenal Volcano, with stays at the Arenal Observatory Lodge; Monteverde Cloud Forest, with stops in Poás and Sarchí; and Corcovado and Manuel Antonio National Parks, with overnight stays at Tiskita Jungle Lodge, Corcovado Tent Camp, Lapa Ríos, and Drake Bay Wilderness Lodge, among other accommodations.

Coast to Coast Adventures ✴✴ (© 506/280-8054; www.ctocadventures.com) has a unique excursion involving no motor vehicles. The company's namesake 2-week trip spans the country, with participants traveling on horses and rafts, by mountain bikes, and on foot. Custom-designed trips (with a minimum of motorized transport) of shorter duration are also available.

Ecole Travel (© 506/223-2240; ecolecr@racsa.co.cr) offers a range of affordable tours and day trips around the country. While the company often uses its own guides for longer trips, many of its day trips are subcontracted out. Its tours are popular with students and European travelers, including a fair number of backpackers.

Fantasy Tours (© 800/272-6654 in the U.S., 800/453-6654 in Canada, or 506/220-2126 in Costa Rica; www.fantasy.co.cr) is not a specifically adventure-oriented operator, but it does offer a comprehensive list of full-day tours to destinations that include Arenal Volcano and Tabacón Hot Springs, Poás and Irazú volcanoes, Manuel Antonio National Park, Carara Biological Reserve, and Bosque de Paz, a private biological reserve. White-water rafting expeditions, mountain-bike and fishing trips, island cruises, and multiday tours are also available. Some of its tours, however, have a cattle-car feel.

Horizontes ✮✮ (℗ **506/222-2022;** www.horizontes.com), while not a specifically adventure-oriented operator, offers a wide range of individual, group, and package tours. The company generally hires responsible and knowledgeable guides.

OTEC Viajes (℗ **506/257-0166;** www.otec.co.cr) offers a range of tour options and specializes in student and discount travel.

Serendipity Adventures ✮✮ (℗ **800/635-2325** in the U.S., or 506/556-2592; www.serendipityadventures.com), an adventure-travel operator, offers everything from ballooning to mountain-biking, sea kayaking to canyoning, as well as most of the popular white-water rafting trips.

Sin Límites (℗ **506/280-5182**) specializes in student and discount travel.

2 Activities A to Z

Each listing in this section describes the best places to practice a particular sport or activity and lists tour operators and outfitters. If you want to focus on only one active sport during your Costa Rican stay, these companies are your best bets for quality equipment and knowledgeable service.

Adventure activities and tourism, by their very nature, carry certain risks and dangers. In the past couple of years there have been several deaths and dozens of minor injuries in activities ranging from mountain-biking to white-water rafting to canopy tours. I try to list only the most reputable and safest of companies. However, if you ever have any doubt as to the safety of the guide, equipment, or activity, it's better to be safe than sorry. Moreover, know your limits and abilities and don't try to exceed them.

BIKING

There are several significant regional and international touring races in Costa Rica each year, but as a general rule, the major roads are dangerous and inhospitable for cyclists. They're narrow, there's usually no shoulder, and most drivers show little care or consideration for those on two wheels. The options are much more appealing for mountain-bikers and off-track riders, however. Fat-tire explorations are relatively new to Costa Rica but growing fast. If you plan to do a lot of biking and are very attached to your rig, bring your own. However, several companies in San José and elsewhere rent bikes, and the quality of the equipment is improving all the time. I've listed rental shops in each of the regional chapters that follows.

The area around **Lake Arenal** and **Arenal Volcano** wins my vote as the best place for mountain-biking in Costa Rica. The scenery's great, with primary forests, waterfalls, and plenty of trails. And nearby Tabacón Hot Springs is a perfect place for those with aching muscles to unwind at the end of the day. (See chapter 6.)

TOUR OPERATORS & OUTFITTERS

BiCosta Rica (℗ **506/446-7585;** www.yellowweb.co.cr/bicostarica.html) runs small group tours around the country; it offers some fixed itineraries, or can custom-design one around your interests.

   Coast to Coast Adventures (© 506/280-8054; www.ctocadventures.com) offers mountain-biking itineraries among its many tour options.
   Experience Plus/Specialty Tours ✶✶ (© 800/685-4565; www.xplus.com) offers guided group and assisted individual bike tours around the country. This is the only company I know of to use touring bikes. It also offers guided group hiking tours.
   Frontiers Spirited Adventures ✶✶ (© 877/603-1989; www.spiritedadventures.com) runs guided multiday mountain-biking trips around Costa Rica.
   Serendipity Adventures (© 800/635-2325 in the U.S., or 506/556-2592; www.serendipityadventures.com) offers several mountain-biking trips among its many other expeditions.

BIRD WATCHING

With more than 850 species of resident and migrant birds identified throughout the country, Costa Rica abounds with great bird-watching sites. Lodges with the best bird watching include **Savegre Lodge,** in Cerro de la Muerte, off the road to San Isidro de El General (quetzal sightings are almost guaranteed); **La Paloma Lodge** in Drake Bay, where you can sit on the porch of your cabin as the avian parade goes by; **Arenal Observatory Lodge,** on the flanks of Arenal Volcano; **La Selva Biological Station,** in Puerto Viejo de Sarapiquí; **Aviarios del Caribe,** just north of Cahuita; **Lapa Ríos** and **Bosque del Cabo,** on the Osa Peninsula; **Rainbow Adventures,** on Playa Cativa along the Golfo Dulce; **La Laguna del Lagarto Lodge,** up by the Nicaraguan border; and **Tiskita Lodge,** down by the Panamanian border.
   Some of the best parks and preserves for serious birders are **Monteverde Biological Cloud Forest Preserve** (for resplendent quetzals and hummingbirds); **Corcovado National Park** (for scarlet macaws); **Caño Negro Wildlife Refuge** (for wading birds, including jabiru storks); **Wilson Botanical Gardens** and the **Las Cruces Biological Station,** near San Vito (the thousands of flowering plants here are bird magnets); **Guayabo, Negritos,** and **Pájaros Islands Biological Reserves** in the Gulf of Nicoya (for magnificent frigate birds and brown boobies); **Palo Verde National Park** (for ibises, jacanas, storks, and roseate spoonbills); **Tortuguero National Park** (for great green macaws); and **Rincón de la Vieja National Park** (for parakeets and curassows). Rafting trips down the Corobicí and Bebedero Rivers near Liberia, boat trips to or at Tortuguero National Park, and hikes in any cloud forest also provide good bird watching.
   In San José, your best bets are to head toward the lush grounds and gardens of the University of Costa Rica, or to Parque del Este, a little further east in the foothills just outside of town.

Tips **A Bird-Watcher's Bible**

Any serious bird-watcher will find *A Guide to the Birds of Costa Rica*, by F. Gary Stiles and Alexander Skutch (Comstock Publishing Associates, a Division of Cornell University Press; Ithaca, NY, 1994), to be essential. For more casual enthusiasts, there's a series of laminated plates covering specific regions, which you'll find for sale at many local bookstores and some gift shops.

Where to See the Resplendent Quetzal

Revered by pre-Columbian cultures throughout Central America, the resplendent quetzal has been called the most beautiful bird on earth. Ancient Aztec and Maya Indians believed that the robin-size quetzal protected them in battle. The males of this species have brilliant red breasts; iridescent emerald green heads, backs, and wings; and white tail feathers complemented by a pair of iridescent green tail feathers that are nearly 2 feet long.

The belief that these endangered birds live only in the dense cloud forests cloaking the higher slopes of Central America's mountains was instrumental in bringing many areas of cloud forest under protection as quetzal habitats (since then, researchers have discovered that the birds do not in fact spend their entire lives here). After nesting, between March and July, resplendent quetzals migrate down to lower slopes in search of food. These lower slopes have not been preserved in most cases, and now conservationists are trying to salvage enough lower-elevation forests to help the quetzals survive. It is hoped that enough land will soon be set aside to ensure the perpetuation of this magnificent species.

Though for many years **Monteverde Biological Cloud Forest Preserve** *was the* place to see quetzals, throngs of people crowding the preserve's trails now make the pursuit more difficult. Other places where you can see quetzals are in the **Los Angeles Cloud Forest Reserve** near San Ramón, in **Tapantí National Wildlife Refuge**, and in **Chirripó National Park.** Perhaps the best place to spot a quetzal is at one of the specialized lodges located along the Cerro de la Muerte between San José and San Isidro de El General.

U.S. TOUR OPERATORS

Field Guides (© 800/728-4953 or 512/263-7295; www.fieldguides.com) is a specialty bird-watching travel operator. Its 16-day tour of Costa Rica costs $3,500, not including airfare. Group size is limited to 14 participants.

Wings (© 888/293-6443 or 520/320-9868; www.wingsbirds.com) is also a specialty bird-watching travel operator with more than 27 years of experience in the field. Its 17-day Costa Rica trip covers all the major bird-watching zones in the country and costs around $3,900, not including airfare. Trip size is usually between 6 and 14 people.

COSTA RICAN TOUR AGENCIES

In addition to the agencies listed below, check in with the **Birding Club of Costa Rica** (© 506/267-7197 or 506/228-2025; http://crbirdingclub. tripod.com), which runs monthly outings and provides you with the opportunity to connect with local English-speaking birders.

Both **Costa Rica Expeditions** (© 506/257-0766; www. costaricaexpeditions.com) and **Costa Rica Sun Tours** (© 506/296-7757; www.crsuntours.com) are well-established companies with very competent and experienced guides who offer a variety of tours to some of the better birding spots in Costa Rica.

BUNGEE JUMPING & BALLOONING

Both of these sports are new to Costa Rica, so as yet there's only one operator who specializes in each activity. The price you'll pay is generally cheaper than in the United States, and the scenery is certainly more lush.

Tropical Bungee (© **506/232-3956;** www.bungee.co.cr) will let you jump off a 265-foot bridge over the Río Colorado for $45; if you want to do it twice, the cost is $70. It is physically located on a small bridge over the Río Colorado about 23 miles northwest of San Jose, just off the Pan American Highway. There are obvious and well-placed signs on the highway. Someone will be there from 9am to 3pm every day. If you need transportation, Tropical Bungee will provide it for $7 per person each way.

Serendipity Adventures (© **800/635-2325** in the U.S., or 506/556-2592; www.serendipityadventures.com) will take you up, up, and away in a hot-air balloon on a variety of single- or multiday tours, either in Turrialba, Naranjo, or near Arenal Volcano. A basic flight costs $900 for up to five people or 800 pounds.

CAMPING

Heavy rains, difficult access, and limited facilities make camping a real challenge in Costa Rica. Nevertheless, a backpack and tent will get you far from the crowds and into some of the most pristine and undeveloped nooks and crannies of the country. Those who relish sleeping out on a beach but wouldn't mind a bit more luxury (beds, someone to prepare meals for you, and running water) might want to consider staying in one of the tent camps on the **Osa Peninsula** ✹✹ (Drake Bay Wilderness Resort or Corcovado Lodge Tent Camp) or down in **Manzanillo** ✹ (Almendros and Corales Tent Camp). See chapters 8 and 9 for details. Camping is forbidden in some national parks, so read through the descriptions for each park carefully before you pack a tent.

If you'd like to participate in an organized camping trip, contact **Coast to Coast Adventures** (© **506/280-8054;** www.ctocadventures.com) or **Serendipity Adventures** (© **800/635-2325** in the U.S., or 506/556-2592; www.serendipityadventures.com).

Another option is to hook up with a **Green Tortoise** (© **800/867-8647** or 415/956-7500 in the U.S.; www.greentortoise.com) tour of Costa Rica. This bus tour/camping outfit runs around five trips each year to Costa Rica, with a 15-day tour of the country costing around $520, not including transportation to Costa Rica.

In my opinion, the best place to pop up a tent on the beach is in **Santa Rosa National Park,** or at the Puerto Vargas campsite in **Cahuita National Park.** The best camping trek is, without a doubt, a hike through **Corcovado National Park,** or a climb up **Mount Chirripó.**

CANOPY TOURS

Canopy tours are taking off in Costa Rica, largely because they are such a unique way to experience tropical rain forests. It's estimated that some two-thirds of a typical rain forest's species live in the canopy (the uppermost, branching layer of the forest). From the relative luxury of Aerial Tram's high-tech funicular to the rope-and-climbing-gear rigs of more basic operations, a trip into the canopy will give you a bird's-eye view of a neotropical forest. There are now canopy-tour operations in Monteverde, Aguas Zarcas (near San Carlos), Tabacón, Punta Islita, Villablanca, Playa Hermosa, and Rincón de la Vieja, as well as on Tortuga Island, around the Osa Peninsula, and at the Iguana Park.

With the exception of the Aerial Tram, most canopy tours involve strapping yourself into a climbing harness and being winched up to a platform some 100 feet above the forest floor, or doing the work yourself. Many of these operations have a series of treetop platforms connected by taut cables. Once up on the first platform, you click your harness into a pulley and glide across the cable to the next (slightly lower) platform, using your hand (protected by a thick leather glove) as a brake. When you reach the last platform, you usually rappel back down to the ground (don't worry, they'll teach even the most nervous neophyte).

While this can be a lot of fun, do be careful, as canopy tours are quite the rage and to date, there is no regulation on the activity. Some of the tours are set up by fly-by-night operators (obviously, I haven't listed any of those). Be especially sure that you feel comfortable and confident with the safety standards, guides, and equipment before embarking. The most reputable operator is **The Original Canopy Tours** (see below), but there are other safe, well-run operations around the country. My favorite canopy tours are the Original Canopy Tour's operation in **Monteverde,** where the ascent goes up the inside of a strangler fig, in the space where the host tree once lived, and its Kazam Cañon tour at Rincón de la Vieja, which zig-zags back and forth through a deep canyon. Before you sign on to any tour, ask whether you have to hoist yourself to the top under your own steam, then make your decision accordingly.

Aerial Tram ✶ (✆ **506/257-5961;** www.rainforesttram.com) is located 50 minutes from San José. For $49.50 (transportation extra), this modern tram takes you on a 90-minute trip through the rain-forest canopy in the comfort and safety of an enclosed cab. The entrance fee includes an additional guided hike and access to its trail system. The best thing here isn't necessarily the tram ride, which I find somewhat disappointing, but the fact that this makes a good spot for a full-day excursion relatively close to San José.

The Original Canopy Tours ✶✶ (✆ and fax **506/257-5149,** or 506/256-7626; www.canopytour.com) is the largest canopy-tour operator, with sites in Monteverde, Aguas Zarcas, Rincón de la Vieja, Tabacón, Iguana Park, and along the banks of the Pacuare River.

CRUISING

Cruising options in Costa Rica range from transient cruisers setting up a quick charter business to converted fishing boats taking a few guests out to see the sunset. For information on the major cruise lines that ply the waters off Costa Rica, see "By Cruise Ship" under "Getting There," in chapter 2.

One popular cruise is a day trip from San José (the boats actually leave from Puntarenas) to **Isla Tortuga** in the Nicoya Gulf (see "Side Trips from San José" in chapter 4). Alternately, you can book a cruise to Tortuga from Playa Montezuma at the tip of the Nicoya Peninsula (see chapter 5 for details). It's much cheaper from here (around $40 per person), but the excursion doesn't include the gourmet lunch that's usually featured on cruises leaving from San José.

One interesting recent entry into the Costa Rican cruising scene is the **Windstar Cruise** ✶ line's (✆ **800/258-7245;** www.windstarcruises.com) 148-passenger, four-masted sail-assist cruise ship, *Wind Song,* which leaves out of Caldera on weeklong trips from January through March. A weeklong cruise runs between $2,500 and $5,500 per person.

Another option is to take a cruise on the *Temptress.* This small cruise ship plies the waters off Costa Rica's Pacific coast from Santa Rosa National Park in the north to Corcovado National Park in the south. The ship has no pool or casino, but it does usually anchor in remote, isolated, and very beautiful spots. Each day you can choose between a natural-history tour and a recreational and cultural tour. For information, contact **Temptress Cruises** (✆ **800/255-3585** in the U.S., or 506/220-1679; www.temptresscruises.org). Weeklong cruises run between $1,995 and $2,995 per person.

If diesel fumes and engine noise bother you, the best places to charter a sailboat are in Playa del Coco, Playa Hermosa, and Playa Flamingo in Guanacaste province (see chapter 5); Playa Herradura and Quepos, along the central Pacific coast (see chapter 7); and Golfito, along the southern Pacific coast (see chapter 8). You can get information about sailboat rides and charters at any one of the larger lodgings in these areas. If you're at Flamingo Beach, head to the marina, where you should be able to find a captain who will take you out. My favorite place to charter a sailboat is **Golfito.** From here, it's a pleasant, peaceful day's sail around the Golfo Dulce (see chapter 8).

DIVING & SNORKELING
Many islands, reefs, caves, and rocks lie off the coast of Costa Rica, providing excellent spots for underwater exploration. Visibility varies with season and location. Generally, heavy rainfall tends to swell the rivers and muddy the waters, even well offshore. Banana plantations and their runoff have destroyed most of the Caribbean reefs, although there's still good diving at **Isla Uvita,** just off the coast of Limón, and in **Manzanillo,** down near the Panamanian border. Most divers choose Pacific dive spots like **Caño Island** ✹✹ , **Bat Island** ✹✹ , and the **Catalina Islands** ✹ , where you're likely to spot manta rays, moray eels, white-tipped sharks, and plenty of smaller fish and coral species. But the ultimate in Costa Rican dive experiences is a week to 10 days spent on a chartered boat, diving off the coast of **Coco Island** ✹✹✹ (see chapter 7).

Snorkeling is not incredibly common or rewarding in Costa Rica. The rain, runoff, and wave conditions that drive scuba divers well offshore tend to make coastal and shallow-water conditions less than optimum. If the weather is calm and the water is clear, you might just get lucky. Ask at your hotel or check the different beach listings to find snorkeling options and operators up and down Costa Rica's coasts. The best snorkeling experience to be had in Costa Rica is on the reefs off **Manzanillo Beach** ✹ in the southern Caribbean coast, particularly in the calm months of September and October.

SCUBA-DIVING OUTFITTERS & OPERATORS
In addition to the companies listed below, check the listings at specific beach and port destinations in the regional chapters.

Aggressor Fleet Limited ✹✹ (✆ **800/348-2628** or 504/385-2628 in the U.S., or 506/289-3333; www.aggressor.com) runs the 120-foot *Okeanos Aggressor* on regular trips out to Coco Island.

Diving Safaris de Costa Rica ✹ (✆ **800/779-0055** in the U.S., or 506/672-0012; www.costaricadiving.net) is perhaps the largest, most professional, and best-established dive operation in the country. Based out of the Sol

---

Beach Blanket, Bingo
If you plan on spending time at the beach, make sure to pack your own beach towel or mat. Only the more upscale hotels in Costa Rica tend to provide them.

Playa Hermosa Hotel in Playa Hermosa, this outfitter is also a local pioneer in nitrox diving.

Mundo Aquatico (© **506/224-9729;** mundoac@racsa.co.cr) offers equipment rental, certification classes, and tours. Tours go to Catalina and Bat Islands, as well as to Isla del Caño.

Undersea Hunter ⚐⚐ (© **800/203-2120** in the U.S., or 506/228-6613; www.underseahunter.com) offers the *Undersea Hunter* and its sister ship, the *Sea Hunter,* two pioneers of the live-aboard diving excursions to Coco Island.

FISHING

Anglers in Costa Rican waters have landed more than 65 world-record catches, including blue marlin, Pacific sailfish, dolphin, wahoo, yellowfin tuna, guapote, and snook. Whether you want to head offshore looking for a big sail, wrestle a tarpon near a Caribbean river mouth, or choose a quiet spot on Arenal Lake to cast for guapote, you'll find it here. You can land a marlin anywhere along the Pacific coast.

Many of the Pacific port and beach towns—Quepos, Puntarenas, Playa del Coco, Tamarindo, Flamingo, Golfito, Drake Bay, Zancudo—support large charter fleets and have hotels that cater to anglers; see chapters 5, 7, and 8 for recommended boats, captains, and lodges. Costs for fishing trips usually range between $400 and $1,500 per day (depending on the size of the boat) for boat, captain, tackle, drinks, and lunch, so the cost per person is dependent on the size of the group.

Costa Rica Outdoors (© **800/308-3394** in the U.S., or 506/282-6743; www.costaricaoutdoors.com) is a well-established operation, run by longtime resident, fisherman, and outdoor writer Jerry Ruhlow, that specializes in booking fishing trips around the country.

FISHING LODGES

For more detailed information about these lodges, see their full listings in chapters 8 and 9.

Aguila de Osa Inn ⚐ (© and fax **506/296-2190,** or 506/232-7722; www.aguiladeosa.com) is a luxury lodge catering to anglers in Drake Bay. See chapter 8.

The **Río Colorado Lodge** (© **800/243-9777** in the U.S. and Canada, or 506/232-4063; www.riocoloradolodge.com), is located at the Barra del Colorado National Wildlife Refuge. See chapter 9.

Roy's Zancudo Lodge (© **877/529-6980** in the U.S., or 506/776-0008; www.royszancudolodge.com) is located in Playa Zancudo. See chapter 8.

Silver King Lodge ⚐⚐ (© **800/847-3474** or 888/682-7766 in the U.S., or 506/381-1403; www.silverkinglodge.com) is a luxury lodge at Barra del Colorado. See chapter 9.

GOLF

Costa Rica is not one of the world's great golfing destinations. Well, not yet, anyway. There are currently five regulation 18-hole courses open to the public and/or visitors, but several others are either under construction or in the planning stages, with a potential boom shaping up in Guanacaste. Very shortly, there should be new courses in operation near the port of Caldera at La Roca Resort, and several new courses in Guanacaste within the next couple of years.

The **Meliá hotel chain** offers two courses. The **Meliá Cariari course** ⚐⚐ (© **800/336-3542** in the U.S. and Canada, or 506/239-0022; cariari@racsa.co.cr) is just outside of San José. Greens fees here are $40, but you

---

Tai Chi in Paradise

For the past 12 years, tai chi master and two-time U.S. national champion Chris Luth has been leading weeklong retreats to Costa Rica, combining intensive classes in this ancient Chinese martial art with rain-forest hikes, river rafting, and just enough beach time. For more information, contact the Pacific School of T'ai Chi (© **800/266-5803** in the U.S., or 858/ 259-1401).

---

have to be a member or a guest at either the Meliá or Herradura hotels. The Meliá chain also runs the **Garra de León course** ☆☆ at the **Meliá Playa Conchal** resort (© **506/654-4123;** mconchal@racsa.co.cr) up in Guanacaste. Greens fees here are $100, including cart. This course is currently open, with advance notice and depending on available tee times, to guests at other hotels in the region. Another option for golfers staying in the metropolitan area is the new 18-hole course **Parque Valle del Sol** ☆ (© **506/282-9222**) in the western sub-urb of Santa Ana. Greens fees here run $50 for 18 holes.

The newest major resort course to open is at the **Los Sueños Marriott Beach & Golf Resort** ☆☆ in Playa Herradura (© **800/228-9290** in the U.S., or 506/630-9000). Greens fees, including cart, run around $100 for guests of the hotel, $150 for the general public.

Another course in operation is **Royal Pacific** (© **506/654-4925**), near Playa Grande, also in Guanacaste. Greens fees there are $50 ($25 for a cart).

Finally, by the time this book goes to press there will be a new course just out-side of Tamarindo called **El Coral** at **Hacienda Pinilla.**

Golfers wanting the most up-to-date information, or interested in a package deal that includes play on a variety of courses, should contact **Costa Rica Golf Adventures** ☆☆ (© **877/258-2688** in the U.S., or 506/239-5176; www. golfcr.com).

HORSEBACK RIDING

Costa Rica's rural roots are evident in the continued use of horses for real work and transportation throughout the country. Visitors will find that horses are eas-ily available for riding, whether you want to take a sunset trot along the beach, ride through the cloud forest, or take a multiday trek through the northern zone.

While most travelers simply saddle up for a couple of hours, those looking for a more specifically equestrian-based visit should check in with the following folks.

Coast to Coast Adventures (© **506/280-8054;** www.ctocadventures.com) specializes in 2-week trips spanning the country via horseback, raft, mountain-bike, and on foot, with no motor vehicles involved. Other trips are also available.

Nature Lodge Finca Los Caballos ☆ (© and fax **506/642-0124;** www. naturelodge.net) has the healthiest horses in the Montezuma area. See chapter 5.

Rancho Savegre Horseback Tours (© **506/777-0528**) offers 1-day and multiday horseback tours based out of its rustic ranch near Quepos. See chapter 7.

Serendipity Adventures (© **800/635-2325** in the U.S., or 506/556-2592; www.serendipityadventures.com) offers many activities, including horseback treks and tours.

ROCK CLIMBING

Although this is a nascent sport in Costa Rica, the possibilities are promising. There are several challenging formations close to San José and along the Cerro de la Muerte, as well as great climbing opportunities on Mount Chirripó. For information on routes, sites, and equipment rentals, contact **Gimnasio Climb X** (© 506/232-4017; www.climbx.com). This gym, in the Sabana Sur section of downtown San José, has a climbing wall and sometimes organizes outings to natural climbing spots. It has one of those complicated Costa Rican addresses, so call for directions.

SPAS & YOGA RETREATS

While Costa Rica still doesn't have any world-class spas, the conditions here are ripe, and some early efforts are beginning to mature and flourish. I expect the trend to boom here in the coming years.

Tara Resort Hotel and Spa, A.P. 1459-1250, Escazú (© **506/228-6992;** www.tararesort.com), is a small hotel and spa located in the hills above Escazú, just 20 minutes from downtown San José. Modern equipment and a wide range of treatments are available. See chapter 4.

Hotel Martino Med-Spa & Resort, La Garita de Alajuela (© **506/ 433-8382;** fax 506/433-9052; www.hotelmartino.com), is a new hotel in the environs of San José that has a top-notch modern spa facility with tons of equipment. The hotel itself is not that noteworthy, so I recommend it for those of you specifically looking for a spa experience.

Pura Vida Retreat ✦✦, Pavas de Carrizal, Alajuela (© **888/767-7375** in the U.S., or 506/483-0033; www.puravidaspa.com), is primarily a yoga retreat, with close ties to the Omega Institute in Rhinebeck, NY. It hosts a steady stream of visiting teachers and groups practicing a wide range of styles and meditations. It's located in a lovely setting in the hills above Alajuela, just outside San José.

Hotel Borinquen, Cañas Dulces (© **506/666-0363;** borinque@racsa.co.cr), has the setting, natural hot springs, and accommodations to be a spectacular spa destination. Now it just needs the facilities and staff. See chapter 5.

Fusion Natural Spa ✦, Playa Ocotal, in the Guanacaste region (© **506/ 670-0250;** www.fusionnaturalspa.com) offers a wide range of massage, aromatherapy, body-wrap, and exfoliating treatments. Half-day, full-day, and multiday packages are available. See chapter 5.

Tabacón Resort ✦✦, Tabacón (© **506/256-1500;** www.tabacon.com), has the setting and potential to become the country's premier spa, with its spectacular hot springs and volcano view. As of press time, the spa services and facilities were on the brink of a big expansion. See chapter 6.

Hotel Occidental El Tucano Resort and Spa ✦ (© **506/460-6000** or 506/ 460-3141; www.occidental-hoteles.com; occhcr@racsa.co.cr), the oldest and most established full-service spa facility in Costa Rica, offers a wide range of treatments in a lush forested setting, with natural hot springs. It's located near Arenal Volcano and La Fortuna; see chapter 6.

Samasati ✦, Puerto Viejo de Talamanca (© **800/563-9643** in the U.S., or 506/224-1870; www.samasati.com), is a lovely new yoga retreat in some dense forest on a hillside above the Caribbean. See chapter 9.

SURFING

When *Endless Summer II,* the sequel to the all-time surf classic, was filmed, the production crew brought its boards and cameras to Costa Rica. Point and

In Search of Turtles

Few places in the world have as many sea-turtle nesting sites as Costa Rica. Along both coasts, five species of these huge marine reptiles come ashore at specific times of the year to dig nests in the sand and lay their eggs. Sea turtles are endangered throughout the world due to overhunting, accidental deaths in fishing nets, development on beaches that once served as nesting areas, and the collection and sale (often illegally) of their eggs. International trade in sea-turtle products is already prohibited by most countries (including the United States), but sea-turtle numbers continue to dwindle.

Among the species of sea turtles that nest on Costa Rica's beaches are the **olive Ridley** (known for their mass egg-laying migrations, or *arribadas*), **leatherback, hawksbill, green,** and **Pacific green turtle.** Excursions to see nesting turtles have become common, and they are fascinating, but please make sure that you and/or your guide do not disturb the turtles. Any light source (other than red-tinted flashlights) can confuse female turtles and cause them to return to the sea without laying their eggs. In fact, as more and more development takes place on the Costa Rican coast, hotel lighting may cause the number of nesting turtles to drop. Luckily, many of the nesting beaches have been protected as national parks.

Here are the main places to see nesting sea turtles: **Santa Rosa National Park** (near Liberia), **Las Baulas National Marine Park** (near Tamarindo), **Ostional National Wildlife Refuge** (near Playa Nosara), and **Tortuguero National Park** (on the northern Caribbean coast).

See the regional chapters for a description of the resident turtles and their respective nesting seasons, as well as listings of local tour operators and companies that arrange trips to see sea turtles nesting.

beach breaks that work almost year-round are located all along Costa Rica's immense coastline. **Playas Hermosa, Jacó,** and **Dominical,** on the central Pacific coast, and **Tamarindo** and **Playa Guiones,** in Guanacaste, are becoming mini–surf meccas. **Salsa Brava** in Puerto Viejo has a habit of breaking boards, but the daredevils keep coming back for more. Crowds are starting to gather at the more popular breaks, but you can still stumble onto secret spots on the **Osa** and **Nicoya Peninsulas** and along the northern Guanacaste coast. Costa Rica's signature wave is still found at **Playa Pavones,** which is reputed to have one of the longest lefts in the world. The cognoscenti, however, also swear by places like **Playa Grande, Playa Negra, Matapalo, Malpais,** and **Witch's Rock.** An avid surfer's best bet is to rent a dependable four-wheel-drive vehicle with a rack and take a surfin' safari around the breaks of Guanacaste.

If you're looking for an organized surf vacation, contact **Tico Travel** (© **800/ 493-8426** in the U.S., or 506/221-3912; www.ticotravel.com). For more general surf information, live wave-cams, and great links pages, point your browser to **www.surfinfo.com, www.swell.com,** or **www.surfline.com.**

WHITE-WATER RAFTING, KAYAKING & CANOEING

Whether you're a first-time rafter or a world-class kayaker, Costa Rica's got some white water suited to your abilities. Rivers rise and fall with the rainfall, but you can get wet and wild here even in the dry season. The best white-water-rafting ride is still the scenic **Pacuare River,** though unfortunately it may be dammed soon. If you're just experimenting with river rafting, stick to Class II and III rivers, like the **Reventazón, Sarapiquí, Peñas Blancas,** and **Savegre.** If you already know which end of the paddle goes in the water, there are plenty of Class IV and V sections to run.

Die-hard river rats should pick up a copy of *The Rivers of Costa Rica,* by Michael W. Mayfield and Rafael E. Gallo (Menasha Ridge Press, 1988), which is loaded with technical data and route tips on every rideable river in the country.

Aventuras Naturales ✵ (✆ **800/514-0411** in the U.S., or 506/225-3939; www.toenjoynature.com) is a major rafting operator running daily trips on the most popular rivers in Costa Rica. Its Pacuare Jungle Lodge is a great place to spend the night on one of its 2-day rafting trips.

Costa Rica White Water ✵ (✆ **506/257-0766;** www.costaricaexpeditions. com) was the first building block in the Costa Rica Expeditions empire. It remains one of the better-run rafting operations.

Canoe Costa Rica (✆ and fax **732/350-3963** in the U.S., or 506/282-3579; www.canoecostarica.com) is the only outfit I know of that specializes in canoe trips; it works primarily with custom-designed tours and itineraries.

If you're out on the Osa Peninsula, hook up with **Escondido Trex** ✵ (✆ and fax **506/735-5210;** www.escondidotrex.com).

Iguana Tours ✵ (✆ and fax **506/777-1262;** www.iguanatours.com) is based in Quepos/Manuel Antonio and specializes in rafting on the Savegre and Naranjo Rivers, as well as ocean and mangrove kayak trips.

Rancho Leona Kayak Tours (✆ **506/761-1019;** www.rancholeona.com) is a small hostel-like roadside hotel in Heredia that caters to both experienced and beginning kayakers looking to ply the Río Sarapiquí. See chapter 6.

Ríos Tropicales ✵ (✆ **506/233-6455;** www.riostropicales.com) is one of the major operators in Costa Rica, operating on most of the runnable rivers. Lodgings include a very comfortable lodge on the banks of the Río Pacuare for the 2-day trips.

WINDSURFING

Windsurfing is still not very popular on the high seas here, where winds are fickle and rental options are limited, even at beach hotels. However, **Lake Arenal** is considered one of the top spots in the world for high-wind boardsailing. During the winter months, many of the regulars from Washington's Columbia River Gorge take up residence around the nearby town of Tilarán. Small boards, water starts, and fancy gibes are the norm. The best time for windsurfing on Lake Arenal is between December and March. The same winds that buffet Lake Arenal make their way down to **Bolaños Bay,** near Santa Cruz, Guanacaste, where you can also get some good windsurfing in. See chapters 5 and 6 for more information.

3 Costa Rica's Top National Parks & Bioreserves

Costa Rica has 32 national parks, protecting more than 12% of the country. They range in size from the 530-acre Guayabo National Monument to the 474,240-acre La Amistad National Park. Many of these national parks are undeveloped tropical forests, with few services or facilities available for visitors. Others, however, offer easier access to their wealth of natural wonders.

After several years of fee hikes, scaled pricing, green passes, and heated controversy, national-park fees seem to have settled on a flat $6-per-person per-day fee for any foreigner. Costa Ricans and foreign residents continue to pay just $1. At parks where camping is allowed, there is an additional charge of $2 per person per day.

The following section is not a complete listing of all of Costa Rica's national parks and protected areas, but rather a selective list of those parks that are of greatest interest and accessibility. They're popular, but they're also among the best. You'll find detailed information about food and lodging options near some of the individual parks in the regional chapters that follow. As you'll see from the descriptions, Costa Rica's national parks vary greatly in terms of attractions, facilities, and accessibility.

If you're looking for a camping adventure or an extended stay in one of the national parks, I recommend **Santa Rosa, Rincón de la Vieja, Chirripó, Corcovado,** or **Cahuita.** Any of the others are better suited for day trips, guided hikes, or in combination with your travels around the country.

For more information, call the national parks office at (C) **506/257-0922.** You can also stop by the **National Parks Foundation office** ((C) **506/257-2239**) in San José, which is located between Calle 23 and Avenida 15. Both offices are open Monday through Friday from 9am to 5pm.

SAN JOSÉ/CENTRAL VALLEY AREA
GUAYABO NATIONAL MONUMENT (★ This is the country's only significant pre-Columbian archaeological site. It's believed that Guayabo supported a population of about 10,000 people some 3,000 years ago. The park is set in a forested area rich in flora and fauna. **Location:** 12 miles (19km) northeast of Turrialba, which is 33 miles (53km) east of San José. See chapter 4.

IRAZÚ VOLCANO NATIONAL PARK (★ Irazú Volcano is the highest (11,260 ft.) of Costa Rica's four active volcanoes and a popular day trip from San José. A paved road leads right up to the crater, and the lookout also allows you a view of both oceans on a clear day. The volcano last erupted in 1963—the same day President John F. Kennedy visited the country. There's an information center, picnic tables, rest rooms, and a parking area here. **Location:** 34 miles (55km) east of San José. See chapter 4.

POÁS VOLCANO NATIONAL PARK (★ Poás is the other active volcano close to San José. The main crater is more than 1 mile wide, and it is constantly active with fumaroles and hot geysers. The area around the volcano is lush, but much of the growth is stunted due to the gasses and acid rain. The park sometimes closes when the gasses get too feisty. There are nature trails, picnic tables, rest rooms, and an information center. **Location:** 23 miles (37km) northwest of San José. See chapter 4.

GUANACASTE & THE NICOYA PENINSULA
BARRA HONDA NATIONAL PARK Costa Rica's only underground national park, Barra Honda features a series of limestone caves that were once part of a coral reef, some 60 million years ago. Today the caves are home to millions of bats and impressive stalactite and stalagmite formations. Only Terciopelo Cave is open to the public. There are a camping area, rest rooms, and an information center here, as well as trails through the surrounding

tropical dry forest. **Location:** 208 miles (335km) northwest of San José. See chapter 5.

PALO VERDE NATIONAL PARK   A must for bird watchers, Palo Verde National Park is one of Costa Rica's best-kept secrets. This part of the Tempisque River lowlands supports a population of more than 50,000 waterfowl and forest bird species. Various ecosystems here include mangroves, savanna brush lands, and evergreen forests. There are camping facilities, an information center, and some nice new accommodations at the Organization for Tropical Studies (OTS) research station here. **Location:** 125 miles (200km) northwest of San José. Be warned that the park entrance is 17½ miles (28km) off the highway down a very rugged dirt road; it's another 5½ miles (9km) to the OTS station and campsites. For more information, call the OTS (© **506/240-6696;** reservas@cro.ots.ac.cr). See chapter 5.

RINCÓN DE LA VIEJA NATIONAL PARK ☀☀   This is a large tract of parkland that experiences high volcanic activity. There are numerous fumaroles and geysers, as well as hot springs, cold pools, and mud pots. There are also excellent hikes to the upper craters, as well as to several waterfalls. You should hire a guide for any hot-spring or mud-bath expeditions, because inexperienced visitors have been burned. Camping is permitted at two separate sites, each of which has an information center, picnic area, and rest rooms. **Location:** 165 miles (266km) northwest of San José. See chapter 5.

SANTA ROSA NATIONAL PARK ☀   Occupying a large section of Costa Rica's northwestern Guanacaste province, Santa Rosa contains the country's largest area of tropical dry forest, as well as important turtle-nesting sites and the historically significant La Casona monument. There are also caves for exploring. The beaches here are pristine and have basic camping facilities, and the waves make them quite popular with surfers. An information center, picnic area, and rest rooms are located at the main campsite and entrance. **Location:** 160 miles (258km) northwest of San José. For more information, you can call the park office at © **506/666-5051.** See chapter 5.

THE NORTHERN ZONE

ARENAL NATIONAL PARK ☀☀   This new park, created to protect the ecosystem that surrounds Arenal Volcano, has few services or attractions. Basically, the government has set up a tollbooth on the access road leading to an up-close view of the volcano's lava flows. Most travelers and tour operators choose to forgo the entrance fee and watch the volcano from spots along the dirt road leading to the Arenal Observatory Lodge, or from the road to Tabacón, where the view is just as good as it is inside. However, there are several excellent hiking trails inside the park that explore cooled-off lava flows and the neighboring rain forest. **Location:** 80 miles (129km) northwest of San José. See chapter 6.

BRAULIO CARRILLO NATIONAL PARK   This park, which occupies a large area of the nation's central mountain range, is the park you pass through on your way from San José to the Caribbean coast. A deep rain forest, Braulio Carrillo receives an average of 177 inches of rain per year. There are beautiful rivers, majestic waterfalls, and more than 6,500 species of plants and animals. The park has an information center, picnic tables, rest rooms, and hiking trails. Camping is allowed, but is not very common or recommended. Be careful here. Make sure you park your car in, and base your explorations from, the park's

Costa Rica's National Parks & Bioreserves

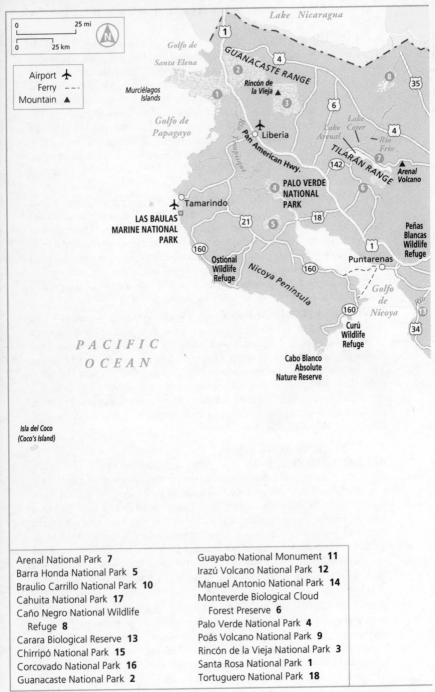

Arenal National Park **7**
Barra Honda National Park **5**
Braulio Carrillo National Park **10**
Cahuita National Park **17**
Caño Negro National Wildlife
    Refuge **8**
Carara Biological Reserve **13**
Chirripó National Park **15**
Corcovado National Park **16**
Guanacaste National Park **2**

Guayabo National Monument **11**
Irazú Volcano National Park **12**
Manuel Antonio National Park **14**
Monteverde Biological Cloud
    Forest Preserve **6**
Palo Verde National Park **4**
Poás Volcano National Park **9**
Rincón de la Vieja National Park **3**
Santa Rosa National Park **1**
Tortuguero National Park **18**

Monkey Business

No trip to Costa Rica would be complete without at least one monkey sighting. Home to four distinct species of primates, Costa Rica offers the opportunity for one of the world's most gratifying wildlife-watching experiences. Just listen for the deep guttural call of a howler or the rustling of leaves overhead—telltale signs that monkeys are in your vicinity.

Costa Rica's most commonly spotted monkey is the white-faced or **capuchin monkey** (*mono cara blanca* in Spanish), which you may recognize as the infamous culprit from the film *Outbreak*. Contrary to that film's plot, however, these monkeys are native to the New World tropics and do not exist in Africa. Capuchins are agile, medium-size monkeys that make good use of their long, prehensile tails. They inhabit a diverse collection of habitats, ranging from the high-altitude cloud forests of the central region to the lowland mangroves of the Osa Peninsula. It's almost impossible not to spot capuchins at Manuel Antonio (see chapter 7), where the resident white-faced monkeys have become a little too dependent on fruit and junk-food feedings by tourists. Please do not feed wild monkeys (and try to keep your food away from them; they're notorious thieves), and boycott establishments that try to attract both monkeys and tourists with daily feedings.

Howler monkeys (*mono congo* in Spanish) are named for their distinct and eerie call. Large and mostly black, these monkeys can seem ferocious because of their physical appearance and deep, resonant howls that can carry for more than a mile, even in dense rain forest.

main entrance, not just anywhere along the highway. There have been several robberies and attacks against visitors reported at trails leading into the park from the highway. This park also seems to have the highest incidence of lost hikers. **Location:** 14 miles (22km) north of San José. See chapter 6.

CAÑO NEGRO NATIONAL WILDLIFE REFUGE A lowland swamp and drainage basin for several northern rivers, Caño Negro is excellent for bird watching. There are a few basic cabinas and lodges in this area, but the most popular way to visit is on a combined van and boat trip from the La Fortuna/Arenal area. **Location:** 12½ miles (20km) south of Los Chiles, near the Nicaraguan border. See chapter 6.

MONTEVERDE BIOLOGICAL CLOUD FOREST PRESERVE
This private reserve might be the most famous patch of forest in Costa Rica. It covers some 26,000 acres of primary forest. Most of it is mid-elevation cloud forest, with a rich variety of flora and fauna. Epiphytes thrive in the cool, misty climate. The most famous resident here is the spectacular resplendent quetzal. There is a well-maintained trail system, as well as some of the best-trained and most experienced guides in the country. Nearby, you can visit both the Santa Elena and Sendero Tranquilo reserves. **Location:** 103 miles (167km) NW of San José. See chapter 6.

Biologists believe that male howlers mark the bounds of their territories with these deep, guttural sounds. In the presence of humans, however, howlers are actually a little timid and tend to stay higher up in the canopy than their white-faced cousins. Howlers are fairly common and easy to spot in the dry tropical forests of coastal Guanacaste and the Nicoya Peninsula (see chapter 5).

Even more elusive are **spider monkeys** (*mono araña* in Spanish). These long, slender monkeys are dark brown to black and prefer the high canopies of primary rain forests. Spiders are very adept with their prehensile tails but actually travel through the canopy with a hand-over-hand motion frequently imitated by their less graceful human cousins on playground monkey bars around the world. I've had my best luck spotting spiders along the edges of Tortuguero's jungle canals (see chapter 9), where howlers are also quite common.

The rarest and most endangered of Costa Rica's monkeys is the tiny **squirrel monkey** (*mono tití* in Spanish). These small, brown monkeys have dark eyes surrounded by large white rings, white ears, white chests, and very long tails. In Costa Rica, squirrel monkeys can be found only in Manuel Antonio (see chapter 7) and the Osa Peninsula (see chapter 8). These seemingly hyperactive monkeys are predominantly fruit eaters and often feed on bananas and other fruit trees near hotels in both of the above-mentioned regions. Squirrel monkeys usually travel in large bands, so if you do see them, you'll likely see quite a few.

CENTRAL PACIFIC COAST

CHIRRIPÓ NATIONAL PARK ✸✸   Home to Costa Rica's tallest peak, 12,536-foot Mount Chirripó, Chirripó National Park is a hike, but on a clear day you can see both the Pacific Ocean and Caribbean Sea from its summit. There are a number of interesting climbing trails here, and camping is allowed. **Location:** 94 miles (151km) southeast of San José. See chapter 7.

MANUEL ANTONIO NATIONAL PARK ✸✸   Though relatively small, Manuel Antonio is the most popular national park and supports the largest number of hotels and resorts. This lowland rain forest is home to a healthy monkey population, including the endangered squirrel monkey. The park is best known for its splendid beaches. **Location:** 80 miles (129km) south of San José. See chapter 7.

THE SOUTHERN ZONE

CORCOVADO NATIONAL PARK ✸✸✸   As the largest single block of virgin lowland rain forest in Central America, Corcovado National Park receives more than 200 inches of rain per year. It's increasingly popular, but still very remote (it has no roads; only dirt tracks lead into it). Scarlet macaws live here, as do countless other neotropical species, including two of the country's largest cats, the puma and endangered jaguar. There are camping facilities and trails throughout the park. **Location:** 208 miles (335km) south of San José, on the Osa Peninsula. See chapter 8.

THE CARIBBEAN COAST

CAHUITA NATIONAL PARK   A combination land and marine park, Cahuita National Park protects one of the few remaining living coral reefs in the country. The topography here is lush lowland tropical rain forest. Monkeys and numerous bird species are common. Camping is permitted, and there are basic facilities at the Puerto Vargas entrance to the park. If you want to visit for only the day, however, enter from Cahuita village, because as of press time, the local community had taken over that entrance and was asking for only a voluntary donation. **Location:** On the Caribbean coast, 26 miles (42km) south of Limón. See chapter 9.

TORTUGUERO NATIONAL PARK 🌟🌟   Tortuguero National Park has been called the Venice of Costa Rica due to its maze of jungle canals that meander through a dense lowland rain forest. Small boats, launches, and canoes carry visitors through these waterways, where caimans, manatees, and numerous bird and mammal species are common. The extremely endangered great green macaw lives here. On the beaches, green sea turtles nest here every year between June and October. The park has a small but helpful information office and some well-marked trails. **Location:** 160 miles (258km) from San José. See chapter 9.

4 Tips on Health, Safety & Etiquette in the Wilderness

Much of what is discussed below is common sense. For more detailed information, see "Health & Insurance" in chapter 2.

While most tours and activities are safe, there are risks involved in any adventure activity. Know and respect your own physical limits before undertaking any strenuous activity. Be prepared for extremes in temperature and rainfall and for wide fluctuations in weather. A sunny morning hike can quickly become a cold and wet ordeal, so it's usually a good idea to carry along some form of rain gear when hiking in the rain forest, or to have a dry change of clothing waiting at the end of the trail. Make sure to bring along plenty of sunscreen when you're not going to be covered by the forest canopy.

If you do any backcountry packing or camping, remember that it really *is* a jungle out there. Don't go poking under rocks or fallen branches. Snakebites are very rare, but don't do anything to increase the odds. If you do encounter a snake, stay calm, don't make any sudden movements, and *do not* try to handle it. Also, avoid swimming in major rivers unless a guide or local operator can vouch for their safety. Though white-water sections and stretches in mountainous areas are generally pretty safe, most mangrove canals and river mouths in Costa Rica support healthy crocodile and caiman populations.

Bugs and bug bites will probably be your greatest health concern in the Costa Rican wilderness, and even they aren't as big a problem as you might expect. Mostly, bugs are an inconvenience, although mosquitoes can carry malaria or dengue (see "Health & Insurance" in chapter 2 for more information). A strong repellent and proper clothing will minimize both the danger and inconvenience; you may also want to bring along some cortisone or Benadryl creme to soothe itching. At the beaches, you'll probably be bitten by sand fleas, or *pirujas*. These nearly invisible insects leave an irritating welt. Try not to scratch, as this can lead to open sores and infections. Pirujas are most active at sunrise and sunset, so you might want to cover up or avoid the beaches at these times.

And remember: Whenever you enter and enjoy nature, you should tread lightly and try not to disturb the natural environment. There's a popular slogan well known to most campers that certainly applies here: "Leave nothing but footprints, take nothing but memories." If you must take home a souvenir, take photos. Do not cut or uproot plants or flowers. Pack out everything you pack in, and *please* do not litter.

5 Ecologically Oriented Volunteer & Study Programs

Below are some institutions and organizations that are working on ecology and sustainable development projects.

Asociación de Voluntarios para el Servicio en las Areas Protegidas (ASVO) (© and fax **506/233-4989;** asvo89@racsa.co.cr) organizes volunteers to work in Costa Rican national parks. A 30-day minimum commitment is required, as are several letters of recommendation and a basic ability to converse in Spanish. Housing is provided at a basic ranger station, and there is a $12-per-day fee to cover food, which is basic Tico fare.

Costa Rica Rainforest Outward Bound School (© and fax **506/777-1222;** www.crrobs.org) is the local branch of this well-respected international adventure-based outdoor-education organization. Courses range from 2 weeks to a full semester and cover everything from surfing, kayaking, and tree-climbing to learning Spanish.

Eco Teach (© **800/626-8992;** www.ecoteach.com) works primarily in facilitating educational trips for high school and college student groups. Trips focus on Costa Rican ecology and culture. Costs run around $1,900 per person for a 10-day trip, including airfare, lodging, meals, classes, and travel.

Global Volunteers (© **800/487-1074** or 651/407-6100; www.globalvolunteers.com) is a U.S.-based organization that offers a unique opportunity to travelers who've always wanted a Peace Corps–like experience but couldn't make a 2-year commitment. For 2 to 3 weeks, you can join one of its working vacations in Costa Rica. A certain set of skills, such as engineering or agricultural knowledge, is helpful but by no means necessary. Each trip is undertaken at a particular community's request, to complete a specific project. However, be warned: These "volunteer" experiences do not come cheap. You must pay for your transportation as well as a hefty program fee, around $1,600 for a 2-week program.

Habitat for Humanity International (© **229/924-6935** in the U.S., or 506/296-8120; www.habitat.org) has several chapters in Costa Rica and sometimes runs organized Global Village programs here.

The **Institute for Central American Development Studies** ★★ (ICADS; © **506/225-0508;** www.icadscr.com) offers internship and research opportunities in the areas of environment, agriculture, human rights, and women's studies. An intensive Spanish-language program can be combined with work-study or volunteer opportunities.

The **Monteverde Institute** (© **506/645-5053;** www.mvinstitute.org) offers study programs in Monteverde and also has a volunteer center that helps in placement and training of volunteers.

The **Organization for Tropical Studies** (© 506/240-6696; www.ots.ac.cr) represents several Costa Rican and U.S. universities. This organization's mission is to promote research, education, and the wise use of natural resources in the tropics. Research facilities include La Selva Biological Station near Braulio Carrillo National Park and Palo Verde and the Wilson Botanical Gardens near San Vito. Housing is provided at one of the research facilities. There's a wide variety of programs, ranging from full-semester undergraduate programs (at around $11,000) to specific graduate courses (of varying duration), to its recently added tourist programs (these are generally being sponsored/run by established operators such as Costa Rica Expeditions, Elderhostel, and others). These range in duration from 3 to 10 days, and costs vary greatly. Entrance requirements and competition for some of these courses can be demanding.

Vida (© 506/233-7203; info@vida.org) is a local nongovernmental organization working on sustainable development and conservation issues that can often place volunteers.

San José

At first blush, San José may seem little more than a chaotic jumble of cars, buses, buildings, and people. The central downtown section of San José is an urban planner's nightmare, where once-quiet streets are now burdened by traffic in a near-constant state of gridlock. Antiquated buses spewing diesel fumes and a lack of emission controls have created a brown cloud over the San José sky. Below the cloud, the city bustles, but it's not particularly hospitable to travelers. Sidewalks are poorly maintained and claustrophobic, and street crime is a problem. Most visitors quickly seek the sanctuary of their hotel room and the first chance to escape the city.

Still, San José is the most cosmopolitan city in Central America. Costa Rica's stable government and the Central Valley's climate have, over the years, attracted people from all over the world. There's a large diplomatic and international business presence here. As a result, there has been a proliferation of small, elegant hotels in renovated historic buildings, as well as innovative new restaurants serving a wide range of international cuisines. Together, these hotels and restaurants provide visitors with one of the greatest varieties of options found anywhere between Mexico City and Bogotá.

San José will invariably serve as a default hub or transfer point for all visitors to Costa Rica (at least until the Liberia airport gets more flights). This chapter will help you plan your time in the capital and help ease your way through the pitfalls inherent in such a rough-and-tumble little city.

IT'S IN THE BEANS San José was built on the profits of the coffee-export business. Between the airport and downtown, you'll pass by working coffee farms. Glance up from almost any street in the city and on the surrounding volcanic mountains and you'll see a patchwork quilt of farm fields, most of which are planted with the *grano de oro* (golden bean), as it's known here. San José was a forgotten backwater of the Spanish empire until the first shipments of the local beans made their way to sleepy souls in Europe late in the 19th century. Soon, San José was riding high. Coffee planters, newly rich and craving culture, imposed a tax on themselves in order to build the Teatro Nacional, San José's most beautiful building. Coffee profits also built the city a university. Today, you can wake up and smell the coffee roasting as you wander the streets near the Central Market (Mercado Central), and in any cafe or restaurant you can get a hot cup of sweet, milky *café con leche* to remind you of the bean that built San José.

Why does coffee grow so well around the city? It's the climate. The Central Valley, in which the city sits, has a perfect climate. At 3,750 feet above sea level, San José enjoys springlike temperatures year-round. This pleasant climate, and the beautiful views of lush green mountainsides, make San José a memorable city to visit. All you have to do is glance up at those mountains to know that this is one of the most beautifully situated capitals in Central America. And if a glance isn't enough for you, you'll find that it's extremely easy to get out into the countryside. Within an hour or two, you can climb a volcano, go white-water rafting, hike through a cloud forest, and stroll through a butterfly garden—among many, many other activities.

1 Orientation

ARRIVING

BY PLANE   **Juan Santamaría International Airport** (© **506/443-2942** for 24-hour airport information) is located near the city of Alajuela, about 20 minutes from downtown San José. A taxi into town will cost between $12 and $15, and a bus is only 55¢. The Alajuela–San José buses run frequently and will drop you off anywhere along Paseo Colón, or at a station near the Parque de la Merced (downtown, between Calles 12 and 14 and Avenidas 2 and 4). There are two separate lines: **Tuasa** buses are red; **Station Wagon** buses are beige/yellow. At the airport you'll find the bus stop directly in front of the main terminal. Make sure to ask whether the bus is going to San José, or you'll end up in Alajuela. If you have a lot of luggage, you should probably take a cab.

There are quite a few car-rental agencies with desks and offices at the airport, although if you're planning on spending a few days in San José itself, a car is a liability. (If you're heading off immediately to the beach, though, it's much easier to pick up your car here than at a downtown office.) Several car-rental agencies already have desks inside the new terminal, right where passengers exit customs and immigration; others are still in limbo awaiting completion of an airport remodeling (see below), so make sure to contact them first to confirm that they will have an agent and/or an office at the airport when you arrive.

At press time, the airport was in the midst of a major renovation and expansion. So far, the section for arriving international passengers is open· and functioning. The new baggage claim and Customs and Immigrations areas are modern and spacious, although not necessarily fast and efficient. Hopefully by the time you read this, the large, new main terminal will be open for departing passengers. Currently, departing passengers must still use the cramped and crowded old terminal. Despite the major remodeling, chaos and confusion still greet arriving passengers the second they step out of the terminal. As in the past, you literally have to fight off scores of aggressive taxi drivers and people offering to carry your bags. Most porters or skycaps wear a uniform identifying them as such, but sometimes "improvised" porters will try to earn a few dollars here (moreover, there's often nowhere for them really to have to carry your bags, as the line of waiting taxis and shuttles is just steps away). Make sure you keep a very watchful eye on your bags, as thieves have historically preyed on newly arrived passengers and their luggage. You should tip porters about 50¢ per bag.

In terms of taxis, you should stick with the official airport taxi service, **Taxis Unidos Aeropuerto** (© **506/221-6865**), which operates a fleet of orange vans and sedans, charging fixed prices according to your destination hotel. Despite the fact that Taxis Unidos has an official monopoly at the airport, you will usually find a handful of regular cabs (in traditional red sedans) and "pirate" cabs, freelance drivers using their own vehicles. In a pinch, you could use either of these latter options, but I recommend using the official service for safety and standardized prices.

You have several options for **exchanging money** when you arrive at the airport. There's an official state bank inside the main terminal. It's open Monday through Friday from 9am to 4pm. When the bank is closed (and even when it's open), there are usually official money-changers (with badges) working both inside and outside the terminal. Outside the terminal, you may be approached by unofficial money-changers. Three things to note: (1) Though black-market money-changing is illegal, it's quite common; (2) there's never much variance between the official bank rate and the street exchange rate; (3) the airport is one of the safer places to try a black-market exchange, though you should be careful wherever and whenever you decide to change money. See "Exchanging Money" in chapter 2 for more details.

If for some reason you arrive in San José via Travelair, private aircraft, or another small commuter or charter airline, you may find yourself at the **Tobías Bolaños International Airport** in Pavas. This small airport is located on the western side of downtown San José, about 10 minutes by car from the center. There are no car-rental desks here, however, so unless you have a car and/or driver waiting for you here, you will have to take a cab into town, which should cost between $10 and $15.

BY BUS   If you're coming to San José by bus, where you disembark depends on where you're coming from. (The different bus companies have their offices, and thus their drop-off points, all over downtown San José. When you buy your ticket, ask where you'll be let off.) Buses arriving from Panama pass first through Cartago and San Pedro before letting passengers off in downtown San José; buses arriving from Nicaragua generally enter the city on the west end of town, on Paseo Colón. If you're staying here, you can ask to be let off before the final stop.

BY CAR   For those of you intrepid readers arriving by car, you will be entering San José via the Interamerican Highway. If you arrive **from Nicaragua and the north,** you will find that the highway brings you first past the airport and the city of Alajuela, to the western edge of the downtown, right at the end of Paseo Colón, where it hits the Parque Sabana. This area is well marked with large road signs, which will either direct you to the downtown (CENTRO) or the western suburbs of Rhomerser, Pavas, and Escazú. If you're heading toward downtown, just follow the flow of traffic and turn left on Paseo Colón.

For those of you entering **from Panama and the south,** things get a little more complicated. The Interamerican Highway first passes through the city of Cartago, and then through the San José suburbs of Curridabat and San Pedro, before reaching downtown. This route is relatively well marked, and if you stick with the major flow of traffic, you should find San José without any problem.

VISITOR INFORMATION

There's an **ICT (Instituto Costarricense de Turismo)** office at Juan Santamaría International Airport, where you can pick up maps and brochures before you head into San José. It's not clear where they'll set up shop once the remodeling is complete, but expect this office to be open Monday through Friday from 8am to 4pm. If you're looking for the **main ICT visitor information center** in San José, it's located below the Plaza de la Cultura, at the entrance to the Gold Museum, on Calle 5 between Avenida Central and Avenida 2 (© **506/222-1090**). The people here are very helpful, although the information they have to offer is rather limited. This office is open Monday through Friday from 9am to 5pm.

CITY LAYOUT

Downtown San José is laid out on a grid. *Avenidas* (avenues) run east and west, while *calles* (streets) run north and south. The center of the city is at **Avenida Central** and **Calle Central.** To the north of Avenida Central, the avenidas have

San José

ACCOMMODATIONS ■

Aurola Holiday Inn **32**
Barceló Amón Plaza **19**
Brittania Hotel **29**
Gran Hotel Costa Rica **37**
Hotel Alóki **23**
Hotel Aranjuez **20**
Hotel Bienvenido **14**
Hotel Cacts **7**
Hotel Del Rey **45**
Hotel Don Carlos **26**
Hotel Grano de Oro **12**
Hotel Le Bergerac **53**

Hotel Petit Victoria **11**
Hotel Rosa del Paseo **10**
Hotel Santo Tomas **31**
Hotel Torremolinos **6**
Joluva Guesthouse **28**
La Casa Verde de Amón **27**
Meliá Confort Corobicí **3**
Pension de la Cuesta **49**
Radisson Europa Hotel **16**
Raya Vida Villa **21**
Taylor's Inn **18**
Toruma Youth Hostel **52**

RESTAURANTS ◆

Aya Sofya **51**
Cafe Britt **39**
Café Mundo **22**
Café Parisien **38**
Chelles **44**
El Chicote **2**
Grano de Oro Restaurant **12**
L'Ile de France **6**
La Cocina de Leña **17**
La Esmeralda **42**
La Masía de Triquel **1**
La Piazzetta **5**

ATTRACTIONS ●

Le Bilboquet **30**

Machu Picchu Bar and Restaurant **8**

Manolo's Restaurante **34**

Pasteleria Francesa Boudsocq **9**

Soda Billy Boy **41**

Soda Coppelia **13**

Tin Jo **47**

Vishnu **33**

Vishnu **36**

Vishnu **48**

Centro Nacional de Arte y Cultura
  (National Arts Center) **24**

Jade Museum (Museo de Jade) **25**

Main Visitor Information Center **43**

Museo de Arte Costarricense **4**

Museo de los Niños (Children's Museum) **15**

Museo de Oro (Gold Museum) **40**

Museo Nacional de Costa Rica
  (National Museum) **50**

Serpentarium **46**

Teatro Melico Salazar **35**

Teatro Nacional (National Theater) **39**

"I know there's got to be a number here somewhere . . .": The Arcane Art of Finding an Address in San José

This is one of the most confusing aspects of visiting Costa Rica in general, and San José in particular. Though there are often street addresses and building numbers for locations in downtown San José, they are almost never used. Addresses are given as a set of coordinates such as "Calle 3 between Avenida Central and Avenida 1." It's then up to you to locate the building within that block, keeping in mind that the building could be on either side of the street. Many addresses include additional information, such as the number of meters or *varas* (an old Spanish measurement roughly equal to a yard) from a specified intersection or some other well-known landmark. (These "meter measurements" are not precise, but are a good way to give directions to a taxi driver. In basic terms, 100 meters = 1 block, 200 meters = 2 blocks, and so on.) These landmarks are what become truly confusing for visitors to the city because they are often simply restaurants, bars, and shops that would be familiar only to locals.

Things get even more confusing when the landmark in question no longer exists. The classic example of this is "the Coca-Cola," one of the most common landmarks used in addresses in the blocks surrounding San José's main market. Trouble is, the Coca-Cola bottling plant it refers to is no longer there; the edifice is long gone, and one of the principal downtown bus depots stands in its place. Old habits die hard, though, and the address description remains. You may also try to find someplace near the *antiguo higuerón* ("old fig tree") in San Pedro. This tree was felled years ago. In outlying neighborhoods, addresses can become long directions such as "50 meters south of the old church, then 100 meters east, then 20 meters south." Luckily for the visitor, most downtown addresses are more straightforward.

Oh, if you're wondering how letter carriers manage, well, welcome to the club. Some folks actually get their mail delivered this way, but most people and businesses in San José use a post-office box. This is called an *apartado,* and is abbreviated "Apdo." or "A.P." in mailing addresses.

odd numbers beginning with Avenida 1; to the south, they have even numbers beginning with Avenida 2. Likewise, calles to the east of Calle Central have odd numbers, and those to the west have even numbers. The main downtown artery is **Avenida 2,** which merges with Avenida Central on either side of the downtown area. West of downtown, Avenida Central becomes **Paseo Colón,** which ends at Sabana Park and feeds into the highway to Alajuela, the airport, and the Pacific coast. East of downtown, Avenida Central leads to San Pedro and then to Cartago and the Interamerican Highway heading south. **Calle 3** will take you out of town to the north and put you on the Guápiles Highway out to the Caribbean coast.

THE NEIGHBORHOODS IN BRIEF

San José is sprawling. Today it's divided into dozens of neighborhoods known as *barrios*. Most of the listings in this chapter fall within the main downtown area, but there are a few outlying neighborhoods you'll need to know about.

Downtown In San José's busiest area, you'll find most of the city's museums. There are also many tour companies, restaurants, and hotels here. Unfortunately, traffic noise and exhaust fumes make this one of the least pleasant parts of the city. Streets and avenues are usually bustling and crowded with pedestrians and vehicular traffic, and street crime is most rampant here.

Barrio Amón/Barrio Otoya These two neighborhoods, just north and east of downtown, are the site of the greatest concentration of historic buildings in San José. In the past few years, some enterprising entrepreneurs have been renovating the old buildings and turning them into hotels. If you're looking for character and don't mind the noise and exhaust fumes, this neighborhood makes a good base for exploring the city.

La Sabana/Paseo Colón Paseo Colón, a wide boulevard west of downtown, is an extension of Avenida Central and ends at La Sabana Park. It has several good, small hotels and numerous excellent restaurants. This is also where many of the city's car-rental agencies have their in-town offices.

San Pedro/Los Yoses Located east of downtown San José, Los Yoses is an upper–middle-class neighborhood that is home to many diplomatic missions and embassies. San Pedro is a little farther east and is the site of the University of Costa Rica. There are numerous college-type bars and restaurants all around the edge of the campus and several good restaurants and small hotels in both neighborhoods.

Escazú/Santa Ana Located in the hills west of San José, Escazú and Santa Ana are two fast-growing suburbs. Although the area is only 15 minutes from San José by taxi, it feels much farther away because of its relaxed atmosphere. This area has a large expatriate community, with so many bed-and-breakfast establishments located here.

Heredia/Alajeula/Airport Area Heredia and Alajuela are two colonial-era cities that lie closer to the airport than San José. Alajeula is the closest city to the airport, with Heredia lying about midway between Alajeula and the capital. For more information on these cities, see "Side Trips from San José" at the end of this chapter. There a several quite nice, high-end boutique hotels in this area. There are also several large hotels and one chain hotel located on, or just off, the Interamerican Highway close to the airport.

2 Getting Around

BY BUS Bus transportation around San José is cheap—the fare is usually somewhere around 15¢ (though the Alajuela–San José buses that run in from the airport cost 55¢). The most important buses are those running east along Avenida 2 and west along Avenida 3. The **Sabana/Cementerio** bus runs from Sabana Park to downtown and is one of the most convenient buses to use. You'll find a bus stop for the outbound Sabana/Cementerio bus near the main post office on Avenida 3 near the corner of Calle 2, and another one on Calle 11 between Avenida Central and Avenida 1. This bus also has stops all along Avenida 2. **San**

Tips Rental-Car Advice

If you know you'll be renting a car, I highly recommend reserving it in advance from home. All of the major international agencies and many of the local companies have toll-free numbers and websites. Sometimes you can even save a bit on the cost by reserving in advance. Costa Rica's car-rental fleet is not sufficient to meet demand during the high season, and rental cars run at a premium. Sometimes this allows the agencies here on the ground to gouge last-minute rental-car shoppers.

Pedro buses leave from Avenida Central between Calle 9 and Calle 11, in front of the Cine Capri, and will take you out of downtown heading east. **Escazú-** bound buses leave from the Coca-Cola bus station, as well as from Avenida 6 and Calle 2, while buses for **Santa Ana** leave only from the Coca-Cola bus station.

Board buses from the front. The bus drivers can make change, although they don't like to receive large bills. Be especially mindful of your wallet, purse, or other valuables, since pickpockets often work the crowded buses.

BY TAXI Although taxis in San José have meters (*marías*), the drivers sometimes refuse to use them, particularly with foreigners, so you'll occasionally have to negotiate the price. Always try to get them to use the meter first (say *"ponga la maría, por favor"*). The official rate at press time is around 80¢ for the first kilometer (0.6 miles) and around 40¢ for each additional kilometer. If you have a rough idea of how far it is to your destination, you can estimate how much it should cost from these figures. After 10pm, taxis are legally allowed to add a 20% surcharge. Some of the meters are programmed to include the extra charge automatically, but be careful: Some drivers will use the evening setting during the daytime, or (at night) try to charge an extra 20% on top of the higher meter setting. **Tipping** taxi drivers is not expected. It's not uncommon for passengers to sit in the front seat with the driver.

Depending on your location, the time of day, and the weather (rain places taxis at a premium), it's relatively easy to hail a cab downtown. You'll always find taxis in front of the Teatro Nacional (albeit at high prices) and around the Parque Central at Avenida Central and Calle Central. Taxis in front of hotels and the El Pueblo tourist complex usually charge more than others, although this is technically illegal. Most hotels will gladly call you a cab, either for a downtown excursion or for a trip back out to the airport. You can also get a cab by calling **Coopetaxi** (© 506/235-9966), **Coopetico** (© 506/224-7979), **Coopeirazu** (© 506/254-3211), or **Coopeguaria** (© 506/226-1366).

ON FOOT Downtown San José is very compact. Nearly every place you might want to go is within a 15-by-4–block area. Because of the traffic congestion, you'll often find it faster to walk than to take a bus or taxi. Be careful when walking the streets any time of day or night. Flashy jewelry, loosely held handbags or backpacks, and expensive camera equipment tend to attract thieves. You should also watch your step: Between the earthquakes, wear and tear, and negligence, the sidewalks in San José have become veritable obstacle courses and the cause of more than one sprained ankle.

Avenida Central is a pedestrian-only street for several blocks around Calle Central toward the Cultural Plaza. It has recently been redone with interesting paving stones and the occasional fountain in an attempt to create a comfortable pedestrian mall.

BY CAR It will cost you between $35 and $85 per day to rent a car in Costa Rica (the higher prices are for four-wheel-drive vehicles). Many car-rental agencies have offices at the airport. If not, they will usually either pick you up or deliver the car to any San José hotel. If you decide to receive your rental car in downtown San José, be prepared for some very congested streets.

The following companies have desks at Juan Santamaría International Airport, as well as offices downtown: **Alamo Rent A Car** (© **506/441-1260** at the airport, or 506/233-7733 in downtown San José; www.alamocostarica.com); **Adobe Rent A Car** (© **506/442-2422** at the airport, or 506/258-4242 in downtown San José; www.adobecar.com); **Avis Rent A Car** (© **800/331-1212** in the U.S., 506/442-1321 at the airport, or 506/293-2222 in downtown San José; www.avis.com); **Budget Rent A Car** (© **800/527-0700** in the U.S., 506/ 441-4444 at the airport, or 506/223-3284 in downtown San José; www.budget. co.cr); **Europcar Rent A Car** (© **506/443-2336** at the airport, or 506/257-1158 in San José; www.europcar.com); **Hertz Rent A Car** (© **800/654-3131** in the U.S., 506/441-0097 at the airport, or 506/221-1818 in downtown San José; www.hertz.com); **National Car Rental** (© **800/328-4567** in the U.S., 506/441-6533 at the airport, or 506/290-8787 in downtown San José; www. natcar.com); **Payless Rent A Car** (© **800/582-7432** in the U.S., 506/441-9366 at the airport, or 506/257-0026 in downtown San José; www.paylesscr.com); **Thrifty Car Rental** (© **800/367-2277** in the U.S., 506/442-8585 at the airport, or 506/257-3434 in downtown San José); **Tropical Rent A Car** (© **506/ 442-8000;** www.tropicalcarrental.com); and **Toyota Rent A Car** (© **506/ 441-1411** at the airport or 506/258-5797 in downtown San José; www. toyotarent.com).

There are dozens of other car-rental agencies in San José, and most of them will arrange for airport or hotel pickup or delivery. Two of the more dependable agencies are **American Rent A Car,** 425 meters north of the Toyota dealership on Paseo Colón (© **506/221-5353**); and **Hola! Rent A Car,** west of Hotel Irazú, La Uruca, San José (© **506/231-5666;** www.hola.net).

To rent a car in Costa Rica, you must be at least 21 years old and have a valid driver's license and a major credit card. For more advice, see the "Getting Around" section in chapter 2.

FAST FACTS: San José

Airport See "Arriving" in section 1 of this chapter.

Bookstores **Seventh Street Books,** Calle 7 between Avenidas 1 and Central (© **506/256-8251**), has a wide range of new and used books in English, with an excellent selection of tropical biology, bird, and flora books; it's open daily from 9am to 7pm. For a wide selection of new books in English and Spanish, you can also check out **Libreria Internacional,** located 300 meters west of the Taco Bell in San Pedro (© **506/253-9553**). It's open Monday through Saturday from 9:30am to 7pm, and Sunday 10am to 6pm. Libreria International also has a store in the Multiplaza mall in Escazú (© **506/288-1138**).

Camera Repair **Equipos Fotográficos Canon,** Avenida 3 between Calles 3 and 5 (© **506/233-0176**), specializes in Canon but may be able to repair other brands. You could also try **Dima,** Avenida Central between Calles 3 and 5 (© **506/222-3969**).

Car Rentals See "Getting Around," earlier in this chapter.

Climate See "When to Go" in chapter 2.

Credit Cards **Credomatic** (℃ **506/257-0155** main office or 506/295-9000 to report lost or stolen cards 24 hours) is the local representative of most major credit cards: American Express, MasterCard, and Visa. It has an office in San José across from the Banco de San José on Calle Central between Avenidas 3 and 5. It's open Monday through Friday from 8am to 7pm, and Saturday from 9am to 1pm. This office also serves as a traditional **American Express Travel Services** office, issuing traveler's checks and providing other standard services. You can call the number above to report all lost or stolen cards. To report lost or stolen American Express traveler's checks within Costa Rica, call ℃ **0-800-011-0080.** To report a lost or stolen American Express card from inside Costa Rica, you can also call **0-800-012-3211.** To report a lost or stolen Diners Club card from inside Costa Rica, call ℃ **506/257-1766,** or call collect ℃ **001-303-799-1504.**

Currency Exchange Most state-run banks will change money, although the lines and bureaucracy can be daunting. The best thing to do is to exchange money at your hotel. If the hotel can't do this for you, or if it is giving a very poor rate of exchange, have someone direct you to a private bank or exchange house (*casa de cambio*) where you won't have to stand in line for hours. Avoid exchanging money on the street. The easiest solution of all is simply to use an ATM and withdraw money from your bank account at home.

Dentists Call your embassy, which will have a list of recommended dentists. Many bilingual dentists also advertise in the *Tico Times*. Because treatments are so inexpensive in Costa Rica, dental tourism has become a popular option for people needing extensive work.

Doctors Contact your embassy for information on doctors in San José, or see "Hospitals," below.

Drugstores There are countless pharmacies and drugstores in San José. Many of them will deliver at little or no extra cost. The pharmacy at the **Hospital Clínica Bíblica** (Avenida 14 between Calle Central and Calle 1; ℃ **506/257-5252**) is open 24 hours every day of the year. **Farmacia Fischel,** Avenida 3 and Calle 2, is across from the main post office (℃ **506/257-7979**). It's open Monday through Saturday from 8am to 7pm. The pharmacy (℃ **506/208-1080**) at the new **Hospital CIMA** in Escazú is also open 24 hours every day.

Embassies/Consulates See "Fast Facts: Costa Rica" in chapter 2.

Emergencies In case of fire, dial ℃ **118;** for the police, an ambulance, or general emergencies, dial ℃ **911.** You can also call the Costa Rican Red Cross directly, by dialing ℃ **128;** this is sometimes the fastest method to get an ambulance and emergency medical support.

Express Mail Services Many international courier and express-mail services have offices in San José, including: **DHL,** on Paseo Colón between Calles 30 and 32 (℃ **506/290-3020;** www.dhl.com); **EMS Courier,** with desks at the principal metropolitan post offices (℃ **506/233-3713**); **FedEx,** represented by the Aerocasillas office at the Yaohan shopping center across from the Hotel Corobicí (℃ **506/255-4567**); and **United Parcel**

Service, in Pavas (© 506/290-2828; www.ups.com). *Beware:* Despite what you may be told, packages sent overnight to U.S. addresses tend to take 3 to 4 days to reach their destination.

Eyeglasses Look for the word *optica*. **Optica Jiménez** (© 506/257-4658 or 506/233-4475) and **Optica Vision** (© 506/255-2266) are two dependable chains, with stores around San José. They can do everything from eye exams to repairs.

Hospitals **Clinica Biblica,** Avenida 14 between Calle Central and Calle 1 (© 506/257-5252 or, for emergencies, 506/257-0466; www.clinicabiblica. org), is conveniently located close to downtown and has several English-speaking doctors. The new **Hospital CIMA** (© 506/208-1000; www.hospitalsanjose.net), located in Escazú on the Fernando Próspero Highway, which connects San José and the western suburb of Santa Ana, has the most modern facilities in the country.

Information See "Visitor Information," in section 1 of this chapter.

Internet Access Internet cafes are popping up around San José at a staggering rate. Many hotels allow guests to send and receive e-mail. If not, you have a number of options: **Racsa,** Avenida 5 and Calle 1 (© 506/287-0087; www.racsa.co.cr); **Cybercafe,** at the Las Arcadas shopping center next to the Gran Hotel Costa Rica (© 506/233-3310); and **Internet Café,** in Plaza San Pedro (© 506/224-7295; www.internetcafecr.com; open 24 hours), with another office in the Centro Colón, on Paseo Colón, all allow Web and e-mail access. Rates run between $1 and $4 per hour.

Laundry/Dry Cleaning **Sixaola,** Avenida 2 between Calles 7 and 9 (© 506/221-2111), open Monday through Friday from 7am to 6pm and Saturday from 8am to 1pm, is a dependable place downtown to get clothes cleaned. Unfortunately, its prices are fairly high. **Cybercafe,** at the Las Arcadas shopping center next to the Gran Hotel Costa Rica (© 506/233-3310), is a popular Internet cafe that has recently added a self-serve Laundromat.

Maps The Costa Rican Tourist Board (ICT) (see "Visitor Information" in section 1 of this chapter) can usually provide you with good maps of both Costa Rica and San José. Other sources in San José are **Seventh Street Books,** Calle 7 between Avenidas Central and 1 (© 506/256-8251); **Librería Lehmann,** Avenida Central between Calles 1 and 3 (© 506/223-1212); and **Librería Universal,** Avenida Central and Calles Central and 1 (© 506/222-2222).

Newspapers/Magazines The *Tico Times* is Costa Rica's principal English-language weekly paper and serves both the expatriate community and visitors. You can also get the *International Herald Tribune, Miami Herald, New York Times, USA Today, TIME,* and *Newsweek,* as well as other English-language publications. You'll find these publications in hotel gift shops and in bookstores that sell English-language books. If you understand Spanish, *La Nación* is the leading daily paper. Its "Viva" section has an extensive listing of current cultural events.

Photographic Needs Film is expensive in Costa Rica, so bring as much as you will need from home. I recommend that you wait to have your film processed at home; but if you must develop your prints down here, try **Fuji**

Foto, Avenida Central between Calle 1 and Calle Central (☏ **506/222-2222**). For more serious photographic needs (equipment, repairs, etc.), try **Dima,** Avenida Central between Calles 3 and 5 (☏ **506/222-3969**).

Police Dial ☏ **911** for the police. They should have someone who speaks English.

Post Office The main post office (*correo*) is on Calle 2 between Avenidas 1 and 3 (☏ **506/223-9766**), and is open Monday through Friday from 7:30am to 6pm and Saturday from 7:30am to noon. At press time, it costs 70 colones (23¢) to mail a letter to the United States; 90 colones (30¢) to Europe; 55 colones (18¢) for a postcard. Given the Costa Rican postal service's track record, I recommend paying an extra 165 colones (55¢) to have anything of any value certified.

Rest Rooms These are known as *sanitarios* or *servicios sanitarios*. You may also see or hear them called *baños.* They are marked *damas* (women) and *hombres* or *caballeros* (men). Public rest rooms are rare to nonexistent, but most big hotels and public restaurants will let you use their bathrooms. If you're downtown, there are public bathrooms at the entrance to the Gold Museum.

Safety Pickpockets and purse slashers are rife in San José, especially on public buses, in the markets, on crowded sidewalks, and near hospitals. Leave your passport, money, and other valuables in your hotel safe and carry only as much as you really need when you go out. It's a good idea to make a photocopy of your passport's opening pages and carry that with you. If you do carry anything valuable with you, keep it in a money belt or special passport bag around your neck. Day packs are a prime target of brazen pickpockets throughout the city. Stay away from the red-light district northwest of the Central Market. Also, be advised that the Parque Nacional is not a safe place for a late-night stroll.

Other precautions include walking around corner vendors, not between the vendor and the building. The tight space between the vendor and the building is a favorite spot for pickpockets. Never park a car on the street, and never leave anything of value in a car, even if it's in a guarded parking lot. Don't even leave your car unattended by the curb in front of a hotel while you dash in to check on your reservation. With these precautions in mind, you should have a safe visit to San José. Also, see "Safety" in "Fast Facts: Costa Rica," in chapter 2.

Taxes All hotels charge 16.3% tax. Restaurants charge 13% tax and also add on a 10% service charge, for a total of 23% more on your bill. There is an airport departure tax of $17.

Taxis See section 2 of this chapter, "Getting Around."

Telegrams/Faxes You can send telegrams and faxes (for about $2 per page to the United States) from the **ICE office** on Avenida 2 between Calles 1 and 3 (open daily from 7am to 10pm). **Radiográfica,** at Calle 1 and Avenida 5 in San José (☏ **506/287-0600**), and **Western Union** (☏ **800/777-7777** or 506/283-6336), with numerous offices around the country, also have telegram services.

Telephones See "Telephones/Faxes" in "Fast Facts: Costa Rica," in chapter 2. There are no city or area codes to dial from within Costa Rica; use the country code, 506, only when dialing a San José number from outside Costa Rica. (To call San José from the United States, dial the international access code [011], then 506, then the seven-digit number.)

Time Zone San José is on central standard time (same as Chicago and St. Louis), 6 hours behind Greenwich mean time.

Useful Telephone Numbers For directory assistance, call ✆ **113**; for international directory assistance, call ✆ **124**; for the exact time, call ✆ **112**.

Water The water in San José is perfectly fine to drink. Nonetheless, travelers sometimes experience stomach discomfort during their first few days in Costa Rica. If you want to be cautious, drink bottled water and *frescos* made with milk instead of water. *Sin hielo* means "no ice," and this is what you'll want to say if you're nervous about the water—just because it's frozen doesn't mean it's not water.

Weather The weather in San José (including the Central Valley) is usually temperate, never getting extremely hot or cold. May to November is the rainy season, though the rain usually falls only in the afternoon and evening.

3 Accommodations

Just a few years back, hotels were popping up all over downtown San José. Though the boom has stopped, there's a distinct glut of accommodations. This can be good for you, the visitor, as it's created a healthy degree of competition—it pays to shop around for special packages or promotions when you plan to visit. Nevertheless, there's been a significant weeding-out process, and the better-run establishments (including those recommended here) are often booked well in advance during the high season.

In San José, your choices range from luxury resorts to budget pensions charging only a few dollars a night. However, these two extremes are the exceptions, not the norm. The vast number of accommodations, and the best deals, are to be found in the $50-to-$100 price range. Within this moderate bracket, you'll find restored homes that have been turned into small hotels and bed-and-breakfasts, modern hotels with swimming pools and exercise rooms, and older downtown business hotels.

CHOOSING WHERE TO STAY   **Downtown hotels,** many of which are in beautifully restored homes, are convenient to museums, restaurants, and shopping, but can be noisy. Many people are also bothered by the exhaust fumes that permeate downtown streets. Moreover, since the streets of downtown are not especially safe, particularly at night, you will often be taking taxis whether you stay downtown or in a close-by neighborhood or suburb. **Barrio Amón** is the downtown neighborhood with the most character and remnants of colonial architecture. If you want clean air and a peaceful night's sleep, consider staying out in the suburbs. **Escazú** and **Santa Ana** are both quiet, yet modern suburbs, and many of the hotels here have great views. Heading east from downtown, **Los Yoses** is fairly close to the center of the action, yet still quiet. If you've rented a car, make sure your hotel provides secure parking, or you'll have to find (and pay for) a nearby lot. If you plan to take some day tours, you can just as easily arrange these from a hotel situated outside the downtown area.

If you're heading out to Guanacaste, the central Pacific, or the northern zone, you might consider a hotel or bed-and-breakfast either near or beyond the airport. Sure, you give up proximity to downtown, but you can cut as much as an hour off your travel time to any of these destinations. Many car-rental companies will even deliver to or pick up cars from these establishments.

ALTERNATIVES TO HOTELS   In the past few years, dozens of bed-and-breakfasts have opened up around the San José area. Most are in residential neighborhoods that are quieter, though less convenient, than downtown locations. You can find out about many B&Bs, both in San José and around the country, by contacting either the **Costa Rica Bed and Breakfast Group** (© 506/228-8726) or the **All Costa Rica Bed and Breakfast Reservation Service** (© 506/223-4168; fax 506/223-4157; rayavida@hotels.co.cr).

If you plan to be in town for a while or are traveling with family or several friends, you may want to consider staying in an *apartotel,* a cross between an apartment complex and a hotel. You can rent by the day, week, or month, and you get a furnished apartment with a full kitchen, plus housekeeping and laundry service. Options include **Apartotel El Sesteo** (© 506/296-1805; fax 506/296-1865; sesteo@racsa.co.cr); **Apartotel La Sabana** (© 506/220-2422; fax 506/231-1786; www.crica.com/hotels/lasabana); **Apartotel Don Carlos** (© 506/221-6707; fax 506/255-0828; www.doncarlos.co.cr); and **Apartotel Los Yoses** (© 506/225-0033; fax 506/225-5595; www.apartotel.com).

DOWNTOWN SAN JOSÉ/BARRIO AMÓN
VERY EXPENSIVE

Aurola Holiday Inn ⚫   Situated directly across the street from the attractive downtown Parque Morazán, this is San José's only high-rise deluxe hotel. The rooms are everything you might expect in this price range—but nothing more. The hotel has been around for quite a few years, and the age is starting to show. Moreover, I've found the service can be somewhat hit-or-miss. However, if you get one of the upper-floor rooms on the north side, you'll have one of the best views in the city.

Avenida 5 and Calle 5 (A.P. 7802-1000), San José. © 800/HOLIDAY [465-4329] in the U.S. and Canada, or 506/222-2424. Fax 506/255-1171. www.aurola-holidayinn.com. 200 units. $125–$150 double, $150 junior suite, $225–$450 suite. AE, DC, MC, V. Free parking. **Amenities:** 2 restaurants (international); 2 bars; casino; indoor pool and poolside snack bar; exercise room; Jacuzzi; sauna; tour desk; car-rental desk; well-appointed business center; 24-hour room service; laundry service; no-smoking rooms. *In room:* A/C, TV, dataport, minibar, coffee maker, hair dryer, iron, safe.

Radisson Europa Hotel ⚫⚫   This hotel is geared primarily to business travelers, but it's a good choice for anyone looking for a big, dependable luxury hotel near downtown San José. Wooden headboards and angular window nooks and other small architectural details give these rooms an edge over those in the Aurola Holiday Inn. An extra $20 buys you an executive room, which is basically a standard room with a coffee maker, scale, terry-cloth bathrobes, and an extra telephone in the bathroom. The junior suites are called CEO Club rooms here and are in an isolated wing with its own comfortable lounge and honor bar. They come with all the above amenities, as well as a desk and chair, in-room fax machine, and small balcony.

Calle Blancos, behind La República building (A.P. 538-2120), San José. © 800/333-3333 in the U.S., or 506/257-3257. Fax 506/257-8221. www.radisson.com. 107 units. $175–$185 double, $250 junior suite, $700 presidential suite. AE, DC, MC, V. Free parking. **Amenities:** 3 restaurants (international, sushi, cafe); 2 bars; 1 lounge; outdoor pool; small gym; casino; tour desk; car-rental agency; full-service business center; small shopping arcade; limited room service; in-room massage; laundry service; nonsmoking rooms. *In room:* A/C, TV, dataport, minibar, hair dryer, iron, safe.

EXPENSIVE

Barceló Amón Plaza ✦✦ Located on the north edge of the historic Barrio Amón neighborhood, this hotel is larger and more luxurious than most of the area's smaller hotels. Moreover, in terms of service, location, and price, this hotel gets my nod over both the nearby Holiday Inn and Radisson Europa. The rooms are spacious and up to international standards, and you are close to several good restaurants.

Avenida 11 and Calle 3 bis (A.P. 4192-1000), San José. ✆ **800/575-1253** in the U.S., or 506/257-0191. Fax 506/257-0284. www.barcelo.com. 90 units. $100 double, $130–$250 suite. AE, DC, MC, V. Free parking. **Amenities:** 2 restaurants (international, 24-hour lobby cafe); 2 bars; casino; small exercise room; Jacuzzi; sauna; tour desk; modest business center; laundry service. *In room:* A/C, TV, coffee maker, hair dryer, safe.

Britannia Hotel ✦✦ *Finds* This is the most luxurious choice among the many hotels that have been created from restored old houses in downtown San José. The large, low building, with its wraparound veranda, is certainly one of the most attractive in the neighborhood. In the lobby, tile floors, large stained-glass picture windows, a brass chandelier, and reproduction Victorian decor all help set a tone of tropical luxury. Along with restoring the old home, the owners have built a four-story addition, which is separated from the original building by a narrow atrium. Rooms in the original home have hardwood floors and furniture, and high ceilings and fans help keep them cool. In the deluxe rooms and junior suites, you get air-conditioning. Though the street-side rooms have double glass, light sleepers will still want to avoid them. The quietest rooms are those toward the back of the new addition.

In what was once the wine cellar, you'll find a casual restaurant. The buffet breakfast is served in the adjacent skylit room. Afternoon tea and happy-hour drinks are also served.

Calle 3 and Avenida 11 (A.P. 3742-1000), San José. ✆ **800/263-2618** in the U.S., or 506/223-6667. Fax 506/223-6411. britania@racsa.co.cr. 23 units. $89–$117 double. AE, MC, V. Parking nearby. **Amenities:** 1 restaurant (international); 1 bar; tour desk; limited room service; laundry services; all rooms no-smoking. *In room:* TV, safe.

Hotel Alóki ✦ This boutique hotel is located in a beautifully restored stucco building with a large central courtyard. It's on a quiet street only a few blocks from the heart of downtown San José, so you get both the convenience of the city and the quiet of a suburban location. Tile floors in the halls and on the veranda surrounding the courtyard provide a touch of old Costa Rica, while European and North American antiques add a bit of international flavor. Guest rooms have high ceilings and either hardwood floors or carpeting. There is a mix of antique and modern furnishings, and though there is no air-conditioning, overhead fans manage to keep the rooms cool. Rooms vary in size. Wrought-iron tables are spread around the covered central patio, which serves as the hotel's restaurant, and dinners are served by candlelight. There's also a quiet and elegant bar located in the back of the building with an open picture window overlooking the Simón Bolívar Zoo.

949 Calle 13, between Avenidas 9 and 11 (A.P. 1040-2050), San José. ✆ **506/222-6702.** Fax 506/221-2533. www.tropicalcostarica.com. 7 units. $90 double, $140 suite. Rates include full breakfast. AE, MC, V. Parking nearby. **Amenities:** 1 restaurant (continental); one bar; concierge; laundry service. *In room:* TV.

Raya Vida Villa ✦ Located behind a big iron gate at the end of a narrow, dead-end lane, this little bed-and-breakfast is so secluded that it seems to be in a world all its own, yet it's in downtown San José. Behind the gate, in a shady old garden, is a miniature villa. The restored old stucco home is furnished with the owners' eclectic collection of crafts from around the world, and in the living room you'll find a grand piano and fireplace. Guest rooms are all different. The upstairs rooms have the largest bathrooms, and one even has a Jacuzzi tub. However, I like the downstairs room that opens onto a small open-air patio with fountain.

A.P. 2209-2100, San José (mailing address in the U.S.: P.O. Box 025216-1638, Miami, FL 33102-5216). ✆ **506/223-4168.** Fax 506/223-4157. rayavida@costarica.net. 4 units. $95 double; slightly lower in the off-season. Rates include full breakfast and round-trip airport transfer. MC, V. Free parking. *In-room:* TV, no phone.

MODERATE

Gran Hotel Costa Rica   Though the Gran Hotel Costa Rica can claim the best location of any downtown hotel (bordering the National Theater and the Plaza de la Cultura), it does not, unfortunately, offer rooms to match the prestigious location or name. Though most of the guest rooms here are fairly large, they have not been well maintained over the decades; there's an adequate but rather run-down feel, especially in the bathrooms.

The **Café Parisien** is the hotel's greatest attribute, and it's memorable not so much for its food as for its atmosphere—it's an open-air patio that overlooks the National Theater, street musicians, and all the activity of the Plaza de la Cultura,

Avenida 2, between Calles 1 and 3, San José. ✆ **506/221-4000.** Fax 506/221-3501. granhcr@ racsa.co.cr. 110 units. $55–$71 double; $84–$144 suite. Rate includes continental breakfast. AE, DC, MC, V. Free parking. **Amenities:** 1 restaurant (international); 1 bar; small and very casual casino; tour desk; 24-hour room service; laundry service. *In room:* TV.

Hotel Del Rey   You can't miss the Del Rey; it's a massive pink corner building with vaguely colonial styling. The lobby continues the façade's theme with pink-tile floors and stone columns. Inside, every guest room is marked by a carved hardwood door. The rooms vary in size and comfort: There are quiet interior rooms that have no windows, and larger rooms with windows (but also street noise). Try for a sixth-floor room with a balcony. The hotel's Del Rey Cafe serves respectable U.S.–style deli sandwiches, seafood, steaks and pasta dishes. Much of the first floor is taken up with a lively casino and the neighboring Blue Marlin Bar, which is very popular with sports fans (and prostitutes).

Avenida 1 and Calle 9 (A.P. 6241-1000), San José. ✆ **888-972-7272** in the U.S., or 506/257-7800. Fax 506/221-0096. www.hoteldelrey.com. 104 units. $68–$85 double, $135 suite. AE, MC, V. Parking nearby. **Amenities:** 1 restaurant (American/international); 1 bar; casino; tour desk; 24-hour room service; laundry service. *In room:* A/C, TV, minibar, safe.

Hotel Don Carlos ★ *(Finds)*   If you're looking for a small hotel that is unmistakably Costa Rican and hints at the days of the planters and coffee barons, this is the place for you. Located in an old residential neighborhood, only blocks from the business district, the Don Carlos is popular with both vacationers and businesspeople. A large reproduction of a pre-Columbian carved-stone human figure stands outside the front door of this gray inn, which was a former president's mansion. Inside, you'll find many more such reproductions, as well as orchids, ferns, palms, and parrots. After a day of exploring the capital, there's nothing like settling down in the lounge, the small courtyard, or the sunny deck, where the wicker furniture, bubbling fountain, and tropical breezes will make you think you're Hope or Crosby on the road to somewhere. The rooms are all distinct and vary greatly in size, so be specific when you reserve, or ask if it's possible to see a few when you check in.

The newest additions here include a 10-person Jacuzzi and an outdoor orchid garden and atrium where breakfast is served. The gift shop here is one of the largest in the country, and the paintings hung throughout the hotel are also for sale.

779 Calle 9, between Avenidas 7 and 9, San José (mailing address in the U.S.: SJO 1686, P.O. Box 025216, Miami, FL 33102). ℂ 506/221-6707. Fax 506/255-0828. www.doncarlos.co.cr. 36 units. $70–$80 double. Rates include continental breakfast. AE, MC, V. Free parking. **Amenities:** 1 restaurant (Costa Rican/international); 1 bar; tour desk; in-room massage; laundry service. *In room:* TV, hair dryer, safe.

Hotel Santo Tomás ⭐

Even though it's on a busy downtown street, this converted mansion is a quiet oasis inside. Built 100 years ago by a coffee baron, the house has been lovingly restored and maintained by its owner, Thomas Douglas. Throughout the hotel you'll enjoy the deep, dark tones of well-aged and well-worked wood. The rooms vary in size, but most are fairly spacious and have a small table and chairs. Skylights in some bathrooms will brighten your morning, and firm beds will provide a good night's sleep. There are a couple of patio areas, as well as a TV lounge and combination breakfast room and outdoor bar. The staff and management are extremely helpful with tour arrangements and any other needs or requests.

Avenida 7, between Calles 3 and 5, San José. ℂ 506/255-0448. Fax 506/222-3950. www.hotelsantotomas.com. 20 units. $60–$90 double. Rates include continental breakfast. MC, V. Parking nearby. **Amenities:** Lounge; 1 bar; tour desk; laundry service. *In room:* TV.

La Casa Verde de Amón

This tropical Victorian house was built around 1910 and was completely renovated between 1989 and 1992. Beautiful old-tile and polished-hardwood floors throughout give the house a patrician air. Off the lobby, there's a small patio and open-air breakfast room. Up on the second floor, there's a large, high-ceilinged central seating area with a 110-year-old baby grand piano and large stained-glass picture windows that bathe the room in a beautiful blue light. Rooms are all different, but most are furnished with antiques. Some have their original porcelain fixtures and brass faucets; you may find a bathtub or only a shower in your bathroom. The Don Carlos suite is huge, with a high ceiling, king-size beds, and a separate seating area. All the rooms have clock radios, but unfortunately, it's more likely that traffic noises will wake you in the morning if you have a room on the street side of the hotel. You shouldn't have any trouble finding this hotel, especially if you remember that *casa verde* translates as "green house"—this one is painted a prominent green. No smoking in any rooms.

Calle 7 and Avenida 9, no. 910, San José (mailing address in the U.S.: Dept. 1701, P.O. Box 025216, Miami, FL 33102-5216). ℂ and fax 506/223-0969. www.zurqui.com/crinfocus/verde/cverde.html. 8 units. $65–$96 double. Rates include continental breakfast. AE, MC, V. Parking nearby. **Amenities:** Lounge; tour desk; laundry service. *In room:* TV, safe.

Taylor's Inn

Here's yet another lovely converted home turned bed-and-breakfast. The rooms are all arranged around the interior courtyard, which features flowering ginger and other tropical flora—a perfect place for breakfast. Most rooms have one single and one double bed, although a few have sleeping lofts and are good for families. All are very clean and feature artwork from prominent Costa Rican artists. The suite is a bit bigger, with a 20-inch television. Don't expect a sense of hermetic privacy here, though—most of the rooms open onto the courtyard, and the old wooden construction guarantees that you hear every footfall and conversation of other guests passing by your door. The hotel has a helpful tour desk.

Avenida 13, between Calle 3 and 3 bis (A.P. 531-1000), San José. (C) **506/257-4333.** Fax 506/221-1475. www.catours.co.cr. 12 units. $60 double; slightly lower in the off-season. Rates include buffet breakfast. AE, MC, V. **Amenities:** Lounge; tour desk; laundry service. *In room:* TV, safe; no phone.

INEXPENSIVE

Hotel Aranjuez *Value*   This is probably the best and deservedly most popular budget option close to downtown. Located on a quiet and safe street in the Barrio Amón neighborhood, this humble hotel is made up of five contiguous houses. The rooms are all simple and clean, although some are little dark. Both the rooms and bathrooms vary greatly in size, so be very specific when reserving, or ask to see a few rooms when you arrive. The nicest features here, aside from the convivial hostel-like atmosphere, are the lush and shady gardens; the hanging orchids, bromeliads, and ferns decorating the hallways and nooks; and the numerous open lounge areas furnished with chairs, tables, and couches—great for lazing around and sharing travel tales with your fellow guests. The hotel has a couple of computers and offers guests free Internet and e-mail services.

Calle 19, between Avenidas 11 and 13 (A.P. 457-2070), San José. (C) **877/898-8663** in the U.S., or 506/256-1825. Fax 506/223-3528. www.hotelaranjuez.com. 30 units. $35–$40 double. Rate includes breakfast buffet. MC, V. Free parking. **Amenities:** 1 bar; several lounge areas; tour desk; laundry service. *In room:* TV, safe.

Hotel Bienvenido   This very basic hotel has historically been popular with travelers on a tight budget, although it's in a terrible and slightly dangerous neighborhood in the heart of downtown. The rooms are clean, though a bit dark. The hotel was created from an old movie theater, and there are still a few architectural details remaining from this incarnation. The place often fills up by early afternoon in the high season, so call ahead for a reservation and ask for a quiet room in the back. The restaurant here serves simple and inexpensive meals.

Calle 10, between Avenidas 1 and 3, San José. (C) **506/233-2161.** Fax 506/221-1872. hotel_ bienvenidocr@hotmail.com. 51 units. $18 double, $27 triple. AE, MC, V. Parking nearby. **Amenities:** 1 restaurant (Costa Rican); laundry service. *In room:* No phone.

Joluva Guesthouse   Though you can find a less expensive hotel, there are few in this price range that offer the old-fashioned architectural detail of the Joluva, with old-tile and hardwood floors throughout and high ceilings (one room offers beautiful plasterwork on the ceiling). However, the rooms are small and a bit dark, and only two have windows that open onto the small courtyard. The breakfast room has skylights, which help brighten it a bit. This hotel caters to a gay clientele, but all guests are welcome.

936 Calle 3B, between Avenidas 9 and 11, San José. (C) **800/298-2418** in the U.S., or 506/ 223-7961. Fax 506/257-7668. www.joluva.com. 7 units, 6 with private bathroom. $27 double without bathroom; $37–$47 double with bathroom. Rates include continental breakfast. AE, MC, V. Parking nearby. **Amenities:** Tour desk; laundry service; all rooms no-smoking. *In room:* TV, safe; no phone.

Pension de la Cuesta *Value*   If you don't mind a clean communal bathroom down the hall from your room, this little bed-and-breakfast on the hill leading up to the Parque Nacional is a real bargain and definitely worth considering. It was once the home of Otto Apuy, a well-known Costa Rican artist, and original artwork abounds. The building itself is a classic example of a tropical wood-frame home and has been painted an eye-catching pink with blue-and-white trim. Some of the rooms can be a bit dark and are very simply furnished, but there's a sunny and cheery sunken lounge/courtyard area in the center of the house. Most of the rooms have one double and a set of bunk beds. Overall, the place feels a lot like a hostel. The owners give you free run of the kitchen and are even offering free use of their Internet connection.

1332 Cuesta de Nuñez, Avenida 1 between Calles 11 and 15, San José. © and fax **506/255-2896.** www.suntoursandfun.com. 9 units, none with private bathroom. $26 double, $34 triple. Children under 12 stay free in parents' room. Rates include continental breakfast. AE, MC, V. Parking nearby. **Amenities:** Lounge with cable TV; tour desk; laundry service. *In room:* No phone.

LA SABANA/PASEO COLÓN
VERY EXPENSIVE

Meliá Confort Corobicí ★ Located just past the end of Paseo Colón and on the edge of Parque La Sabana, the Corobicí offers all the amenities you would expect at a large airport hotel, with one added bonus: It's much closer to downtown. The lobby is a vast expanse of marble floor faced by blank walls, though the art-deco furnishings lend a bit of character. Guest rooms are quite modern and comfortable, with good beds and walls of glass through which, on most floors, you get good views of the valley and surrounding mountains. Joggers will enjoy the nearby Parque La Sabana. The Corobicí claims to have the largest health spa in Central America; here you'll find a well-equipped exercise room, sauna, hot tub, and aerobics classes.

Autopista General Cañas, Sabana Norte (A.P. 2443-1000), San José. © **888/485-2676** in the U.S., or 506/232-8122. Fax 506/231-5834. www.solmelia.com. 203 units. $125 double; $145–$450 suite. AE, MC, V. Free parking. **Amenities:** 3 restaurants (continental, Japanese, coffee shop); 2 bars; 1 lounge; casino; midsize outdoor pool; well-equipped health club and spa; tour desk; car-rental desk; downtown shuttle; business center; shopping arcade; salon; 24-hour room service; in-room massage; laundry service; nonsmoking rooms. *In room:* A/C, TV, dataport, minibar, hair dryer, iron, safe.

MODERATE

Hotel Grano de Oro ★★ (finds) San José boasts dozens of old homes that have been converted into hotels, but few offer the luxurious accommodations or professional service that can be found at the Grano de Oro. Located on a quiet side street off Paseo Colón, this small hotel offers a variety of room types to fit most budgets and tastes. Personally, I prefer the patio rooms, which have French doors opening onto private patios. However, if you want a room with plenty of space, ask for one of the deluxe rooms, which have large, modern, tiled baths with big tubs.

Throughout all the guest rooms, you'll find attractive hardwood furniture, including old-fashioned wardrobes in some rooms. For additional luxuries, you can stay in one of the suites, which have whirlpool tubs. The Vista de Oro suite is the hotel's crown jewel, with its own private staircase and wonderful views of the city and surrounding mountains. If you don't grab a suite, you still have access to the hotel's two rooftop Jacuzzis. The hotel's patio-garden restaurant serves excellent continental cuisine and some of the best desserts in the city.

Calle 30, no. 251, between Avenidas 2 and 4, 150m south of Paseo Colón, San José (mailing address in the U.S.: SJO 36, P.O. Box 025216, Miami, FL 33102). © **506/255-3322.** Fax 506/221-2782. www.hotelgranodeoro.com. 35 units. $85–$115 double; $135–$240 suite. AE, MC, V. Free parking. **Amenities:** 1 restaurant (continental); lounge; 2 rooftop Jacuzzis; concierge; tour desk; limited room service; laundry service; all rooms no-smoking. *In room:* TV, minibar, safe.

Hotel Rosa del Paseo ★ This hotel is housed in one of San José's most beautiful old stucco homes, right on busy Paseo Colón. However, the rooms are all located away from the street and are well insulated against the noise. Built more than 110 years ago, this old home underwent a complete renovation and modernization a few years ago and is now richly appointed and surprisingly evocative of 19th-century Costa Rica. The rooms are all quite comfortable; the master suite even comes with its own balcony and Jacuzzi. I'd definitely try to grab one of the rooms on the second floor, which feature wooden floors and front doors that open onto the open-air central courtyard. There are beautiful details throughout the hotel: transoms, ornate stucco door frames, and polished hardwood floors.

2862 Paseo Colón, between Calles 28 and 30 (A.P. 287-1007, Centro Colón), San José. (C) **506/ 257-3213** or 506/257-3258. Fax 506/223-2776. www.online.co.cr/rosa. 18 units. $70–$80 double, $90 suite; lower in the off-season. Rates include continental breakfast. AE, MC, V. Limited free parking. **Amenities:** 1 bar; 1 lounge; tour desk; airport shuttle; laundry service. *In room:* TV, safe.

Hotel Torremolinos   If you want to be close to downtown, have some of the trappings of a modern business-class hotel, and not spend a fortune, this is your best choice. Located at the west end of Paseo Colón, the Torremolinos is on a fairly quiet street and is built around a colorful and well-tended garden that makes the hotel's pool a wonderful place to while away an afternoon. The rooms are simply furnished and have plenty of space.

Calle 40 and Avenida 5 bis (A.P. 434-1150, La Uruca), San José. (C) **506/222-9129.** Fax 506/ 221-9095. www.occidentaltorremolinos.com. 84 units. $80 double. Rates include breakfast. AE, MC, V. Free parking. **Amenities:** 1 restaurant (international); 1 bar; small outdoor pool; tour desk; downtown shuttle; modest business center; limited room service; laundry service. *In room:* TV, hair dryer, safe.

INEXPENSIVE

Hotel Cacts   This is one of the most interesting and unusual budget hotels I've ever seen. It's housed in an attractive tropical contemporary home on a business and residential street. The original building is a maze of rooms and hallways on several levels (the house is built on a slope). The newer rooms all come with telephones and televisions. My favorite room is the huge bilevel family room with a high-beamed ceiling. There's a third-floor open terrace that serves as the breakfast area. The hotel has even recently added a swimming pool and Jacuzzi. The staff here is very helpful, and the hotel will receive mail and faxes, change money, and store baggage for guests.

2845 Avenida 3 bis, between Calles 28 and 30 (A.P. 379-1005), San José. (C) **506/221-2928** or 506/221-6546. Fax 506/221-8616. www.tourism.co.cr. 30 units. $42–$60 double, $53–$65 triple. Rates include breakfast buffet. AE, MC, V. Free parking. **Amenities:** Small pool; Jacuzzi; tour desk; laundry service. *In room:* TV; no phone.

Hotel Petit Victoria   One of the oldest houses in San José, this tropical Victorian home was once the election campaign headquarters for Oscar Arias Sánchez, Costa Rica's Nobel Prize–winning former president. Today, after extensive remodeling and restoration, it's an interesting little hotel that offers a historic setting at inexpensive rates. The big, covered wraparound veranda is perfect for sitting and taking in the warm sun, and it doubles as the hotel's restaurant. Guest rooms have medium to large tiled bathrooms and high ceilings and fans to keep the air cool. Inside, walls are made of wood, so noise can be a bit of a problem, but this is a small price to pay for such old-fashioned elegance.

Paseo Colón, Frente a la Sala Garbo (A.P. 357-1007), San José. (C) **506/255-8488.** victoria@amnet.co.cr. 16 units. TV. $35 double, $45 triple. Rates include continental breakfast. No credit cards. Free parking. **Amenities:** 1 restaurant (international); 1 bar; tour desk; laundry service. *In room:* TV; no phone.

SAN PEDRO/LOS YOSES
MODERATE

Hotel Le Bergerac ★★ *Finds*   With all the sophistication and charm of a small French inn, the Hotel Le Bergerac has ingratiated itself with business travelers and members of various diplomatic missions. These visitors have found a tranquil environment in a quiet suburban neighborhood, spacious and comfortable accommodations, personal service, and gourmet meals. The hotel is composed of three houses with courtyard gardens in between. Almost all of the rooms are quite large, and each is a little different. My favorite rooms are those with private patio gardens. Some rooms have king-size beds and refrigerators, and in the old master bedroom you'll find a little balcony.

In the evenings, candlelight and classical music set a relaxing and romantic mood. The long-standing **L'Ile de France** restaurant set up shop here several years ago, and gourmet French and continental dinners are available for guests and by reservation.

50 S. Calle 35 (A.P. 1107-1002), San José. ℂ **506/234-7850.** Fax 506/225-9103. www.bergerac. com. 18 units. $68–$88 double. Corporate rates available. Rates include full breakfast. AE, MC, V. Free parking. **Amenities:** 1 restaurant (French); 1 lounge; concierge; tour desk; business and secretarial services; limited room service; laundry service. *In room:* TV, hair dryer, iron, safe.

INEXPENSIVE

D'galah Hotel   If you want to be close to downtown but away from the smog and traffic, this budget hotel is a good choice. Directly across the street from the hotel is the University of Costa Rica, an oasis of greenery that attracts many species of birds, especially among the bamboo groves. Rooms are a bit old-fashioned and dark. But, if you aren't too demanding, for the most part they're quite spacious and acceptable. The largest rooms have kitchenettes and sleeping lofts; the newest rooms have carpets and small private patios.

A.P. 85-2350 (in front of the University of Costa Rica's School of Pharmacy), San José. ℂ and fax **506/280-8092.** dgalah@racsa.co.cr. 25 units. TV TEL. $38–$48 double. Rates include full breakfast. AE, MC, V. Free parking. **Amenities:** Small swimming pool; exercise room; sauna; laundry service. *In room:* No phone.

Toruma Youth Hostel *Value*   This attractive old building, with its long veranda, is the largest hostel in Costa Rica's system of official youth hostels. Although it's possible to find other accommodations around town in this price range, none would likely be as clean. The atmosphere here is convivial and will be familiar to anyone who has hostelled in Europe. There's a large lounge in the center of the building with a high ceiling and a great deal of light. The dorms have four to six beds per room. All of the rooms themselves are no-smoking. The staff here can help you arrange stays at other hostels and trips around the country, and you can store luggage for 25¢ per day.

Avenida Central, between Calles 29 and 31 (A.P. 1352-1002), San José. ℂ **506/234-8186,** or ℂ and fax 506/224-4085. www.hostelling-costarica.com. 95 beds, all with shared bathroom. $10 per person per night with an IYHF card, $13 with student ID, $14 general public. Rates include continental breakfast. MC, V. Free parking. *In room:* No phone.

ESCAZÚ & SANTA ANA

Located about 15 minutes west of San José and about the same distance from the international airport, these affluent suburbs have experienced rapid growth in recent years, as the metropolitan area continues its urban sprawl. Both Escazú and Santa Ana are popular with Costa Rican businessmen and North American retirees and expatriates, and quite a few hotels have sprung up to cater to the needs of their visiting friends. It's relatively easy to commute between Escazú or Santa Ana and downtown via bus or taxi. Taxi fare should run around $9 (each way). A bus costs around 30¢.

VERY EXPENSIVE

Camino Real Inter-Continental 🎯🎯   This is the newest large-scale business and resort hotel to open in the metropolitan area. Three five-story wings radiate off a central hub. The large, open lobby has a flagstone and mosaic floor. The rooms are all well appointed, with either one king or two double beds, a working desk, sitting chair and ottoman, and large armoire housing a 25-inch television. For an extra $25 you can stay on the Club Inter-Continental floor and enjoy personalized concierge and butler services, separate check-in area, an on-floor buffet breakfast, as well as an assortment of refreshments, sweets, hors d'oeuvres, and drinks throughout the day. This floor is where the junior and master suites are located.

The hotel's Casino Real is open nightly from 7pm until the last bettor calls it quits. The hotel is just across from a large, modern shopping-mall complex, which is nice if you want access to more shopping, restaurants, and a six-plex movie theater. Overall, the Inter-Continental offers many of the same features and amenities as the Marriott (see p. 103), although the latter gets the nod in terms of service, restaurants, and ambiance.

Autopista Própero Fernández, across from the Multiplaza shopping complex, Escazú. ✆ 506/ 289-7000. Fax 506/289-8930. www.gruporeal.com. 260 units. $290 double, $500–$1,000 suite. AE, MC, V. Free parking. **Amenities:** 2 restaurants (French/international; continental); 2 bars; 1 lounge; casino; large free-form swimming pool; 1 outdoor tennis court; modest health club and spa; Jacuzzi; concierge; tour desk; car-rental desk; well-appointed business center; small shopping arcade; salon; limited room service; in-room massage; laundry service; no-smoking rooms. *In room:* A/C, TV, minibar, coffee maker, iron, hair dryer, safe.

Hotel Alta 🎯🎯   This small boutique hotel is infused with old-world charm. Curves and high arches abound. My favorite touch is the winding interior alleyway that snakes down from the reception through the hotel. Most of the rooms here have wonderful views of the Central Valley from private balconies; the others have nice garden patios. The rooms are all up to modern resort standards, although some have cramped bathrooms. The suites are considerably larger, each with a separate sitting room with its own television, as well as large Jacuzzi-style tubs (no jets, though) in spacious bathrooms; they're definitely worth the slight splurge. If you opt to rent the entire upper floor, the penthouse becomes a three-bedroom, full-floor extravaganza, with massive living room and open-air rooftop patio. The hotel's **La Luz** restaurant is one of the more elegant and creative in the Central Valley.

Old road to Santa Ana (mailing address in the U.S.: Interlink 964, P.O. Box 02-5635, Miami, FL 33102). ✆ 888/388-2582 in the U.S., or 506/282-4160. Fax 506/282-4162. www.altatravelplanners. com. 23 units. $139 double, $159 suite, $865 penthouse. Off-season discounts available. Rates include continental breakfast. AE, MC, V. Free parking. **Amenities:** 1 restaurant (creative international/fusion); 1 bar; midsize swimming pool; exercise room; Jacuzzi; sauna; tour desk; secretarial services; limited room service; in-room massage; laundry service. *In room:* A/C, TV, minibar, hair dryer, safe.

Tara Resort Hotel and Spa 🎯   Located in San Antonio de Escazú, 600 meters south of the cemetery (once you hit Escazú, just follow the numerous signs), Tara is perched high on a mountainside overlooking the entire Central Valley and surrounding volcanic peaks. The view is breathtaking and so is the setting. The owner has a fixation on *Gone With the Wind,* and everything at this spa/resort follows the theme, from the O'Hara Dining Hall down to one of Rhett's Vitality Baths. It's rich in antebellum Southern grandeur, not local color. The spa is one of the better-equipped facilities in the metropolitan area, and offers a full assortment of treatments, including massage, facials, and aromatherapy.

The suites are all part of the main house, and each has its own balcony (try to get one overlooking the valley). The penthouse suite is on the third floor, and has high ceilings, private Jacuzzi, and 360° views. Villas and bungalows vary in size, but in the larger rooms, you might find a seating area, a big bathroom with two sinks, a tub, a heat lamp, and perhaps even two balconies. Furnishings are traditional American pieces that fit right in with the architecture. My biggest complaint is that service seems to run the gamut from excellent to inattentive to gruff. The Atlanta Dining Gallery is an elegant setting for fine meals; unfortunately, the windows do not do justice to the view. Meals are sometimes served on the large back patio, which has an unobstructed view of the valley.

San Antonio de Escazú (A.P. 1459-1250). ℂ 506/228-6992. Fax 506/228-9651. www.tararesort. com. 14 units. $130 double, $195 bungalow, $160–$250 suite. Rates include continental breakfast. AE, MC, V. Free parking. **Amenities:** 1 restaurant (international); 1 bar; midsize outdoor pool; well-equipped spa; various lawn and indoor games; tour desk; secretarial services; in-room massage; laundry service. *In room:* TV, hair dryer, safe.

MODERATE

Hotel Mirador Pico Blanco There's nothing fancy about the rooms here— in fact, I think they're overpriced—but most offer absolutely fabulous views. Some rooms have high ceilings, creating an appearance of spaciousness, and almost all of them have balconies (albeit small ones) and television sets with cable. A few resident macaws fly around the hillsides during the day but come home here each evening. The restaurant is a popular and inexpensive spot, probably the cheapest "view" restaurant in the valley, and the bar has been getting bigger and more popular over the years as well. A hotel shuttle from the airport will cost you about $15 (per trip, not per person); it holds up to 10 people, so this is a good choice for families or big groups.

Half a mile/1km south of the church in San Antonio de Escazú (A.P. 900), Escazú. ℂ 506/ 289-6197. Fax 506/289-5189. 25 units. $65–$95 double. V. Free parking. **Amenities:** 1 restaurant (international); 1 bar; tour desk; airport shuttle; laundry service. *In room:* No phone.

Villa Escazú *(Finds)* If you're looking for a quiet little inn with a homey feel, this converted private home fits the bill. Service is friendly and personable. The rooms are large and immaculate, with plenty of varnished wood. The upstairs rooms have balconies, and the shared bathroom features a tub. The complimentary breakfasts are extensive and creative. The hotel has well-tended grounds and gardens, with quiet sitting areas. There is a new studio for rent by the week or month.

To find the place, first get yourself to the Banco Nacional in Escazú. (Most any road into Escazu will lead you onto the one-way street along the western edge of the town's central park.) Follow this road uphill (south) until you see the bank on your right. Turn right. Then go 600 meters west, follow the severe dog-leg 300 meters south, and watch for the sign marking the driveway.

Escazú (A.P. 1401-1250). ℂ and fax **506/289-7971.** www.hotels.co.cr. 6 units, 5 with shared bathroom. $65 double; studio $200 per week. Rates lower in the off-season. Rates include full breakfast. No credit cards. *In room:* No phone.

HEREDIA/ALAJUELA/AIRPORT AREA

Alajuela and Heredia are two colonial-era cities that lie much closer to the airport than San José. Alajuela is the closest city to the airport, with Heredia lying about midway between Alajuela and the capital. These are two great places to find small, distinct, and charming hotels. If you'd like to learn more about either of these cities, look under "Side Trips from San José," later in this chapter. If your plans are to get yourself to a remote beach or rain-forest lodge as quickly as possible and use San José and the Central Valley purely as a transportation hub, or you just detest urban clutter, noise, and pollution, you might do well to choose one of the hotels listed below.

VERY EXPENSIVE

Finca Rosa Blanca Country Inn ★★ *(Finds)*   Finca Rosa Blanca is an eclectic architectural confection set amid the lush, green hillsides of a coffee plantation. Square corners seem to have been prohibited in the design of this beautiful home. There are turrets and curving walls of glass, arched windows, and a semi-circular built-in couch. Everywhere the glow of polished hardwood blends with blindingly white stucco walls and brightly painted murals.

Inside, there's original artwork everywhere, and each room is decidedly unique. There's the black-and-white room with a patio and bed made from coffee-tree wood. Another room has a bed built into a corner and a handmade tub with windows on two sides. The view is fabulous. If breathtaking bathrooms are your idea of the ultimate luxury, then consider splurging on the master suite, which has a stone waterfall that cascades into a tub in front of a huge picture window. This suite also has a spiral staircase that leads to the top of the turret. The two separate villas have the same sense of eclectic luxury, with small kitchenettes and quite a bit of space and privacy. No smoking is allowed in any of the rooms.

A four-course gourmet dinner served in the small dining room will run you $30 per person. Be sure to reserve early because there's limited seating. In a tiny space off of the living room, there's an honor bar tucked into a reproduction of a typical Costa Rican oxcart.

Santa Bárbara de Heredia (mailing address in the U.S.: SJO 1201, P.O. Box 025216, Miami, FL 33102-5216). © **506/269-9392.** Fax 506/269-9555. www.fincarosablanca.com. 7 units, 2 villas. $165–$250 double. Extra person $25. Rates include breakfast. AE, MC, V. Free parking. **Amenities:** 1 restaurant (international); small honor bar; lounge; small free-form outdoor pool set in the hillside; Jacuzzi; tour desk; horse rental; limited room service; laundry service. *In room:* minibar, safe.

Hotel Herradura ★★   Big and sprawling, the Herradura possesses San José's largest and most flexible conference facilities, and so it's often bustling with businesspeople and assorted convention traffic. The superior rooms (there are no standard rooms) are all up to snuff, although the bathrooms in these rooms are small, and most have no view. The deluxe rooms, on the other hand, are very attractive and luxurious. The walls of glass let in plenty of light and usually display a good view. The balconies boast marble-topped cafe tables, while the bathrooms feature green-marble counters, phones, and hair dryers.

The main swimming pool (there are three) is one of the largest and most attractive in San José, with a beachlike patio, a swim-up bar, tiled cafe tables in the water, and attractive landscaping around the edges of the pool. The Herradura's wealth of facilities makes it a favorite with families. Guests have access to the neighboring Meliá Cariari's 18-hole golf course, plus its 11 tennis courts, pro shop, and health club.

Autopista General Cañas, Ciudad Cariari (A.P. 7-1880), San José. ℭ **800/245-8420** in the U.S. and Canada, or 506/239-0033 in Costa Rica. Fax 506/239-0210. www.hotelherradura.com. 234 units. $140–$180 double, $220–$850 suite. AE, DC, MC, V. Free parking. **Amenities:** 3 restaurants (Japanese, Spanish, 24-hour coffee shop); 2 bars; 1 lounge; small casino; 3 outdoor swimming pools; tour desk; car-rental desk; well-appointed business center; salon; 24-hour room service; in-room massage; baby-sitting; laundry service. *In room:* A/C, TV, hair dryer, safe.

Marriott Hotel and Resort ✶✶✶   For my money, the Marriott is still the only luxury resort hotel in the San José area that gets everything right. Amenities are plentiful, and service here reaches a level of attention to detail uncommon in Costa Rica. The hotel is designed in a mixed colonial style, with hand-painted Mexican tiles, antique red-clay roof tiles, weathered columns, and heavy wooden doors, lintels, and trim. The centerpiece is a large open-air interior patio, which somewhat replicates Old Havana's Plaza de Armas. The rooms are all comfortable and well appointed, with either a king-size or two double beds, two telephones, a working desk, an elegant wooden armoire holding the large television, plenty of closet space, a comfortable sitting chair and ottoman, and a small "Juliet" balcony. The bathrooms are up to par but seem slightly small for this price.

The elegant La Isabela restaurant is housed in a re-created wine cellar, and features an extensive menu of creative international fare. The more casual Villa Hermosa restaurant serves "nouvelle Costa Rican" and continental dishes. The lobby bar features daily piano music and weekend nights of jazz, as well as a tapas bar, a cigar bar, and both indoor and patio seating.

San Antonio de Belén (A.P. 502-4005). ℭ **800/228-9290** in the U.S. and Canada, or 506/298-0844. Fax 506/298-0844. www.marriott.com. 252 units. $199 double; $229 excecutive level; $450 master suite. Rates include breakfast buffet. AE, DC, MC, V. Free parking. **Amenities:** 4 restaurants (international, continental, outdoor grill, coffeehouse); 1 bar; 1 lounge; 2 adjacent outdoor pools on separate levels of the large outdoor patio area; golf driving range; 3 outdoor tennis courts; small but well-appointed health club and sauna; outdoor Jacuzzi; concierge; tour desk; car-rental desk; free airport and downtown shuttle; business center and secretarial services; small shopping arcade; salon; 24-hour room service; in-room massage; baby-sitting; laundry service; nonsmoking rooms. *In room:* A/C, TV, dataport, minibar, hair dryer, iron, safe.

Meliá Cariari Conference Center and Golf Resort ✶ (Kids)   With its use of stone walls, an open-air lobby, and lush garden plantings, the Cariari has more of a tropical feel than the two luxury hotels mentioned above, although I think both the Marriott and Herradura have better accommodations and service. Still, since the Cariari has come under the management of the large Meliá chain, many of the guest rooms have been remodeled, and all now have plenty of space. The basic rooms have either one king-size or two double beds, and small bathrooms. The suites are more spacious and better appointed. Try to get an upper-floor room; those on the lower floor tend to be a bit dark.

The Cariari is the only resort hotel in the Central Valley with its own golf course, although guests at the Herradura have access to the course, as well. The Cariari does have a sister course at the Meliá Playa Conchal resort, which might make this a must stop for golfers looking for a package tour.

Autopista General Cañas, Ciudad Cariari (A.P. 737-1007, Centro Colón), San José. ℭ **800/227-4274** in the U.S. and Canada, or 506/239-0022. Fax 506/239-2803. www.solmelia.com. 220 units. $150–$170 double, $175–$490 suite. AE, DC, MC, V. Free parking. **Amenities:** 3 restaurants (French/continental, seafood/international, coffee shop); 1 bar; 1 lounge; casino; 1 Olympic-size swimming pool divided into lanes for training, as well as another large pool with plenty of patio space, lounge chairs, and a swim-up bar; 18-hole golf course and pro shop; 11 tennis courts; health club with saunas and Jacuzzis; game room; concierge; tour desk; car-rental desk; complimentary airport and downtown shuttle; business center; salon; 24-hour room service; in-room massage; baby-sitting; laundry service; nonsmoking rooms. *In room:* A/C, TV, dataport, minibar, hair dryer, iron, safe.

Xandari Plantation ⋆⋆ Xandari Plantation is yet another architecturally stunning small hotel not far from the airport. Set on a high hilltop above the city of Alajuela, Xandari Plantation commands wonderful views of the surrounding coffee farms and the Central Valley below. The villas are huge private affairs with high-curved ceilings, stained-glass windows, and handmade fine furniture. All come with both an outdoor patio with a view and private covered palapa, as well as a smaller interior terrace with chaise longues. Most have king-size beds; the rest have two queens (the beds are too soft for my taste). There are spacious living rooms with rattan sofas and chairs, as well as small kitchenettes. The owners are artists, and their original works and innovative design touches abound. The hotel grounds contain several miles of trails that pass by at least five jungle waterfalls, as well as lush gardens and fruit orchards.

A.P. 1485-4050, Alajuela (mailing address in the U.S.: Box 1449, Summerland, CA 93067). **℃ 800/ 686-7879** in the U.S., or 506/443-2020 in Costa Rica. Fax 506/442-4847. www.xandari.com. 16 villas. $150–$250 villa for 2; lower rates off-season. $20 for extra person over age 12; $10 for child ages 3–11; children under age 3 stay free in parent's room. Rates include full breakfast. AE, MC, V. **Amenities:** 1 restaurant (continental); 1 bar; 1 lounge; 2 lap pools, Jacuzzi; small outdoor exercise room; complimentary airport shuttle; in-room massage; laundry service. *In room:* Kitchenette, minibar, safe.

EXPENSIVE

Vista del Valle Plantation Inn ⋆⋆ *(Finds)* If you have little need for San José and would like a comfortable base for exploring the rest of Costa Rica, consider this fine little country inn. It began as a converted private home, and the owners have been adding elegant little cottages around their grounds, which command an impressive view over the Río Grande and its steep-walled canyon. The architecture here has a strong Japanese influence. Most of the accommodations are in independent or duplex cottages or bungalows. The cottages are open and airy, with lots of windows letting in lots of light. You'll also find plenty of varnished woodwork, small kitchenettes (in some), and comfortable wraparound decks.

The grounds are wonderfully landscaped, with several inviting seating areas set among a wealth of flowering tropical plants. Meals are served on the poolside terrace's dining area. The dinner menu varies nightly, featuring fine continental cuisine prepared with fresh local ingredients. The hotel is located 20 minutes north of the Juan Santamaría Airport, and staying here can cut as much as an hour off your travel time to the Pacific coast beaches, Arenal Volcano, and Monteverde Cloud Forest.

A.P. 185-4003, Alajuela. **℃ 506/450-0900**, 506/450-0800, or **℃** and fax 506/451-1165. www.vistadelvalle.com. 12 units. $110–$155 double; lower in the off-season. Rates include full breakfast. V. **Amenities:** 1 restaurant (continental); midsize tile pool with an interesting little fountain/waterfall; Jacuzzi; tennis court; horse rental; laundry service. *In room:* Fridge; no phone.

MODERATE

Hotel Bougainvillea ⋆ *(Value)* The Hotel Bougainvillea is an excellent choice—a great value if you're looking for a hotel in a quiet residential neighborhood not far from downtown. It offers most of the amenities of the more expensive resort hotels around the Central Valley, but charges considerably less. The views across the valley from this hillside location are wonderful, and the gardens are beautifully designed and well tended. Rooms are carpeted and have small triangular balconies oriented to the views. Though there is no air-conditioning, there are fans, and temperatures rarely get too hot here. A complimentary hourly downtown shuttle bus will take you in and out of town.

In Santo Tomás de Santo Domingo de Heredia, 150m west of the Escuela de Santo Tomás (A.P. 69-2120), San José. © **506/244-1414.** Fax 506/244-1313. www.bougainvillea.co.cr. 86 units. $78–$100 double. AE, MC, V. Free parking. **Amenities:** 1 restaurant (continental); 1 bar; midsize outdoor pool in attractive garden; 2 outdoor lighted tennis courts; Jacuzzi; sauna; tour desk; free downtown shuttle; business center; limited room service; baby-sitting; laundry service. *In room:* TV.

Hampton Airport Inn   If familiarity, basic comfort, and proximity to the airport are important to you, then the Hampton Airport Inn is your best bet. The rooms are what you'd expect from a well-known chain, and since the hotel is new, they don't show much wear and tear. Although breakfast is served, there are no other dining options right on the premises. This is a good choice if your plane arrives very late or leaves very early, and you don't plan on spending any time in San José.

Autopista General Cañas, by the airport (A.P. 195-4003), San José. © **800/426-7866** in the U.S., or 506/443-0043. Fax 506/442-9532. www.hamptonhotel.co.cr. 100 units. $92 double. Rates include continental breakfast. AE, DC, MC, V. Free parking. **Amenities:** 1 bar; midsize outdoor pool; tour desk; free airport shuttle; laundry service. *In room:* A/C, TV, safe.

Orquideas Inn   This small country inn is just 10 minutes from the airport on the road heading up to the Poás Volcano. The rooms are all spacious and comfortable, with tile floors, private bathrooms, and colorful Guatemalan bedspreads. There are a few larger minisuites located around the small pool, as well as a separate geodesic dome, with a king-size bed in a loft reached by a spiral staircase, a large sunken tub in the bathroom, and a full kitchen and living-room area. The entire grounds are lush and tropical. The Marilyn Monroe bar serves up good drinks, *bocas,* and some seriously spicy buffalo wings. The hotel recently took over a neighboring property and has grown greatly, with more expansion and remodeling in store.

A.P. 394, Alajuela. © **506/433-9346.** Fax 506/433-9740. www.hotels.co.cr. orchid@racsa.co.cr. 31 units. $59–$99 double, $100–$200 suite. Rates include breakfast buffet. AE, MC, V. No children under the age of 10. **Amenities:** 1 restaurant (international/American); 1 bar; 2 midsize outdoor pools; tennis court; tour desk; laundry service.

4 Dining

For decades, Costa Rican cuisine has been dismissed and disparaged. Rice and beans are served at nearly every meal, the selection of other dishes is minimal, and Ticos generally don't go for spicy food—or so the criticism goes. In recent years, though, some contemporary and creative chefs have been trying to educate and enlighten the Costa Rican palate, particularly in San José, and the early results are promising. Still, most visitors to the capital city quickly tire of Tico fare, even in its more chichi incarnations, and start seeking out the many local restaurants serving international cuisines. They are richly rewarded.

San José has a rather amazing variety of restaurants serving cuisines from all over the world, and you'll never pay much even at the best restaurants. In fact, you really have to work at it to spend more than $40 per person for an extravagant six- or seven-course meal (not including liquor). Most restaurants fall into the moderately priced range. However, service can be indifferent at many restaurants, since the gratuity is already tacked onto the check, and tipping is not common among locals.

LOCAL CUISINE If you'd really like to sample the local flavor, head to a *soda,* the equivalent of a diner in the United States, where you can get good, cheap, and filling Tico food. Rice and beans are the staples here and show up at breakfast, lunch, and dinner (when mixed together, they're called *gallo pinto*). For breakfast, they're garnished with everything from fried eggs to steak. At lunch and dinner, rice and beans are the main components of a *casado* (which means "married"), the Costa Rican equivalent of a "blue-plate special." A casado generally is served with a salad of cabbage and tomatoes, fried bananas, and steak, chicken, or fish. A plate of gallo pinto might cost $2, and a casado might cost $2.50 to $4, usually with a *fresco* (a fresh-fruit drink) thrown into the bargain.

While in Costa Rica, be sure to taste a few of these frescos. They're a bit like a fresh-fruit milkshake without the ice cream, and when made with mangoes, papayas, bananas, or any of the other delicious tropical fruits of Costa Rica, they're pure ambrosia. Frescos can be made with water (*con agua*) or with milk (*con leche*), and preferences vary. Certain fruits like *carambola* (star fruit), *maracuyá* (a type of passion fruit), and *cas* (you'll just have to try it) are used only with water. But remember, while the water in Costa Rica is generally very safe to drink, those with tender stomachs and/or intestinal tracts should stick to frescos made with milk, as it's pasteurized.

FRUIT VENDORS There's a fruit vendor on almost every street corner in downtown San José. If you're lucky enough to be in town between April and June, you can sample more varieties of mangoes than you ever knew existed. I like buying them already cut up in a little bag; they cost a little more this way, but you don't get nearly as messy. Be sure to try a green mango with salt and chile peppers—guaranteed to wake up your taste buds. Another common street food that you might be wondering about is called *pejibaye,* a bright orange palm nut about the size of a plum. They're boiled in big pots on carts, you eat them in much the same way you eat an avocado, and they taste a bit like squash.

LATE-NIGHT BITES San José has quite a few **all-night restaurants,** including La Esmeralda and Café Parisien, both of which are described below. There's also a new **Denny's** (© **506/231-3500**), located at the Best Western Irazú, on the highway out to the airport. Another popular place, which is quite a bit seedier, is **Chelles,** on Avenida Central and Calle 9 (see "San José After Dark," later in this chapter, for more information). Finally, the City Café, at the Hotel Del Rey, is also open 24 hours.

DOWNTOWN SAN JOSÉ
MODERATE

Le Bilboquet ★★ *Finds* FRENCH/BISTRO Le Bilboquet serves up refined nouveau French cuisine with world fusion flourishes in a relaxed, yet lively, bistro environment. It may be too soon to tell, but this could quickly become one of the premier restaurants in San José. French staples include a classic niçoise salad, ratatouille, *pissaladiere,* and fresh profiteroles for dessert. More adventurous entrees include Cajun mahi-mahi served over couscous and coconut-crusted tempura shrimp. The restaurant is housed in a classic old downtown mansion, with dark, aged wainscoting around the interior walls. The tablecloths are simple sheets of heavy blank paper, and each table comes with a jar of crayons for doodling. The bar is a comfortable and dark space with creative post-modern decor, including silk parachutes draped from the high ceiling.

At the corner of Avenida 11 and Calle 3, in front of the Hotel Britannia. ☎ 506/221-2302. Reservations recommended. Main courses $9–$21. AE, MC, V. Tues–Fri and Sun noon–3pm; Tues–Sat 7–11pm.

Café Mundo *✦* INTERNATIONAL   Chef Ray Johnson has a passion for fresh local ingredients prepared with adventurous creativity and classical finesse. The appetizers include vegetable tempura and fried clam cakes alongside more traditional Tico standards like *patacones* and fried yucca. There's a long list of pastas and pizzas, as well as more substantial main courses. The nightly special on my last visit was a macadamia-nut–crusted corvina fillet with a mint-papaya chutney.

This is one of the few places in San José to successfully create an ambiance of casual elegance. Wood tables and art-deco wrought-iron chairs are spread spaciously around several rooms in this former colonial mansion. There's additional seating on the open-air veranda and in the small garden. The tables and chairs here are just plastic lawn furniture, but the lush tropical foliage and small tile fountain make the tradeoff worthwhile, especially during the day. One room here is a lively bar with colorful wall murals by Costa Rican artist Miguel Cassafont that has become the popular hangout for a broad mix of San José's gay, bohemian, theater, arts, and university crowds.

Calle 15 and Avenida 9, 200m east and 100m north of the INS building. ☎ 506/222-6190. Reservations recommended. Main courses $7–$15. AE, MC, V. Mon–Thurs 11am–11pm, Fri 11am–midnight, Sat 5pm–midnight.

Café Parisien INTERNATIONAL   The Gran Hotel Costa Rica is hardly the best hotel in San José, but it does have a picturesque patio cafe right on the Plaza de la Cultura. A wrought-iron railing, white columns, and arches create an old-world atmosphere, while on the plaza in front of the cafe, a marimba band performs and vendors sell handcrafts. It's open 24 hours a day and is one of the best spots in town to people-watch. Stop by for the breakfast buffet ($7) and watch the plaza vendors set up their booths, or peruse the *Tico Times* over coffee while you have your shoes polished. Lunch and dinner buffets are also offered for around $9, or you can simply bask in the tropical sunshine while you sip a beer. This is one of the best spots in town on a sunny afternoon, or just before or after a show at the National Theater.

In the Gran Hotel Costa Rica, Avenida 2 between Calles 1 and 3. ☎ 506/221-4011. Sandwiches $2.50–$5, main courses $5–$20. AE, DC, MC, V. Daily 24 hours.

La Cocina de Leña COSTA RICAN   Located in the El Pueblo shopping, dining, and entertainment center, La Cocina de Leña (The Wood Stove) is designed to create a rustic feel. There are stacks of firewood on shelves above the booths, long stalks of bananas hanging from pillars, tables suspended from the ceiling by heavy ropes, and, most unusual of all, menus printed on paper bags. If you're adventurous, you could try some of the more unusual dishes—perhaps oxtail stew served with yucca and plátano might appeal to you. If not, there are plenty of steaks and seafood dishes on the menu. *Chilasuilas* are delicious tortillas filled with fried meat. Black-bean soup with egg is a Costa Rican standard and is mighty fine here; the corn soup with pork is equally satisfying. For dessert, there's *tres leches* cake as well as the more unusual sweetened *chiverre*, which is a type of squash that looks remarkably like a watermelon.

Centro Comercial El Pueblo. ☎ 506/255-1360 or 506/223-3704. Reservations recommended. Main courses $6–$25. AE, MC, V. Daily 11am–11pm.

Tin Jo ★★ *Finds* CHINESE/THAI/PAN-ASIAN   San José has hundreds of Chinese restaurants, but most simply serve up tired takes on chop suey, chow mein, and fried rice. In contrast, Tin Jo has a wide and varied menu, with an assortment of Cantonese and Szechuan staples as well as a few Thai, Japanese, and Malaysian dishes, and even some Indian food. This is as close to an elegant pan-Asian restaurant as you'll find in these latitudes. The mu shu is so good that you'll forgive the fact that the pancakes are actually thin flour tortillas. Some of the dishes are served in edible rice-noodle bowls, and the pineapple shrimp in coconut-milk curry is served in the hollowed-out half of a fresh pineapple. Other dishes not to miss include the salt-and-pepper shrimp, beef teriyaki, and Thai curries. Tin Jo is also a great option for vegetarians. For dessert, try the sticky rice with mango, or banana tempura. The waiters here are some of the most attentive in Costa Rica. The decor features artwork and textiles from across Asia, and you'll have real tablecloths and cloth napkins. The restaurant has recently expanded quite a bit, and there's a comfortable new bar and lounge area.

Calle 11, between Avenidas 6 and 8. © 506/221-7605. Main courses $4–$12. AE, MC, V. Mon–Sat 11:30am–3pm and 5:30–10:30pm, Sun 11:30am–10pm.

INEXPENSIVE

In addition to the places listed below, a new Turkish restaurant called **Aya Sofya,** Avenida Central and Calle 21 (© **506/221-7185**), is a great place for a light, quick bite.

Café Britt ★ CONTINENTAL/COFFEEHOUSE   The folks at Café Britt recently took over the in-house restaurant at the Teatro Nacional, to good effect. Even if there's no show on during your visit, you can enjoy a light meal, sandwich, dessert, and/or a cup of coffee here, while soaking up the neoclassical atmosphere. The theater was built in the 1890s from the designs of European architects, and the art-nouveau chandeliers, ceiling murals, and marble floors and tables are pure Parisian. There's a daily selection of about three lunch items, as well as sandwiches, quiches, and salads. There are also plenty of desserts and a wide range of coffee drinks. The ambiance is French cafe chic, but the marimba music drifting in from outside the open window and the changing art exhibits by local artists will remind you that you're still in Costa Rica. On sunny days, there's outdoor seating at wrought-iron tables on the side of the theater.

In the Teatro Nacional, Avenida 2 between Calles 3 and 5. © 506/221-3262. Sandwiches $3–$5, main courses $4–$10. AE, MC, V. Mon–Fri 10am–7pm, Sat 10am–5:30pm.

La Esmeralda ★ *Moments* COSTA RICAN   No one should visit San José without stopping in at La Esmeralda at least once—and the later at night, the better. This is much more than just a restaurant serving Tico food: It's Grand Central Station for Costa Rican mariachi bands. In fact, mariachis and other bands from throughout Central America and Mexico hang out here every night waiting for work. While they wait, they often serenade diners in the cavernous open-air dining hall of the restaurant. Friday and Saturday nights are always the busiest, but you'll probably hear lots of excellent music any night of the week. A personal concert will cost you anywhere from $5 to $10 per song, depending on the size of the group, but if you're on a tight budget, you'll still be able to hear just fine by eavesdropping on your neighbors. The classic Tico food is quite good (try the coconut flan for dessert).

Avenida 2 between Calles 5 and 7. © 506/221-0530. Main courses $4–$22. AE, MC, V. Mon–Sat 11am–5am.

Manolo's Restaurante COSTA RICAN   This roomy restaurant, spread out over three floors on a busy corner of Avenida Central, is popular with Ticos and travelers alike. You can grab a first-floor table to check out the action passing by on the street, or catch the live folk-dance performances that are staged nightly upstairs. The open kitchen serves up steaks and fish, but there's also a popular buffet that includes several typical Costa Rican dishes, such as plátanos-and-black-bean soup, for about $5. The ground floor has the feel of a diner. It's a good place for a quick sandwich or perhaps a fried-dough *churro* and a shot of espresso.

There's another Manolo's located on Avenida Central and Calle 11.

Avenida Central, between Calle Central and Calle 2. © **506/221-2041**. All items $3–$10. AE, MC, V. Daily 11:30am–10pm upstairs; 24 hours downstairs.

Soda Billy Boy (Value) COSTA RICAN   Located on the corner across from the Tourist Information Center on the Plaza de la Cultura, this spot is popular with downtown shoppers and office workers. Service is prompt, prices (and noise level) are low, and the food is surprisingly good for a sandwich shop. Slide into a high-backed wooden booth and order the *chalupa de pollo B y B*—it's a toasted tortilla piled high with chicken salad and drenched with sour cream and guacamole.

Calle 5 and Avenida Central. © **506/222-7316**. Breakfast $1.50–$3, sandwiches $2.50–$4, main courses $3–$6. AE, MC, V. Mon–Thurs 8am–9:30pm, Fri–Sat 9am–10pm.

Moments   **Only in the Central Valley: Dining Under the Stars on a Mountain's Edge**

While there are myriad unique experiences to be had in Costa Rica, one of my favorites is dining on the side of a volcano, with the lights of San José shimmering below. These hanging restaurants, called *miradores,* are a resourceful response to the city's topography. Because San José is set in a broad valley surrounded on all sides by volcanic mountains, people who live in these mountainous areas have no place to go but up—so they do, building roadside cafes vertically up the sides of the volcanoes.

While the food at most of these establishments is not usually spectacular, the views often are, particularly at night, when the whole wide valley sparkles in a wash of lights. The town of **Aserri,** 6 miles (10km) south of downtown San José, is the king of miradores, and **Mirador Ram Luna** (© **506/230-3060**; closed Monday) is the king of Aserri. Grab a window seat and, if you've got the fortitude, order a plate of *chicharrones* (fried pork rinds). There's often live music. You can hire a cab for around $9 or take the Aserri bus at Avenida 6 between Calle Central and Calle 2. Just ask the driver where to get off.

There are also miradores in the hills above Escazú and in San Ramón de Trés Ríos and Heredia. One of the best of this bunch is **Le Monestère** (© **506/289-4404**; closed Sunday), an elegant converted church serving fine French and Belgian cuisine in a spectacular setting above the hills of Escazú. The Bar La Cava here is also quite popular and often features live music.

Vishnu VEGETARIAN   Vegetarians will most certainly find their way here. There are booths for two or four people and photo murals on the walls. At the cashier's counter, you can buy natural cosmetics, honey, and bags of granola. However, most people just come for the filling *plato del día* that includes soup, salad, veggies, an entree, and dessert for around $3. There are also bean burgers and cheese sandwiches on whole-wheat bread. This restaurant is part of the Vishnu chain; there are eight sister restaurants spread over the city.

Avenida 1, between Calles 1 and 3. ℂ **506/256-6063**. Main courses $1.50–$4. No credit cards. Daily 8am–9:30pm.

IN LA SABANA/PASEO COLÓN
EXPENSIVE

La Masía de Triquel ⚹ SPANISH   Despite relocation, a healthy field of competitors, and the death of founding chef Francisco Triquel, La Masía de Triquel is still San José's finest Spanish restaurant. Francisco Triquel, Jr., has seen to that. Service is extremely formal, and the regular clientele includes most of the city's upper crust. Although Costa Rica is known for its beef, here you'll also find wonderfully prepared lamb, quail, and rabbit. Seafood dishes include the usual shrimp and lobster, but also squid and octopus. However, there is really no decision to be made when perusing the menu: Start with a big bowl of gazpacho and then spend the rest of the evening enjoying all the succulent surprises you'll find in a big dish of paella.

Sabana Norte, 50m west and 175m north of the Burger King in La Sabana. ℂ **506/296-3528** or 506/232-3584. Reservations recommended. Main courses $10–$18. AE, MC, V. Mon–Sat 11:30am–2pm and 6:30–10:30pm.

La Piazzetta ⚹ ITALIAN   With an amazingly long menu and service by waiters in suits and bow ties, this restaurant harks back to the Italian restaurants of old in the United States, when southern Italian cooking was still an exotic ethnic cuisine. The menu includes quite a few risotto dishes, which is a surprise, since most Italian restaurants in Costa Rica stick to spaghetti. Some other unexpected dishes also make appearances here, including several lobster offerings, and veal scaloppine in a truffle sauce. Salads are colorful and artistically arranged. If you're in no danger of a coronary, try the *baugna cauda*—anchovies and peppers in an olive-oil-based broth. For dessert, sample a classic chocolate mousse, or tiramisu.

Paseo Colón near Calle 40 (opposite Banco de Costa Rica). ℂ **506/222-7896**. Reservations recommended. Main courses $6–$20. AE, MC, V. Mon–Sat noon–2:30pm and 6:30–11pm.

MODERATE

El Chicote ⚹ COSTA RICAN/STEAKHOUSE   This is San José's premier steakhouse. The large room is divided up by half-walls planted with tropical flora and a bevy of hanging ferns. There are heavy wooden beams and plenty of varnished-wood accents all around. True meat aficionados should order the imported rib eye, or pound-and-a-half T-bone. There's an extensive selection of fish and poultry dishes, as well. Everything comes with a choice of baked or mashed potatoes, black beans, and fresh tortillas. The wine list features a broad range of Italian, Spanish, French, and Californian wines. Waiters wear black jackets, white shirts, and black bow ties, and service is unusually formal for Costa Rica.

Avenida Las Américas, 400m west of the ICE building, Sabana Norte. ℂ **506/232-0936** or 506/232-3777. Reservations recommended. Main courses $8–$22 (most dishes around $10). AE, MC, V. Daily 11am–midnight.

Grano de Oro Restaurant ★ 𝘍𝘪𝘯𝘥𝘴 CONTINENTAL   The small restaurant located just off the central courtyard of a wonderful downtown hotel is both elegant and relaxed. The menu features a wide range of meat and fish dishes. The *lomito piemontes* is two medallions of filet mignon stuffed with Gorgonzola cheese in a sherry sauce, while the *lomito Diana* comes with fresh pears and a thick brandy reduction. If you opt for fish, I recommend the macadamia-encrusted corvina, which is served with a light and tangy orange sauce. When the weather's nice, you can grab a table in the courtyard. This is a particularly nice option for lunch.

Calle 30, no. 251, between Avenidas 2 and 4, 150m south of Paseo Colón. ℂ 506/255-3322. Reservations recommended. Main courses $8–$20. AE, MC, V. Daily 6am–10pm.

Machu Picchu Bar and Restaurant ★ PERUVIAN/CONTINENTAL Machu Picchu is an unpretentious little restaurant that has become one of the most popular places in San José. The menu is primarily seafood (especially sea bass), and consequently most dishes tend toward the upper end of the menu's price range. Many of these fish dishes come in thick cream sauces—you're better off sticking with the two-person seafood sampler, combined with different appetizers. One of my favorite entrees is the *causa limeña,* lemon-flavored mashed potatoes stuffed with shrimp. The ceviche here is excellent, as is the *aji de gallina,* a dish of chopped chicken in a fragrant cream sauce, and octopus with garlic butter. Be sure to ask for a pisco sour, a Peruvian specialty drink made from grape brandy.

Calle 32, between Avenidas 1 and 3, 150m north of the Kentucky Fried Chicken on Paseo Colón. ℂ 506/222-7384. Reservations recommended. Main courses $4–$12. AE, DC, MC, V. Mon–Sat 11am–3pm and 6–10pm.

INEXPENSIVE

Pasteleria Francesa Boudsocq PASTRIES/FRENCH   Pastry shops abound in San José, but this little place is worth seeking out. Boudsocq recently celebrated its 20th anniversary, so it must be doing something right. Savory meat-filled pastries make good lunches; unusual sweets are great afternoon snacks. There are only a couple of tables here, so most folks get their goodies to go.

Calle 30 at Paseo Colón. ℂ 506/222-6732. Pastries $1–$3, breakfast $3.50–$4.50, lunch $4–$6. AE, MC, V. Mon–Sat 7am–7pm.

Soda Coppelia COSTA RICAN   If you're looking for a filling, cheap, and quick breakfast in the Paseo Colón area, this is the best *soda* around. You'll find it near the Universal movie theater. The wooden booths and a few tables on the (rather noisy) covered walkway are frequently full of local businesspeople because the meals are so reasonably priced. A thin steak will run you just over $2. For lighter fare, try the burgers, sandwiches, or some of the good-looking pastries such as flaky empanadas or carrot bread.

Paseo Colón, between Calles 26 and 28. ℂ 506/223-8013. Most items $1.75–$5. No credit cards. Daily 7am–8pm.

SAN PEDRO/LOS YOSES

In addition to the restaurants listed below, my vegetarian friends swear by the little **Restaurante El Vegetariano San Pedro** (ℂ 506/224-1163), located 125 meters north of the San Pedro Church.

VERY EXPENSIVE

Le Chandelier ★ FRENCH   Located in a large old house in a quiet residential neighborhood east of downtown San José, Le Chandelier is one of the most elegant restaurants in town. The neighborhood, landscaping, and architectural styling give it the feel of an older Hollywood or Beverly Hills restaurant. The menu includes delicious renditions of French classics such as onion soup, escargots bourguignonne, and chicken à l'orange. There are also some unexpected and less familiar dishes, such as tenderloin with cranberry sauce, carpaccio with smoked salmon and palmito, and roast duck in green-pepper sauce. The fixed-price dinner is a true feast and might start with an appetizer of carpaccio, followed by langostinos Newburg, sorbet, tournedos in cabernet sauvignon and green peppers, cheese and fruit, and a dessert of crème brûlée.

100m west and 100m south of the ICE office in San Pedro. © **506/225-3980.** Reservations recommended. Main courses $15–$25, fixed-price dinner $45. AE, MC, V. Mon–Fri 11:30am–2:30pm; Mon–Sat 6:30–11pm.

MODERATE

Ambrosia ☞ CONTINENTAL This elegant little restaurant is a good choice for lunch or dinner. Greek and Latin mythology make their way onto the menu: Seafood dishes are named after Ulysses, Circe, and Poseidon; Zeus, Apollo, and Orion provide namesakes for the different steaks; and the pasta selections are anchored by Ravioli Romulus. Behind the mythology, you'll find well-prepared meals made with fresh ingredients and interesting spices. The Crepe Aphrodite is a delicate crepe filled with chunks of fish and shrimp in a Gouda cheese sauce. The Corvina Cassiopeia is a grilled sea-bass fillet topped with a light almond sauce. The ambiance is relaxed, and the service can be a bit inattentive. There's a small bar at the center of the restaurant, and live piano music is sometimes offered in the evenings.

Centro Comercial Calle Real. © **506/253-8012.** Sandwiches and salads $3.50–$5, main courses $5–$12. AE, DC, MC, V. Sun–Fri 11:30am–3pm; Mon–Fri 6–10:30pm; Sat 11:30am–10:30pm.

Balalaika INTERNATIONAL This is the biggest and most happening spot in San Pedro; it's like a 300-pound gorilla I can't ignore. The monstrous complex houses two restaurants, two bars, and a pastry shop in about eight separate environments, depending on how you count. The architecture is big and bold, painted in bright primary colors, with giant ferro-cement fruits and vegetables punctuating the huge open spaces. Still, the execution doesn't meet the expectations set. The service frequently falters and the food almost never rises above the level of acceptable.

The most upscale option here, **La Bóveda,** serves up nouvelle Costa Rican and continental cuisine in a formal environment (though unfortunately, you can usually hear the pounding bass of the rowdy second-floor bar). A better bet is the Brazilian *rodizio* plate, the namesake dish in **Rodizio,** the more informal of the two restaurants, which serves a steady stream of succulent and varied grilled meats. The upstairs bars are the liveliest spots here and a good place for a drink and a light bite in the evenings.

75m east of the Fuente de la Hispanidad, San Pedro. © **506/280-0002.** Reservations recommended at La Bóveda. Main courses $7–$28. AE, MC, V. Daily 6:30am–11pm; bars stay open later.

Il Ponte Vecchio ☞ ITALIAN Everyone should have a favorite neighborhood Italian restaurant, and this is mine. Not too formal, but no simple pasteria, Il Ponte Vecchio is consistent, comfortable, and personal. Chef Tony D'Alaimo has years of experience, having cut his teeth in New York's Little Italy before settling in San José. There's a small bar just as you enter, then three separate rooms with tables draped in linen tablecloths and set with glass-lanterned candles. The service is attentive and professional but never overbearing. My favorite dish is the chicken Valdostana, a delicate breast fillet rolled around some fresh mozzarella, Italian prosciutto, and porcini mushrooms, covered in tangy pomodoro sauce and baked in the oven. You might also check out the home-made ravioli in a cream sauce, with hints of nutmeg.

San Pedro, 75m east and 10m north of the Salón de Patines Music. © **506/283-1810.** Reservations recommended in high season. Main courses $5–$14. AE, MC, V. Mon–Sat noon–2:30pm and 6–10:30pm.

ESCAZÚ & SANTA ANA
EXPENSIVE

La Luz ✦✦ *Finds* CALIFORNIAN/PACIFIC RIM/FUSION   La Luz serves up some of the more adventurous food in Costa Rica, mixing fresh local ingredients with the best of a whole host of international ethnic cuisines. The fiery garlic prawns are sautéed in ancho-chili oil and sage and served over a roasted-garlic potato mash. Then the whole thing is served with a garnish of fried leeks and a tequila-lime butterand cilantro-oil sauce. There's also a grilled tenderloin served over champagne risotto, with a strawberry and balsamic vinegar reduction. On top of all this, there are nightly specials, such as fresh-baked rolls and breads, and a wide selection of inventive appetizers and desserts. The glass-walled dining room is one of the most elegant in town, with a view of the city lights. The wait staff is attentive and knowledgeable. La Luz is also open for breakfast and lunch.

In the Hotel Alta, on the old road to Santa Ana. © **506/282-4160.** Reservations recommended. Main courses $6–$22. AE, DC, MC, V. Daily 7am–3pm and 6–10pm.

MODERATE

In addition to the places mentioned below, **Santa Ana Tex Mex** (© **506/ 282-6342**) is one of the most popular places on this side of town. Located a half-block north of the main church in Santa Ana, it serves up Tex-Mex cuisine in a lively atmosphere.

Barbecue Los Anonos ✦ COSTA RICAN/STEAKHOUSE   Good steaks and well-prepared Costa Rican cuisine have made this simple restaurant something of an institution. Most of the seating here is at simple wooden tables covered with red and white checkered table cloths, and long and rustic booths set under the shelter of low interior red-tile roofs. It serves aged Angus beef here, and this is *the* place to come if you're craving a 16-ounce T-bone. There are a host of chicken, pork, and fish options here, and I recommend the mixed grilled plate for two, which comes with a little bit of everything.

600m west of the Los Anonos bridge in San Rafael de Escazú, next to the Sarretto Market. © **506/ 228-0180.** Reservations recommended. Main courses $7–$25. AE, MC, V. Tues–Sat noon–3pm; Tues–Fri 6–10pm, Sat 6–11pm; Sun 11:30am–9pm.

Rincón de la Calle Real ✦ *Finds* INTERNATIONAL/CAFE   Housed in an old adobe home with a low red-tile roof, this restaurant serves up great international cuisine in a lovely setting. Tables are spread through several rooms in this old house, with original artworks hanging on the walls. My favorite tables, though, are outside on the covered patio, where you can listen to the trickle of the bordering stream. The menu features a short but creative mix of appetizers, salads, soups, and entrees. Light bites include falafel, humus, gazpacho, and quiche. If I'm hungry, I opt for one of the meat dishes or the *mariscada de la casa,* a platter of mixed grilled seafood.

San Rafael de Escazú; 150m south of the U.S. Ambassador's residence, on the small st. running parallel to the old Escazú-Santa Ana rd. ⓒ **506/289-5112.** Main courses $5–$15. AE, MC, V. Mon–Sat noon–9pm, Sun 10am–8pm.

5 Seeing the Sights

Most visitors to Costa Rica try to get out of the city as fast as possible so they can spend more time on the beach or off in the rain forests. But if you'll be in San José for longer than an overnight stay, there are a few attractions to keep you busy. Some of the best and most modern museums in Central America are here, with a wealth of fascinating pre-Columbian artifacts. Recent additions include a modern and expansive Children's Museum, as well as a centrally located National Arts Center, featuring yet another museum and several performing-arts spaces. There are also several great things to see and do just outside San José in the Central Valley. If you start doing day trips out of the city, you can spend quite a few days in this region.

ORGANIZED TOURS There really isn't much reason to take a tour of San José. It's so compact that you can easily visit all the major sights on your own, as described below. However, if you want to take a city tour, which will run you between $15 and $20, here are some companies: **Otec Tours,** Edificio Ferencz, Calle 3 between Avenidas 1 and 3 (ⓒ **506/256-0633;** www.otec.co.cr); **TAM,** Calle Central between Avenidas Central and 1 (ⓒ **506/256-0203**); **Horizontes Travel,** ✶ Calle 32 between Avenidas 3 and 5 (ⓒ **506/222-2022;** www.horizontes.com); **Ecole Travel,** Calle 7 between Avenidas Central and 1 (ⓒ **506/223-2240**); and **Swiss Travel Service** (ⓒ **506/282-4898**). These same companies also offer a whole range of day trips out of San José (see section 9, "Side Trips from San José," later in this chapter). Almost all of the major hotels have tour desks, and most of the smaller hotels will also help arrange tours and day trips.

SUGGESTED ITINERARIES

If You Have 1 Day

Start your day on the Plaza de la Cultura. Visit the Gold Museum and see if you can get tickets for a performance that night at the Teatro Nacional. From the Plaza de la Cultura, stroll up Avenida Central to the Museo Nacional. After lunch, head over to the neighboring National Arts Center (if you have the energy for another museum). After all this culture, some shopping at the open-air stalls at the Plaza de la Democracia is in order. Try dinner at either Le Bilboquet or El Chicote before going to the Teatro Nacional. After the performance, you absolutely must swing by La Esmeralda for some live mariachi music before calling it a night.

If You Have 2 Days

On Day 2, visit the Serpentarium, the Children's Museum (a must if you've brought the kids along), or the Spyrogyra Butterfly Garden; do a bit of shopping; and then head out on Paseo Colón to the Museo de Arte Costarricense and La Sabana Park. Alternatively, you could take one of the day trips outside of San José described below.

If You Have 3 Days

On Day 3, head out to Irazú Volcano, the Orosi Valley, Lankester Gardens, and Cartago. Start your day at the volcano and work your way back toward San José. Alternatively you could head to the Poá Volcano and then visit the La Paz Waterfall, returning through the hills of Heredia. If you prefer less strenuous activities, try a cruise around the Gulf of Nicoya or a trip to the Rain Forest Aerial Tram.

If You Have 4 Days or More
Get out of San José. Do a 1- or 2-night trip to Tortuguero, Monteverde, or Arenal. You can go white-water rafting, hiking in a cloud forest, horseback riding near a volcano, or cruising through jungle canals.

THE TOP ATTRACTIONS

In addition to the attractions listed below, the **Jade Museum,** Avenida 7 between Calles 9 and 9B, 11th Floor, INS Building (© **506/287-6034**), has been closed for the past year, and as of press time, no one could say when it would open. Part of the collection has been moved and placed on temporary display at the National Museum (see below). The extensive collection of carved jade objects is definitely well worth seeing, so check to see whether the museum has re-opened for the winter 2001–2002 season.

Centro Nacional de Arte y Cultura (National Arts Center) ★★ (Finds)
Occupying a full city block, this was once the National Liquor Factory (FANAL). Now it houses the offices of the Cultural Ministry, several performing-arts centers, and the Museum of Contemporary Art and Design. The latter has featured several impressive traveling international exhibits since its inception, including large retrospectives by Mexican painter José Cuevas and Ecuadoran painter Oswaldo Guayasamin. If you're looking for modern dance, experimental theater, or a lecture on Costa Rican video, this is the place to check. Allow around 2 hours to take in all the exhibits here.
Calle 13 between Avenidas 3 and 5. © **506/257-7202** or 506/257-9370. Admission $1.50. Museum hours: Tues–Sat 10am–5pm. Any downtown bus.

Museo de Arte Costarricense ★
This small museum at the end of Paseo Colón in Parque La Sabana was formerly an airport terminal. Today it houses a collection of works in all media by Costa Rica's most celebrated artists. On display are some exceptionally beautiful pieces in a wide range of styles, demonstrating how Costa Rican artists have interpreted and imitated the major European movements over the years. In addition to the permanent collection of sculptures, paintings, and prints, there are regular temporary exhibits. If the second floor is open during your visit, be sure to go up and have a look at the conference room's bas-relief walls, which chronicle the history of Costa Rica from pre-Columbian times to the present with evocative images of its people. You can easily spend an hour or two here—more if you take a stroll through the neighboring park.
Calle 42 and Paseo Colón, Parque La Sabana Este. © **506/222-7155**. Admission $1.50 adults; free for children and students. Tues–Sun 10am–4pm. Sabana-Cementerio bus.

Museo de Los Niños (Children's Museum) (Kids)
Recently converted from use as a prison, the museum houses an extensive collection of exhibits designed to edify and entertain children of all ages. Experience a simulated earthquake, or make music by dancing across the floor. Many of the exhibits encourage hands-on play. If you're traveling with children, you'll definitely want to come here, and you may want to visit even if you don't. This museum sometimes features limited shows of "serious" art, and is also the home of the new National Auditorium. You can spend anywhere from 1 to 4 hours here, depending on how

much time your children spend at each exhibit. Be careful, though: The museum is large and spread out, and it's easy to lose track of a family member or friend.

This museum is located a few blocks north of downtown, on Calle 4. It's within easy walking distance, but you might want to take a cab, as you'll have to walk right through the worst part of the red-light district.

Calle 4 and Avenida 9. © 506/233-2734. Admission $2 adults, $1.50 students and children under 18. Tues–Fri 8am–4pm, Sat–Sun 10am–5pm. Any downtown bus.

Museo de Oro Banco Central (Gold Museum) ✦✦ Located directly beneath the Plaza de la Cultura, this unusual underground museum houses one of the largest collections of pre-Columbian gold in the Americas. On display are more than 20,000 troy ounces of gold in more than 2,000 objects. The sheer number of small pieces can be overwhelming and seem redundant, but the unusual display cases and complex lighting systems show off every piece to its utmost. This museum complex also includes a gallery for temporary art exhibits, separate numismatic and philatelic museums (coins and stamps, for us regular folks), a modest gift shop, and a branch of the Costa Rican Tourist Institute's information center. Plan on spending between 1 and 2 hours here.

Calle 5, between Avenida Central and Avenida 2, underneath the Plaza de la Cultura. © 506/243-4202. Admission $4 adults, $1.50 students, 75¢ children under 12. Tues–Sun 10am–4:30pm. Any downtown bus.

Museo Nacional de Costa Rica (National Museum) ✦ Costa Rica's most important historical museum is housed in a former army barracks that was the scene of fighting during the civil war of 1948. You can still see hundreds of bullet holes on the turrets at the corners of the building. Inside this traditional Spanish-style courtyard building, you will find displays on Costa Rican history and culture from pre-Columbian times to the present. In the pre-Columbian rooms, you'll see a 2,500-year-old jade carving that is shaped like a seashell and etched with an image of a hand holding a small animal.

Among the most fascinating objects unearthed at Costa Rica's numerous archaeological sites are many *metates,* or grinding stones. This type of grinding stone is still in use today throughout Central America; however, the ones on display here are more ornately decorated than those that you will see anywhere else. Some of the metates are the size of a small bed and are believed to have been part of funeral rites. A separate vault houses the museum's collection of pre-Columbian gold jewelry and figurines. In the courtyard, you'll be treated to a wonderful view of the city and see some of Costa Rica's mysterious stone spheres. It takes about 2 hours to take in the lion's share of the collection here.

Calle 17, between Avenida Central and Avenida 2, on the Plaza de la Democracia. © 506/257-1433. Admission $1 adults, free for students and children under 10. Tues–Sun 9am–4:30pm. Closed Dec 25 and 31. Any downtown bus.

Parque Zoológico Simón Bolívar (Kids) This zoo has received some upkeep and renovation in recent years. But while it no longer suffers from an overwhelming sense of neglect and despair, the whole thing is still slightly lackluster. Why spend time here when you could head out into the forests and jungles? You won't see the great concentrations of wildlife available in one stop here at the zoo, but you'll see the animals in their natural habitats, not yours. The zoo is really geared toward locals and school groups, with a collection that includes Asian, African, and Costa Rican animals. There's a new children's discovery area, a snake-and-reptile house, and a gift shop. You can easily spend a whole morning or afternoon here.

Avenida 11 and Calle 7, in Barrio Amón. © **506/233-6701**. Admission $1.50 adults, free for children under 3. Mon–Fri 8:30am–3:30pm, Sat–Sun 9am–4:30pm. Any downtown bus, then walk.

Serpentarium *(Kids)*   Reptiles and amphibians abound in the tropics, and the Serpentarium is an excellent introduction to all that slithers and hops through the jungles of Costa Rica. The live snakes, lizards, and frogs are kept in large terrariums that simulate their natural environments. Poisonous snakes make up a large part of the collection, with the dreaded fer-de-lance pit viper eliciting gasps from enthralled visitors. Also fascinating to see are the tiny, brilliantly colored poison arrow frogs. Iguanas and Jesus Christ lizards are two of the more commonly spotted of Costa Rica's reptiles, and both are represented here. Also on display is an Asian import: a giant Burmese python, which is one of the largest I've ever seen. If you show up around 3pm, you may catch them feeding the piranhas and perhaps some of the snakes. It takes only about 30 to 40 minutes to run through this small serpentarium.

Avenida 1, between Calles 9 and 11. & 506/255-4210. Admission $5 adults, $1.50 children under 13. Mon–Fri 9am–6pm, Sat–Sun 10am–5pm. Any downtown bus.

Spyrogyra Butterfly Garden   Though this butterfly garden is smaller and less elaborate than the one listed below, it provides a good introduction to the life cycle of butterflies. Moreover, it's a calm and quiet oasis in a noisy and crowded city, quite close to downtown. Visitors spend anywhere from a half hour to several hours here, depending on whether they have lunch or refreshments at the small coffee shop. You'll be given a self-guided tour booklet when you arrive, and there's an 18-minute video shown continuously throughout the day. You'll find Spyrogyra near El Pueblo, a short taxi ride or 15-minute walk from the center of San José.

100m east and 150m south of El Pueblo Shopping Center. & and fax 506/222-2937. www. infocostarica.com/butterfly. Admission $6. Daily 8am–4pm. Calle Blancos bus from Calle 3 and Avenida 5.

OUTSIDE SAN JOSÉ

The **Juan Santamaría Historical Museum,** Avenida 3 between Calle Central and Calle 2 (© **506/441-4775**), isn't worth a trip of its own, but if you're looking to make an afternoon of it in Alajuela, you might want to make a stop here before or after Zoo Ave. (see below). The museum commemorates Costa Rica's national hero, who gave his life defending the country against a small army led by William Walker, a U.S. citizen who invaded Costa Rica in 1856, attempting to set up a slave state. The museum is open Tuesday through Sunday from 10am to 6pm; admission is free.

Butterfly Farm *✦*   At any given time, you may see around 30 of the 80 different species of butterflies raised at this butterfly farm south of Alajuela. The butterflies live in a large enclosed garden similar to an aviary and flutter about the heads of visitors during tours of the gardens. You should be certain to spot glittering blue morphos and a large butterfly that mimics the eyes of an owl.

The admission includes a 2-hour guided tour. In the demonstration room you'll see butterfly eggs, caterpillars, and pupae. There are cocoons trimmed in a shimmering gold color and cocoons that mimic a snake's head in order to frighten away predators. The last guided tour of the day begins at 3pm.

If you reserve in advance, the Butterfly Farm has three daily bus tours that run from many major San José hotels for $25, including round-trip transportation and admission to the garden. Buses pick up passengers at more than 20 different hotels in the San José area. For a full-day excursion (including lunch and transportation), check out the "Perfect Combination Tour," which takes you first to the Butterfly Farm and then to Café Britt coffee farm (see below) for $60 per person.

In front of Los Reyes Country Club, La Guácima de Alajuela. © **506/438-0400.** www.butterflyfarm.co.cr. Admission $15 adults, $9 students, $7 children ages 5–12, free for children under 5. Daily 9am–5pm.

Café Britt Farm Though bananas are the main export of Costa Rica, most people are far more interested in the country's second most important export crop: coffee. Café Britt is one of the leading brands here, and the company has put together an interesting tour and stage production at its farm, which is 20 minutes outside of San José. Here, you'll see how coffee is grown. You'll also visit the roasting plant to learn how a coffee "cherry" is turned into a delicious roasted bean. Tasting sessions are offered for visitors to experience the different qualities of coffee. There is also a restaurant, and a store where you can buy very reasonably priced coffee and coffee-related gift items. The entire tour, including transportation, takes about 3 to 4 hours. The folks here offer several full-day options that combine a visit to the Britt Farm with a stop at Poás Volcano, the Butterfly Farm (see above), or the Aerial Tram.

North of Heredia on the rd. to Barva. © **506/261-0707.** www.coffeetour.com. Admission $25 per person, including transportation from downtown San José; $20 walk-in. 3 tours daily: 9am, 11am, and 3pm. Tours Nov–Feb during the harvest season; store open daily 8:30am–5pm year-round.

INBio Park Run by the National Biodiversity Institute (Instituto Nacional de Biodiversidad; INBio), this place is part museum, part educational center, and part nature park. In addition to watching a 15-minute informational video, visitors can tour two large pavilions explaining Costa Rica's biodiversity and natural wonders, and hike on trails that re-create the ecosystems of a tropical rain forest, dry forest, and premontane forest. A 2-hour guided hike is available for just $3 per person. Self-guided tour booklets are also available. There's a simple cafeteria-style restaurant here for lunch, as well as a coffee shop and gift shop. You can easily spend 2 to 3 hours here.

400m north and 250m west of the Shell station in Santo Domingo de Heredia. © **506/244-4730.** www.inbio.ac.cr/inbioparque. Admission $18 adults, $9 children 12 and under. Daily 7:30am–4pm. INBio Park can arrange round-trip transportation from downtown for $10 per person.

Lankester Gardens There are more than 1,200 varieties of orchids in Costa Rica, and no fewer than 800 species are on display at this botanical garden in Cartago province. Created in the 1940s by English naturalist Charles Lankester, the gardens are now administered by the University of Costa Rica. The primary goal is to preserve the local flora, with an emphasis on orchids and bromeliads. Paved trails meander from open, sunny gardens into shady forests. In each environment, different species of orchids are in bloom. There's an information center and gift shop, and the trails are well tended and well marked.

Plan on spending at least 2 to 4 hours here if you're interested in flowers and gardening; you could run through it more quickly if you're not. You can easily combine a visit here with an enjoyable tour of Cartago and/or the Orosi Valley and Irazú Volcano. See section 9, "Side Trips from San José," later in this chapter.

Paraíso de Cartago. © **506/552-3247** or 506/552-3151. Admission $5 adults, $1 children. Daily 8:30am–3:30pm. Closed all national holidays. Cartago bus from San José, then the Paraíso bus

Jugglers, dancers and an assortment of acrobats fill the street.

She shoots you a wide-eyed look as a seven-foot cartoon character approaches.

What brought you here was wanting the kids

to see something magical while they still believed in magic.

America Online Keyword: Travel

With 700 airlines, 50,000 hotels and over 5,000 cruise and vaca-

tion getaways, you can now go places you've always dreamed of.

Travelocity.com
A Sabre Company
Go Virtually Anywhere.

"WORLD'S LEADING TRAVEL WEB SITE, 5 YEARS IN A ROW" WORLD TRAVEL AWARDS

I HAVE TO CALL THE TRAVEL AGENCY AGAIN. DARN, OUT TO LUNCH. NOW HAVE TO CALL THE AIRLINE. I HATE CALLING THE AIRLINES. I GOT PUT ON HOLD AGAIN. "INSTRUMENTAL TOP-40" ... LOVELY. I HATE GETTING PUT ON HOLD. TICKET PRICES ARE ALL OVER THE MAP. HOW DO I DIAL INTERNATIONALLY? OH SHOOT, FORGOT THE RENTAL CAR. I'M STILL ON HOLD. THIS MUSIC IS GIVING ME A HEADACHE. I WONDER IF SOMEONE ELSE HAS CHEAPER FLIGHTS. FORGET IT, CAN'T TAKE IT ANYMORE ... I'M HANGING UP.

YAHOO! TRAVEL
100% MUZAK-FREE

Booking your trip online at Yahoo! Travel is simple. You compare the best prices. You click. You go have fun. Tickets, hotels, rental cars, cruises & more. Sorry, no muzak.

YAHOO!
Travel
travel.yahoo.com

from a stop 1 block south and ¾ block west of the Catholic church ruins in Cartago (ride takes 30–40 min.).

La Paz Waterfall Gardens   This new attraction consists of a series of trails through primary and secondary forest alongside the La Paz river, with lookouts over a series of powerful falls, including the namesake La Paz Fall. There's also a large butterfly garden here, an orchid garden, numerous hummingbird feeders, and a large cafeteria-style restaurant. There are plans to add a canopy tour, rooms, and other attractions. I find the admission fee a little steep, but this is a good stop after a morning visit to the Poá Volcano. Plan on spending between 1 and 3 hours here.

6km north of Varablanca on the rd. to San Miguel. ℂ **506/482-2720.** www.waterfallgardens. com. Admission $24 adults, $12 children and students with valid I.D. Daily 8:30am–4pm. Take a Puerto Viejo de Sarapiquí bus from Calle 12 and Avenida 9 (make sure it takes passes through Varablanca and La Virgin), and ask to be let off at the entrance. These buses are infrequent and coordinating your return can be difficult, so it's best to come in a rental car or arrange transport.

Zoo Ave. ⚹   Dozens of scarlet macaws, reclusive owls, majestic raptors, several different species of toucans, and a host of brilliantly colored birds from Costa Rica and around the world make this one exciting place to visit. Bird-watching enthusiasts will be able to get a closer look at birds they may have seen in the wild. There are also large iguana, deer, and monkey exhibits—and look out for the 12-foot-long crocodile. Zoo Ave. houses only injured, donated, or confiscated animals. It takes about 2 hours to walk the paths and visit all the exhibits here.

La Garita, Alajuela. ℂ **506/433-8989.** Admission $9 adults, $1 children under 12. Daily 9am–5pm. Catch one of the frequent Alajuela buses on Avenida 2 between Calles 12 and 14. In Alajuela, transfer to a bus for Atenas and get off at Zoo Ave. before you get to La Garita. The fare is 55¢.

6 Outdoor Activities & Spectator Sports

Due to the chaos and pollution, you'll probably want to get out of the city before undertaking anything too strenuous. But if you want to brave the elements, there are a few activities in and around San José.

La Sabana Park (at the western end of Paseo Colón), formerly San José's international airport, is the city's center for active sports and recreation. Here you'll find everything from jogging trails, soccer fields, and a few public tennis courts to the National Stadium. All the facilities are free and open to the public. Families gather for picnics, people fly kites, and there's even an outdoor sculpture garden. If you really want to experience the local culture, try getting into a pickup soccer game here. However, be careful in this park, especially at dusk or after dark, when it becomes a favorite haunt for youth gangs and muggers.

For information on horseback riding, hiking, and white-water rafting trips from San José, see section 9, "Side Trips from San José," at the end of this chapter.

BIRD-WATCHING   While serious birders will certainly want to head out of San José, it is still possible to see quite a few species in the metropolitan area. Two of the best spots for urban bird watching are the campus at the **University of Costa Rica** in the eastern suburb of San Pedro, and **Parque del Este** ⚹, located a little farther east on the road to San Ramón de Trés Ríos. To get to the University Campus, take any San Pedro bus from Avenida Central between Calle 9 and Calle 11. To get to Parque del Este, take the San Ramón/Parque del Este bus from Calle 9 between Avenida Central and Avenida 2. If you want to hook up with fellow birders, call the **Birding Club of Costa Rica** (✆ 506/ 267-7197 or 506/228-2025), which frequently organizes expeditions around the Central Valley and beyond.

BULLFIGHTING   Although I hesitate to call it a sport, **Las Corridas a la Tica** (Costa Rican bullfighting) is a popular and frequently comic stadium event. Instead of the blood-and-gore/life-and-death confrontation of traditional bullfighting, Ticos just like to tease the bull. In a typical corrida, anywhere from 50 to 150 *toreadores improvisados* (literally, improvised bullfighters) stand in the ring waiting for the bull. What follows is a slapstick scramble to safety whenever the bull heads toward a crowd of bullfighters. The braver bullfighters try to slap the bull's backside as the beast chases down one of his buddies.

You can see a bullfight during the Festejos Populares in Zapote, a suburb east of San José. The corridas run all day and well into the night during Christmas week and the first week in January. Admission is $2 to $5. Take the Zapote bus from Calle 1 between Avenidas 4 and 6. If you're in Costa Rica during the holidays but can't make it out to the stadium, don't despair—the local TV stations show nothing but live broadcasts from Zapote. This is a purely seasonal activity and occurs only during the Festejos.

GOLF & TENNIS   If you want to play tennis or golf in San José, your options are limited. Your best bet is to stay at either the Hotel Meliá Cariari or Hotel Herradura (both reviewed in section 3 of this chapter). Tennis players looking for a real local experience, on some rough concrete courts, can take a racket and some balls down to **Parque La Sabana.** Golfers have a new option with the opening of the new 18-hole course **Parque Valle del Sol** (✆ 506/282-9222) in the western suburb of Santa Ana. This course is open to the public. Greens fees are $40 for 18 holes and a cart will cost you an extra $25. The course at the Meliá Cariari is not technically open to the public, but if there's room, they'll generally let guests at other hotels tee off with advance notice.

HOTEL SPAS & WORKOUT FACILITIES   Most of the higher-end hotels have some sort of pool and exercise facilities. You'll find the best of these at the large Marriott, Meliá Confort Corobicí, Meliá Cariari, and Herradura resorts (see section 3 of this chapter). The Meliá Cariari has the nicest (really the only) Olympic-size lap pool, in addition to 11 tennis courts and a well-equipped exercise room. If you're looking for a good, serious workout, I recommend the **Multi Spa** ✶ (✆ 506/231-5542), located in the Meliá Confort Corobicí. Even if you're not a guest at the hotel, you can use the facilities here and join in any class for $10 per day. Multi Spa has five other locations around the Central Valley.

JOGGING   Try **La Sabana Park** mentioned above, or head to **Parque del Este,** which is east of town, in the foothills above San Pedro. Take the San Ramón/Parque del Este bus from Calle 9 between Avenida Central and Avenida 2. It's never a good idea to jog at night, on busy streets, or alone. Women should be particularly careful about jogging alone. And remember, Tico drivers are not accustomed to sport joggers on residential streets, so don't expect drivers to give you much berth.

SOCCER/FÚTBOL   Ticos take their *fútbol* seriously. Although not up to European or World Cup standards, Costa Rican professional soccer is some of the best in Central America. The soccer season runs from September through June, with the finals spread out over several weeks in late June and early July.

You don't need to buy tickets in advance. Tickets generally run between $2.50 and $12.50. It's worth paying a little extra for *sombra numerado* (reserved seats in the shade). This will protect you from both the sun and the more rowdy afi-cionados. Costa Rican soccer fans take the sport seriously and several violent incidents both inside and outside the stadiums have marred the sport in recent years, so be careful. Other options include *sombra* (general admission in the shade), *palco* and *palco numerado* (general admission and reserved mezzanine), and *sol general* (general admission in full sun).

The main San José team is Saprissa (affectionately called *El Monstro,* or The Monster). **Saprissa's stadium** is in Tibás (take any Tibás bus from Calle 2 and Avenida 5). Games are usually held on Sunday at 11am, but occasionally they are scheduled for Saturday afternoon or Wednesday evening. Check the local newspapers for game times and locations.

SWIMMING   If you aren't going to get to the beach anytime soon and your hotel doesn't have a pool, check out **Waterland** (© 506/239-5770), near the Hotel Herradura. This modern water park has a variety of pools and slides, as well as go-karts, fast food, mini-golf and horse rides. This place has gone bank-rupt and changed hands several times over the past several years and it remains to be seen if this incarnation survives. Your best bet is to take a cab here, or you can take any of the airport or Alajuela-bound buses, getting off at the Mall Cari-ari and then walking 200 meters to the park's entrance. It is open daily 9am to 5pm; admission $8.

Alternatively, head to **Ojo de Agua** (© 506/441-2808), on the road between the airport and San Antonio de Belén. The spring-fed waters are cool and refreshing, and even if it seems a bit chilly in San José, it's always several degrees warmer out here. This place is very popular with Ticos and can get quite crowded on weekends. Unfortunately, you do have to keep an eye on your valu-ables here. Admission is $4.50. Buses leave almost hourly for Ojo de Agua from the Coca-Cola bus terminal at Calle 16 between Avenidas 1 and 3.

7 Shopping

Serious shoppers will be disappointed in Costa Rica. Aside from coffee and oxcarts, there isn't much that's distinctly Costa Rican. To compensate for its own relative lack of goods, Costa Rica does a brisk business in selling crafts and clothes imported from Guatemala, Panama, and Ecuador.

THE SHOPPING SCENE   San José's central shopping corridor is bounded by Avenidas 1 and 2, from about Calle 14 in the west to Calle 13 in the east. For several blocks west of the Plaza de la Cultura, **Avenida Central** is a pedes-trian-only street mall where you'll find store after store of inexpensive clothes for men, women, and children. Depending on the mood of the police that day, you may find a lot of street vendors as well.

Most shops in the downtown district are open Monday through Saturday from about 8am to 6pm. Some shops close for lunch, while others remain open (it's just the luck of the draw for shoppers). When you do purchase something, you'll be happy to find that the sales and import taxes have already been figured into the display price.

International laws prohibit trade in endangered wildlife, so don't buy any plants or animals, even if they're readily for sale. Please do not buy any kind of sea-turtle products (including jewelry); wild birds; lizard, snake, or cat skins; corals; or orchids (except those grown commercially). No matter how unique, beautiful, insignificant and/or inexpensive it may seem, your purchase will directly contribute to the further hunting of endangered species.

Tips **Joe to Go**

Two words of advice: Buy coffee. Lots of it.

Coffee is the best shopping deal in all of Costa Rica. Although the best Costa Rican coffee is supposedly shipped off to North American and European markets, it's hard to beat the coffee that's roasted right in front of you here. Best of all is the price: One pound of coffee sells for between $2 and $3. It makes a great gift and keeps for a long time in your refrigerator or freezer.

Café Britt is the big name in Costa Rican coffee. These folks have the largest export business in the country, and while high-priced, its blends are very dependable. My favorites, however, are the coffees roasted and packaged in Manuel Antonio and Monteverde, by Café Milagro and Café Monteverde, respectively. If you're going to either of these places, definitely pick up their beans.

The best place to buy coffee is in any supermarket. Why pay more at a specialty shop? You can also try **Café Trebol,** on Calle 8 between Avenida Central and Avenida 1 (on the western side of the Central Market; ✆ **506/221-8363**). They're open Monday through Saturday from 7am to 6:30pm, Sunday from 8am to 2pm.

Be sure to ask for whole beans; Costa Rican grinds are often too fine for standard coffee filters. The store will pack the beans for you in whatever size bag you want. If you should happen to buy prepackaged coffee in a supermarket in Costa Rica, the whole beans will be marked either *grano* (grain) or *grano entero* (whole bean). If you opt for ground varieties (*molido*), be sure the package is marked *puro;* otherwise, it will likely be mixed with a good amount of sugar, the way Ticos like it.

One good coffee-related gift to bring home is a coffee sock and stand. This is the most common mechanism for brewing coffee beans in Costa Rica. It consists of a simple circular stand, made out of wood or wire, which holds a sock. Put the ground beans in the sock, place a pot or cup below, and pour boiling water through. You can find the socks and stands at most supermarkets and in the Mercado Central. In fancier craft shops, you'll find them made out of ceramic. Depending on its construction, a stand will cost you between $1.50 and $15; socks run around 30¢, so buy a few spares.

It's especially hard to capture the subtle shades and colors of the rain and cloud forests, and many a traveler has gone home thinking his or her undeveloped film contained the full beauty of the jungle, only to return from the photo developer with 36 bright-green blurs. To avoid this heartache, you might want to buy one of the picture books on Costa Rica mentioned in the "Recommended Books" section of appendix A. Or pick up some postcards of the sights you want to remember forever and send them to yourself.

MARKETS   There are several markets near downtown, but by far the largest is the **Mercado Central,** located between Avenida Central and Avenida 1 and Calles 6 and 8. Although this dark maze of stalls is primarily a food market, inside you'll find all manner of vendors, including a few selling Costa Rican souvenirs, crude leather goods, and musical instruments. Be especially careful about your wallet or purse and any prominent jewelry, because this area is frequented by very skilled pickpockets. All the streets surrounding the Mercado Central are jammed with produce vendors selling from small carts or loading and unloading trucks. It's always a hive of activity, with crowds of people jostling for space on the streets. Your best bet is to visit on Sunday or on weekdays; Saturdays are particularly busy. In the hot days of the dry season, the aromas can get quite heady. If you have a delicate constitution, don't eat any fruit you don't peel yourself (oranges, bananas, mangoes, etc.).

There is also a daily street market on the west side of the **Plaza de la Democracia.** Here you'll find two long rows of temporary stalls selling T-shirts, Guatemalan and Ecuadoran handcrafts and clothing, small ceramic *ocarinas* (a small musical wind instrument), and handmade jewelry. The atmosphere here is much more open here than at the Mercado Central, which I find just a bit too claustrophobic. You may be able to bargain prices down a little bit, but bargaining is not a traditional part of the vendor culture here, so you'll have to work hard to save a few dollars.

SHOPPING A TO Z
ART GALLERIES
Arte Latino   This gallery carries original artwork in a variety of media, featuring predominantly Central American themes. Some of it is pretty gaudy, but this is a good place to find Nicaraguan and Costa Rican "primitive" paintings. The gallery also has storefronts in the Multiplaza Mall in Escazú and at the Mall Cariari, which is located on the Interamerican Highway, about halfway between the airport and downtown, across the street from the Hotel Herradura. Calle 5 and Avenida 1. © 506/258-3306.

Galería Andromeda   This small, personal gallery features contemporary national artists of good quality. There are usually prints and paintings by several artists on display, and prices are very reasonable. Calle 9 at Avenida 9. © 506/223-3529.

Galería 11-12   This outstanding gallery deals mainly in high-end Costa Rican art, from neoclassical painters like Teodorico Quirós to modern masters like Francisco Amighetti and Paco Zuñiga to current stars like Rafa Fernandez, Fernando Carballo, and Fabio Herrera. Avenida 15 and Calle 35. Casa 3506, in Barrio Escalante (from the Farolito, 200m east and 100m north). © 506/280-8441. www.galeria11-12.com.

Galería Jacobo Karpio   This excellent gallery handles some of the more adventurous modern art to be found in Costa Rica. Karpio has a steady stable of prominent Mexican, Cuban, and Argentine artists, as well as some local talent. There's another branch of this gallery downtown, on Avenida 1, between Calles 11 and 13. Paco Shopping Center, on the old rd. to Santa Ana, Escazú. © 506/228-7862.

Galería Kandinsky   Owned by the daughter of one of Costa Rica's most prominent modern painters, Rafa Fernandez, this small gallery usually has a good selection of high-end contemporary Costa Rican paintings, be it the house collection or some specific temporary exhibit. Centro Comercial Calle Real, San Pedro. © 506/234-0478. galkandinsky@yahoo.com.

HANDCRAFTS
As I've said, the quality of Costa Rican handcrafts is generally very low, and the offerings are limited. The most typical items you'll find are hand-painted wooden **oxcarts.** These come in a variety of sizes, and the big ones can be shipped to your home for a very reasonable price. If you want to stick to

downtown San José, try the outdoor market on the **Plaza de la Democracia,** though prices here tend to be high and bargaining can be difficult. If you prefer to do your craft shopping in a flea-market atmosphere, head over to **La Casona** on Calle Central between Avenida Central and Avenida 1.

Notable exceptions to the generally meager craft offerings include the fine wooden creations of **Barry Biesanz** ✶✶ (℗ **506/289-4337;** www. biesanz.com). His work is sold in many of the finer gift shops around, but beware: Biesanz's work is often imitated, so make sure what you buy is the real deal (he generally burns his signature into the bottom of the piece). **Lil Mena** is a local artist who specializes in working with and painting on handmade papers and rough fibers. You'll find her work in a number of shops around San José.

You may also run across **carved masks** made by the indigenous Boruca people of southern Costa Rica. These full-sized balsa-wood masks come in a variety of styles, both painted and unpainted, and run anywhere from $10 to $70, depending on the quality of workmanship. **Cecilia "Pefi" Figueres** ✶ makes practical ceramic ware that is lively and fun. Look for her brightly colored abstract and figurative bowls, pitchers, coffee mugs, and more at some of the better gift shops around the city.

Scores of shops around San José sell a wide variety of crafts, from the truly tacky to the divinely inspired. Here are some that sell more of the latter and fewer of the former.

Angie Theologos's Gallery   Angie makes sumptuous handcrafted jackets from handwoven and embroidered Guatemalan textiles. Her work also includes bolero jackets, plus T-shirts made with Panamanian *molas* (appliquéed panels). San Pedro (call for appointment and directions). ℗ 506/225-6565.

Atmosfera   This place sells high-quality Costa Rican arts and crafts, from primitivist paintings and sculpture to skillfully made turned-wood bowls. It consists of several small rooms spread across two buildings, so be sure you explore every nook and cranny—you'll see some stuff here that's not available anywhere else in town. Calle 5 between Avenidas 1 and 3. ℗ 506/222-4322.

Biesanz Woodworks *Finds*   Biesanz makes a wide range of high-quality items, including bowls, jewelry boxes, humidors, and some wonderful sets of wooden chopsticks. The showroom is adjoined to the artist's house. Biesanz Woodworks is actively involved in reforestation, so you can even pick up a hardwood seedling here. Bello Horizonte, Escazú. ℗ 506/289-4337. www.biesanz.com. Call for directions and off-hour appointments.

Boutique Annemarie *Finds*   Now occupying two floors at the Hotel Don Carlos, this shop has an amazing array of wood products, leather goods, papiermâché figurines, paintings, books, cards, posters, and jewelry. You'll see most of this stuff at the other shops but not in such quantities, nor in such a relaxed and pressure-free environment. Don't miss this shopping experience. At the Hotel Don Carlos, Calle 9, between Avenidas 7 and 9. ℗ 506/221-6063.

Galería Namu *Finds*   This shop has some very high-quality arts and crafts, including excellent Boruca and Huetar carved masks, and "primitive" paintings, many painted by rural women. It also carries a good selection of the ceramic work of Cecilia "Pefi" Figueres. Avenida 7 between Calles 5 and 7. ℗ 506/256-3412. www.galerianamu.com.

Las Garzas Handicraft Market   This is the most appealing artisans' market close to San José (it's a short ride out of town). It includes more than 25 shops selling wood, metal, and ceramic crafts, among a large variety of other items. There's a huge selection, and you can get some really good buys here. Open daily. In Moravia, 100m south and 50m east of the Red Cross Station. ✆ 506/236-0037. Ask a taxi driver to take you to Las Garzas Mercado de Artesenia en Moravia.

Madera Magia   Almost everything is made of wood (*madera* is Spanish for wood). The shop is filled with elegant thin bowls of native hardwood, a big selection of wooden boxes, mirrors framed in wood, and very handsome hand-made furniture. All items are of high quality, created by skilled artisans under the guidance of designer J. Morrison. These folks also have a large showroom in the suburb of Santa Ana. Calle 5 between Avenidas 1 and 3. ✆ 506/233-2630.

Maya-Quiche   Located in the Galería Central Ramírez Valido shopping mall, this shop sells handcrafts from Central American countries, including gaily painted animals, boxes, and wooden letters from El Salvador, and *molas* from Panama. Avenida Central between Calles 5 and 7, Locale #147. ✆ 506/223-5030.

Suraska   Among the selections here are ceramics, mobiles, and jewelry. This store tends to carry higher-quality items than most gift shops downtown. Be warned, however, that the prices here are accordingly more expensive. Calle 5 and Avenida 3. ✆ 506/222-0129.

JEWELRY

Esmeraldas y Diseños   Notice the location given below for this jewelry store—it's truly a classically complicated San José address. Once you find it, however, you'll uncover copies of pre-Columbian jewelry designs in gold, plus jewelry featuring semiprecious stones from Brazil and emeralds from Colombia. Sabana Norte. From the Restaurante El Chicote, go 100m north, 50m west, and 150m north again. ✆ 506/231-4808 or 506/231-5428.

LEATHER GOODS

Malety   The quality of leather products found in Costa Rica is not as good as the quality of those in North America, and prices are high, but take a look and see for yourself. This is one of the outlets in San José where you can shop for locally produced leather bags, briefcases, purses, wallets, and other such items. A second store is located on Calle 1 between Avenida Central and Avenida 2. Avenida 1 between Calles 1 and 3. ✆ 506/221-1670.

LIQUOR

The national drink is *guaro,* a rough, clear liquor made from sugar cane. The most popular brand is **Cacique,** which you'll find at every liquor store and most supermarkets. Costa Ricans drink their guaro straight, or mixed with club soda or Fresca. When drinking it straight, it's customary to follow a shot with a bite into a fresh lime covered in salt.

Costa Ricans also drink a lot of rum. The premier Costa Rican rum is **Centenario,** but I recommend you opt for the Nicaraguan **Flor de Caña** or Cuban **Havana Club,** which are both far superior rums.

Several brands and styles of coffee-based liqueurs are also produced in Costa Rica. **Café Rica** is similar to Kahlúa, and you can also find several types of coffee cream liqueurs. The folks at **Café Britt** produce their own line of coffee liqueurs, which are quite good. You can buy them in most supermarkets, liquor stores, and tourist shops, but the best prices I've seen are at the supermarket chain Mas X Menos. There is a **Mas X Menos** store on Paseo Colón and another on Avenida Central at the east end of town, just below the Museo Nacional de Costa Rica.

MUSIC

A CD of Costa Rican music makes a great souvenir. Many gift shops around the country carry a small selection of Costa Rican music. **Editus** is an inventive trio (guitar, violin, and percussion) that has several albums out. The disc *Tiempos,* on which they accompanied Ruben Blades, won a Grammy for best Latin American album. You should also see discs by **Cantoamerica,** which plays upbeat dance music ranging from salsa to son to calypso to merengue. Jazz pianist **Manuel Obregon** has several excellent albums out, including *Simbiosis,* on which he improvises along with the sounds of Costa Rica's wildlife, waterfalls, and weather.

8 San José After Dark

In order to keep up with the tourism boom and steady urban expansion, San José has made strides to meet the nocturnal needs of visitors and residents alike. You'll find plenty of interesting clubs and bars, a wide range of theaters, and some very lively discos and dance salons.

To find out what's going on in San José while you're in town, pick up a copy of the *Tico Times* (English) or *La Nación* (Spanish). The former is a good place to find out where local expatriates are hanging out; the latter's "Viva" and "Tiempo Libre" sections have extensive listings of discos, movie theaters, and live music.

THE PERFORMING ARTS

Theater is very popular in Costa Rica, and downtown San José is studded with small theaters. However, tastes tend toward the burlesque, and the crowd pleasers are almost always simplistic sexual comedies. The **National Theater Company** (© 506/257-8305) is one major exception, tackling works from Lope de Vega to Lorca to Mamet. Almost all of the theater offerings are in Spanish, though the Little Theater Group is a long-standing amateur group that periodically stages works in English. Check the *Tico Times* to see if anything is running during your stay.

Costa Rica has a strong modern dance scene. Both the **University of Costa Rica** and the **National University** have modern-dance companies that perform regularly in various venues in San José. In addition to the university-sponsored companies, there's a host of smaller independent companies worth catching. **Los Denmedium** is particularly good.

The **National Symphony Orchestra** (© 506/236-5396) is a respectable orchestra by regional standards, though its repertoire tends to be rather conservative. The symphony season runs from March through November, with concerts roughly every other weekend at the **Teatro Nacional,** Avenida 2 between Calles 3 and 5 (© 506/221-1329), and the new **Auditorio Nacional,** located at the **Children's Museum** (see above). Tickets cost between $3 and $15 and can be purchased at the box office.

Visiting artists also stop in Costa Rica from time to time. Recent concerts have featured Spanish pop diva Ana Belen, Argentine legend Mercedes Sosa, salsa legends Celia Cruz and Ruben Blades, and Cuban jazz great Chucho Valdes. Revival tours of aging pop rockers are also popular, with recent visits by Creedence Clearwater Revisted, Yes, and Jethro Tull topping the bill. Many of these concerts and guest performances take place in San José's two historic theaters, the Teatro Nacional (see above) and the **Teatro Melico Salazar,** Avenida 2 between Calle Central and Calle 2 (© 506/222-2653), as well as at the new

Auditorio Nacional (see above). Really large shows are sometimes held at soccer stadiums, or at the amphitheater at the Hotel Herradura.

Costa Rica's cultural panorama changes drastically every March, when the country hosts large arts festivals. In odd-numbered years, **El Festival Nacional de las Artes** reigns supreme, featuring purely local talent. In even-numbered years, the monthlong fete is **El Festival Internacional de las Artes** (www. festivalcostarica.org), which offers a nightly smorgasbord of dance, theater, music, and monologue from around the world. Most nights of the festival, you will have between 4 and 10 shows to choose from. Many are free, and the most expensive ticket is $5. For exact dates and details of the program, you can contact the Ministry of Youth, Culture, and Sports (✆ **506/255-3188**), though you might have trouble getting any info if you don't speak Spanish.

THE CLUB, MUSIC & DANCE SCENE

You'll find plenty of places to hit the dance floor in San José. Salsa and merengue are the main beats that move people here, and many of the dance clubs, discos, and salons feature live music on the weekends. You'll find a pretty limited selection, though, if you're looking to catch some small-club jazz, rock, or blues.

The daily "Viva" and Thursday's "Tiempo Libre" sections of *La Nación* newspaper have weekly performance schedules. A couple of dance bands to watch for are Marfil and Los Brillanticos. El Parque, Ghandi, and Inconsciente Colectivo are popular local rock groups, Expresso is a good cover band, and both Blues Machine and the Blind Pig Blues Band are electric blues outfits. If you're looking for jazz, check out Jazz Expresso, Editus, El Sexteto de Jazz Latino, or pianist Manuel Obregon. Two very good local bands that don't seem to play that frequently are Cantoamerica and Adrian Goizueta's Grupo Experimental.

A good place to sample a range of San José's nightlife is in **El Pueblo,** a shopping, dining, and entertainment complex done up like an old Spanish village. It's just across the river to the north of town. The best way to get there is by taxi; all the drivers know El Pueblo well. Within the alleyways that wind through El Pueblo are a dozen or more bars, clubs, and discos—there's even a roller-skating rink. **Cocoloco** (✆ **506/222-8782**) features nightly "fiestas"; **Discoteque Infinito** (✆ **506/221-9134**) has three different environments under one roof; and **Twister** (✆ **506/222-5746**) is a lively party spot. Across the street you'll find **La Plaza** (✆ **506/222-5143**), one of my favorite dance spots.

Most of the places listed below charge a nominal cover charge; sometimes it includes a drink or two.

El Tobogan (Finds)   The dance floor in this place is about the size of a football field, and yet it still fills up. This is a place where Ticos come with their loved ones and dance partners. It's open only on the weekends (till about 2am), but there's always a live band here, and sometimes it's very good. 200m north and 100m east of the La República main office, off the Guápiles Hwy. ✆ 506/257-3396.

La Plaza   This large, open, upscale disco seems to be the favored dance venue for the young and beautiful of San José. The interior is designed to resemble a colonial plaza. This place gets a younger crowd than many of the other spots around town; they party here from Tuesday to Saturday nights till around 4am. Admission is around $3. Across from the El Pueblo shopping center. ✆ 506/222-5143.

Salsa 54   This is the place to go to watch expert salsa dancers and to try some yourself. You can take formal Latin dance classes here, or you might learn something just by watching. This place is popular with Ticos and tourists are a rare commodity here—tourists who can really dance salsa even more so. Open daily till 4am. Calle 3 between Avenidas 1 and 3. ☎ **506/233-3814**.

THE BAR SCENE

There seems to be something for every taste here. Lounge lizards will be happy in most hotel bars in the downtown area, while students and the young at heart will have no problem mixing in at the livelier spots around town. Sports fans can find plenty of places to catch the most important games of the day, and there are even a couple of brew pubs drastically improving the quality and selection of the local suds.

The best part of the varied bar scene in San José is something called a *boca,* the equivalent of a *tapa* in Spain: a little dish of snacks that arrives at your table when you order a drink. In most bars, the bocas are free, but in some, where the dishes are more sophisticated, you'll have to pay for the treats. You'll find drinks reasonably priced, with beer costing around $1.50 to $2 and mixed drinks $2 to $4.

Beatle Bar   Photos of the Fab Four line the walls here, and the music is a mix of Beatles and other '60s and '70s rock classics. Sit at the bar or take a turn on the dance floor. There are even a couple of outdoor tables at the front of the bar. This place is quite popular with expatriates, and it's a good place for single travelers to meet people. The location is one of the liveliest in the downtown area. Open daily till 2am. Avenida 2 and Calle 15. ☎ **506/389-0562**.

Brew Pub Cabeza Grande   This brew pub, one of my favorites, serves up a wide range of homemade beers. There's some indoor seating near the bar and in plain view of the brewing tanks, but I'd opt for an outdoor table on the large covered patio overlooking Paseo Colón. Open Monday to Saturday till 2am. Paseo Colón, between Calles 22 and 24. ☎ **506/256-6589**.

Chelles *(Finds)*   This classic downtown bar and restaurant makes up for its lack of ambiance with plenty of tradition and its diverse and colorful clientele. The lights are bright, the chairs surround simple Formica-topped card tables, and mirrors adorn most of the walls. Simple sandwiches and meals are served, and pretty good bocas come with the drinks. Open daily, round the clock. Avenida Central and Calle 9. ☎ **506/221-1369**.

El Cuartel de la Boca del Monte   This popular bar, one of San José's best, began life as an artist-and-bohemian hangout, and over the years it's evolved into the leading meat market for the young and well heeled. However, artists still come, as do foreign-exchange students, visitors, and, for some reason, many of the river-rafting guides, so there's always a diverse mix. There's usually live music here on Monday, Wednesday, and Friday nights, and when there is, the place is packed shoulder to shoulder. From Monday to Friday, it's open for lunch and again in the evenings; on weekends, it opens at 4pm. On most nights, it's open till about 1am, though the revelry might continue till about 3am on Friday or Saturday. Avenida 1 between Calles 21 and 23 (50m west of the Cine Magaly). ☎ **506/221-0327**.

Key Largo   Housed in a beautiful old building just off Parque Morazán in downtown San José, Key Largo is the most famous and infamous nightclub in Costa Rica. It's worth a visit just to see the interior of the building, but be warned: This is San José's number-one prostitute pickup spot. This isn't a place for unaccompanied women travelers to pop into. There's a $4 cover charge for men. Open daily till 4am. Calle 7, between Avenidas 1 and 3. ☎ **506/221-0277**.

La Esmeralda   A sort of mariachi Grand Central Station, La Esmeralda is a cavernous open-air restaurant and bar. In the evenings, mariachi bands park their vans out front and wait to be hired for a moonlight serenade or perhaps a surprise party. While they wait, they often fill the restaurant with loud trumpet blasts and the sound of the big bass *guitarón*. This is a great spot for couples. If you've never been serenaded at your table before, this place is a must. A song will cost you anywhere from $3 to $10, depending on the size of the group you hire. Open Monday to Saturday till 5am. Avenida 2 between Calles 5 and 7. 🕿 **506/221-0530**.

Rio   This bar and restaurant is close to the University of Costa Rica, and consequently attracts a younger clientele. At night, Rio is usually packed to overflowing with a rowdy college-age crowd. Open daily till 2am. Avenida Central, Los Yoses. 🕿 **506/225-8371**.

Risa's Bar   This popular restaurant and bar now occupies all four floors of this beautiful old building in the heart of downtown San José. Yet another renovation has created a large disco occupying much of the first two floors, with a variety of different environments spread around the rest of the building. Overall, there are six different bars and a good typical restaurant in this complex. Open Monday to Saturday till 3am. Calle 1, between Avenida Central and Avenida 1. 🕿 **506/223-2803**.

Shakespeare Bar   Located next to the Sala Garbo movie theater, this quiet and classy little spot is a good place to meet after a movie or a show at the Sala Garbo or Laurence Olivier Theater next door. This is good choice if you just want to sit and talk. Open daily till 1am. Avenida 2 and Calle 28. 🕿 **506/257-1288**.

HANGING OUT IN SAN PEDRO

The funky 2-block stretch of **San Pedro** 🌟🌟 just south of the University of Costa Rica is the closest thing to Paris's Left Bank or New York's East Village you'll find here. Bars and cafes are mixed in with bookstores and copy shops. It's one of the few places in town where you can sit calmly at an outdoor table or walk the streets without constantly looking over your shoulder and checking whether your wallet's still with you. You can just stroll the strip until someplace strikes your fancy—you don't need a travel guide to find **Omar Khayyam** (🕿 **506/253-8455**) or **Pizza Caccio** (🕿 **506/224-3261**)—or you can trust me and try one of the following.

You can get here by heading out (east) on Avenida 2, following the flow of traffic. You will first pass through the neighborhood of Los Yoses before reaching a big traffic circle with a big fountain in the center (La Fuente de la Hispanidad). The Mall San Pedro is located on this traffic circle. Heading straight through the circle (well, going around it and continuing on what would have been a straight path), you'll come to the Church of San Pedro about 4 blocks east of the circle. The church is the major landmark in San Pedro. You can also take a bus here from downtown.

All-Star Bar & Grill   This is the closest thing to a U.S.–style sports bar in San José. There's at least one television, and usually more, visible from every seat in the house, as well as one mammoth screen anchoring the main room. There are framed sports jerseys and covers of *Sports Illustrated* on the walls. Upstairs you'll find some billiard and foosball tables. The menu features well-prepared hamburgers, hot dogs, and cheese-steak subs (what else would you expect?). On weekends, there's sometimes live music, for which there's a minimal cover charge. Open daily till 2am. Centro Comercial Cocorí, in front of the Fuente de la Hispanidad, San Pedro. 🕿 **506/225-0838**.

Jazz Café *(Finds)*　Opened by one of the former owners of the popular but now defunct La Maga, the Jazz Café has quickly become one of the more happening spots in San Pedro, and one of my favorites. Wrought-iron chairs, sculpted busts of famous jazz artists, and creative lighting give the place ambiance. There's live music here most nights, and visiting artists have included Chucho Valdes and Tony Perez. Open daily till about 2am. Next to the Banco Popular on Avenida Central. ℂ 506/253-8933.

Mosaikos　The entrance to this popular nightspot is a long, narrow corridor/bar that is generally packed solid. In the back there's a slightly larger room, with another bar, some tables, a couple of televisions, and some funky art. Unlike most bars in San Pedro, these folks actually know how to make a couple of mixed drinks. The crowd here is young and can get quite rowdy. Open Monday to Saturday from 11:30am till 2am, Sunday from 5pm till 2am. 200m east and 150m north of the Church in San Pedro. ℂ 506/280-9541.

Planet Mall　This new place is on the fourth floor of the Mall San Pedro. There are a couple of quiet nooks and corners, but most of the action takes place under the neon lights on and around the immense dance floor, which sometimes features live music. Depending on what's going on here, the cover can be as much $10 here, sometimes even more. Open Thurday through Saturday evenings till 2am. In the San Pedro Mall. ℂ 506/280-4693.

La Villa *(Finds)*　This converted Victorian house holds the ghosts of Che Guevara and Camilo Cienfuegos—or so you'd think from the posters of these and other Latin-American revolutionaries on the walls. Around the tables you'll find poets and painters mixing with a new generation of student activists, all in a lively atmosphere. There's even a foosball table in the far back. Consistent with the revolutionary ethos, everything is priced reasonably and the battered sound sytem plays a steady stream of Silvio Rodriguez, Mercedes Sosa, and other *Nueva Trova* stalwarts. Open Monday to Saturday from 11am to 1am, Sundays from 7pm to 1am. 200m east and 125m north of the Church in San Pedro. ℂ 506/225-9612.

THE GAY & LESBIAN SCENE

Because Costa Rica is such a conservative Catholic country, the gay and lesbian communities here are rather discreet. Homosexuality is not generally under attack, but many gay and lesbian organizations guard their privacy, and the club scene is changeable and not well publicized. For a general overview of the current situation, news of any special events or meetings, and up-to-date information, gay and lesbian travelers should check in at **Uno@Diez,** in the Faisa Building on Calle 1 between Avenidas 9 and 11 (ℂ 506/258-4561; www.1en10.com), a downtown coffeehouse, gallery, and Internet cafe.

The most established and happening gay and lesbian bars and dance clubs in San José are **Déjà Vu,** Calle 2 between Avenidas 14 and 16 (ℂ 506/223-3758), and **La Avispa,** Calle 1 between Avenidas 8 and 10 (ℂ 506/223-5343). The former is predominantly a guys' bar, while the latter is popular with both men and women, although they sometimes set aside certain nights of the week or month for specific persuasions. There's also **Buenas Vibraciones** (ℂ 506/223-4573), out on Paseo de los Estudiantes, and **Bochinche 9** (ℂ 506/221-0500), on Calle 11 between Avenidas 10 and 12. In San Pedro, you'll find **La Tertulia** (ℂ 506/225-0250), a predominantly lesbian hangout.

CASINOS

Gambling is legal in Costa Rica, and there are casinos at virtually every major hotel. However, as in Tico bullfighting, there are some idiosyncrasies involved in gambling *a la Tica.*

If blackjack is your game, you'll want to play "rummy." The rules are almost identical, except the house doesn't pay double on blackjack—instead it pays double on any three of a kind or three-card straight flush.

If you're looking for roulette, what you'll find here is a bingolike spinning cage of numbered balls. The betting is the same, but some of the glamour is lost.

You'll also find a version of five-card-draw poker, but the rule differences are so complex that I advise you to sit down and watch for a while and then ask some questions before joining in. That's about all you'll find. There are no craps tables or baccarat.

There's some controversy over slot machines—one-armed bandits are currently outlawed—but you will be able to play electronic slots and poker games. Most of the casinos here are quite casual and small by international standards. You may have to dress up slightly at some of the fancier hotels, but most are accustomed to tropical vacation attire.

9 Side Trips from San José

San José makes an excellent base for exploring the beautiful Central Valley and the surrounding mountains. For first-time visitors, the best way to make the most of these excursions is usually by taking a guided tour, but if you rent a car, you'll have greater independence. There are also some day trips that can be done by public bus.

GUIDED TOURS & ADVENTURES

A number of companies offer a wide variety of primarily nature-related day tours out of San José. The most reputable include **Costa Rica Expeditions** ✦✦ (© 506/257-0766; www.costaricaexpeditions.com), **Costa Rica Sun Tours** ✦ (© 506/296-7757; www.crsuntours.com), **Ecole Travel** (© 506/223-2240), **Fantasy Tours** (© 800/272-6654 in the U.S., 800/463-6654 in Canada, or 506/220-2126), **Horizontes Tours** ✦ (© 506/222-2022; www. horizontes.com), **Otec Tours** (© 506/256-0633; www.otec.co.cr), **Swiss Travel Service** (© 506/282-4898), and **TAM** (© 506/256-0203; www.tamtravel.com).

Before signing on for a tour of any sort, find out how many fellow travelers will be accompanying you, how much time will be spent in transit and eating lunch, and how much time will actually be spent doing the primary activity. I've had complaints about tours that were rushed, that spent too much time in a bus or on secondary activities, or that had a cattle-car, assembly-line feel to them.

The tours below are arranged by type of activity. In addition to these, there are many other tours, some of which combine two or three different activities or destinations.

BUNGEE JUMPING There's nothing unique about bungee jumping in Costa Rica except for the price—it's a little bit less expensive here than elsewhere. If you've always had the bug, **Tropical Bungee** (© 506/232-3956; www.bungee.co.cr) will let you jump off a 265-foot bridge for $45; two jumps cost $70. Transportation is $7 each way.

CRUISES Several companies offer cruises to the lovely Tortuga Island in the Gulf of Nicoya. These full-day tours generally entail an early departure for the

2½-hour chartered bus ride to Puntarenas, where you board your vessel for a 1½-hour cruise to Tortuga Island. Then you get several hours on the uninhabited island, where you can swim, lie on the beach, play volleyball, or try a canopy tour, followed by the return journey.

The original and most dependable company running these trips is **Calypso Tours** ⚞ (✆ **506/256-2727;** www.calypsotours.com). The tour costs $99 per person and includes round-trip transportation from San José, a basic continental breakfast during the bus ride to the boat, all drinks on the cruise, and an excellent buffet lunch on the beach at the island. Calypso Tours also conducts cruises to a private nature reserve at Punta Coral. Alternatively, you could try **Freedom Cruises** (✆ **506/291-0191**), which also has a 1-day tour to Isla Tortuga for $99. Most of the companies use converted fishing trawlers. Calypso has one of these, which it runs to Punta Coral, as well as a massive motor-powered catamaran, which plies the Isla Tortuga route.

HIKING   Most of the tour agencies listed above offer 1-day guided hikes to a variety of destinations. In general, I recommend taking guided hikes, to really see and learn about the local flora and fauna.

If you don't plan to visit Monteverde or one of Costa Rica's other cloud-forest reserves (see chapter 6), consider doing a day tour to the **Los Angeles Cloud Forest Reserve** ⚞. This full-day excursion and guided walk through the cloud forest is operated by the **Villablanca Hotel** (✆ **506/228-4603;** www. villablanca-costarica.com). The cost is $72, which includes transportation, breakfast, and lunch. It also offers horseback riding and canopy-tour options.

HORSEBACK RIDING   While options are nearly endless outside of San José, it's more difficult to find a place to saddle up in the metropolitan area. The **Valle de Yos-Oy Riding Center** (✆ **506/282-6934** or 506/282-7850) is located in Santa Ana and offers riding classes as well as guided trail rides.

MOUNTAIN-BIKING   The best bicycle riding is well outside of San José—on dirt roads where you're not likely to be run off the highway by a semi, or run head-on into someone coming around a blind curve in the wrong lane. Several companies run a variety of 1-day and multiday tours out of San José. The 1-day tours usually involve a round-trip bus or van ride out of downtown to the primary destination. These destinations include the towns of Sarchí and Turrialba, as well as the Irazú and Poás volcanos. Several of these tours are designed to be either entirely, or primarily, descents. **Velero del Rey Tours** (✆ **506/235-4982;** velrey@racsa.co.cr), **Costa Rica Sun Tours** (✆ **506/296-7757;** www. crsuntours.com), and **BiCosta Rica** (✆ **506/446-7585;** www.yellowweb.co. cr/bicostarica.html) all run a variety of mountain-biking tours. A 1-day trip should cost between $70 and $110 per person.

Another company offering mountain-biking trips is **Coast to Coast Adventures** (✆ **506/225-6055;** www.ctocadventures.com), which, in addition to its 2-week namesake adventure, will also design customized mountain-biking trips of shorter duration.

EXPLORING PRE-COLUMBIAN RUINS   Though Costa Rica lacks the kind of massive pre-Columbian archaeological sites found in Mexico, Guatemala, or Honduras, it does have **Guayabo National Monument,** ⚞ a small excavated town, which today is just a small collection of building foundations, cobbled streets, aqueducts, and a small plaza. **Costa Rica Sun Tours** (✆ **506/296-7757;** www.crsuntours.com) offers a day trip here for around

> ## *Holy Smoke!:*
> ## Choosing the Volcano Trip That's Right for You
>
> Poás, Irazú, and Arenal volcanoes are three of Costa Rica's most popu-
> lar destinations, and the first two are easy day trips from San José (see
> below). Although numerous companies offer day trips to Arenal, I don't
> recommend them because there's at least 3½ hours of travel time in
> each direction. You usually arrive when the volcano is hidden by clouds
> and leave before the night's darkness shows off its glowing eruptions.
> For more information on Arenal Volcano, see chapter 6.
>
> Tour companies offering trips to Poás and Irazú include **Costa Rica
> Expeditions** ✶✶ (© 506/257-0766), **Costa Rica Sun Tours** ✶ (© 506/
> 296-7757), **Horizontes** ✶ (© 506/222-2022), **Otec Tours** (© 506/256-
> 0633), **TAM** (© 506/256-0203), and **Swiss Travel Service** (© 506/282-
> 4898). Prices range from $25 to $35 for a half-day trip and from $50 to
> $90 for a full-day trip.
>
> The 11,260-foot-tall **Irazú Volcano** ✶ is historically one of Costa Rica's
> more active volcanoes, although it's relatively quiet these days. It last
> erupted on March 19, 1963, on the day that President John F. Kennedy
> arrived in Costa Rica. There's a good paved road right to the rim of the
> crater, where a desolate expanse of gray sand nurtures few plants and
> the air smells of sulfur. The landscape here is often compared to that of
> the moon. There are magnificent views of the fertile Meseta Central and
> Orosi Valley as you drive up from Cartago, and if you're very lucky you
> may be able to see both the Pacific Ocean and Caribbean Sea. Clouds
> usually descend by noon, so get here as early in the day as possible.
>
> There's a new visitor center up here with information on the volcano
> and natural history. A short trail leads to the rim of the volcano's two
> craters, their walls a maze of eroded gullies feeding onto the flat floor
> far below. This is a national park, with an admission fee of $6 charged
> at the gate. Dress in layers. This may be the tropics, but it can be cold
> up at the top if the sun's not out. The park restaurant, at an elevation
> of 10,075 feet, with walls of windows looking out over the valley far
> below, claims to be the highest restaurant in Central America.
>
> For those of you who don't want to take an organized tour, buses
> leave for Irazú Volcano Saturday, Sunday, and holidays at 8am from

$110 per person. If you have a car, or are an intrepid bus hound, you can do this
tour on your own—you can usually find a guide at the entrance for $5. See the
section on Turrialba, below.

RAFTING, KAYAKING & RIVER TRIPS ✶✶ Cascading down Costa
Rica's mountain ranges are dozens of tumultuous rivers, several of which have
become very popular for white-water rafting and kayaking. If I had to choose
just one day trip to do out of San José, it would be a white-water rafting trip.
For between $75 and $95, you can spend a day rafting through lush tropical
forests; multiday trips are also available. Some of the more reliable rafting
companies are **Aventuras Naturales** ✶ (© 800/514-0411 in the U.S., or

Avenida 2 between Calles 1 and 3 (in front of the Gran Hotel Costa Rica). The fare is $5 round-trip, with the bus leaving the volcano at 1pm. To make sure the buses are running, call © 506/272-0651. If you're driving, head northeast out of Cartago toward San Rafael, then continue driving uphill toward the volcano, passing the turnoffs for Cot and Tierra Blanca en route.

Poás Volcano ✵ is 23 miles (37km) from San José on narrow roads that wind through a landscape of fertile farms and dark forests. As at Irazú, there's a paved road right to the top, although you'll have to hike in about a kilometer to reach the crater. The volcano stands 8,800 feet tall and is located within a national park, which preserves not only the volcano but also dense stands of virgin forest. Poás's crater, said to be the second-largest in the world, is over a mile across. Geysers in the crater sometimes spew steam and muddy water 600 feet into the air, making this the largest geyser in the world. There's an information center where you can see a slide show about the volcano, and there are marked hiking trails through the cloud forest that rings the crater. About 15 minutes from the parking area, along a forest trail, is an overlook onto beautiful Botos Lake, which has formed in one of the volcano's extinct craters.

Be prepared when you come to Poás: This volcano is often enveloped in dense clouds. If you want to see the crater, it's best to come early, and during the dry season. Moreover, it can get cool up here, especially when the sun isn't shining, so dress appropriately. Admission to the national park is $6 at the gate.

In case you don't want to go on a tour, there's a daily bus ((© 506/222-5325) from Calle 12 and Avenidas 2 and 4, leaving at 8:30am and returning at 2:30pm. The fare is $3.50 round-trip. The bus is usually crowded, so arrive early. If you're driving, head for Alajuela and continue on the main road through town and follow signs for Fraijanes. Just beyond Fraijanes, you will connect with the road between San Pedro de Poás and Poasito; turn right toward Poasito and continue to the rim of the volcano.

506/ 225-3939), **Costa Rica White Water** (© 506/257-0766), and **Ríos Tropicales** ✵ (© 506/233-6455).

These companies all ply a number of rivers of varying difficulties, including the popular Pacuare and Reventazón Rivers. For more information, see "White-Water Rafting, Kayaking & Canoeing" in chapter 3.

The Sarapiquí River is also a popular waterway for day trips out of San José. **Ecoscapes Highlights Tour** (© 506/297-0664; www.ecoscapetours.com) runs a jam-packed trip here that combines a stop at the La Paz waterfall, a visit to a banana plantation, a rain-forest hike, and a boat ride on the river for $80 per person, including round-trip transportation, breakfast, and lunch.

Perhaps the best-known river tours are those that go up to **Tortuguero National Park** ✦✦. Though it's possible to do this tour as a day trip out of San José, it's a long, tiring, and expensive day. You're much better off doing it as a 1- or 2-night trip. See chapter 9 for details.

A RAIN-FOREST AERIAL TRAM   When you first see the **Aerial Tram** ✦ (© **506/257-5961;** www.rainforesttram.com), you may wonder where the ski slopes are. Built on a private reserve bordering Braulio Carillo National Park, the tramway is the brainchild of rain-forest researcher Dr. Donald Perry, whose cable-car system through the forest canopy at Rara Avis helped establish him as an early expert on rain-forest canopies. The tramway takes visitors on a 90-minute ride through the treetops, where they have the chance to glimpse the complex web of life that makes these forests unique. There are also well-groomed trails through the rain forest and a restaurant on site, so a trip here can easily take up a full day.

The cost for tours, including transportation from San José and either breakfast or lunch, is $78.50. Alternatively, you can drive or take one of the frequent Guápiles buses—they leave every half hour and cost $2—from Calle 12 between Avenidas 7 and 9. Ask the driver to let you off in front of the "teleférico." If driving, head out on the Guápiles Highway as if driving to the Caribbean coast. Watch for the tram's roadside welcome center—it's hard to miss. For walk-ins, the entrance fee is $49.50. Students and anyone under 18 pay $25.

CARTAGO & THE OROSI VALLEY

These two regions southeast of San José can easily be combined into one day trip. You might also squeeze in a visit to the Irazú Volcano (see the box, "Holy Smoke!: Choosing the Volcano Trip That's Right for You," for details).

CARTAGO

Located about 15 miles (24km) southeast of San José, **Cartago** ✦ is the former capital of Costa Rica. Founded in 1563, it was Costa Rica's first city, and was in fact its *only* city for almost 150 years. Irazú Volcano rises up from the edge of town, and although it's quiet these days, it has not always been so peaceful. Earthquakes have damaged Cartago repeatedly over the years, so today there are few of the old colonial buildings left standing. In the center of the city, a public park winds through the ruins of a large church that was destroyed in 1910, before it could be finished. Construction was abandoned after the quake, and today the ruins are a neatly manicured park, with quiet paths and plenty of benches.

Cartago's most famous building is the **Basilica de Nuestra Señora de los Angeles** (the Basilica of Our Lady of the Angels), which is dedicated to the patron saint of Costa Rica and stands on the east side of town. Within the walls of this Byzantine-style church is a shrine containing the tiny figure of **La Negrita,** the Black Virgin, which is nearly lost amid its ornate altar. Legend has it that La Negrita first revealed herself on this site to a peasant girl in 1635. Miraculous healing powers have been attributed to La Negrita, and over the years thousands of pilgrims have come to the shrine seeking cures for their illnesses and difficulties. The walls of the shrine are covered with a fascinating array of tiny silver images left as thanks for cures effected by La Negrita. Amid the plethora of diminutive silver arms and legs, there are also hands, feet, hearts, lungs, kidneys, eyes, torsos, breasts, and—peculiarly—guns, trucks, beds, and planes. There are even dozens of sports trophies that I assume were left in thanks for helping teams win big games. Outside the church, vendors sell a wide selection of these trinkets, as well as little candle replicas of La Negrita. August 2 is the day dedicated to La Negrita, and on this day tens of thousands of people walk to Cartago from San José and elsewhere in the country, in devotion to this powerful statue.

A little over a mile (1.6km) east of Cartago, on the road to Paraíso, you'll find **Lankester Gardens** ✷✷ (✆ 506/552-3247 or 506/552-3151), a botanical garden known for its orchid collection. (See p. 118 for a full listing.)

GETTING THERE Buses (✆ 506/233-5350) for Cartago leave San José every 10 minutes between 5am and midnight from Calle 5 between Avenidas 18 and 20. You can also pick up one en route at any of the little covered bus stops along Avenida Central in Los Yoses and San Pedro. The length of the trip is 45 minutes; the fare is about 45¢.

OROSI VALLEY

The Orosi Valley, southeast of Cartago and visible from the top of Irazú on a clear day, is generally considered one of the most beautiful valleys in Costa Rica. The Reventazón River meanders through this steep-sided valley until it collects in the lake formed by the Cachí Dam. There are scenic overlooks near the town of Orosi, which is at the head of the valley, and in Ujarrás, which is on the banks of the lake. Near Ujarrás are the ruins of Costa Rica's oldest church (built in 1693), whose tranquil gardens are a great place to sit and gaze at the surrounding mountains. (In the town of Orosi itself, there is yet another colonial church, built in 1743. A small museum here displays religious artifacts.)

Across the lake is a popular recreation center, called **Charrara** (✆ 506/574-7557), where you'll find a picnic area, swimming pool, hiking trails, and a camping area. Near the town of Cachí, you'll find **La Casa del Soñador** (The House of the Dreamer; ✆ 506/533-3297), which is the home and gallery of the late sculptor Macedonio Quesada and his sons, who carry on the family tradition.

GETTING THERE It would be difficult to explore this whole area by public bus, since this is not a densely populated region. However, there are buses from Cartago to the town of Orosi. During the week, these buses run every hour and leave from a spot 1 block east and 25 meters south of the church ruins in Cartago. Saturday and Sunday, the bus runs roughly every 45 minutes from the same block and will drop you at the Orosi lookout point. The trip takes 30 minutes and the fare is 35¢. If you're driving, take the road to Paraíso from Cartago, head toward Ujarrás, continue around the lake, then pass through Cachí and on to Orosi. From Orosi, the road leads back to Paraíso. There are also guided day tours of this area from San José (call any of the companies listed under "Guided Tours & Adventures," on p. 131).

TURRIALBA

This attractive little town 33 miles (53km) east of San José is best known as the starting point and home base for many popular white-water rafting trips. However, it's also worth a visit if you have an interest in pre-Columbian history or tropical botany.

Guayabo National Monument ✷ is one of Costa Rica's only pre-Columbian sites that has been excavated and is open to the public. It's located 12 miles (19km) northeast of Turrialba and preserves a town site that dates from between 1000 B.C. and A.D. 1400. Archaeologists believe that Guayabo may have supported a population of as many as 10,000 people, but there is no clue yet as to why the city was eventually abandoned only shortly before the Spanish arrived in the New World. Excavated ruins at Guayabo consist of paved roads, aqueducts, stone bridges, and house and temple foundations. There are also grave sites and petroglyphs. The monument is open daily from 8am to 4pm. This is a national park, and admission is $6 at the gate. For more information, see "Costa Rica's Top National Parks & Bioreserves" in chapter 3.

Botanists and gardeners will want to pay a visit to the **Center for Agronomy Research and Development (CATIE),** which is located 3 miles (5km) southeast of Turrialba on the road to Siquirres. This center is one of the world's foremost facilities for research into tropical agriculture. Among the plants on CATIE's 2,000 acres are hundreds of varieties of cacao and thousands of varieties of coffee. The plants here have been collected from all over the world. In addition to trees used for food and other purposes, there are plants grown strictly for ornamental purposes. CATIE is open Monday through Friday from 7am to 4pm. Guided tours are available with advance notice for $25 per person. Call ⓒ **506/556-6431** for reservations.

While you're in the area, don't miss an opportunity to spend a little time at **Turrialtico** (ⓒ **506/556-1111**), a lively open-air restaurant and small hotel high on a hill overlooking the Turrialba Valley. The view from here is one of the finest in the country, with lush greenery far below and volcanoes in the distance. Meals are quite inexpensive; a room will cost you $40. This place is popular with rafting companies that bring groups here for meals and for overnights before, during, and after multiday rafting trips. You'll find Turrialtico about 6 miles (10km) out of Turrialba on the road to Siquirres.

If you're looking for some luxury in this area, check out **Casa Turire** ✦ (ⓒ **506/531-1111;** fax 506/531-1075; www.hotelcasaturire.com), where well-appointed rooms and suites in an elegant country mansion run between $120 and $220.

GETTING THERE Buses (ⓒ **506/556-0073**) leave San José hourly for Turrialba throughout the day from Calle 13 between Avenidas 6 and 8. The fare is $1.50. If you're driving, take the road from Cartago to Paraíso, then through Juan Viñas and on to Turrialba. It's pretty well marked. (Alternatively you can head toward the small town of Cot, on the road to Irazú Volcano, then through the town of Pacayas on to Turrialba, another well-marked route.)

Turrialba itself is a bit of a jumble and you will probably have to ask directions to get to locations out of town. Guayabo is about 12½ miles (20km) beyond Turrialba on a road that is paved the entire way except for the last 2 miles (3km). There are also around three buses daily to Guayabo from the main bus terminal in Turrialba.

HEREDIA, GRECIA, SARCHÍ & ZARCERO

All of these cities and towns are northwest of San José and can be combined into a long day trip (if you have a car), perhaps in conjunction with a visit to Poás Volcano. The scenery here is rich and verdant, and the small towns and scattered farming communities are truly representative of Costa Rica's agricultural heartland and campesino tradition. If you're relying on buses, you'll be able to visit any of the towns listed below, but probably just one or two per day.

The road to Heredia turns north off the highway from San José to the airport. If you're going to Sarchí, take the highway west toward Puntarenas. Turn north to Grecia and then west to Sarchí. There'll be plenty of signs.

HEREDIA

Set on the flanks of the impressive Barva Volcano, this city was founded in 1706. Heredia is affectionately known as "The City of Flowers." A colonial church inaugurated in 1763 stands in the central park. The stone façade leaves no questions as to the age of the church, but the altar inside is decorated with neon stars and a crescent moon surrounding a statue of the Virgin Mary. In the middle of the palm-shaded park is a music temple, and across the street, beside several tile-roofed municipal buildings, is the tower of an old Spanish fort. Of all the cities in the Meseta Central, Heredia has the most colonial feel to it—you'll still see adobe buildings with Spanish tile roofs along narrow streets.

In the center of town you'll find the small **Museo de Cultura Popular** (C 506/260-1619), which is open Monday to Friday from 8am to 4pm, and Saturday and Sunday from 10am to 5pm. Heredia is also the site of the **National Autonomous University,** so you'll find some nice coffee shops and bookstores near the school. Surrounding Heredia are a bevy of picturesque villages and towns, including Santa Barbara, Santo Domingo, Barva, and San Joaquín de Flores. The newest attraction up here is the **InBio Park** ✦ (C 506/244-4730). Located on 5 hectares (12 acres) in Santo Domingo de Heredia, this place is part museum, part educational center, and part nature park. (See "Outside San José," above, for details.)

Buses leave for Heredia almost every 10 minutes from Calle 12 and Avenida 2, and from Calle 1 between Avenidas 7 and 9. Bus fare is 40¢.

GRECIA

The picturesque little town of Grecia is noteworthy for its unusual metal church, which is painted a deep red and has white gingerbread trim. Just off the central park, next to the Palacio Municipal, you'll find the humble **Grecia Regional Museum** (C 506/494-6767), which has some simple exhibits and information about the town's history. About 1½ miles (1km) outside of Grecia, on the old road to Alajuela, you will find the **World of Snakes** (C 506/494-3700). Open daily from 8am to 4pm, this serpentarium has over 150 snakes representing over 50 species. Admission is $11 and includes a guided tour.

Buses leave San José every half-hour for Grecia from the Coca-Cola bus station at Calle 16 between Avenidas 1 and 3. The road to Sarchí is to the left as you face the church in Grecia, but due to all the one-way streets, you'll have to drive around it.

SARCHÍ ✦

Sarchí is Costa Rica's main artisan town. It's here that the colorfully painted miniature **oxcarts** you see all over the country are made. Oxcarts such as these were once used to haul coffee beans to market. Today, though you may occasionally see oxcarts in use, most are purely decorative. However, they remain a well-known symbol of Costa Rica. In addition to miniature oxcarts, many carved wooden souvenirs are made here with rare hardwoods from the nation's forests. There are dozens of shops in town, and all have similar prices.

Aside from handcrafts, the other reason to visit Sarchí is to see its unforgettable **church.** Built between 1950 and 1958, the church is painted pink with aquamarine trim and looks strangely like a child's birthday cake. Buses leave for Grecia every 30 minutes between 7am and 7pm, from the Coca-Cola bus station, at Calle 16 and Avenidas 1 and 3. In Grecia they connect with the Alajuela–Sarchí buses, which leave every 30 minutes from Calle 8 between Avenida Central and Avenida 1 in Alajuela. The fare is 75¢.

ZARCERO

Beyond Sarchí, on picturesque roads lined with cedar trees, you'll find the town of Zarcero. In a small park in the middle of town is a **menagerie of sculpted shrubs** that includes a monkey on a motorcycle, people and animals dancing, an ox pulling a cart, a man wearing a top hat, and a large elephant. Behind all the topiary is a wonderful rural **church.** It's almost worth the drive just to see this park, but it's best to take in Zarcero as a quick stop on the way to La Fortuna and Arenal Volcano.

Buses (ⓒ **506/255-4318**) for Zarcero leave from San José hourly from the Atlantico del Norte bus station at Avenida 9 and Calle 12. This is actually the Ciudad Quesada–San Carlos bus. Just tell the driver you want to get off in Zarcero and keep an eye out for the topiary.

Guanacaste & the Nicoya Peninsula: The Gold Coast

Guanacaste province is Costa Rica's hottest and driest region. The rainy season starts later and ends earlier here, and overall it's more dependably sunny in this region than in other parts of the country. Combine this climate with a coastline that stretches from the Nicaraguan border to the southern tip of the Nicoya Peninsula, and you have an equation that yields beach bliss.

Beautiful **beaches** ✶✶ abound along this coastline. Some are pristine and deserted, some are dotted with new luxury resorts, and still others are backed by little villages where you can still get a clean double room for less than $30 a night. These beaches vary from long, straight stretches of sand to tiny coves bordered by rocky headlands. Whatever your preference in beaches, you're likely to find something that comes close to perfection.

This is Costa Rica's most coveted vacation region and the site of its greatest tourism development. The change is dramatic and ongoing. Large resorts have sprung up, and more are in the works. So far, two regulation golf courses have opened, and several more are under construction. The long-awaited international airport in Liberia is finally getting on its feet, and while charter flights still make up the lion's share of the traffic here, it will soon be possible to fly from major international hubs directly in and out of Liberia—and on to any one of the numerous beaches below—without having to go through San José.

There is one caveat: During the **dry season** (from mid-Nov through Apr), when sunshine is most reliable, the hillsides in Guanacaste turn browner than the chaparral of southern California. Dust from dirt roads blankets the trees in many areas, and the vistas are far from tropical. Driving these dirt roads without air-conditioning and hermetically sealed windows can be extremely unpleasant. But, if you can't tolerate the least bit of rain during your holiday in the sun, the beaches up here are where you'll want to be.

On the other hand, if you happen to visit this area in the **rainy season** (May to mid-Nov), the hillsides are a beautiful, rich green, and the sun usually shines all morning, giving way to an afternoon shower—just in time for a nice siesta.

Guanacaste is also Costa Rica's "Wild West," a dry landscape of cattle ranches and cowboys, who are known here as *sabaneros,* a name that derives from the Spanish word for "savanna" or "grassland." This is big country, with big views and big sky. If it weren't for those rain forest–clad volcanoes in the distance, you might swear you were in Texas. However, Guanacaste hasn't always looked this way. At one time this land was covered with a dense, though fairly dry, forest that was cut for lumber and to create pasturelands for grazing cattle. Today, that dry tropical forest exists only in remnants preserved in several national parks. Up in the mountains, in **Rincón de la Vieja National Park** ✶✶, you'll find not only forests and wildlife, but also hot springs and bubbling mud pots similar to those in Yellowstone National Park in the United States.

1 Liberia ★

134½ miles (217km) NW of San José; 82 miles (132km) NW of Puntarenas

Founded in 1769, Liberia is the capital of Guanacaste province, and though it can hardly be considered a bustling metropolis, it does boast more colonial atmosphere than almost any other city in the country. Its narrow streets are lined with charming old adobe homes, many of which have ornate stone accents on their façades, carved wooden doors, and aged red-tile roofs. Many have beautiful, large, shuttered windows (some don't even have iron bars for protection) opening onto the narrow streets. The central plaza, which occupies 2 square blocks in front of the church, is still the city's social hub and principal gathering spot.

Liberia is best looked upon as a base for exploring this region, or as an overnight stop as part of a longer itinerary. From here, it's possible to do day trips to nearby beaches and three national parks, although only two of them have facilities for visitors. Several moderately priced hotels are located on the outskirts of Liberia at the intersection of the Interamerican Highway and the road to the Nicoya Peninsula and its many beaches.

ESSENTIALS

GETTING THERE & DEPARTING   By Plane   The airstrip in Liberia has been cleared to accept commercial international flights for a couple of years now. But so far, the traffic remains predominantly charter flights. No major airline has regularly scheduled flights to Liberia, although as I've been writing for years, this is expected to change. Check with your travel agent.

Sansa (© **506/221-9414;** reservations@flysansa.com) has daily flights to Liberia leaving at 7:15 and 11:30am, and 2:10 and 5:30pm from San José's Juan Santamaría International Airport. Return flights depart for San José at 8:35am and 12:40, 3:15, and 6:45pm. The one-way fare runs between $60 and $90; duration, 50 minutes.

Travelair (© **506/220-3054;** reservations@travelair-costarica.com) has three flights daily to Liberia at 8:30am, noon, and 3pm from Tobías Bolaños International Airport in Pavas. The afternoon flights stop first in Tamarindo. Return flights leave Liberia at 9:40am, and 1:35 and 4:35pm. Fares are $75 one-way; $150 round-trip. During the low season, the number of flights is often reduced and the schedule changed.

If you plan on flying here and renting a car to continue on to one of the nearby beaches and explore the region, contact the following agencies: **Alamo Rent A Car** (© 506/668-1111), **Budget Rent A Car** (© 506/668-1024), **Economy Rent A Car** (© 506/666-2816), **Toyota Rent A Car** (© 506/666-8190), or **Sol Rent A Car** (© 506/666-2222). You can also reserve with these companies via their San José and international offices (see chapter 4).

By Car   Take the Interamerican Highway west from San José and follow the signs for Nicaragua and the Guanacaste beaches. It takes approximately 4 hours to get to Liberia.

By Bus   Express buses (© **506/222-1650** or 506/666-0458) leave **San José** roughly every hour between 6am and 8pm from Calle 14 between Avenidas 1 and 3. The ride to Liberia is 4 hours. A one-way fare costs $3.50. Buses leave **Puntarenas** for Liberia periodically; it's best to check for a current schedule in town. The ride takes 2½ hours; a one-way fare costs $2.

Buses depart for San José from the Liberia bus station on the edge of town, 200 meters north and 100 meters east of the main intersection on the

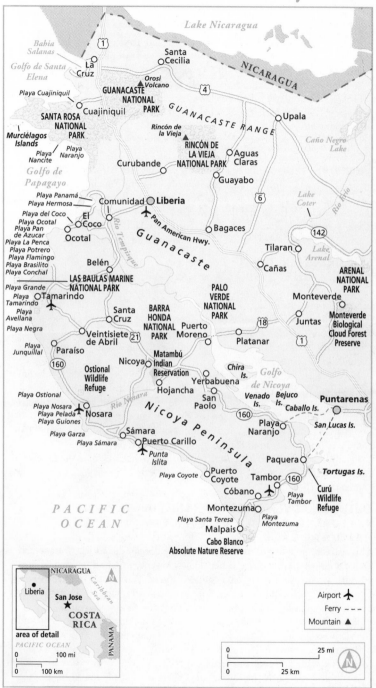

Lake Nicaragua

Bahía Salanas

Golfo de Santa Elena

Santa Cecilia

1

La Cruz

NICARAGUA

Orosi Volcano ▲

Playa Cuajiniquil

GUANACASTE NATIONAL PARK

4

GUANACASTE RANGE

Cuajiniquil

SANTA ROSA NATIONAL PARK

Upala

Rincón de la Vieja ▲

Caño Negro Lake

Murciélagos Islands

Playa Nancite *Playa Naranjo*

RINCÓN DE LA VIEJA NATIONAL PARK

Aguas Claras

Curubande

Golfo de Papagayo

Guayabo

Lake Coter

Playa Panamá
Playa Hermosa

Comunidad ○ **Liberia**

6

Río Tempisque

Río

Playa del Coco
Playa Ocotal
Playa Pan de Azucar

El Coco

Pan American Hwy.

Bagaces

142

Ocotal

Tilaran

Lake Arenal

Playa La Penca
Playa Potrero
Playa Flamingo
Playa Brasilito
Playa Conchal

Belén

G u a n a c a s t e

Cañas

ARENAL NATIONAL PARK

LAS BAULAS MARINE NATIONAL PARK

Playa Grande

PALO VERDE NATIONAL PARK

Monteverde

Playa Tamarindo

Tamarindo

Santa Cruz

BARRA HONDA NATIONAL PARK

Puerto Moreno

Juntas

Monteverde Biological Cloud Forest Preserve

Playa Avellana

Playa Negra

Veintisiete de Abril

21

18

Platanar

1

Playa Junquillal

Paraíso

160

Nicoya ○

Matambú Indian Reservation

Chira Is.

Golfo de Nicoya

Ostional Wildlife Refuge

Río Nosara

Yerbabuena

Hojancha

Venado Is.

Bejuco Is.

Puntarenas

Playa Ostional

San Paolo

Caballo Is.

Playa Nosara
Playa Pelada
Playa Guiones

Nosara

N i c o y a   P e n i n s u l a

160

Playa Naranjo

San Lucas Is.

Playa Garza

Sámara

Playa Sámara

Puerto Carillo

Paquera

Tortugas Is.

Punta Islita

Puerto Coyote

Tambor

160

Playa Coyote

Cóbano

Playa Tambor

Curú Wildlife Refuge

PACIFIC OCEAN

Montezuma

Playa Santa Teresa

Playa Montezuma

Malpais

Cabo Blanco Absolute Nature Reserve

NICARAGUA

Caribbean Sea

N

Liberia ●

San Jose ★

COSTA RICA

area of detail

PACIFIC OCEAN

PANAMA

Airport ✈
Ferry – – –
Mountain ▲

0   100 mi
0   100 km

0   25 mi
0   25 km

N

> **Finds An Interesting Stop on Your Way to Liberia**
>
> If you're driving to or from Guanacaste, be sure to take a brief break to check out the **Catholic Church** ✦ in Cañas. For the past couple years, artist and local prodigal son Otto Apuy has been overseeing the work of enveloping the entire church in colorful mosaic. The work uses whole and broken tiles in glossy, vibrant colors to depict both religious and abstract themes. The church is located in the center of town, just a few blocks off the highway.

Interamerican Highway. Express buses for San José leave roughly every hour between 5am and 8pm. To reach **Monteverde,** take any Puntarenas or San José bus leaving before 1pm. Get off at the Río Lagarto Bridge, walk to the dirt road that leads to Santa Elena, and flag down the Puntarenas/Santa Elena bus, which passes here at approximately 3:15pm. For information on getting to various beaches, see the sections below. The ride takes around 2½ to 3 hours.

EXPLORING THE TOWN

The central plaza in Liberia is a great place to people-watch, especially in the early evenings and on weekends. Grab a seat on one of the many concrete benches, or join the families and young lovers as they leisurely stroll around. If you venture off for a few blocks in any direction, you'll see fine examples of the classic Spanish colonial architecture—adobe buildings with ornate wooden doors, heavy beams, central courtyards, and faded, sagging, red-tile roofs—that abounds in this small city.

It's not much, but you might want to check out the tiny **Sabanero Museum** (© 506/665-0135), which has a small collection of photos and exhibits depicting the life and times, and tools of the trade of the colonial and post-colonial residents of this horse and cattle country. The museum, which doubles as a basic information center for the city and region, is located about 3 blocks south of the church. It's open daily from 8am to 5pm; admission is 50¢.

Finally, if you want to check e-mail or surf the Web, check in at the **Libernet Internet Café** (© 506/666-5095), which is located a half-block east of the church.

OUTDOOR ADVENTURES NEAR LIBERIA
EXPLORING RINCÓN DE LA VIEJA
NATIONAL PARK ✦✦

This national park begins on the flanks of the Rincón de la Vieja Volcano and includes this volcano's active crater. Down lower, you'll find an area of geothermal activity similar to Yellowstone National Park in the United States. Fumaroles, geysers, and hot pools cover this small area, creating a bizarre, otherworldly landscape. In addition to hot springs and mud pots, you can explore waterfalls, a lake, and volcanic craters. The bird watching here is excellent, and the views across the pasturelands to the Pacific Ocean are stunning.

The main entrance is 15½ miles (25km) northeast of Liberia, down a badly rutted dirt road. The park entrance fee is $6 per person per day. Camping will cost you an extra $2 per person per day. There are actually two entrances and camping areas here, the **Santa María** and **Las Espuelas** ranger stations. The latter is by far the more popular and accessible, and it's closer to the action. Here you'll find two small camping areas near each other. I recommend the one closer to the river, although the bathroom and shower facilities are about 100 yards away, at the other site. For those seeking a less rugged tour of the park, there are several lodges located around the perimeter of the park; all offer guided hikes and horseback rides into the park.

GETTING THERE   To reach the Las Espuelas entrance, drive about 3 miles (5km) north of Liberia and turn right on the dirt road to the park. The turnoff is well marked. In about 7½ miles (12km), you'll pass through the small village of Curubandé. Continue on this road for another 3½ miles (6km), until you reach the Hacienda Lodge Guachipelin. The lodge is private property, and the owners have been charging vehicles a $2 toll to pass through their gate and continue on to the park. I'm not sure if this is legal or mandatory, but it's not worth the hassle to protest. Pay the toll, pass through the lodge's gate, and continue for another 2½ miles (4km) until you reach the park entrance.

There are two routes to the **Santa Maria entrance.** The principal route heads out of the northeastern end of Liberia toward the small village of San Jorge. This route is about 15½ miles (25km) long and takes roughly 45 minutes. A four-wheel-drive vehicle is required. Alternatively, you can reach the Santa Maria entrance from a turnoff from the Interamerican Highway at Bagaces. From here, head north through Guayabo, Aguas Claras, and Colonia Blanca. The road is paved up to Colonia Blanca, but again, a four-wheel-drive vehicle is required for the final, very rough, 6 miles (10km) of gravel road.

HIKING IN THE PARK   There are several excellent trails inside the Rincón de la Vieja National Park. More energetic hikers can tackle the 5 miles (8km) up to **the summit** and explore the several craters and beautiful lakes up here. On a clear day, you'll be rewarded with a fabulous view of the plains of Guanacaste and the Pacific Ocean below. The easiest hiking is the gentle **Las Pailas loop** ✦. This 2-mile (3km) trail is just off the Las Espuelas park entrance and passes by several bubbling mud pots and steaming fumaroles. This trail crosses a river, so you'll either have to take off your shoes or get them wet. The whole loop takes around 2 hours.

My favorite hike here is to the **Blue Lake and La Cangrejo Waterfall** ✦✦. This 3-mile (5km) trail passes through several different life zones, including dry forest, transitional moist forest, and open savanna. A variety of birds and mammals are commonly sighted. Pack a lunch; at the end of your 2-hour hike in, you can picnic at the aptly named Blue Lake, where a 100-foot waterfall empties into the small pond, whose crystal-blue hues are amazing.

BIRDING
The **Río Tempisque Basin** ✦, southwest of town, is one of the best places in the country to spot marsh and stream birds by the hundreds. This area is an important breeding ground for gallinules, jacanas, and limpkins, as well as a common habitat for numerous heron and kingfisher species.

Several tour operators offer excursions and a wide range of tours in the region from Liberia. Try **TAM Tours** (✆ **506/668-1059;** www.tamtravel.com), **Swiss Travel Services** (✆ **506/668-1020;** www.swisstravelcr.com), or **Safaris Corobicí** (✆ and fax **506/669-1091;** www.nicoya.com).

One of the more popular tours is a boat tour down the Bebedero River to **Palo Verde National Park** ✦, which is south of Cañas and is best known for its migratory bird populations. Some of the best bird watching requires no more than a little walking around the Biological Station in the park.

RAFTING TRIPS

Leisurely raft trips (with little white water) are offered by **Safaris Corobicí** (② and fax **506/669-1091;** www.nicoya.com), about 25 miles (40km) south of Liberia. It has 2-hour ($37), 3-hour ($45), and half-day ($60) trips that are great for families and bird watchers. Along the way you may see many of the area's more exotic animal residents: howler monkeys, iguanas, caimans, coatimundis, otters, toucans, parrots, motmots, trogons, and many other species of birds. Aside from your binoculars and camera, a bathing suit and sunscreen are the only things you'll need. Safaris Corobicí is based on the main highway, just before the Restaurant Rincón Corobicí (see below). It also runs trips on the Bebedero River.

ACCOMMODATIONS

IN TOWN

Moderate

Best Western El Sitio   Located just out of town, about 75 meters west of the main intersection on the road to Santa Cruz and the beaches, this hotel has a basic Spanish-influenced hacienda style, with an open and modern feel. Throughout the hotel, there are cool tile floors and original paintings of local Guanacaste scenes. There's even one of the famous pre-Columbian stone spheres in the garden (see "Those Mysterious Stone Spheres," p. 287). Beside the large, shady pool (a welcome relief from the strong Guanacaste sun), there's a rancho-style bar/restaurant. This hotel is popular with Costa Ricans both as a conference site and weekend getaway.

Liberia (A.P. 134-5000), Guanacaste. ② **506/666-1211.** Fax 506/666-2059. www.bestwestern. co.cr. 52 units. $70 double; $85 triple; $95 quad. Rates include continental breakfast. AE, MC, V. **Amenities:** 2 restaurants (continental, grill); 2 bars; small casino; large outdoor pool; exercise room; tour desk; car-rental desk; laundry service. *In room:* A/C, TV.

Inexpensive

Hotel Boyeros   This economical hotel isn't as modern or well appointed as the two hotels mentioned above, but it's clearly the most comfortable budget option in town. Arches with turned wooden railings and a red-tile roof give this two-story, motel-style building a Spanish feel. The best and coolest rooms are on the second floor of the east wing. There's a large central courtyard, with the swimming pools, some basic playground equipment, and a massive shade tree.

Liberia (A.P. 85-5000), Guanacaste. ② **506/666-0722** or 506/666-0809. Fax 506/666-2529. www. hotelboyeros.com. 70 units. $40 double; $46 triple. AE, MC, V. **Amenities:** 1 24-hour restaurant (Costa Rican); 1 bar; midsize pool and children's pool; game room; 24-hour room service; laundry service. *In room:* A/C.

Hotel Guanacaste   This basic, economical little choice is primarily a hostel catering to young travelers on a tight budget. In addition to the small and simply furnished rooms—almost all of which have bunk beds with thin foam mattresses—there's a basic *soda* serving cheap Tico meals. The management here can help arrange trips to nearby national parks and tell you about other budget accommodations, including campgrounds, in the area. The two newest rooms are doubles with air-conditioning; these cost slightly more.

A.P. 251-5000 (25m west of the bus station; 1 block north and 2 blocks east of the intersection of the Interamerican Hwy. and the road to the beaches), Liberia, Guanacaste. ② **506/666-0085.** Fax 506/666-2287. www.hostelling-costarica.com. 30 units. $15–$25 double. Discounts for students and those holding a valid hostel ID. MC, V. **Amenities:** 1 restaurant (Costa Rican); mountain-bike rental; laundry service. *In room:* No phone.

Posada del Tope   This humble little pension is nothing fancy, but the rooms and shared bathrooms are clean, the owners are friendly and helpful, and it's a real bargain. Only a couple of rooms have double beds; the rest have either one, two, or three single beds. The nicest thing about Posada del Tope is that it's housed in a wonderfully restored traditional colonial home, with high ceilings, big shuttered windows facing the street, and hefty wooden trim all around. There's safe parking, the hotel offers Internet access, and a few of the rooms here even have televisions. The hotel recently took over another old home, Casa Real, located directly across the street. This annex has more rooms and a simple restaurant serving inexpensive Tico cuisine.

Calle Real, 1½ blocks south of the central park (A.P. 26-5000), Liberia, Guanacaste. ℂ and fax **506/666-3876**. hottope@racsa.co.cr. 15 units, all with shared bathroom. $10 double; $15 triple. AE, MC, V. **Amenities:** 1 restaurant (Costa Rican); mountain-bike rental; tour desk; laundry service. *In room:* No phone.

NEAR RINCÓN DE LA VIEJA NATIONAL PARK

Hacienda Lodge Guachipelin   Located 14¼ miles (23km) northeast of Liberia on the edge of Rincón de la Vieja National Park, this rustic lodge is centered around a 19th-century ranch house and a still-operational cattle and horse ranch. Most of the rooms are housed in new rows of concrete-block buildings. They're all basic and clean, but the newer rooms are definitely nicer and more spacious than those in the original lodge, and come with either a private patio or wide shared veranda.

This is one of the closest lodges to the thermal springs (6.2 miles/10km) and bubbling mud pots (3 miles/5km) of Rincón de la Vieja National Park. Horse-back rides can be arranged to the geothermal areas, as well as to various lakes, the top of a nearby dormant volcano, and some beautiful waterfalls. It isn't easy to get to the lodge, so plan on taking all your meals here and going on a few guided tours. These folks work together with the Original Canopy Tour and their neighboring **Kazam Canyon** ✷✷ attraction ($45 per person); you can sign up for an adventure in which you strap on a climbing harness and ride back and forth over a deep canyon while hanging from a cable—it's one of my favorite "canopy tours" in the country.

Rincón de la Vieja (A.P. 636-4050, Alajuela). ℂ **506/442-2818** or 506/384-2049. Fax 506/442-1910. www.guachipelin.com. 26 units. $48 double. Rates include continental breakfast. MC, V. Follow the directions/signs to Curubandé and Rincón de la Vieja National Park. A 4-wheel-drive vehicle is required in the rainy season (May to mid-Nov) and strongly recommended at other times. **Amenities:** 1 restaurant (Costa Rican); horse rental; laundry service. *In room:* No phone.

Hotel Borinquen ✷ *Finds*   This new place has the potential to be one of the premier spa resorts in Costa Rica. Accommodations are single and duplex bungalows set on a hillside above the main lodge, restaurants, and hot springs. While the single bungalow units are slightly larger, every room is plenty spacious and comes with two double beds, high ceilings, heavy wooden furniture (including a desk and chair and two sitting chairs), a large (by Costa Rican standards) TV, and a comfortable bathroom. Each has an ample wooden deck with a view over the valley and surrounding forests. Here again, the individual bungalow units get the nod, as their decks are covered, thereby providing protection from rain and bright sun.

Down in the foot of the valley are several natural hot-spring pools of differing temperatures; a larger, mineral spring–fed lap pool; a natural sauna; and an area for full-body mud baths given with hot volcanic mud recently collected from steaming volcanic mud pots. The whole thing is set on the edge of the rain forest beside gentle creeks, with trails to the mud pots. There's good hiking and horseback riding here and some nice waterfalls nearby. Since everything is spread out over steep hillsides, each bungalow comes equipped with an electric golf cart for getting around. When I visited, this place had just opened, and a whole host of finishing touches—including the construction of the spa, a large multilevel swimming pool, and additional bungalows—were still in the works.

Cañas Dulces (A.P. 108-5000), Liberia. © 506/666-0363. Fax 506/666-2931. borinque@racsa. co.cr. 33 units. $150 double. Rates include 3 meals daily and unlimited use of the hot springs, sauna, and mud baths. AE, MC, V. Drive 26 km (16 miles) north of Liberia along the Interamerican Hwy., take the turnoff toward Cañas Dulces, and follow the signs. The hotel is approximately 18km from the highway and 3.5km beyond Cañas Dulces. **Amenities:** 2 restaurants (international, Costa Rican/grill); 1 bar; a series of natural hot-spring pools and 1 larger lap pool; tour desk; laundry service. *In room:* A/C, TV, minibar; no phone.

Rincón de la Vieja Mountain Lodge   The closest lodge to the Las Pailas mud pots and the Azufrale hot springs, this place recently changed hands and is receiving a fair amount of remodeling and new construction. Rooms vary in size, but most have hammocks on their verandas, and several back up to a small stream. The newest accommodations here are a series of two-bedroom log cabins, with both front and back balconies. Meals are served in the new, large, open-air rancho in the middle of the project. The lodge offers numerous daylong tours either on foot or on horseback. They also run an extensive canopy tour, which takes you on a high-wire ride over a couple dozen different treetop platforms, beginning with a manual ascent up a towering ceiba tree. Plans here include the building of a small lake to be stocked with tilapia and trout.

Rincón de la Vieja (A.P. 114-5000, Liberia), Guanacaste. © and fax **506/661-8198.** www. rincondelaviejalodge.com. 48 units. $51–$67 double. Student and off-season rates available. AE, MC, V. If you're driving, follow the directions to the Hacienda Lodge Guachipelin and continue driving on this dirt road for another 4¼ miles (7km), bearing right at the turnoff for the park entrance. Transportation from Liberia can be arranged for around $25. **Amenities:** 1 restaurant (Costa Rican); 1 bar; horse rental; laundry service. *In room:* No phone.

DINING

There are plenty of standard Tico dining choices in Liberia. In town, the most popular alternatives are **Pizzeria Pronto,** which is located 100 meters north of the visitor information center (© **506/666-2098**), and **Pizzeria da Beppe,** located near the highway on the road that leads into central Liberia (© **506/ 666-0917**). Both serve a wide range of pizzas and assorted pasta dishes. Just south of Liberia, on the opposite side of the road from Las Espuelas, you'll find thick cuts and fresh meat at the **Steakhouse La Tablita** (© **506/666-7122**). Another alternative is to choose one of the *sodas* around the central park. The best of these is **Restaurante Paseo Real** (© **506/666-3455**).

If you want fast food, you can find both **Burger King** and **Papa John's** in a new shopping complex on the northwest corner of the main intersection of the Interamerican Highway and the road to the beaches.

Restaurante Pókopí CONTINENTAL   It doesn't look like much from the outside, but this tiny restaurant has a surprising amount of class. An even more pleasant surprise is the unusual (for rural Costa Rica) variety of continental dishes on the menu. Order a delicious daiquiri while you peruse the menu, which is presented on a wooden cutting board. You have your choice of mahi-mahi prepared five different ways, chicken cordon bleu, chicken in wine sauce, and other equally delectable dishes. Be sure to dine early if you want a quiet meal; attached to the restaurant is a disco that swings into action most nights at 9pm. If you want to sample the local nightlife, you can combine dinner and disco—and you thought you were out in the sticks.

100m west of the main intersection in Liberia on the road to Santa Cruz, across the street from the Best Western El Sitio. ℂ **506/666-1036.** Main courses $5–$15. AE, MC, V. Sun–Wed 11am–10pm, Thurs–Sat 11am–midnight.

Restaurant Rincón Corobicí COSTA RICAN/INTERNATIONAL   The food here is decidedly mediocre, but the setting, particularly during the day, more than makes up for it. While there's plenty of covered seating in the main open-air dining room, you'll want to choose a table on the wooden deck, which overlooks a beautiful section of the Corobicí River. The sound of rushing water tumbling over the rocks in the riverbed is a soothing accompaniment to the simple but filling meals. The whole fried fish is your best choice here, though you can also have steaks, lobster, shrimp, and sandwiches. This restaurant makes an ideal lunch stop if you're heading to or coming from Liberia, or have just done a rafting trip on the Corobicí River. Be sure to try the fried yucca chips—you may never go back to french fries.

Interamerican Hwy., 3 miles (5km) north of Cañas. ℂ **506/669-1234.** Main courses $4–$25. AE, DC, MC, V. Daily 8am–8:30pm.

2 La Cruz

172 miles (277km) NW of San José; 37 miles (59km) NW of Liberia; 12 miles (20km) S of Peñas Blancas

La Cruz is a tiny hilltop town near the Nicaraguan border. The town itself has little to offer beyond a fabulous view of Bahía Salinas, but it does serve as a gateway to the nearly deserted beaches down below, a few mountain lodges bordering the nearby Santa Rosa and Guanacaste National Parks, and the Nicaraguan border crossing at Peñas Blancas.

There's not really much to do in La Cruz except catch a sunset and some ceviche at the **El Mirador Ehecatl** (ℂ **506/679-9104**). This humble little restaurant holds a commanding **view** ✦✦ of Bahía Salinas and serves up hearty Tico standards at only slightly inflated prices. Similarly, there's not really much reason to stay in La Cruz, but if you must, check out **Amalia's Inn** (ℂ and fax **506/679-9181**), which is a simple little hotel with a small pool and good views of the bay. (Instead of staying in town, check out the listings I've given below for places to stay in the environs of La Cruz.)

ESSENTIALS
GETTING THERE & DEPARTING   By Plane   The nearest airport with regularly scheduled service is in Liberia (see section 1 of this chapter).

By Car   Take the Interamerican Highway west from San José and follow the signs for Nicaragua and the Guanacaste beaches. When you reach Liberia, head straight through the major intersection, following signs to Peñas Blancas and the Nicaraguan border. Allow approximately 5 hours to get from San José to La Cruz.

By Bus   Buses (ℂ **506/256-9072**) leave San José daily for **Peñas Blancas** at 5, 7, 7:45, and 10:30am and 1:30 and 4pm from Calle 14 between Avenidas 3 and 5. These buses stop in La Cruz and will also let you off at the entrance to Santa Rosa National Park. The ride to La Cruz takes 6 hours; a one-way fare costs $5.

Buses leave Liberia for Peñas Blancas at 5:30, 8:30, and 11am, and 2 and 4:30pm. The ride to La Cruz takes about 1 hour and costs $1.75.

Buses depart for San José from Peñas Blancas daily at 5:30, 7:15, and 10:30am, noon, and 1:30 and 3:30pm, passing through La Cruz about 20 minutes later. Buses leave Liberia for San José roughly every hour between 5am and 8pm.

ORIENTATION The highway passes slightly to the east of town. You'll pass the turnoffs to Santa Rosa National Park, Playa Caujiniquil, and Los Inocentes Lodge before reaching the town. To reach the beaches of Bahía Salinas, head into La Cruz to El Mirador Ehecatl and then follow the signs down to the water.

EXPLORING SANTA ROSA NATIONAL PARK

Best known for its remote, pristine beaches (reached by several kilometers of hiking trails or a four-wheel-drive vehicle), **Santa Rosa National Park** ⭐ is a fine place to ramble, surf, or just watch sea turtles nest. Located 18½ miles (30km) north of Liberia and 13 miles (21km) south of La Cruz on the Interamerican Highway, Costa Rica's first national park blankets the Santa Elena Peninsula. Unlike other national parks, it was founded not to preserve the land but to save a building, known as **La Casona,** which played an important role in Costa Rican independence. It was here, in 1856, that Costa Rican forces fought the decisive Battle of Santa Rosa, forcing the U.S.–backed soldier of fortune William Walker and his men to flee into Nicaragua. Inside the restored ranch house you'll find relics from and representations of that historic battle. This small museum and monument is open daily from 8am until 4pm.

It costs $6 per person to enter the park. Camping is allowed at several sites within the park. At times, especially during high season, you must reserve in advance (℃ **506/666-5051**). A campsite costs $2 per person per day. There's camping near the entrance and principal ranger station, as well as at La Casona, and down by Playas Naranjo and Nancite.

THE BEACHES ⭐⭐ Five miles (8km) west of La Casona, down a rugged road that's impassable during the rainy season (it's rough on four-wheel-drive vehicles even in the dry season), is **Playa Naranjo.** Two and a half miles (4km) north of Playa Naranjo, along a hiking trail that follows the beach, you'll find **Playa Nancite. Playa Blanca** is 13 miles (21km) down a dirt road from Caujiniquil, which itself is 12½ miles (20km) north of the park entrance. None of these three beaches has shower or rest-room facilities. (Playa Nancite does have some facilities, but they're in a reservation-only camping area.) Bring along your own water, food, and anything else you'll need, and expect to find things relatively quiet and deserted.

Playa Nancite is known for its *arribadas* ("arrivals"; grouped egg-layings) of Olive Ridley sea turtles, which come ashore to nest by the tens of thousands each year in October. Playa Naranjo is legendary for its perfect surfing waves. In fact, this spot is quite popular with day-trippers who come in by boat from the Playa del Coco area to ride the waves that break around Witches Rock, which lies just offshore.

On the northern side of the peninsula is **Playa Blanca,** a beautiful, remote, white-sand beach with calm waters. This beach is reached by way of the small village of Caujiniquil and is accessible only during the dry season.

If you reach Caujiniquil and then head north for a few kilometers, you'll come to a small annex to the national park system at **Playa Junquillal** (not to be confused with the more-developed beach of the same name farther south in

CENTRAL AMERICA

MIDDLE AMERICA

AT&T Direct® Service

The easy way to call home from anywhere.

Global
connection
with the AT&T
Network

AT&T
direct
service

or the easy way to call home, take the attached wallet guide.

When You Want More Than the Official Line

Over 4 million people rely on the candid star ratings and reviews of the Unofficial Guides for the vacation of a lifetime

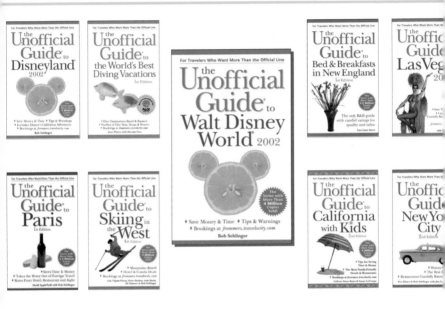

Available at bookstores everywhere.

Guanacaste). This is a lovely little beach that is also often good for swimming. You'll have to pay the park entrance fee ($6) to use the beach, and $2 more to camp here. There are basic bathroom and shower facilities.

ACCOMMODATIONS NEAR LA CRUZ

Ecoplaya Beach Resort ⊛   This is by far the most comfortable, dare I say luxurious, beach hotel in the area. (Aside from a facile attempt to cash in on a trend, I see no reason for the word "eco" in the name.) The rooms are classified as either studios, or junior, master, or luxury suites. Definitely opt for one of the suites, as the studios are a bit cramped. The wide range in prices here reflects the wide range of room sizes. Inside, they all have high ceilings, tile floors, and plenty of varnished wood accents. The beach here is calm and attractive. This is a good option if you're looking to combine some beach time with excursions to Santa Rosa National Park, Los Inocentes Lodge, and/or neighboring Nicaragua. But if you're just looking for a beach-resort vacation, I recommend heading to one of the beaches farther south in Guanacaste.

La Coyotera Beach, Salinas Bay. ℂ **506/289-8920.** Fax 506/289-4563. www.ecoplaya.com. 16 units. $80–$180 double. Rates lower in the off-season, higher during peak weeks. AE, MC, V. From La Cruz, take the dirt road that passes to the right of El Mirador Ehecatl restaurant (as you face the water) and then follow signs to the hotel. **Amenities:** 1 restaurant (Costa Rican/international); 1 bar; midsize outdoor pool; 2 Jacuzzis; limited water-sports-equipment rentals; tour desk; laundry service. *In room:* A/C, TV, kitchenette, fridge, coffee maker.

Los Inocentes Lodge ⊛   Set on a ranch 8½ miles (14km) from La Cruz, near the Nicaraguan border and bordering Guanacaste National Park, Los Inocentes is popular with naturalists interested in exploring the nearby dry and transitional forests. Horseback riding through the ranch ($20 for 2 hr. with guide) is the most popular activity; the ranch does a brisk business in day trips by visitors staying at other hotels.

The rooms are located in the main lodge building, which dates back to 1890. Some have high ceilings, and most open onto large verandas with hammocks and wicker rocking chairs. Each room has access to a private bathroom, but most are not attached to the room (some folks on the second floor even have to go downstairs to their bathroom on the first floor). The cabins, which are located about 100 yards away from the main lodge, are two-bedroom affairs better suited for families and small groups. Meals are simple but filling. There's a great view of Orosi Volcano from the lodge, and the bird watching here is excellent.

On the flanks of the Orosi Volcano (A.P. 228-3000, Heredia). ℂ **506/679-9190.** Fax 506/679-9224. orosina@racsa.co.cr. 11 units, 12 cabins. $74 per person. Rates include all meals, a daily tour, and taxes. AE, MC, V. **Amenities:** 1 restaurant (Costa Rican); small pool; Jacuzzi; tour desk; laundry service. *In room:* No phone.

Three Corners Bolaños Bay   This hotel occupies a beautiful spot in front of Isla Bolaños on Bahía Salinas. But it appeals primarily to windsurfers, due to the strong, steady winds that buffet the bay throughout the Guanacaste dry season and periodically during the rainy season. When these winds are really howling, it makes most other activities here impossible or uncomfortable—even reading quietly by the pool can be quite a challenge. The rooms are acceptable, but uninspired. Eighteen of them have ocean views; all have small patios. The bathrooms have bidets.

The restaurant is located under one of the hotel's two immense peaked thatch roofs, and the reception, gift shop, and tour desk are under the other. Food and service here are inconsistent at best. In addition to full-service windsurfing and scuba-diving centers, the hotel can arrange a wide range of tours and activities, including trips to Nicaragua.

Bahía Salinas (A.P. 1686-1250, Escazú). ℂ **506/289-5561.** Fax 506/228-4205. www. 3cornersbolanosbay.com. 72 units. $55 per person. Rates include food, drinks, lodging, activities, and taxes. AE, MC, V. From La Cruz, take the dirt road that passes to the right of the popular El Mirador Ehecatl restaurant (as you face the water) and then follow the signs to the hotel. You can arrange pickup in La Cruz, or take a cab from the bus station, which should cost around $10. **Amenities:** 1 restaurant (international); 1 bar; small outdoor pool with swim-up bar; Jacuzzi; extensive water-sports-equipment rental; bike rental; tour desk; laundry service. *In room:* No phone.

3 Playa Hermosa & Playa Panamá

160 miles (258km) NW of San José; 25 miles (40km) SW of Liberia

A good destination for families with kids, **Playa Hermosa** ✺ means "beautiful beach," which is an appropriate name for this crescent of sand. Surrounded by dry, rocky hills, this curving gray-sand beach is long and wide and rarely crowded, despite the presence of the Costa del Cacique condo development and the Sol Playa Hermosa Hotel on the hill at the north end of the beach. Fringing the beach is a swath of trees that stays surprisingly green right through the dry season. The shade provided by these trees is a big part of the beach's appeal. Rocky headlands jut out into the surf at both ends of the beach, and at the base of these rocks you'll find fun tide pools to explore.

Beyond Playa Hermosa, you'll find the still undeveloped **Playa Panamá** and, farther on, the calm waters of **Bahía Culebra** ✺. Once one of the most remote and underdeveloped spots in Guanacaste, Bahía Culebra now hosts not one, but two large resort hotels. These hotels let out onto two small, very nice, calm, and essentially private beaches. However, the lack of facilities and misuse by campers and day visitors has turned Playa Panamá, yet another calm and protected stretch of sand, into one of the worst garbage dumps on the coast.

ESSENTIALS

GETTING THERE & DEPARTING   By Plane   The nearest airport with regularly scheduled service is in Liberia. From here you can arrange a taxi to bring you the rest of the way. The ride takes about 45 minutes and should cost around $20.

By Car   Follow the directions for getting to Liberia (see section 1 of this chapter), then head west toward Santa Cruz. Just past the village of Comunidad, turn right. In about 7 miles (11km) you'll come to a fork in the road. Take the right fork. These roads are relatively well marked, and a host of prominent hotel billboards should make it easy enough to find the beach. The drive takes about 5 hours from San José.

By Bus   Express buses (ℂ **506/221-7202**) leave San José daily at 3:10pm from Calle 12 between Avenidas 5 and 7, stopping first at Playa Hermosa and next at Playa Panamá, 2 miles (3km) farther north. One-way fare for the 5-hour trip is $4. Alternatively, you can take a bus from San José to Liberia (see "Liberia," above, for details) and then take a bus from Liberia to Playa Hermosa and Playa Panamá. Buses (ℂ **506/666-0042**) leave Liberia for these two beaches daily at 4:45, 6:30, 7:30, and 11:30am, and 1, 3:30, and 5:30pm. The trip lasts 45 minutes. The one-way fare costs $1.25. During the high season, extra buses from Liberia are sometimes added. Alternatively, you can take a bus to Playa del Coco, from which these beaches are a quick taxi ride away. Taxi fare should run between $5 and $6.

One direct bus departs for San José daily at 5am from Playa Panamá, with a stop in Playa Hermosa along the way. Buses to Liberia leave Playa Panamá at 6, 8:30, and 10am, and 2, 4, 5, and 10pm, stopping in Playa Hermosa a few minutes later. Ask at your hotel where to catch the bus.

ORIENTATION   There are no real towns here, just a few houses and hotels on and near the beach. You'll come to Playa Hermosa first, followed by Playa Panamá a few kilometers farther along the same road. The road ends at the Blue Bay Village Beach Resort.

Playa Hermosa is about a 500-yard stretch of beach, with all the hotels laid out along this stretch. From the main road, which continues on to Playa Panamá, there are about three access roads heading off toward the beach. All the hotels are well marked, with signs pointing guests down the right access road.

VISITOR INFORMATION & EQUIPMENT RENTAL   In the middle of Playa Hermosa you'll find **Aqua Sport** (© 506/672-0050), which is both the visitor information center and water-sports-equipment rental center for Playa Hermosa. Kayaks, sailboards, canoes, bicycles, beach umbrellas, snorkel gear, and parasails are all available for rental at fairly reasonable rates. This is also where you'll find the local post office, public phones, a small supermarket, and a restaurant (see "Dining & After-Dark Diversions," below).

OUTDOOR PURSUITS

Both beaches are usually good for swimming, although Playa Panamá is slightly more protected. You can usually find a nice spot here, though sadly, the beach has a persistent litter problem.

If you want to do some diving while you're here, check in with **Diving Safaris de Costa Rica** ⚓ (© 800/779-0055 in the U.S., or 506/672-0012; www. costaricadiving.net) at the Sol Playa Hermosa Hotel at the north end of the beach. This is a long-established and respected dive operation. It's got a large shop and offers a wide range of trips to numerous dive spots, and also offers night dives, multiday packages, certification classes, and Nitrox dives. Alternatively, you can check out **Resort Divers** (© 506/672-0106; www. resortdiver-cr.com), which has set up shop at the Blue Bay Village Beach Resort. A two-tank dive should run between $70 and $120 per person, depending primarily on the distance traveled to the dive sites.

Since Playa Hermosa is generally flat, **surfers** should look into boat trips to nearby Witch's Rock and Ollie's Point. **Diving Safaris de Costa Rica** (© 506/ 672-0012), **Hotel Finisterra** (© 506/672-0227), and **Aqua Sport** (© 506/672-0050) all offer trips for up to six surfers for between $200 and $250, including lunch. All of these companies also offer fishing trips for between $250 and $800 for groups of two to four anglers.

Both **TAM** (© 506/668-1059) and **Swiss Travel Service** (© 506/668-1020) run a wide range of trips to Santa Rosa or Rincón de la Vieja National Parks. They'll pick you up at any hotel in either Playa Hermosa or Playa Panamá.

ACCOMMODATIONS
EXPENSIVE

Blue Bay Village Resort ⚓ (Kids)   This was the first all-inclusive resort in the Guanacaste region. It has changed its name and management at least twice, but seems to have settled down now as a Blue Bay resort. Most of the independent villas can be separated into two rooms or shared by a family or two couples.

Inside, one room is equipped with a king-size bed, the other with two queen-size beds. All rooms have marble floors, pine ceilings, large bathrooms, and small private patios or balconies. The resort is quite spread out, so if you don't want to do a lot of walking or wait for the minivan shuttles, ask for a room near the main pool and restaurants. If you want a good view, ask for one on the hill overlooking the bay. For those seeking more isolation, there are rooms located in the dry forest behind the resort. The hotel has a host of organized sports and activities, including daily programs for children. All nonmotorized sports equipment, activities, and classes are included. The hotel has its own small crescent-shaped swath of beach, which is very calm and protected for swimming. Extasis, the hotel's dinner theater and disco complex, offers up nightly entertainment revues and late-night dancing.

Playa Arenilla, Guanacaste. ℭ **800/BLUE-BAY** in the U.S., or 506/672-0130. Fax 506/672-0139. www.bluebayresorts.com. 160 units. $130–$190 double; children under 12 $40 per day. Rates include food, drinks, activities, and taxes. Rates higher during peak weeks, lower in the off-season. AE, MC, V. **Amenities:** 3 restaurants (Italian, Costa Rican/international, dinner theater); 3-tiered main pool, a small lap pool and a resistance lap pool; 1 outdoor tennis court; well-equipped fitness center with Nautilus machines, free weights, Jacuzzis, steam room, sauna, health bar, and daily classes; volleyball courts; water-sports equipment; children's programs; tour desk; salon; laundry service. *In room:* A/C, TV, coffee maker, safe.

Sol Playa Hermosa Hotel and Villas *⟨★⟩*　This is the oldest and most established resort in the area. Set on a steep hillside at the north end of the beach, the Sol Playa Hermosa was built with Mediterranean styling. The hotel is at the top of the hill, about 300 yards from the beach—you'll need to be in good shape to stay here. Luckily, the two pools are both at the top of the hill if you want to opt out of the descent to and climb from the beach. The villas are new units located just off the entrance. All have kitchens, satellite TVs, and modern furnishings. Almost half of them have their own small swimming pool or Jacuzzi, although only a few of the newest villas, built high on the hill, have really worthwhile views. The hotel rooms are all well maintained and quite standard for this price range; most have excellent views.

Just so you don't get too confused: This whole complex was formerly the Condovac Hotel and Villas. However, the Sol chain has divorced itself from the older villas, which are spread along the hillside below the main hotel, and now operates only the new villas near the entrance.

Playa Hermosa, Guanacaste. ℭ **800/572-9934** or 506/257-8442. Fax 506/223-3086. www. solmelia.com. 54 units, 106 villas. Dec 1–Apr 15 $131 double, $248–$292 villa; Apr 16–Nov 30 $99 double, $186–$219 villa. AE, DC, MC, V. **Amenities:** 3 restaurants (steakhouse, Italian, continental buffet); 2 bars; 2 outdoor swimming pools, a tennis court; full-service dive shop and limited water-sports-equipment rental; tour desk; laundry service. *In room:* A/C, TV, safe.

MODERATE
El Velero Hotel *⟨★⟩*　This small hotel is the best choice right on the beach in Playa Hermosa. White walls and polished tile floors give El Velero a Mediterranean flavor. The guest rooms are large, and those on the second floor have high ceilings. The furnishings are simple, though, and some of the bathrooms are a bit small. All the rooms have air-conditioning, but the fans alone are usually enough to keep things cool. The hotel has its own popular little restaurant, which offers a good selection of meat, fish, and shrimp dishes, as well as weekly barbecue fests. Various tours, horseback riding, and fishing trips can be arranged through the hotel; however, the most popular excursions are the full-day and sunset cruises on the hotel's 38-foot sailboat.

Playa Hermosa, Guanacaste. ℂ **506/672-0036.** Fax 506/672-0016. www.costaricahotel.net. 22 units. $72 double. Lower rates in the off-season. AE, MC, V. **Amenities:** 1 restaurant (seafood/continental); 1 bar; small pool down by the beach; tour desk; laundry service. *In room:* A/C, safe.

Hotel Finisterra   This hillside hotel offers clean, spacious accommodations on the southern end of Playa Hermosa. The rooms are all located on the second floor and come with either one queen or two double beds. Large picture windows face out onto either a forested hillside or the Pacific Ocean. A large open-air restaurant and lounge takes up most of the first floor, and there's a refreshing little pool with great views. The restaurant here serves a nightly mix of fresh seafood, steaks, and chicken prepared with fusion flare. The owners have a van for beach transfers (the beach is about 300 yards away, down the steep driveway), as well as a couple of boats for fishing and tours.

Playa Hermosa, Guanacaste. ℂ and fax **506/670-0293,** or 506/672-0227. www.finisterra.net. 10 units. $69 double; $79 triple. Rates include full breakfast. Lower rates in the off-season. MC, V. **Amenities:** 1 restaurant (international); 1 bar; small pool with a hillside perch and nice view. *In room:* No phone.

Villa del Sueño ★ (Value)   Although this hotel is not right on the beach (it's about 100 yards from the sand), its well-groomed lawns and gardens feel like an oasis in the dust and heat of a Guanacaste dry season. Villa del Sueño offers clean and comfortable rooms at a good price, and the restaurant here is one of the best in Playa Hermosa. All of the rooms have cool tile floors, high hardwood ceilings, ceiling fans, and well-placed windows for cross ventilation. The second-floor superior rooms have more space, larger windows, and air-conditioning. There's a small pool and open-air bar in the center courtyard. Meals are served in the main building's open-air restaurant, which even has a stage and features live music during much of the high season. The folks here manage a neighboring condominium development, which has additional apartment and efficiency units available for nightly and weekly rental.

Playa Hermosa, Guanacaste (mailing address in the U.S.: Interlink 2059, P.O. Box 025635, Miami, FL 33102). ℂ and fax **506/672-0026.** www.villadelsueno.com. 15 units. $55–$80 double. Lower rates in the off-season. AE, MC, V. **Amenities:** 1 restaurant (international); 1 bar; small pool; tour desk. *In room:* No phone.

INEXPENSIVE

Cabinas Playa Hermosa   This little hotel, tucked away under shady trees, is a sprawling beachfront spread at the south end of Playa Hermosa. Each large room has a pair of Adirondack chairs on its front porch, and the beach is only a few steps away. Rooms 1 through 4 directly face the ocean, but they're also very close to the restaurant and bar and can be noisy. The rest are located in several low buildings that run perpendicular to the beach. Even though most of the rooms are rather dark and can feel run-down, they're large, with two double beds and lots of closet space. The open-air restaurant has a rustic tropical feel, with unfinished tree trunks holding up the roof. Seafood and homemade pasta are the specialties.

Playa Hermosa, Guanacaste. ℂ and fax **506/672-0046,** or 506/672-0019. wifani@racsa.co.cr. 22 units. $40 double, $50 triple; $60 quad. Lower rates in the off-season. No credit cards. Turn left at the first road into Playa Hermosa; the hotel's white archway gate is about ½ mile (1km) down this dirt road. **Amenities:** 1 restaurant (Costa Rican/Italian); 1 bar; laundry service. *In room:* No phone.

DINING & AFTER-DARK DIVERSIONS

In addition to the place listed below, you'll find the best restaurants in Playa Hermosa at the hotel **Villa del Sueño** (ℂ **506/672-0026**) and **Hotel Finisterra**

(© **506/670-0293**). Neither restaurant has a fixed menu, but the nightly selections of blackboard specials will please most palates.

For nightlife, check out **Monkey Bar** (© **506/672-0267**), which is inland, off the main road to Playa Panamá, and has a pool table and a satellite TV, and serves U.S.–style bar food, or **Puerta del Sol** (no phone), a casual place on the beach, near the Sol Playa Hermosa. Also, find out whether there's any live music at **Villa del Sueño.**

Aqua Sport COSTA RICAN/SEAFOOD   Part of the Aqua Sport market and equipment-rental shop is a small open-air restaurant with tables of polished hardwood. The beach is only steps away, the atmosphere is very casual, and the food is better than you'd expect from such a place. The focus is on seafood— grilled lobster for $16, shrimp à la diabla for $7, and huge paella or assorted seafood platters that feed four and cost $45 and $50, respectively.

On the beach in Playa Hermosa. © **506/672-0050**. Main courses $4–$17. AE, MC, V. Daily 6am–10pm (noon–9pm in the rainy season).

4 Playa del Coco & Playa Ocotal

157 miles (253km) NW of San José; 21½ miles (35km) W of Liberia

Playa del Coco is one of the most easily accessible beaches in Guanacaste, with a paved road running right down to the water; it's long been a popular destination with middle-class Ticos and weekend revelers from San José. It's also a prime scuba-diving spot. The beach, which has grayish-brown sand, is quite wide at low tide and almost nonexistent at high tide. In between high and low, it's just right. The crowds that come here like their music loud and constant, so if you're in search of a quiet retreat, stay away from the center of town. Still, if you're looking for a beach with a wide range of inexpensive hotels, lively nightlife, and plenty of cheap food and beer close at hand, you'll enjoy Playa del Coco.

Better still, if you have a car, head over to **Playa Ocotal** ★, which is a couple of kilometers to the south, down a dirt road. This tiny pocket cove features a small salt-and-pepper beach bordered by high bluffs, and is quite beautiful. When it's calm, there's good snorkeling around some rocky islands close to shore here.

ESSENTIALS
GETTING THERE & DEPARTING   By Plane   The nearest airport with regularly scheduled flights is in Liberia. From there you can take a bus or arrange for a taxi to take you to Playa del Coco or Playa Ocotal, which is about a 45-minute drive.

By Car   From Liberia, head west toward Santa Cruz. Just past the village of Comunidad, turn right. In about 7 miles (11km), you'll come to a fork in the road. Take the left fork. It takes about 5 hours from San José.

By Bus   Express buses (© **506/222-1650**) leave San José for Playa del Coco at 8am and 2pm daily from Calle 14 between Avenidas 1 and 3. Allow 5 hours for the trip. A one-way ticket is $5. From Liberia, buses to Playa del Coco leave at 5:30am and 12:30, 2, and 4:30pm. A one-way ticket for the 45-minute trip costs $1.50.

The direct bus for San José leaves Playa del Coco daily at 9am and 2pm. Buses for Liberia leave at 7 and 9:15am, and 2 and 6pm.

Depending on demand, the Playa del Coco buses sometimes go as far as Playa Ocotal; it's worth checking beforehand if possible. Otherwise, a taxi should cost around $5.

ORIENTATION   Playa del Coco is a small but busy beach town. Most of its hotels and restaurants are either on the water, on the road leading into town, or on the road that heads north from San Francisco Treats. Playa Ocotal, which is south of Playa del Coco on a dirt road that leaves the main road about 183 meters (200 yd.) before the beach, is a small collection of vacation homes, condos, and a couple of hotels. It has one bar and one restaurant on the beach.

FUN ON & OFF THE BEACH

There are plenty of boats anchored here at Playa del Coco, and that means plenty of opportunities to go fishing, diving, or sailing. However, the most popular activities, especially among the hordes of Ticos who come here, are hanging out on the beach, hanging out in the *sodas* and bars, and cruising the discos at night. If you're interested, you might be able to join a soccer match (the soccer field is in the middle of town). It's also possible to arrange horseback rides; ask at your hotel.

SCUBA DIVING   Scuba diving is the most popular water sport in the area, and dive shops abound. **Mario Vargas Expeditions** (✆ and fax **506/670-0351;** www.diveexpeditions.com) and **Rich Coast Diving** (✆ **506/670-0176;** www.richcoastdiving.com) are the most established and offer equipment rentals and dive trips. A two-tank dive, with equipment, should cost between $55 and $90 per person. Both also offer PADI certification courses. Mario Vargas offers Nitrox diving.

SPORTFISHING & SAILBOAT CHARTERS   Full- and half-day sportfishing excursions can be arranged through **Papagayo Sportfishing** (✆ and fax **506/670-0354**) or **Agua Rica Yacht Charters** (✆ **506/670-0805;** www.aguaricacharters.com). A half day of fishing, with boat, captain, food, and tackle, should cost between $200 and $400 for two to four passengers; a full day should run between $450 and $800. Papagayo also arranges trips to ferry surfers up to Witches Rock. A boat that carries six surfers for a full day, including lunch and beer, will run around $300.

If you're more interested in wind power, you can take a 6-hour cruise on the catamaran *Spanish Dancer* (✆ **506/670-0518;** dancer@racsa.co.cr). The cost is $55 per person, including lunch and drinks.

A DAY SPA AT THE BEACH   The new **Fusion Natural Spa** ✦ (✆ **506/670-0250;** www.fusionnaturalspa.com) is located on the hillside above Playa Ocotal. The folks here offer a wide range of massage, aromatherapy, body-wrap, and exfoliating treatments. Individual treatments run from $15 to $55, or you could opt for a half-day ($80–$90), full-day ($140), or multiday package.

ACCOMMODATIONS
EXPENSIVE

Ocotal Beach Resort ✦   This is the most luxurious hotel in the Playa del Coco area. Unfortunately, service has consistently been the Achilles' heel here. The guest rooms vary in size, styling, and age. The least expensive rooms are closest to the beach, while the six duplex bungalows are strung along the hillside that climbs toward the reception. In both cases, the rooms are showing their age, although the bungalows are quite spacious. The rooms with the best views and greatest comfort are at the top of the hill, overlooking a dramatic stretch of rocky coastline. These feature pastel-wash painted walls and colorful floral bedspreads. The third-floor suite #520 is the best room in the whole joint, with a large wrap-around balcony and private Jacuzzi. Be forewarned: It's a steep, vigorous hike from top to bottom. Scuba diving and sportfishing are the main draws here, and package tours are available. Diminutive Playa Ocotal is one of the prettiest little beaches along this stretch of coast and offers good swimming.

El Ocotal's **hilltop restaurant** is one of its greatest assets. The large open-air dining room opens onto an expansive, multilevel deck that has more seating, as well as a stunning view of Playa Ocotal and miles of coastline. This is a great place to come for sunset and a drink, and the meals are pretty good as well.

Playa del Coco (A.P. 1), Guanacaste. ℂ **506/670-0321.** Fax 506/670-0083. www.ocotalresort.com. 50 units, 12 bungalows, 9 suites. $92 double; $120 bungalow; $163 suite. Higher rates during peak weeks and lower rates in the off-season. AE, DC, MC, V. **Amenities:** 2 restaurants (continental, seafood/grill); 3 small pools; lighted outdoor tennis court; exercise room; 3 Jacuzzis; full-service dive shop; fishing charters; tour desk; laundry service. *In room:* A/C, TV, coffee maker, safe.

MODERATE

Best Western Coco Verde   This new two-story hotel is the biggest thing in Playa del Coco and a good bet if you're looking for a clean, comfortable, modern room close to the beach and all the action. The rooms are all identical in size, but come equipped with a variety of bedding options for singles, couples, and families. They all share a common veranda, which gets blasted by the hot afternoon Guanacaste sun. You can't miss this green-and-white building on your right, on the main road into Playa del Coco, about 200 yards before you hit the beach.

Playa del Coco (A.P. 61), Guanacaste. ℂ **506/670-0494.** Fax 506/670-0555. www.cocoverde.com. 33 units. $75 double. Rates include breakfast. Lower rates in the off-season. V. **Amenities:** 1 restaurant (Costa Rican/international); 1 bar; small casino; small pool; dive shop; tour desk; limited room service; laundry service. *In room:* A/C, TV, safe.

Hotel Villa Casa Blanca ★   With friendly, helpful owners, beautiful gardens, and attractive rooms, this bed-and-breakfast inn is my favorite option in the area. Located about 500 meters inland from the beach at Playa Ocotal, it's built in the style of a Spanish villa. All the guest rooms have their own distinct characters, and though some are a tad small, others are quite roomy and even have kitchenettes. One room has a canopy bed and a beautiful bathroom with a step-up bathtub. The suites are higher up and have ocean views. My favorite has a secluded patio with lush flowering plants all around.

A little rancho serves as an open-air bar and breakfast area, and beside this is a pretty little lap pool with a bridge over it. Another separate rancho serves as a sort of recreation area and has a satellite television. There's an inviting hot tub set amidst the gardens.

Villa Casa Blanca also manages several rental houses and condos in the area, so if you plan to stay for a week or more, or need lots of room, ask about these.

Playa Ocotal (A.P. 176-5019), Playa del Coco, Guanacaste. ℂ **506/670-0518.** Fax 506/670-0448. www.ticonet.co.cr/casablanca. 15 units. $59–$69 double; $75–$95 suite. Rates include breakfast buffet. AE, MC, V. **Amenities:** 1 outdoor lounge and bar; a small pool; Jacuzzi; tour desk; laundry service. *In room:* No phone.

Villa del Sol B&B   This small bed-and-breakfast, located half a mile (1km) north of Playa del Coco village, is a friendly family-run joint, with four rooms upstairs and three downstairs. All are spacious and clean and receive plenty of light. Several have the option of air-conditioning for an extra $10. The most interesting room has a round queen-size bed, high ceilings, and views of the gardens. When I last visited, there were plans for six new rooms, each with a small kitchenette, private bathroom, air-conditioning, television, and telephone. There's an inviting small pool with a covered barbecue area. Tasty dinners are prepared nightly for guests from a small menu of European-influenced dishes. For me, the hotel's greatest attribute is its location on the quiet northern end of Playa del Coco. To find the hotel, just turn onto the dirt road just beyond the Hotel Coco Verde, before you hit the beach.

Playa del Coco, Guanacaste. ℂ and fax **506/670-0085**. www.villadelsol.com. 13 units, 11 with private bathroom. $45–$60 double, $70 deluxe double. Rates include continental breakfast. Lower rates in the off-season. AE, MC, V. **Amenities:** Small pool; tour desk. *In room:* No phone.

INEXPENSIVE

La Luna Tica This is the classic budget option in Playa del Coco. It's located just south of the soccer field, and the 15 oldest rooms are located right on the beach. These are very basic, have polished concrete floors, and are kept clean. The newer rooms are in the annex just across the street. The nicest rooms are on the second floor; each has hardwood floors and is flanked by a cool veranda. La Luna Tica also houses the Charlie's Marisqueria, serving Tico standards and fish dishes at very reasonable prices.

Playa del Coco (A.P. 67), Guanacaste. ℂ **506/670-0127**. Fax 506/670-0459. 31 units. $20 double; $30 triple; $35 quad. Lower rates in the off-season. V. **Amenities:** 1 restaurant (seafood/Costa Rican); 1 bar. *In room:* No phone.

DINING

There are dozens of cheap open-air *sodas* at the traffic circle in the center of El Coco village. These restaurants serve Tico standards, with an emphasis on fried fish. Prices are quite low—and so is the quality for the most part.

For views and sunsets, you can't beat the restaurant at **El Ocotal Beach Resort.**

In addition to the places listed below, you can get excellent Italian food at the new hotel/restaurant **La Puerta del Sol** (ℂ **506/670-0195**), located 200 meters north and 100 meters east of the main road at the turnoff just beyond the Hotel Coco Verde, before you hit the beach.

Helen's COSTA RICAN/SEAFOOD This is a local favorite, and because Helen's husband is a fisherman, the seafood is always absolutely fresh. The ceviche comes in a big bowl and is enough for a meal. Be sure to try the lobster soup if it's on the menu.

100m south of the ice factory. ℂ **506/670-0121**. Reservations not accepted. Main courses $4.50–$12. No credit cards. Daily 11am–11pm.

L'Angoletto di Roma ITALIAN/PASTA This small Italian-run restaurant is part of the Pato Loco Inn and serves up the best pasta in these parts. Choose spaghetti, penne, linguine, or fettuccine in one of its innumerable fresh sauces, or opt for the nightly special. For vegetarians, the penne *melanzana* (with eggplant) on the regular menu is a standout. Service is friendly and informal at the six tables spread out underneath the exposed red-tile roof. You'll even find a good selection of Italian wines at fair prices here.

800m before the beach on the main rd. ℂ **506/670-0145**. Main courses $3–$8. V. Fri–Wed 6–9pm.

Papagayo Seafood ★★ (Finds) SEAFOOD/CAJUN This simple seafood joint is a definite notch above the rest of the options in town. There are just a dozen or so plastic tables and a couple of crude plywood booths built against one wall, but they fill up fast in the high season. The place doubles as a seafood market, so you know the fish is fresh. In addition to the daily catch cooked to order, you can get seared yellowfin tuna with a ginger-sesame sauce, blackened mahi-mahi, or broiled grouper with green peppercorn sauce. There are also several types of jambalaya, some pasta dishes, and a full complement of meat and poultry selections.

200m before the beach on the main rd. ✆ **506/670-0882.** Reservations recommended. Main courses $5–$18. AE, MC, V. Daily 11am–10pm.

Tequila Bar & Grill ✸ MEXICAN   Run by the same folks who are behind the successful Papagayo Seafood (see above), this is a simple and rustic joint serving good Mexican food and magnificent margaritas. Since this is a fishing town, I'd stick to the seafood tacos and fajitas, although they both come in chicken and beef varieties. Main course meals include pork chops in a chipotle barbeque sauce and grilled chicken with tomatillo and lime. Definitely opt for one of the open-air streetside tables.

150m before the beach on the main rd. ✆ **506/670-0494.** Main courses $3–$12. No credit cards. Daily 11am–10pm.

PLAYA DEL COCO AFTER DARK

Playa del Coco is one of Costa Rica's liveliest beach towns after dark. **Cocomar** (no phone) is the main disco in town. It's located just off the little park right on the beach (if these directions don't get you there, just follow the loud music). Alternatively, you can head across the park to the **Zebra Bar** (✆ **506/670-0272**), a lively nightspot with a crowded dance floor. Just next door, **El Bohio Bar & Yacht Club** (no phone) is popular with expatriates and often shows sporting events on its TV.

On the road into town, you'll find **Banana's Republic** (✆ **506/670-0605**), a comfortable second-floor affair with good bocas and some outdoor tables on the veranda overlooking Coco's main street. A little closer to the beach is the new **Lizard Lounge** (✆ **506/670-0525**), which has a popular pool table. Finally, if you want to test your luck, head to the casino at **La Flor de Itabo** (✆ **506/670-0292**).

5 Playas Flamingo, Potrero, Brasilito & Conchal

173 miles (280km) NW of San José; 41 miles (66km) SW of Liberia

These beaches were among the first in Costa Rica to attract international attention, and are the heart of Guanacaste's "Gold Coast." The Meliá Playa Conchal is still the premier large-scale luxury resort in Costa Rica. Still, with attention and development shifting toward the Papagayo Gulf a little farther north, along with an amazing boom in Tamarindo to the south, this has become a great place to find desolate stretches of beautiful beach and isolated hotels in a wide range of price categories.

Playa Conchal ✸✸ is the first in a string of beaches stretching north along this coast. In 1997, the 310-room Meliá Playa Conchal opened here and forever changed the face of what had been a semiprivate haunt of a few beach cognoscenti. The unique beach here is made up primarily of soft crushed shells. Nearly every place you walk, turn, or lay down your towel is shell-collectors' heaven. Unfortunately, as Conchal's popularity has spread, unscrupulous builders have been bringing in dump trucks to haul away the namesake seashells for landscaping and construction, and the impact is noticeable.

All beaches in Costa Rica are public property. But the land behind the beaches is not, and the Meliá company owns almost all of it in Playa Conchal, so the only public access is along the soft-sand road that follows the beach south from Brasilito (see below). Before the road reaches Conchal, you'll have to ford a small river and then climb a steep, rocky hill, so four-wheel-drive is recommended.

Just beyond Playa Conchal to the north, you'll come to **Playa Brasilito,** a tiny beach town and one of the few real villages in the area. The soccer field is the center of the village, and around its edges you'll find a couple of little *pulperías* (general stores). There's a long stretch of beach, and though it's of gray sand, it still has a quiet, undiscovered feel (at least on weekdays). However, Playa Brasilito is rapidly becoming popular both with Ticos and budget travelers from abroad, and there are a few hotels and a couple of campsites here.

For many years **Playa Flamingo** ☆, on a long spit of land that forms part of Potrero Bay, was *the* beach destination in this neck of the woods. On the ocean side of the peninsula, there's the long white-sand beach, behind which is a dusty road and then a mangrove swamp. At the end of the sand spit is a fortresslike rock outcropping upon which most of Playa Flamingo's hotels and vacation homes are built. There are great views from this rocky hill. In addition to several luxury hotels, Flamingo has a full-service marina, a private airstrip, and a bevy of vacation homes and condo developments. Despite the attention and development all around it on this coast, Playa Flamingo feels sleepy and forgotten. Still, I wouldn't count Flamingo out. The beach here is a beautiful stretch of white sand. If you're not staying here, you should know that there are (unprotected) parking spots all along the beach road where you can park your car for the day. There isn't much shade on the beach, so be sure to use plenty of sunscreen and bring an umbrella if you can. (By the way, don't expect to see any flamingos here.)

If you continue along the road from Brasilito without taking the turn for Playa Flamingo, you'll soon come to **Playa Potrero.** The sand here is a brownish gray, but the beach is long, clean, deserted, and quite calm for swimming. You can see the hotels of Playa Flamingo across the bay. Drive a little farther north and you'll find the still-underdeveloped **Playa La Penca** ☆ and, finally, **Playa Pan de Azúcar (Sugar Beach)** ☆.

ESSENTIALS

GETTING THERE & DEPARTING   By Plane   The nearest airport with regularly scheduled flights is in Tamarindo (see section 6, later in this chapter), although it is also possible to fly into Liberia (see section 1). From either of these places, you can arrange for a taxi to drive you to any one of these beaches. Playas Brasilito and Conchal are about 25 minutes from Tamarindo and 45 minutes from Liberia (add about 5 min. for Flamingo and 10 for Potrero). A taxi from Tamarindo should cost around $25 ($30 from Liberia).

By Car   There are two major routes to these beaches. The most direct is by way of the Tempisque River. By press time or sometime during the 2002 season, a new bridge crossing the river should be operational. In the meantime, you may still have to use the **Tempisque River Ferry** (✆ **506/661-8105**). Take the Interamerican Highway west from San José. Twenty-nine miles (47km) past the turnoff for Puntarenas, turn left for the ferry. The ferry operates continually (at about 20-min. intervals), 24 hours a day. The fare is $3 per car, with an additional fee of 35¢ per passenger. The ferries that ply this crossing are quite small, and on busy days you may have to wait for several crossings before making it onboard. After crossing the Tempisque River, follow the signs for Nicoya, continuing north to Santa Cruz. About 10 miles (16km) north of Santa Cruz, just

---

⎛ **Tips** Driving Tip

Until the new bridge over the Tempisque River is completed and operational, you may find it slightly quicker to drive north all the way to Liberia and head back south, thus avoiding the lines of cars waiting to take the Tempisque River ferry, particularly on Friday and weekends, when beach traffic is heaviest. This also applies if you're heading back to San José. After you reach Liberia, follow the directions for Playa Hermosa but continue on the main road past the town of Filadelfia, until the village of Belén. Turn right here and drive until you reach Huacas, where there will be signs pointing you toward Playa Flamingo. The ride from Liberia should take about an hour.

---

before the village of Belén, take the turnoff for Playas Flamingo, Brasilito, and Potrero. After another 12½ miles (20km), at the town of Huacas, take the right fork to reach these beaches. The drive takes about 6 hours.

Alternatively, you can drive here via Liberia. When you reach Liberia, turn west and follow the signs for Santa Cruz and the various beaches. Just beyond the town of Belén, take the turnoff for Playas Flamingo, Brasilito, and Potrero, and continue following the directions given above. This route also takes around 6 hours.

By Bus   Express buses (© **506/221-7202**) leave San José daily at 8 and 10am from the corner of Calle 20 and Avenida 3, stopping at Playas Brasilito, Flamingo, and Potrero, in that order. The ride takes 6 hours. A one-way ticket costs $7.

Alternatively, you could take the same company's bus to Santa Cruz and connect with either the 6:30am or 3pm bus from Santa Cruz to Playa Potrero. Buses depart San José for Santa Cruz roughly every hour between 7am and 6pm from Calle 20 between Avenidas 1 and 3. Trip duration is around 5 hours; fare, $4. From Santa Cruz, the ride is about 90 minutes; fare, $1.50.

Express buses depart **Playa Potrero** for San José at 9am and 2pm, stopping a few minutes later in Playas Flamingo and Brasilito. Ask at your hotel where to catch the bus. Buses to **Santa Cruz** leave Potrero at 9am and 5pm and take about 90 minutes. If you're heading north toward Liberia, get off the bus at Belén and wait for a bus going north. Buses leave Santa Cruz regularly for San José.

ORIENTATION   These beaches are strung out over several miles of deeply rutted dirt roads. Playa Flamingo is by far the most developed. It's located down a side road, while the villages of Brasilito and Potrero are right on the main road.

GETTING AROUND   **Economy Rent A Car** has an office in Playa Flamingo (© **506/654-4543**); **Budget Rent A Car** has an office at the Meliá Playa Conchal Resort (© **506/654-4381**).

FUN ON & OFF THE BEACH

Though **Playa Flamingo** ❋ is probably the prettiest beach in this area, **Playa Potrero** has the gentlest surf and therefore is the best swimming beach. **Playa Conchal** ❋❋, which is legendary for its crushed seashells, is beautiful, but the drop-off is quite steep, making it notorious for its strong riptides. The water at **Playa Brasilito** is often fairly calm, which makes it another good swimming choice. However, my favorites for a full day of swimming and sunbathing are **Playa La Penca** ⚓ and **Playa Pan de Azúcar (Sugar Beach)** ⚓, both of which are just north of Playa Potrero.

SCUBA DIVING   Scuba diving is quite popular here. The **Edge Adventure Company** (✆ **506/654-4946;** http://edge.virtualave.net) and **Costa Rica Diving** (✆ and fax **506/654-4148;** www.costarica-diving.com) both have shops on the roads into Flamingo. These companies offer trips out to the Catalina and Bat Islands for between $70 and $125. Both also offer PADI certification courses, as well as multiday packages. Alternatively, you can check in at the **Flamingo Marina Resort Hotel and Club** (see below).

SPORTFISHING & SAILBOAT CHARTERS   You have plenty of sportfishing options here. The choices are many and competition is fierce here, so shop around to find the boat, skipper, and price that best fit your needs. At the **Marina Flamingo Yacht Club** (✆ **506/654-4203;** www.marflam.com), you can hook up with a variety of boats based along the docks. A full-day fishing excursion can cost between $475 and $1,300, depending on the size of the boat. Half-day trips cost between $275 and $650.

Alternatively, you can contact the **Edge Adventure Company** (✆ **506/654-4946**) or the **Flamingo Marina Resort Hotel and Club** (✆ **506/654-4141**).

If you're looking for a full- or half-day sail or sunset cruise, check in at the Marina Flamingo (see above), or try to track down the 52-foot cutter ***Shannon*** (✆ **506/654-4537**). Prices range from around $45 to $90 per person, depending on the length of the cruise. Multiday trips are also available.

HORSEBACK RIDING   You can arrange a horseback ride with **Costa Rica Riding Adventures** (✆ **506/654-4106**), **Bo-Mar Tours** (✆ **506/654-4469**), or **Brasilito Excursions** (✆ **506/654-4237**). This last place works out of the Hotel Brasilito. Depending on the size of your group, it should cost between $10 and $20 per person per hour.

MOUNTAIN BIKING & OTHER ADVENTURE TOURS   In addition to the above-mentioned activities, you can rent a mountain bike or sea kayak from **The Edge Adventure Company** (✆ **506/654-4946**). This company can also arrange multiday biking tours to other parts of Costa Rica, as well as hiking and rafting trips. Alternatively, check in with the tour desk at the **Flamingo Marina Resort Hotel and Club** (✆ **506/654-4141**).

LEARN THE LANGUAGE   The **Centro Panamericano de Idiomas** (✆ **506/654-5001;** www.cpi-edu.com), which has schools in San José and Monteverde, recently opened up a branch in Flamingo, next to The Edge Adventure Company, facing Potrero Bay.

ACCOMMODATIONS

If you plan to be here for a while or are coming down with friends or a large family, you might want to consider renting a condo or house. For information and reservations, contact **Sea View Rentals** (✆ **506/654-4007;** fax 506/654-4009), or the **Marina Trading Post** (✆ and fax **506/654-4004;** tpostcr@racsa.co.cr).

VERY EXPENSIVE

Meliá Playa Conchal ⚓⚓⚓   This sprawling hotel is the largest and most luxurious resort in Costa Rica. From the massive open-air reception building down to the free-form swimming pool (the largest in Central America), everything here is on a grand scale. There's a small-village feel to the layout; guest rooms are located in 30 separate low-slung buildings, reached by way of constantly circulating shuttles. All rooms come with either one king or two double beds in a raised bedroom nook. Down below, there's a comfortable sitting area, with a couch, coffee table, and chairs with ottomans. The bathrooms are large and modern, with marble tiles, full tubs, bidets, and even a telephone. Each unit has a garden patio or a small balcony. Only three of the bungalows are actually oceanfront, and two of these contain the master suites, which have double the living area of the standard suites and slightly more luxurious appointments.

The **golf course** ✦✦ is probably the nicest resort course yet opened in Costa Rica, with broad, open holes, rolling hills, and the occasional sea view. Because of the golf course and its ponds and wetlands, there's good bird watching here, with healthy populations of parrots, roseate spoonbills, and wood storks. Because the hotel owns so much land behind Playa Conchal, you'll have almost exclusive access to this crushed-seashell beach. The food has been the least stellar facet of this operation; still, it's a short jaunt into Flamingo or Tamarindo for dinner.

Playa Conchal (A.P. 232-5150, Santa Cruz), Guanacaste. ✆ **888/336-3542** in the U.S., or 506/654-4123. Fax 506/654-4181. www.solmelia.com. 310 suites. $250–$300 suite, $750 master suite. Lower rates in the off-season, higher rates during Christmas and Easter weeks. AE, MC, V. **Amenities:** 5 restaurants (international, Italian, steakhouse, grill, buffet); 3 bars; 2 lounges; small casino and small disco; massive free-form pool with several Jacuzzis; Robert Trent Jones–designed 18-hole golf course; pro shop; 4 lighted tennis courts; exercise room; water-sports-equipment rental; children's programs; concierge; tour and activities desk; car-rental desk; modest business center; shopping arcade; 24-hour room service; in-room massage; baby-sitting; laundry service; no-smoking rooms. *In room:* A/C, TV, minibar, fridge, coffee maker, hair dryer, iron, safe.

EXPENSIVE

Flamingo Beach Resort ✦   Formerly a Holiday Inn, this hotel, located right across the road from the beach at Playa Flamingo, is a large, modern facility with a great location. Nevertheless, it's suffered through years of neglect. The hotel was changing hands and receiving some long-overdue upkeep when I last visited. The hotel is constructed in a horseshoe shape around a large pool and opens out on the ocean. Half of the rooms have clear views of the ocean across a narrow dirt road. All the rooms are clean and cool, with tile floors and comfortable bathrooms. The pool- and beach-view rooms are slightly nicer, and you'll pay more for them. The suites each have a sitting room, wet bar, and VCR. The hotel also rents some slightly less expensive, and much less attractive, rooms in a new annex.

Playa Flamingo, Guanacaste. ✆ **506/654-4010.** Fax 506/654-4060. 91 units. A/C TV TEL. $120–$130 double; $225–$260 suite. Lower rates in the off-season. AE, MC, V. **Amenities:** 2 restaurants (international, grill); 2 bars; large outdoor pool; exercise room; game room; tour desk; laundry service. *In room:* A/C, TV, fridge, safe.

Flamingo Marina Resort Hotel and Club ✦   Located up the hill from the beach, the Flamingo Marina Hotel is a moderately priced midsize resort with a decent mix of facilities and amenities. This place was built in several phases and there's no real sense of coherence or grand plan here. The rooms vary greatly in size, age, comfort, and furnishings. Standard rooms have tile floors and lots of wood accents, while the suites have wet bars in the seating area, mini-fridges, and private whirlpool tubs. There are newer condo units that have full kitchenettes. All the rooms have patios or balconies, and most have pretty good bay views.

Playa Flamingo (A.P. 321-1002, Paseo de los Estudiantes, San José), Guanacaste. ✆ **800/ 276-7501** in the U.S., or 506/290-1858. Fax 506/231-1858. www.FlamingoMarina.com. 45 units, 44 apts. $110 double; $145 suite; $180–$280 apt. Rates slightly higher during peak periods.

AE, DC, MC, V. **Amenities:** 1 restaurant (continental/seafood); 2 bars; snack bar; 4 small pools; 2 Jacuzzis; outdoor tennis court; exercise room; water-sports-equipment rental; tour desk; laundry service. *In room:* A/C, TV, safe.

Hotel Sugar Beach ✦ As the name implies, the Hotel Sugar Beach is located on the white sands. It's one of the few hotels in the area and therefore one of the most attractive, in my opinion, with lots of seclusion and privacy. The beach is on a small cove surrounded by rocky hills. Unfortunately, the hills become very brown and desolate in the dry season, so don't expect the verdant tropics if you come down here in March or April. The hotel itself is perched above the water. Nature lovers will be thrilled to find wild howler monkeys and iguanas almost on their doorsteps. Snorkelers should be happy here, too; this cove has some good snorkeling in the dry season. The newest rooms are set back amid the trees and are quite large. Tile floors, wicker furniture, beautiful carved doors, and big bathrooms all add up to first-class comfort. The oldest rooms are the most basic, though they're in an interesting circular building. Hammocks under the trees provide a great place to while away a hot afternoon.

Playa Pan de Azúcar (A.P. 90, Santa Cruz), Guanacaste. ✆ 800/458-4735 in the U.S., or 506/654-4242. Fax 506/654-4239. www.sugar-beach.com. 29 units. $110–$138 double; $165–$195 suite. AE, MC, V. **Amenities:** 1 restaurant (international); 1 bar; a small kidney-shaped pool set on the hillside; water-sports equipment; tour desk; laundry service. *In room:* A/C, safe.

MODERATE

Fantasias Flamingo Bay Resort ✦ This hot-pink hotel is located up on the bluff, a little bit beyond the Flamingo Marina Hotel and Club. The rooms are all identical, with wall-to-wall carpeting, two double beds, large dressers, and plenty of closet space, plus private bathrooms with tubs. The nicest rooms enjoy a view of Potrero Bay and have large sliding glass doors that open onto either a private patio or a balcony. Several of these patios adjoin the swimming pool and have stairs leading down into the water.

Playa Flamingo (A.P. 12270-1000, San José), Guanacaste. ✆ 506/654-4350 or 506/233-2026. Fax 506/220-4405. www.flamingobayresort.com. 51 units. $99 double. Rate includes breakfast. AE, MC, V. **Amenities:** 1 restaurant (international) with a stunning view of the bay; 1 bar; small casino; small free-form pool with a swim-up bar; tour desk; 24-hour room service; laundry service; no-smoking rooms. *In room:* A/C, TV.

Mariner Inn This small hotel is located close to the marina and is definitely the best bargain in Playa Flamingo. The rooms are cool and comfortable, if a tad on the small side. Most of the rooms come with just one double bed. But all come with air-conditioning, a small television, and a desk. There's one larger, two-bedroom "efficiency" unit with its own private balcony. The Spreaders Bar and small restaurant here are both quite popular with the local expat community.

Playa Flamingo. ✆ 506/654-4081. Fax 506/654-4024. mariner@costarica.net. 12 units. $45–$55 double. AE, MC, V. **Amenities:** 1 restaurant (international); 1 bar; small pool. *In room:* A/C, TV.

INEXPENSIVE

It's possible to camp on Playas Potrero and Brasilito. At the former, contact **Maiyra's** (✆ **506/654-4213**); at the latter, try **Camping Brasilito** (✆ **506/654-4452**). Each charges around $3 per person to make camp and use the basic bathroom facilities, or around $10 per person to stay in a basic cabin.

Cabinas Conchal Located on the south edge of Brasilito, Cabinas Conchal consists of several yellow buildings inside a walled compound. The stucco-and-stone construction gives the buildings a bit of character as well as added security. Some rooms have just a double bed, while others have a double and a pair of bunk beds. All are quite clean. Table fans help keep the rooms cool. The beach is about 200 meters (218 yd.) away.

Playa Brasilito, Santa Cruz, Guanacaste. ☎ **506/654-4257.** Fax 506/654-4489. 9 units. $25 double; $30 triple; $40 quad. Lower rates in the off-season. No credit cards. *In room:* No phone.

Cabinas Cristina (Value) This little place is located on Playa Potrero across the bay from Playa Flamingo and a few kilometers north of Brasilito. Although Cabinas Cristina isn't on the beach, it's a great value in this area of high-priced hotels. The rooms are spacious and very clean. You can opt for a simple room with a couple of beds, a desk, and a fan, or a two-bedroom apartment with kitchenette and air-conditioning. All rooms have small verandas with large rocking chairs. There's a small pool in the middle of a grassy green yard, and a thatch-roofed palapa. Playa Potrero is a 5-minute walk down a dirt road.

Playa Potrero (A.P. 121, Santa Cruz), Guanacaste. ☎ **506/654-4006.** Fax 506/654-4128. www. cabinascristina.co.cr. 6 units. $25–$50 double. AE, MC, V. **Amenities:** Small pool. *In room:* No phone.

Hotel Brasilito This hotel, right in Brasilito and just across a sand road from the beach, offers basic small rooms that are generally quite clean. There's also a bar and big open-air restaurant serving economical meals. This is still one of the best values in town. The higher-priced rooms have nice balconies and ocean views. The hotel rents snorkeling equipment, kayaks, body boards, and horses, and can arrange a variety of tours.

Playa Brasilito, Santa Cruz, Guanacaste. ☎ **506/654-4237.** Fax 506/654-4247. www.brasilito. com. 15 units. $30–$40 double. V (6% surcharge). **Amenities:** Tour desk; laundry service. *In room:* No phone.

DINING

In addition to the places listed below, I've been getting good reports about the Spanish cuisine served up at **Rancho Grande** (☎ **506/654-4494**), which is in Flamingo, on the inland road connecting Playa Potrero and Brasilito.

Amberes CONTINENTAL Not only is this the most upscale restaurant outside of a hotel, but it also boasts a bar, an open-air disco, and even a tiny casino. You can come for dinner and make it an evening. Though the menu changes nightly, you'll always find a wide selection, with an emphasis on seafood. Fresh fish served either meunière or Provence style are two of the best dishes here. Unfortunately, the music can become way too loud at dinner, but if you dine early, it should be no problem—the disco doesn't usually get cranking until 10pm.

Playa Flamingo, near the Flamingo Marina Hotel. ☎ **506/654-4001.** Reservations recommended in high season. Main courses $6–$20. AE, MC, V. Daily 5–10pm.

Marie's ★ COSTA RICAN/SEAFOOD Right in the middle of all the luxury hotels at Playa Flamingo is a great little place for a snack or a full meal. The menu primarily offers sandwiches and other lunch foods, but on the blackboard behind the bar you'll find daily specials, which usually feature the freshest catch, such as mahi-mahi (called *dorado* down here), marlin, and red snapper. You'll also find such Tico favorites as casados and ceviche. Tables in the open-air restaurant are made from slabs of tree trunks. Be sure to try the *tres leches,* or three-milks cake (a Nicaraguan specialty), which just might be the moistest cake on earth.

Playa Flamingo. ☎ **506/654-4136.** Sandwiches $3–$6, main courses $5–$17. V. Daily 6:30am–9:30pm.

PLAYA FLAMINGO AFTER DARK

If you don't head to the disco and casino at Amberes, check out the poolside bar at the **Mariner Inn** ✶ (① **506/654-4081**), which seems to be the liveliest spot in town. Over in Playa Potrero, the **Tucan Jungle Sports Bar** (① **506/654-4014**) is the most happening joint.

6 Playa Tamarindo & Playa Grande

183 miles (295km) NW of San José; 45 miles (73km) SW of Liberia

Tamarindo ✶✶ is a bit of a boomtown, perhaps too much of a boomtown. So far, the development is a mixture of predominantly small hotels in a variety of price ranges, and an eclectic array of restaurants. The most recent development seems to be creeping up the hills inland from the beach and south beyond Punta Langosta. The beach itself is a long, wide swath of white sand that curves gently from one rocky headland to another. Behind the beach are low, dry hills that can be a dreary brown in the dry season but instantly turn green with the first brief showers of the rainy season.

Though there's only one major resort hotel in town, the proximity to great surfing and an abundance of stylish smaller hotels have made Tamarindo one of the most popular beaches on this coast. Fishing boats bob at their moorings at the south end of the beach, and brown pelicans fish just outside the breakers. A sandy islet offshore makes a great destination if you're a strong swimmer; if you're not, it makes a great foreground for sunsets. Tamarindo is popular with surfers, who ply the break right here or use the town as a jumping-off place for Playas Grande, Langosta, Avellana, and Negra.

Just to the north of Tamarindo lies **Playa Grande** ✶✶, one of the principal nesting sites for the giant leatherback turtle, the largest turtle in the world. This beach is often too rough for swimming, but the well-formed and consistent beach break is very popular with surfers. I almost hate to mention places to stay in Playa Grande, because the steady influx of tourists and development could doom this beach as a turtle-nesting site.

ESSENTIALS

GETTING THERE & DEPARTING   By Plane   Sansa (① **506/221-9414;** reservations@flysansa.com) flies to Tamarindo from San José's Juan Santamaría International Airport daily at 5:15, 8:30, and 11:35am, and 1, 2:30, and 3:50pm. The flight takes 55 minutes. The fare is $66 each way.

Travelair (① **506/220-3054;** reservations@travelair-costarica.com) flies to Tamarindo daily at 8:30am, noon, and 3pm from Tobías Bolaños International Airport in Pavas. The fare is $70 each way. The flight takes 55 minutes direct, about 20 minutes extra when stopping first in Liberia. During the low season, there is only one flight daily at 8am. Whether you arrive on Sansa or Travelair, there are always a couple of cabs or minivans waiting for arriving flights. It costs around $5 for the ride into town.

Sansa flights leave Tamarindo for San José at 6:20 and 9:35am, and 12:40, 2:05, 3:35, and 4:55pm daily. Travelair flights leave for San José at 10am, and 1:10 and 4:10pm daily during the high season; 9:10am only during the low season.

By Car   The most direct route is by way of the Tempisque River. By press time or sometime during the 2002 season, a new bridge crossing the river should be operational. In the meantime, you may still have to use the **Tempisque River Ferry** (① **506/661-8105**). Take the Interamerican Highway west from San José, and 29 miles (47km) past the turnoff for Puntarenas, turn left toward the ferry. The ferry operates 24 hours a day (at approximately 20-min. intervals) and costs about $3 per car and driver, with a nominal 35¢ fee per passenger. On busy days (especially Friday nights and Saturday mornings) you may have to wait for several crossings before making it onboard. After crossing the Tempisque River, follow the signs for Nicoya and Santa Cruz. About 10 miles (16km) north of Santa Cruz, just before the village of Belén, take the turnoff for Tamarindo. In another 12½ miles (20km), take the left fork for Playa Tamarindo. The drive takes about 6 hours.

Until the bridge is open, particularly on weekends and holidays when beach traffic is heavy, it's often quicker to drive all the way north to Liberia and then come back south, thus avoiding the lines of cars waiting to take the ferry. This also applies if you're heading back to San José. See the "Driving Tip" on p. 162.

By Bus An express bus ((C) **506/222-2666**) leaves San José daily for Tamarindo at 3:30pm, departing from Calle 14 between Avenidas 3 and 5, and takes 5½ hours. The one-way fare is $5.

Alternatively, you can catch a bus to Santa Cruz from the same station. Buses ((C) **506/221-7202**) leave San José for Santa Cruz roughly every hour between 7am and 6pm. The trip's duration is 5 hours; the one-way fare is $4. Buses leave Santa Cruz ((C) **506/680-0392**) for Tamarindo daily at 10:30am, and 1:30, 3:30, and 8pm. The trip lasts 1½ hours; the one-way fare is $1.50.

A direct bus leaves Tamarindo for San José daily at 5:45am. Buses to Santa Cruz leave at 6 and 9am, noon, and 3pm. In Santa Cruz you can transfer to one of the frequent San José buses.

Finally, there's a new alternative: **Fantasy Tours/Gray Line** ((C) **506/220-2126**) runs a daily shuttle from most major hotels in San José, leaving between 6:30 and 7:30am and arriving in Tamarindo at around noon; the return trip leaves Tamarindo at 2pm and arrives in San José at 6pm. This shuttle costs $19 per person each way.

ORIENTATION The unpaved road leading into town runs parallel to the beach and ends in a small cul-de-sac, just past Cabinas Zully Mar. There are a couple of side roads off this main road that lead farther on to Playas Langosta, Avellana, and Negra. You'll find several of the newer hotels mentioned below off of these side roads.

GETTING AROUND **Elegante Rent A Car** ((C) **506/653-0015**) has an office at the Pueblo Dorado Hotel. **Alamo Rent A Car** ((C) **506/653-0727**) and **Economy Rent A Car** ((C) **506/653-0728**) both have offices on the beach side of the main road into Tamarindo, before the Tamarindo Diriá hotel.

FUN ON & OFF THE BEACH

Tamarindo is a long beach, and though it can sometimes be great for swimming, it's often too rough. You also have to be careful when and where you swim. There are rocks just offshore in several places, some of which are exposed only at low tide. An encounter with one of these rocks could be nasty, especially if you're bodysurfing. You should also avoid swimming near the estuary mouth, where the currents can carry you out away from the beach. That said, the best swimming is always down at the southern end of the beach, toward Punta Langosta.

If you just want to laze on the beach, you can pick up beach chairs, umbrellas, and mats at **Tamarindo Tour/Rentals** ((C) and fax **506/653-0078**), located on the right as you come into town. It's open daily. There's a little storefront and

---

Para Bailar La Salsa

If you want to brush up on your Spanish or learn how to dance salsa, check in with the folks at **Wayra Instituto de Español** (© and fax **506/653-0359;** www.Spanish-wayra.co.cr). This place is located up a side street from Iguana Surf.

---

gift shop here, which doubles as a local information center and clearinghouse for condo and apartment rentals around the area.

Finally, if you're sore and worn out from all the activities listed below, call **Shannon Vacca** (© **506/653-0291**) for professional sports and/or Swedish massage. Shannon is based out of the Coral Reef, but she'll come to any hotel in the area. A 1-hour massage costs $55; half-hour, $35.

BIKING   Bikes are available for rent at **Iguana Surf** (© **506/653-0148;** iguanasurf@aol.com). These folks have one shop on the main road into Tamarindo, but their main office is a little bit out of "downtown" Tamarindo, on the road to Playa Langosta. This outfit also rents gear for other active pursuits; see "Other Water Sports," below.

FOUR-WHEELING   Tamarindo Adventures (© **506/653-0640;** www. tamarindoadventure.com) has a fleet of four-wheel-drive all-terrain vehicles. They're available for the day ($75) and half day ($55). This company also offers a wide range of guided tours around the region, and rents snorkel equipment, surf and boogie boards, and Jet Skis.

GOLF   Golf has come to this region in a big way, with not one, not two, but three regulation courses. The best course and facilities are at the **Meliá Playa Conchal Resort** ✦✦ (© **506/654-4123**). This Robert Trent Jones–designed course is still open to the walk-in public, but as the resort itself gets more and more popular, it may restrict public access. Currently, it will cost you $100 in greens fees for 18 holes, including a cart and a bucket of balls for the driving range. If you tee off after 1pm, it's just $70.

Just north of Tamarindo, in Playa Grande, you'll find the **Royal Pacific** ✦ (© **506/654-4925**), a Ron Garl–designed 18-hole course, which charges $50 in greens fees plus $20 for the cart. While this is actually a nice course, and locals love it, it's almost always deserted.

The newest entry into the fray is **Hacienda Pinilla,** a new 18-hole course located south of Tamarindo, slated to open in late 2001.

HORSEBACK RIDING   You'll probably see plenty of horses and riders running up and down the beach. You can flag down one of these and ask about rates, or set up a riding date with **Tamarindo Tour/Rentals** or **Papagayo Excursions** (© **506/653-0254** or 506/653-0227; papagayo@racsa.co.cr). Rates for horse rental, with a guide, are around $10 to $15 per hour. Both companies, as well as **Iguana Surf** (see "Biking," above) also offer boat or kayak tours of the nearby estuary for around $20 per person. Papagayo Excursions offers the widest selection of full-day and multiday trips, including excursions to Santa Cruz and Guaitíl ($45), raft floats on the Corobicí River ($85), tours to Palo Verde and Rincón de la Vieja National Parks ($85), and tours to Arenal Volcano and Tabacón Hot Springs ($100).

SAILBOAT CHARTERS   The folks who run the **Finca Monte Fresco** (© **506/394-4152**), just outside of Tamarindo, also own the 52-foot ketch

Samonique III. They charter this boat for anything from sunset cruises to week-long trips out to Cocos Island. A half-day cruise costs $60 per person, and a full day is just $90 per person. This includes an open bar and snacks on the half-day cruise, lunch on the full-day trip. Beyond this, it runs a sunset cruise for $45 per person, and charter rates are around $225 per person per day, including board, and vary depending on the size of your group.

SCUBA   If you want to do any scuba diving while you're here, check in with **Agua Rica** (© 506/653-0094; www.tamarindo.com), which you'll find on the main road, near Cabinas Marielos. It has a full-service dive shop and offers day trips, multiday dive cruises, and the standard resort and full-certification courses.

SPORTFISHING   **Papagayo Excursions** (see "Horseback Riding," above), which has its office and a small gift shop in the commercial center across from the Tamarindo Diriá hotel, offers folks a chance to go after the "big ones" that abound in the waters offshore. From here it takes only 20 minutes to reach the edge of the continental shelf and the waters preferred by marlin and sailfish. Although fishing is good all year, the peak season for billfish is between mid-April and August. Alternatively, you can contact **Tamarindo Sportfishing** (© 506/653-0090; www.tamarindosportfishing.com), **Warren Sellers Sportfishing** (© 506/653-0186; www.wssportfishing.com), or **Capullo Sport-fishing** (© 506/653-0048; www.capullo.com). All offer half-day trips for between $250 and $500 and full-day trips for between $400 and $1,000.

OTHER WATER SPORTS   If you want to try snorkeling, surfing, or sea kayaking while in Tamarindo, **Iguana Surf** (© 506/653-0148) is your one-stop source for equipment. These folks are open daily and rent snorkeling equipment ($15 per day), boogie boards ($10 per day), sea kayaks ($35 per day), and surf-boards ($20 per day). They have half-day and hourly rates for many of these items. You can also rent similar equipment of slightly lesser quality, and at slightly lower rates, from Tamarindo Tour/Rentals.

Tamarindo Adventures (see "Four-Wheeling," above) also rents water-sports equipment.

WATCHING NESTING SEA TURTLES   On nearby **Playa Grande,** leatherback sea turtles nest between late September and mid-March. The only time to see this activity is at night. During the nesting season, you'll be inundated with opportunities to sign up for the nightly tours, which usually cost around $25 to $35 per person. If your hotel can't set it up for you, you'll see signs all over town offering tours. Make sure you go with someone licensed and reputable. No flash photography is allowed because any sort of light can confuse the turtles and prevent them from laying their eggs; guides must use red-tinted flashlights.

In Tamarindo, there are two main organizations running the tours: a local cooperative of guides called **Coopetamarindo** (no phone; office located on the road into town) and **Papagayo Excursions** (see "Horseback Riding," above).

Playa Grande is just north of Tamarindo across a small river mouth. The tours either drive you around to the Playa Grande entrance or simply ferry you across the Tamarindo estuary in small *pangas* (outboard-driven boats), where you begin your trek up Playa Grande in search of a nesting mother. In both cases, you will probably be shown a brief introductory video before hitting the beach. If you are driven to Playa Grande, you will probably tour the small turtle museum there (see below).

A few words of warning: Turtle nesting is a natural, unpredictable, and increasingly rare event. You may have to wait your turn for hours while sitting on the concrete floor of the turtle museum, hike quite a ways, and even accept the possibility that no nesting mothers will be spotted at all that evening. Moreover, with the vast development in this area, the numbers of nesting turtles have dropped, while the number of tourists has skyrocketed. Do not expect an intimate experience.

Do-it-yourselfers can drive over to Playa Grande, where tours are offered by the **Matapalo Conservation Association.** These local folks operate out of a small shack next to the Las Tortugas Hotel. Part of the money goes to support local schools and a medical clinic. Try to arrive early (the shack opens at 6pm) to sign up for a tour ($15), because only a limited number of people are allowed on the beach at one time. The list fills up fast, and if you arrive late, you may have to wait until really late.

If the turtles are not nesting, or you've got some time to kill before your turtle tour, check out **El Mundo de la Tortuga** (© and fax **506/653-0471**), a small turtle museum/exhibit at Playa Grande. Visitors take the half-hour, self-guided tour by picking up a cassette player and choosing a tour cassette in English, Spanish, German, or Italian. The museum opens each afternoon at 4pm and stays open until the turtle tours are done for the night. Admission $5.

ACCOMMODATIONS
IN TOWN
Very Expensive
Hotel and Villas Cala Luna ★★   If you're looking for serious luxury in Tamarindo, stay in one of the two- or three-bedroom villas here, which are the size of a small home and just as well equipped. The living rooms are huge, with high-peaked ceilings, couches, tables and chairs, satellite televisions, and complete sound systems. The full kitchens come with microwave ovens and cappuccino machines—even washing machines. If this isn't enough, each villa has its own private swimming pool. The bedrooms are spacious and elegant, with either a king or two double beds. Everything is done in soft pastels with hand-painted accents, and the red-tile roofs and Mexican tile floors add elegance while keeping things cool. Rooms in the hotel are similarly spacious and well done, with their own terraces, but you'll have to share the hotel's main swimming pool with the rest of the guests. The biggest drawback is that the attention and service fall far short of measuring up to the surroundings. The hotel isn't right on the beach; you have to cross the street and walk a short path to reach the ocean.

Playa Tamarindo, Guanacaste. © **506/653-0214.** Fax 506/653-0213. www.calaluna.com. 20 units, 21 villas. $160 double; $300–$380 villa. Slightly lower rates in the off-season. AE, MC, V. **Amenities:** 1 restaurant (Italian/continental); 1 bar; large free-form pool with a poolside bar; Jacuzzi; water-sports-equipment rental; bike rental; tour desk; limited room service; laundry service. *In room:* A/C, TV, hair dryer, safe.

Expensive
Hotel Capitan Suizo ★★ *(Kids)*   This well-appointed beachfront hotel is located on the quiet southern end of Tamarindo. The rooms are located in a series of two-story buildings. The lower rooms have air-conditioning and private patios; the upper units have plenty of cross ventilation and small balconies. All have large bathrooms and sitting rooms with fold-down futon couches. In effect, all the rooms are really suites, with their separate sitting/living room area. The spacious bungalows are spread around the shady grounds. These all come with a tub in the bathroom and an inviting outdoor shower among the trees.

The hotel's free-form pool is quite nice. The shallow end slopes in gradually, imitating a beach, and there's also a separate children's pool. Perhaps this hotel's greatest attribute is the fact that it's just steps from one of the calmer and more isolated sections of Playa Tamarindo.

Playa Tamarindo, Guanacaste. © **506/653-0353** or 506/653-0075. Fax 506/653-0292. www. hotelcapitansuizo.com. 22 units, 8 bungalows. $110–$130 double; $155 bungalow. Rates include continental breakfast. Lower rates in the off-season. AE, MC, V. **Amenities:** 1 restaurant (international); 1 bar; midsize outdoor pool; small exercise room; tour desk; horse rental; laundry service. *In room:* Fridge, safe.

Hotel El Jardín del Eden ✱   Though it isn't right on the beach, this is one of the most luxurious and comfortable hotels in Tamarindo. The Italian owners bring a touch of sophistication that's often lacking at beach hotels in Costa Rica. There are splendid views from many of the guest rooms, which are in Mediterranean-style buildings on a hill 150 yards from, and high above, the beach. Almost all have balconies or private terraces with views of the Pacific. The large stone-tiled terraces, in particular, give you the sense of staying at your own private villa. The honeymoon room has a large bathroom with a tub, while other rooms have showers only.

Playa Tamarindo, Guanacaste. © **506/653-0137**. Fax 506/653-0111. www.jardindeleden.com. 18 units, 2 apts. $125–$145 double. Rates include breakfast. Lower rates in the off-season. AE, MC, V. **Amenities:** 1 restaurant (international/seafood); 1 bar; 2 small adjoining pools; Jacuzzi; small exercise room; tour desk; laundry service. *In room:* A/C, TV, safe.

Sueño del Mar ✱✱ *(Finds)*   This place is such a gem I was hesitant to let the secret out—now it's nearly impossible to get a room. Located at the south end of Tamarindo Beach on Punta Langosta, the hotel features rooms that are a bit small. But it's the little touches and innovative design that set Sueño del Mar apart: four-poster beds made from driftwood, African dolls on the windowsills, Kokopeli candleholders, and open-air showers with sculpted angelfish, hand-painted tiles, and lush tropical plants. Fabrics are from Bali and Guatemala. Somehow, all this works well together, and the requisite hammocks nestled under shade trees right on the beach add the crowning touch.

The separate small casita has its own kitchen, veranda, and sleeping loft, while the suite is a spacious second-floor room, with wraparound screened-in windows, a delightful open-air bathtub and shower, and an ocean view. The beach right out front is rocky and a bit rough but does reveal some nice, quiet tidal pools at low tide; it's one of the better sunset-viewing spots in Costa Rica.

Breakfasts are huge and creative and have earned local renown. In fact, co-owner Susan Money has even published her own breakfast cookbook. In 2000, the hotel began serving dinners. The menu varies nightly and has a creative, fusion flair. Reservations are recommended.

Playa Tamarindo, Guanacaste. © and fax **506/653-0284**. www.tamarindo.com/sdmar. 4 units, 1 casita. $105–$128 double; $125–$160 suite or casita. Rates include full breakfast. V. **Amenities:** 1 well-regarded restaurant (eclectic); small pool; free use of snorkel equipment and boogie boards; tour desk. *In room:* A/C, safe.

Tamarindo Diriá ✱   This is Tamarindo's oldest and largest beachfront resort. Constant remodeling and new construction has kept it in pretty good shape. Wedged into a narrow piece of land between a dusty road and the beach, the Diriá manages to create its own little world of tropical gardens and palm trees. The newest addition rises three stories over the main entrance and lobby. The rooms are done in contemporary pastel colors with red-tile floors. Some have separate seating areas, and most have hair dryers, clock radios, and a basket of toiletries in the small bathroom. The central beachfront location and attractive gardens make this hotel a nice choice. When I last visited, the management was planning to remodel and enlarge the pool.

Playa Tamarindo (A.P. 476-1007, San José), Guanacaste. ⓒ 506/653-0031. Fax 506/653-0208. www.tamarindodiria.co.cr. 123 units. $120–$160 double. Rates include breakfast buffet. Lower rates in the off-season. AE, MC, V. **Amenities:** 2 restaurants (continental, Costa Rican/seafood); 2 bars; small outdoor swimming pool; water-sports-equipment rental; game room; tour desk; car-rental desk; laundry service. *In room:* A/C, TV, safe.

Villa Alegre ✸ This small bed-and-breakfast on Playa Langosta is a well-run and homey option. The owners' years of globe-trotting has inspired them to decorate each room in the theme of a different country. The Guatemalan and United States rooms share a large bathroom; however, these can easily be joined to form one larger suite. The Mexican room is wheelchair accessible. Each room has its own private patio. The villas are quite spacious and luxurious, with kitchenettes. My favorite is the Japanese unit, with its subtle design touches and great woodwork. The Russian villa is truly wheelchair-accessible and -equipped. The beach is about 100 yards or so away through the trees.

Playa Tamarindo, Guanacaste. ⓒ **506/653-0270.** Fax 506/653-0287. www.tamarindo.com. vialegre@racsa.co.cr. 5 units, 3 with private bathroom; 2 villas. $110–$125 double; $155–165 villa. Rates include full breakfast. Lower rates in the off-season. AE, MC, V. **Amenities:** Small pool; horseshoe and shuffleboard courts. *In room:* A/C, safe; no phone.

Moderate

Best Western Tamarindo Villas Hotel & Resort This place was originally conceived of as a condo project, then converted into a hotel and taken over by the Best Western chain. Nevertheless, it overwhelmingly attracts and caters to surfers. There's a wide range of accommodations here, from the simple garden-view rooms to the Tropical and Corona suites. The former are basic budget motel-like affairs. The latter are split-level one-bedroom affairs with full kitchens, large living rooms (with two couches that can double as single beds), and either a private patio or a balcony with fabulous views of the Pacific Ocean.

Playa Tamarindo, Guanacaste. ⓒ **506/653-0118.** Fax 506/653-0115. www.bestwestern.co.cr. 32 units. $89–$119 double; $139–$209 suite. Rates include continental breakfast. AE, MC, V. **Amenities:** 1 restaurant (international); 1 bar; a midsize free-form pool with a swim-up bar and a waterfall that is sometimes turned on; tour desk; laundry service. *In room:* A/C, TV/VCR, safe.

Hotel El Milagro This place started out as a restaurant but has expanded into an attractive little hotel on the edge of town. It's located across the road from the beach, and the rooms are lined up in two long rows facing each other behind the restaurant. The front wall of each room is made of louvered doors that open onto small semicircular patios. Pretty gardens and some big old shade trees make El Milagro even more attractive. The restaurant serves well-prepared seafood and continental dishes.

Playa Tamarindo (A.P. 145-5150, Santa Cruz), Guanacaste. ⓒ **506/653-0042.** Fax 506/653-0050. www.elmilagro.com. 32 units. $75–$85 double with fan, $85–$95 double with A/C; lower rates in the off-season. Rates include breakfast buffet. AE, MC, V. **Amenities:** 1 restaurant (continental/seafood); small outdoor pool and children's pool, placed a little too close to the street; tour desk; laundry service. *In room:* Safe; no phone.

Hotel Pasatiempo *Value* A great value, this hotel is set back from the beach a couple of hundred yards in a grove of shady trees. Most of the rooms are housed in duplex buildings, but each room has its own private patio with a hammock or chairs. There's plenty of space in every room, and some even sleep five people. Each room bears the name of a different beach, and the bedroom walls all have hand-painted murals. A small yet very inviting pool sits in the center of the five duplexes.

Pacho's Restaurant and Bar serves excellent fresh fish, as well as Cajun, Thai, and Tex-Mex specialties. This popular rancho-style affair also has a pool table, nightly happy hour, cable television with live sporting events, good snacks, and occasional live music. It gets loud and lively, especially on weekends, so it may be hard to get an early night's sleep if you're staying in one of the rooms close by.

Playa Tamarindo, Santa Cruz, Guanacaste. ℂ **506/653-0096.** Fax 506/653-0275. www. hotelpasatiempo.com. 14 units. $59–$79 double. Lower rates in the off-season. AE, MC, V. **Amenities:** 1 popular restaurant (international); 1 bar; midsize pool; exercise room; tour desk. *In room:* A/C; no phone.

Inexpensive

In addition to the cabinas listed below, there's **Tito's Camping,** located out toward the Hotel Capitan Suizo in Tamarindo. It costs $2.50 per person.

Cabinas Marielos This place is located down a palm-shaded driveway across the road from the beach. Rooms are clean and fairly new, though small and simply furnished. Patios have tile floors and wooden chairs. Some of the bathrooms don't have doors, but they're clean. There's a kitchen that guests can use, and the garden provides a bit of shade. All in all, this is probably the best budget option in town.

Playa Tamarindo, Guanacaste. ℂ and fax **506/653-0141.** cabinasmarielos@hotmail.com. 20 units. $30 double; $40 triple; $50 quad. V. **Amenities:** Tour desk; surfboard rentals; laundry service. *In room:* No phone.

Cabinas Zully Mar The Zully Mar has long been a favorite of budget travelers. The newer rooms, which are in a two-story, white-stucco building with a wide, curving staircase on the outside, have air-conditioning and are more comfortable. These rooms also have tile floors, long verandas, overhead or standing fans, large bathrooms, and doors that are hand-carved with pre-Columbian motifs. The older, less expensive rooms are smaller, darker, and have soft foam mattresses. The newest addition here is a small free-form pool, although there's not much landscaping or shade around it. Miles of beach are just across the street.

Tamarindo, Guanacaste. ℂ **506/653-0140** or 506/226-4732. Fax 506/653-0028. zullymar@ racsa.co.cr. 46 units. $30–$55 double; $40–$65 triple. AE, MC, V. **Amenities:** Small outdoor pool; laundry service. *In room:* No phone.

IN PLAYA GRANDE

Hotel El Bucanero This new hotel is a decent, but overpriced, choice in Playa Grande, about 100 yards from the beach. The rooms are all clean and cool, with tile floors and private bathrooms. The rooms come in several sizes and a mix of bed arrangements. Three of the rooms have air-conditioning. The hotel's restaurant and bar, which is located on the second floor of the octagonal main building, serves reasonably priced seafood dishes and Tico standards; but the best part about it is the fact that it's an open-air affair and gets a nice breeze.

Playa Grande, Guanacaste. ℂ and fax **506/653-0480.** 8 units. $80 double; $90 triple; $100 quad. V (add 6% surcharge). **Amenities:** 1 restaurant (Costa Rican/seafood); 1 bar. *In room:* No phone.

Las Tortugas Hotel ★ *(Finds)* Playa Grande is best known for the leatherback turtles that nest here, and much of the beach is now part of Las Baulas National Park, which was created to protect the turtles. However, this beach is also very popular with surfers, who make up a large percentage of the clientele at this beachfront hotel. Several of the rooms are quite large, and most have interesting stone floors and shower stalls. The upper suite has a curving staircase that leads up to its second room. A few canoes on the nearby estuary are available for gentle paddling among the mangroves. Las Tortugas also manages some nearby houses for longer stays.

The owners led the fight to have the area declared a national park and continue to do everything possible to protect the turtles. As part of the hotel's turtle-friendly design, a natural wall of shrubs and trees shields the beach from the restaurant's light and noise.

Playa Grande (A.P. 164, Santa Cruz), Guanacaste. © and fax 506/653-0458, or 506/653-0423. www.cool.co.cr/usr/turtles. 11 units. $58–$85 double. Slightly higher during peak weeks, lower rates in the off-season. V (add 5% surcharge). **Amenities:** 1 restaurant (Costa Rican/international); one bar; small pool; Jacuzzi; canoes. *In room:* A/C; no phone.

DINING

In addition to the restaurants listed below, **Nogui's Sunset Café** (© **506/653-0029**) is one of the most popular places in town—and rightly so. This simple open-air cafe is just off the beach on the small traffic circle and serves hearty breakfasts and well-prepared salads, sandwiches, and quiche for lunch.

I've gotten rave reviews on a brand new spot called the **Lazy Wave** (© **506/653-0737**), located in a new mini-comercial center, just before Hotel Pasatiempo, which serves creative international fare.

Stella's (© **506/653-0127**), located about 200 yards beyond Pasatiempo, is a local favorite for Italian food and fresh-baked pizzas. **Soda Natural,** next to Coconut Café, is also a good, inexpensive spot for breakfast and lunch.

Finally, there's **Pedro's Fish Shack,** just a basic wooden shanty on the beach, just beyond Nogui's, where I've had some of the freshest fish dinners of my life.

In addition, I've been getting raves about the five-course dinners being cooked up at **Sueño del Mar,** located on Playa Langosta (© **506/653-0284**). The menu changes nightly, and you'll definitely need a reservation in the high season.

Cantina Las Olas ✷ MEXICAN   A real bargain, this casual open-air restaurant is painted in light blue pastel, with bright geometric designs for trim. There's a large and popular bar in the back and a pool table off to the side. Dining is at one of the three wooden picnic tables or several smaller bare-wood tables. The tacos, burritos, and fajitas are all well-prepared Tex-Mex standards and come with a very spicy hot sauce on the side. There are even several vegetarian entrees. I recommend the fish burritos, but ask about the nightly specials, which might feature blackened fish tacos or shrimp enchiladas. Wash the whole thing down with some mango margaritas. Since this is a surfer hangout, you can expect surf videos and loud rock-and-roll or reggae music, and the occasional live band.

On the side road toward Punta Langosta before Iguana Surf. No phone. Main courses $3–$8. No credit cards. Sun–Fri 6pm–midnight (kitchen closes at 10pm).

Fiesta del Mar SEAFOOD/COSTA RICAN   Another bargain spot, the Fiesta del Mar is located across the circle from the beach and specializes in steaks and seafood cooked over a wood fire. Try the grilled steak in garlic sauce for $7 or the whole fried fish for $5. The open-air dining area is edged with greenery and has a thatch roof, so it feels very tropical. There's even live music several nights a week.

At the end of the main road. No phone. Main courses $4–$15. No credit cards. Daily 8am–11pm.

La Meridiana ✦ ITALIAN   Loosen your belt a notch and prepare for some very good Italian food at this casually elegant family-run place. The restaurant, which takes up most of the terraced outdoor patio of a large house, is surrounded by lush gardens and a pool down below. Ceiling fans keep things cool. The extensive menu covers all the bases with a wide range of antipasti, pasta, meat, and seafood to choose from. The fish is fresh (dorado, tuna, and snapper are usually on hand) and can be done *al limone, alla siciliana,* or *al vino bianco.* The *filetto tartufato* is a tender piece of tenderloin in a truffle-butter sauce.

But don't rush past the pastas. The house tagliatelle is a delicious seafood pasta in a light cream sauce, the gnocchi come in delicate medallions, and the homemade ravioli with lobster is to die for. The wine list features a wide range of Italian vintages including some very high-end offerings. Whether or not you choose one of the delicious desserts, you should definitely wash everything down with a glass of *grappa,* which is a contraband brew made by an uncle somewhere in northern Italy.

About 100m off the main road (turn left just before Zully Mar). ✆ and fax **506/653-0230.** Reservations recommended in the high season. Main courses $12–$24. AE, MC, V. Daily 6–11pm.

Pachanga ✦✦ (Finds) SEAFOOD/INTERNATIONAL   This funky little restaurant serves up an eclectic mix of seafood and pasta dishes in a casual open-air setting. The menu changes periodically and is displayed on a big blackboard. I had a wonderful seared tuna with wasabi and red onions served over a fresh salad. Blackened snapper, fresh baked mussels, and mahi-mahi in a Dijon-mustard sauce were also on the menu. Heavy wooden tables and chairs are spread over the cement floor, and you can watch the kitchen hum behind the open bar.

Across the street from Hotel Pasatiempo. No phone. Main courses $5–$18. No credit cards. Daily 6–11pm.

EN ROUTE SOUTH: PLAYA AVELLANAS & PLAYA NEGRA

As you head south from Tamarindo, you'll come to several as-yet-underdeveloped beaches, most of which are quite popular with surfers. Beyond Tamarindo and Playa Langosta are **Playa Avellanas** and then **Playa Negra,** both of which have a few basic cabinas catering to surfers.

ACCOMMODATIONS

Hotel Playa Negra   This collection of thatch-roofed bungalows is right in front of the famous Playa Negra point break. Even if you're not a surfer, the beach and coast along this area are beautiful, with coral and rock outcroppings and calm tide pools. The round bungalows each have one queen and two single beds, two desks, a ceiling fan, and a private bathroom. Although they have concrete floors, everything is painted in contrasting pastels and feels quite comfortable. The restaurant is close to the ocean in a large open-air rancho, and serves as a social hub for guests and surfers staying at more-basic cabinas inland from the beach.

Playa Negra (A.P. 31, Santa Cruz), Guanacaste. ✆ **506/382-1301.** Fax 506/382-1302. www.playanegra.com. 10 bungalows. $60 double; $70 triple; $80 quad. AE, MC, V. The hotel is closed Sept. 15–Nov. 15. **Amenities:** 1 restaurant (Costa Rican/international); 1 bar; midsize oval pool; laundry service. *In room:* No phone.

Mono Congo Lodge ✦   This overgrown jungle house has morphed into a popular surf and nature lodge. The main house is a huge three-story affair that is almost entirely open—no exterior walls—and has the feel of a giant treehouse. There are ample open areas for lounging on both the second and third floors, where you'll find the basic but clean and comfortable rooms; the beds have mosquito netting. Off the main building you'll find the separate two-bedroom guest house, which is more swank, with its arched door and rounded windows, full kitchen, and tile floors. The owners are friendly and have horses available for riding. The hotel is about a 10-minute walk from Playa Negra through Pacific dry forest.

Playa Negra (A.P. 177-5150, Santa Cruz), Guanacaste. ℂ and fax **506/382-6926.** wsurf@racsa.co.cr. 6 units, 5 with private bathroom. $45–$50 double; $80 guest house. No credit cards. **Amenities:** 1 restaurant (international); 1 bar; tennis court; horse rental; laundry service. *In room:* No phone.

7 Playa Junquillal 🏄

18½ miles (30km) W of Santa Cruz; 12½ miles (20km) S of Tamarindo

Playa Junquillal (pronounced Hoon-key-*al*) is a long, windswept beach that, for most of its length, is backed by grasslands. This gives it a very different feel from other beaches on this coast. There's really no village to speak of here, so if you're heading out this way, plan on getting away from it all. In fact, if you're looking to leave the madding crowds behind and want some unfettered time on a nearly deserted beach, this is a great choice. The long stretch of sand is great for strolling, and the sunsets are superb. When the waves are up and the sea is rough, this beach can be a little dangerous for swimming. When it's calm, jump right on in.

ESSENTIALS

GETTING THERE & DEPARTING   By Plane   The nearest airport with regularly scheduled flights is in Tamarindo (see section 6 of this chapter). You can arrange a taxi from the airport to Playa Junquillal. The ride should take 45 minutes and costs about $40.

By Car   Take the Interamerican Highway from San José. Twenty-nine miles (47km) past the turnoff for Puntarenas, turn left toward the Tempisque River. By press time or sometime during the 2002 season, a new bridge crossing the river should be operational. In the meantime, you may still have to use the **Tempisque River Ferry** (℃ **506/661-8105**). The ferry operates continually (at about 20-min. intervals), 24 hours a day. The fare is $3 per car, with an additional fee of 35¢ per passenger. The ferries that ply this crossing are quite small, and on busy days you may have to wait for several crossings before making it onboard. After crossing the Tempisque River, continue north through Nicoya to Santa Cruz. In Santa Cruz, head west 8½ miles (14km) to the town of 27 de Abril, which is where the pavement ends. From here, it's another rough 11 miles (18km) to Playa Junquillal.

By Bus   An express bus (℃ **506/221-7202**) leaves San José daily at 2pm from the corner of Calle 20 and Avenida 3. The trip takes 5½ hours; the one-way fare is $5.

   Alternatively, you can take a bus to Santa Cruz (see section 5, "Playas Flamingo, Potrero, Brasilito & Conchal," earlier in this chapter, for details), and from there, take a bus to Playa Junquillal. Buses leave Santa Cruz for Junquillal at 10am, and 12:30, 2:30, and 5:30pm. The ride takes 1½ hours, and the one-way fare is $1.25.

   The one express bus to San José departs Playa Junquillal daily at 5am. There are also daily buses to Santa Cruz departing at 5 and 6am, noon, and 2pm.

WHAT TO DO IN JUNQUILLAL

Other than walking on the beach, swimming when the surf isn't too strong, and exploring tide pools, there isn't much to do here—which is just fine with me. This beach is ideal for anyone who just wants to relax without any distractions. Bring a few good books. The larger hotels here—**Antumalal, Iguanazul,** and **Villa Serena**—all offer plenty of activities and facilities, including volleyball, swimming pools, and/or tennis courts. At the Iguanazul, guests can rent bikes, which is a good way to get up and down to the beach; horseback-riding tours are also popular.

If you're a surfer, the beach break right in Junquillal is sometimes pretty good. I've also heard that if you look hard enough, there are a few hidden reef and point breaks around.

Several sportfishing boats operate out of Playa Junquillal. Inquire at your hotel, or ask for **Captain Gene,** who works out of the Iguanazul Hotel.

Finally, if you want to do some **diving,** check in with Micke and Maarten at **El Lugarcito** (© and fax **506/658-8442;** lugarcito@racsa.co.cr). These folks offer day trips to the Catalina Islands as well as resort and full-certification courses.

ACCOMMODATIONS & DINING

Most of the hotels listed below have their own restaurants. You can also get good Italian meals, homemade pasta, and fresh seafood at **La Puerta del Sol** (© **506/ 658-8442**), which is located right in front of the beach as you come into Junquillal.

EXPENSIVE

Hotel Antumalal ✯   Located at the end of the road into Playa Junquillal, the Antumalal is the oldest and most extensive hotel on the beach. Everything is well maintained. The big, old shade trees and lush gardens create a world of tropical tranquillity that's perfect for romance and relaxation. Guest rooms are all in duplex buildings with stucco walls on the outside and murals on the inside. Out front, you'll find a big patio with a hammock, while inside there are brick floors and big bathrooms. The suites are located in a large two-story building closer to the beach; each suite has a sitting room, kitchenette, and lots of space. Oddly, the views are best from those on the ground floor, at least until the many coconut palms grow a bit more. Right now, the second-floor balconies put you right at the level of the palm fronds, which largely block the view of the sea.

Playa Junquillal (A.P. 49-5150, Santa Cruz), Guanacaste. © and fax **506/658-8426,** or 506/ 281-2610. www.westnet.com/costarica/lodging/antumalal.html. 30 units. $95 double; $110 suite. AE, MC, V. **Amenities:** 1 restaurant (international/Italian/seafood); 2 bars; midsize swimming pool with swim-up bar; tennis court; horse rental; tour desk; laundry service. *In room:* No phone.

MODERATE

Hotel Villa Serena   Villa Serena is directly across the street from the beach and has long been a popular choice in Playa Junquillal. The hotel changed owners a couple of years ago and received a major refurbishing. Each of the individual bungalows is surrounded by neatly manicured lawns and gardens. The rooms are quite spacious and have ceiling fans, dressing rooms, and large bathrooms. Each has its own covered patio, and only steps away is the small pool. The second-floor Land Ho Restaurant, which serves filling and tasty continental and Tico dishes, has an enticing view of the sea.

Playa Junquillal (A.P. 37-5150, Santa Cruz), Guanacaste. © and fax **506/658-8430.** serenaho@ racsa.co.cr. 12 units. $70 double. Lower rates in the off-season. MC, V. **Amenities:** 1 restaurant (continental/Costa Rican); 1 bar; small pool; in-room massage; laundry service. *In room:* No phone.

Iguanazul Hotel ★ Set on a windswept, grassy bluff above a rocky beach, Iguanazul is far from the crowds. Originally catering to surfers, this is definitely a spot for sun worshippers who like to have a good time; the clientele tends to be young and active. The pool is large, as is the surrounding patio area, and there's a volleyball court. If you're feeling mellow, head down to one of the quiet coves or grab a hammock set in a covered palapa on the hillside. Guest rooms are spacious and nicely decorated with basket lampshades, wicker furniture, red-tile floors, high ceilings, and blue-and-white–tile bathrooms. The higher prices are for air-conditioned rooms, and two of these even have televisions. Even if you're not staying here, this is a good place to dine; the food is excellent and the sunset views ★★ are phenomenal.

Playa Junquillal (A.P. 130-1550, Santa Cruz), Guanacaste. ℂ and fax **506/658-8123,** or 506/658-8124. www.iguanazul.com. 24 units. $70–$90 double; $80–$100 triple. Rates include continental breakfast. AE, MC, V. **Amenities:** 1 recommended restaurant (international/seafood); 1 bar; large outdoor pool set on a high hill; water-sports-equipment rental; bike rental; horse rental; game room; tour desk; laundry service. *In room:* No phone.

INEXPENSIVE

In addition to the lodgings listed below, **Camping Los Malinches** (ℂ **506/658-8429**) has wonderful campsites on fluffy grass, amid manicured gardens, set on a bluff above the beach. Camping will run you $5 per person, and the fee entitles you to bathroom and shower privileges. You'll see a sign on the right as you drive toward Playa Junquillal, a little bit beyond the Iguanazul Hotel. The campground is located about half a mile (1km) down this dirt road.

Hibiscus Hotel *Value* Though the accommodations here are very simple, the friendly German owner makes sure that everything is always clean and in top shape. The grounds are pleasantly shady, and the beach is just across the road. The rooms have cool Mexican-tile floors and firm beds. For years now, I've been getting glowing reports about both the service and general ambiance. A restaurant has recently been added, specializing in fresh seafood at reasonable prices.

Playa Junquillal (A.P. 163-5150, Santa Cruz), Guanacaste. ℂ and fax **506/658-8437.** 5 units. $40 double; $50 triple. Rates include continental breakfast. V. **Amenities:** 1 restaurant (seafood/international); laundry service. *In room:* No phone.

Hotel El Castillo Divertido This fanciful hotel, built by a young German, is a tropical rendition of a classic medieval castle (well, sort of). Ramparts and a turret with a rooftop bar certainly grab the attention of passersby. Guest rooms here are fairly small, though rates are also some of the lowest in the area. Ask for an upstairs room with a balcony. If you don't get one of these, you'll still have a good view from the hotel's rooftop bar, which sometimes features live music. The hotel is about 500 meters (545 yd.) from the beach.

Playa Junquillal, Santa Cruz, Guanacaste. ℂ and fax **506/658-8428.** 7 units. $35 double. Lower rates in the off-season. AE, MC, V. **Amenities:** 1 restaurant (international); 1 bar. *In room:* No phone.

8 Playa Nosara ★★

34 miles (55km) SW of Nicoya; 165 miles (266km) W of San José

Playa Nosara is actually several beaches, almost all of which are nearly deserted most of the time. Because the village of Nosara is several kilometers from the beach, and because the land near the beach has been turned into a sprawling resort and residential community, Nosara has been spared the sort of ugly, uncontrolled growth characteristic of many other Guanacaste beaches. All of the hotels are small and spread out, with most tucked away down side roads. There's none of the hotels-piled-on-top-of-hotels feeling that you get at Playas Flamingo, Tamarindo, and Coco. In fact, on first arriving here, it's hard to believe there are any hotels around at all. Nosara has long been popular with North American retirees and a handful of Hollywood celebs, and they too have made sure that their homes are not crammed cheek-by-jowl in one spot, hiding them instead among the profusion of trees that make Nosara one of the greenest spots on the Nicoya Peninsula. So, if you're looking for reliably sunny weather and a bit of tropical greenery, this is a good bet.

The best way to get to Nosara is to fly, but, with everything so spread out, that makes getting around difficult once you've arrived. The roads to and in Nosara are in horrendous shape, and though there has long been talk of some sections being widened and paved, it will probably still be quite a few years before the blacktop reaches here.

ESSENTIALS
GETTING THERE & DEPARTING   By Plane   Sansa (© **506/221-9414;** reservations@flysansa.com) has one flight daily to Nosara, departing from San José's Juan Santamaría International Airport at 11:40am. The fare for the 50-minute flight is $66 each way. Taxis are waiting for every arrival; fares range between $4 and $7 to most hotels.

The return Sansa flight to San José departs Nosara daily at 12:30pm.

By Car   Follow the directions for getting to Playa Sámara (see section 9, later in this chapter), but watch for a well-marked fork in the road a few kilometers before you reach that beach. The right-hand fork leads, after another 13½ miles (22km) of terrible road, to Nosara.

By Bus   An express bus (© **506/222-2666**) leaves San José daily at 6am from Calle 14 between Avenidas 3 and 5. The trip's duration is 6½ hours; the one-way fare is $6.50.

You can also take a bus from San José to Nicoya (see section 9 of this chapter, on Playa Sámara, for details) and then catch a second bus from Nicoya to Nosara. Buses leave Nicoya for Nosara daily at 10am and 2pm. Trip duration is 3 hours; the one-way fare is $1.25.

The bus to San José leaves daily at 12:45pm. Buses to Nicoya leave Nosara daily at 6am and 12:15pm. Buses leave Nicoya for San José daily at 5, 7, and 9am, noon, and 2:30 and 5pm.

ORIENTATION   The village of Nosara is about 3 miles (5km) inland from the beach. The small airstrip ends practically in town; however, most of the hotels listed here are on, or near, the beach itself. You'll find the post office and police station right at the end of the airstrip. There's an Internet cafe right in the village, and another at Café de Paris (see below).

FUN ON & OFF THE BEACH
There are several beaches at Nosara, including the long, curving **Playa Guiones** ✺✺, **Playa Nosara** ✺, and, my personal favorite, diminutive **Playa Pelada** ✺✺. Pelada is a short white-sand beach with three deep scallops, backed by sea grasses and mangroves. There isn't too much sand at high tide, so you'll want to hit the beach when the tide's out. At either end of the beach there are rocky outcroppings that reveal tide pools at low tide. Surfing and bodysurfing are both good here, particularly at Playa Guiones, which is garnering quite a

reputation as a consistent and rideable beach break. Because the village of Nosara is several miles inland, these beaches are very clean, secluded, and quiet.

FISHING CHARTERS & OTHER OUTDOOR ACTIVITIES   Most of the hotels in the area can arrange fishing charters for $250 to $400 for a half day, or $450 to $950 for a full day. These rates are for one to four people and vary according to boat size and accoutrements. You can also contact **Grand Slam Charters** (ⓒ **506/682-0012**) or **Black Marlin Sportfishing** (ⓒ **506/682-0059;** www.blackmarlinfishing.com).

HORSEBACK RIDING   The folks at **Casa Rio Nosara Excursions** (ⓒ **506/682-0117**) have a large stable of well-cared-for horses and a range of beach, jungle, and waterfall rides to choose from. Rates run around $15–$20 per hour per person.

KAYAK TOURS   Based out of the Gilded Iguana restaurant, **Iguana Expeditions** ☆ (ⓒ and fax **506/682-0259;** www.nosara-costa-rica.com) offers a range of full- and half-day tours around the area. Explore the inland coastal mangroves, or combine some open-water paddling with a snorkel break at San Juanillo. A half-day tour with picnic lunch costs between $35–$40; full-day tours run between $60–$90. These folks can also arrange inexpensive fishing outings in a *panga,* or small craft, with a local fisherman.

BIRD & SEA TURTLE WATCHING   Bird watchers should explore the mangrove swamps around the estuary mouth of the Río Nosara. Just walk north from Playa Pelada and follow the riverbank; explore the paths into the mangroves.

If you time your trip right, you can do a night tour to nearby **Playa Ostional** to watch nesting Olive Ridley sea turtles. These turtles come ashore by the thousands in a mass egg-laying phenomenon known as an *arribada.* These arribadas take place 4 to 10 times between July and November; each occurrence lasts between 3 and 10 days. Consider yourself very lucky if you happen to be around during one of these fascinating natural phenomena. Even if it's not turtle-nesting season, you might still want to look into visiting Playa Ostional, just to have a long, wide expanse of beach to yourself. However, be careful swimming here, as the surf and riptides can be formidable. During the dry season (mid-Nov through Apr), you can usually get here in a regular car, but during the rainy season you'll need four-wheel-drive. This beach is part of Ostional National Wildlife Refuge. At the northwest end of the refuge is **India Point,** which is known for its tide pools and rocky outcrops.

The arribadas are so difficult to predict that no one runs regularly scheduled turtle-viewing trips, but when the arribada is in full swing, several local tour guides and agencies will offer tours. Your best bet is to ask the staff at your hotel, or check in with **Harbor Reef Lodge** (ⓒ **506/683-0059**) or **Iguana Expeditions** (ⓒ and fax **506/682-0259;** www.nosara-costa-rica.com).

ACCOMMODATIONS

Almost Paradise (Value)   Located on the hill above Playa Pelada, this delightful little hotel is aptly named. This older wood building is a welcome relief from all the concrete and cinder block so common in Costa Rican construction. The rooms are simple and clean and feature colorful local artwork. Most have some ocean view. My favorites are those just off the restaurant, which have access to a broad, inviting covered veranda with hammocks, sitting chairs, and a great view. These folks also rent a separate fully equipped apartment, which is great for longer stays.

Playa Nosara (A.P. 15-5233, Bocas de Nosara), Guanacaste. ℭ and fax **506/682-0173**. www. nosara.net. 9 units. $35–$45 double. Rates include breakfast. V (6% surcharge). **Amenities:** 1 restaurant (international); 1 bar; small lap pool; laundry service. *In room:* No phone.

Café de Paris ✶ Located on the main road into Nosara, where it branches off to Playa Guiones, this popular little bakery and restaurant has some equally popular rooms out back, set behind the restaurant and pool in a series of duplex buildings. About half have kitchenettes, and a few have air-conditioning. All have high ceilings and plenty of room. There are a few shady ranchos spread around the grounds. These folks also rent a couple of luxury villas atop a steep hill across the street.

Playa Nosara, Guanacaste. ℭ **506/682-0087**. Fax 506/682-0089. www.cafedeparis.net. 12 units. $39–$69 double. Rates include buffet breakfast. AE, MC, V. **Amenities:** 1 restaurant (bakery/bistro); 1 bar; small pool; game room; tour desk; laundry service. *In room:* No phone.

Harbor Reef Lodge ✶ The home base of Black Marlin Sportfishing, this place caters primarily to fishermen and surfers, with clean, spacious rooms close to the beach (about 200 yd. inland from Playa Guiones). Several of the units come with kitchenettes and separate sitting rooms. There's a cool, oasislike feel to the lush grounds.

Playa Nosara, Guanacaste. ℭ **506/683-0059**. Fax 506/682-0060. www.harborreef.com. 10 units. $49–$65 double; $75–$93 suite. AE, MC, V. **Amenities:** 1 restaurant (international); 1 bar; small pool; water-sports-equipment rental; tour desk; laundry service. *In room:* A/C, fridge; no phone.

Hotel Villa Taype This sprawling hotel is located down a side road that leads from the main road to Playa Guiones. The room decor is simple but attractive, with white-tile floors, high ceilings, overhead fans, and well-designed bathrooms. All the rooms have patios, but the bungalows are a little larger, and each has its own little *ranchito*, with a sitting area and hammock. Best of all, the beach is only about 100 yards away. During the high season, it even opens a small disco here, which can get quite lively.

Playa Nosara (A.P. 8-5233, Bocas de Nosara), Guanacaste. ℭ **506/682-0188**. Fax 506/682-0187. www.villataype.com. 12 units, 7 bungalows. $60 double; $80 bungalow. Rates include breakfast buffet. Lower rates in the off-season. AE, MC, V. **Amenities:** 1 restaurant (Costa Rican/International); 1 bar; midsize pool with a swim-up bar and children's pool; 1 outdoor tennis court; water-sports-equipment rental; game room; tour desk; free laundry service. *In room:* A/C.

Lagarta Lodge Located on a hillside high over the Nosara River, this small lodge is an excellent choice for bird watchers and other travelers more interested in the flora and fauna than the beach. The rooms are Spartan but acceptable. The lodge borders its own private reserve, which has trails along the riverbank and through the mangrove and tropical humid forests here. There are spectacular views from the restaurant and most rooms over the river and surrounding forest, with the beaches of Nosara and Ostional in the distance. You'll want to have your own vehicle if you're staying here, as the beach is a good 10- to 15-minute hike away, and it's uphill on the way back.

Playa Nosara (A.P. 18-5233), Guanacaste. ℭ **506/682-0035**. Fax 506/682-0135. www.lagarta. com. $60 double. Lower rates in the off-season. V. **Amenities:** 1 restaurant (international); 1 bar; midsize outdoor pool; tour desk; laundry service. *In room:* No phone.

Nosara Beach Hotel Perched high on a hill above both Playa Pelada and Playa Guiones, this hotel has the best views in the area, if not necessarily the best accommodations. In the 8 years I've been visiting, the place has always had the feeling of someone's unfinished backyard project, and it still does. There's a six-story tower with an onion-dome on top, looking something like "Gaudí Goes Russian Orthodox." While this is the best place to take in the amazing sunsets, it's not yet finished. However, the large kidney-shaped pool is finally open and work is actually nearing completion on most of the rooms and surrounding landscaping. Most of the rooms have balconies overlooking either Playa Guiones or Playa Pelada. They are simple and clean, and most are quite spacious. The restaurant holds a high perch over Playa Pelada and serves good cuisine.

Playa Nosara (A.P. 4, Bocas de Nosara), Guanacaste. © 506/682-0121. Fax 506/682-0123. www. nosarabeachhotel.com. 20 units. $30–$60 double. MC, V. **Amenities:** 1 restaurant (seafood/ continental); 1 bar; midsize outdoor pool; tour desk; laundry service. *In room:* No phone.

DINING & AFTER-DARK DIVERSIONS

In addition to the place mentioned below, I've been getting rave reviews of the Italian food at **La Dolce Vita** (© **506/682-0107**), located on the main road into town, about 1¼ miles (2km) before the BIENVENIDOS A PLAYAS DE NOSARA sign. When I last visited, **Marlin Bill's** (© **506/682-0458**) was setting up shop in a new and massive open-air haunt on a hillside on the main road, just across from Café de Paris. You can expect to get good, fresh seafood and American classics here.

When evening rolls around, don't expect a major party scene. Nightlife near the beach seems to center around the Café de Paris, Marlin Bill's, and the Gilded Iguana. In "downtown" Nosara, you'll probably want to check out either **Las Iguanas Locas,** a German-run restaurant/bar, or **Tropicana,** the town's disco. Both are on the streets fronting the soccer field.

Café de Paris ★ *Finds* BAKERY/BISTRO   This popular little place has wonderful fresh-baked goods and a wide assortment of light bites and full-on meals. You can get pizza or nachos or filling sandwiches on fresh baguettes. There are also hearty salads, as well as fish, meat, and chicken dishes. I enjoy stopping in for a cup of espresso and a fresh almond croissant. Sporting events or movie videos are shown nightly, and there's even a pool table and Internet cafe here.

On the main road into Nosara. © **506/682-0087**. Baked goods 50¢–$2, main courses $4–$11. AE, MC, V. Daily 7am–11pm.

Doña Olga's COSTA RICAN   Little more than a roof over a concrete slab, Olga's is still one of the most popular restaurants in Nosara. Gringos and Ticos alike hang out here, savoring fried-fish casados, sandwiches, and breakfasts that include huge helpings of bacon. On the weekends, the cavernous structure beside the restaurant becomes a lively disco.

On the beach at Playa Pelada. No phone. Main courses $3–$15. No credit cards. Daily 6:30am–10pm.

The Gilded Iguana ★ SEAFOOD/GRILL   This simple restaurant serves fish so fresh it's still wiggling, as the owner's husband is a local fisherman. There are also great burgers, Costa Rican casados, and a short list of nightly specials. If you're in town fishing yourself, they'll cook your catch. Sporting events are shown on a not-quite-big-enough television. Overall, the vibe is sociable and lively.

About 100 yd. inland from the beach at Playa Guiones. (C) **506/682-0259.** Main courses $5–$12. No credit cards. Tues–Sun 10am–10pm.

9 Playa Sámara ✦

21¹⁄₂ miles (35km) S of Nicoya; 152 miles (245km) W of San José

Playa Sámara is a pretty beach on a long, horseshoe-shaped bay. Unlike most of the rest of the Pacific coast, the water here is excellent for swimming, since an off-shore island and rocky headlands break up most of the surf. Because Playa Sámara is easily accessible along a well-paved road, and because there are quite a few cheap cabinas, *sodas,* and raging discos here, this beach is popular both with families seeking a quick and inexpensive getaway and with young Ticos out for a weekend of beach partying. Given this heavy traffic and party atmosphere, this wouldn't be my first choice for a relaxing beach getaway. Still, the calm waters and steep cliffs on the far side of the bay make this a very attractive spot, and the beach is long, wide and protected. Moreover, if you drive along the rugged coastal road in either direction, you'll come to some truly spectacular beaches.

ESSENTIALS

GETTING THERE & DEPARTING   By Plane   Sansa ((C) **506/221-9414;** reservations@flysansa.com) flies to Carillo (15 min. south of Sámara) daily at 7am and 11:40am from San José's Juan Santamaría International Airport. The flight stops first at either Punta Islita or Nosara and takes approximately 1 hour; the fare is $66 each way.

Travelair ((C) **506/220-3054;** reservations@travelair-costarica.com) flies to Carillo daily at 1pm from Tobías Bolaños International Airport in Pavas. The flight takes 40 minutes; the fare is $65 each way.

Most hotels will arrange to pick you up in Carillo. If not, you'll have to hire a cab for between $8 and $10.

Sansa flights leave Carillo for San José at 8:10am and 12:50pm. Travelair flies out of Carillo daily at 1:50pm.

By Car   Take the Interamerican Highway from San José. Twenty-nine miles (47km) past the turnoff for Puntarenas, turn left toward the Tempisque River. By press time or sometime during the 2002 season, a new bridge crossing the river should be operational. In the meantime, you may still have to use the **Tempisque River Ferry** ((C) **506/661-8105**). The ferry operates 24 hours a day (at approximately 20-min. intervals) and costs about $3 per car and driver, with a nominal 35¢ fee per passenger. The ferries that ply this crossing are quite small, and on busy days you may have to wait for several crossings before making it onboard. After crossing the Tempisque River, continue north to Nicoya. In Nicoya, head more or less straight through town until you see signs for Playa Sámara. From here it's a paved road almost all the way to the beach (rumor has it that the road is paved because an important government official has a beach house here). Alternatively, you can go via Liberia. This route is longer but comes in handy when the ferry is down or extremely busy.

By Bus   An express bus ((C) **506/222-2666**) leaves San José daily at 12:30pm from Calle 14 between Avenidas 3 and 5. The trip lasts 6 hours; the one-way fare is $6.

Alternatively, you can take a bus from this same San José station to Nicoya and then catch a second bus from Nicoya to Sámara. Buses leave San José for Nicoya daily at 6:30, 8, and 10am, and 1, 2, 3, and 5pm. The trip takes 5 hours;

the fare is $4. Buses leave Nicoya for Sámara and Carillo daily at 8 and 10am, noon, and 3 and 4:30pm. The trip's duration is 1½ hours. The fare to Sámara is $1.50; fare to Carillo is $1.75.

The express bus to San José leaves daily at 4:30am. Buses for Nicoya leave daily at 5:30, 6:30, 7 and 11:30am, and 1:30 and 4:30pm. Buses leave Nicoya for San José daily at 4, 5, 7, and 9:30am, noon, and 2:30 and 5pm.

ORIENTATION   Sámara is a busy little town at the bottom of a steep hill. The main road heads straight into town, passing the soccer field before coming to an end at the beach. Just before the beach is a road to the left that leads to most of the hotels listed below. This road also leads to Playa Carillo and Hotel Punta Islita.

FUN ON & OFF THE BEACH

Aside from sitting on the sand and soaking up the sun, the main activities in Playa Sámara seem to be hanging out in the bars and *sodas* and dancing into the early-morning hours. But if you're looking for something more, there's horseback riding, either on the beach or through the bordering pastureland and forests. Other options include sea kayaking in the calm waters off of Playa Sámara, sportfishing, snorkeling and scuba diving, boat tours, and tours to Playa Ostional to see the mass nestings of olive Ridley turtles. You can inquire about any of these tours at your hotel, or call **Sámara Adventures** (© **506/656-0655**).

The newest adventure available here is one of the popular zip-line and harness "canopy tours." The folks at **Wingnuts Canopy Tours** (© **506/656-0153**) offer a 2-hour outing for $40 per person. You'll find their office by the giant strangler fig tree, or *matapalo,* toward the southern end of the beach.

You'll find that the beach is nicer and cleaner down at the south-end hotel. Better yet, head about 8 kilometers (5 miles) south to **Playa Carillo** ⚘⚘ , a long crescent of soft white sand. There's almost no development here, so the beach is almost always deserted and there are loads of palm trees providing shade. If you've got a good four-wheel-drive vehicle, ask for directions at your hotel and set off in search of the hidden gems of **Playa Buena Vista** ⚘ and **Playa Barrigona** ⚘⚘ , which are north of Sámara, less than a half-hour drive away. A taxi to Playa Carillo should cost about $5 to $6 each way. Because it's a bit farther and the roads are a little rougher, expect to pay a little more to reach Playa Buena Vista, and even more for Playa Barrigona.

Cavers will want to head 38½ miles (62km) northeast of Playa Sámara on the road to the Tempisque ferry. If you don't have a car, your best bet is to get to Nicoya, which is about half an hour away by bus, and then take a taxi to the park, which should cost about $12. Here, at **Barra Honda National Park** ⚘ , there's an extensive system of caves, some of which reach more than 200 meters in depth. Human remains and indigenous relics have been found in other caves, but these are not open to the public. Since this is a national park, you'll have to pay the $6 entrance fee. If you plan to descend the one publicly accessible cave, you'll also need to rent (or bring your own) equipment and hire a local guide at the park entrance station. Expect to pay around $30 to $50 per person for a visit to the Terciopelo Cave, including the guide, harness, helmet, and flashlight. Furthermore, the cave is open only during the dry season (mid-Nov to Apr). Inside, you'll see plenty of impressive stalactites and stalagmites, while visiting several chambers of varying sizes. Even if you don't descend, the trails around Barra Honda and its prominent limestone plateau are great for hiking and bird watching. Camping is permitted for around $1.50 per person, and the simple *soda* here offers up filling, inexpensive meals.

ACCOMMODATIONS

EXPENSIVE

Hotel Isla Chora ✶   This mini-resort hotel is located a couple hundred yards north of town, but feels like a world apart. A half-dozen two-story buildings ring the free-form pool here. Rooms are spacious and clean. The bathrooms are comfortable and have lots of natural light. The suites are located on the second floor of each building, and are twice the size, with living rooms that contain two fold-out futon sofas and small kitchenettes. The nicest feature of these rooms is the wraparound balcony. While the facilities and amenities here are acceptable, I don't think they justify the prices.

Playa Sámara, Guanacaste. ② **506/656-0174.** Fax 506/656-0173. hechombo@racsa.co.cr. 14 units. $100–$120 double; $180 suite. Rates include continental breakfast. AE, MC, V. **Amenities:** 1 restaurant (Italian/Costa Rican); 1 bar; disco; midsize outdoor pool; tour desk; laundry service. *In room:* A/C, safe; no phone.

Villas Playa Sámara   Located 5 minutes south of town, right on the beach, this place has the nicest setting and grounds around Playa Sámara, if not the best facilities. Built to resemble a small village, the hotel consists of numerous villas varying in size from one to three bedrooms. The spacious rooms are outfitted with bamboo furniture and have tiled bathrooms. All the villas have kitchens and patios, and are finished with colorful bedspreads and artwork, basket lampshades, and vertical blinds on the windows. White-stucco exterior walls and red-tile roofs give the whole thing a Mediterranean look. However, the upkeep and maintenance have been spotty, and service can be downright bad.

Playa Sámara (A.P. 111-1007, Centro Colón, San José), Guanacaste. ② **506/656-0100.** Fax 506/ 656-0109. htlvilla@racsa.co.cr. 57 units. $169 double; $240–$350 2- to 3-room villa. Lower rates in the off-season. AE, MC, V. **Amenities:** 1 restaurant (international/Costa Rican); 1 bar; midsize outdoor pool; exercise room; Jacuzzi; bike rental; tour desk; laundry service. *In room:* Kitchenette; no phone.

MODERATE

Hotel Las Brisas del Pacífico ✶   Located on the southern end of Playa Sámara, this hotel is set amid very shady grounds right on a quiet section of the beach, and backs up on a steep hill. Most of the rooms are found in the three-story building, up a long and steep flight of stairs at the top of the hill. These have comfortable balconies and walls of glass that provide an excellent view of the bay. The third-floor rooms are the largest here, but the second-floor rooms actually have the best views. At the base of the hill, there are rooms in stucco duplexes with steeply pitched tile roofs and red-tile patios. The range in prices reflects the range in room size, location, and amenities. Some of the rooms have air-conditioning. Depending on the season and demand, either one or both of the restaurants here will be open. Regardless, you'll find excellent fresh seafood and perfectly prepared Italian pastas and entrees.

Playa Sámara (A.P. 11917-1000, San José), Guanacaste. ② **506/656-0250.** Fax 506/656-0076. www.brisas.net. 34 units. $55–$115 double. Lower rates in the off-season, higher rates during peak weeks. AE, MC, V. **Amenities:** 2 restaurants (international; seafood/Italian); 2 bars; 2 midsize outdoor pools; 2 unheated Jacuzzis; limited water-sports-equipment rental; tour desk; massage; laundry service. *In room:* Safe; no phone.

INEXPENSIVE

You'll find a slew of very inexpensive places to stay along the road into town and around the soccer field. Many of the rooms at these places are less accommodating than your average jail cell. As an alternative, you can pitch a tent right by the beach for a few dollars at **Camping Cocos,** which has basic showers and bathrooms. You'll find Camping Cocos about 400 meters north of the center of town. It can be reached from the beach or from the beach-access road beside Hotel Isla Chora.

Casa del Mar   Located on the inland side of the beach-access road, 1 block south of "downtown," Casa del Mar is just 50 meters from the beach. The rooms here are immaculate, and most of them are quite spacious. Despite the fact that the postage-stamp-sized plunge pool is barely large enough for two adults, the place feels like a cool oasis from the harsh Guanacaste sun, with its shady central courtyard and open-air restaurant. While the units with shared bathrooms are the best bargains here, I'd opt for a second-floor room with a private bathroom. Several rooms come with air-conditioning, and a few even have small fridges.

Playa Sámara, Nicoya, Guanacaste. ✆ **506/656-0264.** Fax 506/656-0129. www. casadelmarsamara.com. 11 units, 6 with shared bathroom. $35–$50 double. Rates include continental breakfast. Lower rates in the off-season. AE, MC, V. **Amenities:** 1 restaurant (Costa Rican/international); 1 bar; tiny pool; tour desk; laundry service. *In room:* No phone.

Casa Valeria   This is the best beachfront super-budget option in town. The rooms are quite basic, and much more rustic than those at either Giada or Casa del Mar, but they are just steps away from the sand and surf. The best bets here are the four individual bungalows. There's a basic restaurant, as well as some tables, chairs, and hammocks set in the shade of some tall coconut palms. This place is popular with European backpackers, and there's a hostel feel to the whole operation.

Playa Sámara, Nicoya, Guanacaste. ✆ **506/656-0511.** Fax 506/656-0317. 9 units. $20–$30 double. Rates include breakfast. No credit cards. **Amenities:** 1 restaurant (Costa Rican/seafood). *In room:* No phone.

Hotel Giada *Value*   This neat little Italian-owned hotel is located on the left-hand side of the main road into town, about 150 meters before the beach. The rooms are all very clean and comfortable and even have a small balcony. Breakfast is served in a cool, shady central gazebo. The management is very helpful and can arrange diving or fishing expeditions and horseback-riding trips.

Playa Sámara, Nicoya, Guanacaste. ✆ **506/656-0132.** Fax 506/656-0131. www.hotelgiada.net. 13 units. $38–$44 double; $48–$50 triple; $56–$60 quad. Rates include breakfast. AE, MC, V. **Amenities:** 1 restaurant (pizza); 1 bar; small pool; tour desk; laundry service. *In room:* No phone.

A NEARBY LUXURY HOTEL

Hotel Punta Islita ★★★ *Finds*   This is one of the most exclusive and romantic small luxury resorts in Costa Rica. It's isolated on a high bluff between two mountain ridges that meet the sea. The rooms here are done in a Santa Fe style, with red Mexican floor tiles, neo-Navajo-print bedspreads, and adobe-colored walls offset with sky-blue doors and trim. Each room has a king-size bed and a private patio with a hammock. The suites come with a separate sitting room and a private two-person plunge pool; the villas have two or three bedrooms, their own private swimming pools, and full kitchens.

The beach below the hotel is a small crescent of gray-white sand with a calm, protected section at the northern end. It's about a 10-minute hike, but the hotel will shuttle you up and back if you don't feel like walking. You can take the hotel's small "canopy tour," which leaves from just below the small exercise room and ends just steps from the beach. There's a rancho bar and grill down there for when you get hungry or thirsty.

Although it's possible to drive here, most guests opt to fly into the nearby airstrip. Punta Islita is just two beaches south of Sámara, but if you do drive, it's best to come over on the Naranjo ferry from Puntarenas and then up through Jicarral and Coyote.

Playa Islita (A.P. 242-1225, Plaza Mayor, San José), Guanacaste. ✆ 800/525-4800 in the U.S., or 506/231-6122 in Costa Rica. Fax 506/231-0715. www.hotelpuntaislita.com. 37 units, 3 villas. $180 double; $245 junior suite, $300–$350 suite; $400–$600 villa. Rates include breakfast. AE, MC, V. **Amenities:** 2 restaurants (international/beachfront grill); 1 bar; small tile pool set on the edge of the bluff; 2 tennis courts; driving range; small exercise room; Jacuzzi; water-sports equipment, bicycle, horse and 4-by-4 rentals; game room; free beach shuttle; tour desk; in-room massage; spa treatments; laundry service. *In room:* A/C, TV, minibar, fridge, hair dryer; no phone.

DINING & AFTER-DARK DIVERSIONS

There are numerous inexpensive *sodas* in Sámara, and most of the hotels have their own dining rooms. If you want to eat overlooking the water, check out either **El Ancla** or **El Delfin**, for seafood and Tico cuisine. These two places are right next to each other on the beach, a little bit to the left (or south) of where the main road dead-ends at the beach. On the main road into town about 100 meters before the beach, you'll find the **Sandwicheria** (no phone), a simple kiosk serving hearty sandwiches on fresh baguette bread, bagels, or croissants, as well as hamburgers, hot dogs, and fresh pastries.

After dark, the most happening place in town is **La Gondola Bar,** which has a pool table, dartboards, and board games. **Hotel Isla Chora** also has a popular bar and disco, but I prefer the slightly funkier atmosphere at **El Lagarto,** a beachfront bar and disco, just beyond Isla Chora. Still, my favorite evening activity is walking the long, wide expanse of beach and watching the stars.

Las Brasas ★ *Finds* SPANISH/SEAFOOD This two-story, open-air affair serves authentic Spanish cuisine and well-prepared fresh seafood. The whole fish à la Catalana is excellent, as is the paella, but my favorite dish here is the gazpacho Ándaluz, a refreshing lunch choice on a hot afternoon. There's a good selection of Spanish wines here, a rarity in Costa Rica. Service is attentive, yet informal.

On the main road into Sámara, about 100 yd. before the beach. ✆ 506/656-0546. Reservations recommended in the high season. Main courses $7–$18. V. Daily noon–11pm. Closed Mon in low season.

10 Playa Tambor

93–104 miles (150–168km) W of San José (not including ferry ride); 12¹⁄₂ miles (20km) S of Paquera; 23¹⁄₂ miles (38km) S of Naranjo

Playa Tambor itself is a long scimitar of beach protected on either end by rocky headlands. These headlands give the waters a certain amount of protection from Pacific swells, making this a good beach for swimming. However, the sand is a rather hard-packed, dull gray-brown color, which often receives a large amount of flotsam and jetsam brought in by the sea. I find this beach much less attractive than those located farther south along the Nicoya Peninsula. There has been a bit of development here, with Costa Rica's first all-inclusive beach resort, the Barceló Playa Tambor Beach Resort, opening in 1993, followed by a condominium project and a nine-hole golf course. But despite this development, the Tambor still has a forgotten, isolated feel.

All the hotels listed below offer horseback riding and tours around this part of the peninsula and can arrange dive trips.

Curú Wildlife Refuge ⭑, 10 miles (16km) north of Tambor (☏ **506/ 661-2392**), is a private reserve that has several pretty, secluded beaches, as well as forests and mangrove swamps. This area is extremely rich in wildlife. Howler and white-faced monkeys are often spotted here, as are quite a few species of birds. Admission for the day is $10 per person. Camping is also permitted for a nominal fee, and there are some very rustic cabins available with advance notice for around $25. If you don't have a car, you should arrange pickup with the folks who manage this refuge. Or you could hire a taxi in Paquera to take you there for around $7.

ESSENTIALS

GETTING THERE & DEPARTING   By Plane   Sansa (☏ **506/221-9414;** reservations@flysansa.com) flies twice daily to Tambor from San José's Juan Santamaría International Airport at 10am and 3:45pm. These flights depart for San José at 10:40am and 4:25pm. Flight duration is 30 minutes; the fare is $55 each way.

Travelair (☏ **506/220-3054;** reservations@travelair-costarica.com) flies to Tambor daily at 11:30am from Tobías Bolaños International Airport in Pavas. Flight duration is 30 minutes; the fare is $50 each way. The return flight leaves at 12:10pm.

By Car   Take the Interamerican Highway from San José to Puntarenas and catch either the Naranjo ferry or the Paquera ferry.

In 1998, a new company was given permission to operate a car ferry between Puntarenas and Paquera, easing some of the load on this popular route. Lines and waits are much shorter now, but I still recommend arriving a little bit early during the peak season and on weekends. **Ferries to Paquera** (Naviera Tambor: ☏ **506/661-2084;** Paquera Ferry: ☏ **506/661-3674**) leave daily at 5 and 8:45am and 12:30, 2, 5, and 8:15pm. The trip takes 1½ hours. The fare is around $10 for a car and driver; $1.50 for additional adults, $4 for adults in first class; $1 for children, and $2 for children in first class.

The **Naranjo ferry** (☏ **506/661-1069**) leaves daily at 3, 7, and 10:50am, and 2:50 and 7pm. The trip takes 1½ hours. The fare is $10 for cars, $1.50 for adults, and 75¢ for children.

The car ferry from Paquera to Puntarenas leaves daily at 6, 8, and 11:45am, and 2:30, 6, and 8:30pm. The car ferry from Naranjo leaves at 5:10 and 8:50am and 12:50, 5, and 9pm.

Tambor is about 45 minutes south of Paquera and 2 hours south of Naranjo. The road from Paquera to Tambor was upgraded when the resort was built, and taking the Paquera ferry will save you time and some rough, dusty driving. The road from Naranjo to Paquera is all dirt and gravel and in very bad shape.

By Bus & Ferry   If you're traveling from San José by public transportation, it takes two buses and a ferry ride to get to Tambor. If you miss your connections, you might have to spend the night in Puntarenas, so plan ahead and give yourself plenty of time.

Express buses (☏ **506/222-0064**) leave for Puntarenas from San José daily every 30 minutes between 6am and 9pm from Calle 16 and Avenida 12. Trip duration is 2 hours; the fare is $2.50.

From Puntarenas, take the passenger launch **Paquereña** (☏ **506/661-2830**), which leaves from the pier behind the market at 6 and 11am, and 3pm. This passenger launch (*la lancha*) should not be confused with the several car ferries that also leave from Puntarenas, and you should always check the schedule before making plans. Ferry-trip duration is 1½ hours; the fare is $2. The bus south to Montezuma (this will drop you off in Tambor) will be waiting to meet the lancha when it arrives in Paquera. The bus ride takes about 45 minutes; the fare is $2.

When you're ready to head back, the Paquera bus, which originates in Montezuma, passes through Tambor at approximately 6 and 10:45am, and 2:45pm to meet the Paquereña ferry, which leaves for Puntarenas at 8am, and 12:30 and 5pm. Total trip duration is 3½ hours. Buses to San José leave Puntarenas daily every 30 minutes between 5:30am and 7pm.

ORIENTATION   Though there's a small village of Tambor, through which the main road passes, the hotels themselves are scattered along several kilometers. You'll see signs for these hotels as the road circles around Playa Tambor.

ACCOMMODATIONS

Aside from the hotels listed here, there are a few inexpensive cabinas available near the town of Tambor, at the southern end of the beach. Your two best bets are **Cabinas El Bosque** (© 506/683-0039) on the main road, and **Hotel Dos Largatos** (© and fax **506/683-0236**), on the beach next to Tambor Tropical.

The **Barceló Playa Tambor Beach Resort** was Costa Rica's first all-inclusive resort, but its beach is mediocre at best, and the Barceló company has been accused of violating Costa Rica's environmental laws, ignoring zoning regulations, and mistreating workers. So while this resort is a major presence here, I don't recommend it.

Tambor Tropical ⚡   This is one of the more architecturally interesting hotels around. The rooms here are located in five two-story octagonal cabins, and the whole place is an orgy of varnished hardwoods, with purpleheart and cocobolo offsetting each other at every turn. The rooms are enormous and come with large, complete kitchens and a spacious sitting area. The walls are in effect nothing but shuttered picture windows, which give you the choice of gazing out at the ocean or shutting in for a bit of privacy. The upstairs rooms have large wraparound verandas, while the lower rooms have garden-level decks. The beach is only steps away. Plenty of coconut palms and flowering plants provide a very tropical feel.

Tambor, Puntarenas (mailing address in the U.S.: P.O. Box 12945, Salem, OR 97309). © 506/683-0011. Fax 506/683-0013. www.tambortropical.com. 10 units. $125–$150 double. Rates include breakfast. AE, MC, V. No children under 16. **Amenities:** 1 restaurant (seafood/international); 1 bar; a small free-form tile pool and Jacuzzi; tour desk; laundry service. *In room:* Kitchenette, fridge; no phone.

Tango Mar Resort ⚡   Before the Playa Tambor Beach Resort was built, Tango Mar was *the* luxury resort in this neck of the woods. Today, it's still a great place to get away from it all. With only 18 rooms and scattered suites and villas, there are never any crowds. The water is wonderfully clear, and the beach is fronted by coconut palms and luxuriant lawns. If you choose to go exploring, you'll find seaside cliffs and a beautiful nearby waterfall that pours into a tide pool. The hotel rooms all have big balconies and glass walls to soak up the ocean views; some even have their own Jacuzzis. The suites are set back among shade trees and flowering vegetation. Most come with carved four-poster canopy beds and indoor Jacuzzis. The villas are all different, but all are spacious and relatively secluded. Some of the suites and villas are a bit far from the beach and main hotel, so you'll either need your own car or one of the hotel's gas-powered golf carts. The suites closest to the beach are the five octagonal Tiki suites.

Playa Tambor, Puntarenas (mailing address in the U.S.: SJO 684, Box 025216, Miami, FL 33102). ℂ **506/683-0001**. Fax 506/683-0003. www.tangomar.com. 18 units, 17 suites, 4 villas. $165 double; $165–$210 suite; $350–$1,150 villa. Rates include breakfast. AE, DC, MC, V. **Amenities:** 1 restaurant (international); 1 bar; 2 small swimming pools; 9-hole par-3 golf course ($30 greens fee) with wonderful sea views; 2 lighted tennis courts; limited water-sports-equipment rental; bike rental; tour desk; limited room service; in-room massage; laundry service. *In room:* A/C, TV, minibar, safe.

11 Playa Montezuma ★★

103–114 miles (166–184km) W of San José (not including the ferry ride); 22½ miles (36km) SE of Paquera; 33½ miles (54km) S of Naranjo

For years, Montezuma has enjoyed near-legendary status among backpackers, UFO seekers, hippie expatriates, and European budget travelers. This fame and tourist traffic have taken their toll. The haphazard collection of budget lodgings that sprung up were generally pretty ratty; long-term campers were trashing the beach; and Montezuma earned a reputation for noise, sewage, and drug problems. In recent years, local businesspeople and hotel owners have joined together and addressed most of these issues. Now the town has a well-tended feel, and there are lodgings of value and quality in all price ranges. The local community even passed an ordinance shutting down all loud discos in the town center, so it's now possible to get a good night's sleep as well.

Still, it's the natural beauty, miles of almost abandoned beaches, rich wildlife, and jungle waterfalls that first made Montezuma famous, and they continue to make this one of my favorite beach towns in Costa Rica.

ESSENTIALS

GETTING THERE & DEPARTING   By Plane   The nearest airport is in Tambor, 10½ miles (17km) away. See section 10 of this chapter for flight details. Some of the hotels listed below may be willing to pick you up in Tambor for a reasonable fee. If not, you'll have to hire a taxi, which could cost anywhere between $10 and $20. **Taxis** are generally waiting to meet most regularly scheduled planes, but if they aren't, you can call Gilberto Rodríguez (ℂ **506/642-0241**) for a cab. Budget travelers can walk the 50 meters (55 yd.) out to the main road and hitchhike or flag down the next bus.

By Car   Take the Interamerican Highway from San José to Puntarenas and catch either the Naranjo ferry or the Paquera ferry. The Paquera ferry will save you a lot of time and a lot of driving on the rough road from Naranjo to Paquera.

In 1998, a new company was given permission to operate a car ferry between Puntarenas and Paquera, easing some of the load on this popular route. Lines and waits are much shorter now, but I still recommend arriving a little bit early during the peak season and on weekends. **Ferries to Paquera** (Naviera Tambor: ℂ **506/661-2084;** Paquera Ferry: ℂ **506/661-3674**) leave daily at 5 and 8:45am, and 12:30, 2, 5, and 8:15pm. The trip takes 1½ hours. The fare is around $10 for a car and driver; $1.50 for additional adults, $4 for adults in first class; $1 for children, and $2 for children in first class.

The **Naranjo ferry** (ℂ **506/661-1069**) leaves daily at 3, 7, and 10:50am, and 2:50 and 7pm. The trip takes 1½ hours. The fare is $10 for cars, $1.50 for adults, and 75¢ for children.

The car ferry from Paquera to Puntarenas leaves daily at 6, 8, and 11:45am, and 2:30, 6, and 8:30pm. The car ferry from Naranjo leaves at 5:10 and 8:50am, and 12:50, 5, and 9pm.

Montezuma is about 1½ hours south of Paquera and 2¾ hours south of Naranjo. The road from Paquera to Tambor has been upgraded with the arrival of the resort hotel. Beyond Tambor, it's approximately another 50 minutes to Montezuma.

By Bus & Ferry   If you're traveling from San José by public transportation, it takes two buses and a ferry ride to get to Montezuma. If you miss your connections, you might have to spend the night in Puntarenas, so plan ahead and give yourself plenty of time.

Express buses (℡ **506/222-0064**) leave for Puntarenas from San José daily every 30 minutes between 6am and 9pm from Calle 16 and Avenida 12. Trip duration is 2 hours; the fare is $2.50.

From Puntarenas, take the passenger launch **Paquereña** (℡ **506/661-2830**), which leaves from the pier behind the market at 6 and 11am, and 3pm. This passenger launch should not be confused with the several car ferries that also leave from Puntarenas, and you should always check the schedule before making plans. Ferry-trip duration is 1½ hours; the fare is $2. The bus south to Montezuma will be waiting to meet the launch when it arrives in Paquera. The bus ride takes 1½ hours; the fare is $3.

When you're ready to return, the bus for Paquera leaves Montezuma daily at 5am and 10am, and 2pm and meets the Paquereña ferry, which leaves for Puntarenas at 8am, and 12:30 and 5pm. Buses to San José leave Puntarenas daily every 30 minutes between 5:30am and 7pm.

Buses these days are met by hordes of locals trying to corral you to one of the many budget hotels. Remember, they are getting a small commission for every body they bring in, so their information is biased.

ORIENTATION   As the winding mountain road that descends into Montezuma bottoms out, you turn left onto a small dirt road that defines the village proper. On this 1-block road, you will find the Sano Banano restaurant, and across from it a small park with its own brand-new basketball court. The bus stops at the end of this road. From here, hotels are scattered up and down the beach and around the village's few sand streets.

FUN ON & OFF THE BEACH

In Montezuma, mostly you just hang out at the beach, a restaurant, a bar, or in a hammock. The ocean here is a gorgeous royal blue, and beautiful beaches stretch out along the coast on either side of town. Be careful, though: The waves can occasionally be too rough for casual swimming, and you need to be aware of stray rocks at your feet. Be sure you know where the rocks and tide are before doing any bodysurfing. The best places to swim are a couple hundred yards north of town in front of the Soda Momaya, or several kilometers farther north at Playa Grande.

> **Buy the Book . . . or Just Borrow It**
>
> If you came unprepared, or run out of reading material, check in at **Libreria Topsy** (℡ **506/642-0576**), which, in addition to selling books, also runs a lending library.

If you're interested in more than just hanging out, head for the waterfall just south of town—it's one of those tropical fantasies where water comes pouring down into a deep pool. It's a popular spot, but it's a bit of a hike up the stream. There are actually a couple of waterfalls up this stream, but the upper falls are by far the more spectacular. You'll find the trail to the falls just over the bridge south of the village (on your right just past Las Cascadas restaurant). At the first major outcropping of rocks, the trail disappears, and you have to scramble up the rocks and river for a bit. A trail occasionally reappears for short stretches. Just stick close to the stream, and you'll eventually hit the falls.

HORSEBACK RIDING   Several people around the village will rent you horses for around $7 to $10 an hour, though most people choose to do a guided 4-hour horseback tour for $30 to $40. The longer rides usually go to a second waterfall 5 miles (8km) north of Montezuma. This waterfall cascades straight down into a deep tide pool at the edge of the ocean. The pool here is a delightful mix of fresh- and seawater, and you can bathe while gazing out over the sea and rocky coastline. When the water is clear and calm, this is one of my favorite swimming holes in all of Costa Rica. However, the pool here is dependent upon the tides—it disappears entirely at very high tide. You can also ride a horse to Cabo Blanco (see below). Luis, whose rental place is down the road that leads from town out to the beach, is a reliable source for horses, as is "Roger the horse guy"—any local can direct you to him. However, you'll find the best-cared-for and -kept horses at **Finca Los Caballos** (℘ (℗ 506/642-0124), which is located up the hill on the road leading into Montezuma.

OTHER ACTIVITIES   There are some rental shops in the center of the village where you can rent a bicycle by the day or hour, as well as boogie boards and snorkeling equipment (although the water must be very calm for snorkeling).

Your best one-stop resource is **Aventuras en Montezuma** (℗ and fax **506/642-0050**), which functions as a tour and information clearinghouse. Located next to El Sano Banano restaurant, Aventuras en Montezuma can arrange boat tours and rafting trips; car and motorcycle rentals; airport transfers; international phone, fax, and Internet service; and currency exchange. However, since this is pretty much the only game in town, the service can be gruff and indifferent.

Montezuma Expeditions/Cabo Blanco Divers (℗ and fax **506/642-0467**) has set up shop across the street from Chico's Bar and offers most of the same tours as Aventuras, as well as diving trips and certification classes. One of the more popular excursions is a day trip to Tortuga Island ($40, including lunch). Most hotels can also arrange most of these tours and services.

AN EXCURSION TO CABO BLANCO NATURE RESERVE

As beautiful as the beaches around Montezuma are, the beaches at **Cabo Blanco Absolute Nature Reserve** ℘℘, 6¾ miles (11km) south of the village, are even more stunning. Located at the southernmost tip of the Nicoya Peninsula, Cabo Blanco is a national park that preserves a nesting site for brown pelicans, magnificent frigate birds, and brown boobies. The beaches are backed by lush tropical forest that is home to howler monkeys. You can hike through the preserve's lush forest right down to the deserted, pristine beach. This is Costa Rica's oldest official bioreserve and was set up thanks to the pioneering efforts of conservationists Karen Mogensen and Nicholas Wessberg. Admission is $6; the reserve is closed on Monday and Tuesday.

On your way out to Cabo Blanco, you'll pass through the tiny village of **Cabuya.** Some very basic cabinas and hotels have sprung up out here. There are nice deserted stretches of beach and very few travelers.

There are usually shared taxis heading out this way from Montezuma in the morning. The fare is around $4 per person. Taxis here are generally red four-by-fours, clearly marked. They tend to hang around Montezuma center. Some enterprising locals also function as pirate taxis. The general rule is, "Don't call us, we'll find you." However, the most dependable *taxista* is **Gilberto Rodríguez** (© **506/642-0241**).

ACCOMMODATIONS

In addition to the places listed below, **Horizontes de Montezuma** (© and fax **506/642-0534;** www.horizontes-montezuma.com) is a new hotel up on the hill above the beach.

Now that camping on the beach is discouraged (although many folks still get away with it), most campers make do at **El Rincón de Los Monos** (© **506/ 642-0048**), which is about 100 yards north of town along the beach at the Soda Momaya. They charge about $3 per tent, and provide showers and bathrooms. Others head south toward Cabuya and Cabo Blanco. Finally, I've been getting good reports about **El Pargo Feliz** (© **506/642-0064**), a new budget option right in town.

MODERATE

Amor de Mar ★ *(Finds)* It would be difficult to imagine a more idyllic spot in this price range—or in *any* price range. With its wide expanse of neatly trimmed grass sloping down to the sea, tide pools (one of which is as big as a small swimming pool), and hammocks slung from the mango trees, this is the perfect place for anyone who wants to do some serious relaxing. The rooms are all housed in a beautifully appointed two-story building, which abounds in varnished hardwoods. Most of the rooms have plenty of space and receive lots of sunlight. The big porch on the second floor is a great place for reading or just gazing out to sea. Only breakfast is served here, but it's served all day; the specialties include big banana pancakes and fresh homemade whole-wheat French bread.

Montezuma, Cóbano de Puntarenas. © and fax **506/642-0262**. shoebox@racsa.co.cr. 11 units, 9 with private bathroom. $35–40 double with shared bathroom, $50–$75 double or triple with private bathroom. Slightly lower rates in the off-season. V (7% surcharge). **Amenities:** 1 restaurant (breakfast only); laundry service. *In room:* No phone.

El Sano Banano ★★ *(Finds)* El Sano Banano is the sort of tropical retreat many travelers dream about finding. If you walk down the beach (toward your left as you face the water), after about 15 minutes you'll find it on the left. From the front porch of your cabin you can sit and listen to the waves crashing on the beach a few feet away. (Please don't try to drive up the beach, even if you have a four-wheel-drive vehicle—seclusion and quiet are the main offerings of this place, and cars would ruin the atmosphere. If you don't want to carry all your bags, the hotel will be pleased to bring them to your room.)

The choice accommodations here are the individual cabins. Most are white ferroconcrete geodesic domes that look like igloos; there's also one octagonal, hardwood Polynesian-style bungalow. Most of the showers are outdoor garden affairs, which match the surroundings perfectly. There are also two hostel-style rooms, three standard rooms, and one large apartment in a separate building. Most of the rooms have refrigerators, coffee makers, and hot plates, enticing many guests to opt for extended stays. There's a beautiful little swimming pool with a sculpted waterfall, and the whole operation is set amid lush gardens planted with lots of banana, heliconia, and elephant-ear plants. When I last visited, they were planning on opening up a few rooms either alongside or above their popular in-town restaurant.

Montezuma, Cóbano de Puntarenas. © and fax **506/642-0068**, or © 506/642-0638. www.elbanano.com. 6 units, 8 bungalows, 1 apt. $65 double; $80 bungalow; $120 apt. Lower rates in the off-season. AE, MC, V. **Amenities:** 1 restaurant (international/vegetarian), though it's in town, about a 15-min.walk away); tour desk; in-room massage; laundry service. *In room:* Safe; no phone.

Nature Lodge Finca Los Caballos ⭐   This remote lodge is located on a high ridge about 1¾ miles (3km) above Montezuma. The rooms are in two separate concrete-block buildings. Each room has either one double or one double and one single bed, a private bathroom, and polished cement floors. Spanish-style tile roofs, hardwood trim, and some nice paintings add accents. I prefer the end rooms of each building, as they have open gables (screened, of course) that allow for more cross ventilation. Every room has a small patio, and there are plenty of hammocks strung around. There's a small pool here, with a wonderful view of rolling hills down to the Pacific Ocean. The restaurant serves creative, well-prepared meals using fresh and natural ingredients.

Finca Los Caballos translates to "horse ranch," and riding is taken seriously here. The owners have 40 acres of land and access to many neighboring ranches and trail systems. The horses are well tended and trained. The standard trips to Montezuma's waterfalls are available, as well as a host of other adventure-tour options.

Cóbano de Puntarenas (A.P. 22). ✆ and fax **506/642-0124.** www.naturelodge.net. 8 units, 1 apt. $50–$65 double. No credit cards. **Amenities:** 1 restaurant (international); small pool; horse rental and tours; tour desk; laundry service. *In room:* No phone.

INEXPENSIVE

Hotel La Aurora   Just to the left as you enter the village of Montezuma, you'll see this large, white house. The rooms are spread around the spacious three-story building, which also features a small library of books, some hammocks and comfortable chairs, and flowering vines growing up the walls. In fact, there are plants and vines all over La Aurora, which give it a tropical yet Gothic feel. Most rooms are of average size and have wooden walls that don't go all the way to the ceiling, which improves air circulation but reduces privacy. There are two rooms on the third floor with balconies and an ocean view over the treetops. Fresh coffee, tea, and hearty breakfasts are served each morning, and there are communal refrigerators located on each floor, as well as a kitchen available for guests' use.

Montezuma (A.P. 2), Cóbano de Puntarenas. ✆ and fax **506/642-0051.** www.auroroa-costa-rica. com. 16 units. $12–$22 double with shared bath, $25–$50 double with bathroom. Lower rates in the off-season. AE, MC, V. **Amenities:** Laundry service. *In room:* No phone.

Hotel Lucy (Value)   Situated on a pretty section of beach a bit south of town, in front of Los Mangos, this converted two-story home has the best location of any budget lodging in Montezuma. If you can snag a second-floor room with an ocean view, you'll be in budget heaven. The beach here is a bit rough and rocky for swimming, but the sunbathing and sunsets are beautiful. There's a small restaurant here serving Tico standards and fresh seafood at very reasonable prices all day long.

Montezuma, Cóbano de Puntarenas. ✆ **506/642-0273.** 10 units, all with shared bathroom. $10 double; $15 triple. No credit cards. **Amenities:** 1 restaurant (Costa Rican/seafood); laundry service. *In room:* No phone.

Los Mangos   Situated across the road from the water a bit before the waterfall on the road out toward Cabo Blanco, this place takes its name from the many mango trees under which the bungalows are built. (If mango is your passion, come in May, when they're in season.) The rooms are fairly basic, and those in the older building close to the road are a good value. However, the octagonal bungalows built of Costa Rican hardwoods are the nicest accommodations here. Each has a small porch with rocking chairs, a thatched roof, a good amount of space, and ceiling fans. The swimming pool is built to resemble a natural pond—there's even an artificial waterfall flowing into it—and there's a separate Jacuzzi.

Montezuma, Cóbano de Puntarenas. ℂ **506/642-0076.** Fax 506/642-0259. www. losmangoshotel.com. 10 units, 6 with private bathroom; 10 bungalows. $30 double without bathroom; $55 double with bathroom; $70 bungalow. Lower rates in the off-season. V. **Amenities:** 1 bar; small pool; Jacuzzi; laundry service. *In room:* No phone.

DINING

In addition to the places listed below, you'll find several basic *sodas* and casual restaurants right in the village. For a midday break, the try **Iguana Café** (ℂ **506/393-8006**) for homemade ice cream and sorbets, delicious baked goods, and hearty sandwiches. There's also **The Bakery** (ℂ **506/642-0458**), which serves breakfast and is a great place to pick up a snack, something sweet, or the makings of a bag lunch.

El Sano Banano ★★ VEGETARIAN/INTERNATIONAL   Delicious vegetarian meals, including nightly specials, sandwiches, and salads, are the specialty of this ever-popular Montezuma restaurant, although there's also a variety of fish and chicken dishes. Lunches feature hefty sandwiches on whole-wheat bread, pita pizzas, and filling fish and vegetarian casados for around $5. The yogurt fruit shakes are fabulous, but I like to get a little more decadent and have one of the mocha shakes.

El Sano Banano also doubles as the local movie house. Nightly laser-disc and DVD releases are projected on a large screen; the selection ranges from first-run to quite artsy, as there's a constantly growing library of more than 800 movies. The movies begin at 7:30pm and require a minimum purchase of $5.

On the main road into the village. ℂ **506/642-0272.** Main courses $5–$9. AE, MC, V. Daily 7am–9:30pm.

Las Cascadas COSTA RICAN/SEAFOOD   This little open-air restaurant is built on the banks of the stream just outside of the village and takes its name from the nearby waterfalls. The menu sometimes includes fresh-fish fillets, whole red snapper, or shrimp in salsa ranchera. Las Cascadas even added a few vegetarian items recently (as well as some budget rooms). This is one of the more enjoyable places in Costa Rica to have a meal—you can sit for hours beneath the thatched roof listening to the stream rushing past.

On the road out of town toward Cabo Blanco. ℂ **506/642-0057.** Reservations accepted. Main courses $3–$12. V. Daily 7am–10pm.

Playa de los Artistas ★★ *Finds* ITALIAN/MEDITERRANEAN   This popular open-air restaurant is beside an old house fronting the beach, and there are only a few tables, so arrive early. If you don't get a seat and you feel hearty, try the low wooden table surrounded by tatami mats on the sand. Meals are served in large, broad wooden bowls set on ceramic-ringed coasters and come with plenty of fresh bread for soaking up the sauces. The menu changes nightly but always features several fish dishes. The fresh grouper in a black-pepper sauce is phenomenal. The new outdoor grill is great for grilled fish and seafood.

Across from Hotel Los Mangos. No phone. Main courses $6–$18. No credit cards. Mon–Sat 5–10:30pm.

MONTEZUMA AFTER DARK

Montezuma has had a tough time coming to terms with its nightlife. For years, local businesses had banded together to force most of the loud, late-night activity out of town. This has eased somewhat and there's currently quite an active nightlife in Montezuma proper. The local action seems to base itself either at **Chico's Bar** or at the bar at the **Hotel Moctezuma.** Both are located on the main strip in town facing the water. A nicer option, however, is **Luz de Mono,** a new place nestled in some trees across from the school. This large open-air restaurant and bar has been featuring some interesting live music. I also enjoy **Cocolores,** which has natural-wood tables set in the sand under thatch-roofed palapas and offers great appetizers to go along with the drinks. If your evening tastes are mellower, **El Sano Banano** restaurant also doubles as the local movie house. See the listing under "Dining," above, for more information.

For real raging nightlife, some folks have been heading to the large disco at the **Playa Tambor Beach Resort.** Another option is **Las Manchas,** which is located about half a mile (1km) outside of town on the road to Cabo Blanco. It's open nightly during the high season, but during the off-season it has a sporadic schedule. Both Playa Tambor Beach Resort and Las Manchas have been known to offer free round-trip taxi service in order to lure the crowds.

12 Malpais/Santa Teresa ★ ★

93 miles (150km) W of San José; 7½ miles (12km) S of Cóbano

Malpais translates as "badlands," and I can't decide whether this is an accurate description or a deliberate local ploy to keep this place private. The beach here is a long, wide expanse of light sand dotted with rocky outcroppings. Sure, it can get rough here, but the surfers seem to like it. The road out here from Cóbano used to be even rougher than the surf, but it's gradually being tamed. This place is on the verge of becoming the next hot spot and hotels and restaurants are opening up at an increasing pace. Still, it should take some time before this area becomes yesterday's news. What you'll find in Malpais and Santa Teresa today is a scattering of beach hotels and simple restaurants, miles of nearly deserted beach, and easy access to some nice jungle and the nearby **Cabo Blanco Reserve** (see p. 193).

If you do decide to do anything here besides sunbathing on the beach and playing in the waves, your primary options include nature hikes and horseback riding, which most hotels can help arrange.

ESSENTIALS

GETTING THERE & DEPARTING   By Car   Follow the directions above to Montezuma (see section 11 of this chapter). At Cóbano, follow the signs to Malpais and Playa Santa Teresa. It's another 7½ miles (12km) or so down a very rough dirt road that pretty much requires four-wheel-drive year-round and is sometimes impassable during the rainy season.

By Bus & Ferry   Follow the directions above for getting to Montezuma, but get off the Montezuma bus in Cóbano. From Cóbano there are three buses daily for Malpais and Santa Teresa at 10:30am, noon, and 2:30, 3:15 and 6pm (fare: $1.50). In theory these buses wait for passengers getting off of the above Montezuma buses. Buses return daily to Cóbano at 7, 9 and 11:45am, and 1 and 4pm. *Be forewarned:* These bus schedules are subject to change according to demand, road conditions, and the whim of the bus company, so it pays to check with your hotel in advance.

If you miss this bus connection, you can hire a cab for around $12.

ORIENTATION   Malpais and Santa Teresa are two tiny beach villages. As you reach the ocean, the road will fork; Malpais is straight ahead and to your left; Santa Teresa is to your right. If you continue on beyond Santa Teresa, you'll come to the even more deserted beaches of Playa Hermosa and Manzanillo (not to be confused with beaches of the same names to be found elsewhere in the country).

ACCOMMODATIONS

In addition to the hotels listed below, budget travelers should probably head over to **Cabinas Bosque Mar** (© 506/640-0074), which is on the Malpais road and has a few basic rooms. You may also be able to pitch a tent. Look for camping signs; you should get bathroom and shower access for a few bucks. For a nicer, more isolated option, head north beyond Santa Teresita to **Milarepa** (© 506/640-0023; fax 506/640-0168).

When I last visited, the owners of **Sueño del Mar** (© and fax **506/653-0284;** see the "Playa Tamarindo & Playa Grande " section, earlier in this chapter), were well underway on construction of their new **Sueño del Sur** (no phone, yet) just beyond Milarepa. The luxurious private bungalows here are expected to open in January 2002, and will be huge, luxurious and, judging by their track record in Tamarindo, tastefully done.

Blue Jay Lodge   This new hotel isn't right on the beach, but the individual raised bungalows built amidst tall trees on a gentle, reforested hillside might make the 5-minute walk to the water worthwhile. The bungalows are all spacious and feature huge, open, screened windows to take in the views and the wildlife (actually, I'm not sure I'd call them windows—rooms really have screened half-walls on three sides). Each room comes with one single and one double bed and a comfortable deck with a hammock or two strung up for afternoon siestas. If you choose one of the bungalows highest up the hillside, you'll even get a glimpse of the ocean.

Malpais. © **506/640-0089.** Fax 506/640-0141. www.bluejaylodgecostarica.com. 7 units. $70 double. AE, MC, V. **Amenities:** 1 restaurant (Costa Rican/international); 1 bar; laundry service. *In room:* No phone.

Mal País Surf Camp & Resort   There's a wide range of accommodations here, reflected in the equally wide range of prices. The most basic rooms are open-air ranchos with gravel floors, lathe and bamboo walls, bead curtains for a door, and shared bathrooms. From here your options get progressively more comfortable, ranging from shared-bathroom bunk-bed rooms, to new deluxe poolside villas, to private houses with all the amenities. You can also pitch a tent. There's a refreshing free-form tile pool in the center of the complex, and the large open main lodge area serves as a combination restaurant, bar, lounge, and surfboard-storage area. There's satellite TV and surf videos playing most of the day, as well as pool, Ping-Pong, and foosball tables, and even a mechanical bull—the first I've found in Costa Rica. As the name implies, this place is run by and caters to surfers. The restaurant serves filling, fresh, and at times quite creative cuisine, depending on how accomplished the itinerant surf-chef-of-the-month is. Surf rentals, lessons, and video sessions are all available.

Malpais, Cóbano de Puntarenas. © and fax 506/640-0061. www.malpaissurfcamp.com. 16 units, 8 with shared bathroom. $20–$85 double; $7.50 per person camping. AE, MC, V (7% surcharge). **Amenities:** 1 restaurant (international); 1 bar; midsize pool; small exercise room; water-sports-equipment rental; bike rental; game room; tour desk; baby-sitting; laundry service. *In room:* No phone.

Star Mountain Eco Resort 🌟   If you don't mind being a few rough kilometers away from the beach, this mountain lodge is an excellent place to escape it all and get very close to nature. The hotel has 86 hectares of its own land and basically borders the Cabo Blanco Reserve. The rooms are all wonderfully done in lively pastel colors, with cool tile floors, Indian bedspreads, and nice artwork on the walls. The bunkhouse is clean and comfortable, and good for groups or students. Guests can either hike or ride horseback through the surrounding jungle. The restaurant features French/Belgian cuisine, and a full dinner should run you between $10 and $15.

Malpais, Cóbano, Puntarenas. 🕾 and fax **786/242-4996** in the U.S., or 506/640-0102. Fax 506/640-0101. www.starmountaineco.com. 5 units, 4 with private bathroom. $25 per person with shared bathroom, $75 double with private bathroom. Rates include breakfast. No credit cards. Head toward Malpais and turn left at the sign for the lodge. It's another 2 miles (3km) or so up a dirt road, and you'll have to ford a river, so come by four-wheel-drive vehicle or horse. **Amenities:** 1 restaurant (French/Belgian); 1 bar; small pool; Jacuzzi; horse rental; laundry service. *In room:* No phone.

Trópico Latino Lodge ⭐   This simple beach hotel is still a good choice. Its rooms, housed in three duplex bungalows, are huge—the king-size bamboo bed barely makes a dent in the floor space. There's also a separate sofa bed, as well as a small desk, a wall unit of shelves, and closet space galore. The bathrooms are modern and comfortable. Although none of the rooms has any ocean view to speak of, they do all have private patios with a hammock; best of all, the beach is less than 100 meters away. You'll find more hammocks and some chaise longues on the beach. The shady grounds are rich in the native pochote tree, which is known for its spiky trunk. The small restaurant here has excellent fresh fish and plenty of pasta dishes, probably just to please the palate of the Italian owners. A wide range of tours and activities can be arranged, as well as transport to Cóbano or the Tambor airport.

Playa Santa Teresa, Cóbano, Puntarenas. 🕾 and fax **506/640-0062.** www.centralamerica.com/cr/hotel/tropico.htm. 6 units. $52 double. Lower rates in the off-season. No credit cards. **Amenities:** 1 restaurant (international/Italian); 1 bar; small free-form swimming pool; Jacuzzi; laundry service. *In room:* No phone.

DINING

If you venture away from the rather dependable restaurants located at the hotels listed above, you'll probably end up at **Dulce Magia** (🕾 **506/640-0073**), a homey Italian restaurant located across the street from Cabinas Bosque Mar, or **Frank's Place** (🕾 **506/640-0096**), which is located at the crossroads where you enter town. Frank's is a notch above most *sodas* and seems to be the most happening spot in town. For breakfasts and light lunches, try the **Mambo Café** (🕾 **506/640-0110**), which is located right off the beach, near Frank's Place. The cinnamon buns here are locally famous. Alternatively, you can head to **Café Concoco** (🕾 **506/640-0196**), which serves wonderful crepes and the best coffee in town.

6

The Northern Zone: Mountain Lakes, Cloud Forests & a Volcano

The northern zone, roughly defined here as the area north of San José, between Guanacaste province on the west and the lowlands of the Caribbean coast on the east, is a naturalist's dream come true. Small, isolated lodges abound, and the sheer diversity of terrain, flora, and fauna is astounding. Slight changes in elevation create unique microclimates and ecosystems throughout the region. There are rain forests and cloud forests, jungle rivers, mountain lakes, lowland marshes, and an unbelievable wealth of birds and other wildlife.

In addition to its reputation for muddy hiking trails and crocodile-filled rivers, the northern zone claims one of the best windsurfing spots in the world (on **Lake Arenal** ⋆, which is free of crocodiles, by the way) and Costa Rica's most active volcano. **Arenal Volcano** ⋆⋆, when free of clouds, puts on spectacular nighttime light shows. Adding a touch of comfort to a visit to the northern zone are several hot springs and a variety of hotel options that vary in their levels of luxury.

1 Puerto Viejo de Sarapiquí ⋆

51 miles (82km) N of San José; 63¼ miles (102km) E of La Fortuna

The Sarapiquí region, named for the river that drains this area, lies at the foot of the Cordillera Central mountain range. To the west is the rain forest of **Braulio Carrillo National Park,** and to the east are **Tortuguero National Park** ⋆⋆ and **Barra del Colorado National Wildlife Refuge** ⋆. In between these protected areas lie thousands of acres of banana, pineapple, and palm plantations. Here you can see the great contradiction of Costa Rica: On the one hand, the country is known for its national parks, which preserve some of the largest tracts of rain forest left in Central America; on the other hand, nearly every acre of land outside of these parks, save a few private reserves, has been clear-cut and converted into plantations—and the cutting continues.

Within the remaining rain forest, there are several lodges that attract naturalists (both amateur and professional). Two of these lodges, La Selva and Rara Avis, have become well known for the research that's conducted on their surrounding reserves. Bird watching and rain-forest hikes are the primary attractions, but more adventure-oriented travelers will find plenty of activities available here, including canopy tours and boating and rafting trips along the Sarapiquí River.

ESSENTIALS
GETTING THERE & DEPARTING   By Car   The Guápiles Highway, which leads to the Caribbean coast, heads north out of downtown San José on Calle 3 before heading east. Turn north before reaching Guápiles on the road to Río Frío and continue north through Las Horquetas, passing the turnoffs for Rara Avis, La Selva, and El Gavilán lodges, before reaching Puerto Viejo.

The Northern Zone

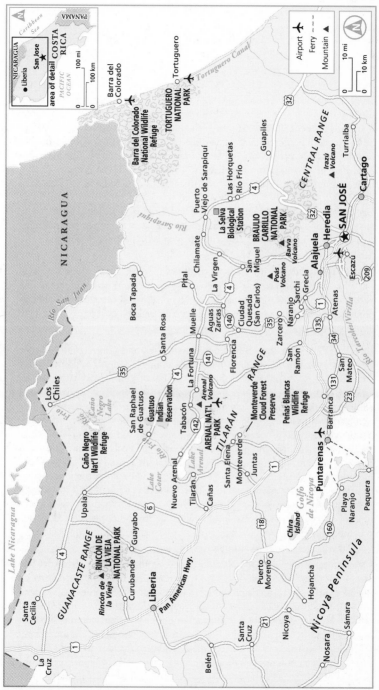

Airport ✈ Ferry - - - Mountain ▲

10 mi
10 km

Caribbean Sea
PANAMA
NICARAGUA
COSTA RICA
Liberia
San José
area of detail
PACIFIC OCEAN
100 mi
100 km

**Main map labels:**
NICARAGUA

Lake Nicaragua

Río San Juan

Río Frío

Caño Negro Lake

Lake Arenal

Lake Coter

Río Frío

Río Sarapiquí

Tortuguero Canal

Barra del Colorado

Tortuguero

TORTUGUERO NATIONAL PARK

Barra del Colorado National Wildlife Refuge

Guápiles

32

CENTRAL RANGE

Turrialba

Irazú Volcano ▲

Cartago

Las Horquetas
Río Frío

4

Puerto Viejo de Sarapiquí

La Selva Biological Station

BRAULIO CARRILLO NATIONAL PARK

Barva Volcano ▲

32

SAN JOSÉ

Heredia

Alajuela

Escazú

209

Chilamate

La Virgen

San Miguel

Poás Volcano ▲

Sarchí

Grecia

1

Atenas

Pital

4

Ciudad Quesada (San Carlos)

Naranjo

Zarcero

135

Boca Tapada

Muelle

Aguas Zarcas

140

35

34

Santa Rosa

141

Florencia

San Ramón

San Mateo

131

La Fortuna

RANGE

Peñas Blancas Wildlife Refuge

23

Barranca

Los Chiles

35

San Raphael de Guatuso

Guatuso Indian Reservation

Tabacón

4

142

Arenal Volcano ▲

ARENAL NAT'L PARK

TILARÁN

Monteverde Cloud Forest Preserve

Puntarenas

Río Tárcoles/Virilla

Caño Negro Nat'l Wildlife Refuge

Nuevo Arenal

Tilarán

Santa Elena

Monteverde

Juntas

1

Cañas

18

Chira Island

Golfo de Nicoya

160

Playa Naranjo

Paquera

Upala

GUANACASTE RANGE

RINCÓN DE LA VIEJA NATIONAL PARK

Rincón de la Vieja ▲

Guayabo

6

Puerto Moreno

Hojancha

Nicoya Peninsula

Santa Cecilia

4

Curubande

Liberia

Pan American Hwy.

Santa Cruz

21

Nicoya

Sámara

La Cruz

1

Belén

Nosara

201

A more scenic route goes through Heredia, Barva, Varablanca, and San Miguel before reaching Puerto Viejo. This route passes very close to the Poás Volcano and directly in front of the La Paz waterfall. If you want to take this route, head west out of San José and then turn north to Heredia and follow the signs for Varablanca.

By Bus   Express buses (© **506/257-6854**) leave San José daily at 6:30, 8, 10, and 11:30am, and 1, 1:30, 2:30, 3:30, and 6pm from the **Gran Terminal del Caribe,** on Calle Central, 1 block north of Avenida 11. The buses will be marked RÍO FRÍO, PUERTO VIEJO, or both. There are two routes to Puerto Viejo de Sarapiquí. The faster heads out on the Guápiles Highway, through Braulio Carrillo National Park and then past Las Horquetas. The slower, but more scenic, route heads out through Heredia, Varablanca, and La Virgen, passing between the Barva and Poás volcanoes. If you're heading to La Selva, Rara Avis, or El Gavilán lodges, be sure you're on a bus going through Braulio Carrillo and Las Horquetas. The trip takes between 2 and 4 hours, depending on the route taken, the condition of the roads, and the frequency of stops; the fare is $2.50.

Buses for San José leave Puerto Viejo daily at 5:30, 7, 8, and 11am, and 1:30, 3:30, 5:30, and 7pm.

ORIENTATION   Puerto Viejo is a small town, at the center of which is a soccer field. If you continue past the soccer field on the main road and stay on the paved road, then turn right at the Banco Nacional, you'll come to the Río Sarapiquí and the dock, where you can look into arranging a boat trip.

WHAT TO SEE & DO
BOAT TRIPS   For the adventurous, Puerto Viejo is a jumping-off point for trips down the Río Sarapiquí to Barra del Colorado National Wildlife Refuge and Tortuguero National Park on the Caribbean coast. Boat trips can be arranged at most hotels in town. A boat for up to 10 people will cost you around $200 to $250 to Barra del Colorado, and $250 to $350 to Tortuguero.

Alternatively, you can head down to the town dock on the bank of the Sarapiquí and see if you can arrange a less expensive boat trip on your own, by tagging on with another group, or better yet, with a bunch of locals. It's worth checking at your hotel, or with either **Oasis Nature Tours** (© **506/766-6108**) or **Aventuras Sarapiquí** (© **506/766-6846**). In addition to the longer trips, these two companies also offer shorter trips on the river for between $15 and $20. A trip down the Sarapiquí, even if it's for only an hour or two, provides opportunities to spot crocodiles, caimans, monkeys, sloths, and dozens of bird species.

RAFTING & KAYAKING   If you want a faster, wilder ride on the river, check in with **Aguas Bravas** (© **506/292-2072;** www.aguas-bravas.co.cr), a white-water-rafting company that has its local base at the very basic **Islas del Río Hotel** (© **506/766-6575**). You'll find this hotel on the main road between Puerto Viejo and Chilamate on the left, a little before Selva Verde. Aguas Bravas runs trips on a variety of sections of the Sarapiquí River, ranging from Class III to Class V. Trips cost between $50 and $75 per person. Aguas Bravas also runs mountain-biking tours in the area. Located just off the main road about 1¼ miles (2km) west of La Virgen, the **Sarapiquí Outdoor Center** (© **506/ 761-1123;** sarapiquioutdoor@hotmail.com) offers similar tours at similar prices. Both companies also rent kayaks and offer kayak trips for more experienced and/or daring river rats.

Another option is to take a kayak trip with the folks at **Rancho Leona,** in La Virgen de Sarapiquí (© and fax **506/761-1019;** www.rancholeona.com).

Rancho Leona is a small stained-glass workshop, kayaking center, and rustic guest house on the banks of the Río Sarapiquí in the village of La Virgen. Its trips are offered as a package that includes 2 nights' lodging in simple dormitory-style accommodations and an all-day kayak trip with some basic instruction and lunch on the river. The cost for the 2-day trip is $85 per person. No experience is necessary, and the river here is very calm. Trips for experienced kayakers can be arranged.

THE AERIAL TRAM ✿ If you're driving to Puerto Viejo de Sarapiquí via the Guápiles Highway, you might want to stop here. You'll see the entrance to the Aerial Tram on your right, a little bit after passing through the Zurquí tunnel. For more information, see "Side Trips from San José," in chapter 4, p. 131.

HIKING & GUIDED TOURS Anyone can take advantage of the 35 miles (56km) of well-maintained **trails at La Selva** ✿✿ (see below). If you're not staying there, however, you'll have to take a guided hike, led by experienced and well-informed naturalists. Half-day ($25) and full-day ($45) hikes are offered daily, but you must reserve in advance (© **506/766-6565;** laselva@sloth.ots. ac.cr). The half-day tours leave at 8am and 1:30pm daily.

My favorite hike starts off with the Cantarana ("singing frog") trail, which includes a section of low bridges over a rain-forest swamp. From here you can join up with either the near or far circular loop trails—**CCC** and **CCL.**

Finally, if you want to visit the Sarapiquí region on a day trip from San José, call either **Costa Rica Fun Adventures** (© **506/290-6015**) or **Ecoscapes Highlights Tour** (© **506/297-0664**), which runs jam-packed day trips up here that combine a bus ride and stop at the La Paz waterfall, a visit to a banana plantation, a rainforest hike, and a boat ride on the river for around $75 to $80 per person.

BUGGING OUT Located at the La Quinta de Sarapiquí Country Inn (see below), entomologist Richard Whitten's **"Jewels of the Rainforest" insect museum** is a lively, educational, and aesthetic display of part of his massive collection of insect species from around the world. Admission is $8 for the general public and $5 for hotel guests.

A NATURAL-HISTORY THEME PARK IN THE MAKING The **Centro Neotrópico Sarapiquís** (see below) is working toward the creation of the most comprehensive natural-history project in the region. The "Alma Ata" Archaeological Park is basically an ongoing dig of a modest pre-Colombian grave site; so far, 12 graves, some petroglyphs, and numerous pieces of ceramic and jewelry have been unearthed. Plans for the park include the reconstruction of a small indigenous village. Slated to open in September 2001, the hotel will have a large indoor exhibition space for the display of the ceramics, tools, and carvings found here, as well as other natural-history exhibits. There will also be a small theater showing educational videos. Just across the hotel's driveway, you'll find the Chester Field Biological Gardens, which feature well-tended and displayed examples of local medicinal and ornamental plants and herbs, as well as food crops. Across the Sarapiquí River is the 750-acre private **Tirimbina Biological Reserve** ✿, which features a small network of trails and several impressive suspension bridges, both over the river and through the forest canopy.

This is a new and ongoing project, and entrance fees are still being ironed out. As of press time, the center was charging $7 admission for the archaeological park. An unguided walk of the bridges and trails of the reserve runs between $3 and $10 depending on how far into the reserve you go, while guided tours run around $15 to $20 per person. A walk through the botanical gardens is free.

ACCOMMODATIONS & DINING

All of the lodges listed below arrange excursions throughout the region, including boat trips on the Sarapiquí, guided hikes in the rain forest, and horseback or mountain-bike rides. Also, note that the rates for all of lodges in the "Expensive" category include all meals, taxes, and usually a tour or two, greatly reducing their real cost.

EXPENSIVE

La Selva Biological Station Located a few kilometers south of Puerto Viejo, La Selva Biological Station caters primarily to students and researchers but also accepts visitors seeking a rustic rain-forest adventure. The atmosphere is definitely that of a scientific research center. La Selva, which is operated by the Organization for Tropical Studies (OTS), covers 3,700 acres and is contiguous with Braulio Carrillo National Park. There are miles of well-maintained hiking trails to explore. Researchers estimate that more than 2,000 species of flora exist in this private reserve, and 400-plus species of birds have been identified here, making this a great choice if you want to do some serious **bird watching** . Rooms are basic but large, and the high ceilings help keep them cool. Most have bunk beds and all share bathrooms. The dining hall is a big, bright place where students and scientists swap data over fried chicken or fish with rice and beans.

Because scientific research is the primary objective of La Selva, researchers receive priority over casual, short-term visitors. However, very informative guided tours are available most days, even if you are staying at another hotel in the area. Call the local number (© **506/766-6565**) at least a day in advance to arrange one of these. If you wish to stay overnight at La Selva, you must have a reservation with the San José office—you can't just drop in and check for a vacancy. Since there are very few rooms here, it pays to book well in advance. The rates here are quite high for the actual accommodations, but you can take some solace in the fact that you're helping to support valuable and valiant research and conservation efforts.

Puerto Viejo (A.P. 676-2050, San Pedro, Costa Rica; mailing address in the U.S.: Box 90630, Durham, NC 27708). © **506/240-6696** or 506/766-6565. Fax 506/240-6783. www.ots.ac.cr. reservas@ots.ac.cr. 10 units, all with shared bathroom. $66 per person double occupancy. Rates include all meals, a half-day tour, and taxes. Lower rates for researchers and student groups. MC, V. **Amenities:** 1 restaurant (Costa Rican); kayak rentals; laundry service. *In room:* No phone.

Rara Avis Once the exclusive stomping grounds of scientists and students, Rara Avis is one of the most responsible, biologically rich, and isolated ecolodge operations in Costa Rica. There are several lodging options here, but the Waterfall Lodge is by far the most comfortable and popular. It has rustic but comfortable rooms in a two-story building near the main lodge and dining room and just a couple hundred yards from its namesake two-tiered waterfall. Each unit here is a corner room with a wraparound porch. For those wanting closer communion with nature, Rara Avis has a comfortable two-room cabin set deep in the forest beside a river, about a 10-minute hike from the main lodge, as well as four more rustic two-bedroom cabins with shared bathrooms, located in a small clearing about a 5-minute walk from the lodge. Meals are basic Tico-style dishes with lots of beans and rice.

The grounds of Rara Avis are adjacent to Braulio Carrillo National Park, and together the two areas have many miles of trails for you to explore. Bird watchers, take note: More than 362 species of birds have been sighted here.

When making reservations, be sure to get directions for how to get to Las Horquetas, and information on coordinating your ride on the lodge's tractor.

The tractor leaves around 9am each day for the 3-hour/9½-mile (15km) ride to the lodge.

15km from Las Horquetas (A.P. 8105-1000, San José). ℂ **506/253-0844** or 506/764-3131. Fax 506/257-0438. www.rara-avis.com. 14 units, 10 with private bathroom. $90 double with shared bathroom, $150–$160 double with private bathroom. Rates include transportation from Las Horquetas (you can't get here by car), guided hikes, all meals, and taxes. AE, MC, V. **Amenities:** 1 restaurant (Costa Rican). *In room:* No phone.

Selva Verde Lodge ★ *Kids*   For years, this was one of the showcase ecotourist lodges in Costa Rica. Frankly, I think the success has gone to their heads. Expansion and remodeling have included the building of a new reception area and a covered bus port for the numerous tour buses that come here. Service, food, and personal attention have all suffered, and there's now an assembly-line feel to the whole operation. But you can't beat the location: It's right between the main road (a few km west of Puerto Viejo) and by the Río Sarapiquí. Across the river is a large rain-forest preserve.

Overall, these are still probably the nicest rooms in the area. They're all connected by covered walkways that keep you dry even though this area receives more than 150 inches of rain each year. The lodge buildings are all made of varnished hardwoods, inside and out, and are built on pilings so that the rooms are on the second floor. The bungalows are located across the road and 500 meters (545 yd.) into the forest and are not nearly as comfortable as the rooms in the main compound, but they do offer somewhat more privacy. Meals are served buffet style in a beautiful, large dining room that overlooks the river; they're well prepared and filling, but not too creative. There are several trails on the grounds, a wonderful suspension bridge across the Sarapiquí River to more trails, and modest butterfly and botanical gardens.

Chilamate (A.P. 55-3069), Sarapiquí. ℂ **800/451-7111** in the U.S. and Canada, or 506/766-6800. Fax 506/766-6011. www.selvaverde.com. 40 units, 5 bungalows. $136 double; $145 triple. Rates include 3 meals daily and taxes. Slightly lower rates during the off-season (May–Nov). MC, V. **Amenities:** 1 restaurant (Costa Rican/international); 1 bar; tour desk; laundry service. *In room:* No phone.

MODERATE

Casa Río Blanco   This small nature lodge is located about 1¼ miles (2km) up a gravel road just off the Guápiles Highway, in a small but dense patch of rain forest on a steep hill overlooking the Río Blanco. The atmosphere is rustic but comfortable. There are two rooms in the main lodge building and four separate cabins. The cabins, with their wood floors, clapboard walls, and private balconies, are the best bet. Numbers 1 and 4 have the best views. There are trails through the rain forest, a covered lookout point, and several swimming holes on the premises. Located close to the Aerial Tram and La Selva, and en route to the Caribbean coast, this hotel makes a good stopover point for a night or two as part of a larger itinerary.

A.P. 241-7210, Guápiles. ℂ **506/382-0957**. Fax 506/710-2264. www.casarioblanco.com. 6 units. $60 double; $75 triple. Rates include breakfast. Lower rates in the off-season (May–Nov). No credit cards. **Amenities:** 1 restaurant (Costa Rican/international). *In room:* No phone.

Centro Neotrópico Sarapiquís ★   Located on a high bluff fronting the Sarapiquí River, this new complex is the most unique project in the Sarapiquí region. The rooms are housed in three large, round buildings, or "palenques." Based on the traditional pre-Colombian constructions of the area, each of the three palenques has a towering thatch roof rising some 18 meters. The rooms are all comfortable and spacious, although a little dark, and they each have a door leading out to the shared veranda that encircles the building.

The hotel has several interesting attractions, including a small natural-history museum, an on-site excavation of a pre-Colombian graveyard, and a well-marked botanical garden. Just across the river lies the 750-acre Tirimbina Biological Reserve, with a small network of trails and several impressive suspension bridges, both over the river and through the forest canopy. Tours of the museum and reserve cost extra and are open to guests at other hotels in the area.

No smoking is permitted in any of the rooms, or on any of the terraces, though smokers can light up in the bar and restaurant.

La Virgen de Sarapiquí. (C) 506/761-1004. Fax 506/761-1415. www.sarapiquis.org. 24 units. $77–$85 double. V. **Amenities:** 1 restaurant (Costa Rican/international); 1 bar; tour desk; limited room service; baby-sitting; laundry service; no-smoking rooms.

El Gavilán Lodge   Located on the banks of the Río Sarapiquí just south of Puerto Viejo on the road to Río Frío, El Gavilán is surrounded by 250 acres of forest reserve (secondary forest) and 25 acres of gardens planted with lots of flowering ginger, heliconia, orchids, and bromeliads. Guest rooms are basic and simply furnished. Still, all have fans and hot water, and there are always fresh-cut flowers. Most have one single and one double bed, but there are variations. What El Gavilán lacks in luxurious comfort, it makes up for in friendliness and attentive service. There's an unheated Jacuzzi in the garden and several open-air ranchos, some of which have hammocks strung up for afternoon siestas. Tico and continental meals are served buffet style, and there are always plenty of fresh fruits and juices. Breakfast will run you $7; lunch, $9; and dinner, $12. Guided hikes through the forest, horseback rides, and river trips are all offered for around $20 per person.

Puerto Viejo de Sarapiquí (A.P. 445-2010, San José). (C) **506/234-9507.** Fax 506/253-6556. www.gavilanlodge.com. 13 units. $50 double. Lower rates in the off-season (May–Nov). MC, V. **Amenities:** 1 restaurant (Costa Rican); 1 bar; Jacuzzi; laundry service. *In room:* No phone.

Hotel El Bambú   This is the most luxurious hotel right in the town of Puerto Viejo, although that's not saying much. The best rooms here are up on the second floor facing away from the main road. They all have high ceilings, tile floors, and attractive bamboo furniture. Downstairs, just off the lobby, you'll find a big, open-air restaurant that overlooks a dense grove of bamboo. The hotel is directly across the street from the soccer field in the middle of town. Tours around the region, as well as boat trips down the Río Sarapiquí as far as Barra del Colorado and Tortuguero, can be arranged.

A.P. 1518-2100, Puerto Viejo de Sarapiquí. (C) **506/766-6005.** Fax 506/766-6132. www.elbambu. com. 14 units. $55 double; $70 triple; $85 quad. Rates include continental breakfast. AE, MC, V. **Amenities:** 1 restaurant (Costa Rican); 1 bar; small outdoor pool; laundry service; no-smoking rooms. *In room:* A/C, TV, safe.

La Quinta de Sarapiquí Country Inn *(Value)*   This small, family-run lodge makes a good base for exploring the Sarapiquí region. Located on the banks of the Sardinal River about 15 minutes west of Puerto Viejo, La Quinta caters primarily to nature lovers and bird watchers. The rooms are located in a half-dozen buildings dispersed around the grounds among richly flowering gardens and connected by covered walkways. They're simple but clean, with good lighting and comfortable bathrooms. Each room has a small patio with a sitting chair or two for gazing out into the garden. There's a small pool, and it's even safe to swim in the river. There's also a small gift shop, a small butterfly garden, a small frog garden, and a vegetable garden and reforestation project on hand. If you don't have a car, call the hotel to see if you can arrange a pickup in Puerto Viejo. Meals are served family style in the main lodge and will run you an extra $25 per day.

Chilamate (A.P. 11021-1000, San José), Sarapiquí. ✆ 506/761-1300. Fax 506/761-1395. www. quintasarapiqui.com. 23 units. $50 double. Children under 12 stay free in parent's room. MC, V. **Amenities:** 1 restaurant (Costa Rican); 1 bar; small pool; tour desk; laundry service. *In room:* No phone.

INEXPENSIVE

Mi Lindo Sarapiquí   This little family-run lodging is located in the center of town overlooking the soccer field. The rooms are on the second floor above the large restaurant and bar. There's nothing fancy (in fact, it's downright depressing), but still, this is still the most popular budget lodging in town. Be warned that the bar/restaurant is popular with locals and can be noisy.

Puerto Viejo de Sarapiquí. ✆ and fax **506/766-6074.** lindo@sarapiquirainforest.com. 8 units. $17 double; $27 triple. AE, MC, V. **Amenities:** 1 restaurant (Costa Rican); 1 bar. *In room:* TV; no phone.

A REMOTE NATURE LODGE

La Laguna del Lagarto Lodge ★ (Finds)   It's hard to get much more remote than this. Located near the Nicaraguan border, La Laguna del Lagarto Lodge is bordered by over 1,200 acres of virgin rain forest that is home to a rich variety of tropical flora and fauna. The accommodations are simple yet comfortable. Most rooms open onto a balcony or veranda with sitting chairs and hammocks. Meals, which will run you around $24 per person per day, are served family style in the open-air dining room, and are filling affairs.

The hotel is named after the two man-made lagoons that sit below the lodge buildings; canoes are available for paddling around these and several other nearby jungle waterways. There are over 6 miles (10km) of well-maintained hiking trails, and the lodge offers trips on the San Carlos and San Juan Rivers ($30), touching ground briefly in Nicaragua. Over 365 species of birds have been spotted here, and the hotel is involved in efforts to preserve the rare great green macaw, two of which I spotted soon after my arrival. In addition to the rain forest, the lodge also sits on a small pepper plantation and has other lands planted with palmito, pineapple, and other tropical fruits.

To get here, you head first to Pital and then continue on dirt roads to the town of Boca Tapada. It's another 4 miles (6km) to the lodge on more bumpy dirt roads. It's also possible to get here on public transportation (call for directions), or you can arrange for the lodge to handle your transportation from San José. The lodge's transfers cost $180 round-trip for two or three people, or $50 per person for more than three. But anyone with a four-wheel-drive can make the trip here independently, so you're best off driving on your own.

Boca Tapada (A.P. 995-1007, San José). ✆ **506/289-8163.** Fax 506/289-5295. http:// adventure-costarica.com/laguna-del-lagarto/. 20 units, 18 with private bathroom. $57 double with shared bathroom, $68 double with private bathroom. V (5% surcharge). **Amenities:** 1 restaurant (Costa Rican/international); 1 bar. *In room:* No phone.

2 Arenal Volcano & La Fortuna ★★

87 miles (140km) NW of San José; 37³⁄₄ miles (61km) E of Tilarán

If you've never experienced them firsthand, the sights and sounds of an active volcano erupting are awesome. **Arenal** is one of the world's most regularly active volcanoes. In July 1968, the volcano, which had lain dormant for hundreds of years, surprised everybody by erupting with sudden violence. The nearby village of Tabacón was destroyed, and nearly 80 of its inhabitants were killed. Since that eruption, 5,358-foot Arenal has been Costa Rica's most active volcano. Frequent powerful explosions send cascades of red-hot lava rocks tumbling down the western slope, and during the day, the lava flows steam and rumble. However, it's at night that the volcano puts on its most mesmerizing show. If you are lucky enough to be here on a clear and active night, you'll see the night sky turned red by lava spewing from Arenal's crater. In the past few years, the forests to the south of the volcano have been declared Arenal National Park. Eventually, this park should stretch all the way to Monteverde Biological Cloud Forest Preserve.

Lying at the eastern foot of this natural spectacle is the tiny farming community of **La Fortuna.** In recent years, this town has become a magnet for volcano watchers from around the world. There's a host of moderately priced hotels in and near La Fortuna, and from here you can arrange night tours to the best volcano-viewing spots, which are 10½ miles (17km) away on the western slope, past Tabacón Hot Springs.

ESSENTIALS

GETTING THERE & DEPARTING   By Plane   Travelair (🕻 **506/220-3054;** reservations@travelair-costarica.com) flies to La Fortuna daily at 8:30am from Tobías Bolaños International Airport in Pavas. Flight duration is 30 minutes; the fare is $50 each way.

Sansa (🕻 **506/221-9414;** reservations@flysansa.com) used to fly here, but cancelled this route in December 2000, following the crash of one of its flights. I expect that by the time this book goes to press, it may have resumed service to La Fortuna.

The **airport** (🕻 **506/469-1080**) is actually located in El Tanque, a few kilometers outside of La Fortuna. A taxi or airport shuttle should cost around $5 to the center of La Fortuna, around $15 to Tabacón.

By Car   There are several routes to La Fortuna from San José. The most popular is to head west on the Interamerican Highway and then turn north at Naranjo, continuing north through Zarcero to Ciudad Quesada (Zarcero is a nice place to make a brief stop on the way; see p. 140 in chapter 4). From Ciudad Quesada, one route goes through Jabillos, while the other goes through Muelle. The former route is more popular and better maintained. However, the severe weather and heavy traffic quickly take their toll, and the roads up here can be notoriously bad for long stretches.

I personally recommend staying on the Interamerican Highway until San Ramón (west of Naranjo), then heading north through La Tigra, which is very scenic and passes the hotels Villablanca and Valle Escondido and is currently the fastest route to La Fortuna. The travel time on any of the above routes will be between 3 and 4 hours.

Finally, if you're combining your visit here with a stop at the Poás Volcano and La Paz waterfall, or if you're staying at one of the lodges closer to Aguas Zarcas, you can go first to Alajuela or Heredia and then head north to Varablanca before continuing on to San Miguel, where you turn west toward Río Cuarto and Aguas Zarcas. From Aguas Zarcas, continue west through Muelle to the turnoff for La Fortuna. This is the longest route.

By Bus   Buses (🕻 **506/255-4318**) leave San José for La Fortuna daily at 6:15, 8:40, and 11:30am from the Atlántico del Norte bus station at Avenida 9 and Calle 12. The trip's duration is 4½ hours; the fare is $3.

Boats, Horses & Taxis

You can travel between La Fortuna and Monteverde on a combination boat, horseback, and taxi trip. After a quick boat ride across the lake, participants are saddled up for a 4-hour ride up and over the mountains to the town of San Gerardo, which is just a short taxi ride from Santa Elena and Monteverde.

Be forewarned: The riding is often rainy, muddy, and steep. Many find it much more arduous than awe-inspiring. Moreover, I've received numerous complaints about the condition of the trails and the treatment of the horses, so be very careful and demanding before signing on for this trip. **Desafio Raft** (📞 506/479-9464; www.desafiocostarica.com) offers this trip for $65 per person. They will even drive your car around for you while you take the scenic (and sore) route.

Alternatively, you can take a bus to Ciudad Quesada from the same location in San José and then take a local bus from Ciudad Quesada to La Fortuna. Ciudad Quesada buses leave San José roughly every hour from 5am to 7:30pm, and "roughly" is the operative word. Buses are sometimes added or canceled depending on demand, and hours may vary, though you'll never have to wait more than an hour for the next bus. If you want to be sure, call 📞 506/255-4318. The fare for the 2½-hour trip is $2.50. The bus you take may be labeled TILARÁN. Make sure it is passing through Ciudad Quesada. If it is, you're in luck, because it will also pass through La Fortuna. If it's not, you'll end up in Tilarán via the Interamerican Highway, passing through the Guanacaste town of Cañas. Local buses between Ciudad Quesada and La Fortuna run regularly through the day, though the schedule changes frequently depending on demand. The trip lasts 1 hour; the fare is $1.75.

Buses depart **Monteverde/Santa Elena** for Tilarán every day at 7am. This is a journey of only 22 miles (35km), but the trip lasts 2½ hours because the road is in such horrendous condition. Pregnant women and people with bad backs should think twice about making this trip, especially by bus. The return bus from Tilarán to Santa Elena leaves at 1pm. The fare is $2. Buses from Tilarán to La Fortuna depart daily at 7am and 12:30pm (hence, a person coming from Monteverde would have to wait for the 12:30pm bus) and make the return trip at 8am and 2:30pm. The trip is 3 to 4 hours; the fare is $2.50.

Buses depart La Fortuna for San José daily at 12:45 and 2:45pm. Buses to Ciudad Quesada leave at 5 and 8am, and 12:15, 2, and 3:30pm daily. From there, you can catch one of the hourly buses to San José.

Jacamar Tours (📞 506/479-9456; jacamar@racsa.co.cr) runs daily shuttles leaving La Fortuna at 8:30am for Tilarán ($10), continuing on to Liberia ($20), Monteverde ($25), and Tamarindo ($25). And another leaves at 10am for San José ($20).

ORIENTATION As you enter La Fortuna, you'll see the massive volcano directly in front of you. La Fortuna is only a few streets wide, with almost all the hotels, restaurants, and shops clustered along the main road that leads out of town toward Tabacón and the volcano. There are several small information and tour-booking offices across the street from the soccer field, as well as a Laundromat. There's a Banco de Costa Rica as you enter La Fortuna, just over the Río Burío bridge, and a Banco Nacional in the center of town, across the park from the church. Both have ATMs.

GETTING AROUND   If you don't have a car, you'll need to either take a cab or go on an organized tour if you want to visit the hot springs or view the volcano eruption. One alternative is to rent a car. **Elegante,** behind the Hotel San Bosco (© 506/479-8055), and **Alamo,** on the main road beside the church (© 506/479-9090), both have offices in La Fortuna. There are tons of taxis in La Fortuna (you can flag one down practically anywhere), and there is always a line of them ready and waiting along the main road beside the central park. A taxi between La Fortuna and Tabacón should cost around $5.

WHAT TO SEE & DO
EXPERIENCING THE VOLCANO
The first thing you should know is that you can't climb Arenal Volcano; it's not safe due to the constant activity. Several foolish people who have ignored this warning have lost their lives, and others have been severely injured. The most recent fatalities occurred in August 2000.

The second thing you should know is that Arenal Volcano borders a region of cloud and rain forests, and the volcano's cone is often socked in by fog. Many people come to Arenal and never get to see the exposed cone. Moreover, the volcano does go through periods when it is relatively quiet.

Still, waiting for and watching Arenal's nearly constant eruptions is the main activity in La Fortuna and is best done at night when the orange lava glows against the starry sky. Though it's possible simply to look up from the middle of town and see Arenal erupting, the view is best from the north and west sides of the volcano along the road to Tabacón and toward the national-park entrance. If you have a car, you can drive along this road, but if you've arrived by bus, you will need to take a taxi or tour.

Arenal National Park ✸✸ constitutes an area of more than 7,200 acres, which includes the viewing and parking areas closest to the volcano. The park is open from 8am to 10pm daily and charges $6 admission per person. The trails through forest and over old lava flows inside the park are gorgeous and fun (be careful climbing on those volcanic boulders). However, at night, the view from inside the park is no better than on the roads just outside it.

If you don't have a car and are staying in La Fortuna, every hotel in town and several tour offices offer night tours of the volcano (they don't actually enter the park; rather, they stop on the road that runs between the park entrance and the Arenal Observatory Lodge). Most tours, which cost $7 to $15 per person, include a stop at one of the hot springs (not Tabacón).

OTHER ADVENTUROUS PURSUITS IN THE AREA
Aside from the impressive volcanic activity, the area around Arenal Volcano is packed with other natural wonders.

HIKING & HORSEBACK RIDING   Leading the list of side attractions in the area is the impressive **Río Fortuna waterfall** ✸, located about 3½ miles (5.5km) outside of town in a lush jungle setting. There's a sign in town to indicate the road that leads out to the falls. Depending on recent rainfall, you can drive or hike to just within viewing distance. Once you get to a makeshift entrance to the lookout, you'll have to pay the $3 entrance fee to actually check out the falls. It's another 15- to 20-minute hike down a steep and often muddy path to the pool formed by the waterfall. You can swim, but stay away from the turbulent water at the base of the falls—several people have drowned here. Instead, check out and enjoy the calm pool just around the bend. If this seems like too much exercise, you can rent a horse and guide for transportation.

ⓒ Taking a Soothing Soak in Hot Springs

Arenal Volcano has bestowed a terrific fringe benefit on the area around it: several naturally heated thermal springs. Located at the site of the former village that was destroyed by the 1968 eruption, **Tabacón Hot Springs** ✸✸✸ (ⓒ **506/256-1500**; www.tabacon.com) is the most extensive and luxurious spot to soak your tired bones. It feels like a playground for adults: A series of variously sized pools, fed by natural springs, are spread out among lush gardens. At the center is a large, warm, spring-fed swimming pool with a slide, a swim-up bar, and a perfect view of the volcano. One of the stronger streams flows over a sculpted waterfall, with a rock ledge underneath that provides a perfect place to sit and receive a free hydraulic shoulder massage. The resort also has a small spa on the grounds offering professional massages, mud masks, and other treatments at very reasonable prices (make appointments in advance).

The Ave de Paraíso restaurant here serves well-prepared Tico and international cuisine, and there is also a more informal grill serving burgers and sandwiches. You can sign a credit-card voucher when you enter and charge your food and drinks throughout your stay. This sure beats pulling soggy bills from your bathing suit.

Entrance fees are $17 for adults and $10 for children under 9. The hot springs are open daily from 10am to 10pm. The management recently instituted a policy of limiting the number of visitors at any one time, so reservations are recommended during the high season (late Nov–late Apr).

Across the street from the resort and down a gravel driveway is another bathing spot fed by the same springs and run by the same folks. You'll find several large pools here, but far more basic facilities and no view. Admission is $5. There are changing rooms and showers, but you won't find the Disneyland atmosphere, pampering spa treatments, or magnificent gardens that prevail at the Tabacón resort.

There's a popular free public spot located in a densely forested section of the road between Tabacón and the park entrance. This area has some very rudimentary dams set in a section of a warm side-stream. To find it, keep going past the Tabacón Hot Springs Resort away from La Fortuna. You'll soon enter the forested section. After a few tight turns, the path leading down to the springs is on your left. There's a small sign and this is a well-known and popular spot, so you'll usually see several cars parked on the side of the road here.

Finally, there's a new entry in the hot-springs field. **Baldi Termae** (ⓒ **506/479-9652**), next to the Volcano Look Disco, are the first hot springs you'll come to as you drive from La Fortuna toward Tabacón; however, I find this place far less attractive than the options you'll find a little farther on down the road. The main attraction here is the swim-up bar set in the center of the circular concrete pool. Admission is $7.

Another good ride is up to **Cerro Chato,** a dormant volcanic cinder cone on the flank of Arenal. There's a pretty little lake up here. Either of these tours should cost around $20 to $25 per person. You can arrange either tour through your hotel, or through **Aventuras Arenal** (✆ 506/479-9133) or **Sunset Tours** ✶ (✆ 506/479-9800; www.sunset-tours.com). In addition to the above tours, each of these companies offers most of the tours listed below, as well as fishing trips and sightseeing excursions on the lake.

CANOPY TOURS   The **Original Canopy Tour** ✶✶ company (✆ 506/257-5149; www.canopytour.com) has an operation set up right at the Tabacón Hot Springs Resort. The 2½-hour tour leaves right from the hot springs. You strap on a climbing harness, ascend more than 100 feet up to a treetop platform, and careen from tree to tree while hanging from a pulley on a skinny cable. It's exhilarating. This same company has another canopy tour at **Termales del Bosque** (see "Accommodations & Dining Farther Afield," below) just outside of Aguas Zarcas.

As this is a new and quite popular activity, several other canopy-adventure tour operations have been opened recently around the area. Be sure that you feel confident with any company's safety standards, guides, and equipment before embarking. There have been at least two deaths on these types of tours. Overall, I recommend sticking with the folks at the Original Canopy Tour, as they seem to have the most dependable safety standards.

WHITE-WATER RAFTING   For adventurous tours of the area, check out **Desafío Raft** ✶ (✆ 506/479-9464; www.desafiocostarica.com) or **Aguas Bravas** (✆ 506/479-9025; www.aguas-bravas.co.cr). Both of these companies offer daily raft rides of Class I to II, III, and IV to V on different sections of the Peñas Blancas and Sarapiquí Rivers. A half-day trip on the Peñas Blancas leaving from La Fortuna costs just $37 per person; a full day of rafting costs $60 to $80 per person. Both of these companies also offer mountain-biking and most of the standard local guided trips.

FISHING   With Lake Arenal just around the corner, fishing is a popular activity here. The big action is guapote, a South American species of rainbow bass. Most hotels and adventure-tour companies can arrange fishing excursions. Costs run around $100 to $150 for a half day, and $200 to $250 for a full day.

SIDE TRIPS FROM LA FORTUNA

La Fortuna is a great place from which to make a day trip to the **Caño Negro National Wildlife Refuge** ✶. This vast network of marshes and rivers is 62 miles (100km) north of La Fortuna near the town of Los Chiles. This refuge is best known for its amazing abundance of bird life, including roseate spoonbills, jabiru storks, herons, and egrets, but you can also see caimans and crocodiles. Birdwatchers should not miss this refuge, though keep in mind that the main lake dries up in the dry season (mid-Apr to Nov), which reduces the number of wading birds. Full-day tours to Caño Negro average between $40 and $60 per person.

You can also visit the Venado Caverns, a 45-minute drive away. In addition to plenty of stalactites, stalagmites, and other limestone formations, you'll see bats and cave fish. Tours here cost around $35.

Aventuras Arenal (✆ 506/479-9133), **Sunset Tours** (✆ 506/479-9800; www.sunset-tours.com), **Desafío Raft** (✆ 506/479-9464; www.desafiocostarica.com), and **Aguas Bravas** (✆ 506/479-9025; www.aguas-bravas.co.cr) all offer trips to Caño Negro and Venado Caverns. Ask at your hotel for more information.

Kids and the young at heart may enjoy the pool, fountain, and water slide at **Jungla y Senderos Los Lagos** (ⓒ **506/479-9126**). I personally come here more for the network of trails and small lakes that are also on this property. It recently added a small crocodile hatchery and tilapia farm, a canopy tour, and some basic hot springs. You'll find Los Lagos on the road to Tabacón, a few kilometers out of La Fortuna. It charges $8 for daily use of its facilities.

ACCOMMODATIONS IN LA FORTUNA

La Fortuna is a tourist boomtown; basic hotels have popped up here at a phenomenal rate. Right in La Fortuna you'll find a score of budget options. If you have time, it's worth walking around and checking out a couple. If you have a car, drive a little bit out of town toward Tabacón, and you'll find several more basic cabins, some that even offer views of the volcano. There are a couple places both in town and right on the outskirts of La Fortuna that allow camping, with access to basic bathroom facilities, for around $5 to $7 per person per night.

Hotel La Fortuna   Located 1 block south of the gas station, this perennial budget travelers' favorite has risen from the ashes. A 1997 fire destroyed most of the original hotel, but reconstruction was quick. Most of the rooms are on the original site, but there are three rooms in a new annex across the street. Accommodations are very basic, but what do you expect at these prices? At least the rooms are clean and have private bathrooms. There is a popular open-air restaurant at the front of the hotel, and the helpful owners can arrange a wide variety of tours.

La Fortuna, San Carlos. ⓒ and fax **506/479-9197**. 13 units. $10–$15 per person. Rates include breakfast. MC, V. **Amenities:** 1 restaurant; 1 bar; tour desk. *In room:* No phone.

Hotel Las Colinas   This three-story building in the center of town offers clean but basic rooms. You'll need to be in good shape if you stay in one of the third-floor rooms, but it's worth it if you can snag room 33, which has a private balcony and an unobstructed view of the volcano. However, most of the other rooms are probably overpriced, considering the wear and tear they've received over the years. There are a few rooms on the ground floor, but they don't even have windows to the outside and are very dark.

La Fortuna (A.P. 06), San Carlos. ⓒ and fax **506/479-9107**. hcolinas@racsa.co.cr. 19 units. $25 double; $35 triple. AE, MC, V. *In room:* No phone.

Hotel San Bosco   Located a block off La Fortuna's main street, the San Bosco has two styles of rooms. The older units all received a recent facelift and now feature tile floors and fans. Nevertheless, the newer rooms are still much more attractive and are probably the nicest options right in town. These have stone walls, tile floors, air-conditioning, reading lights, televisions, and benches on the veranda in front. There's an observation deck for volcano viewing on the top floor of the hotel.

La Fortuna, San Carlos (200m north of the gas station). ⓒ **506/479-9050**. Fax 506/479-9109. www.arenal-volcano.com. 34 units. $40–$50 double. Lower rates in the off-season. AE, MC, V. **Amenities:** Small outdoor pool; Jacuzzi; small exercise room; tour desk; laundry service. *In room:* No phone.

Luigi's Lodge   This small, in-town hotel has a lively, hostel-like atmosphere. The rooms are all comfortable and clean; those on the second floor have the best views of the volcano, although those on the first floor have higher ceilings. All open onto a long shared veranda or porch. Despite the name and the fact that the restaurant here is a pizza and pasta joint, the owners are actually Costa Rican, not Italian.

La Fortuna, San Carlos. ℂ **506/479-9909,** or ℂ and fax 506/479-9898. www.luigislodge.com. 22 units. $40–$50 double. MC, V. **Amenities:** 1 restaurant (Costa Rica/Italian); 1 bar; small outdoor pool; Jacuzzi; tour desk; laundry service. *In room:* A/C, coffee maker, hair dryer; no phone.

DINING IN & AROUND LA FORTUNA

Dining in La Fortuna is nowhere near as spectacular as volcano viewing. Most folks either eat at their hotel or go to any one of a number of basic *sodas* serving Tico standards. The favorite meeting places in town are the **El Jardín Restaurant** (ℂ **506/479-9360**), **Luigi's Pizza** (ℂ **506/479-9909**), and **Lava Rocks** (ℂ **506/479-9231**); all are on the main road, right in the center of La Fortuna. Other choices include **La Choza de Laurel** (ℂ **506/479-9231**), **Rancho La Cascada** (ℂ **506/479-9145**), and **La Pradera** (ℂ **506/479-9167**).

Heading out of town, you'll find **El Vagabundo** (ℂ **506/479-9565**), an Italian pizza and spaghetti joint. After dark, the area's biggest attraction is the volcano, but the new **Volcano Look Disco** (ℂ **506/479-9690**) on the road to Tabacón is hoping to compete. If you get bored of the eruptions and seismic rumbling, head here for heavy dance beats and mirrored disco balls.

El Novillo ✴ *Finds* STEAKHOUSE/COSTA RICAN   This place is the definition of "nothing fancy." In fact, it's just some lawn furniture (tables and chairs) set on a concrete slab, underneath a high, open, zinc roof. Still, it's garnered a well-deserved reputation as the best steakhouse in the area. The steaks are big and tender and well prepared. The chicken and fish dishes are huge as well, and also nicely done. Meals come with garlic bread, fries, and some slaw. If you want a real local treat, order some fried yucca as a side. If the night is clear, you can get a good view of any volcanic activity from the parking lot here.

On the rd. to Tabacón, 10km outside of La Fortuna. ℂ **506/460-6433.** Main courses $5–$9. No credit cards. Daily 10am–midnight.

ACCOMMODATIONS NEAR THE VOLCANO
EXPENSIVE

Arenal Lodge ✴   Located high on a hillside above Lake Arenal, this lodge has a direct view of Arenal Volcano (some 6 miles/9.5km away) over a forested valley. Although it's not as close to the volcano as some of the other lodges mentioned below, the view is still stunning. The standard rooms, though attractively decorated, have no views at all, although it's only a few steps to a large viewing deck. If you reserve one of the huge junior suites, you can lie in bed and gaze out at the volcano through a wall of glass. These rooms have two queen-size beds, balconies, large picture windows, and lots of space. The matrimonial suite comes with its own private Jacuzzi. Five separate buildings on a hill behind the main building house the 10 new chalet rooms. These rooms all have plenty of space, small kitchenettes, and good views from their balconies or patios, although they feel a little bit Spartan.

Meals are served in a dining room with a glass wall facing the volcano. After dinner, you can retire to the library, where there's a huge stone fireplace and a pool table, or soak in the outdoor Jacuzzi. A separate lounge has a TV and VCR. Situated on a macadamia plantation between two strips of virgin forest, the lodge has several trails that are great for bird watching.

Lake Arenal (A.P. 1139-1250, Escazú). ℂ **506/228-3189.** Fax 506/289-6798. www.arenallodge. com. 35 units. $70 double; $115–$145 suites and chalet rooms. Rates include buffet breakfast and a 1-hour horseback ride. Slightly higher rates during peak weeks, lower rates in the off-season

(May–Nov). AE, MC, V. Drive west from La Fortuna past Tabacón and the National Park. About 200m (218 yd.) past the dam over Lake Arenal, you'll see a steep driveway. The lodge is a couple of km up the driveway. **Amenities:** 1 restaurant; 1 bar; Jacuzzi; mountain-bike rental; free shuttle to Tabacón Hot Springs 4 times daily; tour desk; laundry service. *In room:* Fridge, coffee maker; no phone.

Tabacón Resort ✦✦   This new hotel is by far the most upscale option in the Arenal area. Guests here enjoy privileges at the spectacular hot springs complex and spa across the street (see the box called "Taking a Soothing Soak in Hot Springs," above). Most rooms here have excellent, direct views of the volcano. Those on the upper floors of the 300-block building have the best vistas. They're all spacious and new, with nice wooden furniture; each has a private terrace or balcony with a table and a couple of chairs for volcano viewing. Nine of the rooms here are truly designed to be accessible to travelers with disabilities. Another nine are suites, with separate sitting rooms and a private volcano-view Jacuzzi. There's a large hot-spring-fed pool and separate Jacuzzi right at the hotel.

As you drive along the main road between La Fortuna and Lake Arenal, you'll see the lodge on your right, and then about 100 yards or so later, around a sharp bend, the hot springs and spa will be on your left.

On the main rd. between La Fortuna and Lake Arenal, Tabacón (P.O. Box 181-1007, Centro Colón, San José). ✆ **506/256-1500.** Fax 506/221-3075. www.tabacon.com. 82 units. $130 double; $170 suite. Rates include buffet breakfast. Slightly lower rates in the off-season (May–Nov). AE, DC, MC, V. **Amenities:** 2 restaurants (Costa Rican, international); 2 bars; 1 large pool with swim-up bar; extensive hot springs and spa facilities; Jacuzzi; mountain-bike rental; tour desk; free shuttle to the spa and hot springs; small business center; in-room massage; laundry service. *In room:* A/C, TV, coffee maker, hair dryer, safe.

MODERATE

Arenal Observatory Lodge ✦✦ *(Finds)*   This once-rustic lodge was originally built for the use of volcanologists from the Smithsonian Institute but has turned into one of my favorite choices in the Arenal area. The hotel is only 2½ miles (4km) from the volcano and is built on a high ridge, with a spectacular view of the cone. Lying in bed at night listening to the eruptions, it's easy to think you're in imminent danger (don't worry—you're not). The superior rooms feature massive picture windows, with a direct view of the volcano. The nicest of these are the four new rooms in the Observatory Block. Room 29 even has a view of both the lake and the volcano. There are even a couple of rooms for disabled travelers. The most basic rooms are in the original *casona* (big house) and are located about 500 meters (545 yd.) from the main lodge; bathrooms are shared.

Surrounding the lodge is Arenal National Park, which includes thousands of acres of forest and many kilometers of excellent trails. The lodge offers a number of guided and unguided hiking options, including a free morning trip to one of the cooled-off lava flows, as well as a wide range of other tours. Meals are served in a well-placed dining room, with a full wall of glass facing the volcano. The newest addition here is an outdoor swimming pool and Jacuzzi. The only downside here is that due to the shifting of vents and a major blowout on the side of the main crater, you now get better views of lava flows from the Tabacón side of the volcano.

To get here, head to the national park entrance, stay on the dirt road past the entrance, and follow the signs to the Observatory Lodge. A four-wheel-drive vehicle used to be required for the 5½-mile (9km) dirt road up to the lodge, but two bridges now eliminate the need to ford any major rivers, and a two-wheel-drive vehicle will usually make it in the dry season (Dec–Apr)—although you'll always be better off with the clearance afforded by a four-wheel-drive or SUV.

On the flanks of Arenal Volcano (A.P. 13411-1000, San José). *©* **506/290-7011.** Fax 506/290-8427. www.arenal-observatory.co.cr. 32 units, 28 with private bathroom. $52 double with shared bathroom; $76–$108 double with private bathroom. Rates include breakfast buffet. Lower rates in the off-season (May–Nov). AE, MC, V. **Amenities:** 1 restaurant (Costa Rican/international); 1 bar; outdoor pool; Jacuzzi; tour desk; laundry service. *In room:* No phone.

Montaña de Fuego Inn   This place started out as a small collection of cabins with a great view and great prices. As its popularity grew, the prices and a whole host of new cabins have quickly gone up. Still, these individual cabins have wonderful volcano views from their spacious glass-enclosed porches. Inside, the cabins are all varnished wood, with sparse but new appointments. The junior suites all have air-conditioning and minifridges, and some even have back balconies overlooking a forested ravine, in addition to the volcano-facing front porch. There's a large, glass-walled restaurant, Acuarelas, that serves overpriced international cuisine. The newest addition here is a pool, Jacuzzi, and spa facility with a modest exercise room and massage-treatment rooms.

If this place is full, check next door at the **Cabañas Arenal Paraíso** (*©* **506/479-9006**), which has very similar accommodations at slightly lower prices and is run by the same family (the owners of the two lodges are brothers). Both of these hotels are located 5 miles (8km) outside La Fortuna on the road to Tabacón.

La Palma de la Fortuna (A.P. 82-4417), San Carlos. *©* **506/460-1220.** Fax 506/460-1455. www.montanadefuego.com. 40 units. $60–$80 double. MC, V. **Amenities:** 1 restaurant (international); 2 bars; 1 small pool; Jacuzzi; exercise room; tour desk; massage; laundry service. *In room:* No phone.

Volcano Lodge   This new lodge is a collection of 10 duplexes across the road from and facing the volcano. All of the rooms come with two double beds, a private bathroom, two wicker chairs inside, and a small terrace with a couple of wooden rocking chairs for volcano viewing outside. The appointments are simple, but the rooms are spacious and get plenty of light through big picture windows. Rooms 1 through 12 have the best views. A wide range of tours is available. The hotel also provides free shuttle service to La Fortuna and Tabacón Hot Springs.

La Fortuna de San Carlos. *©* **506/460-6080** or 506/460-6022. Fax 506/460-6020. www.costaricavolcanolodge.com. 20 units. A/C. $75 double. Rates include continental breakfast. Lower rates in the off-season. AE, MC, V. **Amenities:** 1 restaurant; 1 bar; small free-form outdoor pool; Jacuzzi; tour desk; laundry service. *In room:* No phone.

ACCOMMODATIONS & DINING FARTHER AFIELD

All of the hotels listed in the following two sections are at least a half-hour drive from La Fortuna and the volcano. Most if not all offer both night and day tours to Arenal and Tabacón, but also hope to attract you with their own natural charms.

EAST OF LA FORTUNA

Hotel La Garza   This comfortable, small nature lodge is set on a large working ranch just south of Muelle. La Garza means "the egret," and you'll see plenty of these birds here, as they roost nearby. Also, the ranch includes 750 acres of primary rain forest, where many other species of birds can be spotted. Built on the banks of the San Carlos River, the hotel consists of six duplex bungalows, each of which has a deck overlooking the river. Large trees provide shade, and the sound of the river lulls you to sleep at night. High ceilings and overhead fans help keep the rooms cool, and all the rooms are attractively decorated and have views of Arenal Volcano in the distance. The hotel's restaurant and bar are reached via a small suspension bridge over the lazy little river that runs through the property. You can arrange tours of the region, or wander around the ranch observing the day-to-day activities.

Plantanar, San Carlos (A.P. 100-2250, Tres Ríos). ℂ 506/475-5222. Fax 506/475-5015. www. hotel-lagarza-arenal.com. 12 units. $75 double; $87 triple. Lower rates off-season (May–Nov). AE, DC, MC, V. **Amenities:** 1 restaurant (Costa Rican/international); 1 bar; small outdoor pool; outdoor tennis court; Jacuzzi; tour desk; laundry service.

Hotel Occidental El Tucano Resort and Spa ⭐

Located 5¼ miles (8.5km) north of Ciudad Quesada (San Carlos) on the road to Aguas Zarcas, El Tucano is one of the most elegant spa facilities in Costa Rica, with natural hot springs, Jacuzzis, indoor and natural steam rooms, a small gym, and a wide range of massage and spa treatments. The resort is located in a steep-walled valley and faces a lush rain forest. The rooms are set into the hillside and are connected by narrow, winding alleys and stairways. Most rooms are carpeted and very comfortable, with attractive decorations. The two presidential suites have private terraces, in-room Jacuzzis, and large-screen TVs. This is a great place just to kick back and relax for a day or two.

There are hiking trails on the property, and you can arrange a variety of tours around the region, including some on horseback. Just hanging around, you should see plenty of colorful toucans, the hotel's namesake, as well as many other birds.

The dining room is large and formal, with excellent service and a continental menu that includes chicken à l'orange and pasta with shrimp. The best tables here, when the weather is nice, are on an outdoor balcony overlooking the river.

Aguas Calientes de San Carlos (A.P. 114-1017, San José). ℂ **506/460-6000** or 506/460-3141. Fax 506/460-1692. www.occidental-hoteles.com. occhcr@racsa.co.cr. 90 units. $83 double; $136 junior suite, $188 suite. AE, DC, MC, V. **Amenities:** 1 restaurant (international); 1 bar; large natural-spring-heated outdoor pool and several smaller pools; Jacuzzi; 2 outdoor tennis courts; health club and spa; sauna; minigolf course; tour desk; salon; limited room service; massage; laundry service. *In room:* TV, hair dryer, safe.

Termales del Bosque

This new place packs a lot of ecotourism punch for the buck. Most of the rooms are in duplex buildings set on a small hill. Each comes with two double beds, or a double and a single, and front and back patios. The rooms are clean and spacious. There is also a three-bedroom bungalow with a shared bathroom and kitchenette. Meals will run you around $20 per day.

It's nowhere near as fancy as the neighboring El Tucano Resort, but Termales del Bosque does have some truly wonderful **natural hot springs** ⭐⭐ set in rich rain forest. The series of sculpted pools is set on the banks of a small river. Down by the pools, there's a natural steam room (scented each day with fresh eucalyptus), a massage room, and a snack-and-juice bar. The trail down here winds through the thick forest and, if you want to keep on walking, you can take guided or self-guided tours on a network of well-marked trails. You can rent horses right at the lodge, and there's even a canopy tour. If you aren't staying here, you can use the pools and hike the trails for $8, or do the canopy tour for $45. You'll find Termales del Bosque on the road from San Carlos to Aguas Zarcas, just before El Tucano.

Ciudad Quesada (A.P. 243-4400), San Carlos. ℂ **506/460-4740** or 506/257-5149. Fax 506/460-1356. termales@racsa.co.cr. 19 units. $45 double; $55 triple. Rates include breakfast. AE, MC, V.

Amenities: 1 restaurant (Costa Rican); several hot-spring pools set beside a forest river; canopy tour; tour desk; massage; laundry service. *In room:* No phone.

Tilajari Hotel Resort ☽ *Kids* This sprawling 30-acre resort just outside the farming community of Muelle (17.4 miles/28km from La Fortuna) makes a good base for exploring this area, and offers terrific **bird watching** ☽☽. Built on the banks of the San Carlos River, the Tilajari Hotel offers some of the more luxurious accommodations in the region. Most of the rooms have views of the river (some even have balconies), while others open onto rich flowering gardens. Each suite comes with a separate living room and kitchenette. Large iguanas are frequently sighted on the grounds, and crocodiles live in the San Carlos River. There's also an orchid garden, tropical fruit-and-vegetable garden, medicinal herb garden, and well-maintained butterfly garden. The large open-air dining room has both formal and informal sections and a bar.

The lodge arranges tours around the region, including trips to Caño Negro, Arenal Volcano and Tabacón Hot Springs, and Fortuna Falls, for around $45 per person. Trips into the nearby rain forest, on foot, on horseback, or by tractor, can also be arranged, as can gentle floats on the Peñas Blancas River.

To reach Tilajari from San José, drive first to Ciudad Quesada; from there continue on to Florencia. In Florencia, turn north on the road to Muelle (marked). In Muelle, turn left (head west) toward Tanque and follow the signs for Tilajari, which will be on your right a mile (1.6km) from this last turn.

Muelle (A.P. 81-4400), San Carlos. ℂ **506/469-9091.** Fax 506/469-9095. www.tilajari.com. 76 units. $85 double; $105 junior suite, $110 family suite. Slightly lower rates in the off-season (May–Nov) and 15% higher over Christmas holidays. AE, MC, V. **Amenities:** 1 restaurant (Costa Rican/international); 1 bar; large outdoor pool; 6 lighted tennis courts (2 indoors); exercise room; Jacuzzi; sauna; kayak rental; mountain-bike rental; racquetball court; soccer field; game room with pool tables and table tennis; tour desk; laundry service. *In room:* A/C, TV, hair dryer, safe.

SOUTH OF LA FORTUNA

Hotel Valle Escondido This modest ecolodge, which provides access to some of the region's rain forests, is south of La Fortuna, just off the road between San Ramón and La Fortuna. Valle Escondido (Hidden Valley) is situated on a 990-acre farm that includes primary and secondary forest as well as fields of ornamental plants grown for export. The rooms are located in long low rows of buildings, with good views over a forested valley. All are spacious and comfortable. Some are carpeted, but I prefer those with hardwood floors. In front of the rooms run long verandas where you can sit and enjoy the tranquillity of the surroundings.

There are miles of well-maintained trails here. Hiking, horseback riding ($10 per hr.), mountain-biking ($4 per hr.), and bird watching are the primary activities here; a wide range of tours is available for an additional charge. There's a new canopy tour ($40) here, but be aware that it claimed the life of a guide early on in its operation.

San Ramón (A.P. 452-1150, La Uruca). ℂ **506/231-0906.** Fax 506/232-9591. www.valleescondido. com. 35 units. $70 double; $85 triple. AE, MC, V. **Amenities:** 1 restaurant (Costa Rican/international); 1 bar; small pool; Jacuzzi; mountain-bike and horse rental; tour desk; laundry service. *In room:* No phone.

Villablanca Hotel Owned and operated by a former president of Costa Rica, this lodge consists of a series of Tico-style *casitas*, or little houses, surrounded by 2,000 acres of farm and forest. Each casita is built of adobe and has traditional tile floors and whitewashed walls with deep-blue trim (this is the classic color scheme of 19th-century adobe homes throughout the country). Inside, you'll find a rounded fireplace in one corner, window seats, comfortable hardwood chairs, colorful curtains, and two twin beds covered with colorful bedspreads. The "family" casitas have two bedrooms and two baths. Most rooms come with electric teapots and some have small refrigerators. In several rooms the bathrooms have tubs that look out through a wall of windows onto lush gardens.

The dining room, which offers a simple but filling buffet, is in the hacienda-style main lodge. A central atrium garden, library, TV room/lounge, gift shop, and small bar round out the hotel. Villablanca is off the beaten track, but it is relatively close to San José, and if you're interested in bird watching or exploring a cloud forest and want to avoid the crowds of Monteverde, this is a good choice.

Adjacent to the lodge are 6¾ miles (11km) of trails through the **Los Angeles Cloud Forest Reserve.** Admission to the reserve is $24 per person and includes a guided hike. You can also rent horses ($12 per hr.) or take an adventurous swing through the canopy on their new canopy tour ($39). If you're driving, head west out of San José to San Ramón and then head north, following the signs to Villablanca. Or you can take a public bus from San José to San Ramón and then take a taxi for around $15.

San Ramón (A.P. 247-1250), Alajuela. ℂ **506/228-4603** or 506/661-1600. Fax 506/228-4004. www.villablanca-costarica.com. 48 units. $99 double; $119 triple; $163 family casita for up to 6. AE, DC, MC, V. **Amenities:** 1 restaurant (Costa Rican/buffet); 1 bar; horse rental; laundry service. *In room:* No phone.

3 Along the Shores of Lake Arenal ⟨⭑⟩

124 miles (200km) NW of San José; 12½ miles (20km) NW of Monteverde; 43½ miles (70km) SE of Liberia

This remains one of the least-developed tourism regions in Costa Rica but not for lack of resources or charms. It does, after all, have Lake Arenal, a man-made lake with an area of 33 square miles (85.5km; making it the largest lake in Costa Rica), surrounded by rolling hills that are partly pastured and partly forested. The perfect cone of Arenal Volcano lies at the opposite (east) end of the lake from the small towns of Tilarán and Nuevo Arenal. The volcano's barren slopes are a stunning sight from here, especially when reflected in the waters of the lake. The northwest side of Lake Arenal is a dry region of rolling hills and pastures, distinctly different from the lusher landscape near La Fortuna.

People around here used to curse the winds, which often come blasting across this end of the lake at 60 knots or greater. However, since the first sailboarders caught wind of Lake Arenal's combination of warm, fresh water, steady blows, and spectacular scenery, things have been changing quickly. Although the towns of Tilarán and Nuevo Arenal are little more than a quiet rural communities, hotels are proliferating all along the shores of the lake. Even if you aren't a fanatical sailboarder, you still might enjoy hanging out by the lake, hiking in the nearby forests, and catching glimpses of Arenal Volcano.

The lake's other claim to fame is its rainbow-bass fishing. These fighting fish are known in their native South America as *guapote* and are large members of the cichlid family. Their sharp teeth and fighting nature make them a real challenge.

ESSENTIALS

GETTING THERE & DEPARTING   By Car From San José, take the Interamerican Highway west toward Puntarenas and then continue north on this road to Cañas. In Cañas, turn east toward Tilarán. The drive takes 4 hours. If you're continuing on to Nuevo Arenal, follow the signs in town, which will put you on the road that skirts the shore of the lake. Nuevo Arenal is about a half-hour drive from Tilarán. You can also drive here from La Fortuna, along a scenic road that winds around the lake. From La Fortuna, it's approximately 1 hour to Nuevo Arenal and 1½ hours to Tilarán.

By Bus   Express buses (© **506/222-3854**) leave San José for Tilarán daily at 7:30 and 9:30am, and 12:45, 3:45, and 6:30pm from Calle 12 between Avenidas 7 and 9. The trip lasts from 4 to 5½ hours, depending on road conditions; the fare is $3.

There are also morning and afternoon buses from **Puntarenas** to Tilarán. The ride takes about 3 hours; the fare is $2.50. To get to Puntarenas, see the information on getting to Puntarenas in chapter 5. From **Monteverde** (Santa Elena), there is a bus daily at 7am. The fare for the 3-hour trip is $2. Buses from **La Fortuna** leave for Tilarán daily at 8am and 2:30pm, returning at 7am and 12:30pm. The trip is 3 to 4 hours; the fare is $2.50.

From Tilarán, direct buses to San José leave daily at 5, 7, and 7:45am and 2 and 5pm. Buses to Puntarenas leave at 6am and 1pm daily. The bus to Santa Elena (Monteverde) leaves daily at 1pm. Buses also leave regularly for Cañas, where you can catch buses north or south along the Interamerican Highway. Buses for La Fortuna, at the south end of Lake Arenal, leave daily at 7am and 3pm.

ORIENTATION   Tilarán is about 3 miles (5km) from Lake Arenal. All roads into town lead to the central park, which is Tilarán's main point of reference for addresses. If you need to exchange money, check at one of the hotels listed here, or go to the Banco Nacional. If you need a taxi to get to a lodge on Lake Arenal, call **Taxis Unidos Tilarán** (© **506/695-5324**).

WHAT TO SEE & DO

WINDSURFING ✸✸   If you want to try windsurfing, you can rent equipment from **Tilawa Windsurfing Center** (© **506/695-5050**), which has its facilities on one of the lake's few accessible beaches, about 5 miles (8km) from Tilarán on the road along the west end of the lake. Boards rent for $45 to $55 per day, and lessons are also available. You can also ask at **Tico Wind** (© **506/ 383-2694;** www.ticowind.com; info@ticowind.com), which sets up shop on the shores of the lake each year when the winds blow, and rents equipment for $350 per week, including daily lunch.

SWIMMING & HIKING   Up above Lake Arenal on the far side of the lake from Tilarán, you'll find the beautiful little heart-shaped **Lake Coter.** This lake is surrounded by forest and has good swimming. (UFO watchers also claim that this is a popular pit stop for extraterrestrials.) A taxi to Lake Coter will cost around $12.

If you feel like strapping on your boots, there are some hiking trails on the far side of Lake Arenal, near the smaller Lake Coter.

MOUNTAIN-BIKING   This is a great area to explore on a mountain-bike. **Rock River Lodge** (© **506/695-5644;** www.rokriverlodge.com) has some high-end mountain-bikes, which will run you around $35 per day. You can also rent bikes in the town of Tilarán at **La Carreta** restaurant (© **506/695-6654**).

FISHING   If you want to try your hand at fishing for rainbow bass, contact **J.J.'s Fishing and Outdoor Tours** (© **506/695-5825**). A half-day fishing trip will cost around $175, and a full day goes for $200 (this is a flat fee, but can be split between two people). J.J.'s can also arrange nonfishing boat trips out on the lake and other outdoor tours.

HORSEBACK RIDING   The folks at **Tilawa** (see "Windsurfing," above) or **Rock River Lodge** (⟁ 506/695-5644; www.rokriverlodge.com) can arrange for you to rent a horse for around $10 to $15 per hour.

ARENAL BOTANICAL GARDENS 🖈   Continuing clockwise on the road around the lake will bring you to the town of Nuevo Arenal, where the pavement ends. If you continue another 2½ miles (4km) on the dirt road, you'll come to the Arenal Botanical Gardens (⟁ **506/694-4273;** open daily 9am–5pm; $8 admission). This private garden was started only in 1991, but it's already quite beautiful and extensive. Not only are there many tropical plants and flowers to be seen, but there are always butterflies and hummingbirds here.

ARTS, CRAFTS & DOWNHOME COOKING   If you're in the area, don't miss **Toad Hall** 🖈 (⟁ **506/381-3662;** www.toadhall-gallery.com). Located 9 kilometers outside of Nuevo Arenal, toward La Fortuna, this roadside gallery and cafe serves up excellent breakfasts, light lunches, and a wide range of coffee drinks and desserts. It also has one of the better-stocked galleries in the country. You'll find the works of Lil Mena, Cecilia Figueres, Patricia Erickson, and Barry Biesanz, among others, as well as a good selection of craftworks.

ACCOMMODATIONS
MODERATE
Chalet Nicholas _Value_   This friendly American-owned bed-and-breakfast is located 1½ miles (2½km) west of Nuevo Arenal and sits on a hill above the road. There are great views from the garden, and all three rooms have a view of Arenal Volcano. This converted home is set on 15 acres and has pretty flower gardens, an organic vegetable garden, and an orchid garden. Behind the property are acres of forest through which you can hike in search of birds, orchids, butterflies, and other tropical beauties. The upstairs loft room is the largest unit, with its own private deck. No smoking is allowed in the house or on the grounds. A 3-hour horseback-riding tour costs $25 per person. Owners John and Catherine Nicholas go out of their way to make their guests feel at home, although their three Great Danes might intimidate you when you first drive up. All around, it's a really good deal.

Tilarán (A.P. 72-5710), Guanacaste. ⟁ and fax **506/694-4041.** nicholas@racsa.co.cr. 3 units. $59 double. Rates include full breakfast. No credit cards. _In room:_ No phone.

Hotel Tilawa   Built to resemble the Palace of Knossos on the island of Crete, the Hotel Tilawa sits high on the slopes above the lake and has a sweeping vista down to the water. It's primarily a windsurfers' hangout. Unusual colors and antique paint effects give the hotel a weathered look; inside there are wall murals and other artistic paint treatments throughout. Rooms have dyed cement floors, Guatemalan bedspreads, and big windows. Some have kitchenettes. For a fee, the Tilawa can arrange windsurfing, mountain-biking, horseback-riding, and fishing trips (with or without meals and/or equipment). It also offers a 5-hour boat tour across the lake, with a visit to Tabacón Hot Springs, for $49.

Tilarán (A.P. 92-5710), Guanacaste. ⟁ **800/851-8929** in the U.S., or 506/695-5050. Fax 506/695-5766. www.hotel-tilawa.com. tilawa@racsa.co.cr. 28 units. $77 double; $100 triple; $148 suite. Children under age 5 stay free in parents' room; children ages 5–18 $12 to stay in parents' room. AE, DC, MC, V. **Amenities:** 1 restaurant (Costa Rican/international); 1 bar/disco; small outdoor swimming pool; outdoor tennis court; sailboard and mountain-bike rentals at well-equipped windsurfing center down by the lake; tour desk; laundry service.

Rock River Lodge 🖈 _Value_   Set high on a grassy hill above the lake, this small lodge is _the joint_ for serious windsurfers. The rooms are in a long, low lodge set on stilts. Walls and floors are made of hardwood, and there are bamboo railings along the veranda. Wind chimes let you know when the breezes are kicking up, and there are sling chairs on the porch. Rooms are of medium size; each has one double bed and a bunk bed, and a small tiled bathroom. Though fairly simple in style, this is one of the most attractive lodges in the area. The newer bungalows, which are farther up the hill, offer more privacy and space and have small sculpted bathtubs in larger bathrooms. It's a long walk down to the lake (not to mention the walk back up), so a car is recommended. Meals will cost you around $25 per person per day and are served in the spacious open-air restaurant, where there's a large stone fireplace. When the wind isn't up, owner Norman List offers mountain-biking trips and horseback and hiking adventures to a nearby waterfall.

Tilarán (A.P. 95), Guanacaste. ℂ and fax **506/695-5644**. www.rokriverlodge.com. rokriver@ racsa.co.cr. 6 units, 8 bungalows. $53 double; $76 bungalow for 2. Extra person $12. AE, MC, V. **Amenities:** 1 restaurant; 1 bar; sailboard and mountain-bike rental; laundry service. *In room:* No phone.

Villa Decary ☆ *(Finds)*   Named after a French explorer (and a rare palm species he discovered and named), this small bed-and-breakfast is nestled on a hill above Lake Arenal, midway between the town of Nuevo Arenal and the Arenal Botanical Gardens. Each room comes with two double beds, large picture windows, and a spacious private balcony with a lake view. The rooms get plenty of light, and the bright Guatemalan bedspreads and white-tile floors create a vibrant look. The separate casitas, or little houses, have full kitchens, more room, and even better views of the lake from their slightly higher perches. Breakfasts are extravagant and memorable, with a steady stream of fresh fruits; fresh juice; strong coffee; homemade pancakes, waffles, or muffins; and usually an excellent omelet or soufflé. There's great bird watching on the hotel grounds, and howler monkeys are common guests here as well.

Nuevo Arenal, 5717 Tilarán, Guanacaste. ℂ **506/383-3012**. Fax 506/694-4330. www. villadecary.com. 5 units, 3 casitas. $69 double; $79–$119 casita for 2. Extra person $15. Rates include full breakfast. No credit cards. *In room:* No phone.

INEXPENSIVE

Cabinas Mary   Located right on Tilarán's large and sunny central park, Cabinas Mary is a very basic but fairly clean lodging. It's upstairs from the restaurant of the same name and has safe parking in back. Rooms are large, and most have plenty of windows. You even get hot water here, which is a surprise at this price. The restaurant downstairs is a popular hangout. It's open daily from 6am to 10pm; meals cost between $3 and $7.

Tilarán (A.P. 89), Guanacaste. ℂ and fax **506/695-5479**. 18 units. $20 double. No credit cards. **Amenities:** 1 restaurant (Costa Rican); 1 bar. *In room:* No phone.

Hotel Naralit   This budget hotel is a good bet in Tilarán. The rooms are clean and comfortable, and some even come with cable TV, albeit with very small television sets. There are three second-floor rooms that have a nice shared balcony, more natural light, and views of the town's church.

Tilarán, Guanacaste. ℂ **506/695-5393**. Fax 506/695-6767. 26 units. $16–25 double; $25–$32 triple. V. *In room:* No phone.

Mystica *(Value)*   Set on a high hill above Lake Arenal, about midway between Nuevo Arenal and Tilarán, this is my favorite budget option in the area. The rooms are all simple, but spacious and cheery. The painted cement floors are kept immaculate, and the rooms get good ventilation from their large windows. All units open onto a long and broad shared veranda with a great view of the lake. See "Dining," below for a review of the restaurant's recommended Italian restaurant.

On the road between Tilarán and Nuevo Arenal. (℃ **506/382-1499.** mystica@racsa.co.cr. 6 units. $45 double. Rates include breakfast. V. **Amenities:** 1 restaurant (Italian); 1 bar; laundry service. *In room:* No phone.

DINING

There are numerous inexpensive places to eat in Tilarán, including the restaurant at Cabinas Mary, as well as **La Carreta** (℃ **506/695-6654**), a popular restaurant and bar around the corner. If you're staying outside of town, it's likely you'll eat in your hotel's dining room, since there are few restaurants around the shores of the lake.

In Nuevo Arenal, try the pizzas and pastas at **Tramonti** (℃ **506/694-4282**). Also worth mentioning is **Equus BBQ,** a small open-air restaurant in front of Xiloe Lodge that has a view of the lake. It specializes in roast chicken and steaks.

Mystica ⊛ PIZZA/ITALIAN   The restaurant in this Italian-run hotel has a wonderful setting high on a hill overlooking the lake. The large dining room features rustic wooden chairs and tables, varnished wood floors, colorful tablecloths, and abundant flower arrangements. The most striking features, aside from the view, are the large open fireplace on one end, and the large brick oven, in the shape of a small cottage, on the other, which turns out pizzas. The pastas and delicious main dishes are authentically northern Italian. Whenever possible, Mystica uses fresh ingredients from its own garden.

On the rd. between Tilarán and Nuevo Arenal. (℃ **506/382-1499.** Main courses $3–$9. V. Daily 7:30am–9pm.

Willy's Caballo Negro ⊛ *Finds* GERMAN/EUROPEAN   The German owners of this attractive little roadside cafe serve up three different types of schnitzel, both chicken and veal cordon bleu, and a host of other old-world meat dishes. Try the Zigeuner Schnitzel, a tender veal cutlet in a slightly spicy sauce of onions and bell peppers, served with spätzle. Despite the emphasis on meats and sausages, vegetarians will find several tasty and filling options here, including stuffed potatoes and eggplant Parmesan. Wooden tables are set around the edges of the round dining room, with a high peaked roof. Candles and creative lighting give the place a cozy and warm feel. There's a small, picturesque lake behind the restaurant and a small but interesting gift shop.

Nuevo Arenal (about 3km out of town on the road to Tilarán). (℃ **506/694-4515.** Main courses $4.50–$11. No credit cards. Daily 9am–9pm.

4 Monteverde ⊛⊛

103 miles (167km) NW of San José; 51 miles (82km) NW of Puntarenas

Next to Manuel Antonio, this is Costa Rica's most internationally recognized tourist destination. The fame and accompanying traffic have led me to dub it the Monteverde Crowd Forest. Nevertheless, the preserve itself and the extensive network of private reserves around it are incredibly rich in biodiversity, and a well-organized infrastructure helps guarantee a rewarding experience for both first-time and experienced eco-adventurers.

Monteverde translates as "green mountain," and that's exactly what you'll find at the end of the steep and windy rutted dirt road that leads here. Along the way, you'll pass through mile after mile of often dry, brown pasturelands. All of these pastures were once covered with dense forest, but now only small pieces of that original forest remain.

The village of Monteverde was founded in 1951 by Quakers from the United States who wished to leave behind a constant fear of war as well as an obligation to support continued militarism through paying U.S. taxes. They chose Costa Rica primarily because it had no standing army. Although Monteverde's founders came here to farm the land, they wisely recognized the need to preserve the rare cloud forest that covered the mountain slopes above their fields, and to that end they dedicated the largest adjacent tract of cloud forest as the Monteverde Biological Cloud Forest Preserve. Perched on a high mountain ridge, this tiny, scattered village and surrounding cloud forest are well known both among scientific researchers and ecotravelers.

Cloud forests are a mountaintop phenomenon. Moist, warm air sweeping in off the nearby ocean is forced upward by mountain slopes, and as this moist air rises, it cools, forming clouds. The mountaintops of Costa Rica are blanketed almost daily in dense clouds, and as these clouds cling to the slopes, moisture condenses on forest trees. This constant level of moisture has given rise to an incredible diversity of innovative life-forms and a forest in which nearly every square inch of space has some sort of plant growing. Within the cloud forest, the branches of huge trees are draped with epiphytic plants: orchids, ferns, and bromeliads. This intense botanic competition has created an almost equally diverse population of insects, birds, and other wildlife. Monteverde Biological Cloud Forest Preserve covers 26,000 acres of forest, including several different life zones that are characterized by different types of plants and animals. Within this small area are more than 2,000 species of plants, 400 species of birds, and 100 different species of mammals. It's no wonder that the preserve has been the site of constant scientific investigations since its founding in 1972.

The preserve was originally known only to the handful of researchers who came here to study different aspects of life in the cloud forest. However, as the beauty and biological diversity of the area became known outside of academic circles, casual visitors began arriving. For many, the primary goal was a chance to glimpse the rare and elusive **quetzal,** a bird once revered by the pre-Columbian peoples of the Americas. As the number of visitors began to grow, lodges began opening, word spread, more lodges opened, and so on. Today Monteverde is a place of great and fragile beauty whose popularity threatens to destroy the very beauty that draws people to it. That said, and despite the hordes of ecotourists traipsing its trails, Monteverde is still a beautiful place and offers a glimpse into the life of one of the world's most threatened ecosystems. However, if your primary goal is to sight a quetzal, you should also consider visiting

---

Tips   **Driving Note**

All roads to Monteverde are rugged, especially the one from Tilarán, which is riddled with potholes and rough gravel. Pregnant women or people with bad backs should think twice before embarking on these painful, poorly maintained roads. It's usually possible to make the trip in a standard two-wheel-drive vehicle in the dry season (Dec–Mar), but even so, you might want the extra clearance afforded by four-wheel-drive. In the rainy season (Apr–Nov), four-wheel-drive is a must.

Monteverde

HOTELS
Arco Iris Lodge **7**
El Bosque **25**
El Establo **15**
El Sapo Dorado **11**
Hotel Belmar **22**
Hotel Camino Verde **4**
Hotel De Montaña Monteverde **20**
Hotel El Tucan **6**
Hotel Fonda Vela **33**
Hotel Heliconia **14**
Hotel Villa Verde **34**
La Colina Lodge **32**
Monteverde Lodge **17**
Pension Flor de Monteverde **10**
Pension Monteverde Inn **19**

ATTRACTIONS, ETC. ●
Bajo del Tigre Trail **28**
Banco Nacional **1**
Bromelias **27**
Butterfly Garden **18**
Canopy Tours **2**
Centro Panamericano de Idiomas **21**
Chunches **5**
Galeria Extasis **23**
Hummingbird Gallery **35**
Meg's Riding Stables **24**
Monteverde Conservation League **28**
Monteverde Studio of the Arts **31**
The Orchid Garden **13**
Reserva Sendero Tranquilo **30**
Serpentarium Santa Elena **9**
Sky Trek/Sky Walk **8**

RESTAURANTS ◆
El Sapo Dorado **11**
Monteverde Cheese Factory **29**
Morphos Café **3**
Pizzeria de Johnny **12**
Restaurante De Lucia **16**
Stella's Bakery **26**

other cloud-forest areas around Costa Rica. In particular, consider the Tapantí National Wildlife Refuge, near Cerro de la Muerte, which has several specialty lodges (see chapter 7, section 5), where you'll find far fewer crowds and usually better chances of seeing the famed quetzal.

ESSENTIALS
GETTING THERE & DEPARTING   By Car   Take the Interamerican Highway toward Nicaragua. About 19 miles (31km) past the turnoff for Puntarenas, just before the Río Lagarto Bridge, there's the turnoff for the principal route up to Santa Elena and Monteverde. It takes about 2 hours and 15 minutes from San José to this point. Be careful—this turnoff isn't always well marked.

From this turnoff, it's another 23½ miles (38km) and 1½ to 2 hours to Monteverde. Why is the going so slow? Because the road is so bad, with such deep and frequent potholes. Many people are told that this road is not passable without four-wheel-drive, but I've been driving it in regular cars for years, albeit in the dry season. Don't try it in the rainy season (mid-Apr to Nov) unless you have four-wheel-drive. Also, be careful where you turn: There's an alternate route to Monteverde that turns off the highway near the Río Sardinal (before the Río Largato), and this road is in even worse shape.

By Bus   Express buses (© **506/222-3854** or 506/645-5159) leave San José daily at 6:30am and 2:30pm from Calle 12 between Avenidas 7 and 9. The trip takes between 3½ and 5 hours, depending on road conditions; the fare is $5.50.

There's also a daily bus that departs Puntarenas for Santa Elena, only a few kilometers from Monteverde, at 2:15pm. The bus stop in Puntarenas is across the street from the main bus station. The fare for the 2½-hour trip is $2.50.

There is a daily bus from Tilarán (Lake Arenal) at 1pm. Trip duration, believe it or not, is 2 hours (for a 25-mile/40km trip); the fare is $2.

Another option is to take **Costa Rica Expeditions'** van (© **506/257-0766**) from San José. You must have a reservation. The fare is $40 each way.

The express bus departs for San José daily at 6:30am and 2:30pm. The bus from Santa Elena to Puntarenas leaves daily at 6am. If you are heading to Manuel Antonio, take the 6am Santa Elena/Puntarenas bus and transfer in Puntarenas. To reach Liberia, take any bus down the mountain and get off at the Río Lagarto Bridge, where you hit the paved road. You can then flag down a bus bound for Liberia (almost any bus heading north). The Santa Elena/Tilarán bus leaves daily at 7am.

ORIENTATION   As you approach Santa Elena, take the right fork in the road if you're heading directly to Monteverde. If you continue straight, you'll come into the little village of **Santa Elena,** which has a bus stop, a health clinic, a bank, a general store, and a few simple restaurants, budget hotels, souvenir shops and tour offices. There's a laundry located on the road out toward the preserve entrance, just beyond the Hotel Sapo Dorado.

Monteverde, on the other hand, is not a village in the traditional sense of the word. There's no center of town, only dirt lanes leading off from the main road to various farms. This main road has signs for all the hotels and restaurants mentioned here, and dead-ends at the reserve entrance.

The telephone number for the **local clinic** is © **506/645-5076;** for the **Red Cross,** © **506/645-6128;** and for the **local police,** © **117.**

GETTING AROUND   A taxi between the town of Santa Elena and either the Monteverde Biological Cloud Forest Preserve or the Santa Elena Cloud Forest

> **Tips** **Seeing the Forest for the Trees, Bromeliads, Monkeys, Hummingbirds . . .**
>
> Since the entrance fee to Monteverde is valid for a full day, I recommend taking an early-morning walk with a guide and then heading off on your own either directly after that hike or after lunch. A guide will certainly point out and explain a lot, but there's also much to be said for walking quietly through the forest on your own or in very small groups. This will also allow you to stray from the well-traveled paths in the park.

Reserve will cost around $8. Count on paying between $4 and $8 for the ride from Santa Elena to your lodge in Monteverde. Your lodge can call a cab for you.

EXPLORING THE MONTEVERDE BIOLOGICAL CLOUD FOREST PRESERVE

The **Monteverde Biological Cloud Forest Preserve** ✹✹✹ (② **506/645-5122;** www.cct.or.cr/english.htm) is one of the most developed and well-maintained natural attractions in Costa Rica. The trails are clearly marked, regularly traveled, and generally gentle in terms of ascents and descents. The cloud forest here is lush and largely untouched. Still, keep in mind that most of the birds and mammals you've been reading about are rare, elusive, and nocturnal. Moreover, to all but the most trained of eyes, those thousands of exotic ferns, orchids, and bromeliads tend to blend into one large mass of indistinguishable green. However, with a guide hired through your hotel, or on one of the preserve's official guided 2- to 3-hour hikes, you can see and learn far more than you could on your own. At $15 per person, the preserve's tours may seem expensive, especially after you pay the entrance fee, but I strongly recommend that you go with a guide.

Perhaps the most famous resident of the cloud forests of Costa Rica is the quetzal, a robin-size bird with iridescent green wings and a ruby-red breast, which has become extremely rare due to habitat destruction. The male quetzal also has two long tail feathers that can reach nearly 2 feet in length, making it one of the most spectacular birds on earth. The best time to see quetzals is early to mid morning, and the best months are February through April (mating season).

Other animals that have been seen in Monteverde include jaguars, ocelots, and tapirs. After the quetzal, Monteverde's most famous resident was the golden toad (*sapo dorado*), a rare, native species. However, the golden toad seems to have disappeared from the forest and is feared extinct. Competing theories of the toad's demise include adverse effects of a natural drought cycle, the disappearing ozone layer, pesticides, or acid rain. Photos of the golden toad abound in Monteverde (I particularly like the shots of amphibian group sex). I'm sure you'll be as saddened as I was by the disappearance of such a beautiful creature.

ADMISSION, HOURS & TOURS   The preserve is open daily from 7am to 4pm, and the entrance fee is $10 per person, $5.50 for students and children. Because only 150 people are allowed into the preserve at any one time, you may be forced to wait for a while. Most hotels can reserve a guided walk and entrance to the preserve for the following day for you, or you can get tickets in advance directly at the preserve entrance.

The trails can be very muddy, depending on the season, so ask about current conditions. If the mud is heavy, you can rent rubber boots at the preserve entrance for $1.50 per day. They may make your hike much more pleasant.

Before venturing into the forest, have a look around the information center. There are several guidebooks available, as well as posters and postcards of some of the preserve's more famous animal inhabitants.

WHAT TO SEE & DO OUTSIDE THE PRESERVE
BIRD WATCHING & HIKING

Ample bird-watching and hiking opportunities can also be found outside the preserve boundaries. You can avoid the crowds at Monteverde by heading 3 miles (5km) north from the village of Santa Elena to the **Santa Elena Cloud Forest Reserve** ✦✦ (© 506/645-5390). This 900-acre reserve has a maximum elevation of 5,600 feet, which makes it the highest cloud forest in the Monteverde area. There are 5 miles (8km) of hiking trails as well as an information center. As it borders the Monteverde Preserve, a similar richness of flora and fauna is to be found here, although quetzals are not nearly as common. The $8 entry fee at this reserve goes directly to support local schools. The reserve is open daily from 7am to 9pm. Guided tours are available for $15 per person, not including the entrance fee (call the number above to make a reservation for the tour).

To learn even more about Monteverde, stop in at the **Monteverde Conservation League** (© 506/645-5003 or 506/645-5305), which has its operations at the welcome center at the trailhead of the Bajo del Tigre trail. In addition to being a good source for information, they also sell books, T-shirts, and cards, and all proceeds go to purchase more land for the Bosque Eterno de Los Niños (Children's Eternal Forest).

The **Bajo del Tigre Trail** ✦ is a 2-mile-long (3.5km) trail that's home to several different bird species not usually found within the reserve. There are several different loops you can take, lasting anywhere from 1 to several hours. The trail starts a little past the CASEM artisans' shop (see "Shopping," below) and is open daily from 8am to 5pm. Admission is $5 general, $2 students.

You can also go on guided 3-hour hikes at the **Reserva Sendero Tranquilo** ✦ (© 506/645-5010), which has 200 acres of land, two-thirds of which is in virgin forest. This reserve is located up the hill from the cheese factory, charges $20 for its tours, and is open daily from 7am to 3pm seasonally.

CANOPY TOURS

For an elevated look at the cloud forest, check out the local branch of **Canopy Tours** ✦✦ (© 506/645-5243; www.canopytour.co.cr), which has an office right in the center of Santa Elena. This is one of my favorite canopy tours in Costa Rica, since the ascent is made by climbing up the hollowed-out interior of a giant strangler fig. This is no educational walk through the woods. You strap on a climbing harness, clip into a pulley, and hurl yourself from tree to tree along a wire cable. At the final tree, you rappel down to the ground. Anybody in average physical condition can do it, but it's not for the faint-hearted or acrophobic. The 2½-hour tours run three times daily and cost $45 for adults, $35 for students, and $25 for children under 12.

Another new canopy tour has opened up near the Santa Elena Reserve. The **Sky Trek/Sky Walk** (© 506/645-5238; www.skywalk.co.cr) is a growing complex of aerial adventures. Like most other canopy tours in Costa Rica, the **Sky Trek** ✦ ($35 per person) consists of a series of platforms connected by cables strung through the canopy. (There's no strangler-fig ascent, however, just a walk to the top of a hill.) The **Sky Walk** ✦✦ ($12) is a network of forest paths and suspension bridges that provides visitors with a view previously reserved for birds, monkeys, and the much more adventurous tourist. The bridges reach

130 feet above the ground at their highest point, so acrophobia is still an issue, but at least the faint-hearted won't be flying along a cable. The Sky Trek/ Sky Walk is located about 2 miles (3.5km) outside of the town of Santa Elena, on the road to the Santa Elena Cloud Forest Reserve. It is open daily from 7am to 4pm. For an extra $12, a knowledgeable guide will point out the diverse flora and fauna on the Sky Walk. Reservations are recommended for the Sky Trek.

The newest entry into the aerial fray is **Aerial Adventures** (© 506/645-5960), a two-person chairlift that winds through some secondary forest and open spaces for about a mile (1.6km). I find this ride a bit tacky—it's my least favorite canopy tour in the country. The cost is $12.

HORSEBACK RIDING

Meg's Riding Stables (© 506/645-5419) and **La Estrella Stables** (© 506/645-5075) are two of the more established operators, offering guided rides for around $10 per hour. As I mentioned earlier in this chapter (see p. 000 for details), there are now popular horseback/boat trips linking Monteverde/Santa Elena with La Fortuna. This is certainly an exciting and adventurous means of connecting these two popular destinations, but I've received numerous complaints about the state of the trails and the treatment of the horses, so be very careful before undertaking this trip.

OTHER ADVENTURES IN MONTEVERDE

Birds are not the only colorful fauna in Monteverde. Butterflies abound here, and the **Butterfly Garden** ✸ (© 506/645-5512), located near the Pensión Monteverde Inn, displays many of Costa Rica's most beautiful species. Besides the hundreds of preserved and mounted butterflies, there's a garden and a greenhouse where you can watch live butterflies. The garden is open daily from 9:30am to 4pm, and admission is $7 for adults and $3 for children, which includes a guided tour. The best time to visit is between 11am and 1pm, when the butterflies are most active.

If you've had your fill of birds and snakes and butterflies, you might want to stop at the **Orchid Garden** (© 506/645-5510), on the main road toward the preserve. This new attraction boasts more than 400 species of orchids. Admission is $5 general, $3 students. It's open daily from 8am to 5pm.

If your taste runs toward the slithery, you can check out the **Serpentarium Santa Elena** (© 506/645-5772) on the road to the preserve. Personally, I find the condition of the enclosures and their residents rather depressing. It's open daily from 8am to 5pm and charges $3 for admission.

Because the vegetation in the cloud forest is so dense, most of the forest's animal residents are rather difficult to spot. If you were unsatisfied with your sightings, even with a naturalist guide leading you, you might want to consider attending a slide show of photographs taken in the preserve. There is a host of daily slide shows around Monteverde. The longest running of these take place at the **Monteverde Lodge, El Sapo Dorado, Hotel Belmar** (see "Accommodations," below, for phone numbers), and **Hummingbird Gallery** (see "Shopping," below). Dates, show times, and admissions vary, so inquire at your hotel or one of the places mentioned above.

The **Centro Panamericano de Idiomas** ✸ (© 888/682-0054 in the U.S. and Canada, or 506/645-5441; www.cpi-edu.com; anajarro@racsa.co.cr) offers immersion language classes in a wonderful setting. A 2-week program, with 4 hours of class per day and a homestay with a Costa Rican family, costs $700.

Almost all of the area hotels can arrange a wide variety of other tours and activities, including night trips to the Arenal Volcano (a grueling 4-hr. ride away) and guided night tours of the cloud forest.

SHOPPING

If you're in the mood to do some shopping, stop in at **CASEM,** on the right side of the main road, just past Restaurant El Bosque (© **506/645-5190**). This crafts co-operative sells embroidered clothing, T-shirts, posters, and postcards with photos of the local flora and fauna, Boruca weavings, locally grown and roasted coffee, and many other items to remind you of your visit to Monteverde. CASEM is open Monday through Saturday from 8am to 5pm and Sunday from 10am to 4pm (closed Sunday from May–Oct). There is also a well-stocked **gift shop** at the entrance to the preserve. You'll find plenty of T-shirts, postcards, and assorted crafts here, as well as a well-stocked selection of science and natural-history books.

Perhaps the best-stocked gift shop in Monteverde is the **Hummingbird Gallery** (© **506/645-5030**). You'll find the gallery just outside the preserve entrance. Hanging from trees around it are several hummingbird feeders that attract more than seven species of these tiny birds. At any given moment, there might be several dozen hummingbirds buzzing and chattering around the building and your head. Inside, you will, of course, find a lot of beautiful color prints of hummingbirds and other local flora and fauna, as well as a wide range of craft items, T-shirts, and other gifts. The Hummingbird Gallery is open daily from 8:30am to 4:30pm.

Over the years, Monteverde has developed a nice little community of artists. Around town, you'll see paintings by local artists like Paul Smith and Meg Wallace, whose works are displayed at the Fonda Vela Hotel and Stella's Bakery, respectively. You might also check out **Galería Extasis** (© **506/645-5548**), off the main road to the reserve, which sells the intriguing wooden sculptures of artist Marco Tulio Brenes. **Bromelias** (© **506/645-6093**) is a new gallery-cum-gift-shop-cum-coffee-shop run by the folks who own the Hummingbird Gallery. It has a good, slightly higher-end selection of artwork and crafts, housed in a wonderfully open and light two-storied building, located up the hill from Stella's Bakery.

If you're interested in taking a class or workshop with one of the many local artists, check in with the newly formed **Monteverde Studio of the Arts** (© **506/645-5434;** www.mvstudios.com).

ACCOMMODATIONS

When choosing a place to stay in Monteverde, be sure to check whether the rates include a meal plan. In the past, almost all the lodges included three meals a day in their prices, but this practice is on the wane. Check before you assume anything.

EXPENSIVE

Monteverde Lodge   Operated by Costa Rica Expeditions, the Monteverde Lodge is one of the most upscale hotels in Monteverde. It's located 3 miles (5km) from the preserve entrance in a secluded setting near Santa Elena. Guest rooms are large and comfortable and have angled walls of glass with chairs and a table placed so that avid bird watchers can do a bit of birding without leaving their rooms. The gardens and secondary forest surrounding the lodge have some gentle groomed trails and are also home to quite a few species of birds. Perhaps the lodge's most popular feature is the large hot tub in a big atrium garden just off the lobby. After hiking all day, you can soak your bones under the stars.

The hotel's dining room offers great views, good food, and excellent formal service provided by bow-tied waiters. The adjacent bar is a popular gathering spot, and there are regular evening slide shows focusing on the cloud forest. Scheduled bus service to and from San José is available ($40 each way), as is a shuttle to the preserve ($6 each way), horseback riding, and a variety of optional tours.

Monteverde (mailing address in the U.S.: Dept. 235, P.O. Box 025216, Miami, FL 33102). © **506/ 257-0766.** Fax 506/257-1665. www.costaricaexpeditions.com. 27 units. Dec 15–Apr 30 $115 double, $132 triple; May 1–Dec 14 $100 double, $115 triple. AE, MC, V. **Amenities:** 1 restaurant (Costa Rican/international); 1 bar; Jacuzzi; tour desk; laundry service. *In room:* No phone.

MODERATE

El Sapo Dorado ✦✦ *Finds*   Located on a steep hill between Santa Elena and the preserve, El Sapo Dorado (named for Monteverde's famous "golden toad") offers the most charming and comfortable accommodations in Monteverde. The spacious cabins are built of hardwoods both inside and out and are surrounded by a grassy lawn. Big windows let in lots of light, and high ceilings keep the rooms cool during the day. Some of the older cabins have fireplaces, which are a welcome feature on chilly nights and during the peak parts of the rainy season. My favorite rooms are the sunset suites, which have private terraces with views to the Gulf of Nicoya and wonderful sunsets.

There's an excellent restaurant here (see "Dining," below), and the quiet yet jovial bar stays open until 10pm. The hotel has a massage room with a local therapist on call, as well as a conference room, where it sometimes shows slide shows at night. Not only does El Sapo Dorado own and manage the Reserva Sendero Tranquilo, but it also has a network of well-maintained trails into primary forest. To find the hotel and restaurant, watch for the sign on the left-hand side of the main road to the preserve, just as you're leaving Santa Elena.

Monteverde (A.P. 9-5655), Puntarenas. © **506/645-5010.** Fax 506/645-5180. www.cool.co.cr/ usr/sapodorado/. 30 cabin suites. $89–$99 double; $95–$109 triple. Lower rates in the off-season (May–Nov) rates. AE, MC, V. **Amenities:** 1 highly recommended restaurant (international); 1 bar; tour desk; massage; laundry service. *In room:* No phone.

Hotel Belmar ✦   You'll think you're in the Alps when you stay at this beautiful Swiss chalet–style hotel. Set on the top of a grassy hill, the Belmar has stunning views of the Nicoya Gulf and the Pacific. Afternoons in the dining room or lounge are idyllic, with bright sunlight streaming in through a west-facing glass wall. Sunsets are spectacular. Most of the guest rooms are fitted with wood paneling, French doors, and little balconies that open onto splendid views. There are actually two buildings here. My favorite rooms are in the main building; those in the "Chalet" building are a bit smaller. The restaurant serves a mix of well-prepared Tico and international cuisine; a full meal plan runs around $23 per person per day. The Belmar is up a road to the left of the gas station as you come into the village of Monteverde.

Monteverde (A.P. 17-5655), Puntarenas. © **506/645-5201.** Fax 506/645-5135. www.hotelbelmar. com. 34 units. $60–$75 double. Lower rates in the off-season (May–Nov). V. **Amenities:** 1 restaurant (Costa Rican/international); 1 bar; game room; tour desk; laundry service. *In room:* No phone.

Hotel de Montaña Monteverde   This long, low motel-style building is one of the oldest hotels in Monteverde and is frequently filled with tour groups. The hotel is surrounded by 37 acres of farm and woods. Older rooms are rustic and have wood paneling. Newer rooms have queen-size beds, more light, and great views of the Nicoya Gulf. There are deluxe suites, and one master suite with its own whirlpool tub and a view. There is a lot of variation in room size, age, and quality. I find the newer standard rooms much nicer than some of the older suites. For family privacy, there are four cabins across the lawn from the main lodge. The rustic glass-walled dining room offers excellent views. Attached to the restaurant is a small bar that's busy in the evening, when people sit around swapping stories of their day's adventures and wildlife sightings. Meals will run you around $36 per person per day. On cold nights, you can warm up in the hotel's sauna or hot tub.

Monteverde (A.P. 2070-1002, Paseo Los Estudiantes, San José). © **506/645-5046.** Fax 506/645-5320. www.ticonet.co.cr/monteverde. 34 units, 8 family cabins. $76 double; $94 family or deluxe suite. AE, MC, V. **Amenities:** 1 restaurant (international); 1 bar; Jacuzzi; sauna; horse rental; tour desk; laundry service. *In room:* Safe; no phone.

Hotel Fonda Vela ✴   Although it's one of the older hotels here, Fonda Vela is still one of the nicer choices in Monteverde. Guest rooms are in a half-dozen buildings scattered among the forests and pastures of this former farm, and most have views of the Nicoya Gulf. Lots of hardwood has been used throughout. Most of the rooms have bathtubs, which is a rarity in Costa Rica. The suites, two of which have sleeping lofts, are the most spacious accommodations available, but unfortunately, several of these do not have views. But the dining room has great sunset views, and it sometimes even features live music. There's a large and popular bar here, as well as a small system of private trails. Meals will run you around $36 per person per day. Throughout the hotel, you'll see paintings by owner Paul Smith, who also handcrafts violins and cellos and is a musician himself.

Monteverde (A.P. 70060-1000, San José). © **506/257-1413** or 506/645-5125. Fax 506/257-1416. www.centralamerica.com/cr/hotel/fondavel.htm. 40 units. $85 double; $94 junior suite for 2, $103 suite for 2. Extra person $9. Children under age 8 stay in parents' room for $4.50; older children charged at regular extra-person rate. AE, MC, V. **Amenities:** 1 restaurant (international); 1 bar; horse rental; tour desk; shuttle to the preserve; laundry service. *In room:* No phone.

Hotel Heliconia ✴   The Heliconia is another comfortable and semi-luxurious hotel. The new main lodge building is a three-story behemoth, located high on a hill behind the rest of the hotel's several buildings. Here you'll find most of the suites and junior suites, which are immense rooms featuring varnished wood walls, carpeted floors, two king-size beds, and huge private balconies. All of the rooms on the second and third floors here get great sunset views. Rooms in the older buildings down by the road are also done in floor-to-ceiling hardwoods that give them the rustic feel of a mountain resort. Some of these have large picture windows facing dense forest. All around, there are paths that lead through attractive gardens and to a hot tub in a bamboo grove; additional trails lead from the hotel up to and through a 600-acre private reserve of virgin forest with scenic views of the Nicoya Gulf. Meals will run about $35 a day.

Monteverde (A.P. 10921-1000, San José). © **506/645-5109.** Fax 506/645-5007. www.centralamerica.com/cr/hotel/heliconia.htm. 32 units. $80 double; $90 junior suite, $106 suite. V. **Amenities:** 1 restaurant (international/Mediterranean); 1 bar; Jacuzzi; tour desk; laundry service. *In room:* No phone.

Hotel Villa Verde   This hotel's greatest asset is that it is one of the closest lodgings to the preserve entrance. The main lodge features a huge dining room with floor-to-ceiling windows that reach all the way to the two-story-high roof.

Each suite has a living room and a fireplace and is identified not by a number but by the likeness of a specific bird carved into the door. Standard rooms are spacious and Spartan, and the textured sand bathroom walls and pale-blue tiles are an aesthetic affront.

Monteverde (A.P. 16-5655), Puntarenas. ℰ **506/645-5025.** Fax 506/645-5115. estefany@racsa.co.cr. 21 units. $54 double; $66 suite. Rates include breakfast. AE, MC, V. **Amenities:** 1 restaurant (Costa Rican/international); 1 bar; game room; tour desk; laundry service. *In room:* No phone.

INEXPENSIVE

In addition to the hotels listed below, there are quite a few pensiónes and backpacker specials in Santa Elena and spread out along the road to the preserve. The best of these are **Hotel Camino Verde** (ℰ and fax **506/645-5916**), **Pensión Flor de Monteverde** (ℰ and fax **506/645-5236**), and **Pensión Monteverde Inn** (ℰ **506/645-5156**). All three charge around $8 to $10 per person.

Finally, it is possible to stay in one of the very basic dormitory rooms right at the **Monteverde Biological Cloud Forest Preserve** (ℰ **506/645-5122;** www.cct.or.cr). A bunk bed and three meals per day here run $26 per person. Admission to the preserve is extra.

Arco Iris Lodge ✦ *(Finds)* This is by far the nicest hotel right in Santa Elena, and one of the nicest hotels in the area regardless of price. The rooms are spread out in eight separate buildings (so, in effect, most are individual cabins). All have wood or tile floors and plenty of wood accents. My favorite is the "honeymoon cabin," which has its own private balcony with a forest view and good bird watching. Real budget travelers can inquire about the two rooms here equipped with bunk beds (for $17 single, $27 double). The management here is extremely helpful, speaks five languages, and can arrange a wide variety of tours. Although it recently stopped serving lunch and dinner, there's a breakfast buffet for $6.50; and beer, wine, and other refreshments are available throughout the day and evening.

Monteverde (A.P. 003-5655), Puntarenas. ℰ **506/645-5067.** Fax 506/645-5022. www.arcoirislodge.com. 10 units. $45–$65 double. AE, MC, V. **Amenities:** 1 restaurant (breakfast buffet only); tour desk; laundry service. *In room:* No phone.

El Bosque *(Value)* Hidden down the hill behind El Bosque restaurant (on the main road to the preserve) is one of Monteverde's better values. Though the rooms are very basic, they're clean and fairly large and have high ceilings, picture windows, and double beds. The cement floors and simple furnishings are what help keep the rates down. The rooms are arranged in a semicircle around a minimally landscaped garden. The setting may not be spectacular, but if you're going to spend all day in the preserve, this shouldn't bother you too much. The hotel's restaurant is some 100 yards up a dirt road and down a path that crosses a junglelike ravine by footbridge, which turns going for breakfast into a morning bird-watching trip.

Monteverde (A.P. 27-5655), Puntarenas. ℰ **506/645-5221** or 506/645-5158. Fax 506/645-5129. www.bosquelodge.com. 26 units. $40 double; $47 triple; $57 quad. AE, MC, V. **Amenities:** 1 restaurant (Costa Rican/Italian); 1 bar; tour desk; laundry service. *In room:* No phone.

El Establo *(Value)* Horses are an integral part of Costa Rican culture and a common sight in Monteverde. El Establo, as its name implies, is a working stable and incorporates this theme in its architectural design. Though the hotel is next to the road, there are 120 acres of farm behind it, and half of this area is in primary forest. Most of the rooms are situated off a large enclosed porch that contains plenty of comfortable chairs and a fireplace. Guest-room doors look as if they were salvaged from a stable, but inside, the rooms are carpeted and have orthopedic mattresses and modern bathrooms. The second-floor rooms are my favorites here, and those on the end of the hall even have a bit more light than others. There's a large new restaurant off the main hotel, by the road, where meals will run you about $27 a day. When I last visited, there were plans to add 30 new junior suites. Of course, the hotel also has plenty of horses for rent at $10 per hour, with a guide.

Monteverde (A.P. 549-2050, San Pedro). ✆ **506/645-5110** or 506/645-5033. Fax 506/645-5041. www.establo.com. 22 units. $40–$50 double; $60 triple. AE, MC, V. **Amenities:** 1 restaurant (Costa Rican/international); 1 bar; tour desk; horse rental; laundry service. *In room:* No phone.

Hotel El Tucan   This very basic lodging is located on the edge of Santa Elena (on the back road from the village's main street that leads to Monteverde) and consequently does not have the rural feel of many of the area's other accommodations. Though the rooms without bathrooms are only slightly larger than closets, they are fairly clean. Rooms with private bathrooms are slightly larger; some are in a separate building across the street. Very inexpensive Costa Rican–style meals are served in a very basic dining room. Keep in mind that this hotel is 3 miles (5km) from the preserve, so if you don't have a car, transportation to and from the preserve by taxi is going to add a bit to the cost of the room.

Santa Elena, Puntarenas. ✆ **506/645-5017**. Fax 506/645-5462. 14 units, 7 with private bathroom. $14 double without bathroom, $20 double with bathroom. No credit cards. **Amenities:** 1 restaurant (Costa Rican); laundry service. *In room:* No phone.

La Colina Lodge   The folks who run the La Colina bed & breakfast in Manuel Antonio have remodeled and renamed this old pensión. The rooms are housed in two separate buildings. Everything is still quite simple here. Most rooms each have one double and one single bed, although a couple still have bunk beds. When I last visited, there were plans to install a Jacuzzi and open a bar. Sporting events and videos are shown on a large-screen satellite TV in a lounge area. Service is friendly and attentive, and they even allow camping here, with access to the shared bathrooms. The lodge is pretty close to the reserve, which is a plus for budget travelers without a car.

Monteverde. ✆ **506/645-5009**. Fax 506/645-5580. www.lacolina.com. 11 units, 6 with private bathroom. $35 double with shared bathroom, $45 double with private bathroom; $15 per person bunk; $5 per person camping. Rates include full breakfast. V. **Amenities:** 1 restaurant (international); laundry service. *In room:* No phone.

DINING

Most lodges in Monteverde have their own dining rooms, and these are the most convenient places to eat, especially if you don't have a car. Because most visitors want to get an early start, they usually grab a quick breakfast at their hotel. It's also common for people to have their lodge pack them a bag lunch to take with them to the preserve, although there's now a decent little *soda* at the preserve entrance. If you're in the mood to eat out, there are several inexpensive restaurants scattered along the road between Santa Elena and Monteverde.

A good choice for lunch is **Stella's Bakery** (✆ **506/645-5560**), across the road from the CASEM gift shop. Stella's is open daily from 6am to 6pm and has a small cafe and a few outdoor tables, where you can pile your plate with an assortment of fresh foods served cafeteria style. The selection changes, but might include vegetarian quiche, eggplant Parmigiana, and different salads. It also has fresh-baked breads and muffins and a daily supply of other deliciously decadent baked goods.

Take a Break

If all of the activities in Monteverde have worn you out, stop in at **Chunches** (© **506/645-5147**), a new coffee/espresso bar and bookstore in Santa Elena, which also doubles as a Laundromat. Chunches is open Monday through Saturday from 9am to 6pm.

It's also worth stopping by the **Monteverde Cheese Factory** (© **506/645-5136**) to pick up some of the best cheese in Costa Rica (you can even see it being made). The cheese factory is open Monday through Saturday from 7:30am to 4pm and Sunday from 7:30am to noon. You can also get homemade ice cream at the Cheese Factory.

In Santa Elena, you might want to check out **Morphos Café** (© **506/645-5818**), which specializes in vegetarian meals, fresh-fruit juices, and ice-cream desserts.

El Sapo Dorado ♥♥ INTERNATIONAL   Located high on a hill above the main road, El Sapo Dorado provides great sunsets and good food. The menu is a little bit more imaginative than at most restaurants in Monteverde, which makes it well worth a visit even if you miss the sunset. The regularly changing menu might include grilled corvina in heart-of-palm sauce, fettuccine in peanut-squid sauce, and/or filet mignon in pepper-cream sauce. The emphasis is on fresh ingredients and healthy preparation, and there are always vegetarian and vegan options, as well. If you come for lunch, or a sunset dinner, definitely grab a table in the new, large, covered dining room, which has full walls of picture windows for taking in the views.

On the left as you go from Santa Elena toward the preserve. © 506/645-5010. Reservations recommended during high season (late Nov–late Apr). Main courses $6–$15. AE, MC, V. Daily 6:30–9:30am, noon–3pm, and 6–9pm.

Pizzeria de Johnny PIZZA/ITALIAN   This popular pizza joint has grown from a little hole-in-the-wall to a near institution here in Monteverde. The thin-crust wood-oven pizzas are delicious, and there's a large menu of meat, chicken, and pasta dishes as well. You can start things off with a bruschetta or mussels Parmesan. Its signature pizza Traviesa comes with artichoke hearts, onions, mushrooms, garlic, and marinated tomatoes. There's a modest little gift shop and a quiet bar off the large open dining room, but the nicest tables are on the covered veranda out back.

On the rd. to the preserve, a little beyond El Sapo Dorado, on your right. © 506/645-5066. Reservations recommended during high season. Small pizzas $3.50–$6, medium pies $8–$12, large pies $14–$21; other main courses $5–$10. V. Daily 11:30am–10pm.

Restaurante De Lucía COSTA RICAN/INTERNATIONAL   In just a few years here, De Lucía's has earned some local renown. There's really no menu, but your waiter will bring out a platter with the nightly selection of meats and fresh fish, which are then grilled to order. One of the more interesting dishes is the chicken in orange sauce. All meals come with fresh homemade tortillas and a full accompaniment of side orders and vegetables. The sweet plátanos prepared on the open grill are delicious. Service is informal and friendly. The heavy wood tables and chairs are spread comfortably around the large dining room.

On the rd. down to the Butterfly Farm, on your right. © 506/645-5337. Reservations recommended during high season (late Nov–late Apr). Lunch $2.50–$6; main courses $8–$12. AE, MC, V. Daily 11am–9pm.

7 The Central Pacific Coast: Where the Mountains Meet the Sea

The central Pacific coast is home to some of the most accessible beaches in Costa Rica. They range from the somewhat seedy Puntarenas and the cut-rate, fun-in-the-sun Jacó to the jungle-clad hillsides of Manuel Antonio and Dominical. For the most part, this coast is not as spectacular or varied as that of the Nicoya Peninsula and Guanacaste, but on the bright side, in the dry season, it doesn't get as brown and desolate-looking. The climate here is considerably more humid than that farther north, but it's not nearly as steamy as along the south Pacific or Caribbean coasts.

Jacó and Manuel Antonio are Costa Rica's two most developed beaches, while Puntarenas, a former seaport, offers the most urban beach setting in the country (it's just a short day trip away from San José). If you're looking to get away from it all, without traveling too far or spending too much, Dominical should be your top choice on this coast.

This is also where you'll find some of Costa Rica's most popular and spectacular national parks and biological reserves: **Manuel Antonio National Park** ⋆⋆, home of three-toed sloths and white-faced monkeys; **Chirripó National Park** ⋆, a misty cloud forest that becomes a barren *páramo* (a region above 10,000 ft.) at the peak of its namesake, **Mount Chirripó**; and **Carara Biological Reserve** ⋆⋆, one of the last places in Costa Rica where you can see the disappearing dry forest join the damp, humid forests that extend south down the coast. You might even glimpse an occasional scarlet macaw.

1 Puntarenas

71 miles (115km) W of San José; 118 miles (191km) S of Liberia; 47 miles (75km) N of Playa de Jacó

Some see Puntarenas as a fallen jewel with vast potential; others see nothing more than a run-down, rough-and-tumble port town best seen through a rearview mirror. I tend to hold the latter view.

A 10-mile-long (16km) spit of land jutting into the Gulf of Nicoya, Puntarenas was once Costa Rica's busiest port, but that changed drastically when the government inaugurated nearby Puerto Caldera, a modern container port facility. After losing its shipping business, the city survived primarily on commercial fishing. Watching the tourist boom bring big bucks to other cities, Puntarenas decided to try to grab its piece of the pie. After decades of decay and neglect, Puntarenas has recently received some long-overdue attention. In 1998, Puntarenas initiated a large public works and renovation project that has so far yielded a new cruise-ship docking facility, a convention-and-recreation center, a modest maritime museum, and an artisans' row where visitors can stock up on regional arts and crafts.

There's a good highway leading all the way from San José, so Puntarenas can be reached (on a good day, with no traffic) in about 2 hours by car, which makes

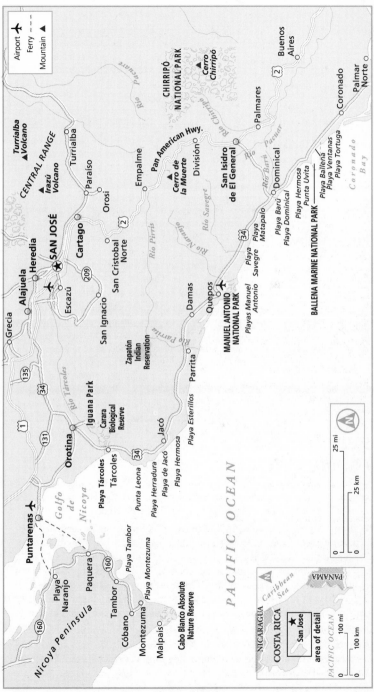

it one of the closest beaches to San José(at least in elapsed time, if not in actual mileage. Because Puntarenas is a city, a former port town, and a commercial fishing center, this beach has a very different character from any other in Costa Rica.

A long, straight stretch of sand with gentle surf, the beach is backed for most of its length by the **Paseo de los Turistas** (Tourist Walk). Across a wide boulevard from the paseo are hotels, restaurants, bars, discos, and shops. The sunsets and the views across the Gulf of Nicoya are quite beautiful, and there's almost always a cooling breeze blowing in off the water. All around town you'll find unusual old buildings, reminders of the important role Puntarenas once played in Costa Rican history. It was from here that much of the Central Valley's coffee crop was once shipped, and while the coffee barons in the highlands were getting rich, so too were the merchants of Puntarenas.

A Colorful Festival

If you're in Puntarenas on the Saturday closest to July 16, you can witness the **Fiesta of the Virgin of the Sea.** During this festival, a regatta of colorfully decorated boats carries a statue of Puntarenas's patron saint.

If you're in Costa Rica for only a short time and want to get in some time on the beach, Puntarenas is certainly an option, though I recommend driving (or being driven) the extra hour or so that it takes to reach some of the nicer beaches farther south. Swimming here still seems more the exception than the rule, and Puntarenas is still primarily a place to spend the night during transit. It is here you must pick up the ferries to the southern Nicoya Peninsula, and many folks like to arrive the night before and get an early start. It's also a good place to break up the longer trip up to, or back from, Guanacaste. Puntarenas is most popular as a weekend holiday spot for Ticos from San José and is at its liveliest on weekends.

One final note: In 1997 and 1998, Puntarenas was the site of Costa Rica's worst outbreak of dengue fever (see chapter 2 for more information). This has subsided, but this is still one of the country's areas of highest risk, and you should take precautions in Puntarenas, especially during the day, since dengue is spread by a mosquito that is active only during the daytime.

ESSENTIALS

GETTING THERE & DEPARTING   By Car   Head west out of San José on the Interamerican Highway, passing the airport and Alajuela, and follow the signs to Puntarenas. The drive takes between 2 and 2½ hours.

By Bus   Express buses (© **506/222-0064**) leave San José daily every half hour between 6am and 9pm from Calle 16 and Avenida 12. Trip duration is 2½ hours; the fare is $2.50.

The main Puntarenas bus station is a block east of the Hotel Imperial, which is in front of the old main dock on the Paseo de los Turistas. Buses to **San José** leave daily every half hour between 5:30am and 7pm. The bus to **Santa Elena** leaves daily at 2:15pm from a stop across the railroad tracks from the main bus station. Buses to **Quepos** (Manuel Antonio) leave daily at 4:30 and 10:30am, and 3pm.

By Ferry   See the "Playa Tambor" or "Playa Montezuma" sections of chapter 5 for information on crossing to and returning from Puntarenas from Paquera or Naranjo on the Nicoya Peninsula.

ORIENTATION   Puntarenas is built on a long, narrow sand spit that stretches 10 miles (16km) out into the Gulf of Nicoya and is marked by only five streets at its widest. The ferry docks for the Nicoya Peninsula are near the far end of town, as are the bus station and market. The north side of town faces an estuary, while the south side faces the mouth of the gulf. The Paseo de los Turistas is on the south side of town, beginning at the pier and extending out to the point.

FAST FACTS   Check out the new **Millennium Cibercafe** (© **506/661-4759**), right on the Paseo de los Turistas, if you need to send or check e-mail. If you need a taxi, call **Coopetico** (© **506/663-2020**).

WHAT TO SEE & DO

Take a walk along the **Paseo de los Turistas,** which feels rather like a Florida beach town out of the 1950s. The hotels across the street range in style from converted old wooden homes with bright gingerbread trim to modern concrete monstrosities to tasteful art-deco relics needing a new coat of paint.

If you venture into the center of the city, be sure to check out the **central plaza around the Catholic Church.** The church itself is interesting, as it has portholes for windows, reflecting the city's maritime tradition. Here you'll also find the city's new cultural center, **La Casa de la Cultura** (© **506/661-1394**), and a small museum.

If you want to go swimming, the ocean waters are now said to be perfectly safe (pollution was a problem for many years), although the beach is still not very attractive. Your best bet is to head back down the spit, and just a few kilometers out of town you'll find **Playa Doña Aña,** a popular beach with picnic tables, bath- and changing rooms, and a couple of *sodas.* Surfers will want to head to the mouth of the Barranca River, which boasts an amazingly long left break, although surfers often complain about the polluted waters emptying out of the river here.

Puntarenas isn't known as one of Costa Rica's prime sportfishing ports, but there are usually a few charter boats available. Check at your hotel, near the docks, or call **Latii Express Travel** (© **506/296-1146;** www.costaricalatiiexpress. com), which maintains a fleet here in Puntarenas. Rates are usually between $250 and $400 for a half day and between $400 and $800 for a full day. These rates are for up to four people.

You can also take a yacht cruise through the tiny, uninhabited islands of the Guayabo, Negritos, and Pajaros Islands Biological Reserve. These cruises include a lunch buffet and relaxing stop on beautiful and undeveloped **Tortuga Island,** where you can swim, snorkel, and sun. The water is clear blue, and the sand is bright white. However, as this trip has surged in popularity, the tours have begun to have a cattle-car feel. Several San José–based companies offer these excursions, with round-trip transportation from San José, but if you're already in Puntarenas, you might receive a slight discount by boarding here.

Calypso Tours ✦ (© **506/256-2727;** info@calypsotours.com) is the most reputable company that cruises out of Puntarenas. In addition to Tortuga Island trips, Calypso Tours takes folks to their own private nature reserve at Punta Coral, and even on a sunset cruise that includes dinner and some guided stargazing. Any of these cruises will run you $99 per person from San José, or $94 from Puntarenas. If you check down at the docks, you might find some other boats that ply the waters of the Nicoya Gulf. Some of these companies also offer sunset cruises with live music, snacks, and a bar.

ACCOMMODATIONS
MODERATE

Hotel Las Brisas   Out near the end of the Paseo de los Turistas, you'll find this clean hotel with large air-conditioned rooms, a small pool out front, and the beach right across the street. All the rooms have tile floors, double or twin beds,

Diving Trips to Isla del Coco (Cocos Island)

This little speck of land located some 300 miles (480km) off the Pacific coast was a prime pirate hideout and refueling station. Robert Louis Stevenson most likely modeled *Treasure Island* on Cocos. Sir Francis Drake, Captain Edward Davis, William Dampier, and Mary Welch are just some of the famous corsairs who dropped anchor in the calm harbors of this Pacific pearl. They allegedly left troves of buried loot, though scores of treasure-hunters over several centuries have failed to unearth more than a smattering of the purported bounty. The Costa Rican flag was first raised here on September 15, 1869. Throughout its history, Cocos Island has provided anchorage and fresh water to hundreds of ships, and entertained divers and dignitaries (Franklin Delano Roosevelt visited it three times). In 1978, it was declared a national park and protected area.

The clear, warm waters around Cocos are widely regarded as one of the most rewarding **dive destinations** ★★★ on this planet. This is a prime place to see schooling herds of scalloped hammerhead sharks. On a recent shallow-water checkout dive—normally, a perfunctory and uninspiring affair—I spotted my first (12-ft.) hammerhead lurking just 15 feet below me within 15 seconds of flipping into the water. Soon there were more, and soon they came much, much closer.

Other denizens of the waters around Cocos Island include white- and silver-tipped reef sharks; marbled, manta, eagle, and mobula rays; moray and spotted eels; octopi; spiny and slipper lobsters; hawksbill turtles; squirrel fish, trigger fish, and angelfish; surgeon fish, trumpet fish,

and small televisions and tables. Large picture windows keep the rooms sunny and bright during the day. There's complimentary coffee and a secure parking lot. However, the prices have gone up considerably here, and I'm not sure it's worth it anymore. The hotel's small open-air restaurant serves well-prepared continental dishes. The bouillabaisse is excellent, and there's always a Greek-style fish special or homemade moussaka on the menu.

Paseo de los Turistas (A.P. 83-5400), Puntarenas. ℂ 506/661-4040. Fax 506/661-2120. hbrisas@racsa.co.cr. 20 units. $60–$80 double. Rates include breakfast. Lower rates in the off-season. AE, MC, V. **Amenities:** 1 restaurant (continental); 1 bar; small pool. *In room:* A/C, TV, safe; no phone.

Hotel Tioga   This 1950s modern-style hotel is probably your best choice on the Paseo de los Turistas. The beach is across the street, and there are plenty of nearby restaurants. When you walk through the front door, you enter a court-yard with a pool that's been painted a brilliant shade of blue. In the middle of the pool, there's a tiny island with a palm tree growing on it. Rooms vary in size and view. The larger, most expensive rooms are attractive, with huge closets, modern bathrooms, and private balconies with a view of the ocean. The smaller, less-expensive rooms have louvered, frosted-glass windows to let in lots of light and air while maintaining some privacy. The garden-sector rooms, however, have only cold-water showers. There's a breakfast room and lounge on the fourth floor, so you can look out across the water over breakfast.

Paseo de los Turistas (A.P. 96-5400), Puntarenas. ℂ **506/661-0271** or 506/255-3115. Fax 506/661-0127. www.hoteltioga.com. 46 units. $65–$130 double. Rates include breakfast. AE, MC, V. **Amenities:** 1 restaurant (international); 1 bar; small pool; modest casino. *In room:* A/C, TV.

grouper, grunts, snapper, jack, tangs, and more. Two of the more spec-tacular underwater residents here include the red-lipped batfish and the frog fish.

Most diving at Cocos is relatively deep (between 85 and 120 ft.), and there are often strong currents and choppy swells to deal with—not to mention all those sharks. This is not a trip for novice divers.

The perimeter of Cocos Island is ringed by steep, forested cliffs punc-tuated by dozens of majestic waterfalls cascading down in stages or steady streams for hundreds of feet. The island itself has a series of trails that climb its steep hills and wind through its rain-forested inte-rior. There are several endemic bird, reptile, and plant species here, including the ubiquitous Cocos finch, which I spotted soon after land-ing onshore, and the wild Cocos Island pig.

With just a small ranger station housing a handful of national-park guards, Cocos Island is essentially uninhabited. Visitors these days come on private or charter yachts, fishing boats, or one of the few live-aboard dive vessels making regular voyages out here. It's a long trip: Most dive vessels take 30 to 36 hours to reach Cocos. Sailboats are even slower.

Both the **Aggressor Fleet Limited** (© **800/348-2628** or 504/385-2628 in the U.S., or © 506/289-3333; www.aggressor.com) and **Undersea Hunter** (© **800/203-2120** in the U.S., or © 506/228-6613 in Costa Rica; www.underseahunter.com) regularly run dive trips to Cocos Island from Puntarenas.

Yadran Hotel   Located at the far end of Puntarenas, at the tip of the spit, this is the most luxurious in-town choice, which isn't exactly saying much. I find it over-priced for what you get, but you are close to the Paseo de los Turistas and most restaurants. Also, the car-ferry dock is only a few blocks away. The range in room prices reflects whether you get an ocean, estuary, or no view. I like the upper-floor rooms, with a balcony and a sea view, but even the priciest rooms can seem a bit dreary. The hotel's disco gets going nightly at 6pm. It's located underground, so the beat won't keep you awake if you decide not to dance the night away.

At the end of the Paseo de los Turistas (A.P. 14-5400), Puntarenas. © **506/661-2662.** Fax 506/661-1944. yadran@racsa.co.cr. 42 units. $90–$105 double. AE, DC, MC, V. **Amenities:** 2 restau-rants (international); 1 bar; 1 disco; casino; small pool and children's pool; bike rental; tour desk; laundry service. *In room:* A/C, TV.

INEXPENSIVE

Hotel Ayi Con   Centrally located near the market and close enough to the ferryboat docks, the Ayi Con is your basic low-budget Tico accommodation. It's above a row of shops in a very busy shopping district of Puntarenas and is fre-quented primarily by Costa Ricans. Backpackers will find that this is probably the best and the cleanest of the cheap hotels in Puntarenas. If you're just passing through and have to spend a night in town, this place is convenient and acceptable.

Puntarenas (50m south of the market). © **506/661-0164** or 506/661-1477. 44 units, 22 with pri-vate bathroom. $12 double without private bathroom, $18 double with private bathroom, $22 double with private bathroom and A/C. No credit cards. *In room:* No phone.

DINING

Since you're in a seaport, try some of the local catch. **Corvina,** or sea bass, is the most popular offering, and it's served in various forms and preparations. My favorite dish on a hot afternoon is **ceviche,** and you'll find that just about every restaurant in town serves this savory marinated seafood concoction.

The most economical option is to pull up a table at one of the many open-air snack bars along the Paseo de los Turistas. They have names like **Soda Rio de Janeiro** and **Soda Acapulco,** and serve everything from sandwiches, drinks, and ice cream to ceviche and whole fish meals. Sandwiches are priced at around $1.50, and a fish fillet with rice and beans should cost around $4. If you want a slightly more formal atmosphere, try the open-air **Restaurant Aloha,** or the new **Capitán Moreno,** which are also both located on the Paseo de los Turistas.

Jardin Cervecero Bierstube SEAFOOD   This Tico beer garden is a popular drinking spot that also happens to serve decent seafood. The restaurant is a huge, open room with a high ceiling; louvered windows swing open and provide fresh breezes and a view of the bay. The tuna and marlin hung on the walls and from the ceiling are either the world's worst examples of taxidermy, or pretty good papier-mâché. This is a good place to grab a window seat, order some ceviche, and kick back. There's beer on tap and good, hearty meals.

Paseo de los Turistas, between Calles 21 and 23. (©) **506/661-0330.** Main courses $3–$9. AE, DC, MC, V. Wed–Mon noon–1am.

La Caravelle FRENCH   For more than 19 years, La Caravelle has been serving fine French dinners in an eclectically decorated cafe atmosphere. The restaurant's walls are decorated with a curious assortment of paintings, as well as a carousel horse, which imparts a very playful feel. The menu, however, is strictly traditional French, with such flavorful and well-prepared dishes as tenderloin with bourguignon sauce or a tarragon béarnaise. There are quite a few good seafood dishes, as well as a salade Niçoise. There's a modest assortment of both French and Chilean wines to accompany your meal.

Paseo de los Turistas, between Calles 21 and 23. (©) **506/661-2262.** Reservations recommended in high season and on weekends. Main courses $5.50–$15. AE, MC, V. Tue 6–10:30pm; Wed–Sun noon–2:30pm and 6–10:30pm.

La Yunta Steakhouse (★) (Finds) STEAKS/SEAFOOD   This airy place bills itself as a steakhouse, but it has an ample menu of seafood dishes as well. Most of the tables are located on a two-tiered covered veranda at the front of the restaurant, overlooking the street and the ocean just beyond. Overall, this restaurant has the nicest ambiance in town. The portions are immense, and the meat is tender and well prepared.

Paseo de los Turistas. (©) **506/661-3216.** Reservations recommended. Main courses $4–$20. AE, MC, V. Daily 10:30am–midnight.

2 Playa de Jacó (★)

73 miles (117km) W of San José; 47 miles (75km) S of Puntarenas

Playa de Jacó is the closest thing in Costa Rica to Daytona Beach during spring break. This long stretch of beach is strung with a dense hodgepodge of hotels in all price categories, cheap souvenir shops, seafood restaurants, pizza joints, and even a miniature-golf course. Surfers love the consistent beach break here (and at neighboring Playa Hermosa). The number-one attraction is the surf, and this is definitely a surfer-dominated beach town. Still, if you're looking for a cheap place not far from San José where you can spend a few days in the sun, Jacó continues to be a top choice.

However, the beach here is not particularly appealing. It's made of dark-gray sand with lots of little rocks and it's often very rough. Charter flights arrive weekly from Montréal and Toronto, and consequently many of the hotels here are owned and populated by Canadians. Jacó is also now gaining popularity with Germans and young Ticos. This is the most touristy beach in Costa Rica and is a prime example of what happens when rapid growth hits a beach town. However, on the outskirts of town and close to the beach, there's still plenty of greenery to offset the excess of cement along the town's main street. In fact, after the dryness of Guanacaste, this is the first beach on the Pacific coast to have a tropical feel. The humidity is palpable, and the lushness of the tropical forest is visible on the hillsides surrounding town. In hotel gardens, flowers bloom profusely throughout the year.

ESSENTIALS
GETTING THERE & DEPARTING   By Car   There are two main routes to Jacó. The easier, though longer, route is to take the Interamerican Highway west out of San José and get off at the Puntarenas exit. From here, head south on the Costanera, the coast road. Alternatively, you can take the narrow and winding, though more scenic, old highway, which turns off the Interamerican Highway just west of Alajuela near the town of Atenas. This highway meets the Costanera a few kilometers west of Orotina.

By Bus   Express buses (🕾 **506/223-1109** or 506/643-3135) leave San José daily at 7:30 and 10:30am, and 3:30pm from the Coca-Cola bus terminal at Calle 16 between Avenidas 1 and 3. The trip takes between 2½ and 3 hours; the fare is $2.50. On weekends and holidays, extra buses are often added, so it's worth calling to check.

Buses from San José to **Quepos** and Manuel Antonio also pass by Jacó (they let passengers off on the highway about half a mile/1km from town). These buses leave San José daily at 6, 7, and 10am; noon; and 2, 4, and 6pm. Trip duration is 3 hours; the fare to Jacó is $2.50 on the indirect bus to Quepos, $5 on the direct bus to Manuel Antonio. However, during the busy months, some of these buses will refuse passengers getting off in Jacó, or accept them only if they pay the full fare to Quepos or Manuel Antonio.

From **Puntarenas,** there are two buses daily to Jacó at 5am and 3pm, or you can catch Quepos-bound buses daily at 5 and 11am, and 2pm, and get off in Jacó. Either way, the trip's duration is 1 hour; the fare is $1.50.

The Jacó bus station is at the north end of town, at a small mall across from the Jacó Fiesta Hotel. Buses for San José leave daily at 5 and 11am, and 3pm. Buses returning to San José from Quepos pass periodically and pick up passengers on the highway. Since schedules can change, it's best to ask at your hotel about current departure times.

ORIENTATION   Playa de Jacó is a short distance off the southern highway. One main road runs parallel to the beach, with a host of arteries heading toward the water; it's off these roads that you'll find most of the hotels and restaurants.

GETTING AROUND   While almost everything is within walking distance in Jacó, you can rent a bicycle or scooter from several shops on the main street or call **Jacó Taxi** (🕾 **506/643-3030**). For longer excursions, you can rent a car from **Economy** (🕾 **506/643-1719**), **Elegante** (🕾 **506/643-3224**), or **Zuma** (🕾 **506/643-3207**). Expect to pay approximately $50 for a 1-day rental. You might also consider talking to any of the local taxi drivers, who would probably take you wherever you wanted to go for the same $50 per day, thus saving you some hassle and headache.

FAST FACTS Both the **Banco Nacional** (© 506/643-3072) and the **Banco de Costa Rica** (© 506/643-3334) have branches in town on the main road and are open Monday through Friday from 8:30am to 3pm. **Farmacia Jacó** (© 506/ 643-3205), the town's pharmacy, is down the street from the Banco Nacional. There's a gas station out on the main highway, at the south end of town. The **health center** and **post office** are at the Municipal Center at the south end of town, across from El Naranjal restaurant. A **public phone office,** from which you can make international calls, is located in the ICE building on the main road. This office is open Monday through Saturday from 8am to noon and from 1 to 5pm. The **Aguamatic Laundry** (© 506/643-2083) is located on the main strip across from the Red Cross and is open Monday through Saturday from 7am to 5pm. Same-day service is available. Finally, there's a **Western Union office** in a small strip mall across from La Hacienda restaurant.

FUN ON & OFF THE BEACH

Unfortunately, this beach has a nasty reputation for riptides (as does most of Costa Rica's Pacific coast). Even strong swimmers have been known to drown in the power rips. At times, storms far offshore cause huge waves to pound on the beach, making it impossible to go into the water much beyond your waist. If this is the case, you'll have to be content with the hotel pool.

After you've spent some time on Playa de Jacó, you might want to visit some of the other nearby beaches. **Playa Esterillos,** 13½ miles (22km) southeast of Jacó, is long and wide and almost always nearly deserted. **Playa Hermosa,** 6.2 miles (10km) southeast of Jacó, where sea turtles lay eggs from July through December, is also well known for its great surfing waves. **Playa Herradura,** about 4 miles (6½km) northwest of Jacó, is a hard-packed brown-sand and rock beach ringed by lush hillsides. For years this was an almost deserted beach with just a few basic cabins and campgrounds. Now, it's home to the Marriott Los Sueños Beach & Golf Resort. The luxury hotel and 18-hole golf course are open, and work is ongoing to complete a full-service marina, as well as large condo-minium and vacation-home projects. However, the Marriott occupies only one end of the beach here, and despite its presence, Playa Herradura still feels a lot

---

Day of the Iguana

The nearby **Iguana Park** (© 506/428-7776) is actually an iguana preserva-tion project, and makes a good day trip from Jacó. Don't let the iguana burgers and tacos on sale at the restaurant here or the iguana "leather" wallets and belts on sale at the gift shop fool you. When you're not eat-ing and buying iguana products, you can take a walk through a forest trail in an area massively repopulated with green iguanas, or visit the park's education center (where you can touch and hold iguanas).

The park is also the site of one of the country's original canopy-tour operations. The canopy tour here takes 3½ hours and costs $45, including the separate $8 entrance fee for Iguana Park. You'll find Iguana Park about 6.2 miles (10km) from Orotina. To get here from Jacó, head back toward San José via Orotina. In Orotina, follow the signs to Iguana Park, which is about 20 minutes south.

more isolated and deserted than Jacó. All of these beaches are easily reached by car, moped, or bicycle—if you've got a lot of energy. All are signposted, so you'll have no trouble finding them.

In addition to the activities listed below, you could spend an enjoyable hour or so visiting **Butterfly Fantasy** (© **506/643-2081**), a good-sized butterfly garden, located across the street from the Best Western Jacó Beach Hotel. Admission is $7 and includes an informative tour.

If you try to do any shopping in Jacó, you'll be overrun with shops selling T-shirts, cut-rate souvenirs, and handmade jewelry and trinkets. Two exceptions are **Guacamole** (© **506/643-1120**), a small clothing store that produces its own line of batik beachwear, and **La Galería Heliconia** ☞ (© **506/643-3613**), which carries a good selection of artworks and pottery.

BIKING   You can rent a bike for around $8 per day or $1.50 per hour. Bikes are available from a slew of shops along the main road. One of the better choices is **Maravillas Naturales** (© **506/643-1113**).

A CANOPY TOUR   **Chiclets Tree Tour** (© **506/643-3222**) offers up a canopy adventure ($55 per person) just outside Jacó in nearby Playa Hermosa. You'll spend 3 hours in climbing gear, zipping across cables from one tree plat-form to another in this transitional forest, with some sweeping views of the Pacific. There's also another canopy tour at Iguana Park (see below).

HORSEBACK RIDING   Horseback-riding tours give you a chance to get away from all the development in Jacó and see a bit of nature. Contact **Fantasy Tours** (© **506/643-3231**), **Jacó Equestrian Center** (© **506/643-1569**), or **Hermanos Salazar** (© **506/643-3203**) to make a reservation. Down in Playa Hermosa, check in with **Diana's Trail Rides** (© **506/643-3808**). Tours lasting 3 to 4 hours cost around $25 to $45.

KAYAKING   **Kayak Jacó** (© **506/643-1233;** www.kayakjaco.com) runs a couple of different trips on stable, hard-plastic, sit-on-top kayaks. The first is a gentle float on the Tulín River. The second is a combination ocean-kayaking/snorkel trip on calm Herradura Bay. Both options run around 4 hours and include transportation to and from the put-in, as well as fresh fruit and soft drinks during the trip. The tours cost between $40 and $60 per person depend-ing on where you are staying.

LEARNING THE LANGUAGE   **Escuela del Mundo** (© **506/643-1064;** www.speakcostarica.com) offers a variety of course options from 1 to 4 weeks in length that focus on language, culture, and even surfing. A 1-week course costs $295, with lodging an extra $95 per person, double occupancy.

A SPA   The **Serenity Spa** (© **506/643-1624**) offers massage, as well as mud packs, face and body treatments, and manicures and pedicures. The spa is located on the first floor, among a tiny little cul-de-sac of shops next to Zuma Rent-A-Car. These folks are also in charge of spa services at the new Los Sueños Marriott resort.

SPORTFISHING, SCUBA DIVING & SUNSET CRUISES   With the open-ing of the new Los Sueños Marriott resort and the ongoing construction of its adjacent 250-slip marina, expect much of the local maritime activity to shift over here. If you're interested in doing some sportfishing, scuba diving, or any other waterborne activity, I'd recommend you check with your hotel or at the marina.

Alternatively, you can call **J. D. Watersports** (© **506/257-3857**), which operates out of Punta Leona, or ask at **Hotel Club del Mar** (© **506/643-3194**).

A half-day fishing trip for four people will cost around $250 to $400, and a full day will cost between $450 and $900. J. D. Watersports also offers scuba-diving trips and sunset cruises.

SURFING   The same waves that make Playa de Jacó unsafe for swimming make it one of the most popular beaches in the country with surfers. Nearby **Playa Hermosa** and **Playa Escondida** are also excellent surfing beaches. Those who want to challenge the waves can rent surfboards for around $3 an hour or $10 to $15 per day, and boogie boards for $2 an hour, from any one of the numerous surf shops along the main road.

ORGANIZED TOURS FARTHER AFIELD   If you'll be spending your entire Costa Rican visit in Jacó but would like to see some other parts of the country, you can arrange tours through the local offices of **Explorica** (© 506/643-3586) or **Fantasy Tours** (© 506/643-3231). Both companies offer day tours to Arenal, Poás, and Irazú Volcanoes, white-water rafting trips, cruises to Tortuga Island, and trips to Braulio Carrillo National Park and other places. Overnight trips are also available. Rates range from $45 to $90 for day trips. Thanks to improvements to the road, you can now reach Manuel Antonio in about 1 hour from Jacó. Both of the companies mentioned above offer a host of tour options in Manuel Antonio, including trips to the national park, Rainmaker reserve, and Isla Damas estuary.

CARARA BIOLOGICAL RESERVE ★★

A little over 9 miles (15km) north of Jacó is Carara Biological Reserve, a world-renowned nesting ground for **scarlet macaws.** It has several miles of trails open to visitors. There's a loop trail that takes about an hour and another trail that's open only to tour groups. The macaws migrate daily, spending their days in the park and their nights among the coastal mangroves. It's best to view them in the early morning when they arrive, or around sunset when they head back to the coast for the evening, but a good guide can usually find them for you during the day. Whether or not you see them, you should hear their loud squawks. Among the other wildlife you might see here are caimans, coatimundis, armadillos, pacas, peccaries, river otters, kinkajous, and, of course, hundreds of species of birds.

Be sure to bring along insect repellent, or, better yet, wear light cotton long sleeves and pants. (I was once foolish enough to attempt a quick hike while returning from Manuel Antonio, still in beach clothes and flip-flops—not a good idea.) The reserve is open daily from 8am to 4pm. Admission is $6 per person at the gate.

There are several companies offering tours to Carara Biological Reserve for around $30 to $40. Check at your hotel or contact **Fantasy Tours** (© 506/643-3231) for schedules and more information. If you're looking for a more personalized tour, check out Lisa Robertson, a knowledgeable and amiable guide, who calls her small tour company **Happy Trails** (© 506/643-1894). You can hike the trails of Carara independently, but my advice is to take the guided tour; you'll learn a lot more about your surroundings.

The muddy banks of the Tárcoles River are home to a healthy population of American crocodiles, and just north of the entrance to the Carara Biological Reserve is a bridge that's a prime spot for viewing both the crocs and the macaw migrations. It's worth a stop, but be careful: Thieves and pickpockets work this spot regularly. Don't leave your car or valuables unguarded, and be wary if yours is the only car parked here. Once you're in Jacó, you'll find several operators who run daily crocodile tours on the Tárcoles River. Most of these companies bring along plenty of freshly killed chicken to attract the reptiles and pump up the adrenaline. Expect to pay between $40 and $50 per person for the trip.

Finally, just beyond Carara National Park on the Costanera Sur in the direction of Jacó, you'll find a turnoff for some spectacular waterfalls (including a 600-ft. fall) around the town of **Bijagual.** A local family here runs the **Complejo Ecologico La Catarata** (no phone), which features a basic restaurant and a campground. They charge a nominal fee to visit the falls on foot and also run horseback tours. To get here, turn off at the signs for Hotel Villa Lapas. From here you can either drive the very rough 5 miles (8km) up to the entrance to the falls, or arrange for them to pick you up at Villa Lapas.

ACCOMMODATIONS IN PLAYA DE JACÓ

Since Punta Leona, Playa Herradura, and Playa Hermosa de Jacó (not to be confused with Playa Hermosa in Guanacaste) are close by, many people choose accommodations in these beach towns as well. Selected listings for these towns follow this section.

EXPENSIVE

Club del Mar Condominiums and Resort 🖈🖈 *(Kids)*   This has long been my favorite Playa de Jacó hotel because of its location, friendly owners, and attractively designed rooms. A major expansion and remodeling—in full swing on my last visit—should only serve to make this an even more attractive option. Club del Mar is at the far southern end of the beach where the rocky hills meet the sand. Most of the rooms will actually be one- or two-bedroom condo units, with full kitchens. All are spacious and feature private balconies or porches. There will also be nine luxurious rooms in the new main building. All units come with an ocean view, although some are more open and expansive than others. The grounds are lush and chock-full of flowering heliconia and ginger.

Playa de Jacó (A.P. 107-4023), Puntarenas. 🕿 and fax **506/643-3194.** www.clubdelmarcostarica. com. 31 units. $120–$250 double. Lower rates in the off-season. AE, MC, V. **Amenities:** 1 restaurant (international); 2 bars; large free-form pool; 3 Jacuzzis; exercise room; water-sports equipment rental; tour desk; concierge; limited room service; massage; laundry service; no-smoking rooms. *In room:* A/C, TV, minibar, fridge, hair dryer, safe.

Hotel Barceló Amapola 🖈   This place was taken over by the Spanish Barceló chain and converted into an all-inclusive resort. While it's one of the nicer accommodations in town, it has an unenviable location, some 500 meters (about 545 yd.) inland from the beach, toward the southern end of Jacó. The rooms are new, cool, and comfortable, with white-tile floors, two double beds, plenty of closet and shelf space, a desk and chair, and either a small patio or balcony. The bathrooms have sleek European fixtures and a bidet. The suites have an extra living/sitting room with a foldout sofa bed and just a king-size bed in the master bedroom. The villas come with two bedrooms, living room, full kitchen, and small patio, but frankly, I find the rooms much nicer and more comfortable, particularly those on the second floor. Meals are all served buffet style, and the hotel, which is often filled with Spanish and/or Tico groups, has a lively party atmosphere.

Playa de Jacó (A.P. 133), Puntarenas. 🕿 **506/643-2225.** Fax 506/643-3668. www.barcelo.com. 106 units. $170–$200 double. Rates include all meals, beverages, and taxes. Lower rates in the off-season. AE, MC, V. **Amenities:** 1 restaurant (international/buffet); 2 bars; casino; disco; a midsize pool with a swim-up bar and 2 Jacuzzis; bike rental; tour desk; laundry service. *In room:* A/C, TV, hair dryer, minibar, safe.

Hotel Cocal 🖈   Located right on the beach, the building is done in colonial style, with arched porticos surrounding a courtyard that contains two medium-size pools, a few palapas for shade, and a thatch-roofed bar. Each guest room is good-sized, with a tile floor, a double and a single bed, a desk, and a porch or a balcony. The beachfront location here and the modest array of amenities are the hotel's greatest attributes, but I don't think it warrants the rates they're charging. The Cocal is on one of the nameless streets leading down to the beach from the main road through Jacó; watch for its sign in the middle of town.

Playa de Jacó (A.P. 54), Puntarenas. ℂ **506/643-3067.** Fax 506/643-3082. www. hotelcocalandcasino.com. 44 units. $95–$140 double. Rates include breakfast buffet. Lower rates in the off-season. AE, MC, V. **Amenities:** 2 restaurants; 2 bars; 2 small pools; small casino; laundry service. *In room:* A/C, safe; no phone.

MODERATE

Best Western Jacó Beach Hotel   This has long been Jacó's most popular Canadian charter-flight hotel. Situated right on the beach, this five-story hotel offers all the amenities and services you could want at this price. The hotel is often packed throughout the high season, and a party atmosphere pervades the place. The open-air lobby is surrounded by lush gardens, and there are covered walkways connecting the hotel's buildings. Rooms are adequate and have tile floors and walls of glass facing onto balconies; however, not all of the rooms have good views (some face another building), and many of them show their age. Ask for a view room on a higher floor and with an ocean view, if possible. Bathrooms tend to be a bit battered, but they do have bathtubs. If you'd like more space and a kitchen, ask about the Villas Jacó Princess, managed by the same company and located just across the road.

Playa de Jacó (A.P. 962-1000, San José), Puntarenas. ℂ **506/643-1000.** Fax 506/643-3246. www. bestwesterncostarica.com. 120 units. $80–$110 double. AE, DC, MC, V. **Amenities:** 2 restaurants (continental, international); 2 bars; too-small circular pool; outdoor tennis court; volleyball court; water-sports equipment rental; complimentary bicycle rental; tour desk; car-rental desk; room service; laundry service. *In room:* A/C, TV, safe.

Hotel Copacabana   This Canadian-owned hotel is right on the beach and is popular with sport-fishers and sports lovers. It recently received a major remodeling and new construction. The basic standard rooms are on the second floor of the older building, and each has one double and one single bed, a ceiling fan, and little bay windows with bamboo shades. On the shared veranda, strung hammocks alternate with small tables and chairs. Although they have the benefit of air-conditioning and kitchenettes, most of the rooms on the first floor are a bit claustrophobic. The nicest rooms here are the new oceanfront suites, which are spacious and come with air-conditioning, televisions, kitchenettes, and private balconies facing the waves. Most of the activity here is centered around the pool and its neighboring bar and restaurant. A 24-foot satellite dish ensures a steady stream of televised sports events, and the food is surprisingly good.

Playa de Jacó (A.P. 150), Puntarenas. ℂ **506/643-1005.** Fax 506/643-3131. www. copacabanahotel.com. 32 units. $49 double; $79–$99 suite, $119 ocean-front suite. Lower rates in the off-season. AE, MC, V. **Amenities:** 1 restaurant (international/American); 1 bar; small pool; tour desk; limited room service. *In room:* Fridge, safe.

Pochote Grande 🌟   Named for a huge old pochote tree on the grounds, this well-kept and attractive hotel is located right on the beach at the far north end of Jacó. The grounds are shady and lush, and there's a refreshing pool. All of the rooms are quite large and have white-tile floors, one queen and one single bed, a small fridge, and a balcony or patio. I prefer the second-floor rooms, which are blessed with high ceilings. The modest restaurant and snack bar serve a mixture of Tico, German, and American meals (the owners are German by way of Africa).

Playa de Jacó (A.P. 42), Puntarenas. ✆ **506/643-3236**. Fax 506/220-4979. www.centralamerica. com/cr/hotel/pochote.htm. 24 units. $55 double to quad. Lower rates in the off-season (May–Nov). AE, MC, V. **Amenities:** 1 restaurant (Costa Rican/international); 1 bar; small pool. *In room:* Fridge, safe; no phone.

INEXPENSIVE

There are several campgrounds in or near Playa de Jacó. **Madrigal** (✆ **506/643-3851**), at the south end of town at the foot of some jungly cliffs, is my favorite. You can also try **El Hicaco** (✆ **506/643-3004**), which is close to the beach but also pretty close to the Disco La Central, so don't expect to get much sleep if you stay here. Campsites run between $2 and $5 per night.

Flamboyant Hotel   The Flamboyant doesn't quite live up to its name, but it's still a good value. The rooms are arranged around a small swimming pool and are only a few steps from the beach. They're all spacious, with simple furnishings, and most have kitchenettes. The newer and more expensive rooms have air-conditioning, televisions, and private balconies. You'll find the hotel down a narrow lane toward the ocean, down from the Wishbone Cafe, which is on the main road in the middle of Jacó.

Playa de Jacó (A.P. 18), Puntarenas. ✆ **506/643-3146**. Fax 506/643-1068. flamboya@racsa.co.cr. 15 units. $40–$70 double. AE, MC, V. **Amenities:** Outdoor pool; unheated Jacuzzi. *In room:* Safe; no phone.

Hotel Mar de Luz 𝄞 (Value)   This is one of Playa de Jacó's best deals and a comfortable alternative to the typical string of cut-rate cabinas you'll find crowding this popular beach town. All the rooms are immaculate and comfortable. Some feature stone walls, small sitting areas, and either one or two double beds placed on a raised sleeping nook. My only complaint is that the windows are too small and mostly sealed, so you're forced to use the air-conditioning. In the gardens just off the pools, there are a couple of grills available for guest use. There is also a comfortable common sitting area, with a selection of magazines and books in several languages. Dutch owners Victor and Carmen Keulen seem driven to offer as much comfort, quality, and service as they can for the price. You'll find the hotel 50 meters (55 yd.) east of the Hotel Tangeri, right in the center of Jacó.

Playa de Jacó (A.P. 143), Puntarenas. ✆ and fax **506/643-3259**. www.mardeluz.com. 29 units. $50 double. Lower rates in the off-season. V. **Amenities:** 2 small to midsize adult pools, 1 children's pool; Jacuzzi; tour desk; laundry service. *In room:* A/C, TV, kitchenette (some rooms), coffee maker, safe; no phone.

Hotel Zabamar   The Zabamar is set back from the beach in a shady compound. The older rooms have red-tile floors, small refrigerators, ceiling fans, hammocks on their front porches, and showers in enclosed private patios. There are also 10 newer rooms with air-conditioning. There are even *pilas* (laundry sinks) in little gravel-and-palm gardens behind the older rooms. Some have rustic wooden benches and chairs. The shallow swimming pool stays quite warm. Travelers on tight budgets will appreciate the size of the older, less-expensive rooms.

Playa de Jacó, Puntarenas. ✆ and fax **506/643-3174**. 20 units. $30–$50 double; $45 triple. A/C extra. Lower rates in the off-season; discounts for long-term stays. MC, V. **Amenities:** 1 restaurant (Costa Rican/international); 1 bar; small outdoor pool. *In room:* No phone.

ACCOMMODATIONS JUST NORTH OF PLAYA DE JACÓ
VERY EXPENSIVE

Los Sueños Marriott Beach & Golf Resort ⟨★★★⟩ ⟨Kids⟩   This is closest large-scale resort to San José, and one of the nicest in the country. The hotel is a massive, four-story horseshoe facing the beach. The whole thing is done in a Spanish colonial style, with stucco walls, heavy wooden doors, and red-clay roof tiles. The rooms are all spacious and tastefully done. They come with either one king or two queen-size beds, a large armoire, a desk, and a sitting chair with ottoman. The bathrooms are large and have plenty of counter space. Every room has a balcony, but all are not created equal. Most have only small Juliet-style balconies. Those facing the ocean are clearly superior, and a few of the ocean-facing rooms even have large, comfortable balconies with chaise longues and tables and chairs (you'll have to specifically request one of these).

The expansive lobby area opens out on a large terrace and the Puesta del Sol bar, with its panoramic views of the beach and the bluffs bordering Playa Herradura. The pool is a vast, intricate maze built to imitate the canals of Venice (in miniature), with private nooks and grottos. The beach here is calm and good for swimming, although it's one of the least attractive beaches on this coast, with a mix of rocks and hard-packed, dark-brown sand. The Ted Robinson–designed 18-hole golf course winds through some of the neighboring forest and is an excellent, if not particularly challenging, resort course. The **Stellaris casino** is the largest and most comfortable I've found at a beach resort in Costa Rica.

Playa Herradura (A.P. 502-4005), San Antonio de Belén. ℂ **800/228-9290** in the U.S.; 506/298-0000 or 506/630-9000 in Costa Rica. Fax 506/298-0033. www.marriotthotels.com. 211 units. $250–$280 double; $600 suite, $1,100 presidential suite. AE, MC, V. **Amenities:** 4 restaurants (continental, international, grill, "New Latin"); coffee shop; 2 bars; 1 lounge; casino; large outdoor pool; golf course and pro shop; 4 outdoor tennis courts; health club and spa; water-sports-equipment rentals; children's program; game room; concierge; tour desk; car-rental desk; salon; 24-hour room service; in-room massage; baby-sitting; laundry service; no-smoking rooms. *In room:* A/C, TV, dataport, minibar, coffee maker, hair dryer, iron, safe, bathrobes.

Villa Caletas ⟨★★★⟩ ⟨Finds⟩   It's hard to find a luxury hotel in Costa Rica with a more spectacular setting. Perched 350 meters above the sea, Villa Caletas enjoys commanding **views of the Pacific** ⟨★★⟩ over forested hillsides. While the regular rooms are all elegantly appointed and spacious, you'll want to stay in a villa here. Each individual villa is situated on a patch of hillside facing the sea or forests. Inside, you'll find a main bedroom with a queen-size bed and a comfortable sitting room with couches that convert into two single beds. The villas feature white-tile floors, modern bathrooms, and a private terrace for soaking up the views. The junior suites are even larger, while the suites and master suites are larger still—and even come with their own private swimming pools. There are only two master suites here, and one is a vigorous hike downhill from the main hotel building and restaurants. The same is true of some of the villas and juniors. While most guests are happy to lounge around and swim in the free-form "infinity" pool that seems to blend into the sea below and beyond, Villa Caletas also offers periodic shuttle service to its own little private beach, as well as a host of tour options.

A.P. 12358-1000, San José. ℂ **506/637-0606.** Fax 506/637-0404. www.hotelvillacaletas.com. 21 units, 12 villas. $140–$170 double; $180 villa; $215–$330 suite. Slightly lower rates in the off-season. Extra person $25. AE, MC, V. Amenities: 2 restaurants (international, French); 1 bar; Greek-style amphitheater that sometimes hosts sunset concerts of jazz and classical music; midsize swimming pool with spectacular view; exercise room; concierge; tour desk; beach shuttle; laundry service. *In room:* A/C, TV, minibar, coffee maker, hair dryer, safe.

Villas Lapas *⚜*   Located on a lush piece of property along the Río Tarcolitos and bordering Carara National Park, Villa Lapas is a decent choice if you're looking to combine a bit of eco-adventure and bird watching with some beach time. However, the all-inclusive nature of the hotel tends to appeal mostly to Tico weekend revelers and large party-hungry groups, and I find its rates on the high side for what it offers. The rooms here are all spacious, with two double beds, cool red-clay tile floors, ceiling fans, and a shady veranda with some plastic chairs. Most of the rooms have air-conditioning, at no extra cost. The hotel's nicest feature is its massive, open-air restaurant and deck overlooking the river, where buffet-style meals are served. Hopefully the spectacular setting will take your mind off the mediocre meals. Villa Lapas has 543 acres of land with excellent trails, a series of suspended bridges crossing the river, and a butterfly garden. You'll see the signs for Villa Lapas on the left, just after passing Carara National Park. The hotel is about 15 to 20 minutes from the beaches of Jacó, Hermosa, and Herradura.

Tárcoles (A.P. 419-4005), Puntarenas. ℂ **506/293-4821**. Fax 506/293-4104. www.villalapas.co.cr. 47 units. $105–$140 per person. Rates include all meals and taxes. AE, MC, V. **Amenities:** 1 restaurant (international/buffet); 1 bar; small pool; 2 Jacuzzis; miniature golf, laundry service. *In room:* A/C, safe.

MODERATE

Punta Leona Beach Hotel *(Overrated)*   Located 6.2 miles (10km) north of Jacó, this gated resort and residential community was the first large-scale resort complex in Costa Rica. A private forest reserve, white-sand beaches (two of them), and a rocky promontory jutting out into the Pacific give Punta Leona more natural charms than anything this side of Manuel Antonio. However, due to its status as a popular Tico weekend party resort and its haphazard development planning, these natural charms are often drowned out by the blare of Jet Skis, all-terrain vehicles, and nightly discos. The main guest rooms are not as luxurious as one would hope, and in fact some of them are downright run-down. The standard hotel rooms are in Spanish-style buildings with red-tile roofs and white stucco walls. Inside, you'll find that the beds and bedspreads are a bit dated and worn, but otherwise the rooms are comfortable and clean. In addition to these rooms, there is a variety of different apartment types, including some unusual small chalets and some converted railroad cars (which feel a lot like mobile homes).

Punta Leona (A.P. 8592-1000, San José). ℂ **506/231-3131**. Fax 506/232-0791. www. hotelpuntaleona.com. 108 units, 72 apts. $82 double; $92–$200 apt or suite (4–8 people). Lower off-season rates. AE, DC, MC, V. **Amenities:** 3 restaurants (Costa Rican, international, seafood); 2 bars; 2 snack bars; 4 swimming pools; outdoor tennis court; miniature golf; water-sports equipment rentals; bike rental; tour desk; beach shuttle; laundry service. *In room:* A/C, TV, safe.

DINING

Playa de Jacó has a wide range of restaurants. Most cater to surfers and budget travelers. Budget travelers who really want to save money on meals can always stay at a hotel that provides kitchenettes for its guests, shop at the local *supermercado,* and fix their own meals. Even the most inexpensive lodgings have restaurants, so if you don't want to cook, you won't have to venture far.

   If you end up walking the strip and want to eat in town, I've recommended some places below. In addition, the **Terraza El Hicaco** (ℂ **506/643-3226**), **Colonial Restaurant** (ℂ **506/643-3326**), and **Pancho Villa** (ℂ **506/643-3571**) are all local favorites. If you're looking for simply prepared, fresh seafood,

El Recreo (✆ **506/643-1172**) and **Restaurante Santimar** (✆ **506/643-3605**) are both good bets, serving standard Tico beach fare—fresh seafood, sandwiches, chicken, and steak. For a filling American-style breakfast, try **Chatty Cathy's** (✆ **506/643-1039**).

On the main road to Jacó, at the first main entrance into town, you'll find **Lighthouse Point** (✆ **506/643-3083**), a new steakhouse, seafood restaurant, and raw bar, which is open 24 hours daily and also has an extensive gift shop. **Steve & Lisa's** (✆ **506/637-0106**), located several miles outside of town, around Tárcoles, is a good place for lunch. The food here is standard Tico fare, but the ocean-side setting and views set it apart from other simple *sodas*.

Caliche's Wishbone ⚔ ⓕⁱⁿᵈˢ SEAFOOD/MEXICAN   This casual spot, popular with surfers, offers Tex-Mex standards and homemade pizzas. However, you can also get excellent fresh fish and perfectly prepared seafood dishes, as well as hearty stuffed potatoes and a variety of sandwiches served in homemade pita bread. The portions are huge. It almost always has fresh tuna lightly seared and served with a soy-wasabi dressing. The nicest tables are street-side on a covered veranda. Inside there are more tables, as well as a bar with television sets showing surf videos.

On the main rd. in Jacó. ✆ **506/643-3406.** Main courses $4–$12. V. Thurs–Tues 11:30am–3pm and 5:30–10pm.

El Nuevo Latino ⚔⚔ LATIN FUSION   This restaurant offers creative and modern takes on local and regional dishes. The dozen or so tables are set in a narrow room, which features a glass wall running its length, fronting a gorgeous pool fed by a series of spouts from a story-high aqueduct. The service and setting are semiformal, but there's no dress code—they realize you're at the beach and on vacation here. Standout dishes include the plantain-crusted red snapper and the guava-glazed baby-back ribs. Be sure to start things off with the Honduran tuna ceviche (a unique ceviche flavored with coconut milk and served in a coconut shell), or the lobster-and-shrimp croquettes, which come with a roasted-corn and pepper salsa.

At the Los Sueños Marriott Resort. ✆ **506/630-9000.** Reservations recommended. Main courses $20–$34. AE, MC, V. Daily 6–11pm; closed Mon during the low season.

Rioasis PIZZA/MEXICAN   Rioasis serves hearty burritos, simple pasta dishes, and a wide array of freshly baked wood-oven pizzas. My favorite item is the Greek pizza, with olives, feta cheese, and anchovies, but the barbecued chicken pizza is also delicious. There are both indoor and terrace seating, as well as a bar area, complete with pool table, dartboards, and a couple of TVs for sports events and surf videos.

On the main rd. in Jacó. ✆ **506/643-3354.** Main courses $3–$12. V. Wed–Mon noon–midnight.

PLAYA DE JACÓ AFTER DARK

Playa de Jacó is the central Pacific's party town, and the **Disco La Central** (✆ **506/643-3076**) is packed every night of the high season and every weekend during the low season. La Central is right on the beach near the south end of town. There's a huge open-air hall, which features the requisite '70s flashing lights and suspended mirrored ball, as well as a garden bar in a thatch-roofed building that's a slightly quieter place to have a drink. The disco charges a nominal cover charge.

If you're looking for a surfer hangout, check out **La Hacienda** (✆ **506/643-3191**), a second-floor bar with a laid-back feel, a beat-up pool table, a dartboard, and surf videos on the TVs. Lately, live rock bands perform here on weekends. La Hacienda is located on the main drag toward the north end of town.

Sports freaks can catch the latest games at **Hotel Copacabana** (© **506/643-3131**) or **El Zarpe** (© **506/643-3473**). The latter serves up good, reasonably priced burritos, burgers, and other assorted bar food. The very late-night crowd always seems to end up at the **Pancho Villa Restaurant** (© **506/643-3571**).

EN ROUTE SOUTH TO MANUEL ANTONIO: PLAYA HERMOSA

Playa Hermosa is the first beach you'll hit as you head south from Playa de Jacó. This is primarily a surfers' beach, but it is still a lovely spot to spend some beach time. In addition to the hotels listed below, **Safari Surf Cabinas** (© **506/643-3508**) and **Cabinas Vista Hermosa** (© **506/643-3422**) are two popular surfer hotels, with basic rooms for between $15 and $20 per person.

If you're looking for something even more remote and undeveloped, head farther south to Playa Esterillos Este for the **Auberge du Pelican** (fax **506/779-9236**).

Most folks at Playa Hermosa find their way to **The Backyard** (© **506/643-3936**), a lively surfer bar with a pool table, darts, and hearty food.

ACCOMMODATIONS

Cabinas Las Olas Playa Hermosa is a renowned surfing beach, and this is its most popular surfer hotel. The main building is on a hill by the road. Three of the rooms are located upstairs and have a mix of double and single beds, a veranda with a hammock, and ocean views; downstairs are a couple of smaller budget rooms that are fine for a single traveler. The rooms are all basic but comfortable. Closer to the beach are three A-frame cabins or *ranchos,* each of which have a roomy bedroom on the second floor (in the peak of the A) and a single bed, bunk bed, kitchenette, and bathroom on the ground floor. The nicest room here is the "Skybox Suite," located on the top floor of the main building, with a great view. Between the main building and the cabins is a pool with a small stone waterfall. Out by the ocean there's the Hard Charger's Cafe, which serves three meals daily. The breakfast burritos provide just the carbo load needed for a full day of surfing. If you don't surf, there's a thatch palapa strung with hammocks for watching the waves, the sunsets, and the surfers. The folks at Las Olas can also arrange a wide variety of tours and activities.

A.P. 258, Jacó, Puntarenas. © and fax 506/643-3687. www.cabinaslasolas.com. 8 units. $50–$90 double to quad. MC, V. **Amenities:** 1 restaurant (international); 1 bar; small pool. *In room:* Fridge, safe; no phone.

Terraza del Pacífico ☆ Located just over the hill at the start of Playa Hermosa, this hotel has a wonderful setting on a mostly undeveloped section of beach. In recent years, it's received major renovation and repairs. Rooms are built so that they all have ocean views. In the middle of the complex is a circular pool with a swim-up bar and plenty of chaise longues for sunbathing and siestas. Red-tile roofs and faux-stucco walls give the buildings a very Mediterranean look, while hardwood balcony railings add a touch of the tropics. Each guest room has two double beds, a private bathroom, and either a patio or balcony. The hotel's restaurant is located within a few feet of the high-tide mark and serves Costa Rican and international cuisine. The hotel offers a range of tours, including a nearby canopy tour. Surfing is still the major draw here, and Terraza has even installed klieg lights on the beach for night surfing.

Playa Hermosa de Jacó (A.P. 168), Jacó, Puntarenas. ℂ **506/643-3222.** Fax 506/643-3424. www. terraza-del-pacifico.com. 43 units. $90 double or triple. Lower rates in the off-season. AE, MC, V. **Amenities:** 1 restaurant (seafood/international); 1 bar; outdoor pool with swim-up bar; pool bar; laundry service. *In room:* A/C, TV, safe.

3 Manuel Antonio National Park (★★)

87 miles (140km) SW of San José; 43 miles (69km) S of Playa de Jacó

No other destination in Costa Rica has received more international attention than Manuel Antonio. Many first-time visitors to Costa Rica plan their vacation around seeing it, and it's no surprise why: The views from the hills overlooking Manuel Antonio are spectacular, the beaches (particularly those inside the national park) are idyllic, and its jungles are crawling with white-faced and squirrel monkeys, among other forms of exotic wildlife. The flip side is that you'll have to pay more to see it, and you'll have to share it with more fellow travelers than in other parts of this coast. Moreover, development here is leaving a noticeable footprint. What was once a smattering of small hotels tucked into the forested hillside has become a long string of lodgings along the 4¼ miles (7km) of road between Quepos and the national-park entrance. Hotel roofs now regularly break the tree line, and there are numerous architectural and environmental anomalies, including a retired cargo plane recently converted into a roadside bar.

Still, this is one of the most beautiful locations in the entire country. Gazing down on the blue Pacific from high on the mountainsides of Manuel Antonio, it's almost impossible to hold back a gasp of delight. Offshore, rocky islands dot the vast expanse of blue, and in the foreground, the rich deep green of the rain forest sweeps down to the water. Even cheap Instamatics regularly produce postcard-perfect snapshots. It's this superb view that the numerous hotels at Manuel Antonio sell, and that keeps people transfixed on decks, patios, and balconies.

One of the most popular national parks in the country, Manuel Antonio is also one of the smallest, covering fewer than 1,700 acres. Its several nearly perfect small beaches are connected by trails that meander through the rain forest. The mountains surrounding the beaches quickly rise as you head inland from the water; however, the park was created to preserve not its beautiful beaches, but its forests, home to endangered squirrel monkeys, three-toed sloths, purple-and-orange crabs, and hundreds of other species of birds, mammals, and plants. Once this entire stretch of coast was a rain forest teeming with wildlife, but now, only this small rocky outcrop of forest remains.

The popularity of Manuel Antonio has brought increased development and ever-growing crowds of beachgoers. In just the last few years, these factors have turned what was once a remote and pristine spot into an area full of crowded parking areas, overpriced hotels, and noisy crowds. In many respects, Manuel Antonio has been victimized by adoring throngs, some of whom have taken to feeding the wild animals (monkeys and pizotes, in particular), which is a dangerous distortion of what ecotourism should be. On weekends, the beaches are filled with people, and the disco near the park entrance blares its music until early morning, drowning out the sounds of crickets and frogs that once lulled visitors to sleep here. A shantytown of snack shacks and makeshift parking lots line the road just outside the park, which makes the entrance road look more like a slum than a national park.

Those views that are so bewitching also have their own set of drawbacks. If you want a great view, you aren't going to be staying on the beach and, in fact,

To San José ↖
Estuario Boca Vieja

↑ To ✈ Airport, Hospital and Dominical

area of inset at right

Quepos

PACIFIC OCEAN

Quepos

1

2 Banco Nacional
3
4 7 8 **Market & Bus Terminal**
5
6 Banco de Costa Rica Soccer Field ✉ ✝

To Airport →

9

To Manuel Antonio ↘

0 ___ 1/2 mi
0 ___ 0.5 km

10 12 11

12

14

15

16
17
18 22
21 23
19 24 25 26
20 27

Quebrada Camaronera

28
29
30 32
31 33

Playa Espadilla

PARQUE NACIONAL MANUEL ANTONIO

Park Entrance

Playa Espadilla Sur

Playa Puerto Escondido

Isla Olocuita

Playa Manuel Antonio

Punta Quepos

Punta Catedral

Punta Surrucho

NICARAGUA
COSTA RICA ★ San Jose
● Quepos
area of detail
PACIFIC OCEAN PANAMA
Caribbean Sea
0 ___ 100 mi
0 ___ 100 km

HOTELS ■

Cabinas Pedro Miguel **10**
Cabinas Vela-Bar **33**
El Mono Azul Hotel **12**
El Parador **20**
Hotel and Cabinas Playa Espadilla **32**
Hotel Casitas Eclipse **26**
Hotel Costa Verde **27**
Hotel Malinche **8**
Hotel Plinio **11**
Hotel Quepos **9**
Hotel Sí Como No **25**
Karahé **28**
La Colina **14**
La Mariposa **22**
Makanda-by-the-Sea **19**
Tulemar Bungalows **16**
Verde Mar **30**
Villas Nicolas **24**

Church ✝
Post Office ✉
Trails •••••

RESTAURANTS ◆

Barba Roja **17**
Cafe Milagro **2** & **23**
El Gato Negro **26**
El Gran Escape **3**
Karola's **18**
Plinio Restaurant **11**
Restaurant Vela-Bar **33**
Sunspot Bar and Grill **19**

ATTRACTIONS, ETC. ●

Botica Quepos **6**
Disco Arco Iris **1**
El Banco Bar **7**
Epicentro **3**
Fish Head Bar **3**
Hotel Divisamar Casino **21**
Hotel Kamuk Casino **4**
Jardín Gaia **13**
L'Aventura Boutique **5**
La Buena Nota **29**
Mar y Sombra Restaurante & Disco **31**
Stable Equus **15**

you probably won't be able to walk to the beach. This means that you'll be driving back and forth, taking taxis, or riding the public bus a lot. Also keep in mind that it's hot and humid here, and it rains a lot. However, the rain is what keeps Manuel Antonio lush and green, and this wouldn't be the tropics if things were otherwise.

If you're traveling on a rock-bottom budget or are mainly interested in sportfishing, you might end up staying in the nearby town of **Quepos,** which was once a quiet banana port—the land to the north was used by Chiquita to grow its bananas. Disease wiped out most of the banana plantations, and now the land is planted with African oil-palm trees. To reach Quepos by road, you must pass through miles and miles of these oil-palm plantations. More and more, Quepos is filling up with a wide variety of restaurants, souvenir and craft shops, and lively bars.

ESSENTIALS
GETTING THERE & DEPARTING   By Plane   Sansa (© 506/221-9414; reservations@flysansa.com) flies to Quepos daily at 7:50, 9, and 10:30am; and 12:30, 2, 3, and 4:30pm from San José's Juan Santamaría International Airport. The flight's duration is 30 minutes; the fare is $44 each way.

Travelair (© 506/220-3054; reservations@travelair-costarica.com) also flies to Quepos daily at 8:10 and 9am, and 1 and 4pm from Tobías Bolaños International Airport in Pavas. Flight duration is 30 minutes; the fare is $40 each way.

There's an airport-transfer service that charges $4 per person to any hotel in Manuel Antonio and Quepos. Speak to a gate agent at either Sansa or Travelair to arrange a ride. Taxis occasionally meet incoming flights as well. Expect to be charged between $8 and $12 per car for up to four people, depending on the distance to your hotel and your bargaining abilities.

When you're ready to depart, **Sansa** (© 506/777-0683 in Quepos) has daily flights to San José leaving at 8:30, 9:40, and 11:10am; and 1:10, 2:40, 3:40, and 5pm.

Travelair flights leave for San José daily at 8:45 and 10:45am, and 1:35 and 4:40pm.

By Car   Despite being one of the most traveled routes in Costa Rica, the roads between San José and Manuel Antonio have historically been a national disgrace. Massive repair work has left them in good shape for the start of this millennium, but it's not clear how long that will remain the case. From San José, the most popular route is to take the narrow and winding old highway, which

---

Tips   Travel Tips

Despite the above caveats, Manuel Antonio is still worth visiting. If you plan carefully, you can escape many of the problems that detract from its appeal. If you steer clear of the peak months (Dec–Mar), you'll avoid most of the crowds. If you must come during the peak months, try to avoid weekends, when the beach is packed with families from San José. If you stay at a hotel partway up the hill from the park entrance, you'll have relatively easy access to the beach, you may get a view, and best of all, you'll be out of earshot of the disco. If you visit the park early in the morning, you can leave when the crowds begin to show up at midday. In the afternoon, you can lounge by your pool or on your patio.

turns off the Interamerican Highway just west of Alajuela near the town of Ate-nas and joins the Costanera near Orotina. Just follow the many signs to hotels in either Jacó or Manuel Antonio. When you reach Jacó, it's a straight shot and another hour to Manuel Antonio.

Alternatively, you can take the Interamerican Highway west to the Puntare-nas turnoff and head south on the Costanera, the coastal road through Jacó. This is your best bet if heading to Manuel Antonio from Puntarenas or any point north.

By Bus   Express buses (© **506/223-5567** or 506/777-0101) to Manuel Antonio leave San José daily at 6am, noon, and 6pm from the Coca-Cola bus terminal at Calle 16 between Avenidas 1 and 3. Trip duration is 3½ hours; the fare is $5.50. These buses go all the way to the park entrance and will drop you off at any of the hotels along the way.

Regular buses (© **506/223-5567**) to Quepos leave San José daily at 6, 7, and 10am; and noon, 2, 4, and 6pm. Trip duration is 4 hours; the fare is $4.50. These buses stop in Quepos. From here, if you're staying at one of the hotels on the road to Manuel Antonio, you must take a local bus or taxi to your hotel.

Buses leave **Puntarenas** for Quepos daily at 5 and 11am, and 2:30pm. The ride takes 3½ hours; the fare is $3.

Many of the buses for Quepos stop to unload and pick up passengers in **Playa de Jacó.** If you're in Jacó heading toward Manuel Antonio, you can try your luck at one of the covered bus stops out on the Interamerican Highway (see the sec-tion on Playa de Jacó, above).

From Quepos, buses leave for Manuel Antonio daily, roughly every half-hour, from 6am to 7pm, with one late bus at 10pm. The fare is 35¢. The ride takes about 15 minutes.

When you're ready to depart, the Quepos bus station is next to the market, which is 3 blocks east of the water and 2 blocks north of the road to Manuel Antonio. Express buses to San José leave daily at 6am, noon, and 3 and 5pm. Local buses to San José (duration is 4 hr.) leave at 5 and 8am, and 2 and 4pm.

In the busy winter months, tickets sell out well in advance, especially on weekends; if you can, purchase your ticket several days in advance. However, you must buy your Quepos-bound tickets in San José and your San José return tickets in Quepos. If you're staying in Manuel Antonio, you can buy your return ticket for a direct bus in advance in Quepos and then wait along the road to be picked up. There is no particular bus stop; just make sure you are out to flag the bus down and give it time to stop—you don't want to be standing in a blind spot when the bus comes flying around some tight corner.

Buses for **Puntarenas** leave daily at 4:30 and 10:30am, and 3pm. Any bus headed for San José or Puntarenas will let you off in Playa de Jacó.

ORIENTATION   Quepos is a little port town at the mouth of the Boca Vieja Estuary. After crossing the bridge into town, take the lower road (to the left of the high road). In 4 blocks, turn left, and you'll be on the road to Manuel Anto-nio. This road winds through town a bit before starting over the hill to all the hotels and the national park.

GETTING AROUND   A taxi from Quepos to Manuel Antonio (or any hotel along the road toward the park) costs around $4. The return trip from the park to your hotel should cost only 75¢ per person. I know this system doesn't make much sense, but this is a fixed price, so watch out for drivers who try to charge more. If the taxi must leave the main road (for hotels like La Mariposa,

El Parador, and Makanda), the charge is a little higher. If you need to call a taxi, dial © **506/777-1693** or 506/777-0425.

The bus between Quepos and Manuel Antonio takes 15 minutes each way, and runs roughly every half hour from 6am to 7pm daily, with one late bus leaving Quepos at 10pm and returning from Manuel Antonio at 10:25pm. The buses, which leave from the main bus terminal in Quepos, near the market, go all the way to the National Park entrance before turning around and returning. You can flag down these buses from any point on the side of the road. The fare is 35¢.

You can also rent a car from **Elegante Rent-a-Car** (© **506/777-0115**) for around $50 a day. It's located in downtown Quepos, on the left just as you cross the bridge into town. With advance notice, someone will meet you at the airport with your car for no extra charge.

If you rent a car, never leave anything of value in it unless you intend to stay within sight of the car at all times. Car break-ins are commonplace here. There are now a couple of parking lots just outside the park entrance, which cost around $3 for the whole day. You should definitely keep your car in one of these while exploring the park or soaking up sun on the beach. And while these lots do offer a modicum of protection and safety, you should still not leave anything of value exposed in the car. The trunk is probably safe.

FAST FACTS   **Botíca Quepos** (© **506/777-0038**) is the main pharmacy in town. It's on the corner of the main street where you make the turn for Manuel Antonio and is open daily from 7am to 8pm. The telephone number of the **Quepos Hospital** is © **506/777-0922;** and for the **Rural Guard** (local police), call © **506/777-0196.**

There are a handful of Internet cafes around Quepos and along the road to Manuel Antonio, and many hotels are providing this service as well.

EXPLORING THE NATIONAL PARK

Manuel Antonio is a small park with only three major trails. Most visitors come primarily to lie on one of the beaches and check out the white-faced monkeys, which sometimes seem as common as tourists. A guide is not essential here, but as I've said before, unless you're experienced in rain-forest hiking, you'll see and learn a lot more with one. A 2- or 3-hour guided hike should cost between $25 and $35 per person. Almost any of the hotels in town can help you set up a tour of the park. If you decide to explore the park on your own, a basic map is available at the park entrance.

ENTRY POINT, FEES & REGULATIONS   The park is closed on Monday, but open Tuesday through Sunday from 8am to 4pm year-round. You'll find the park entrance at **Playa Espadilla,** the beach at the end of the road from Quepos. To reach the park station, you must cross a small, sometimes polluted stream that's little more than ankle-deep at low tide but can be knee- or even waist-deep at high tide. Just after crossing the stream, you'll come to a small ranger station. You will have to pay a fee of $6 per person to enter. This is where you can pick up the small map of the park I mentioned above. The Parks Service allows only 600 visitors to enter each day, which may mean that you won't get in if you arrive in mid-afternoon during the high season. Camping is not allowed.

THE BEACHES   **Playa Espadilla Sur** (as opposed to Playa Espadilla, which is just outside the park; see "Hitting the Water," below) is the first beach you come to within the actual park boundaries. It's usually the least-crowded beach in the park and one of the best places to find a quiet shade tree to plant yourself under. If you want to explore further, you can walk along this soft-sand beach or follow a trail through the forest parallel to the beach. At the far end, there's a short connecting trail to **Playa Manuel Antonio,** which is sometimes clear enough to offer good snorkeling along the rocks at either end. At low tide, Playa Manuel Antonio shows a very interesting relic: a circular stone turtle trap left by its pre-Columbian residents. From Playa Manuel Antonio, there's another slightly longer trail to **Puerto Escondido,** where there's a blowhole that sends up plumes of spray at high tide.

THE HIKING TRAILS   From either Playa Espadilla Sur or Playa Manuel Antonio, you can take a circular hike around a high promontory bluff. The far-thest point on this hike, which takes about 25 minutes round-trip, is **Punta Catedral** (Cathedral Point), where the view is spectacular. The trail is a little steep in places, but anybody in average shape can do it. I have done it in sturdy sandals, but you might want to wear good hiking shoes. This is a good place to spot monkeys, though you're more likely to see a white-faced monkey than a rare squirrel monkey.

Another good place to see monkeys is the **trail inland** from Playa Manuel Antonio. This is a linear trail, and mostly uphill, but not too taxing. It's great to spend hours exploring the steamy jungle and then take a refreshing dip in the ocean.

Finally, there's a trail that leads first to Puerto Escondido (see above) and **Punta Surrucho,** where there are some sea caves. Be careful when hiking beyond Puerto Escondido: What seems like easy beach hiking at low tide becomes treacherous to impassable at high tide. Don't get trapped. Two other trails wind their way inland from the trail between Playa Manuel Antonio and Puerto Escondido.

HITTING THE WATER

BEACHES OUTSIDE THE PARK   **Playa Espadilla,** the gray-sand beach just outside the park boundary, is often perfect for board surfing and bodysurf-ing. At times, it can be a bit rough for casual swimming, but because there's no entrance fee, it's the most popular beach with locals and visiting Ticos. There are some shops by the water that rent boogie boards, beach chairs, and beach umbrellas. A full-day rental of a beach umbrella and two chaise longues will cost around $10 (these are not available inside the park).

BOATING, KAYAKING, RAFTING & SPORTFISHING TOURS   **Iguana Tours** (ⓒ and fax **506/777-1262;** www.iguanatours.com) is the most established and dependable tour operator in the area, offering river rafting, sea kayaking, mangrove tours, and guided hikes. These folks have an office on the main road, just as you begin to head out of Quepos toward Manuel Antonio. One of its offerings, among my favorite tours in the area, is a mangrove estuary tour of Damas Island. These trips generally include lunch, a stop on Damas Island, and roughly 3 to 4 hours of cruising the waterways. You'll see loads of wildlife. The cost is $65.

There are several rafting companies in Quepos that ply the same rivers. Among them are Iguana Tours (see above) and **Amigos del Río** (ⓒ **506/ 777-0082;** www.amigosdelrio.com). All offer full-day rafting trips for around $70 to $90. Large multiperson rafts are used during the rainy season, and single-person "duckies" are broken out when the water levels drop. Both of the above companies also offer sea-kayaking trips for around $65.

Among the newer options around Quepos/Manuel Antonio are boat excursions in search of dolphins and simple sunset cruises. In addition to **Iguana Tours** (see above), **Sunset Sails** (© 506/777-1304; www.sunsetsails.net), **Planet Dolphin** (© 506/777-1647; www.planetdolphin.com), and **Taximar** (© 506/777-1647) all offer these tours for between $40 and $60 per person. **Waverunner Safaris** (© 506/777-1706) offers 2-hour Jet Ski tours for $125 per person.

Quepos is one of Costa Rica's billfish centers, and sailfish, marlin, and tuna are all common in these waters. If you're into sportfishing, try hooking up with **Blue Fin Sportfishing** (© 506/777-1676; www.bluefinsportfishing.org), **Blue Water II** (© 506/777-1596; www.bluewaterii.com), **Costa Rican Dreams** (© 506/777-0593; www.crdreams.com), or **Poseidon Adventures** (© 506/ 777-0935; cksibus@racsa.co.cr). A full day of fishing should cost between $450 and $1,500, depending on the size of the boat. There's a lot of competition here, so it pays to shop around and investigate. Try asking at **El Gran Escape** restaurant and also down at the **Manuel Antonio Marina.**

OTHER ACTIVITIES IN THE AREA

BIKING   If you want to do some mountain-biking while you're here, check in with **Cycling Estrella** (© and fax 506/777-1286; estrellatour@ queposcostarica.com), which is in downtown Quepos. Well-maintained bikes rent for around $25 per day. You can also do a number of different guided tours according to skill level for between $40 and $80 per day, as well as multiday expeditions.

CANOPY & CANYONING ADVENTURES   About 20 minutes outside of Quepos is **Rainmaker Nature Refuge** (★). This place has been caught up in legal wrangling over ownership, but the last I heard, it was up and running again. Aside from a small network of trails and some great swimming holes, the main attraction here is a system of connected suspension bridges strung through the forest canopy, crisscrossing a deep ravine. There are eight bridges; the longest is 300 feet across. A half-day tour, including a light breakfast, buffet lunch, round-trip transportation from Quepos, and a guide costs $65 per person. Tours leave every morning, and most hotels in the area can book it for you.

There are also two new canopy tours in the area, offered by **Canopy Safari** (© 506/777-0100; www.canopy-tour.com) and **Dream Forest Canopy Tour** (© 506/777-3030; www.canyoningtours.com). Both consist of a series of platforms connected by zip lines. Adventurers use a harness and pulley system to "zip" between platforms, using a leather-gloved hand as their only brake. A half-day canopy tour should run you around $50 to $65 per person.

The folks at Canopy Safari also offer **ATV tours** ($80–$95 half-day) through some private forests, while the folks at Dream Forest Canopy Tour will take you on a local version of the new adventure craze, **canyoning.** Their canyoning tour ($55 half-day; $75 full day) is, in effect, a series of rappels down the face and in the cascading waters of a jungle waterfall. These rappels are combined with climbs back up and refreshing swims in the natural pools at the bottoms of the falls.

HORSEBACK RIDING   If your tropical fantasy is to ride a horse down a beach between jungle and ocean, contact **Stable Equus** (© 506/777-0001), which charges $35 for a 2-hour ride in Manuel Antonio. This stable allegedly treats its animals more humanely than other stables in the area and is also concerned with keeping horse droppings off the beaches. Full-day horseback-riding excursions to a typical Costa Rican farm are provided by **Rancho Savegre Tours** (© 506/ 777-0528). Tours cost $50 per person and include hotel transfers, lunch, and several swimming stops. Another interesting tour that passes through both primary and secondary forest and includes a swimming stop at a jungle waterfall is offered by **Brisas del Nara** (✆ **506/777-1889**). A full-day tour with these folks, including breakfast and lunch, costs $48 per person (a half day is $38).

A WILDLIFE REHABILITATION CENTER For a closer look at some exotic birds and other assorted wildlife, check out **Jardín Gaia** (✆ **506/777-0535**), a wildlife rescue center that rehabilitates and breeds injured and confiscated animals, many of them endangered. The center is located on the road between Quepos and Manuel Antonio. Jardín Gaia runs daily guided tours at 9am and 4pm. Currently, you can visit Jardín Gaia only on one of the tours. Admission is $5 for adults, $2 for children.

SHOPPING

If you're looking for souvenirs, you'll find plenty of beach towels, beachwear, and handmade jewelry in a variety of small shops in Quepos and at impromptu stalls down near the national park. For a good selection in one spot, try **La Buena Nota** (✆ **506/777-1002**), which is on the road to Manuel Antonio, right near the Hotel Karahé. This shop is jam-packed with all sorts of beachwear, souvenirs, used books, and U.S. magazines and newspapers. They recently put in a few basic rooms upstairs, and if you'd like to find out about renting a house, this is a good place to ask.

If you're looking for higher-end gifts, check out **L'Aventura Boutique** (✆ **506/777-1019**) on Avenida Central in Quepos. This small shop has a nice collection of woodwork by Barry Biesanz, banana-fabric works by Lil Mena, and pottery by Cecilia "Pefi" Figueres.

The Hotel Sí Como No's **Regalame** gift shop is pretty well stocked and now has two locations, one at the small shopping center in front of the hotel, and another down in Quepos, on the main road just as you cross the bridge into town.

One of my favorite hangouts has always been the **Cafe Milagro** ✦✦ (✆ **506/777-1707**; www.cafemilagro.com), a homey coffeehouse in downtown Quepos. The folks here roast their own beans and also have a mail-order service to keep you in Costa Rican coffee year-round. You'll find local art for sale on the walls and a good selection of Cuban cigars, too. There's another branch on the main road to Manuel Antonio right near La Mariposa, which is just as nice, and even serves a full breakfast menu.

ACCOMMODATIONS

Take care when choosing your accommodations in Quepos/Manuel Antonio. There are very few true beachfront hotels in Manuel Antonio, so you won't have much luck finding a hotel where you can walk directly out of your room and onto the beach. In fact, most of the nicer hotels here are half a mile (1km) or so away from the beach, high on the hill overlooking the ocean.

If you're traveling on a rock-bottom budget, you'll get more for your money by staying in Quepos and taking the bus to the beaches at Manuel Antonio every day. The rooms in Quepos may be small, but they're generally cleaner and more appealing than those available in the same price category closer to the park.

VERY EXPENSIVE

El Parador ⟨⟨ What is luxurious opulence to one person can seem blindingly ostentatious to another. I lean toward the latter in this case. The hotel itself is spread out over more than 12 acres of land on a low peninsula, down a dirt road from La Mariposa. Its design aims to imitate Spanish Mediterranean grandeur, and the main building is loaded with antiques, including 17th-century Dutch and Flemish oil paintings, a 300-year-old carved wooden horse, and 16th-century church and castle doors. The standard rooms are well appointed, but far too small for this price range. All have private patios, but few have any view to speak of. Most look out on the miniature-golf course. Deluxe rooms offer slightly more space, and the second-floor units have private balconies.

The spacious junior suites are located on the top of a hill, giving a good view of the sea and Cathedral Point in the distance. Be forewarned: It's an arduous hike up to these units, although it does offer an on-call golf-cart shuttle service. The new premium rooms, located in a three-story building built on a high spot on the grounds, have the best views and would be my first choice here. The hotel runs a shuttle van to the national park, and there's a small, secluded beach about 500 meters (545 yd.) from the hotel.

Manuel Antonio (A.P. 284, Quepos). ⟨⟨ **506/777-1414.** Fax 506/777-1437. www.hotelparador. com. 89 units. $185 standard double; $235 deluxe double; $285 premium double; $335 junior suite; $750 presidential suite. Rates include breakfast buffet. Rates slightly higher during peak weeks, significantly lower in the off-season. AE, MC, V. **Amenities:** 2 restaurants (continental, international); 2 bars; midsize free-form pool with a swim-up bar and central fountain; modest fitness center; Jacuzzi; steam room; outdoor tennis court; private helipad; concierge; tour desk; laundry service. *In room:* A/C, TV, minibar, hair dryer, safe.

Hotel Sí Como No ⟨⟨⟨ ⟨Finds⟩ This small resort complex, a good choice for families with kids, seeks to combine modern amenities with an ecologically conscious attitude. They've done a great job of creating a lively, upscale hotel that blends in with and respects the rain forests and natural wonders of Manuel Antonio. All the wood used is farm grown, and although all the rooms have energy-efficient air-conditioning units, guests are asked to use them only when necessary. The standard rooms (housed in the hotel's main building or in the ground floor of a villa) are quite acceptable, but it's worth the small splurge for a superior or deluxe room. Most of these are on the top floors of the two-to-three–story villas, with spectacular treetop views out over the forest and on to the Pacific. These rooms all have a bedroom with an adjoining living room, private balcony, and either a kitchenette or a wet bar. The newest rooms here are a series of deluxe suites, with tons of space and huge garden bathrooms, some of which have private Jacuzzis. There's a separate building set on a high patch of land that has a more art-deco style to it. This building features a penthouse suite with a wonderful outdoor Jacuzzi.

Manuel Antonio (mailing address in the U.S.: Mail Stop SJO 297, P.O. Box 025216, Miami, FL 33102). ⟨⟨ **506/777-0777.** Fax 506/777-1093. www.sicomono.com. 60 units. $160–$250 double. Rates include breakfast. Lower rates in the off-season. Extra person $25. Children under 6 stay free in parents' room. AE, MC, V. **Amenities:** 2 restaurants (international, grill); 2 bars; 2 midsize pools, including 1 with a small waterslide; 2 outdoor Jacuzzis; exercise room; 50-seat laser-projection theater with nightly movies; game room; concierge; tour desk; in-room massage; free beach shuttle; baby-sitting; laundry service. *In room:* A/C, minibar, coffee maker, hair dryer, iron, safe.

La Mariposa (★) While this is still one of Manuel Antonio's premier accommodations, I think it's been coasting on its reputation for some time. Perched on a ridge at the top of the hill between Quepos and Manuel Antonio, La Mariposa (The Butterfly) commands a **mountains-to-the-sea vista** (★)(★) of more than 270°. Needless to say, the sunsets here are knockouts, and the daytime views are pretty captivating themselves. Overall, La Mariposa offers spacious and attractively designed and decorated rooms, but there are better options in Manuel Antonio in this price range.

The nicest accommodations are the bilevel villas and suites. Each has a large bedroom and bathroom on the upper floor and a spacious living room and deck on the lower floor. There are painted tropical murals behind the two queen-size beds in the bedrooms, plus high ceilings, skylights, blue-and-white-tile counters, and shelves of plants. The bathrooms are spacious, and most even have small atrium gardens. Several of these villas have recently been split into separate junior suites and deluxe rooms. The junior suites each have a Jacuzzi out on the small balcony or just inside its sliding glass door. There are new rooms in the four-story addition to the hotel's main building; they're quite spacious and have great views, but don't have much charm or personality. There are also a few standard rooms, which are certainly comfortable, but have no view to speak of.

Manuel Antonio (A.P. 4, Quepos). ℂ **800/416-2747** in the U.S., or 506/777-0355. Fax 506/777-0050. www.lamariposa.com. 41 units. $130–$150 double; $195–$280 suite or villa. Lower rates in the off-season. Extra person $30. AE, MC, V. **Amenities:** 1 restaurant, 1 bar; 3 small pools; concierge; tour desk; complimentary shuttle to and from the national park; in-room massage; baby-sitting; laundry service. *In room:* A/C, minibar, safe.

Makanda-by-the-Sea (★)(★) (*Finds*) Located halfway down the road to El Parador and Punta Quepos, Makanda is a wonderfully luxurious collection of studio apartments and private villas. Each is individually decorated with flair and a sense of style. If you combine Villa 1 with the three studios, you get one very large four-bedroom villa, great for a family or small group (although children under 16 are not allowed, unless you rent out the whole hotel). Every choice comes with a full kitchenette and either a terrace or a balcony. The grounds are well tended, intermixed with tropical flowers and Japanese gardens. A continental breakfast is delivered to your room each morning. The hotel's pool and Jacuzzi combine intricate and colorful tile work with a view of the jungle-covered hillsides and the Pacific Ocean.

Makanda's **Sunspot Bar & Grill** (★) is one of the better restaurants in Manuel Antonio, with just a few tables set under open-sided cloth tents, serving creative continental dishes and rich desserts. Be sure to make reservations in the high season.

Manuel Antonio (A.P. 29, Quepos). ℂ **506/777-0442.** Fax 506/777-1032. www.makanda.com. 11 units. $200 studio; $250–$300 villa. Rates include continental breakfast. Lower rates in the off-season. AE, MC, V. No children under age 16. **Amenities:** 1 excellent restaurant (continental); 1 bar; midsize outdoor pool; Jacuzzi; concierge; tour desk; room service 6am–11pm; in-room massage and spa services; laundry service. *In room:* Kitchenette, coffee maker, safe.

Tulemar Bungalows (★) These individual octagonal bungalows are some of the more enticing and exclusive accommodations in Manuel Antonio. Each bungalow has a spacious living room, full kitchenette, two queen-size beds, and 180° views over jungle and ocean. The couches in the living room fold out into beds, and extra cots for children can be placed in the rooms. The furnishings are acceptable, but a bit sparse and lacking in style.

A private road winds steeply down to a small cove and semiprivate beach where you'll find chaise longues, kayaks, boogie boards, and a snack bar. The pool here is small yet elegant, with its infinity effect blending in with the Pacific Ocean and the breathtaking view.

Manuel Antonio (mailing address in the U.S.: SJO 042, P.O. Box 025369, Miami, FL 33102). ℂ **506/ 777-0580** or 506/777-1325. Fax 506/777-1579. www.tulemar.com. 14 bungalows. $250 double. Rates include full breakfast. Rates higher during peak weeks and lower off-season. AE, MC, V. **Amenities:** 1 restaurant (Mediterranean/international); beachside grill; 2 bars; 1 small pool with a wonderful view and landscaping; free water-sports equipment; laundry service. *In room:* A/C, TV/VCR, kitchenette, minibar, coffee maker, safe.

EXPENSIVE

Hotel Casitas Eclipse ✦ Located close to the top of the hill between Quepos and Manuel Antonio, these beautiful casitas are some of the most boldly styled structures in the area. While the villas have a distinctly Mediterranean flavor, the owner swears they're inspired by Mesoamerican and Pueblo Indian villages. Their styling makes them seem much larger than they actually are, although they're certainly plenty roomy. All are painted a blinding white and are topped with red-tile roofs. Though simply furnished, the rooms are quite comfortable and attractive inside.

You can rent either the entire casita or split it up. The larger downstairs suites have tile floors, built-in banquettes, high ceilings, large patios, and full kitchens. If you don't need all that space, you can opt for the upstairs room, which has a separate entrance, private bathroom, and balcony of its own. There are three attractive tiled pools spread out among the lush grounds. Only the **restaurant** ✦ (see "Dining," below) and a couple of villas have ocean views here, and even these are rather blocked by trees. I personally prefer the units farther from the road, where you're more likely to hear and see squirrel monkeys passing by than trucks and buses.

Manuel Antonio (A.P. 11-6350, Quepos). ℂ **506/777-0408.** Fax 506/777-1738. www. casitaseclipse.com. 30 units. Dec 16–Apr 15 $112–$172 double, $275 2-bedroom casita; Apr 16–Dec 15 $86–$116 double, $172 2-bedroom casita. AE, MC, V. **Amenities:** 1 good restaurant (Italian); 1 bar; 3 outdoor swimming pools; exercise room; concierge; tour desk; laundry service. *In room:* A/C, TV, fridge, safe.

MODERATE

Hotel and Cabinas Playa Espadilla   These are actually two separate, sister projects located across the street from each other. The newer hotel has rooms with air-conditioning and cable television, and most have full kitchenettes. There's a tennis court here, and a bordering private reserve with a small trail system. The older (and less expensive) cabinas are more basic, although most have been well maintained, and a few even have air-conditioning. Ask about bed distribution before you take or reserve a room, as there are a fair amount of rooms with one double and a bunk bed. There's a small swimming pool and well-tended green areas at each site. This place started out as a popular budget option down near the national park entrance. Despite the expansion and improvements, I'm not sure the facilities and amenities merit the prices it's now charging. You'll find both of these places down the side road that runs inland, perpendicular to Playa Espadilla, the first beach outside the national park.

Manuel Antonio (A.P. 195, Quepos). ℂ and fax **506/777-0416,** or 506/777-0903. www.espadilla. com. 28 units. $65–$96 double. Lower rates in the off-season. AE, MC, V. **Amenities:** 1 restaurant;

1 bar; 2 small outdoor pools; tennis court; tour desk; laundry service. *In room:* Fridge, safe; no phone.

Hotel Costa Verde

This is one of the older hotels in Manuel Antonio, and it has consistently offered up good values, ocean views, and reasonably close proximity to the beaches and national park. Located more than halfway down the hill to Manuel Antonio, about a 10-minute walk from the beach, Costa Verde has continued to add new rooms and new buildings over the years. Today, there are rooms in a wide range of sizes and prices. Some of the buildings are located quite a hike from the hotel's pools and restaurants, so be sure you know exactly what type of room you'll be staying in and where it's located. The nicest rooms here have ocean views, kitchenettes, private balconies, and loads of space. There is also a huge penthouse suite, which has a commanding view of the spectacular surroundings. There are two small pools set into the hillside, with views out to the ocean, and the hotel has a couple of miles of private trails through the rain forest.

I have one major complaint here: The folks at Costa Verde are notorious for feeding the monkeys each evening around sunset, which is a particular pet peeve of mine and a blatant violation of the basic tenets of ecotourism.

Manuel Antonio (mailing address in the U.S.: SJO 1313, P.O. Box 025216, Miami, FL 33102). © **888/234-5565** in the U.S. and Canada, or 506/777-0584. Fax 506/777-0570. www. hotelcostaverde.com. 43 units. $79–$129 double; $155 penthouse. Lower rates in the off-season. AE, MC, V. **Amenities:** 2 restaurants (international, grill); 2 bars; 2 small outdoor pools; laundry service. *In room:* No phone.

Hotel Plinio *Value*

The Plinio was for many years a favorite of budget travelers visiting Manuel Antonio, and although its room rates have crept up over the years, it's still a good value. The hotel is built into a steep hillside, so it's a bit of a climb from the parking lot up to the guest rooms and restaurant (roughly the equivalent of three flights of stairs). Once you're up top, though, you'll think you're in a treehouse. Floors and walls are polished hardwood, and there are even rooms with tree-trunk pillars.

The hotel's suites are the best value. These are built on either two or three levels. Both have sleeping lofts, while the three-story rooms also have rooftop decks. My favorite room is known as the "jungle house" and is set back in the forest. Behind the hotel there's a private reserve with 9 miles (15km) of trails and, at the top of the hill, a 50-foot-tall observation tower with an incredible view. In addition to the popular restaurant (see "Dining," below), there's also a poolside grill, where lunches are served. Plinio is located just outside of Quepos on the road toward the national park, so it is a fair distance from the park entrance and beaches.

Manuel Antonio (A.P. 71-6350, Quepos). © **506/777-0055** or 506/777-0077. Fax 506/777-0558. www.hotelplinio.com. 13 units. Dec–Apr $50–$65 double, $80–$100 suite or house; lower rates May–Nov. Rates include breakfast buffet in high season. AE, MC, V (6% surcharge). **Amenities:** 1 restaurant (international); 1 bar; small outdoor pool in lush garden setting; laundry service. *In room:* No phone.

Karahé

The Karahé has long been one of the better beachfront hotels in Manuel Antonio, but competition is increasing, and in order to keep up, the hotel has had to lower its rates, which is good news for travelers. Note that if you opt for one of the villas (the cheapest and oldest rooms in the hotel), you'll have a steep uphill climb from the beach. On the other hand, a couple of these have great views. If you stay in one of the more expensive beachfront units, you'll have a new room with cool tile floors, two double beds, air-conditioning, and a small patio. The least-expensive rooms are located just off the reception and offer neither views nor easy access to the ocean. The gardens here are quite lush and are planted with flowering ginger that often attracts hummingbirds.

The hotel can arrange a wide variety of tours and charters, including sportfishing ($800 for a full day). Karahé is located on both sides of the road about 500 yards before you reach Playa Espadilla.

Manuel Antonio (A.P. 100-6350, Quepos). ℂ **506/777-0170.** Fax 506/777-0175. www.karahe. com. 24 units, 9 villas. $80–$100 double. Rates include continental breakfast. Lower rates in the off-season. AE, MC, V. **Amenities:** 1 restaurant; 1 bar; small outdoor pool and Jacuzzi; exercise room; tour desk; laundry service. *In room:* A/C; no phone.

La Colina *Value* This casual little place is operated by Colorado natives who moved to Manuel Antonio several years ago and converted their home into a B&B. Although the original rooms here are fairly small, they're decorated with style. They have black-and-white-tile floors, louvered French doors, and a good writing desk. Outside each room, there's a small patio area with a few chairs. The new suites are built on the highest spot on this property and have front and back balconies with views of both the ocean and the mountains. The suites are large and comfortable, and several come with cable television. All of the suites and a couple of the rooms have air-conditioning. There's a two-tiered swimming pool with a swim-up bar. La Colina also rents out two fully equipped apartments and can accommodate longer-term stays. The hotel is on your right as you head out of Quepos toward Manuel Antonio, right at a sharp switchback on a steep hill, hence the name, La Colina (The Hill).

Manuel Antonio (A.P. 191, Quepos). ℂ **506/777-0231.** Fax 506/777-1553. www.lacolina.com. 13 units. Dec–Apr $45–$80 double, slightly higher on peak holiday weeks; May–Nov $29–$70 double. Rates include full breakfast. AE, MC, V. **Amenities:** 1 restaurant (international/seafood); 1 bar; small pool; laundry service. *In room:* No phone.

Verde Mar This new hotel is one of the better choices for proximity to the national park and the beach. From your room, it's just a 50-meter (55-yd.) walk to the beach (Playa Espadilla) via a raised wooden walkway. All but two of the rooms come with a basic kitchenette; six of them have air-conditioning. All have plenty of space, nice wrought-iron queen-size beds, red-tile floors, a desk and chair, a fan, and a small porch. Some of the larger rooms even have two queen-size beds. The hotel has no restaurant, but there are plenty within walking distance. There's a small pool here, for when the surf is too rough. You'll find Verde Mar on the beach side of the road just before the Mar y Sombra.

Manuel Antonio (A.P. 348-6350), Quepos. ℂ **506/777-1805** or 506/777-2122. Fax 506/777-1311. www.maqbeach.com/verdemar/html. 20 units. $65–$85 double. Lower rates in the off-season. A/C $10 extra. AE, MC, V. **Amenities:** Small pool; laundry service. *In room:* No phone.

Villas Nicolas *Value* These large villas offer bang for your buck. Built as terraced units up a steep hill in deep forest, they really give you the feeling you're in the jungle. Most are quite spacious and well appointed, with wood floors, throw rugs, and comfortable bathrooms; some rooms even have separate living rooms and full kitchenettes, which make longer stays comfortable. My favorite features, though, are the balconies, which come with sitting chairs and a hammock. Some of these balconies are massive and have incredible views. In fact, the rooms highest up the hill have views I'd be willing to pay a lot more for, and a few of them even have air-conditioning. During the high season, the hotel usually opens up an informal restaurant/bar near the pool serving breakfast, lunch, and sunset cocktails.

Manuel Antonio (A.P. 236, Quepos). © 506/777-0481. Fax 506/777-0451. www.villasnicolas. com. 20 units. $65–$105 double. Weekly, monthly, and low-season (May–Nov) rates available. AE, MC, V. **Amenities:** Small outdoor pool; laundry service. *In room:* Fridge; no phone.

INEXPENSIVE

Cabinas Pedro Miguel   Located a kilometer outside Quepos on the road to Manuel Antonio (across from Hotel Plinio), these cabinas are very basic, with cement floors and cinder-block walls, but at least they're away from the fray and surrounded by forest. The second-floor rooms are newer and cleaner and have carpeting, as well as a glimpse of the water from the common veranda. One of them is huge, with a kitchen, and a back wall made entirely of screen. From it, guests can look out over a lush stand of trees. During the high season (late Nov–late Apr), there's a breakfast buffet, which will run you about $5. In the evening you can dine at the restaurant, which serves Costa Rican standards; the owners encourage guests to participate in meal preparation.

Manuel Antonio (A.P. 17, Quepos). © and fax 506/777-0035. pmiguel@racsa.co.cr. 16 units. $25–$30 double; $50 quad. AE, MC, V. **Amenities:** 1 restaurant (Costa Rican); postage stamp–sized swimming pool. *In room:* No phone.

Cabinas Vela-Bar   You'll find this little hotel up the narrow road that leads off to the left just before the end of the road to Manuel Antonio National Park. It has a wide variety of room choices: If you're on an exceedingly tight budget, you can stay in a tiny room, or if you have a little more money to spend, you can opt for a spacious one-bedroom house that has tile floors and arched windows. There are double beds and tiled bathrooms in all rooms. Quite a few rooms come with air-conditioning and small refrigerators, and a couple have full kitchenettes. The open-air restaurant/bar is deservedly popular; check the chalkboard for the day's special. If you can bear the soft beds, this is one of the best budget options in Manuel Antonio, and it's only 100 meters from the beach.

Manuel Antonio (A.P. 13, Quepos). © 506/777-0413. Fax 506/777-1071. www.velabar.com. 11 units. $40–$70 double. Lower rates in the off-season. AE, MC, V. **Amenities:** 1 restaurant (Costa Rican); 1 bar; laundry service. *In room:* No phone.

El Mono Azul Hotel *(Value*   "The Blue Monkey" has quickly become a budget favorite. Located on the road to Manuel Antonio, just outside of Quepos, it offers clean and comfortable budget rooms. These are some of the best rooms in this price range, and for about $10 extra, you can get air-conditioning and a small television with cable. One room even has a Jacuzzi tub. The whole place has a lively, hostel-like feel. The owner is active in a children's arts program aimed at helping preserve the local rain forest and the endangered squirrel monkey. In fact, 10% of your bill goes to this program.

Manuel Antonio (A.P. 297, Quepos). © 506/777-1548, or © and fax 506/777-1954. www. monoazul.com. 20 units. $40 double ($10 extra for room with A/C and TV). Lower off-season rates. DC, V. **Amenities:** 1 popular restaurant (international/pizza); 1 bar; 2 small pools; small exercise room; laundry service. *In room:* No phone.

Hotel Malinche   A good choice for budget travelers, the Hotel Malinche is located on the first street to your left as you come into Quepos. You can't miss the hotel's arched brick entrance. Inside, you'll find bright rooms with louvered windows. The rooms are small but have hardwood or tile floors and clean bathrooms. The more expensive rooms are newer and larger, and have air-conditioning, TVs, and carpets.

Quepos. © and fax 505/777-0093. 24 units. $20–$45 double. AE, MC, V. *In room:* No phone.

Hotel Quepos This little budget hotel is both comfortable and clean, offering hardwood floors, ceiling fans, a large and sunny TV lounge, and a protected parking lot. The management is very friendly, and there's an interesting souvenir shop and a charter-fishing office on the first floor. This hotel is hard to miss—it's directly across from the soccer field on the way out of town toward Manuel Antonio, and it's painted hot pink with green trim.

Quepos. ℂ **506/777-0274.** 20 units, 11 with private bathroom. $12 double without private bathroom, $17 double with private bathroom. No credit cards. **Amenities:** Laundry service. *In room:* No phone.

DINING

There are scores of dining options around Manuel Antonio and Quepos, and almost every hotel has some sort of restaurant. My favorites of these are the small restaurants at **Makanda-by-the-Sea** ✦ and **Tulemar Bungalows** (see "Accommodations," above).

For the cheapest meals around, try a simple *soda* in Quepos, or head to one of the open-air shacks near the side of the road just before the circle at the entrance to the national park. The standard Tico menu prevails, with prices in the $3-to-$8 range. Though these little places lack atmosphere, they do have views of the ocean. In Quepos, **La Marquesa** (ℂ **506/777-1545**), on the main road, is a good bet—the fish is caught fresh daily, the portions are large, and the prices are bargains.

If you have a room with a kitchenette, you can shop at one of several supermarkets in Quepos, or brave the cluttered stalls of its central market, right next to the bus station. For a picnic lunch, complete with cooler, check out **Pickles Deli** in the small shopping center next to Hotel Sí Como No. Another option for light meals and well-prepared sandwiches is **L'Angelo Italian Deli** in Quepos, located 1 block west of the bus terminal.

Barba Roja SEAFOOD/CONTINENTAL Perched high on a hill, with stunning views over jungle and ocean, the Barba Roja has long been one of the more popular restaurants in Manuel Antonio. The rustic interior is done with local hardwoods and bamboo, which gives the open-air dining room a warm glow, and there's an outdoor patio where you can sit for hours taking in the view or the stars. There's even a gallery attached to the restaurant, displaying original art by local artists. On the blackboard, there are daily specials such as grilled fish steak served with a salad and a baked potato. Portions here are massive. The restaurant is open for breakfast and serves delicious whole-wheat French toast. For lunch, there are a number of different sandwiches, all served on whole-wheat bread. If you're in the mood to hang out and meet some locals and other fellow travelers, spend some time at the bar sipping piña coladas or margaritas.

Manuel Antonio Rd. ℂ **506/777-0331.** Reservations not accepted. Main courses $5–$20; sandwiches $3–$6. AE, MC, V. Tues–Sun 7am–10pm; Mon 4–10pm.

El Gato Negro ✦ ITALIAN Perched at the highest part of the Hotel Casitas Eclipse, this place serves the best Italian food in the area. Fresh fillets of tuna and dorado come either grilled or in light sauces. The *grigliata mista* is an ample plate of mixed grilled seafood, and the *penne mare e monti* is a plate of *al dente* penne with fresh shrimp in a Gorgonzola sauce. There are plenty of meat and chicken choices, as well as a healthy and reasonably priced selection of wines for the area. The restaurant is an open-air affair with rattan tables and chairs, cloth tablecloths, and candles. You can also get breakfast and light lunches here.

In the Hotel Casitas Eclipse, Manuel Antonio. ℂ and fax **506/777-1728**. Reservations recommended during high season. Main courses $8–$25. AE, MC, V. Daily 6am–11pm.

El Gran Escape ✵✵ *Finds* SEAFOOD This Quepos landmark is a favorite with locals and fishermen—for good reason. The fish is fresh and expertly prepared, and the prices are reasonable. If that's not enough of a recommendation, the atmosphere is lively, and the service is darn good for a beach town in Costa Rica. The popularity has translated into a major expansion, with covered outdoor seating nearly doubling the original dining capacity. Sturdy wooden tables and chairs fill up the large indoor dining room, and sportfishing photos and an exotic collection of masks fill up the walls. If you venture away from the fish, there are hearty steaks, giant burgers, and a wide assortment of delicious appetizers, including fresh tuna sashimi. El Gran Escape's Fish Head Bar is usually crowded and lively, and if there's a game going on, it will be on the television here.

On the main rd. into Quepos, on your left just after the bridge. ℂ **506/777-0395**. Reservations recommended in the high season. Main courses $6–$16. V. Wed–Mon 6am–11pm.

Karola's ✵ SEAFOOD/INTERNATIONAL The steep driveway leading down to this open-air restaurant is within a few feet of the Barba Roja parking lot but is easily overlooked (watch closely when you're up at the top of the hill). The restaurant is across a footbridge from its parking lot and is set against a jungle-covered hillside. Far below, you can see the ocean if you're here during the day. Grilled seafood is the specialty, but there's also a wide range of international treats including sashimi, fish burritos, and Caribbean chicken. I highly recommend starting things off with the Honduran tuna ceviche. Desserts are decadent, and you can order a variety of margaritas by the pitcher. As at the Barba Roja, there's a separate art gallery here as well.

Manuel Antonio Rd. ℂ **506/777-1557**. Reservations recommended. Main courses $10–$22. V. Daily 11am–11pm.

Plinio Restaurant INTERNATIONAL This is a long-standing, popular restaurant in Manuel Antonio, located at an equally popular hotel. The open-air restaurant is about three stories above the parking lot, so be prepared to climb some steps. It's worth it, though. The basket of bread that arrives at your table shortly after you sit down is filled with delicious treats; the menu that follows is an enticing mix of international dishes. The chef uses organically grown herbs and veggies. Thai and Indonesian dishes are found alongside German and Italian fare, and there are always vegetarian options and a nightly special. Breakfasts are served in the high season. At lunchtime, a separate chef takes over the restaurant at the poolside snack bar, preparing German sausages and schnitzel.

In the Hotel Plinio, 0.62 miles (1km) out of Quepos toward Manuel Antonio. ℂ **506/777-0055**. Reservations recommended in the high season. Main courses $5–$17. AE, MC, V (6% surcharge). Daily 5–10pm.

Restaurant Vela-Bar INTERNATIONAL The Vela-Bar is a small and casual place that serves some of the more creative cuisine in Manuel Antonio. This is also the best of the restaurants closest to the park entrance. Seafood and vegetarian meals are the specialties. The most interesting dishes are almost always the specials posted on the blackboard. A typical day's choice might include fresh fish in sherry or wine sauce with curried vegetables.

100m down the side rd. near the park entrance. ℂ **506/777-0413**. Reservations recommended in the high season. Main courses $5–$15. AE, MC, V. Daily 7–10pm.

MANUEL ANTONIO AFTER DARK

Discos are becoming almost as common in Manuel Antonio as capuchin monkeys. Night owls and dancing fools have their choice. The local favorite appears to be the **Arco Iris,** which is located just over the bridge heading out of town. Admission is usually around $2.50. Down near the beach, folks get going at the restaurant **Mar y Sombra** ✻ (© **506/777-0510**). This is my favorite spot—you can walk off the dance floor and right out onto the beach, and there's usually no cover.

The bars at the **Barba Roja** restaurant (© **506/777-0331**) and the **Hotel Sí Como No** (© **506/777-0777**) are also good places to hang out and meet people in the evenings. You can also hang out at the **Vela-Bar** (© **506/777-0413**), which seems to be popular with gay men. Back in Quepos, **El Banco Bar** (© **506/777-0478**), the new **Epicentro** (no phone; next door to El Gran Escape), and the **Fish Head Bar** at **El Gran Escape** (© **506/777-0395**) are the most popular gringo hangouts.

If you enjoy the gaming tables, the **Hotel Kamuk** (© **506/777-1500**) in Quepos has a small casino and will even foot your cab bill if you try your luck and lay your money down. You'll also find a small casino at the **Hotel Divisamar** (© **506/777-0371**) on the Manuel Antonio Road, across from the Barba Roja.

If you want to see a flick, check what's playing at **Hotel Sí Como No's** little theater, although you have to eat at the restaurant or spend a minimum at the bar to earn admission.

EN ROUTE TO DOMINICAL: PLAYA MATAPALO

Playa Matapalo is a long expanse of flat beach that's about midway between Quepos and Dominical. It's an easy, but bumpy, 16 miles (26km) south of Quepos on the Costanera Sur. It's nowhere near as developed as either of those two beaches, but that's part of its charm. The beach here seems to stretch on forever, and it's usually deserted. The surf and strong riptides frequently make Matapalo too rough for swimming, although boogie boarding can be good. Foremost among this beach's charms are peace and quiet.

ACCOMMODATIONS

Matapalo is basically a little village; the beach is about half a mile (1km) away. There are a few very small and intimate lodges right on the beach. Of these, the **Jungle House** (© **506/779-9255;** www.junglehouse.com) is the nicest.

El Silencio *(finds)*   A bit before you reach Matapalo, you'll pass one of the more interesting tourism developments in Costa Rica. El Silencio is a project run by the 60 or so families of an agricultural cooperative. There are 10 simple rooms in thatch-roofed cabins here. Each comes with two single beds on the ground floor and another two in a sleeping loft. All have private bathrooms, and some even have water. This is a new, grassroots tourism venture, and not many of the folks here, not even the guides, speak much English. A stay here, however, allows you to mix hikes in the forest and horseback rides with a look into the rural life of Costa Rica. El Silencio is located about 3¾ miles (6km) inland from the Coastal Highway, about 14¼ miles (23km) south of Quepos. Volunteer stays are available.

Cooperativa El Silencio (A.P. 6939-1000, San José). © and fax **506/779-8250,** or © 506/777-1938. cooprena@racsa.co.cr. 10 units. $30 per person. Rates include 3 meals, tour, and taxes. No credit cards. **Amenities:** 1 restaurant (Costa Rican); 1 bar; laundry service. *In room:* No phone.

4 Dominical (

18 miles (29km) SW of San Isidro; 26 miles (42km) S of Quepos; 99 miles (160km) S of San José

This area may not be the best-kept secret in Costa Rica any longer, but Dominical and the coastline just south of it remain excellent places to find isolated beaches, spectacular views, remote jungle waterfalls, and abundant budget lodgings. The beach at Dominical itself has both right and left beach breaks, which means there are usually plenty of surfers in town. In fact, the beach in Dominical really has appeal only to surfers; it's generally too rough and rocky for regular folks. However, you will find excellent swimming, sunbathing, and strolling beaches just a little farther south at **Dominicalito, Playa Hermosa,** and **Ballena Marine National Park** (.

Leaving Manuel Antonio, the road south to Dominical runs by mile after mile of oil-palm plantations. However, just before Dominical, the mountains once again meet the sea. From Dominical south, the coastline is dotted with tide pools, tiny coves, and cliff-side vistas. Dominical is the largest village in the area and has several small lodges both in town and along the beach to the south. The village enjoys an enviable location on the banks of Río Barú, right where it widens considerably before emptying into the ocean. There's good bird watching along the banks of the river and throughout the surrounding forests.

ESSENTIALS

GETTING THERE & DEPARTING   By Plane   The nearest airport with regular service is in Quepos (see "Essentials" in section 3 of this chapter, on Manuel Antonio). From there you can hire a taxi, rent a car, or take the bus.

By Car   From San José, head south (toward Cartago) on the Interamerican Highway. Continue on this road all the way to San Isidro de El General, where you turn right and head down toward the coast. The entire drive takes about 4 hours.

You can also drive here from Manuel Antonio/Quepos. Just take the road out of Quepos toward the hospital and airport. Follow the signs for Dominical. It's a straight, albeit bumpy, shot. However, the road is slated to be paved, and if that happens, it should no longer take over an hour to cover the mere 25 miles (40km).

By Bus   To reach Dominical, you must first go to San Isidro de El General or Quepos. Buses ((**506/222-2422** or 506/771-3829) leave San José for San Isidro roughly every hour between 5am and 5pm from Calle 16 between Avenidas 1 and 3. Leave no later than 9:30am if you want to catch the 1:30pm bus to Dominical. The trip takes 3 hours; the fare is $3.

From San Isidro de El General, buses ((**506/257-4121** or 506/771-2550) leave for Dominical at 7 and 9am and 1:30 and 4pm. The bus station for Dominical is 1 block south of the main bus station and 2 blocks west of the church. Trip duration is 1½ hours; the fare is $1.50.

From **Quepos,** buses leave daily at 5am and 1:30pm. Trip duration is 2 hours; the fare is $3.50.

When you're ready to leave, buses depart Dominical for San Isidro at 6:45 and 7:30am, and 2:30 and 3:30pm. If you want to get to San José the same day, you should catch the morning bus. Buses leave San Isidro for San José roughly every hour between 5am and 5pm. Buses to Quepos leave Dominical at approximately 7am and 1:30pm

ORIENTATION   Dominical is a small village on the banks of Río Barú. The village is to the right after you cross the bridge and stretches out along the main road parallel to the beach. As you first come into town, there's a soccer field and general store, where there are a couple of public telephones.

FAST FACTS   You can purchase stamps and send mail from the **San Clemente Bar & Grill.** Taxis tend to congregate in front of the soccer field, or you can ask around for Beto. The gas station is located about 1¼ miles (2km) north of town on the road to Quepos.

EXPLORING THE BEACHES & BALLENA MARINE NATIONAL PARK

Because the beach in the village of Dominical itself is unprotected and at the mouth of a river, it's often too rough for swimming; however, you can go for a swim in the calm waters at the mouth of the Río Barú, or head down the beach a few kilometers to the little sheltered cove at **Roca Verde.**

If you have a car, you should continue driving south, exploring beaches as you go. You will first come to **Dominicalito,** a small beach and cove that shelters the local fishing fleet and can be a decent place to swim, but still, continue on a bit. You'll soon hit **Playa Hermosa,** a long stretch of desolate beach with fine sand. As in Dominical, this is unprotected and can be rough, but it's a nicer place to sunbathe and swim than Dominical.

At the village of Uvita, 10 miles (16km) south of Dominical, you'll reach the northern end of the **Ballena Marine National Park** ✦, which protects a coral reef that stretches from Uvita south to Playa Piñuela and includes the little Isla Ballena, just offshore. To get to **Playa Uvita** (which is inside the park), turn in at the village of Bahia and continue until you hit the ocean. The beach here is actually well protected and good for swimming. At low tide, an exposed sand-bar allows you to walk about and explore another tiny island. This park is named for the whales that are sometimes sighted close to shore in the winter months. If you ever fly over this area, you'll also notice that this little island and the spit of land that's formed at low tide compose the perfect outline of a whale's tail. There's a parks office at the entrance here that regulates the park's use and even runs a small turtle-hatching shelter and program. Although this is a national park, for some reason, they've never charged the standard $6 entrance fee here, and camping is allowed. A small donation is recommended both for daily use and camping.

OTHER ACTIVITIES IN THE AREA

Although the beaches stretching south from Dominical should be beautiful enough to keep most people content, there are lots of other things to do. Several local farms offer horseback tours through forests and orchards, and at some of these farms you can even spend the night. **Hacienda Barú** ✦ (© **506/ 787-0003;** fax 506/787-0004; www.haciendabaru.com) offers several different hikes and tours, including a walk through mangroves and along the riverbank (for some good bird watching), a rain-forest hike through 200 acres of virgin jungle, an all-day trek from beach to mangrove to jungle that includes a visit to some Indian petroglyphs, an overnight camping trip, and a combination horseback-and-hiking tour. It even has tree-climbing tours and a small canopy platform 100 feet above the ground. Tour prices range from $20 (for the mangrove hike) to $60 (for the jungle overnight). If you're traveling with a group, you'll be charged a lower per-person rate, depending on the number of people in your group. Hacienda Barú also has six comfortable cabins with two bedrooms each, full kitchens, and even a living room ($60 double, $70 triple). Hacienda Barú is located about a mile (1.6km) north of Dominical on the road to Manuel Antonio.

The jungles just outside of Dominical are home to two spectacular waterfalls. The most popular and impressive is the **Santo Cristo** or **Nauyaca Waterfalls** ⍟, a two-tiered beauty with an excellent swimming hole. Most of the hotels in town can arrange for the horseback ride up here, or you can call **Don Lulo** at ✆ **506/ 771-3187.** A half-day tour, with both breakfast and lunch, should cost around $40 per person. This site has become so popular that Don Lulo has set up a lit- tle welcome center at the entrance (just off the road into Dominical from San Isidro) and even allows camping here. **Bellavista Lodge** (✆ **506/388- 0155**) also runs tours to these falls, although they've begun calling them the **Barú River Falls,** as there seems to have been a copyright battle over the name Nauyaca. This tour ($40) leaves from the lodge up on the Escaleras road. Round-trip car transportation can be arranged for a nominal charge. It is also possible to reach these falls by horseback from an entrance near the small village of Tinamaste (you will see signs on the road). Similar tours (at similar prices) are offered to the **Diamante Waterfalls,** which are a three-tiered set of falls with a 1,200-foot drop, but not quite as spacious and inviting a pool as the one at Santo Cristo.

If you're sore from surfing, hiking, or horseback riding, or just interested in some massage, meditation, or yoga, head to **Om Massage & Meditation** (✆ **506/787-0101**), located on the beach at Dominical. A full-hour massage should run you just $40. Alternatively, you could see what's happening at **Cabañas Escondidas** (✆ **506/282-3848;** www.crdirect.com/retreats). This place has nine individual cabins on the hillside and beach, about 6 kilometers south of Dominical. Cabañas Escondidas specializes in tai chi and chi kung retreats and private groups seeking some body/mind enrichment.

ACCOMMODATIONS
MODERATE
Bella Vista Lodge *Bella Vista* means "beautiful view," and that's exactly what you get when you stay at this small rustic lodge high in the hills south of Dominical. The simple rooms have recently been renovated, and each now has a private, tiled bathroom with heated-water showers. The corner room (number 4) is the best unit here, offering greater privacy. There are two separate cabins, located a little below the main lodge, both of which come with fully equipped kitchens. The owners here are friendly, and the location is magnificent. Simple meals are served ($4 for breakfast, $6 to $9 for lunch and dinner). Guests' favorite activity is an all-day horseback ride through the rain forest to a beauti- ful waterfall. The price of $40 per person includes your horse, guide, breakfast, and lunch. The lodge is located 1¾ miles (3km) up the steep Escaleras road, just south of Dominical. You'll need a four-wheel-drive vehicle to get up here, or arrange a pickup in Dominical.

Dominical (c/o Selva Mar, A.P. 215-8000, Pérez Zeledón). ✆ **506/771-4582** or 506/395-7832. www.bellavistalodge.com. 4 units, 2 cabins. $45–$60 double. AE, MC, V. **Amenities:** 1 restaurant. *In room:* No phone.

Cabinas Punta Dominical   Located about 2½ miles (4km) south of Dominical on a rocky point, this place has a stony cove on one side and a sandy beach on the other. The cabins and restaurant are set among shady old trees high above the surf and have excellent views of both coves. All the cabinas have good views, but the best are to be had from the ones higher up the hill. The cabins, built on stilts and constructed of dark, polished hardwood, all have big porches with chairs and hammocks. Screened and louvered walls are designed to catch the breezes. The bathrooms are large and have separate changing areas.

A.P. 196-8000, Dominical. 🕿 **506/787-0016.** Fax 506/787-0241. puntadominical@racsa.co.cr. 4 cabins. $50 double; $58 triple; $64 quad. V. **Amenities:** 1 open-air restaurant (seafood/ Mediterranean); 1 bar; laundry service. *In room:* No phone.

Costa Paraiso Lodge   This new hotel offers spacious and clean rooms on a rocky point at the north end of Dominicalito beach. All but one of the rooms come with either a full kitchen or kitchenette, and most have high ceilings and plenty of light and ventilation. Dolphin Lodge and Pelican Roost are the two nicest rooms here, with spacious living and dining areas. Though it's not quite as large and lacks the cooking facilities, the Toucan Nest is the most private of the accommodations, with an inviting shaded patio. There's no restaurant here, but breakfast is served on the terrace of the owner's home. There are some tide pools right in front of the hotel, and the beach is just a short walk away.

2km south of Dominical, just off the coastal hwy., Dominicalito (A.P. 578-8000, Pérez Zeledón). 🕿 and fax **506/787-0025.** costapar@racsa.co.cr. 5 units. $73–$83 double. V. *In room:* Fridge; no phone.

Hotel Roca Verde 🖈   This newly rebuilt hotel offers the nicest beachfront accommodations in this area. The setting is superb—on a protected little cove with rocks and tide pools. The rooms are located in a two-story building, beside the swimming pool. Each room comes with one queen and one single bed, and a small patio or balcony. There's a large open-air restaurant with a popular bar that keeps folks dancing most weekend nights. The rooms are a bit close to the bar, so it can sometimes be hard to get an early night's sleep, especially during the high season, and especially on weekends. These folks rent out some stunning luxury villas located in the hills behind the hotel.

½ mile (1km) south of Dominical, just off the coastal hwy. 🕿 **506/787-0036.** Fax 506/787-0013. www.hotelrocaverde.com. 10 units. $85 double. Lower rates in the off-season. MC, V. **Amenities:** 1 restaurant (international); 1 bar; small pool; tour desk; laundry service. *In room:* A/C; no phone.

Villas Río Mar   This is the closest thing to a resort in this neck of the woods. The bamboo-accented rooms are in 20 separate thatch-roofed duplex bunga-lows. While the rooms themselves seem a bit overwhelmed by the queen-size beds, each has a small couch, coffee table, wet bar, and mini-fridge, plus a spa-cious and comfortable porch with several chairs. At night, you can drop the tulle drapes that enclose each patio for some privacy and mosquito protection. The grounds have beautiful flowering plants, and the bird watching is excellent. A wide range of tours is offered, including inner-tube floats on the nearby Río Barú.

Up a dirt rd. a few hundred m up the Río Barú, just on the right as you enter Dominical; Dominical, Pérez Zeledó. 🕿 **506/787-0052** or 506/787-0053. Fax 506/787-0054. www.villasriomar.com. 40 units. Dec 15–Apr 24 $80 double; Apr 25–Dec 14 $65 double. Children under 12 stay free in parents' room. AE, MC, V. **Amenities:** 1 open-air restaurant (international/seafood); 1 bar; large outdoor pool with swim-up bar; tennis court; exercise room; Jacuzzi; bike rental; tour desk; laun-dry service. *In room:* Mini-fridge, hair dryer; no phone.

INEXPENSIVE

In addition to the places listed here, if you continue south another 10 miles (16km) you'll find a campground at Playa Ballena and a couple of basic cabinas in Bahia and Uvita. The most popular of these is **Cabinas El Cocotico** (no phone, $20 double), owned and operated by Jorge Díaz, a local legend and enjoyable raconteur who also arranges trips to a nearby waterfall. You'll see a sign for Cabinas El Cocotico on your left as you reach Uvita, traveling south from Dominical. Turn here; the hotel is 500 meters (545 yd.) up the dirt road. Closer to the beach, in Bahia, **Cabinas Hegalva** (no phone) offers clean, basic rooms costing $15 for a double.

Cabinas San Clemente *Value*   In addition to running the town's most popular restaurant and serving as the social hub for the surfers, beach bums, and expatriates passing through, this place offers a variety of accommodations to fit most budgets. The cheapest rooms are all located above the restaurant, which is on the main road in the center of town. These are very basic budget affairs, with wood walls and floors, shared bathrooms, and floor or ceiling fans. About a kilometer (⅔ mile) away, at the beach, San Clemente has much nicer rooms in two separate buildings. Some of the newer second-floor rooms have wood floors and wraparound verandas and are a real steal in this price range. The grounds are shady, and there are plenty of hammocks.

The **Snack Shack** is a beachside cafe serving up filling sandwiches, refreshing fresh-fruit juices, and a host of other light lunch items. San Clemente also serves as the local post office and information center, and the owner makes, bottles, and sells a very serious hot sauce.

Dominical (A.P. 703-8000, Pérez Zeledón). ✆ **506/787-0026** or 506/787-0055. Fax 506/787-0158. 21 units, 16 with bathroom. $14 double with shared bathroom, $20–$65 double with private bathroom. AE, MC, V. **Amenities:** 2 restaurants (seafood/Tex-Mex, sandwiches/salads); 1 bar; surf- and boogie-board rental; tour desk; laundry service. *In room:* No phone.

El Mono Loco   This long-standing surfer hotel is a good budget option on the beach, especially if all of the best rooms at San Clemente are booked. There are several styles of rooms located in a cluster of buildings, including older rooms with fans, older rooms with air-conditioning, and newer rooms with air-conditioning, skylights, carved wooden headboards, and louvered windows. I recommend the second-floor rooms with ocean views but no air-conditioning. Since the rooms differ so much in size and comfort levels, you should definitely take a look at a few of them before choosing.

Dominical. ✆ and fax **506/787-0033**. tortflats@racsa.co.cr. 18 units. $30–$40 double or triple. Lower off-season rates. AE, MC, V (7% surcharge). **Amenities:** 1 restaurant (continental/Costa Rican); 1 bar; laundry service. *In room:* No phone.

Pacific Edge 🌤 *Finds*   This place is away from the beach, but the views from each individual bungalow are so breathtaking that you may not mind. Spread along a lushly planted ridge on the hillside over Dominical, these comfortable cabins have wood floors, solar-heated water, and solar reading lights. Their best feature is surely the private porch with a comfortable hammock in which to laze about and enjoy the view. The restaurant serves breakfast and dinner daily, which will run you around an extra $25 per person per day. A wide range of tours and activities can be arranged here. Pacific Edge is 2½ miles (4km) south of Dominical and then another three-quarter miles (1.2km) up a steep and rocky road; four-wheel-drive vehicles are highly recommended—I'd say required.

Dominical (A.P. 531-8000, Pérez Zeledón). ✆ **506/381-4369** or 506/771-4582. Fax 506/771-8841. pacificedge@pocketmail.com. 4 units. $50–$75 double; $50 triple. MC, V (10% surcharge added). **Amenities:** 1 restaurant. *In room:* No phone.

DINING & AFTER-DARK FUN

The social center of Dominical is definitely the **San Clemente Bar & Grill** 🌤 (✆ **506/787-0055**), located right at the entrance to town beside the soccer field.

This gringo/surfer hangout and sports bar specializes in massive breakfasts, nightly dinner specials (usually seafood), and a regular menu of hefty sandwiches and tasty Mexican-American food (expect main courses to run between $5 and $15). One interesting (and sobering) thing here is the ceiling full of broken surfboards. If you break a board out on the waves, bring it in, and they'll hang it and even buy you a bucket of beer. If you head a little bit south of town, you can check out the restaurants at either Roca Verde or Punta Dominical. **Thrusters** (© 506/787-0150), a couple of hundred yards south of San Clemente, is another surfer bar with pool tables and dartboards.

Right in town, in front of the soccer field, there's the **Su Raza** (© 506/787-0105), which serves basic Tico meals and good seafood at great prices, and even has a nice view of the river mouth. A little farther on down the main road is the **Soda Nanyoa.** Dishes at these places range in price from $2 to $8.

Don't come to Dominical expecting a raging nightlife. But occasionally there are roving discos that set up shop at one bar or another on weekends. If so, you'll hear about it—and hear it.

SOUTH OF DOMINICAL

The beaches south of Dominical are some of the nicest and most unexplored in Costa Rica. Basic cabinas and hotels are starting to pop up all along this route. This is a great area to roam in a rental car—it's a **beautiful drive** ✸✸. The southern highway **(Costanera Sur)** is still not paved, but it is relatively well graded and maintained. One good itinerary is to make a loop from San Isidro to Dominical, down the Costanera Sur, hitting several deserted beaches and then returning along the Interamerican Highway.

Among the beaches you'll find are **Playa Ballena, Playa Piñuela, Playa Ventanas,** and **Playa Tortuga.** There's a bit of development in the area around Playa Tortuga and Ojochal, and some in the works around Playas Piñuela and Ventanas.

A REMOTE NATURE LODGE

Hotel Villas Gaia   Located just off the Costanera Sur just before the town of Ojochal, this small hotel has the nicest accommodations down in this neck of the woods. All the rooms are separate, spacious wood bungalows. Each has one single and one double bed, a private bathroom, a ceiling fan, and a small veranda with a jungle view. I prefer the bungalows furthest from the restaurant, up on the high hill by the swimming pool. The pool can accommodate scuba instruction— Villa Gaia hopes to lure divers with its close proximity to Isla del Caño. There's a large, open-air dining room down by the parking lot, which is too close to the highway for my taste. A wide range of tours is available, including Isla del Caño, Corcovado National Park, and Wilson Botanical Gardens.

Playa Tortuga (A.P. 11516-1000, San José). © and fax **506/256-9996.** hvgaia@racsa.co.cr. 15 units. $60 double. V. **Amenities:** 1 restaurant (international); 2 bars; small outdoor pool with a wonderful ocean view; tour desk; laundry service. *In room:* No phone.

5 San Isidro de El General: A Base for Exploring Chirripó National Park

74 miles (120km) SE of San José; 76 miles (123km) NW of Palmar Norte; 18 miles (29km) NE of Dominical

San Isidro de El General is the largest town in this region and is located just off the Interamerican Highway in the foothills of the Talamanca Mountains. Although there isn't much to do right in town, this is the jumping-off point for

Little Devils

If you're visiting this area in February, head out to nearby **Rey Curré** village for the **Fiesta of the Diablitos,** where costumed Boruca Indians perform dances representative of the Spanish conquest of Central America. There are fireworks and an Indian handcraft market. The date varies, so it's best to call the **Costa Rica Tourist Board** (© **800/327-7033**) for more information.

trips to **Chirripó National Park** ✶✶. This is also the principal transfer point if you're coming from or going to Dominical, and most buses traveling the Interamerican Highway stop here.

ESSENTIALS

GETTING THERE & DEPARTING By Car The long and winding stretch of the Interamerican Highway between San José and San Isidro is one of the most difficult sections of road in the country. Not only are there the usual car-eating potholes and periodic landslides, but you must also contend with driving over the 11,000-foot-high Cerro de la Muerte (Mountain of Death). This aptly named mountain pass is legendary for its dense afternoon fogs, blinding torrential downpours, steep drop-offs, severe switchbacks, and unexpectedly breathtaking views. (Well, you wanted adventure travel, so here you go!) Drive with extreme care, and bring a sweater or sweatshirt—it's cold up at the top. It'll take you about 3 hours to get to San Isidro.

By Bus Two companies, **Musoc** (© **506/222-2422** or 506/771-3829) and **Tuasur** (© **506/222-9763** or 506/771-0419) run express buses between San José and San Isidro leaving roughly every hour between 5am and 5pm from Calle 16 between Avenidas 1 and 3. Trips take 3 hours; the fare is $3. There are buses from **Quepos** to San Isidro daily at 5am and 1pm. Trip duration is 3½ hours; the fare is $3. Buses to or from **Golfito** and **Puerto Jiménez** will also drop you off in San Isidro.

Buses depart San Isidro for **San José** roughly every hour between 5am and 5pm. Buses to **Dominical** (onward to **Quepos**) leave daily at 7am and 1:30pm. Buses to **Dominical** and **Uvita** leave daily at 9am and 4pm. Buses to **Puerto Jiménez** leave San Isidro daily at 6am and noon. The San José bus to **Puerto Jiménez** passes through San Isidro at around 9am and 3pm. Buses to **Golfito** pass through San Isidro at around 10am, and 2 and 6pm.

ORIENTATION Downtown San Isidro is just off the Interamerican Highway. There's a large church that fronts the central park. The main bus station is 2 blocks west of the north end of the central park.

EXPLORING CHIRRIPÓ NATIONAL PARK ✶✶

At 12,530 feet in elevation, Mount Chirripó is the tallest mountain in Costa Rica. If you're headed up this way, come prepared for chilly weather. Actually, dress in layers and come prepared for all sorts of weather: Because of the great elevations, temperatures frequently dip below freezing, especially at night. However, during the day, temperatures can soar—remember, you're still only 9° from the equator. The elevation and radical temperatures have produced an environment here that's very different from the Costa Rican norm. Above 10,000 feet, only stunted trees and shrubs survive in regions known as *páramos.*

If you're driving the Interamerican Highway between San Isidro and San José, you'll pass through a páramo on the Cerro de la Muerte.

Hiking up to the top of Mount Chirripó is one of Costa Rica's great adventures. On a clear day (usually in the morning), an unforgettable **view** ★★ is your reward: You can see both the Pacific Ocean and the Caribbean Sea from the summit. You can do this trip fairly easily on your own if you've brought gear and are an experienced backpacker. While it's possible to hike from the park entrance to the summit and back down in 2 days (in fact, some daredevils even do it in 1 day), it's best to allow 3 to 4 days for the trip, to give yourself time to enjoy your hike fully and spend some time on top, since that's where the glacier lakes and páramos are. For much of the way you'll be hiking through cloud forests that are home to abundant tropical fauna, including the spectacular **quetzal,** Costa Rica's most beautiful bird. These cloud forests are cold and damp, so come prepared for rain and fog.

There are several routes to the top of Mount Chirripó. The most popular, by far, leaves from **San Gerardo de Rivas.** However, it's also possible to start your hike from the nearby towns of **Herradura** and **Canaan.** All these places are within a mile or so of each other, reached by the same major road out of San Isidro. San Gerardo is the most popular because it's the easiest route to the top and has the greatest collections of small hotels and lodges, as well as the National Parks office. Information on all of these routes is available at the parks office.

Once you're at the summit lodge, there is a number of hiking options. The most popular is to the actual summit (the lodge itself is a bit below), which is about a 2-hour hike passing through the Valle de los Conejos (Rabbit Valley) and the Valle de los Lagos (Valley of Lakes). There are other hikes and trails leading off from the summit lodge, and it's easy to spend a couple of days hiking around here. A few trails will take you to the summits of several neighboring peaks. These hikes should be undertaken only after carefully studying an accurate map and talking to park rangers and other hikers.

ENTRY POINT, FEES & REGULATIONS   Although it's not that difficult to get to Chirripó National Park from nearby San Isidro, it's still rather remote. And to see it fully, you have to be prepared to hike. To get to the trailhead, you have three choices: car, taxi, or bus. If you choose to drive, take the road out of San Isidro, heading north toward San Gerardo de Rivas, which is some 12½ miles (20km) down the road. Otherwise, you can catch a bus in San Isidro that will take you directly to the trailhead in San Gerardo de Rivas. Buses leave daily at 5am from the western side of the central park in San Isidro. It costs 85¢ one-way and takes 1½ hours. Another bus departs at 2pm from a bus station 200 meters south of the park. Buses return to San Isidro daily at 7am and 4pm. A taxi from town should cost around $15 to $20. Because the hike to the summit of Mount Chirripó can take between 6 and 12 hours, depending on your physical condition, I recommend taking the earlier bus so that you can start hiking when the day is still young, or, better still, arriving the day before and spending the night in San Gerardo de Rivas (there are inexpensive cabinas there), before setting out early the following morning.

Park admission is $6 per day. Before climbing Mount Chirripó, you must check in with the National Parks office in San Gerardo de Rivas. The office is open from 6am to 5pm daily. I highly recommend checking in the day before you plan to climb, if possible. If you plan to stay at the lodge near the summit, you must make reservations in advance, since accommodations there are limited (see "Staying at the Summit Lodge," below). Note that camping is not allowed in the park. It's possible to have your gear carried up to the summit by horse-back during the dry season (Dec–Apr). Guides work outside the park entrance in San Gerardo de Rivas. They charge between $20 and $25 per pack, depending on size and weight. In the rainy season, the same guides work, but they take packs up by themselves, not by horseback. The guides like to take the packs up well before dawn, so arrangements are best made the day before.

STAYING AT THE SUMMIT LODGE   Reservations for lodging on the summit of Mount Chirripó must be made with the **National Parks office** in San Gerardo de Rivas (© and fax **506/771-3155** or 506/771-5116). In 1998, the old buildings were torn down, and two new ones were erected. Helicopters and lots of pack horses were used in the construction. This is an increasingly popular destination, and you must reserve well in advance during the dry season. The new lodge holds only 60 people and it fills up quite frequently. There are bunk beds, bathrooms, and a common kitchen area, complete with pots, pans, plates, and silverware. There is good drinking water at the lodge and blankets, lanterns, and cook stoves for rent, although you'll certainly have to pack in your own food. Be forewarned: It gets cold up here at night, and the new lodge seems to have been designed to be as cold, dark, and cavernous as possible. No consideration was made to take advantage of the ample passive solar potential. The showers are freezing. It costs $6 per person per night to stay here, in addition to the $6 park entrance fee.

WARNING   It can be dangerous for more inexperienced or out-of-shape hikers to climb Chirripó, especially by themselves. It's not very technical climbing, but it is a long, arduous hike. If you're not sure you're up for it, you can just take day hikes out of San Isidro and/or San Gerardo de Rivas, or ask at your hotel about guides.

OTHER ADVENTURES IN SAN ISIDRO

If you want to undertake any other adventures while in San Isidro, contact **Brunca Tours** (© **506/771-3100;** www.ecotourism.co.cr) or **Selva Mar** (© **506/771-4582;** www.chirripo.com). Among its varied offerings, Brunca Tours' main operation is white-water rafting on the Río General, which has Class III and IV sections. Rafting trips run around $65 to $75 per person.

Just 4½ miles (7km) from San Isidro is **Las Quebradas Biological Center** (© and fax **506/771-4131**), a community-run private reserve with 1¾ miles (2.7km) of trails through primary rain forest. Camping is permitted. There's an information center here and a small souvenir store. Admission is $6. From San Isidro, you can take a local bus to Quebradas, but you'll have to walk the last mile to the entrance. You can also take a taxi for around $8. If you're driving, take the road to Morazán and Quebradas. The center is open from 8am to 2pm Tuesday to Sunday.

ACCOMMODATIONS & DINING

The following section lists only hotels because there are no notable restaurants in San Isidro. The town has its fair share of local joints, but most visitors are content at their hotel restaurant.

Hotel Chirripó   This budget hotel is fine in a pinch if you need to spend the night in San Isidro. It's located on the central square within a couple of blocks of all the town's bus stations. Rooms vary considerably, so ask to see some first. Some have windows (and street noise), and some have no windows or street noise. Stay away from the rooms in front, since these are the noisiest. There's a large, popular restaurant at the front of the lobby.

San Isidro de El General (south side of the church). ✆ 506/771-0529. 41 units, 24 with private bathroom. $9 double without private bathroom, $14 double with private bathroom; $20 triple with private bathroom. No credit cards. **Amenities:** 1 restaurant (Costa Rican); 1 bar. *In room:* No phone.

Hotel del Sur   This midsize hotel has far better facilities and a wider range of services than anything within several hours of here, but it's seen better days. Rooms are generally large. The nicer (and more expensive) rooms have air-conditioning, loads of space, plenty of light, and tile floors; the cheaper rooms have worn carpeting and feel cramped and dingy. The whole place has the feel of a cut-rate country club. There's a large pool, as well as a basketball court, tennis court and pro shop, playground equipment, and Ping-Pong table.

About 3¾ miles (6km) south of San Isidro, right on the Interamerican Hwy. (A.P. 4-8000), San Isidro de El General. ✆ 506/771-3033. Fax 506/771-0527. www.hoteldelsur.com. 55 units. $40–$80 double. AE, MC, V. **Amenities:** 2 restaurants (international; grill); 2 bars; small casino; large outdoor pool; tennis court and pro shop; game room; tour desk; laundry service. *In room:* TV.

Hotel Iguazu   This is a good, clean, safe choice in San Isidro. The rooms are basic and come in different sizes, with a different arrangement of beds, but all have small televisions. The rooms are definitely in better shape than those at the Hotel Chirripó. The hotel is a half block away from the Musoc bus station. Some may find this convenient; others might find it too noisy. The hotel is actually on the second and third floors of the Super Lido department store.

San Isidro de El General. Above the Super Lido department store. ✆ 506/771-2571. Fax 506/771-4451. 21 units, 16 with private bathroom. $12 double without private bathroom, $18 double with private bathroom. No credit cards. *In room:* TV.

ACCOMMODATIONS CLOSER TO THE TRAILHEAD

If you're climbing Mount Chirripó, you'll want to spend the night as close to the trailhead as possible. As mentioned above, there are several basic cabinas right in San Gerardo de Rivas that charge between $5 and $10 per person. The best of these is **El Descanso** (✆ 506/771-1866). If you're looking for a little more comfort, check out one of the two lodges listed below.

Río Chirripó Pacífico Mountain Lodge   This new lodge is located on a beautiful bend in the Río Chirripó, just 500 meters (545 yd.) before the National Parks office. The rooms are in two side-by-side, two-story buildings. All have one single and one double bed, painted cement floors, and a small veranda, with some interesting natural wood latticework on the railings. I prefer the rooms on the second floor, as they have a slightly better view. There's a large open-air rancho that serves as the restaurant here. If you have time before or after your ascent of the big mountain, you can climb on some impressive river-polished rocks or swim in a couple of natural pools.

San Gerardo de Rivas, Pérez Zeledón. No phone. 8 units. $40 double. Rates include breakfast. No credit cards. **Amenities:** 1 restaurant (Costa Rican); 1 bar. *In room:* No phone.

Rest Your Weary Muscles Here

If you're tired and sore from so much hiking, be sure to check out the small natural hot springs located a short hike off the road between San Gerardo de Rivas and Herradura. The entrance to the springs is about half a mile (1km) beyond San Gerardo de Rivas. From here you'll have to hike about 10 minutes and pay a $2 entrance fee before getting in to soak.

Talari Mountain Lodge ✱   This small mountain getaway, though nothing fancy, is one of the nicer options right around San Isidro and also makes a good base for exploring or climbing Mount Chirripó. The eight rooms are in two separate concrete-block buildings. Most come with one double and one single bed, although one room can handle a family of four in one double and two single beds. Each of the rooms comes with a small fridge and a small patio. I prefer the four rooms that face the Talamanca Mountains. There are plenty of fruit trees around and good bird watching right on the grounds (they've identified 179 bird species here). The hotel borders the Rió General and maintains some forest trails. Talari is located 5 miles (8km) outside of San Isidro, and a staff member picks you up in town for free with advance notice. Remember, if you're here just to climb the mountain, this lodge is about 7 miles (11km) from San Gerardo de Rivas, so you'll probably also have to arrange transportation to and from the park entrance.

Rivas, San Isidro (A.P. 517-8000), Pérez Zeledón. ℂ and fax **506/771-0341.** talaripz@racsa.co.cr. 8 units. $52 double; $62 triple. Rates include full breakfast. Closed Sept 15–Oct 31. AE, MC, V. **Amenities:** 1 restaurant (international); 1 bar; small pool and separate children's pool; tour desk; laundry service. *In room:* Mini-fridge; no phone.

EN ROUTE TO SAN JOSÉ:
THREE PLACES TO SEE QUETZALS IN THE WILD

Between San Isidro de El General and San José, the Interamerican Highway climbs to its highest point in Costa Rica and crosses over the Cerro de la Muerte. This area has recently acquired a newfound importance as one of the best places in Costa Rica to see quetzals. March, April, and May is nesting season for these birds, and this is usually the best time to see them, but it's often possible to spot them year-round. On one 2-hour hike here, without a guide, our small group spotted eight of these amazing birds.

All of the lodges listed below, along with some new ones, are located along a 12½-mile (20km) stretch of the Interamerican Highway, between the cities of Cartago and San Isidro. You'll probably start seeing their billboards and quetzal-painted placards long before you see any birds.

In addition to the lodges listed below, if you're looking for a rustic (although not cheap) escape on a private reserve, check in with the folks at **Genesis II Cloudforest Preserve** (ℂ and fax **506/381-0739;** www.genesis-two.com). This place recently opened a canopy tour, which combines suspension bridges and treetop platforms connected by cables (you hang from the cable as you ride from tree to tree). Day tours of the preserve cost $45 per person, including a simple lunch. You'll see signs for this place along the Interamerican Highway. The road down into Genesis is very rugged and a four-wheel-drive vehicle is necessary. If you want to stay here ($85 per person, including three meals), there are only five rooms, so reservations are highly recommended.

Albergue de Montaña Tapantí   If you want easy access to both the highway and the cloud forest, this cross between a mountain lodge and roadside motel might be your best bet. The buildings at Tapantí are built to resemble Swiss chalets—and you may come to believe you're in Switzerland when you feel how cold it gets here at night. The lodge is at 10,000 feet and frost is not uncommon, but there's a fireplace in the lounge to warm your bones. Most of the guest rooms are actually suites with separate bedrooms and living rooms, although the furnishings are both sparse and dated. Luckily, the rooms do have heaters. The nicest rooms have private balconies that provide views of the neighboring forests. The lodge's dining room serves such Swiss specialties as beef fondue and raclette, as well as other continental dishes. Guided hikes, horseback rides, trout fishing, and bird-watching walks are all available through the lodge.

Km 62, Carretera Interamericana Sur, Macho Gaff, Cartago (A.P. 461-1200, Pavas). © and fax **506/ 232-0436**, or © 506/290-7641. adriandiaz@sosthome.net. 10 units. $60 double; $70 triple; $80 quad. Rates include breakfast. MC, V. **Amenities:** 1 restaurant (continental/Costa Rican); 1 bar. *In room:* No phone.

Albergue Mirador de Quetzales   This family-run lodge is also known as Finca Eddie Serrano. The rooms in the main lodge are quite basic, with wood floors, bunk beds, and shared bathrooms. Four newer A-frames provide a bit more comfort and a private bathroom. Meals are served family style in the main lodge. But quetzals, not comfort, are the main draw here, and if you come between December and May, you should have no trouble spotting plenty of them. There are good hiking trails through the cloud forest, and the Serrano family are genial hosts and good guides. The newest addition here is a hilltop lookout. On a clear day, you can see the peaks of five volcanoes from here (but it's not that clear too often). The lodge is located about 700 meters down a dirt road from the main highway.

Km 70, Carretera Interamericana Sur (A.P. 985-7050, Cartago). © and fax **506/381-8456**. 10 units, 8 with private bathroom. $35 per person. Rate includes breakfast, dinner, a 2-hr. tour, and taxes. No credit cards. **Amenities:** 1 restaurant (Costa Rican); 1 bar. *In room:* No phone.

Savegre Mountain Lodge ✸ *(Finds)*   This working apple-and-pear farm, which also has more than 600 acres of primary forest, has acquired a reputation for superb **bird watching** ✸✸—it's one of the best places in the country to see quetzals. The rustic farm has long been popular as a weekend vacation and pic-nicking spot for Ticos, but now people from all over the world are searching it out. The rooms are basic, but if you're serious about birding, this shouldn't mat-ter. In addition to the quetzals, some 150 other species have been spotted. Hearty Tico meals are served, and if you want to try your hand at trout fishing, you might luck into a fish dinner. You'll find this lodge 5½ miles (9km) down a dirt road off the Interamerican Highway. This road is steep and often muddy, and four-wheel-drive is recommended. (Some of the signs pointing to the lodge may still read CABINAS CHACÓN—the place is run by the Chacón family.)

Km 80, Carretera Interamericana Sur, San Gerardo de Dota (A.P. 482), Cartago. © and fax **506/ 771-1732**. www.costaricasavegrehoteldemontana.com. 26 cabins. $70 per person. Rates include all meals and taxes. AE, MC, V. **Amenities:** 1 restaurant (Costa Rican/international); 1 bar. *In room:* No phone.

8

The Southern Zone

The southern zone is an area of rugged beauty, with vast expanses of virgin lowland rain forest and few cities or settlements. Lushly forested mountains tumble into the sea, streams still run clear and clean, scarlet macaws squawk raucously in the treetops, and dolphins frolic in the Golfo Dulce. The Osa Peninsula is the most popular attraction in this region, and one of the premier ecotourism destinations in Costa Rica. It's home to **Corcovado National Park** ⟨★★★⟩, the largest single expanse of lowland tropical rain forest in Central America, and its sister, **Piedras Blancas National Park** ⟨★⟩. Scattered around the edges of these national parks and along the shores of the Golfo Dulce are some of the country's finest nature lodges. These lodges, in general, offer comfortable to nearly luxurious accommodations, attentive service, knowledgeable guides, and a wide range of activities and tours, all in close proximity to the area's many natural wonders.

But this beauty doesn't come easy. You must have plenty of time (or plenty of money—or preferably both) and a desire for adventure. Because it's so far from San José (it's an 8-hour drive from San José to Golfito or Puerto Jiménez) and there are so few roads, most of the really fascinating spots can be reached only by small plane or boat, although hiking and four-wheeling will get you into some memorable surroundings as well. In many ways this is Costa Rica's final frontier, and the cities of Golfito and Puerto Jiménez are nearly as wild as the jungles that surround them. Tourism is still underdeveloped here; there are no resorts in this neck of the woods. Moreover, the heat and humidity are more than many people can stand. So it's best to put some forethought into planning a vacation down here, and it's usually wise to book your rooms and transportation in advance.

1 Drake Bay ⟨★★⟩

90 miles (145km) S of San José; 20 miles (32km) SW of Palmar

Located on the northern end of the Osa Peninsula, Drake Bay is what adventure travel is all about. Little more than a small collection of lodges catering to naturalists, anglers, scuba divers, and assorted vacationers, Drake Bay is a good place to get away from it all. Accommodations vary from tents on wooden platforms and cement-walled cabinas to very comfortable lodges that border on the luxurious. There are few conventional phones and no power lines in Drake Bay, so most lodges make do with radio and cellular phones and gas-powered electrical generators.

Until 1997, there was no road into Drake Bay and no airstrip in town. Currently both exist, but how reliable they are is another story—the road is often closed by heavy rains and mudslides, and the airstrip is serviced only by charter flights. Because of the bay's remoteness, development has been very slow here.

Unfortunately, it's starting to increase and it could someday change the face of this pristine destination. The town itself is starting to grow a bit, and massive logging is underway all along the road into Drake Bay and around—and even in—the national park.

The bay is named after Sir Francis Drake, who is believed to have anchored here in 1579. Emptying into the bay is the tiny **Río Agujitas,** which acts as a protected harbor for small boats and is a great place to do a bit of canoeing or swimming. It's here that many of the local lodges dock their boats. Stretching south from Drake Bay are miles and miles of deserted beaches. Adventurous explorers will find tide pools, spring-fed rivers, waterfalls, forest trails, and some of the best bird watching in all of Costa Rica. If a paradise such as this appeals to you, Drake Bay makes a good base for exploring the peninsula.

South of Drake Bay lie the wilds of the **Osa Peninsula,** including **Corcovado National Park.** This is one of Costa Rica's most beautiful regions, yet it's also one of its least accessible. Corcovado National Park covers about half of the peninsula and contains the largest single expanse of virgin lowland rain forest in Central America. For this reason, Corcovado is well known among naturalists and researchers studying rain-forest ecology, and if you come here you'll learn firsthand why they call them rain forests—some parts of the peninsula receive more than 250 inches of rain per year. In addition to producing lush forests, this massive amount of rain produces more than a few disgruntled visitors.

Puerto Jiménez (see section 2 of this chapter) is the best base to choose if you want to spend a lot of time hiking in and camping inside Corcovado National Park. Drake Bay is really just a collection of mostly high-end hotels, very isolated and mostly accessible only by boat. Travelers using these hotels can have great day hikes and guided tours into Corcovado park, but Puerto Jiménez is the place if you want to have more time in the park or explore independently (it has a range of budget hotels, the parks office, and "taxi/bus" service to Carate and Los Patos, from where visitors can hike into the various stations). From the Drake Bay side, you're much more dependent on a boat ride/organized tour from one of the lodges to explore the park; these lodges also offer many other guided outings in addition to visits to the park.

ESSENTIALS

Because Drake Bay is so remote, it's highly recommended that you have a room reservation and transportation arrangements (usually arranged with your hotel) before you arrive. The lodges listed here are scattered along several kilometers of coastline, and it is not easy to go from one to another looking for a room.

A flashlight and rain gear are always useful to have on hand in Costa Rica; they're absolutely essential in Drake Bay.

GETTING THERE   Depending on your temperament, getting to Drake Bay may be half the fun, or it may be torture. Despite the new road into—and airstrip in—Drake Bay, the traditional route is still the most dependable and popular. Most guests still fly first (or take a bus) to **Palmar Sur.** From here, it's a 15-minute bus or taxi ride over dirt roads to the small town of **Sierpe.** This bumpy ride takes you through several banana plantations and quickly past some important archaeological sites. In Sierpe, you board a small boat for a 25-mile (40km) ride to Drake Bay (see "By Taxi & Boat [from Sierpe]," below). The first half of this trip snakes through a maze of mangrove canals and rivers before heading out to sea for the final leg to the bay. Be warned: Entering and exiting the Sierpe River mouth is often treacherous, and I've had several very white-knuckle moments here.

The Southern Zone

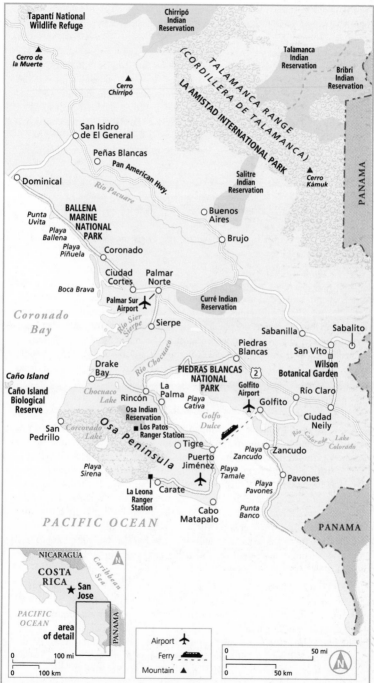

Tapantí National Wildlife Refuge

Chirripó Indian Reservation

Talamanca Indian Reservation

Bribri Indian Reservation

Cerro de la Muerte ▲

Cerro Chirripó ▲

TALAMANCA RANGE (CORDILLERA DE TALAMANCA)

LA AMISTAD INTERNATIONAL PARK

San Isidro de El General

Peñas Blancas

Pan American Hwy.

Salitre Indian Reservation

Cerro Kámuk ▲

PANAMA

Dominical

Río Pacuare

Buenos Aires

Punta Uvita

Playa Ballena

BALLENA MARINE NATIONAL PARK

Brujo

Playa Piñuela

Coronado

Ciudad Cortes

Palmar Norte

Boca Brava

Currí Indian Reservation

Palmar Sur Airport

Coronado Bay

Río Sier Sierpe

Sierpe

Sabanilla

Sabalito

Piedras Blancas

San Vito

Wilson Botanical Garden

Río Chocuaco

PIEDRAS BLANCAS NATIONAL PARK

Golfito Airport

Río Claro

Caño Island

Drake Bay

Chocuaco Lake

Rincón

La Palma

Playa Cativa

Golfo Dulce

Golfito

Caño Island Biological Reserve

Corcovado Lake

Osa Indian Reservation

Los Patos Ranger Station

Ciudad Neily

Río Colorado

Lake Colorado

San Pedrillo

Osa Peninsula

Tigre

Puerto Jiménez

Playa Zancudo

Zancudo

Playa Sirena

Playa Tamale

Playa Pavones

Pavones

La Leona Ranger Station

Carate

Cabo Matapalo

Punta Banco

PACIFIC OCEAN

PANAMA

NICARAGUA

COSTA RICA

San Jose

Caribbean Sea

PACIFIC OCEAN

area of detail

PANAMA

0 ___ 100 mi

0 ___ 100 km

Airport ✈

Ferry 🚢

Mountain ▲

0 ___ 50 mi

0 ___ 50 km

N

By Plane The airstrip in Drake Bay itself is currently operating only by char-ter. Most lodges include transportation in their packages, so check with them about where you will be flying into. The closest regularly serviced airport to Drake Bay is in **Palmar Sur,** a taxi and boat ride away. **Sansa** (✆ **506/221-9414;** reservations@flysansa.com) flies to Palmar Sur daily at 9:30am from San José's Juan Santamaría International Airport. The flight takes 50 minutes; the fare is $66 each way. Note that Sansa frequently alters its schedule and routing; this flight may stop in Quepos on the way down and thus take slightly longer.

 Travelair (✆ **506/220-3054;** reservations@travelair-costarica.com) has flights to Palmar Sur that depart daily at 9am from Tobías Bolaños International Airport in Pavas. This flight stops at Quepos en route. Flight duration is 55 min-utes; fare is $68 each way.

By Bus **Tracopa** (✆ **506/221-4214**) express buses leave San José daily for Palmar Norte at 5, 7, 8:30, and 10am, and 1, 2:30, and 6pm from Avenida 5 and Calle 14. Bus trips take 6 hours; the fare is $4.50.

 You can also catch any Golfito-bound bus from this same station and get off in Palmar Norte. Once in Palmar Norte, ask when the next bus goes out to Sierpe. If it doesn't leave for a while (they aren't frequent), consider taking a taxi (see below).

By Taxi & Boat (from Sierpe) Once you arrive at either the Palmar Norte bus station or the Palmar Sur airstrip, you'll most likely need to take a taxi to the vil-lage of Sierpe. The fare should be between $10 and $15. If you're booked into one of the main lodges, chances are your transportation is already included—via a guy named Rainer and his minibus, whom most of the lodges use. Even if you're not booked into one of the lodges, Rainer (or another driver—there are always some hanging around) will probably have room for you. Once you get to Sierpe, head to the dock and try to find space on a boat. This should run you another $15 to $20. Make sure you feel confident about the boat and skipper and, if possible, try to find a spot on a boat from one of the established lodges in Drake Bay.

By Car Driving is still not a recommended way to get to Drake Bay. But if you insist, you should drive down the Interamerican Highway, past Palmar to the turnoff for Puerto Jiménez (at the town of Chacarita; clearly marked). Then at Rincón, turn onto the rough road leading into Drake Bay. I'm getting mixed reports as to the viability of this road and I'm not sure whether it remains pass-able during the rainy season. It certainly reaches only into the small heart of the village of Drake Bay, whereas almost all of the hotels I've listed are farther out along the peninsula, where only boats reach. In fact, the only hotels that you can actually drive up to are very basic cabins in town. For the rest, you'd have to find someplace secure to leave your car and either haul your bags quite a way or get picked up in a boat.

DEPARTING Have your lodge arrange a boat trip back to Sierpe for you. Be sure the lodge also arranges for a taxi to meet you in Sierpe for the trip to Pal-mar Sur or Palmar Norte. (If you're on a budget, you can ask around to see whether a late-morning public bus is still running from Sierpe to Palmar Norte.) In the two Palmars, you can make onward plane and bus connections. At the Palmar Norte bus terminal, almost any bus heading north will take you to San José, and almost any bus heading south will take you to Golfito.

WHAT TO SEE & DO
Beaches, forests, wildlife, and solitude are the main attractions of Drake Bay. While Corcovado National Park (covered in section 2 of this chapter) is the

Those Mysterious Stone Spheres

While Costa Rica lacks the great cities, giant temples, and bas-relief carvings of the Maya, Aztec, and Olmec civilizations of northern Mesoamerica, its pre-Columbian residents did leave a unique legacy that continues to cause archaeologists and anthropologists to scratch their heads and wonder. Over a period of several centuries, hundreds of painstakingly carved and carefully positioned granite spheres were left by the peoples who lived throughout the Diquis Delta, which flanks the Terraba River in southern Costa Rica. The orbs, which range from grapefruit-size to more than 7 feet in diameter, can weigh up to 15 tons, and many reach near-spherical perfection.

Archaeologists believe that the spheres were created during two defined cultural periods. The first, called the Aguas Buenas period, dates from around A.D. 100 to 500. Few spheres survive from this time. The second phase, during which spheres were created in apparently greater numbers, is called the Chiriquí period, and lasted from approximately A.D. 800 to 1500. The "balls" believed to have been carved during this time frame are widely dispersed along the entire length of the lower section of the Terraba River. To date, only one known quarry for the spheres has been discovered, in the mountains above the Diquis Delta, which points to a difficult and lengthy transportation process.

Some archaeologists believe the spheres were hand-carved in a very time-consuming process, using stone tools, perhaps aided by some sort of firing process. However, another theory holds that granite blocks were placed at the bases of powerful waterfalls, and the hydraulic beating of the water eventually turned and carved the rock into these near-perfect spheres. And not a few proponents have credited extraterrestrial intervention for the creation of the stone balls.

Most of the stone balls have been found at the archaeological remains of defined settlements and are associated with either central plazas or known burial sites. Their size and placement have been interpreted to have both social and celestial importance, although their exact significance remains a mystery. Unfortunately, many of the stone balls have been plundered and are currently used as lawn ornaments in the fancier neighborhoods of San José. Some have even been shipped out of the country. The **Museo Nacional de Costa Rica** (see chapter 4) has a nice collection, including one massive sphere in its center courtyard. It's a never-fail photo op. You can also see the stone balls near the small **airport in Palmar Sur** and on **Caño Island** (which is located 12 miles/19km off the Pacific coast near Drake Bay).

area's star attraction, there's plenty to soak up in Drake Bay. The **Osa Peninsula** is home to an unbelievable variety of plants and animals: more than 140 species of mammals, 267 species of birds, and 117 species of amphibians and reptiles. While you aren't likely to see a high percentage of these animals, you can expect to see quite a few, including several species of monkeys, coatimundis, scarlet macaws, parrots, and hummingbirds. Other park inhabitants include jaguars, tapirs, sloths, and crocodiles. If you're lucky, you might even see one of the region's namesake *osas,* the giant anteaters.

Around Drake Bay and within the national park there are many miles of trails through rain forests and swamps, down beaches, and around rock headlands. All of the lodges listed below offer guided excursions into the park. It's also possible to begin a hike around the peninsula from Drake Bay.

You can do some sportfishing while you're in the area—all of the lodges listed below either run their own fishing trips or can arrange a charter boat for you.

One of the most popular excursions from Drake Bay is a trip out to **Caño Island** and the **Caño Island Biological Reserve** ✺ for a bit of exploring and snorkeling or scuba diving. The island is located about 12 miles (19km) offshore from Drake Bay and was once home to a pre-Columbian culture about which little is known. A trip to the island will include a visit to an ancient cemetery, and you'll also be able to see some of the stone spheres that are commonly believed to have been carved by the people who once lived in this area (see the box, above). Few animals or birds live on the island, but the coral reefs just offshore teem with life and are the main reason most people come here. This is one of Costa Rica's prime scuba spots. Visibility is often quite good, and there's even easily accessible snorkeling from the beach. All of the lodges listed below offer trips to Caño Island.

ACCOMMODATIONS & DINING

Given the remote location and logistics of reaching Drake Bay, as well as the individual isolation of each hotel, almost all of the hotels listed below deal almost exclusively in package trips that include transportation, meals, tours, and taxes. I've listed the most common packages, although all of the lodges will work with you to accommodate longer or shorter stays. I've listed nightly room rates only where they're available and practical, generally at the more moderately priced hotels.

All of the lodges listed below offer a host of half- and full-day tours and activities, including hikes in Corcovado National Park, trips to Caño Island, horseback rides, and sportfishing. In some cases, tours are included in your room rate or package; in others, they must be bought a la carte. Other options include mountain-biking, night tours, and sea kayaking. Most of these tours run between $60 and $90, depending on the activity, with scuba diving ($100–$120 for a two-tank dive) and sportfishing ($450–$1,200 depending on the size of the boat and other amenities) costing a bit more.

VERY EXPENSIVE

Aguila de Osa Inn ✺ This luxurious hillside lodge has long been a popular choice for serious sportfishermen. Situated high on a hill overlooking Drake Bay and the Pacific Ocean, the Aguila de Osa Inn offers large, attractively decorated rooms (with hardwood or tile floors, ceiling fans, large bathrooms, and excellent views), located a vigorous hike up a steep hillside. This could pose a problem for older guests, or those with heart or health problems, since the restaurant, reception, and docks are located far below, around river level. There's a bar built atop some rocks on the bank of the Río Agujitas, and the dining room has a good view of the bay. Meals are simply prepared, but tasty and filling, and the kitchen leaves a fresh Thermos of coffee outside each room every morning.

Since most folks are out for the day fishing or taking one of the organized tours, lunches are often picnic affairs on the boat, in Corcovado National Park, or on Caño Island. Dinners feature fresh fish, meat, and chicken, often prepared with a tropical or Caribbean flair.

Drake Bay (mailing address in the U.S.: Interlink 898, P.O. Box 025635, Miami, FL 33102). ℂ 506/
296-2190. Fax 506/232-7722. www.aguiladeosa.com. 14 units. $521 per person for 3 days/
2 nights with 1 tour; $666 for 4 days/3 nights with 2 tours. Rates are based on double occupancy
and include round-trip transportation from San José, all meals, park fees, and taxes. AE, MC, V (5%
surcharge). **Amenities:** 1 restaurant (international); 1 bar; modern fleet of sportfishing and dive
vessels; laundry service. *In room:* No phone.

Casa Corcovado Jungle Lodge ⭐

This very isolated jungle lodge is the
closest accommodation to Corcovado National Park from this end of the Osa
Peninsula. The rooms are all private bungalows built on the grounds of an old
cacao plantation on the jungle's edge. The bungalows are all spacious, with one
or two double beds (each with mosquito netting) and a large tiled bathroom.
Electricity and hot water are supplied by a combination solar and hydroelectric
energy system. Family-style meals are served in the main lodge, although most
guests take lunch with them to the beach or on one of the various tours available. Late afternoons are usually enjoyed from a high point overlooking the sea
and sunset, with your beverage of choice in hand. Access is strictly by small boat
here, and sometimes the beach landing can be a bit rough, so it's recommended
that guests be in decent physical shape. When the sea's not too rough, the beach
is great for swimming. When it is rough, it's a great place to grab a hammock in
the shade and read a book. There's also a small conference room equipped with
a TV and a VCR. A wide range of tours and activities is available.

Osa Peninsula (mailing address in the U.S.: Interlink 253, P.O. Box 526770, Miami, FL 33152).
ℂ 888/896-6097 in the U.S., or 506/256-3181. Fax 506/256-7409. www.casacorcovado.com.
10 units. $640–$685 per person for 3 days/2 nights with 1 tour; $795–$895 for 4 days/3 nights
with 2 tours. Rates are based on double occupancy and include round-trip transportation from San
José, all meals, park fees, and taxes. AE, MC, V. **Amenities:** 1 restaurant (international); 2 bars;
small, spring-fed swimming pool surrounded by lush jungle; laundry service. *In room:* "Dry" (no
fridge) stocked minibar, safe; no phone.

La Paloma Lodge ⭐⭐ (Finds)

Set on a steep hill overlooking the Pacific, with
Caño Island in the distance, the individual bungalows at La Paloma offer expansive ocean views that, combined with the attentive and amiable service, make
this my choice in Drake Bay. The main lodge building is a large, open-air structure with a long veranda that has a sitting area and swing chairs, where you can
mingle with other guests. All of the cabins are built on stilts, feature private
verandas, and are set among lush foliage facing the Pacific. I prefer the three
older cabins, simply for their spaciousness and seclusion. Four screen walls keep
you in touch with nature and let the ocean breezes blow through. The newer
cabins are a little smaller, but provide amazing ocean views from their main
sleeping lofts. The standard rooms, which were recently remodeled, are much
smaller and less private than the cabins, but they're still quite attractive and have
good views from their verandas (which, like the cabins, have hammocks). The
beach is about a 10-minute hike down a winding jungle path, and the lodge also
offers scuba certification courses. There are single and double kayaks free for
guests to use.

Hearty and delicious meals are served family style, and the kitchen will
accommodate vegetarians or those with special dietary needs with advance warning. There's scrumptious fresh-baked bread served with almost every meal here.

Drake Bay (mailing address in the U.S.: SJO Dept. 229, Box 025216, Miami, FL 33102-5216).
ℂ 506/239-2801, or ℂ and fax 506/239-0954. www.lapalomalodge.com. 9 units. Nov 16–
Apr 30 $750–$850 per person for 4 days/3 nights with 2 tours; $845–$950 per person for 5 days/
4 nights with 2 tours. Rates are based on double occupancy and include round-trip transportation
from San José, all meals, park fees, indicated tours, and taxes. Slightly lower rates May 1–Nov 15.

MC, V (6% surcharge added). **Amenities:** 1 restaurant (international); 1 bar; small tile pool with spectacular view; dive shop offering PADI certification courses; free use of sea kayaks; laundry service. *In room:* No phone.

EXPENSIVE/MODERATE

Cabinas Jinetes de Osa This perennial budget hotel in the village of Drake Bay has been spruced up, expanded, and turned into a hotel for serious divers. While it's now far from a budget lodging, it does offer a reasonable alternative to the more upscale options in the area (although the Drake Bay Wilderness Resort has far more charm and a much better location at almost the same price). Nevertheless, the wooden construction and location directly above the beach give Jinetes an edge over other lodgings right in the village of Drake Bay. The nicest rooms here are quite comfortable and even have a view of the bay. The hotel is pretty close to the docks on the Río Agujitas, which is nice for those traveling independently or with heavy bags. A wide range of tours and activities is available, as are dive packages, weekly packages, and PADI certification courses.

Drake Bay (mailing address in the U.S.: P.O. Box 833, Conifer, CO 80433). ✆ **800/317-0333**, 303/838-0969 in the U.S. and Canada, or 506/385-9541 in Costa Rica. Fax 303/838-1914. www.costaricadiving.com. 9 units, 5 with private bathroom. $120–$150 double. Rates include 3 meals daily and taxes. Dive packages available. DISC, MC, V. **Amenities:** 1 open-air restaurant (international/Costa Rican) serving basic meals; 1 bar. *In room:* No phone.

Drake Bay Wilderness Resort ⨯ This is one of the most convenient and best-located lodges at Drake Bay. It backs onto the Río Agujitas and fronts onto the Pacific. Travelers who want to rough it a bit or economize can opt for a large tent with a double bed, small table and lamp, and nearby communal bathroom and shower. Those seeking more comfort should opt for one of the basic rooms, which have ceiling fans, small verandas, good mattresses on the beds, and private bathrooms.

The family-style meals are filling, with an emphasis on fresh seafood and fresh fruits. My favorite treats here are the fresh-baked chocolate-chip cookies frequently served for dessert.

Because it's on a rocky spit, there isn't a good swimming beach right here (it's about a 15-min. walk away), but there's a new saltwater pool in front of the bay and, depending on the tide, you can bathe in a beautiful small tide pool formed by the rocks. The resort offers a wide range of tour options. The lodge runs a small butterfly farm and iguana-breeding project on some land inland from Drake Bay, and you can even spend the night here if you want. The resort is also one of the principal movers behind the small airstrip here, and almost all their charters fly directly to Drake Bay.

Drake Bay (A.P. 98-8150, Palmar Norte, Osa). ✆ and fax **506/770-8012**, or ✆ 506/256-7394. Fax 506/221-4948. www.drakebay.com. 7 tents, all with shared bathroom; 20 rooms. $120 tent for 2; $160 double room. Rates include all meals and taxes. $710 per person for 4 days/3 nights with 3 tours, including round-trip transportation from San José, all meals and taxes, and lodging in a room. MC, V. **Amenities:** 1 restaurant (international); 1 bar; small saltwater pool; free same-day laundry service; free use of canoes. *In room:* No phone.

Río Sierpe Lodge This lodge is located on the south bank of the Río Sierpe near the river mouth and is best known as a fishing lodge, with various fishing packages available. You won't be right on the beach if you stay here, but the lodge will ferry you to one of two nearby beaches. All the Drake Bay excursions are available here at comparable prices, making this an economical alternative to the lodges located there. Naturalists, anglers, and scuba divers are all catered to. Adventurous types can do a 2-day horseback trek that includes camping in the rain forest. The lodge also specializes in overnight trips into Panama. Río Sierpe is surrounded by forests, and there are hiking trails on the property.

On the Sierpe River (A.P. 85, Palmar Norte). ✆ **506/283-5573,** or 506/384-5595. Fax 506/786-7366. www.riosierpelodge.com. 15 units. $275 per person for 4 days/3 nights. Rates include 3 meals daily, 2 tours, taxes, and transportation to and from Palmar. AE, MC, V (7% surcharge). **Amenities:** 1 restaurant (international), 1 bar. *In room:* No phone.

2 Puerto Jiménez ✦ : Gateway to Corcovado National Park

21½ miles (35km) W of Golfito by water (56 miles/90km by road); 53 miles (85km) S of Palmar Norte

Despite its small size and languid pace, Puerto Jiménez is a double boomtown, where rough jungle gold panners mix with wealthy ecotourists, budget backpackers, and a surprising number of celebrities seeking a small dose of anonymity and escape. Located on the southeastern tip of the Osa Peninsula, the town itself is just a couple of gravel streets, with the ubiquitous soccer field, a block of general stores, some inexpensive *sodas,* a butcher shop, and several bars. Scarlet macaws fly overhead, and mealy parrots provide wake-up calls.

On first glance, it's hard to imagine anything ever happening here, but looks are often deceiving. Signs in English on walls around town advertise a variety of tours, with most of the excursions going to nearby Corcovado National Park. The national park has its headquarters here, and this town makes an excellent base for exploring this vast wilderness. If the in-town accommodations are too budget-oriented, you'll find several far more luxurious places farther south on the Osa Peninsula. However, not only the highbrow are making their way to this remote spot: You will also find a burgeoning surfer community. It's no secret any longer—**Cabo Matapalo** (the southern tip of the Osa Peninsula) is home to several very dependable right point breaks.

If you're worried the nightlife is going to be too sleepy for you, don't forget about all those gold miners lurking about. As the home base and resupply station for miners (most of them panning illegally) seeking to strike it rich in the jungles in and around the park, Puerto Jiménez can actually get pretty rowdy at night, especially when panners cash in a find.

ESSENTIALS

GETTING THERE & DEPARTING   By Plane   Sansa (✆ **506/221-9414;** reservations@flysansa.com) has flights departing for Puerto Jiménez daily at 8am and 1:40pm from San José's Juan Santamaría International Airport. The flight takes 55 minutes; the cost is $66 each way.

Travelair (✆ **506/220-3054;** reservations@travelair-costarica.com) has flights to Puerto Jiménez departing from Tobías Bolaños International Airport in Pavas at 6 and 9:30am, and 1pm daily. The flight takes between 55 minutes and 1½ hours depending on whether it stops en route; the fare is $68 each way.

Sansa flights depart Puerto Jiménez daily at 9:05am and 2:45pm. The Travelair flights leave for San José daily at 7:30 and 10:40am, and 2:30pm.

Note that due to the remoteness of this area and the unpredictable flux of traffic, both Sansa and Travelair frequently improvise on scheduling. Sometimes this means an unscheduled stop in Quepos or Golfito either on the way down from or back to San José, which can add some time to your flight. Less frequently it may mean a change in departure time, so it's always best to confirm.

By Car   Take the Interamerican Highway east out of San José (through San Pedro and Cartago) and continue south on this road. In about 3 hours, you'll pass through San Isidro de El General. In another 3 hours or so, take the turnoff for La Palma and Puerto Jiménez. This road is paved at first, but at Rincón it turns to gravel. The last 22 miles (35km) are slow and rough, and, if it's the rainy season (mid-Apr through Nov), it'll be too muddy for anything but a four-wheel-drive vehicle.

By Bus An express bus (© **506/257-4121**) leaves San José daily at noon from Calle 12 between Avenidas 7 and 9. The trip takes 9 hours; the fare is $8.

The bus departs Puerto Jiménez for San José daily at 5am.

By Boat There is daily passenger launch service from **Golfito** to Puerto Jiménez at 11:30am. The boat leaves from the municipal dock. Trip duration is 1½ hours; the fare is $4. It's also possible to charter a water taxi in Golfito for the trip across to Puerto Jiménez. You'll have to pay between $40 and $55 for an entire launch, some of which can carry up to 12 people. The return trip departs Puerto Jiménez for Golfito from the public dock at 6am; the fare is $4.

ORIENTATION Puerto Jiménez is a dirt-lane town on the southern coast of the Osa Peninsula. The public dock is over a bridge past the north end of the soccer field; the bus stop is 2 blocks east of the center of town.

EXPLORING CORCOVADO NATIONAL PARK ✸✸✸

Although a few gringos have, over the years, come to Puerto Jiménez to try their luck at gold panning, the primary reason for coming here these days is to visit Corcovado National Park. Within a couple of hours of the town (by four-wheel-drive vehicle) there are several entrances to the park; however, there are no roads in the park, so once you reach any of the entrances, you'll have to start hiking.

Exploring Corcovado National Park is not something to be undertaken lightly, but neither is it the expedition that some people make it out to be. The weather is the biggest obstacle to overnight backpacking trips through the park. The heat and humidity are often unbearable, and frequent rainstorms cause the trails to be quite muddy. Should you choose the alternative—hiking on the beach—you'll have to plan your hiking around the tides. Often there is no beach at all at high tide, and some rivers are impassable at high tide.

Because of its size and remoteness, Corcovado National Park is best explored over several days; however, it is possible to enter and hike a bit of it for day trips. The best way to do this is to book a tour with your lodge on the Osa Peninsula, from a tour company in Puerto Jiménez, or through a lodge in Drake Bay (see "Accommodations & Dining" in section 1 of this chapter).

GETTING THERE & ENTRY POINTS There are four primary entrances to the park, which are really just ranger stations reached by rough dirt roads. Once you've reached them, you'll have to strap on a backpack and hike. Perhaps the easiest one to reach from Puerto Jiménez is **La Leona ranger station,** accessible by car, bus, or taxi.

Trail Distances in Corcovado National Park

It's 10 miles (16km) from La Leona to Sirena. From Sirena to San Pedrillo, it's 15½ miles (25km) along the beach. From San Pedrillo, it's 5½ miles (9km) to Marenco Biological Reserve. It's 11¾ miles (19km) between La Sirena and Los Patos.

If you choose to drive, take the dirt road from Puerto Jiménez to Carate (Carate is at the end of the road). From Carate, it's a 2-mile (3km) hike to La Leona. To travel there by bus, pick up one of the collective buses (actually a four-wheel-drive pickup truck with a tarpaulin cover and slat seats in the back) that leave Puerto Jiménez for Carate daily at 6am (and return at 9am). Remember, these "buses" are very informal and change their schedules regularly to meet demand or avoid bad weather, so always ask in town. One-way fare is around $7. A small fleet of these pickups leaves from the main road in town, more or less in front of the Soda Carolina, and will stop to pick up anyone who flags them down along the way. Your other option is to hire a taxi, which will charge approximately $60 each way to Carate.

En route to Carate, you will pass several campgrounds and small lodges as you approach the park. If you are unable to get a spot at one of the campsites in the park, you can stay at one of these and hike the park during the day.

You can travel to **El Tigre,** about 8¾ miles (14km) by dirt road from Puerto Jiménez, where there's another ranger station. But note that trails from El Tigre go only a short distance into the park.

The third entrance is in **Los Patos,** which is reached from the town of La Palma, northwest of Puerto Jiménez. From here, there's an 11¾-mile (19km) trail through the center of the park to **Sirena,** a ranger station and research facility (see "Beach Treks & Rain-Forest Hikes," below). Sirena has a landing strip that is used by charter flights.

⟨*Tips* **Important Corcovado Tips**

If you plan to hike the beach trails from La Leona or San Pedrillo, be sure to pick up a tide table at the park headquarters' office in Puerto Jiménez. The tide changes rapidly; when it's high, the trails and river crossings can be impassable.

If you plan to spend a night or more in the park, you'll want to stock up on food, water, and other essentials while you're in Puerto Jiménez, too. There's a mini-market in Carate, but the selection is limited.

The northern entrance to the park is **San Pedrillo,** which you can reach by hiking from Sirena or by taking a boat from Drake Bay or Sierpe (see "Beach Treks & Rain-Forest Hikes," below). It's 8¾ miles (14km) from Drake Bay.

FEES & REGULATIONS   Park admission is $6 per person per day. Most of the ranger stations have dormitory-style lodgings, campsites, and simple *sodas,* but all must be reserved in advance through **Osa Natural** in Puerto Jiménez (© **506/735-5440;** osanatur@racsa.co.cr). Its office is on the main drag in Puerto Jiménez. If this doesn't work, you can try contacting the Parks Service in Puerto Jiménez (© **506/735-5036** or 506/735-5282). Its offices are adjacent to the airstrip. Only a limited number of people are allowed to camp at each ranger station, so make your reservations well in advance. There is an extra $2-per-day fee for camping, and meals can be prepared for you at around $17 more per day, but you must also reserve your meals in advance.

BEACH TREKS & RAIN-FOREST HIKES   There are quite a few good hiking trails in the park. Two of the better-known ones are the beach routes, starting at either the La Leona or San Pedrillo Ranger Station. None of the hikes is easy, but the forest route from the Los Patos ranger station to Sirena, while long, is less taxing than either of the beach treks, which can be completed only when the tide is low. The route between the Los Patos/Sirena hike is 11¾ miles (19km) through beautiful rain forest.

Sirena is a fascinating destination. As a research facility and ranger station, it's frequented primarily by scientists studying the rain forest. One of the longest hikes, from San Pedrillo to Sirena, can be done only during the dry season. Between any two stations, the hiking is arduous and will take all day, so it's best to rest for a day or so between hikes, if possible.

Remember, this is quite a wild area. Never hike alone and take all the standard precautions for hiking in the rain forest. In addition, be especially careful about swimming in any isolated rivers or river mouths, as most rivers in Corcovado are home to crocodiles.

ACCOMMODATIONS & DINING IN THE PARK: CAMPSITES, CABINS & CANTINAS   Reservations are essential at the various ranger stations if you plan on eating or sleeping inside the park (see "Fees & Regulations," above). The **La Leona** and **San Pedrillo** ranger stations each have a campground, some very basic dormitory-style cabins, and a *soda.* There is also camping and a *soda* at **Los Patos** ranger station. **Sirena** has a modern new research facility with dormitory-style accommodations, as well as a campground, *soda,* and landing strip for charter flights. Every ranger station has potable water, but it's advisable to pack in your own; whatever you do, don't drink stream water. Campsites in the park are $2 per person per night. A dorm bed will run you $6, and meals are around $17 per day.

ACTIVE PURSUITS OUTSIDE THE PARK

Closer to Puerto Jiménez, **kayaking trips** ✵✵ around the estuary and up into the mangroves and out into the gulf are popular. Contact **Escondido Trex** ✵ (© **506/735-5210;** www.escondidotrex.com), which has an office in the Soda Carolina (see "Dining in Puerto Jiménez," below). There are daily paddles through the mangroves, as well as sunset trips, where you can sometimes see dolphins. These folks also do guided rain-forest hikes and can have you rappelling down the face of a jungle waterfall. More adventurous multiday kayak and camping trips are also available, in price and comfort ranges from budget to luxury (staying at various lodges around the Golfo Dulce and Matapalo). They'll even take you gold panning (although no guarantees your panning will pay for the trip).

Osa Aventura (© and fax **506/735-5670;** www.osaaventura.com) and **Osa Natural** (© **506/735-5440;** osanatur@racsa.co.cr) also offer a host of guided tours around the Osa Peninsula and into Corcovado National Park.

If you're interested in doing some **billfishing or deep-sea fishing,** you'll probably want to stay at or fish with **Crocodile Bay Lodge** (© **506/735-5631;** fax 506/735-5633; www.crocodilebay.com). This is a new, upscale fishing lodge close to the Puerto Jiménez airstrip. If you want a more budget-oriented fishing outing, check around the public dock for notices put up by people with charter boats, or call **Marco "Taboga" Loaiciga** (© **506/735-5265**). Rates usually run between $250 and $700 for a full day, or between $100 and $350 for a half day, depending on the boat and tackle.

If you're not into hiking in the heat, you can charter a plane in Puerto Jiménez to take you to Carate, Sirena, Drake Bay, or even Tiskita Jungle Lodge (see "Accommodations & Dining" in section 5 of this chapter, on Playa Pavones), which is across the gulf, south of Playa Pavones. A five-passenger plane should cost around $150 to $200 one-way, depending on your destination. Contact **Alfa Romeo Aero Taxi** (© **506/775-1515** or © and fax 506/735-5178) for details.

ACCOMMODATIONS IN PUERTO JIMÉNEZ
MODERATE

Doña Leta's Bungalows   This collection of individual cabins is located on a spit of land jutting out into the gulf, just east of town and the airstrip. The smaller cabins are octagonal and have just one double bed, while the larger ones each feature a sleeping loft with a double and single bed above and a double bed below. Each cabin comes with a refrigerator, two-burner stove, private bathroom, and carved-wood door. There's a small restaurant and bar here and a large central deck built under and around a large fig tree that's frequented by scarlet macaws. The grounds also include a small patch of beach and a semi-groomed trail through the mangroves.

A.P. 91, Puerto Jiménez. © **506/735-5568,** or © and fax 506/735-5180. www.donaleta.com. 7 units. $85 double. Lower rates in the off-season. V. **Amenities:** 1 restaurant (international); 1 bar; limited water-sports-equipment rental; volleyball court; free use of kayaks; laundry service. *In room:* Kitchenette, fridge; no phone.

INEXPENSIVE

Agua Luna ⟨Value⟩   These very reasonable rooms are the nicest of the in-town lodgings in Puerto Jiménez. Agua Luna is located right at the foot of the town's public dock and backs up to a mangrove forest. The six older rooms directly face the gulf across a fenced-in gravel parking area. The most surprising feature in each of these rooms is the bathroom, which includes both a shower and a tub facing a picture window that looks into the mangroves. (The most disappointing feature is that these windows let you watch the gray water discharge directly into the mangroves.) There are two double beds in each room, and on the tiled veranda out front you'll find hammocks for lounging. The newer rooms are located a half block away and are smaller and less attractive than those in the original building. Most of the rooms have televisions. The higher prices are for the larger rooms, which have tubs and mini-refrigerators.

In front of the public dock, Puerto Jiménez. ✆ **506/735-5034.** Fax 506/735-5393. agualu@ racsa.co.cr. 14 units. $45–$55 double. V. **Amenities:** 1 restaurant (seafood/international); laundry service. *In room:* A/C; no phone.

Cabinas Oro Verde   The rooms at this budget hotel are on the second floor of a basic restaurant of the same name. The rooms are kept clean and have fans and fresh sheets. The five rooms in the front of the hotel share a narrow veranda over a sleepy street in Puerto Jiménez. The owners can help arrange a variety of tour and adventure options.

On a cross st. in the center of town, 50m east of the main rd., Puerto Jiménez. ✆ **506/735-5241.** oroverde@racsa.co.cr. 10 units. $20 double; $30 triple. No credit cards. **Amenities:** 1 restaurant (Costa Rican); laundry service. *In room:* No phone.

Cabinas Puerto Jiménez   Located right on the waterfront at the north end of the soccer field, this inexpensive accommodation even offers one room with a view of the bay. The exterior of the building, with its varnished wood, is more appealing than the guest rooms. Though large, the basic rooms have cement floors, and either a floor or table fan. However, they're kept clean and are the best choice in town for travelers on a real shoestring budget.

50m (55 yd.) north of Bar y Restaurant El Rancho, Puerto Jiménez. ✆ **506/735-5090** or 506/735-5215. 10 units. $16 double; $24 triple. No credit cards. *In room:* No phone.

DINING IN PUERTO JIMÉNEZ

Bar Restaurant Agua Luna COSTA RICAN/SEAFOOD   The first restaurant you come to after arriving in Puerto Jiménez by boat is also one of the best. The restaurant is a large, mostly open building built between the dirt road and the mangroves. I recommend a table overlooking the mangroves. Seafood is plentiful and fresh, and prices for fish dinners are low even for Costa Rica. The bar and its dance floor are popular, and the music is usually loud, so don't expect a quiet, romantic dinner for two.

25m north of the public pier. ✆ **506/735-5033.** Main courses $3–$17. No credit cards. Daily 10am–10pm.

Soda Carolina COSTA RICAN   Set in the center of the town's main street, and otherwise known as the "Bar, Restaurante y Cabinas Carolina," this is the town's budget travelers' hangout and also serves as an unofficial information center. The walls are painted with colorful jungle and wildlife scenes. As for the fare, seafood is the way to go. There's good fried fish as well as a variety of ceviches. The black-bean soup is usually tasty, and the casados are filling and cost less than $3.

If you need a place to stay, there are five basic rooms with cement floors and private bathrooms behind the kitchen. The rooms cost around $10 per person and front a very unattractive yard.

On the main st. ✆ **506/735-5185.** Main courses $3–$8. V. Daily 7am–10pm.

ACCOMMODATIONS & DINING ELSEWHERE AROUND THE OSA PENINSULA

As with most of the lodges in Drake Bay, the accommodations listed in this section include three meals a day in their rates and do a large share of their business in package trips. Per-night rates are listed, but the price categories have been adjusted to take into account the fact that all meals are included. Ask about package rates if you plan to take several tours and stay a while: They could save you money.

In addition to the lodges listed below, there are several other options, ranging from small bed-and-breakfasts to fully equipped home rentals. Surfers, in particular, might want to inquire into one of the several rental houses located close to the beach at Matapalo. Your best bet for any of the above is to contact Isabel at **Osa Tropical** (© 506/735-5062). In addition to being the local Sansa agent, Isabel arranges bookings via radio with a host of small remote lodges around the area.

Finally, there's a new, very isolated option up in the hills above Carate. **Luna Lodge** (© 888/409-8448 in the U.S., or 506/380-5036 in Costa Rica; www.lunalodge.com) has five rustically luxurious cabins, with great views over the jungle.

VERY EXPENSIVE

Bosque del Cabo Wilderness Lodge ★★ *(Finds)*   This secluded jungle lodge is my favorite option in this neck of the woods. The cabins are all spacious and attractively furnished, have wooden decks or verandas to catch the ocean views, and are set amid beautiful gardens. Bosque del Cabo is located 500 feet above the water at the southern tip of the Osa Peninsula, where the Golfo Dulce meets the Pacific Ocean. The deluxe cabins come with king-size beds and slightly larger deck space. Cabin 6 is my choice for its spectacular view of the sunrise from your bed. All of the cabins have indoor bathrooms, although the tiled showers are set outdoors amid flowering heliconia and ginger.

There's a trail down to a secluded beach that has some tide pools and ocean-carved caves. Another trail leads to a jungle waterfall, and several others wind through the rain forests of the lodge's private reserve. If you're too lazy to hike down to the beach, there's a small pool by the main lodge. Surfing is a popular activity here, as are hiking and horseback riding. The newest attraction here is a canopy platform 120 feet up a Manu tree, reached along a 300-foot zip line. Trips to the national park or fishing excursions can be arranged, as well as guided hikes, sea kayaking, and a host of other activities and tours. These folks also rent out two separate, fully equipped houses that are quite nice and popular.

Osa Peninsula (mailing address in the U.S.: Interlink 528, P.O. Box 025635, Miami, FL 33152). © and fax **506/735-5206**, or 506/381-4847. www.bosquedelcabo.com. 9 units. $250–$270 double. Rates include 3 meals daily and taxes. $20 round-trip transportation from Puerto Jiménez. V. **Amenities:** 1 restaurant (international); 1 bar; small pool; nature trails; laundry service. *In room:* No phone.

Lapa Ríos ★★   This is Costa Rica's most upscale ecolodge. However, keep in mind that there are no TVs, no telephones, no air-conditioning, no discos, no shopping, no paved roads, and no crowds. Moreover, the beach is a good 15-minute hike away, and it's not the best for swimming. In fact, other than a beautiful little pool, miles of hiking trails, an array of adventure tours and activities, and a quiet tropical bar, there is nothing around to distract your attention from the stupendous views of the rain forest all around and the ocean far below.

The hotel consists of seven duplex buildings perched along a steep ridge. Each spacious room is totally private and oriented toward the view. Walls have open screening, and the ceiling is a high-peaked thatched roof. Mosquito nets drape languidly over the two queen-size beds. A large deck and small tropical garden, complete with outdoor shower, more than double the living space of each room. Be warned: It's a bit of a hike back and forth from the main lodge to the rooms located farthest down the ridge.

The centerpiece of the lodge's large open-air dining room is a 50-foot-tall spiral staircase that leads to an observation deck tucked beneath the peak of the building's thatched roof. Lapa Ríos is surrounded by its own 1,000-acre private rain-forest reserve, which is home to scarlet macaws, toucans, parrots, hummingbirds, monkeys, and myriad other wildlife. Tour and activity options include guided walks, horseback riding, boat tours, sportfishing, sea kayaking, as well as day trips to Corcovado National Park, Casa Orquideas, and Wilson Botanical Gardens.

Osa Peninsula (mailing address in the U.S.: Box 025216, SJO-706, Miami, FL 33102). (C) **506/735-5130.** Fax 506/735-5179. www.laparios.com. 14 units. $200–$230 per person. Rates are based on double occupancy and include 3 meals daily and taxes. Discounts for children up to 10 years old; lower rates in the off-season. $20 for round-trip transportation from Puerto Jiménez. AE, MC, V. **Amenities:** 1 restaurant (international); 1 bar; small pool; body-board and surfboard rentals; nature trails; laundry service. *In room:* No phone.

EXPENSIVE

Corcovado Lodge Tent Camp ⭐ If you're looking for a balanced blend of comfort and adventure, check out Corcovado Lodge Tent Camp, which is built on a low bluff right above the beach. Forested mountains rise up behind the tent camp, and just a few minutes' walk away is the entrance to the national park. Accommodations are in large tents pitched on wooden decks. Each tent has two twin beds, a table, a couple of plastic garden chairs on the front deck, and an ocean view. Toilets and showers are a short walk away, but there are enough so that there's usually no waiting.

Meals are served family-style in a large open-air dining room furnished with picnic tables. A separate screen-walled building is furnished with hammocks, a small bar, a Ping-Pong table, and a few board games. Services at the lodge include guided walks and excursions, including hikes through the national park and horseback rides on the beach. The newest addition to the lodge is a canopy platform located 120 feet up an ancient Guapinol tree. If you're truly adventurous, you can spend the night in a tent atop the platform (just don't wake up on the wrong side of the tent). Package rates that include transportation and tours are also available and are the way most people come here.

Just reaching this lodge is an adventure in itself. Most guests take a five-seat chartered plane to the gravel landing strip at Carate and then walk for around 30 minutes along the beach to the lodge. Don't worry: Your bags are hauled in on a mule-drawn cart. If you have a four-wheel-drive vehicle, you can get as far as Carate, arrange for safe parking, and then walk the remaining mile (1.6km). Once you're there, you have a real sense of being very away from it all.

Osa Peninsula (mailing address in the U.S.: SJO 235, P.O. Box 025216, Miami, FL 33102). (C) **506/257-0766.** Fax 506/257-1665. www.costaricaexpeditions.com. 20 tents. $135 double. Rates include 3 meals daily and all taxes. 3-day/2-night package $1,398 double, including air transportation (pickup and delivery from any San José hotel), 3 meals daily, 1 treetop/canopy tour, park entrance fee, and all taxes. Add $67 per person per day for extra days. AE, MC, V. **Amenities:** 1 restaurant (international); 1 bar; nature trails; laundry service. *In room:* No phone.

3 Golfito: Gateway to the Golfo Dulce

54 miles (87km) S of Palmar Norte; 209 miles (337km) S of San José

Golfito is an odd and unlikely destination for foreign travelers. In its prime, this was a major banana port, but United Fruit pulled out in 1985 following a few years of rising taxes, falling prices, and labor disputes. Now, Ticos come here in droves on weekends and throughout December to take advantage of cheap prices on name-brand goods and clothing sold at the duty-free zone, and some-times all these shoppers make finding a room difficult.

Golfito is also a major sportfishing center and a popular gateway to a slew of nature lodges spread along the quiet waters, isolated bays, and lush rain forests of the Golfo Dulce, or "Sweet Gulf." In 1998, much of the rain forest border-ing the Golfo Dulce was officially declared the **Piedras Blancas National Park,** which includes 30,000 acres of primary forests, as well as newly protected sec-ondary forests and pasturelands.

Golfito is set on the north side of the Golfo Dulce, at the foot of lush green mountains. The setting alone is enough to make this one of the most attractive cities in the country, but Golfito also has a certain charm all its own. Sure, the areas around the municipal park and public dock are kind of seedy and the "downtown" section is quite run-down, but if you go a little bit farther along the bay, you come to the old United Fruit Company housing. Here you'll find well-maintained wooden houses painted bright colors and surrounded by neatly manicured gardens. Toucans are commonly sighted. It's all very lush and green and clean—an altogether different picture from that painted by most port towns in this country. These old homes are experiencing a sort of renaissance as they become small hotels catering to shoppers visiting the adjacent duty-free shopping center.

Sportfishing cognoscenti know that Golfito's real draw is the marlin and sail-fish just beyond its bay. Arguably one of the best fishing spots in Costa Rica, it provides pleasant, uncrowded surroundings in which die-hard sportfishers can indulge their greatest fantasies of landing the great one to end all great ones. Landlubbers, take heed: Golfito has great opportunities for bird watching and is also close to some lovely botanical gardens that you can easily spend a day or more touring.

ESSENTIALS

GETTING THERE & DEPARTING   By Plane   Sansa (© **506/221-9414;** reservations@flysansa.com) has three daily flights to Golfito departing at 6 and 9:40am, and 2:15pm from San José's Juan Santamaría International Air-port. Trip duration is 1 hour; fare is $66 each way. Sansa flights return to San José daily at 7:10 and 10:50am, and 3:25pm. **Travelair** (© **506/220-3054;** reservations@travelair-costarica.com) has one flight to Golfito daily at 6am from Tobías Bolaños International Airport in Pavas. The flight returns to San José at 7:10am. The flight takes 1 hour; the fare is $70 each way.

By Car   The Interamerican Highway goes almost all the way to Golfito from San José, but even the main highway is a long and arduous trip. In the 8 hours it takes to drive the 209 miles (337km) from San José, you'll pass over the Cerro de la Muerte, which is famous for its dense fog and torrential downpours. Also, you'll have to contend with potholes of gargantuan proportions for almost the entire length of this road. Just remember, if the road is suddenly smooth and in great shape, you can bet that around the next bend there will be a bottomless pothole that you can't swerve around. Take it easy. When you get to Río Claro, you'll notice a couple of gas stations and quite a bit of activity. Turn right here and follow the signs to Golfito. If you end up at the Panama border, you've missed the turnoff by about 20 miles (32km).

By Bus   Express buses leave San José daily at 7am and 3pm from the Tracopa station at Avenida 5 and Calle 14 (© **506/222-2666**). The trip takes 8 hours; the fare is $6.

Buses depart Golfito for San José daily at 5am and 1:30pm from the bus station near the municipal dock.

By Boat   A passenger launch leaves **Puerto Jiménez,** on the Osa Peninsula, daily at 6am. The trip takes 1½ hours; the fare is $4. You can also hire a boat to take you across the Golfo Dulce to Golfito. However, as there are not very many available in Puerto Jiménez, you're likely to have to pay quite a bit ($40 to $55 each way) for such a service. The passenger launch departs Golfito for Puerto Jiménez daily at 11:30am.

GETTING AROUND   If you can't get to your next destination by boat, bus, or car, **Alfa Romeo Aero Taxi** (© **506/775-1515** or © and fax 506/735-5178) runs charters to most of the nearby destinations, including Carate, Drake Bay, Sirena, and Puerto Jiménez. A regular taxi ride anywhere in town should cost around 75¢.

FAST FACTS   You can **exchange money** at the gas station, or "La Bomba," in the middle of town. There's a **Laundromat** on the upper street of the small downtown that charges $3 for a 5-pound load. If you drop off your clothes in the morning, they'll be ready in the afternoon.

EXPLORING THE AREA

There aren't any really good swimming beaches right in Golfito. The closest spot is **Playa Cacao,** a short boat ride away, although this is not one of my favorite beaches in Costa Rica. You should be able to get a ride here for around $5 per person from one of the boat taxis down at the public docks, however, you might have to negotiate hard, as these boatmen like to gouge tourists whenever possible. If you really want some beach time, I recommend staying at one of the hotels in the Golfo Dulce (see below) or heading over to **Playa Zancudo** (see section 4, later in this chapter).

The waters off Golfito also offer some of the best **sportfishing** ☆☆ in Costa Rica. If you'd like to try hooking into a possible world-record marlin or sailfish, contact **Banana Bay Marina** (© 506/775-0838; www.bananabaymarina.com). You could also try either **Golfito Sportfishing** (© 506/776-0007; www. costaricafishing.com) or **Roy's Zancudo Lodge** (© 506/776-0008; www.royszancudo.com). Both of these operations are based in nearby Playa Zancudo, but they can arrange pickup in Golfito. A full-day fishing trip will cost between $450 and $800.

There's no steady charter fleet here, but itinerant sailors often set up shop here for a season or so. If you're looking to charter a sailboat, you should check with the **Banana Bay Marina** (© 506/775-0838) or **Las Gaviotas Hotel** (© 506/775-0062).

About 30 minutes by boat out of Golfito, you'll find **Casa Orquídeas** ☆☆, a private botanical garden lovingly built and maintained by Ron and Trudy MacAllister. Most hotels in the area offer trips here, including transportation and a 2-hour tour of the gardens. During the tour, you'll sample a load of fresh fruits picked right off the trees. If your hotel can't, you can book a trip out of Golfito with **Land Sea Tours** (© 506/775-1614), which charges $80 for up to four people, including the boat transportation and tour.

If you have a serious interest in botanical gardens or bird watching, consider an excursion to **Wilson Botanical Gardens** ✮✮✮ (© 506/240-6696; fax 506/240-6783; nat-hist@ots.ac.cr), located just outside the town of San Vito, about 40 miles (65km) to the northeast. The gardens are owned by the Organization for Tropical Studies and include more than 7,000 species of tropical plants from around the world. Among the plants grown here are many endangered species, which make the gardens of interest to botanical researchers. Despite the scientific aspects of the gardens, there are so many beautiful and unusual flowers amid the manicured grounds that even a neophyte can't help but be astounded. All this luscious flora has attracted at least 330 species of birds. Entrance to the gardens is $6 per person. A full-day guided walk, including lunch, will cost you $38; a half-day guided walk costs $15. If you'd like to stay the night here, there are 12 well-appointed rooms and 4 cabins. Rates, which include three meals and taxes, run around $60 per person; you need to make reservations beforehand if you wish to spend the night. You'll find the gardens about 3¾ miles (6km) before San Vito. To get here from Golfito, drive back out to the Interamerican Highway and continue south toward Panama. In Ciudad Neily, turn north. A taxi from Golfito should cost between $30 and $40 each way.

GUIDED TOURS   If you're interested in having a guide for any of the above activities, or for a hike in some nearby rain forest, check in with either the **Golfo Dulce Eco-Tourist Guide Association** (© 506/775-1813) or **Land Sea Tours** (© 506/775-1614). The latter offers kayaking and camping trips out on the gulf.

ACCOMMODATIONS

In addition to the listings below, the **Wilson Botanical Gardens** offer moderately priced rooms and cabins. See "Exploring the Area," above.

IN GOLFITO

Complejo Turístico Samoa del Sur ⟨Value⟩   It's hard to miss the two giant thatched spires that house this popular hotel, restaurant, and bar. The rooms are spacious and clean. Varnished wood headboards complement two firm and comfortable double beds. With red-tile floors, modern bathrooms, and carved-wood doors, the rooms all share a long, covered veranda that's set perpendicular to the gulf, so the views aren't great. If you want to watch the water, you're better off grabbing a table at the restaurant. On my last visit, there were big plans to expand and develop this hotel, adding on a full-service marina, swimming pool, tennis and volleyball courts, and more rooms.

100m north of the public dock, Golfito. © 506/775-0233. Fax 506/775-0573. samoa@golfito.net. 14 units. $50 double. AE, MC, V. **Amenities:** 1 restaurant (international); 1 bar; laundry service. *In room:* A/C, TV.

Golfo Azul   Azul offers clean rooms and a quiet location in the most attractive part of Golfito. Most of the guests here are Ticos in town to shop at the nearby Depósito Libre (free port). Unfortunately, service can range from inattentive to downright rude. The smallest rooms are cramped, but there are larger rooms, some with high ceilings, making them feel even more spacious. Bathrooms are tiled and have hot water. The hotel's restaurant serves only breakfast.

Barrio Alameda, 300m south of the Depósito Libre, Golfito. © 506/775-0871. Fax 506/775-1849. golfoazul@racsa.co.cr. 20 units. $24 double; $27 triple; $30 quad. V. *In room:* A/C; no phone.

Las Gaviotas Hotel   Situated just at the start of Golfito proper—a short taxi or bus ride from the "downtown"—Las Gaviotas has long been a popular choice. The waterfront location is this hotel's greatest asset. There is a long pier that attracts the sailboat and sportfishing crowd. For landlubbers, there's a small pool built out near the gulf. Guest rooms, which are set amid attractive gardens, all face the ocean, and though they're quite large, they're a bit Spartan and definitely show their age. There are small, tiled patios in front of all the rooms, and the cabanas have little kitchens. A large, open-air restaurant looks over the pool to the gulf; it's a great view, but the food leaves much to be desired. Just around the corner is a large, open-air bar.

A.P. 12-8201, Golfito. (℃ **506/775-0062.** Fax 506/775-0544. lasgaviotas@hotmail.com. 18 units, 3 cabanas. $40–$55 double; $45–$60 triple; $84 cabana. AE, DC, MC, V. **Amenities:** 1 restaurant (seafood/international); 1 bar; small outdoor pool; limited water-sports equipment rental; tour desk; laundry service. *In room:* A/C, TV.

FARTHER AFIELD ON THE GOLFO DULCE

The lodges listed here are all located on the shores of the Golfo Dulce. There are no roads into this area, so you must get to the lodges by boat. I recommended that you have firm reservations when visiting this area, so your transportation should be arranged. If worse comes to worst, you can hire a boat taxi at the *muellecito* (little dock), which is located on the water just beyond the gas station, or "La Bomba," in Golfito, for between $25 and $35 depending on which lodge you are staying at.

In addition to the places listed below, **Dolphin Quest** (℃ **506/383-8630;** www.dolphinquestcostarica.com) is the closest thing to a budget option in this area. They have a variety of lodging options, and even allow camping. They are particularly hard to contact, but you can try booking them through **Osa Tropical** (℃ **506/735-5062**).

Expensive

Caña Blanca Beach & Rainforest Lodge ★★ *(Finds)*   This small, isolated nature lodge is perfect for a romantic getaway and/or some serious relaxation. The three individual cabins are nestled on the edge of a 900-acre private reserve. All are spacious, wooden affairs, built on stilts, with private bathrooms and outdoor-garden showers. From your balcony, you can watch the waters of the Golfo Dulce lap onto Caña Blanca's palm-lined black-sand beach. There are kayaks for paddling around the gulf, as well as several miles of trails and a resident naturalist guide. Gourmet meals are prepared by your hosts, Earl and Carol Crews, featuring fresh fruits, herbs and vegetables, and quite often fresh fish. There are no TVs and only an erratic cellular phone connection out here, so be prepared to get away from it all. However, the bird watching is fabulous, and you're guaranteed to see some monkeys, pizotes, and much more of the rich local fauna.

Golfo Dulce (A.P. 48, Puerto Jiménez). (℃ **506/383-5707** or 506/735-5062. Fax 506/735-5043. www.canablanca.com. 3 units. $250 double. Rates include all meals, drinks, daily tours, taxes, and transfers to and from either Golfito or Puerto Jiménez. 3-day minimum stay. V (with a 5% surcharge). **Amenities:** 1 restaurant (international); 1 bar; limited water-sports equipment; nature trails; laundry service. *In room:* No phone.

Golfo Dulce Lodge ★   This small, Swiss-run lodge is just down the beach from Casa Orquideas, about a 30-minute boat ride from Golfito. The five separate cabins and main lodge buildings are all set back away from the beach about 500 meters (545 yd. or so) into the forest. The cabins are spacious, airy, and feature either a twin and a double bed or three single beds. In addition, there are large modern bathrooms, solar hot-water showers, a small sitting area, and a porch with a hammock. The rooms are all comfortable and well appointed, and even feature private verandas, but they are not nearly as nice as the cabins. Meals are served in a two-story open rancho with an observation deck, located beside the small swimming pool. The lodge offers jungle hikes, river trips, and other guided tours.

Golfo Dulce (A.P. 137-8201, Golfito). ℂ **506/391-9840.** Fax 506/280-8635. www. golfodulcelodge.com. 8 units. $190–$210 double; $225–$255 triple. Lower rates in the off-season. Rates include 3 meals daily and taxes. Add $15 per person for transportation to and from Golfito or Puerto Jiménez. No credit cards. **Amenities:** 1 restaurant (international); 1 bar; small outdoor pool; nature trails; laundry service. *In room:* No phone.

Rainbow Adventures 🏵🏵 *(Finds)* The open architecture, varnished hardwoods, four-poster beds and scattered antiques, stained glass, and oriental rugs make this one of the more unique jungle lodges in Costa Rica. The grounds immediately surrounding the lodge are neatly manicured gardens planted with exotic fruit trees, flowering shrubs, and palms from around the world. The second-floor rooms in the main lodge are the smallest and least expensive. But for just a little more, you can have the penthouse, a large third-floor room with four open walls and treetop views of the gulf. The individual cabins, which are set off a hundred yards or so from the main building, have open living rooms and a large bedroom that can be divided into two small rooms.

Days are spent lounging in hammocks, swimming, sunning, exploring the jungle, reading, bird watching, wild-animal–watching, and maybe fishing a bit. A private (albeit rocky) beach provides protected swimming and, when it's calm, there's some good snorkeling nearby (equipment is available at no charge). Boat charters and guided tours to neighboring attractions are available. The hotel has an air-conditioned library and reading room, with one of the most extensive collections of natural-history books I've ever seen. There are several well-maintained trails through primary rain forest, with jungle waterfalls and wonderful swimming holes. Creative and tasty meals are served either family or buffet style.

The owner has eight more rooms in the sister lodge, Buena Vista, located several hundred meters/yards up Playa Cativa, but the level of comfort, service, and general ambiance are not quite as appealing there.

Playa Cativa (mailing address in the U.S.: Michael Medill, 5875 NW Kaiser Rd., Portland, OR 97229). ℂ **800/565-0722,** 503/690-7750 in the U.S., or ℂ and fax 506/775-0220 in Costa Rica. Fax 503/690-7735 in the U.S. www.rainbowcostarica.com. 4 units, 2 cabins. $310–$350 double. Extra person $65. Rates include 3 meals daily, round-trip transportation between the lodge and Golfito, all nonalcoholic drinks, snacks, and taxes. AE, DC, MC, V. **Amenities:** 1 restaurant (international); small outdoor spring-fed pool; limited water-sports equipment; nature trails; laundry service. *In room:* No phone.

DINING

In addition to the restaurants listed below, the **Coconut Cafe,** across from the gas station (ℂ **506/775-0518**), is a popular hangout. Open for breakfast and lunch, this place specializes in espresso and exotic coffee concoctions as well as desserts. It's a good place to gather information on trips and tours around the gulf, and also offers Internet access.

Bar & Restaurant La Cubana COSTA RICAN This small, open-air restaurant with a basic menu commands a good view of the gulf from its location on the bluff of a small hill. It serves hearty meals at rock-bottom prices. A fresh whole fish in garlic sauce costs around $4. The bar is a quiet spot to have a drink in the evening.

150m east of the gas station, on the upper rd. through downtown Golfito. No phone. Main courses $3–$8. No credit cards. Tues–Sun 6am–10pm.

Samoa del Sur CONTINENTAL   It's hard to miss the Samoa del Sur: It's that huge twin-towered rancho just north of the public dock. This oversized jungle structure seems out of place in a town where cinder blocks are the preferred construction material, but its tropical atmosphere is a welcome change from the rather rundown ambiance that pervades the rest of this town. The restaurant's biggest surprise, however, is its extensive menu of familiar continental and French dishes (the owners are French), such as onion soup, salad Niçoise, fillet of fish meunière, and paella. There are also pizzas and spaghetti. The view of the gulf makes this a great spot for a sunset drink. In addition to the food, the giant rancho houses a pool table, several high-quality dartboards, and a big-screen TV. The bar sometimes stays open all night.

100m north of the public dock. ℂ 506/775-0233. Main courses $3–$18. AE, MC, V. Daily 7am–midnight.

GOLFITO AFTER DARK

Golfito is a rough-and-tumble port town, and it pays to be a bit careful here after dark. Most folks stick pretty close to their hotel bar and restaurant. Of these, the bar/restaurants at **Las Gaviotas** and **Samoa del Sur** are by far the liveliest. Right in town, about a block inland and slightly uphill from the *muellecito*, **El Balcón** is the most popular spot. The second-floor, open-air bar attracts a regular crowd of resident expatriates, itinerant sailors, and tourists.

4 Playa Zancudo

12 miles (19km) S of Golfito (by boat); 22 miles (35km) S of Golfito (by road)

Although word has leaked out in recent years, Playa Zancudo remains one of Costa Rica's most isolated beach getaways. It's a popular backpacker hangout, which means there are plenty of cheap rooms, some cheap places to eat, and lots of young gringos and Europeans around. These factors alone are enough to keep Zancudo jumping through the winter months. The beach itself is long and flat, and because it's protected from the full force of Pacific waves, it's one of the calmest beaches on this coast and relatively good for swimming, especially toward the northern end. There's a splendid view across the Golfo Dulce, and the sunsets are hard to beat. Because there's a mangrove swamp directly behind the beach, mosquitoes and biting sand flies can be a problem, so be sure to bring insect repellent.

ESSENTIALS

GETTING THERE   By Plane   The nearest airport is in Golfito. See the Golfito section, above, for details. To get from the airport to Playa Zancudo, you can take a boat (see "By Boat," below) or a taxi (see "By Car," below).

By Boat   Water taxis can be hired in Golfito to make the trip out to Playa Zancudo; however, trips depend on the tides and weather conditions. When the tide is high, the boats take a route through the mangroves. This is by far the calmest and most scenic way to get to Zancudo. When the tide is low, they must stay out in the gulf, which can get choppy at times. Currently it costs around $10 per person for a water taxi, with a minimum charge of $20. If you can round up any sort of group, be sure to negotiate. The ride takes about 30 minutes.

Also, there's a passenger launch from the *muellecito* (little dock) in Golfito, which normally leaves twice daily at around 4:30am and noon. Because the schedule sometimes changes, be sure to ask in town (ask for "Makarela") about current departure times. The trip lasts 40 minutes; fare is $2.

If you plan ahead, you can call **Zancudo Boat Tours** (© **506/776-0012**) and arrange for pickup in Golfito. The trip costs $12.50 per person each way, with a $25 minimum.

By Car   If you've got a four-wheel-drive vehicle, you should be able to make it out to Zancudo even in the rainy season, but be sure to ask in Golfito before leaving the paved road. The turnoff for Playas Zancudo and Pavones is at El Rodeo, about 2½ miles (4km) outside of Golfito, on the road in from the Interamerican Highway. Pretty quickly after the turnoff, you'll have to wait and take a small diesel-operated crank ferry (fare is $2 per vehicle). A four-wheel-drive taxi will cost around $30 from Golfito. It takes about 1 hour when the road is in good condition, about 2 hours when it's not. To get here from San José, see "By Car" under "Getting There," above, in section 3 of this chapter, on Golfito.

By Bus   It's possible to get to Zancudo by bus, but I recommend the above waterborne routes. If you insist, though, you can catch the 2pm Pavones bus in front of the gas station "La Bomba" in downtown Golfito and get off in the village of Conte (at around 3:30pm). A Zancudo-bound bus should be there waiting. The whole trip takes about 3 hours; the fare is $3.

DEPARTING   The public launch to Golfito leaves twice daily at 5am and noon from the dock near the school, in the center of Zancudo. You can also arrange a water taxi back to Golfito, but it's best to work with your hotel owner and make a reservation at least 1 day in advance. **Zancudo Boat Tours** (© **506/776-0012**) will take you for $12.50 per person with a two-person minimum. If you're heading to **Pavones** or the **Osa Peninsula** next, **Zancudo Boat Tours** will also take you to these two places. It costs around $15 per person, with a minimum charge of $30. The bus to Golfito leaves Zancudo each morning at 5:30am. You can catch the bus anywhere along the main road.

ORIENTATION   Zancudo is a long, narrow peninsula (sometimes only 100 yd. or so wide) at the mouth of the Río Colorado. On one side is the beach; on the other is a mangrove swamp. There is only one road that runs the length of the beach, and it's along this road, spread out over several kilometers of long, flat beach, that you'll find the hotels I mention here. It's about a 20-minute walk from the public dock near the school to the popular Cabinas Sol y Mar.

WHAT TO SEE & DO (OR HOW NOT TO DO ANYTHING)

The main activity at Zancudo is relaxing, and people take it seriously. There are hammocks at almost every lodge, and if you bring a few good books, you can spend quite a number of hours swinging slowly in the tropical breezes. The beach along Zancudo is great for swimming. It's generally a little calmer on the northern end and gets rougher (good for bodysurfing) as you head south. There are a couple of bars, and even a disco, but visitors are most likely to spend their time just hanging out in restaurants, meeting like-minded folks, or playing board games.

Susan and Andrew Robertson, who run Cabinas Los Cocos, also operate **Zancudo Boat Tours** (© **506/776-0012**), which offers snorkeling trips, trips to the Casa Orquideas Botanical Garden, a trip up the Río Coto to watch birds and wildlife, and others. Tour prices are $40 per person per tour, with discounts available for larger groups.

For fishing, contact **Arena Alta Sportfishing** at Cabinas Sol y Mar (© **506/ 776-0115;** arenaalta@aol.com). You can also check out **Golfito Sportfishing** (© **506/776-0007**), which, despite the name, is located in Zancudo, or **Roy's Zancudo Lodge** (© **506/776-0008**). A full-day of fishing with lunch and beer should cost between $500 and $800 per boat.

ACCOMMODATIONS
EXPENSIVE
Roy's Zancudo Lodge ★★ Primarily a fishing lodge, this comfortable hotel is located at the north end of Zancudo. All of the rooms look out onto a bright green lawn of soft grass and the small swimming pool and Jacuzzi; the beach is just a few steps beyond. The rooms are in several long row buildings on stilts. All have hardwood floors; small, clean bathrooms; ceiling fans; air conditioners; and small verandas. There are four suites that have separate sitting rooms and stocked mini-fridges. The lodge offers many different types of fishing excursions and packages, and boasts more than 40 world-record catches.

Playa Zancudo (A.P. 41, Golfito). © **877/529-6980** in the U.S., or 506/776-0008 in Costa Rica. Fax 506/776-0011. www.royszancudolodge.com. 14 units. $90 per person nonfishing, $395 per person double occupancy for full-day fishing. Rates include all meals, beer, and taxes. Multiday packages available. V. **Amenities:** 1 restaurant (international); 1 bar; pool; Jacuzzi; laundry service. *In room:* A/C.

INEXPENSIVE
Cabinas Sol y Mar ★ *Finds* Although there are only four rooms here, this is the most popular lodging in Zancudo. Two of the rooms are modified geodesic domes with tile floors, verandas, and tin roofs. The bathrooms have unusual showers that feature a tiled platform set amid smooth river rocks and translucent roofs that flood them with light. The other two rooms are larger and newer but aren't as interesting. You'll have to decide between space and character. The hotel's open-air restaurant is one of the most popular places to eat in Zancudo. Seafood dishes are the specialty here (the whole fried fish is good), and prices are very reasonable. There's a small gift shop, and the hotel can provide e-mail and fax services.

Playa Zancudo (A.P. 87, Golfito). © **506/776-0014.** Fax 506/776-0015. www.zancudo.com. 4 units. $31 double. Lower rates in the off-season. V (6% surcharge). **Amenities:** 1 restaurant (international/seafood), 1 bar. *In room:* No phone.

Los Cocos ★ *Finds* If you've ever pondered throwing it all away and setting up shop in a simple house by the beach, these kitchen-equipped cabins might be a good place for a trial run. Set under the trees and only a few yards from the beach, the four cabins are quiet and semi-isolated from one another. Two of them served as banana-plantation housing in a former life, until they were salvaged and moved here. These wood houses have big verandas and bedrooms, and large eat-in kitchens. Bathrooms are down a few steps in back and have hot water. The two newer cabins also offer plenty of space, small kitchenettes, and a private veranda, as well as comfortable sleeping lofts. If you plan to stay in Zancudo for a while, this is a perennially good choice. The owners, Susan and Andrew Robertson, also run Zancudo Boat Tours, so if you want to do some exploring or need a ride into Golfito or Puerto Jiménez, they're the folks to see.

Playa Zancudo (A.P. 88, Golfito). ℂ and fax 506/776-0012. www.loscocos.com. 4 units. $40–$45 double. Lower rates in the off-season and weekly discounts available. No credit cards. **Amenities:** Free use of boogie boards and kayaks. *In-room:* Kitchenette; no phone.

DINING

The most popular restaurant in Zancudo has traditionally been at **Cabinas Sol y Mar** (ℂ 506/776-0014). This small open-air spot is a classic hangout for resident gringos as well as travelers. You might also try the tasty Italian meals at **Restaurante Maconda** (ℂ 506/776-0157). And if you want basic Tico fare and some local company, head to **Soda Suzy** (ℂ 506/776-0107) or **Soda Catherine** (ℂ 506/776-0124).

5 Playa Pavones: A Surfer's Mecca

25 miles (40km) S of Golfito

Touted as the world's longest rideable left break, Pavones is a legendary destination for **surfing** ✹✹. It takes around 6 feet of swell to get this wave cranking, but when the surf's up, you're in for a long, long ride—so long, in fact, that it's much easier to walk back up the beach to where the wave is breaking than to paddle back. The swells are most consistent during the rainy season, but you're likely to find surfers here year-round. Locals tend to be pretty possessive around here (both the wave and local properties have engendered bitter disputes), so don't be surprised if you receive a cool welcome in Pavones.

Other than surfing, nothing much goes on here; however, the beach is quite nice, with some rocky areas that give Pavones a bit more visual appeal than Zancudo. If you're feeling energetic, you can go for a horseback ride or hike into the rain forests that back up this beach town, or stroll south on the beaches that stretch toward Punta Banco and beyond, all the way to the Panamanian border. Various lodges are starting to sprout up, but so far most accommodations are very basic—Pavones is a tiny village with few amenities.

For the past 20 or so years, Pavones has been the site of some fierce and ongoing land battles among locals, foreign investors, and squatters. In 1997 the conflict turned bloody, and one foreign landholder and one squatter were killed in a gun battle. The U.S. State Department quickly issued a traveler's advisory. This has since been rescinded. If you stick to tourism and stay away from wave hogging and real-estate speculation, you should have no problems.

Pavones is so overwhelmingly a surf destination that other tour options are just starting to be offered. Still, this area is surrounded by vast stands of virgin rain forest and has miles of deserted beaches stretching all the way down to Panama. You can hike the forests or the beaches, visit a jungle waterfall, or go for a horseback ride. If you're looking for an organized or guided tour, check in with **Boruca Adventures** (ℂ 506/388-3630; www.borucaadventures.com), which offers a range of day tours.

ESSENTIALS

GETTING THERE & DEPARTING   By Plane   The nearest airport with regularly scheduled flights is in Golfito (see section 3, earlier in this chapter). See "By Car," and "By Bus," below, for how to get to Pavones from the Golfito airport. There is a private strip at Tiskita Lodge (see below). Depending on space, you may be able to arrange transportation to Pavones on one of their charter flights even if you are not staying with them.

By Car If you have a four-wheel-drive vehicle, you should be able to get to Pavones even in the rainy season, but be sure to ask in Golfito before leaving the paved road. The turnoff for Playas Zancudo and Pavones is at El Rodeo, about 2½ miles (4km) outside of Golfito, on the road in from the Interamerican Highway. Pretty quickly after the turnoff, you'll have to wait and take a small diesel-operated crank ferry (the fare is $2 per vehicle). A four-wheel-drive taxi from Golfito to Pavones will cost between $30 and $40. It takes around 2 hours.

By Bus There is one bus (© 506/775-0365) to Pavones from Golfito daily at 3pm. Trip duration is 3 hours; the fare is $2. A bus to Golfito departs Pavones daily at 4am. This is a very remote destination, and the bus schedule is subject to change, so it always pays to check in advance.

ACCOMMODATIONS & DINING

Right in Pavones, there are several very basic lodges catering to itinerant surfers and renting rooms for between $10 and $20 per night for a double room. There are also a couple of *sodas* where you can get Tico meals. The most popular of these is **Esquina del Mar,** which is located right on the beach's edge, in front of the fattest part of the surf break.

EXPENSIVE

Casa Siempre Domingo   This small hillside inn offers up the nicest accommodations right in Pavones. The rooms all feature high ceilings, tile floors, and two double beds (one room has two doubles and a twin). The high beds are custom-made constructions, and they're uncommonly high off the ground. The owner says the design helps capture every bit of breeze from the picture windows. Meals are served on picnic tables in the large interior common space, and there is also a separate sitting room with satellite TV. The nicest feature is the huge deck, with its ocean view. Casa Siempre Domingo is located several hundred yards south and then several hundred more uphill from downtown Pavones.

Pavones (A.P. 91, Golfito). © **506/775-0131.** Fax 506/775-0631. www.casa-domingo.com. 4 units. $120 double. Rate includes breakfast and dinner. No credit cards. *In room:* No phone.

Tiskita Jungle Lodge ★★   This small lodge is nearly on the Panamanian border, with the beach on one side and rain-forest–clad hills behind. Originally an experimental fruit farm growing exotic tropical fruits from around the world, Tiskita has also become a great place to get away from it all. The lodge itself is set on a hill a few hundred yards from the beach and commands a superb view of the ocean. There's a dark-sand swimming beach, tide pools, jungle waterfalls, a farm and forest to explore, and great bird watching (285 species have been sighted). Of the 400 acres here, 250 are in primary rain forest, while the rest are in secondary forest, reforestation projects, orchards, and pastures.

Accommodations are in deluxe rustic cabins with screen walls and verandas. Constructed of local hardwoods, the cabins have a very tropical feel. If you're a bird watcher, you can just sit on the veranda and add to your life list. My favorite cabin is no. 6, which has a great view and ample deck space. Some of the cabins have two or three rooms, making them great for families but less private for couples. Most of the bathrooms are actually outdoors, although private and protected, allowing you to take in the sights and sounds as you shower and shave.

Meals are served family style in the open-air main lodge. While they're not fancy, they're certainly tasty and filling, and you'll be eating plenty of ingredients straight from the gardens.

The lodge is well over 8 hours from San José by car, so most guests take advantage of the package tours, which include air transportation to Tiskita's private landing strip. If you've already driven all the way to Pavones, Tiskita is only 3¾ miles (6km) farther down the road.

Pavones (A.P. 13411-1000, San José). ✆ **506/296-8125.** Fax 506/296-8133. www.tiskita-lodge.co.cr. 14 units. $355 per person for 2 nights; $455 per person for 3 nights. Rates are based on double occupancy and include round-trip air transportation from Golfito or Puerto Jiménez, all meals, guided walks, and taxes. AE, MC, V. **Amenities:** 1 restaurant (international); 1 bar; small outdoor pool; limited water-sports equipment; laundry service. *In room:* No phone.

9

The Caribbean Coast

Costa Rica's Caribbean coast feels a world apart from the rest of the country. The pace is slower, the food is spicier, the tropical heat is more palpable, and the rhythmic lilt of patois and reggae music fill the air.

Although Christopher Columbus landed here in 1502 and christened Costa Rica (Rich Coast), this region has until recently remained terra incognita. The Guápiles Highway between San José and Limón was not completed until 1987. Before that, the only routes down to this region were the famous jungle train (which is no longer in operation) and the narrow, winding road from Turrialba to Siquirres. More than half of this coastline is still inaccessible except by boat or small plane. This inaccessibility has helped preserve large tracts of virgin lowland rain forest, which are now set aside as **Tortuguero National Park** ⊛⊛ and **Barra del Colorado National Wildlife Refuge** ⊛. These two parks, on the northern reaches of this coast, are among Costa Rica's most popular destinations for adventurers and ecotravelers. Of particular interest are the sea turtles that nest along this stretch of coast. Another popular national park in this area is in Cahuita, a beach town. It was set up to preserve 500 acres of coral reef, but its palm-tree-lined beaches are stunning.

So remote was the Caribbean coast from Costa Rica's population centers in the Central Valley that it developed a culture all its own. The original inhabitants of the area included people of the Bribri, Cabécar, and Kéköldi tribes, and these groups maintain their cultures on indigenous reserves in the Talamanca Mountains. In fact, until the 1870s, there were few non-Indians in this area. However, when Minor Keith built the railroad to San José and began planting bananas, he brought in black laborers from Jamaica and other Caribbean islands to lay the track and work the plantations. These workers and their descendants established fishing and farming communities up and down the coast. Today, dreadlocked Rastafarians, reggae music, Creole cooking, and the English-based patois of this Afro-Caribbean culture give this region a distinctly Jamaican flavor. Many visitors find this striking contrast with the Spanish-derived Costa Rican culture fascinating.

Over the past few years, the Caribbean coast has garnered a reputation as being a dangerous, drug-infested zone, rife with crime and danger. Part of this reputation is deserved, as there have been several high-profile crimes; marijuana, cocaine, and crack are readily available in Limón and at the beach towns here. However, part of this reputation is exaggerated. The same crime and drug problems exist in San José and some of the more popular beach destinations on the Pacific coast. Use common sense and take normal precautions, and you should have no problems on the Caribbean coast.

The Caribbean Coast

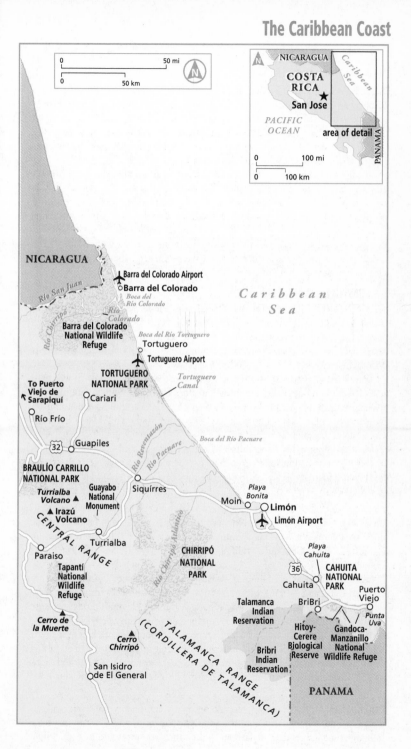

0 50 mi
0 50 km

NICARAGUA

COSTA RICA

San Jose ★

PACIFIC OCEAN

Caribbean Sea

area of detail

PANAMA

0 100 mi
0 100 km

NICARAGUA

Rio San Juan

Rio Chirripó

Barra del Colorado Airport
Barra del Colorado
Boca del Rio Colorado

Rio Colorado

Barra del Colorado National Wildlife Refuge

Boca del Rio Tortuguero

Tortuguero

Tortuguero Airport

Caribbean Sea

TORTUGUERO NATIONAL PARK

Tortuguero Canal

To Puerto Viejo de Sarapiquí

Cariari

Río Frío

32 Guapiles

Rio Reventazón

Rio Pacuare

Boca del Rio Pacuare

BRAULÍO CARRILLO NATIONAL PARK

Turrialba Volcano ▲

Guayabo National Monument

Siquírres

Playa Bonita

Moin   Limón

▲ Irazú Volcano

Limón Airport

CENTRAL RANGE

Turrialba

Paraiso

Tapantí National Wildlife Refuge

Rio Chirripó Atlántico

CHIRRIPÓ NATIONAL PARK

Playa Cahuita

36

CAHUITA NATIONAL PARK

Cahuita

Puerto Viejo

BriBri

▲ Cerro de la Muerte

Cerro Chirripó

TALAMANCA RANGE (CORDILLERA DE TALAMANCA)

Talamanca Indian Reservation

Hitoy-Cerere Biological Reserve

Punta Uva

Gandoca-Manzanillo National Wildlife Refuge

San Isidro de El General

Bribri Indian Reservation

PANAMA

1 Barra del Colorado ⟨★⟩

71 miles (115km) NE of San José

Named for its location at the mouth of the Río Colorado up near the Costa Rica–Nicaragua border, Barra del Colorado is an isolated little town, accessible only by boat or small plane. There are no roads in or to Barra del Colorado. The town itself is a small, ramshackle collection of raised stilt houses, and supports a diverse population of Afro-Caribbean blacks, Miskito Indians, Nicaraguan emigrants, and transient commercial fishermen.

Visitors come here for the fishing. Tarpon and snook fishing are world-class, or you can head farther offshore for some deep-sea action. Barra del Colorado is part of the same ecosystem as Tortuguero National Park (see section 2 of this chapter) and, as in Tortuguero, there's an abundance of wildlife and rainforest fauna in the rivers and canals, which are accessible only by small boat. It's hot and humid here most of the year, and it rains a lot, so while some of the lodges have at times risked offering a "tarpon guarantee," they're generally hesitant to promise anything in terms of the weather.

ESSENTIALS

GETTING THERE & DEPARTING By Plane Sansa (℗ 506/221-9414) has a daily flight departing at 6am for Barra del Colorado from San José's Juan Santamaría International Airport. The return flight to San José leaves Barra del Colorado daily at 6:45am. Flight duration is 35 minutes; the fare is $55 each way.

Travelair (℗ 506/220-3054; reservations@travelair-costarica.com) will have its 6:15am Tortuguero flight stop in Barra del Colorado, with a minimum of two passengers. Flight duration is between 35 and 55 minutes, depending on which stop is first. Fare is $50 each way. The return flight would leave Barra del Colorado at approximately 7:10am.

Most folks come here on multiday fishing packages, and most of the lodges in this area either operate charter flights as part of their package trips or will book you a flight.

By Boat It is also possible to travel to Barra del Colorado by boat from **Puerto Viejo de Sarapiquí** (see chapter 6). Expect to pay $200 to $250 each way for a boat that holds up to 10 people. Check at the public dock in Puerto Viejo de Sarapiquí or ask at the Hotel El Bambú if you're interested. **Río Colorado Lodge** (℗ 800/243-9777 in the U.S. and Canada, or 506/232-4063 in Costa Rica) runs its own launch, the *Tucan,* between Barra del Colorado and Puerto Viejo de Sarapiquí (and sometimes between Barra and Limón), including land transportation between Puerto Viejo de Sarapiquí and San José. If you're staying at the Río Colorado Lodge, be sure to ask about this option (for at least one leg of your trip) when booking; the hotel doesn't discriminate—you can arrange transportation even if you aren't staying there. For $196 per person, you can arrange a pickup in San José, a minibus to the boat, a trip down the river to Barra, overnight accommodations at Río Colorado Lodge, and a return trip the next day, all meals and taxes included.

ORIENTATION The Río Colorado neatly divides the town of Barra del Colorado in two. The airstrip is in the southern half of town, as are most of the lodgings. The lodges that are farther up the canals will meet you in a small boat at the airstrip.

FISHING, FISHING & MORE FISHING

Almost all of the lodges here specialize in fishing and fishing packages. If you don't fish, you might wonder just what in the world you are doing here. Even though there are excellent opportunities for bird watching and touring the jungle waterways, most lodges are still merely paying lip service to ecotourists and would rather see you with a rod and reel.

Fishing takes place year-round. You can do it in the rivers and canals, in the very active river mouth, or offshore. Most anglers come in search of the tarpon, or silver king. **Tarpon** can be caught year-round, both in the river mouth and to a lesser extent in the canals; however, they are much harder to land in July and August—the two rainiest months—probably because the river runs so high and is so full of runoff and debris. **Snook,** an aggressive river fish, peak in April, May, October, and November, while fat snook, or **calba,** run heavy from November through January. Depending on how far out to sea you venture, you might hook up with **barracuda, jack, mackerel (Spanish and king), wahoo, tuna, dorado, marlin,** or **sailfish.** In the rivers and canals, fishermen regularly bring in **mojarra, machaca,** and **guapote** (rainbow bass).

Following recent developments in fishing, anglers have been using traditional rod-and-reel setups, as well as fly rods, to land just about all the fish mentioned above. To fish here, you'll need both salt- ($10) and fresh- ($40) water fishing licenses. The lodges here either include these in your packages or can readily provide the licenses for you.

Nonfishers should see whether their lodge has a good naturalist guide and/or canoes or kayaks for rent or use.

ACCOMMODATIONS & DINING

Almost all of the hotels here specialize in package tours, including all your meals, fishing and tackle, taxes, and usually your transportation and liquor, too, so rates are high. There are no dependable budget hotels here, and Barra remains a remote and difficult destination for independent and budget travelers.

VERY EXPENSIVE

Río Colorado Lodge ✦   This rustic old lodge, one of the country's best-known fishing lodges, was founded and built more than a quarter of a century ago by local legend Archie Fields. The rooms are comfortable but rustic, with some showing the wear and tear of the years. Several have televisions, and two are wheelchair accessible. There's even a "honeymoon suite," which is basically a standard room with a small mirror hung by ropes over the bed. As at Silver King Lodge, the whole complex is tied together by covered walkways.

The nicest feature here is the large covered deck out by the river, where breakfast is served. Dinner is served family style in the second-floor dining room. There's also a large bar (where lunch is served), with satellite TV, pool table, and dartboard, as well as a conference room and well-stocked tackle shop. The most disappointing aspect for me here is the sad little zoo, which houses a wide range of local birds and mammals in small chicken-wire cages.

This lodge runs the *Tucan* riverboat (see "Essentials," above) for those interested in cruising to either Puerto Viejo de Sarapiquí or Limón, as well as several other smaller launches for a variety of tours and outings.

Barra del Colorado (A.P. 5094-1000, San José). ✆ **800/243-9777** in the U.S. and Canada, or 506/232-4063 in Costa Rica. Fax 506/231-5987. www.riocoloradolodge.com. 19 units. $1,797 per person for 7 days/6 nights/4 full days of fishing, including 2 nights' lodging in San José, all meals at the lodge, boat, guide, fuel, licenses, and taxes. Nonfishing guests $100 per person per day.

AE, MC, V. **Amenities:** 1 restaurant (international); 1 bar; Jacuzzi; free coffee all day; free rum and soft drinks during happy hour; laundry service. *In room:* A/C; no phone.

Silver King Lodge ★★ (Finds) This is by far the most upscale lodge in Barra del Colorado. They take their fishing seriously here—there's a large selection of modern boats and equipment, as well as a full tackle shop—but Silver King also emphasizes comfort. The rooms are immense, with two double beds, desk and chair, luggage racks, fishing racks, an overhead fan, and a roomy closet. The floors and walls are all varnished hardwood, and the ceilings are finished in bamboo. The entire complex is built on raised stilts and connected by covered walkways (useful during the frequent downpours).

The meals here are truly exceptional, by far the best buffet-style lodge cooking I've ever had. Each all-you-can-eat meal is anchored with at least two main dishes and a wide variety of appetizers, salads, side dishes, and dessert. You should be eating plenty of fish during your stay—coconut-battered snook nuggets with a pineapple-wasabi dip was just one of the highlights of my culinary indulgences here.

Barra del Colorado (mailing address in the U.S.: Interlink 399, P.O. Box 02-5635, Miami, FL 33102). ℂ **800/847-3474** or 888/682-7766 in the U.S., 506/381-1403 in Costa Rica. Fax 506/381-0849. www.silverkinglodge.com. 10 units. $2,195 per person double occupancy for 4 full days of fishing, air transportation to and from Barra del Colorado from San José, all meals at the lodge, liquor, taxes, and up to 2 nights' lodging in San José; $435 per person per day, including all fishing, meals, liquor, and taxes. AE, MC, V. **Amenities:** 1 restaurant (international); 1 bar and lounge with satellite TV; small outdoor swimming pool and enclosed Jacuzzi; tackle shop; free daily laundry service. *In room:* No phone.

MODERATE

Samay Lagoon Lodge This is the only lodge in the Barra del Colorado area that doesn't specifically cater to hard-core fishermen. You can fish here, but Samay Lagoon Lodge is geared more toward backpackers and ecotourists, and is quite popular with European budget travelers and student groups. The hotel is actually about halfway between Barra and Tortuguero on a small spit of land between its namesake lagoon and the Caribbean Sea. The rooms come in a variety of shapes and sizes. The beds are all just soft foam mattresses, but they have mosquito netting. There is a separate lounge, dining room, and bar where buffet-style meals are served. The lodge has 12 canoes and several boats for tours. If that's too active for you, there are plenty of hammocks for just hanging out.

Barra del Colorado (mailing address in the U.S.: SJO 1650, P.O. Box 025216, Miami, FL 33102). ℂ **506/384-7047.** Fax 506/383-6370. www.samay.com. 22 units. $278 per person for 3 days/ 2 nights, including ground and boat transportation to and from San José, meals, taxes, and several tours. AE, MC, V. **Amenities:** 1 restaurant (international); 1 bar; laundry service. *In room:* No phone.

2 Tortuguero National Park ★★

155 miles (250km) NE of San José; 49 miles (79km) N of Limón

"Tortuguero" comes from the Spanish name for the giant sea turtles (*tortugas*) that nest on the beaches of this region every year from early March to mid-October. The chance to see this nesting attracts many people to this remote region, but just as many come to explore the intricate network of jungle canals that serve as the region's main transportation arteries. This stretch of coast is connected to Limón, the Caribbean coast's only port city, by a series of rivers and canals that parallel the sea, often running only about 100 yards or so from the beach. This aquatic highway is lined for most of its length with a dense rain forest that is home to howler and spider monkeys, three-toed sloths, toucans, and great green macaws. A trip up the canals is a bit like cruising the Amazon, but on a much smaller scale.

Very important: Consider the climate in this region. More than 200 inches of rain fall annually, so you can expect a downpour at any time of the year. Most of the lodges in the area will provide you with sturdy rain gear (including ponchos and rubber boots), but it can't hurt to carry your own.

Independent travel is difficult in this area. You'll have to rely on your lodge for boat transportation through the canals, and unless you stay at one of the accommodations on the beach side of the canal, you won't even be able to walk into town. At most of the lodges around Tortuguero, almost everything (bus rides to and from, boat trips through the canals, even family-style meals) is done in groups. Depending on a variety of factors, this group feeling can be intimate and rewarding, or overwhelming and impersonal.

ESSENTIALS

GETTING THERE & DEPARTING By Plane Travelair (② **506/220-3054;** reservations@travelair-costarica.com) has one flight departing daily at 6:15am for Tortuguero from Tobías Bolaños International Airport in Pavas. The flight takes 35 minutes; the fare is $50 each way. The return flight leaves Tortuguero daily at 7:10am for San José.

Sansa (② **506/221-9414;** reservations@flysansa.com) has a daily flight departing at 6am for Tortuguero from San José's Juan Santamaría International Airport. Flight duration is 35 minutes; the fare is $55 each way. The return flight leaves Tortuguero daily at 6:45am for San José.

It always pays to check with both Sansa and Travelair. Additional flights are often added during the high season, and departure times can vary according to weather or the whim of the airline.

In addition, many lodges in this area operate charter flights as part of their package trips.

By Car It is not possible to drive to Tortuguero. If you have a car, your best bet is to either leave it in San José and take an organized tour, or drive it to Limón or Moín, find a secure hotel or public parking lot, and then follow the directions for arriving by boat below.

In 1996, local citizens and certain municipal officials began work on a road to Tortuguero, via the village of Cariari. A large swath was cut to within almost 0.6 miles (1km) of the village, with several kilometers of the construction passing through protected parklands. When the project was publicly discovered, it caused a minor local and regional scandal. Work was halted, and several parties are under indictment, but much of the damage is done. There are actually road signs declaring TORTUGUERO at the turnoffs for both Cariari and Caño Blanco Marina. Ignore them unless you have prior arrangements to take a boat out of one of these secondary embarkation points. There is no reliable road route to Tortuguero and probably won't be for some time.

By Boat Flying to Tortuguero is convenient if you don't have much time, but a boat trip through the canals and rivers of this region is often the highlight of any visit to Tortuguero. However, be forewarned: While this trip can be stunning and exciting, it can also be uncomfortable. You'll first have to ride by bus or minivan from San José to Moín or one of the other nearby embarkation points; then it's 3 hours on a boat, usually with hard wooden benches or plastic seats. All of the more expensive lodges listed offer their own bus and boat transportation packages, which include the boat ride through the canals. However, if you're coming here on the cheap and plan to stay at one of the less-expensive lodges or at a budget cabina in Tortuguero, you will have to arrange your own transportation. In this case, you have a few options.

The most popular method is to get yourself first to Limón (see section 3, later in this chapter) and then to the public docks in **Moín,** just north of Limón, and try to find a boat on your own. You can reach Limón easily by public bus from San José (see "Getting There & Departing" in the Limón section). If you're coming by car, make sure you drive all the way to Limón or Moín, unless you have prior arrangements out of Cariari or Caño Blanco Marina. *Ignore the signs for Tortuguero* that turn off the highway near Guápiles and Siquirres. These will just take you to secondary and infrequent embarkation points for boats to Tortuguero Village.

To get to the docks from Limón, there's a bus that runs from a stop in front of the prominent Radio Casino building, 1 block north of Limón's central market; it costs 45¢. Otherwise, you can take a taxi for around $5 (for up to four people). Once at the docks, you should be able to negotiate a fare of between $40 and $70, depending on how many people you can round up to go with you. These boats tend to depart between 8 and 10am every morning. Usually, the fare you pay covers the return trip as well, and you can arrange with the captain to take you back when you're ready to leave. Search out **Modesto Watson** (© 506/ **226-0986;** www.tortuguerocanals.com; fvwatson@racsa.co.cr), who owns a boat named after his wife, Francesca. The couple offers overnight and multiday packages to Tortuguero. They've been doing this for a long time and are wonderful guides. The trip from **Moín** to Tortuguero takes between 3 and 4 hours. **Laura's Tropical Tours** (© **506/758-2410**) also offers boat tours to Tortuguero from Moín.

As I mentioned above, it is possible to get to Tortuguero by bus and boat from Cariari. This is the cheapest and most adventurous means of reaching Tortuguero from San José, but it's also more work. There's only one boat per day from Cariari to Tortuguero, and if you miss it or it doesn't run that day, you'll have to spend the night at some very basic cabinas in this small town, or head back toward Guápiles. To take this route, begin by catching the 9am direct bus to Cariari from the **Gran Terminal del Caribe,** on Calle Central, 1 block north of Avenida 11 (© **506/222-0610**). The fare is $2. This bus will actually drop you off in a new terminal in Cariari, from which you'll have to walk 5 blocks north to catch the noon bus to "La Geest Casa Verde." The fare is $1.75. Take this bus to the very end of the line. Tell the driver you are going to Tortuguero. A boat should be waiting to meet the bus at the dock at the edge of the river at around 1:30pm. The fare to Tortuguero is $10. This boat leaves Tortuguero every morning at 7am and makes all the return bus connections. If you have doubts, or want to check on the current state of this route, try to contact Daryl Loth in Tortuguero (© **506/392-3201;** safari@racsa.co.cr).

Finally, it's also possible, albeit expensive, to travel to Tortuguero by boat from **Puerto Viejo de Sarapiquí** (see chapter 6). Expect to pay $250 to $350 each way for a boat that holds up to 10 people. Check at the public dock in Puerto Viejo de Sarapiquí or ask at the Hotel El Bambú if you're interested. The ride usually takes about 3 to 4 hours and the boats tend to leave in the morning.

ORIENTATION Tortuguero is one of the most remote locations in Costa Rica. There are no roads into this area and no cars in the village, so all transportation is by boat or foot. Most of the lodges are spread out over several kilometers to the north of the village of Tortuguero on either side of the main canal; the small airstrip is at the north end of the beachside spit of land. At the far northern end of the main canal you'll see the **Cerro de Tortuguero** (Turtle Hill), which, at some 350 feet, towers over the area. The hike to the top of this hill is a popular half-day tour and offers some good views of the Tortuguero canals and village, as well as the Caribbean Sea.

Tortuguero Village is a tiny collection of houses connected by footpaths. The village is spread out on a thin spit of land, bordered on one side by the Caribbean Sea and on the other by the main canal. At most points, it's less than 300 meters (over 300 yd.) wide. In the center of the village you'll find a small children's playground and a soccer field, as well as a kiosk that has information on the cultural and natural history of this area. There's also a new information center in town across from the Catholic church. This is a good place to go if you're desperate for an Internet connection and e-mail services.

If you stay at a hotel on the ocean side of the canal, you'll be able to walk into and explore the village at your leisure; if you're across the canal, you'll be dependent on the lodge's boat transportation. However, some of the lodges across the canal have their own network of jungle trails that may appeal to naturalists.

EXPLORING THE NATIONAL PARK

According to existing records, sea turtles have frequented Tortuguero National Park since at least 1592, largely due to its extreme isolation. Over the years, turtles were captured and their eggs harvested by local settlers; by the 1950s, this practice became so widespread that the turtles faced extinction. Regulations controlling this mini-industry were passed in 1963, and in 1970, Tortuguero National Park was established.

Today, four different species of sea turtles nest here: the green turtle, the hawksbill, the loggerhead, and the giant leatherback. The prime nesting period is from **July to mid-October** (with Aug and Sept being the peak months). The park's beaches are excellent places to watch sea turtles nest, especially at night. Appealingly long and deserted, however, the beaches are not appropriate for swimming. The surf is usually very rough, and the river mouths have a nasty habit of attracting sharks that feed on the turtle hatchlings and many fish that live here.

Green turtles are perhaps the most common turtle found in Tortuguero, so you're more likely to see one of them than any other species if you visit during the prime nesting season. **Loggerheads** are very rare, so don't be disappointed if you don't see one. The **giant leatherback** is perhaps the most spectacular sea turtle to watch laying eggs. The largest of all turtle species, the leatherback can

---

Tips **Turtle Tips**

- Visitors to the beach at night must be accompanied by a licensed guide. Tours generally last between 2 and 4 hours.
- Sometimes you must walk quite a bit to encounter a nesting turtle. Wear sneakers or walking shoes, rather than sandals. The beach is very dark at night, and it's easy to trip or step on driftwood or other detritus.
- Wear dark clothes. White T-shirts are not permitted.
- Flashlights, cameras, and video cameras are prohibited on turtle tours.
- Smoking is prohibited on the beach at night.

grow to 6½ feet long and weigh well over 1,000 pounds. It nests from early March to mid-April, predominantly in the southern part of the park.

You can also explore the park's rain forest, either by foot or by boat, and look for some of the incredible varieties of wildlife that live here: jaguars, anteaters, howler monkeys, collared and white-lipped peccaries, some 350 species of birds, and countless butterflies, among others. Boat tours are far and away the most popular way to visit this park, although there is one frequently very muddy trail here that starts at the park entrance and runs for about 2km through the coastal rain forest and along the beach.

ENTRY POINT, FEES & REGULATIONS   The Tortuguero National Park entrance and ranger station are at the south end of Tortuguero Village. Admission to the park is $6. A 4-day pass can be purchased for $10. However, there are some caveats: Most people visit Tortuguero as part of a package tour. Be sure to confirm whether the park entrance is included in the price. Moreover, only certain canals and trails leaving from the park station are actually within the park. Many hotels and private guides take their tours to a series of canals that border the park, and are very similar in terms of flora and fauna, but don't require a park entrance. When the turtles are nesting, you will have to arrange a night tour in advance either with your hotel or one of the private guides working in town. These guided tours generally run between $10 and $15. Flashlights and flash cameras are not permitted on the beach at night, since the lights discourage the turtles from nesting.

ORGANIZED TOURS   Most visitors come to Tortuguero on an organized tour. All of the lodges listed below, with the exception of the most budget accommodations in Tortuguero Village, offer complete package tours that include various hikes and night tours, and this is generally the best way to visit the area.

In addition, there are several San José–based tour companies that offer budget 2-day/1-night excursions to Tortuguero, which include transportation, all meals, and limited tours around the region. Prices for these trips range between $100 and $200 per person, and—depending on price—guests are lodged either in one of the basic hotels in Tortuguero Village or one of the nicer lodges listed below. There are even 1-day trips that allow time for a quick tour of the canals and lunch in Tortuguero. These trips are good for travelers who like to be able to say, "Been there, done that," and generally run between $80 and $95 per person. Companies offering these excursions include **Ecole Travel** (© **506/223-2240;** ecolecr@racsa.co.cr), **Caño Blanco Marina** (© **506/256-9444**), and **Arenas Tours** (© **506/221-6839**). However, if you really want to experience Tortuguero, I recommend staying for at least 2 nights and booking directly with one of the lodges.

BOAT CANAL TOURS   Aside from watching the turtles nest, the unique thing to do in Tortuguero is tour the canals by boat, keeping your eye out for tropical birds and native wildlife. Most of the lodges can arrange a canal tour for you, but you can also arrange a tour through one of the operators in Tortuguero Village. I recommend **Ernesto Castillo,** who can be reached through Cabinas Sabina or by just standing anywhere in the village and shouting his name—Tortuguero's that small. **Daryl Loth** (© **506/392-3201;** safari@racsa.co.cr), who runs a small B&B in the center of the village, and **Albert Taylor,** who can be reached through Cabinas Miss Junie (© **506/710-0523**), are also very good. If none of these guides is available, ask for a recommendation at the **Jungle**

Shop (© 506/391-3483) or at the **Caribbean Conservation Corporation's Museum** (© 506/710-0547). Most guides charge between $10 and $15 per person for a tour of the canals. If you travel through the park, you'll also have to pay the park entrance fee ($6 per person).

EXPLORING THE VILLAGE

The most popular attraction in town is the small **Caribbean Conservation Corporation's Visitors' Center and Museum** (© 506/710-0547; ccc@cccturtle.org). While the museum has information and exhibits on a whole range of native flora and fauna, its primary focus is on the life and natural history of the sea turtles. Most visits to the museum include a short, informative video on the turtles. There's a small gift shop here, and all the proceeds go toward conservation and turtle protection. The museum is open daily from 10am to noon and 2 to 5:30pm. On Sunday the museum closes a half hour earlier, at 5pm. There's a $1 admission charge, but more-generous donations are encouraged.

In the village, you can also rent dugout canoes, known in Costa Rica as *cayucos* or *pangas*. Be careful before renting and taking off in one of these; they tend to be heavy, slow, and hard to maneuver, and you may be getting more than you bargained for.

There are a couple of souvenir shops on the main footpath near the center of the village. The **Jungle Shop** (© 506/391-3483) donates 10% of its profits to local schools and is open from 9am to 5pm. **Paraiso Tropical Gift Shop** (© 506/710-0323) is open from 8:30am to 6pm.

ACCOMMODATIONS & DINING

Although the room rates below appear quite high, keep in mind that they usually include round-trip transportation from San José (which amounts to approximately $100–$150 per person), all meals, and taxes. When broken down into nightly room rates, most of the lodges are really only charging between $50 and $90 for a double room.

Most visitors take all their meals, as part of a package, at their hotel. There are a couple of simple *sodas* and local restaurants in town. The best of these is **La Caribeña** (no phone). There's also a nice little coffee shop, **The Vine** (© 506/391-3483), just across from The Jungle Shop.

EXPENSIVE

Tortuga Lodge ★★ *Finds*   This is Costa Rica Expeditions' oldest hotel, but thanks to several years of renovations and additions, it's not just aged well, but it has improved over time. The nicest feature here is the long multilevel deck, where you can sit and dine, sip a cool tropical drink, or just take in the view as the water laps against the docks at your feet. There's also a small pool, built by the water's edge and designed to create the illusion that it blends into Tortuguero's main canal. All the rooms are considered standards, with one double and one single bed, ceiling fans, and a comfortable private bathroom. I'd opt for the second-floor rooms, which feature varnished wood walls and floors and come with a small, covered veranda.

Despite the high rates (considerably higher than at other area lodgings), the rooms are not substantially larger or more luxurious than those at the Mawamba, Laguna, or Pachira Lodges; what you're paying for is all the years of experience that Costa Rica Expeditions brings to Tortuguero. Service here is generally quite good, as are the family-style meals. There are several acres of forest behind the lodge, and a few kilometers of trails wind their way through the trees. This is a great place to look for howler monkeys and colorful poison-arrow frogs.

Tortuguero (mailing address in the U.S.: SJO 235, P.O. Box 025216, Miami, FL 33102). © **506/257-0766.** Fax 506/257-1665. www.costaricaexpeditions.com. 24 units. $578 double for 2 days/1 night; $758 double for 3 days/2 nights. Rates include round-trip transportation (bus and boat one-way, charter flight the other) from San José, tours, taxes, and 3 meals daily. AE, MC, V. **Amenities:** 1 restaurant (international); 1 bar; small pool; nature trails; laundry service. *In room:* No phone.

MODERATE

Laguna Lodge ⚲   This small lodge is a good choice, located 1¼ miles (2km) north of Tortuguero Village, on the ocean side of the main canal (which allows you to walk along the beach and into town, at your leisure). The rooms are all spacious and attractive. Most have wood walls, waxed hardwood floors, and tiled bathrooms with screened upper walls to let in air and light. The newest rooms are made of concrete and stucco, but are similarly spacious and well appointed. Each room also has a little shared veranda.

The large dining room, where basic family-style meals are served, is located on a free-form deck that extends out over the Tortuguero Canal. Another covered deck, also over the water, is strung with hammocks for lazing away the afternoons. Several covered palapa huts have also been built among the flowering ginger and hibiscus and strung with hammocks. All the standard Tortuguero tours are available.

Tortuguero (A.P. 173-2015, San José). © **506/225-3740.** Fax 506/283-8031. www.lagunalodgetortuguero.com. 52 units. $374 double for 2 days/1 night; $468 double for 3 days/2 nights. Rates include round-trip transportation from San José, tours, taxes, and 3 meals daily. AE, DC, MC, V. **Amenities:** 1 restaurant (Costa Rican/international); 2 bars; large and inviting free-form pool; butterfly garden; frog garden; laundry service. *In room:* No phone.

Mawamba Lodge ⚲   Located about 500 meters (about 545 yd.) north of Tortuguero Village on the ocean side of the canal, Mawamba is quite similar to Laguna Lodge (in fact, they are owned by brothers), but slightly larger and with more of an impersonal feel. Rooms have varnished wood floors, twin beds, hot-water showers, ceiling fans, and verandas with rocking chairs. The gardens are lush and overgrown with flowering ginger, heliconia, and hibiscus. There are plenty of hammocks around for anyone who wants to kick back, and a beach volleyball court for those who don't.

The family-style meals here are above average for Tortuguero, and might include pasta with shrimp or chicken in béchamel sauce. Plus there's usually good, fresh bread. Tours included in the rates include a 4-hour boat ride through the canals and a guided forest hike. There's a small gift shop on the premises and nightly lectures and slide shows that focus on the natural history of this area.

Tortuguero (A.P. 10980-1000, San José). © **506/223-7490** or 506/223-2421. Fax 506/222-5463. www.grupomawamba.com. 54 units. $402 double for 2 days/1 night; $504 double for 3 days/2 nights. Rates include round-trip transportation from San José, 3 meals daily, taxes, and some tours. AE, MC, V. **Amenities:** 2 restaurants (international); 1 bar; freeform pool; laundry service. *In room:* No phone.

Pachira Lodge ⚲   The rooms in this new lodge are in a series of buildings perched on stilts and connected by covered walkways in a dense section of secondary forest set in a little bit from the main canal. Each room is spacious and clean, with varnished wood floors, painted wood walls, two double beds, ceiling fans, and plenty of cross-ventilation. The covered walkways come in handy when it rains. Meals are served family style in a large, screened-in dining room. Bilingual guides and all the major tour options are available.

Tortuguero (A.P. 1818-1002, San José). ℂ **506/256-7080.** Fax 506/223-1119. www.pachiralodge. com. paccira@racsa.co.cr. 40 units. $352 double for 2 days/1 night; $478 double for 3 days/ 2 nights. Rates include round-trip transportation from San José, 3 meals daily, taxes, and tours. AE, MC, V. **Amenities:** 1 restaurant (Costa Rican/international); 1 bar; laundry service. *In room:* No phone.

INEXPENSIVE

There are several basic lodges in the village of Tortuguero, offering budget lodgings for between $7 and $15 per person. **Cabinas Miss Junie** (ℂ **506/710-0523**) and **Cabinas Sabinas** (no phone) are the traditional favorites, although the best of this batch is the new **Cabinas Tortuguero** (no phone), located at the south end of the village on the way to the national-park entrance. If you choose one of these, you'll likely be taking your meals at one of the several small *sodas* in town and will have to make your own arrangements for touring the canals or renting a canoe. One new option I expect to be open by press time is **Casa Marbella,** a small bed-and-breakfast run by longtime resident and guide Daryl Loth (ℂ **506/392-3201;** www.safari.jumptravel.com).

El Manati Lodge *Value*   For budget travelers looking for some of the trappings of an ecolodge experience, this is a good choice. El Manati is located across the canal from Laguna Lodge, about 1¼ miles (2km) north of Tortuguero Village. Most of the rooms are fairly basic, with cement floors and floor fans, but they're kept clean and painted. There's even hot water. Some of the cabins have several rooms, with a variety of sleeping arrangements, including bunk beds. These are a good deal for families. The owners live here and have slowly built the lodge themselves over the years; they're also very active in a local project to protect the manatees that inhabit these waters. Canal tours and turtle-watching walks can be arranged, and there are canoes you can rent for $5 per hour. The honor bar is housed in a separate screened-in building and features a dartboard and Ping-Pong table.

Tortuguero, Limón. ℂ and fax **506/383-0330.** 8 units. $33 double. Rates include breakfast. No credit cards. **Amenities:** 1 restaurant, 1 bar. *In room:* No phone.

3 Limón: Gateway to Tortuguero National Park & Southern Coastal Beaches

99 miles (160km) E of San José; 34 miles (55km) N of Puerto Viejo

It was just offshore from present-day Limón, in the lee of Isla Uvita, that Christopher Columbus is believed to have anchored in 1502, on his fourth and last voyage to the New World. He felt that this was potentially a very rich land and named it Costa Rica (Rich Coast), but it never quite lived up to his expectations.

The spot where he anchored, however, has proved over the centuries to be the best port on Costa Rica's Caribbean coast, so his judgment wasn't all bad. It was from here that the first bananas were shipped to North America in the late 19th century. Today, Limón is primarily a rough-and-tumble port city that ships millions of pounds of bananas northward every year and accepts a fair share of the country's ocean-borne imports and a modest number of cruise-ship callings.

Limón is not generally considered a tourist destination, and I don't recommend it except during Carnaval, or as a brief logistical stop on your way to someplace else. Most travelers use it primarily as a gateway to Tortuguero to the north or the beaches of Cahuita and Puerto Viejo to the south.

A Fall Festival

The biggest event of the year in Limón, and one of the liveliest festivals in Costa Rica, is the annual **Carnaval,** which is held for a week around Columbus Day (Oct 12). For a week, languid Limón shifts into high gear for a nonstop bacchanal orchestrated to the beat of reggae, soca, and calypso music. During the revelries, residents don costumes and take to the streets in a dazzling parade of color. In recent years, the central government has tried to rein in Carnaval, citing health and safety concerns. The effort has somewhat dampened the party, but the city still gets pretty boisterous. If you want to experience Carnaval, make your reservations early, as hotels fill up fast (this advice goes for the entire coast).

If you do spend some time in Limón, you can take a seat in Parque Vargas along the seawall and watch the city's citizens go about their business. There are even some sloths living in the trees here—maybe you'll spot them. Take a walk around town if you're interested in architecture. When banana shipments built this port, many local merchants erected elaborately decorated buildings, several of which have survived the city's many earthquakes. There's a certain charm in the town's fallen grace, drooping balconies, rotting woodwork, and chipped paint. Just be careful, particularly after dark and outside of the city center— Limón has earned a reputation for frequent muggings and robberies.

If you want to get in some beach time while you're in Limón, hop in a taxi or a local bus and head north a few kilometers to **Playa Bonita,** a small public beach. Although the water isn't very clean and is usually too rough for swimming, the setting is much more attractive than downtown. This beach is popular with surfers.

ESSENTIALS

GETTING THERE & DEPARTING   By Car   The Guápiles Highway heads north out of San José on Calle 3 before turning east and passing close to Barva Volcano and through the rain forests of Braulio Carrillo National Park, en route to Limón. The drive takes about 2½ hours, and is spectacularly beautiful, especially when it's not raining or misty. Alternately, you can take the old highway, which is also scenic, though much slower. This highway heads east out of San José on Avenida Central and passes through San Pedro before reaching Cartago. From Cartago on, the road is narrow and winding and passes through Paraiso and Turrialba before descending out of the mountains to Siquirres, where the old highway meets the new. This route will take you around 4 hours, more or less, to get to Limón.

By Bus   Buses (ⓒ **506/221-2596**) leave San José roughly every half hour daily, between 5am and 7pm, from the new Caribbean bus terminal (Gran Terminal del Caribe) on Calle Central, 1 block north of Avenida 11. Trip duration is 2½ to 3 hours. The buses are either direct or local (*corriente*), and they don't alternate in any particularly predictable fashion. The local buses are generally older and less comfortable and stop en route to pick up passengers from the roadside. I highly recommend taking a direct bus if possible. The fare is $2.50 for the local, $3.50 for the direct.

Buses leave Limón for San José roughly every half hour between 5am and 7:30pm and similarly alternate between local and direct. The bus stop is 1 block east and half a block south of the municipal market. Buses to **Cahuita** and

Puerto Viejo leave daily at 5, 7, 8, and 10am, and 1, 4, and 6pm. The Cahuita/ Puerto Viejo bus stop is on Avenida 4, near the Radio Casino building, 1 block north of the municipal market. Buses to **Punta Uva** and **Manzanillo,** both of which are south of Puerto Viejo, leave Limón daily at 6am and 2:30 and 6pm, from the same block.

ORIENTATION   Nearly all addresses in Limón are measured from the central market, which is aptly located smack-dab in the center of town, or from Parque Vargas, which is at the east end of town fronting the sea. The stop for buses out to Moín and Playa Bonita is located in front of the prominent Radio Casino building, just to the north of the Cahuita/Puerto Viejo bus stop.

ACCOMMODATIONS & DINING

Two of the hotels listed here are actually a few kilometers out of town toward Playa Bonita, and I recommend them over the options you'll find in Limón proper.

Cabinas Cocori   Located on the water just before you reach Playa Bonita, this hotel commands a fine view of the cove, a small beach, and crashing surf. The grounds are in need of landscaping, and the rooms are a bit run-down. A pair of two-story, peach-colored buildings house the rooms, most of which are small and basic. Ten rooms have air-conditioning, and a few more even have televisions. Those on the second floor have better sea breezes and views. A long veranda runs along both floors. The restaurant serves basic Tico fare, but has a great setting overlooking the sea.

Playa Bonita, Limón. ℂ **506/798-1670.** Fax 506/758-2930. 22 units. $40–$45 double. Rates include breakfast. AE, MC, V. **Amenities:** 1 restaurant (Costa Rican). *In room:* No phone.

Hotel Acon   This older in-town choice is a decent bet in Limón proper, if you can't get a room at the Park. The rooms are clean, each with two twin beds with bright yellow bedspreads. The architecture and decor could best be described as art-deco decay. The restaurant on the first floor just off the lobby is a cool, dark haven on steamy afternoons. The second-floor disco here is open every night and particularly lively on weekends, so if your room is anywhere near it, don't count on a quiet night.

Avenida 3 and Calle 3 (A.P. 7300-528), Limón. ℂ **506/758-1010.** Fax 506/758-2924. 39 units. $25 double, $30 triple. AE, MC, V. **Amenities:** 1 restaurant (Costa Rican/Chinese), 1 bar/disco. *In room:* A/C, TV.

Hotel Maribu Caribe   Located on top of a hill overlooking the Caribbean and built to resemble an Indian village, the Maribu Caribe is a pleasant, if not overly luxurious, choice if you're looking to spend some time close to Limón. The hotel is popular with Tico families from San José because it's easy to get to for weekend trips. The guest rooms are in circular bungalows with white-tile floors and varnished wood ceilings. The furnishings are comfortable but a bit old.

The hotel's restaurant has the best view in or around Limón. It's built out over the edge of a steep hill, with tide pools and the ocean below. In addition to the formal dining room, there are tables outside on a curving veranda that make the most of the view. The Maribu Caribe can help you with tour arrangements and has a gift shop.

Playa Bonita, Limón (mailing address: A.P. 623-7300, San José). ℂ **506/758-4543,** 506/758-4010, or 506/253-1838 in San José. Fax 506/758-3541, or 506/234-0193 in San José. 52 units. $78 double; $88 triple. AE, DC, MC, V. **Amenities:** 1 restaurant (international); 1 bar; attractive outdoor pool; laundry service. *In room:* A/C.

Park Hotel   You can't miss this pastel peach building facing the ocean, across the street from the fire station. It's certainly seen better years, but in Limón there aren't too many choices, so I often end up staying here. This place is periodically painted (last year it was pink) and spruced up, but the climate and sea breezes really take their toll. Still, part of what makes this hotel memorable is the aging tropical ambiance. Try to see the room you'll be getting before putting down any money. Ask for a room on the ocean side of the hotel, because these are brighter, quieter, and cooler than those that face the fire station, although they're also slightly more expensive. The suites are generally kept in much better condition and have private ocean-view balconies and larger bathrooms with tubs. The large, sunny dining room off the lobby serves standard Tico fare at very reasonable prices.

Avenida 3, between Calles 1 and 3 (A.P. 35), Limón. ✆ **506/758-3476** or 506/798-0555. Fax 506/758-4364. 32 units. $35 double; $45 triple; $55 suite. AE, MC, V. **Amenities:** 1 restaurant (Costa Rican/international). *In room:* A/C, TV.

EN ROUTE SOUTH

Staying at one of the places below is a great way to combine some quiet beach time on the Caribbean coast with a more active ecolodge or bird-watching experience into one compact itinerary.

Aviarios del Caribe ✦   If you prefer **bird watching** ✦✦ to beaching, this B&B, located on the edge of a small river delta, is the place to stay on this section of the Caribbean coast. The lodge's owners have spotted more than 315 species within the immediate area. You can work on your life list from the lawns, the second-floor open-air dining room and lounge, or a canoe paddling around the nearby canals. This small hotel is surrounded by a private wildlife sanctuary, comprised mainly of the estuary, mangroves, and an uninhabited island, but it also includes several well-groomed forest trails adjacent to the main building.

The guest rooms are all large and comfortable and have fans, tile floors, potted plants, fresh flowers, and modern bathroom fixtures. Some rooms even have king-size beds.

In the lounge area you'll find an interesting collection of mounted insects, as well as terrariums that house live poison-arrow frogs. You'll also certainly make friends with Buttercup, the resident three-toed sloth. In fact, you're guaranteed of seeing sloths, as they run a sloth rehabilitation and breeding program here. Only breakfast is served, so you'll have to take your other meals in Cahuita or at a roadside *soda* along the way.

18½ miles (30km) south of Limón, or 5½ miles (9km) north of Cahuita, just off the main rd. (A.P. 569-7300, Limón). ✆ and fax **506/382-1335.** http://members.nbci.com/aviarios. 6 units. $70–$90 double. Rates include full breakfast. AE, MC, V. *In room:* No phone.

Selva Bananito Lodge ✦✦ (Finds)   This remote nature lodge is a welcome addition to the Caribbean coast, allowing you to combine some rain-forest adventuring with some serious beach time in Cahuita or Puerto Viejo. The individual raised-stilt cabins are all spacious and comfortable, with an abundance of varnished woodwork. Inside you'll find two double beds, a desk and chair, and some fresh flowers, as well as a large private bathroom. Outside, there's a wraparound veranda with a hammock and some chairs. It all adds up to what I call rustic luxury. Half the cabins have views of the Bananito River and a small valley; the other half have views of the Matama Mountains, part of the Talamanca mountain range.

There are no electric lights at Selva Bananito, but each evening as you dine by candlelight, your cabin's oil lamps are lit for you. Hot water is provided by solar panels. Tasty family-style meals are served in the large, open rancho, which is also a great spot for morning bird watching. There's a wide range of tours and activities, including rain-forest hikes and horseback rides in the jungle, tree climbing, self-guided trail hikes, and even the opportunity to rappel down the face of a jungle waterfall. The owners are very involved in conservation efforts in this area, and approximately two-thirds of the 2,100 acres here are primary forest managed as a private reserve. You'll need a four-wheel-drive vehicle to reach the lodge, or arrange pickup in Bananito beforehand. You can also arrange to be picked up in San José.

Bananito (mailing address in the U.S.: 850 Juniper Ave., Kellogg, IA 50135). ℂ and fax **506/253-8118**, or 506/284-4278. www.selvabananito.com. 11 units. $200 double. Rates include 3 meals daily and all taxes. Lower rates in the off-season. No credit cards. **Amenities:** 1 restaurant (international); laundry service. *In room:* No phone.

4 Cahuita ⟨★⟩

124 miles (200km) E of San José; 26 miles (42km) S of Limón; 8 miles (13km) N of Puerto Viejo

Cahuita is a sleepy Caribbean beach village and the first "major" tourist destination you'll reach heading south out of Limón. The boom going on in Puerto Viejo and the beaches south of Puerto Viejo has in many ways passed Cahuita by. Any way you slice it, Cahuita is one of the most laid-back villages in Costa Rica. The few dirt and gravel streets here are host to a languid parade of pedestrian traffic, parted occasionally by a bicycle, car, or bus. After a short time, you'll find yourself slipping into the heat-induced torpor that affects anyone who ends up here.

The village traces its roots to Afro-Caribbean fishermen and laborers who settled in this region in the mid-1800s, and today the population is still primarily English-speaking blacks whose culture and language set them apart from other Costa Ricans.

People come to Cahuita for its miles of pristine beaches, which stretch both north and south from town. The southern beaches, the forest behind them, and the coral reef offshore (one of just a handful in Costa Rica) are all part of **Cahuita National Park** ⟨★⟩. Silt and pesticides washing down from nearby banana plantations have taken a heavy toll on the coral reefs, so don't expect the snorkeling to be world-class. But on a calm day, it can be pretty good, and the beaches are idyllic every day. It can rain almost any time of year here, but the most dependably dry season is in September and October.

In recent years, the influx of visitors and an apparently robust drug trade have changed the face and feel of this quiet little town. A few notorious crimes against tourists and businesses have had a serious impact here. Local citizens and business owners have responded to the problem and even organized civilian patrols to monitor the park paths during the day (and unlit streets at night). Still, it's highly recommended that you take every possible precaution against robbery and avoid walking alone outside of downtown at night.

ESSENTIALS

GETTING THERE & DEPARTING   By Car   Follow the directions above for getting to Limón, and as you enter Limón, about 500 meters (about 545 yd.) from the busiest section of downtown, watch for a paved road to the right, just before the railroad tracks. Take this road south to Cahuita, passing the airstrip and the beach on your left as you leave Limón. Alternatively, there's a turnoff with signs for Sixaola and La Bomba several miles before Limón. This winding shortcut skirts the city and puts you on the coastal road several miles south of town. I recommend this latter route.

By Bus   Express buses (© 506/257-8129) leave San José daily at 6 and 10am, and 1:30 and 3:30pm from the new Caribbean bus terminal (Gran Terminal del Caribe) on Calle Central, 1 block north of Avenida 11. The trip's duration is 4 hours; fare is $5. During peak periods, extra buses are often added. However, it's wise to check, as this bus line (**Mepe**) is one of the most fickle.

Alternatively, you can catch a bus to **Limón** (see section 3, earlier in this chapter) and then transfer to a Cahuita- or Puerto Viejo–bound bus in Limón. These latter buses leave daily at 5, 8, and 10am, and 1, 4, and 6pm from Radio Casino, which is 1 block north of the municipal market. Buses from Limón to Manzanillo also stop in Cahuita and leave daily at 6am and 2:30pm. The trip takes 1½ hours; the fare is $1.25.

Buses departing **Puerto Viejo** and Sixaola (on the Panama border) stop in Cahuita at approximately 7, 8, 9:30 and 11:30am and 4:30pm en route to San José. However, this schedule is far from precise, so it's always best to check with your hotel. Moreover, these buses are often full, particularly on weekends and throughout the high season. To avoid standing in the aisle all the way to San José, it is sometimes better to take a bus first to Limón and then catch one of the frequent Limón/San José buses. Buses to Limón leave daily at 6:30 and 9am, noon, and 3, 4:30, and 6pm.

Another tactic I've used is to take a morning bus to Puerto Viejo, spend the day down there, and board a direct bus to San José at its point of origin, thereby snagging a seat.

ORIENTATION   There are only about eight dirt streets in Cahuita. The highway runs parallel to the ocean/coast, with three main roads running perpendicular. The northernmost of these bypasses town and brings you to the northern end of Playa Negra. It's marked with signs for the Magellan Inn and other hotels up on this end. The second road in brings you to the southern end of Playa Negra, a half-mile closer to town. Look for signs for Atlantida Lodge. The third road is the principal entrance into town. The village's main street in town, which runs parallel to the highway, dead-ends at the entrance to the national park (a footbridge over a small stream).

Buses usually drop their passengers in front of Coco's Bar, which is still sometimes called Salon Vaz, its legendary prior incarnation. If you come in on the bus and are staying at a lodge on Playa Negra, head out of town on the street that runs between Coco's Bar and the small park. This road curves to the left and continues a mile or so out to Playa Negra.

FAST FACTS   You can wash your clothes at the self-service **Laundromat** in front of Cabinas Vaz (about 1½ blocks south of the former Salon Vaz). One load in the washer or dryer will cost $1.50. The **police station** is located where the road from Playa Negra turns into town. The **post office,** next door to the police station, is open Monday through Friday from 8am to 5pm. If you can't find a **cab** in town, try calling **René** (© 506/755-0243), **Wayne** (© 506/755-0078), or **Dino** (© 506/755-0012).

EXPLORING CAHUITA NATIONAL PARK ☞

On arrival, you'll immediately feel the call of the long scimitar of beach that stretches south from the edge of town. This beach can be glimpsed through the trees from Cahuita's sunbaked main street and extends a promise of relief from the heat. While the lush coastal forest and picture-perfect palm lines are a tremendous draw, the park was actually created to preserve the 600-acre **coral reef** that surrounds it. The reef contains 35 species of coral and provides a haven for hundreds of brightly colored tropical fish. You can walk on the beach itself, or follow the trail that runs through the forest just behind the beach to check out the reef.

The best place to swim is just before or beyond the **Río Peresoso** (Lazy River), several hundred yards inside Cahuita National Park. The trail behind the beach is great for bird watching, and if you're lucky, you might see some monkeys or a sloth. The loud grunting sounds you hear off in the distance are the calls of howler monkeys, which can be heard from more than a mile away. Nearer at hand, you're likely to hear crabs scuttling amid the dry leaves on the forest floor—there are half a dozen or so species of land crabs living in this region. My favorites are the bright orange-and-purple ones.

The trail behind the beach stretches a little more than 4 miles (6.4km) to the southern end of the park at **Puerto Vargas,** where you'll find a beautiful white-sand beach, the park headquarters, and a primitive campground with showers and outhouses. It's a nice, flat walk, but a rewarding one, since there's good wildlife viewing and access to the beach. The reef is off the point just north of Puerto Vargas, and you can snorkel here. If you don't dawdle, the hike to Puerto Vargas should take no more than 2 hours each way. Bring plenty of mosquito repellent, as this area can be buggy.

Although there's snorkeling at Puerto Vargas, the nicest coral heads are located several hundred yards offshore, and it's best to have a boat take you out. A 3-hour **snorkel trip** should cost between $15 and $25 per person with equipment. These can be arranged with any of the local tour companies listed below. Be warned: These trips are best taken when the seas are calm—for safety's sake, for visibility, and for comfort.

ENTRY POINTS, FEES & REGULATIONS The **in-town park entrance** is just over a footbridge at the end of the village's main street. It has bathroom facilities, changing rooms, and storage lockers. This is the best place to enter if you're just interested in spending the day on the beach and maybe taking a little hike in the bordering forest.

The main park entrance is at the southern end of the park in **Puerto Vargas.** This is where you should come if you plan to camp at the park, or if you don't feel up to hiking a couple of hours to reach the good snorkeling spots. The road to Puerto Vargas is approximately 3 miles (5km) south of Cahuita on the left.

Officially, **admission** is $6 per person per day, but the last time I visited, the fee was being collected only at the Puerto Vargas entrance, and it was possible to enter the park from the town of Cahuita with just a voluntary contribution.

The park is open from dawn to dusk for day visitors.

There is an extra $1.50 per person charge for **camping.** The 50 campsites at Puerto Vargas stretch along for several kilometers and are either right on, or just a few steps from, the beach. My favorite campsites are those farthest from the entrance. There are basic shower and bathroom facilities at a small ranger station, but these can be a bit far from some of the campsites.

GETTING THERE   By Car   The turnoff for the Puerto Vargas entrance is clearly marked, 4½ miles (7km) south of Cahuita.

By Bus   Your best bet is to get off of a Puerto Viejo– or Sixaola-bound bus at the turnoff for the Puerto Vargas entrance (well marked, but tell the bus driver in advance). The actual guard station/entrance is only about 500 meters (about 545 yd.) down this road. However, the campsites are several kilometers farther on, so it's a long hike with a heavy pack.

BEACHES & ACTIVITIES OUTSIDE THE PARK

Outside the park, the best place for swimming is **Playa Negra.** The stretch right in front of the Atlantida Lodge is my favorite spot.

If you want to take advantage of any organized adventure trips or tours while in Cahuita, there are plenty of options. I recommend **Cahuita Tours and Adventure Center** (© 506/755-0232), on the village's main street heading out toward Playa Negra. Cahuita Tours offers glass-bottom-boat and snorkeling trips ($20 per person), jungle tours ($25), white-water rafting trips ($95), and Jeep tours to the Bribri Reservation ($60). Cahuita Tours has a decent little gift shop, provides e-mail access, and functions as a Western Union office.

Turistica Cahuita Information Center (© and fax **506/755-0071**), also on the main road heading toward Playa Negra, and **Roberto Tours** (© **506/755-0117**), a block away from Coco's Bar toward the national park, offer similar tours at similar prices. Most of the companies offer multiday trips to Tortuguero, as well as to Bocas del Toro, Panama.

Brigitte (watch for the sign on Playa Negra) rents horses for $8 per hour (you must have experience) and also offers guided horseback tours for $25 to $35.

Bird watchers who have cars should head north 5½ miles (9km) to the **Aviarios del Caribe Bed-and-Breakfast Lodge** ✦ (© and fax **506/382-1335**), where guided canoe tours of the Estrella Estuary are available. More than 315 species of birds have been sighted in the immediate area. The 3½-hour tour costs $30 per person and leaves throughout the day, but it's best to leave very early or very late in the afternoon, and to make reservations in advance. If you'd just like to walk the grounds and bird-watch from its covered deck, there's a $5 entrance fee.

SHOPPING

For a wide selection of beachwear, local crafts, cheesy souvenirs, and batik clothing, try **Boutique Coco Miko** or **Boutique Bambata,** which are both on the main road near the entrance to the park. The latter is also a good place to have your hair wrapped in colorful threads and strung with beads. Out toward Playa Negra, similar wares are offered at the gift shop at **Cahuita Tours.** Handmade jewelry and crafts are sold by local and itinerant artisans in makeshift stands near the park entrance.

Ask around town and you should be able to pick up a copy of Paula Palmer's *What Happen: A Folk-History of Costa Rica's Talamanca Coast* (Publications in English, 1993). The book is a history of the region, based on interviews with many of the area's oldest residents. Much of it is in the traditional Creole language, from which the title is taken. It makes fun and interesting reading, and you just might bump into someone mentioned in the book.

ACCOMMODATIONS

MODERATE

Atlantida Lodge ✦ This quiet, comfortable hotel is your best bet if you want to be just steps away from the beach, with a nice pool and a few basic amenities. The guest rooms are clean and comfortable, with pale-yellow stucco walls, red-tile floors, a ceiling fan, and plenty of bamboo trim. Each has a small patio with a bamboo screen divider for privacy, which opens onto the hotel's lush gardens. A host of different tours can be arranged here, from snorkeling to horseback riding to white-water rafting.

Beside the soccer field on the rd. to Playa Negra, about a mile (1.6km) north of town, Cahuita, Limón. ℂ 506/755-0115. Fax 506/755-0213. www.atlantida.co.cr. 30 units. $55 double; $65 triple or quad. Lower rates in the off-season. AE, MC, V. **Amenities:** 1 restaurant (international); 1 bar; small gym; midsized tile pool; Jacuzzi; laundry service. *In room:* No phone.

Chalet Hibiscus   If you're planning a long stay in Cahuita, I advise checking into this place. The largest house has two bedrooms and sleeps up to six people. There's hardwood paneling all around, a full kitchen, hot water, red-tile floors, a *pila* (wash basin) for doing your laundry, and even a garage. A spiral staircase leads to the second floor, where you'll find the bedrooms, as well as hammocks on a balcony that looks over a green lawn to the ocean. The other houses are similarly simple yet elegant, and the setting is serene and beautiful. The small cabins are much more basic, and have wicker furniture and walls of stone and wood. Be sure to ring the bell outside the gate—there are guard dogs on the grounds. You're a kilometer north of Playa Negra here, on a section of exposed coral coastline, so you'll have to walk, ride a bike, or drive a bit to enjoy the beach.

A.P. 943, Limón. ℂ **506/755-0021.** Fax 506/755-0015. hibiscus@racsa.co.cr. 7 units. Dec–Apr $40–$50 cabin, $50–$100 house; lower rates May–Nov. AE, MC, V. **Amenities:** 1 bar; tiny pool; volleyball court. *In room:* No phone.

Magellan Inn ⭐   This small inn is the most sophisticated hotel in the area. The rooms are all carpeted and have French doors, vertical blinds, tiled bathrooms with hardwood counters, and two joined single beds. Although there's a ceiling fan over each bed, the rooms could use a bit more ventilation. Each unit has its own spacious tiled veranda with another overhead fan, Persian rug, and bamboo chairs. The combination bar/lounge and sitting room features even more Persian-style rugs and wicker furniture. Most memorable of all are the hotel's sunken pool and lush gardens, both of which are built into a crevice in the ancient coral reef that underlies this entire region—which leads to good bird watching. Quiet breakfasts are served overlooking the gardens, and the sister restaurant, Casa Creole, is just next door.

At the far end of Playa Negra (about 1¼ miles/2km north of Cahuita), Cahuita (A.P. 1132), Limón. ℂ and fax **506/755-0035.** www.betaweb.com/tropinet/magellan1.htm. 6 units. $69 double; $81 triple. Rates include continental breakfast. AE, MC, V. **Amenities:** 1 bar/lounge; small pool; laundry service. *In room:* No phone.

INEXPENSIVE

Alby Lodge ⭐ *Value*   With the feel of a small village, Alby Lodge is a fascinating little place hand-built by its German owners. Though the four small cabins are close to the center of the village, they're surrounded by a large lawn and feel secluded. The cabins are quintessentially tropical, with thatched roofs, mosquito nets, hardwood floors and beams, big shuttered windows, tile bathrooms, and a hammock slung on the front porch. There's no restaurant here, but there is a communal kitchen area if you want to cook your own meals. The turnoff for the lodge is on your right just before you reach the national park entrance; the hotel is located about 150 yards down a narrow, winding lane from here.

Cahuita (A.P. 840), Limón. ℂ and fax **506/755-0031.** 4 units. $40 double; $45 triple; $50 quad. Children under 12 stay free in parents' room. No credit cards. *In room:* No phone.

Cabinas Arrecife   Located near the water, next to Restaurant Edith (see "Dining," below), this new row of basic rooms is an excellent budget choice in Cahuita. Each room comes with a double and a single bed, table fan, and tile floors. There's not a lot of room to move around, but things are pretty clean and new for this price range. There's a shared veranda with some chairs for sitting, where you can catch a glimpse of the sea through a dense stand of coconut palms. If you want to be closer to the sea, grab one of the hammocks strung on those palms, or sit in the small, open restaurant, which serves breakfast every day and dinners according to demand.

Cahuita (about 100m east of the post office), Limón. ✆ and fax **506/755-0081.** 12 units. $20 double; $25 triple. AE, MC, V. **Amenities:** 1 restaurant (Costa Rican). *In room:* No phone.

El Encanto Bed and Breakfast *(Value)*   The individual bungalows at this new bed-and-breakfast are set in from the road, on spacious and well-kept grounds. The bungalows themselves are also spacious and have attractive touches such as wooden bed frames, arched windows, Mexican-tile floors, Guatemalan bed-spreads, and framed Panamanian molas hanging on the walls. There are three new rooms in a separate two-story, two-bathroom house with a full kitchen, at the rear of the grounds. Hearty breakfasts are served in the open dining room of the owner's other separate two-story house.

Cahuita (A.P. 1234), Limón. Just outside of town on the rd. to Playa Negra. ✆ and fax **506/755-0113.** encanto@racsa.co.cr. 5 units. $40–$55 double. Rates include full breakfast. Slightly lower off-season rates. MC, V. *In room:* No phone.

Jenny's Cabinas   This place has been popular for years, and the rooms, while decidedly basic, have arguably the best views and location in town, just a few yards away from and overlooking the Caribbean Sea. All of the rooms have shut-tered windows, and there are sling chairs and hammocks on their porches. The more expensive rooms are on the second floor, and I think it's worth a few extra dollars for the added elevation and private balcony. There are hammocks strung up between palms, and a few tables and chairs around the grounds in front of the hotel, where you'll likely spend hours trading tales with fellow travelers.

Cahuita, Limón. ✆ **506/755-0256.** jennys@racsa.co.cr. 9 units. $20–$30 double. Slightly lower rates in the off-season. No credit cards. *In room:* No phone.

DINING

Coconut meat and milk figure in a lot of the regional cuisine. Most nights, local women cook up pots of various local specialties and sell them from the front porches of the two discos or from street-side stands around town; a full meal will cost you around $2 to $4. For snacks, there's the **Pastry Shop,** a tiny bakery on the left side of the main road as you head toward Playa Negra. The coconut pie, brownies, gingersnaps, banana bread, and corn pudding are all delicious. Prices range from 50¢ to $1.

Casa Creole 🌟🌟 FRENCH/CREOLE   While the rest of Cahuita may feel like a misplaced piece of Bob Marley's Jamaica, this new restaurant takes its inspiration from islands a little farther south in the Caribbean—and far more French. The restaurant is an outgrowth of the neighboring Magellan Inn. Tables in the open first-floor dining room are set with linen tablecloths and candles in glass lanterns. The building is painted a lively pastel pink, with plenty of painted gingerbread and varnished wood trim. There's a sense of informal elegance about it. Start with a dish of the pâté maison or a shrimp, coconut, and pineapple cocktail. The spiced shrimp martiniquaise and the jumbo coconut shrimp soup are both excellent, as is the fresh fish, seasoned and baked inside a banana leaf. The emphasis here is on seafood, but the ample menu includes meat, chicken, and pasta dishes. Top it off with some fresh raspberry coulis, homemade prof-iteroles, or exquisite homemade fresh-fruit sherbet.

Adjacent to the Magellan Inn, Playa Negra Rd., 1½ miles (2.5km) north o
0104. Reservations recommended during the high season. Main course
Mon–Sat 6–9pm.

Cha Cha Cha ✦ SEAFOOD/INTERNATIONAL Fresh se
meats, simply and expertly prepared. What more could you as....... a casual,
open-air restaurant in a funky beach town? In addition to the fresh catch of the
day and filet mignon, the menu here is an eclectic mix, including everything
from jerk chicken and Thai shrimp salad to pasta primavera and fajitas. The
grilled squid salad with a citrus dressing is one of the house specialties and a
great light bite. The restaurant occupies the ground floor of an old wooden
building. Everything is painted pure white, with some blue trim and accents.
There are only a half-dozen or so tables, so the place fills up fast.

On the main rd. in town, 200 yd. north of Coco's Bar. ⓒ 506/394-4153. Reservations recommended during the high season. Main courses $4.50–$15. MC, V. Tues–Sun 2–10pm.

Restaurant Edith ✦ (Finds) CREOLE/SEAFOOD This place has become a
tradition, and deservedly so. Quite some years ago, Miss Edith decided to start
serving home-cooked meals to all the hungry visitors hanging around. If you
want a taste of the local cuisine in a homey sit-down environment, this is the
place. While Miss Edith's daughters take the orders, Mom cooks up a storm out
back. The menu, when you can get hold of it, is long, with lots of local seafood
dishes and Creole combinations such as yucca in coconut milk with meat or vegetables. The sauces here have spice and zest and are a welcome change from the
typically bland fare served up throughout the rest of Costa Rica. After you've
ordered, it's usually no more than 45 minutes until your meal arrives. It's often
crowded here, so don't be bashful about sitting down with total strangers at any
of the big tables. Miss Edith's place is at the opposite end of town from the park
entrance; just turn right at the police station/post office.

By the police station, Cahuita. ⓒ 506/755-0248. Main courses $4–$12. No credit cards. Mon–Sat
8am–10pm; Sun 6–10pm. Sometimes closed without warning.

CAHUITA AFTER DARK

Coco's Bar, a classic Caribbean watering hole, has traditionally been the place
to spend your nights (or days, for that matter) if you like cold beer and very loud
reggae and soca music. **Casa de Locos,** located just across the street, is giving
Coco's a run for its money. Check them both out; on any given night you may
be more drawn to one or the other. There are usually local women hanging out
on the front porches of each establishment, selling fresh *pati* pies or bowls of
rundown stew (see "That Rundown Feeling," later in this chapter). Toward the
park entrance, the **National Park Restaurant** (ⓒ 506/755-0244) has a popular bar and disco most nights during the high season and weekends during the
low season. **Sobre Las Olas** (no phone) is a restaurant-bar with a stunning location, just north of town, right on the water. However, it's gone through owners
like wildfire, and I can't yet vouch for the most recent incarnation.

5 Puerto Viejo ✦✦

124 miles (200km) E of San José; 34 miles (55km) S of Limón

Though Puerto Viejo is farther down the road from Cahuita, it's become
increasingly more popular and has a livelier atmosphere, due in part to the many
surfers who come here from around the country (and around the world) to ride

village's famous Salsa Brava wave. For nonsurfers, there are also some good swimming beaches, plenty of active vacation options, nearby rain-forest trails, and some great local and international restaurants. This area gets plenty of rain, just like the rest of the coast (Sept and Oct are your best bets for sun, though it's not guaranteed even in those months).

Moreover, if you head still farther south, you will come to the most beautiful beaches on this coast, with white sand and turquoise seas. When it's calm (between Aug and Oct), the waters down here are some of the clearest anywhere in the country, with good snorkeling among the nearby coral reefs. The recent paving of the road, at least as far as Punta Uva, has made these beaches much more accessible, and there's been a slew of small, moderately priced and budget hotels built along this stretch of coast.

This is the end of the line along Costa Rica's Caribbean coast. After the tiny town of Manzanillo, some 15km south of Puerto Viejo, a national wildlife reserve stretches a few final kilometers to the Panamanian border.

You may notice, as you make your way into town from the highway, that there are cacao trees planted along the road. Most of these trees continue to suffer from a blight that has greatly reduced the cacao-bean harvest in the area. However, there is still a modest harvest, and you can get delicious, locally made cocoa candies here.

As in Cahuita and Limón, Puerto Viejo has had its peaceful image tarnished over the years by periodic violent incidents, including drug trafficking and endemic petty theft. The murder of two young American tourists in 2000 received lots of international media attention. Locals and Caribbean coast lovers say the region is getting a bad rap, based on sensationalism, fear, and racial prejudice, and that the area is no better nor worse than anywhere else in Costa Rica. There's some truth to their claims. Still, be careful here, especially at night, and do not get involved in the local drug culture.

ESSENTIALS

GETTING THERE & DEPARTING **By Car** To reach Puerto Viejo, continue south from Cahuita for another 10 miles (16km). Watch for a prominent fork in the highway. The right-hand fork continues on to Bribri and Sixaola. The left-hand fork (it actually appears to be a straight shot) takes you into Puerto Viejo on 3 miles (5km) of paved road.

By Bus Express buses (© **506/257-8129**) to Puerto Viejo leave San José daily at 6 and 10am, and 1:30 and 3:30pm from the new Caribbean bus terminal (Gran Terminal del Caribe) on Calle Central, 1 block north of Avenida 11. The trip's duration is 5 hours; fare is $5.50. During peak periods, extra buses are sometimes added. Always ask if the bus is going into Puerto Viejo (you do not want to end up getting dropped off at the turnoff for Sixaola), and if it's continuing on to **Manzanillo** (especially helpful if you're staying in a hotel south of town). Regardless, don't be surprised if it doesn't do exactly what you were told.

Alternatively, you can catch a bus to **Limón** (see the Limón section, above, for details) and then transfer to a Puerto Viejo–bound bus in Limón. These latter buses leave daily at 5, 8, and 10am, and 1, 4, and 6pm from Radio Casino, which is 1 block north of the municipal market. Buses from Limón to Manzanillo also stop in Puerto Viejo and leave daily at 6am and 2:30pm. The trip takes 1½ hours; the fare is $1.50.

If you arrive by bus, be leery of hucksters offering you hotel rooms. In most cases, they just work on a small commission from whatever hotel or cabina is hiring, and in some cases they'll steer you away from one of my recommended hotels, or falsely claim that it is full.

Express buses leave Puerto Viejo for San José daily at 9 and 11am, and 4pm. Buses for Limón leave daily at 6 and 9am, and 1, 4, and 5pm. Buses to **Punta Uva** and **Manzanillo** leave Puerto Viejo daily around 7am and 4pm. These buses return from Manzanillo at 8:15am and 5:15pm.

ORIENTATION   The road in from the highway runs parallel to Playa Negra, or Black Sand Beach, for a couple hundred meters before entering the village of Puerto Viejo, which has all of about ten dirt streets. The sea will be on your left and forested hills on your right as you come into town. It's another 9 miles (15km) road south to Manzanillo. This road was recently paved as far south as Punta Uva (around 5 miles, or 8km), and should be paved all the way to Manzanillo by the time this book goes to press.

The last time I visited, a little information center was about to open in a portable trailer placed right at the end of Playa Negra, just before the little bridge at the start of town. However, the ATEC office (see below) is still your best bet for local information.

FAST FACTS   **Public phones** are located at Hotel Maritza, El Pizote lodge, the Manuel Leon general store (next to Johnny's Place), and the **ATEC office** (*C* **506/ 750-0398;** *C* and fax 506/750-0191; www.greencoast.com), across the street from the Soda Tamara. The nearest **bank** is in **Bribri,** about 6 miles (10km) away, although rumors are swirling that Banco Nacional will soon open a branch here. Rumor has it that a **post office** will soon open here as well, but for the time being, you'll have to post letters and cards at your hotel or the ATEC office. There is a **Guardia Rural police** (*C* **506/750-0230**) post on the beach, near Johnny's Place.

In addition to the ATEC office, which sometimes works as an Internet cafe, there's the new **Cibercafe** (*C* **506/750-0067**), located 1 block inland from El Bambú. The town's main **taxi** driver is named **Bull** (*C* **506/750-0112**), and he drives a beat-up old Isuzu Trooper. You might find him hanging around the *parquecito* (little park), or you can ask a local to point you to his house. If Bull's not around or he's busy, you could try **Delroy** (*C* **506/750-0132**).

WHAT TO SEE & DO
SUNNING & SURFING   **Surfing** has historically been the main draw here, but increasing numbers of folks are coming here for the miles of beautiful and uncrowded **beaches** *✶✶*, lush rain forests, and laid-back atmosphere. If you aren't a surfer, the same activities that prevail in any quiet beach town are the norm here as well—sunbathe, go for a walk on the beach, read a book, or take a nap. If you have more energy, there's a host of tours and hiking options, or you can rent a bicycle or a horse (watch for signs). For swimming and sunbathing, locals like to hang out on the small patches of sand in front of Stanford's Disco and Johnny's Place. There are small, protected tide pools in front of each of these bars for cooling off.

If you want a more open patch of sand and sea, head north out to **Playa Negra** (this is not the same one I talked about in Cahuita), along the road into town, or, better yet, to the beaches south of town around Punta Uva and all the way down to Manzanillo, where the coral reefs keep the surf much more manageable (see below).

Just offshore from the tiny village park is a shallow reef where powerful storm-generated waves sometimes reach 20 feet. **Salsa Brava,** as it's known, is the prime surf break on the Caribbean coast. Even when the waves are small, this spot is recommended only for very experienced surfers because of the danger of the reef. There are also popular beach breaks south of town on Playa Cocles.

Atlántico Tours (© 506/750-0004) rents boogie boards, snorkel gear, and bicycles (all for $10 per day). **Reef Runners Dive Shop** (© 506/750-0480) rents dive equipment and mask and fins (around $10); see below for details on their dive trips. Right in the heart of town, there's a makeshift stand facing the water, with no name and no phone, that rents full-size surfboards.

CULTURAL & ADVENTURE TOURS   The **Asociación Talamanqueña de Ecoturismo y Conservacion (ATEC)** office, across the street from the Soda Tamara (© 506/750-0398; © and fax 506/750-0191; www.greencoast.com), is concerned with preserving both the environment and the cultural heritage of this area and promoting ecologically sound development. (If you're looking to stay in Puerto Viejo for an extended period of time and would like to contribute to the community, you can ask here about volunteering.) In addition to functioning as the local information center and traveler's hub, ATEC runs a little shop that sells T-shirts, maps, posters, and books.

ATEC also offers quite a few tours, including **half-day walks** that focus on nature and either the local African-Caribbean culture or the indigenous Bribri culture. These walks pass through farms and forests, and along the way you'll learn about local history, customs, medicinal plants, and Indian mythology, and have an opportunity to see sloths, monkeys, iguanas, keel-billed toucans, and other wildlife. There are four different walks through the nearby Bribri Indians' Kékoldi Reserve; there are also more strenuous hikes through the primary rain forest. **Bird walks** and **night walks** will help you spot more of the area wildlife; there are even overnight treks. The local guides who lead these tours have a wealth of information and make a hike through the forest a truly educational experience. Half-day walks (and night walks) are $15, and a full-day runs between $25 and $40. ATEC can arrange snorkeling trips to the nearby coral reefs, as well as snorkeling and fishing trips in dugout canoes. A half day of snorkeling or fishing will cost around $20 to $40 per person.

ATEC can also help you arrange overnight and multiday **camping trips** into the Talamanca Mountains and through neighboring indigenous reserves, as well as trips to Tortuguero, and even a 7-to-10-day transcontinental trek to the Pacific coast. Some tours require minimum groups of 5 or 10 people and several days' advance notice. The ATEC office is open Monday through Friday from 8am to 9pm, and Saturday and Sunday from 8am to noon and 4 to 8pm.

Both **Atlántico Tours** (© 506/750-0004) and **Terraventuras** (© 506/750-0426) offer a whole host of half- and full-day adventure tours into the jungle or sea for between $30 and $90 per person. Scuba divers can check in with the **Reef Runners Dive Shop** (© 506/750-0480); these folks charge $55 for a two-tank dive including all your equipment and a guide. They frequent about 10 different dive sites between Punta Uva and Manzanillo, and when the seas are calm and visibility good, this is some good diving.

A TROPICAL GARDEN   One of the nicer ways to spend a day in Puerto Viejo is to visit the local **Botanical Gardens** ☞☞ (© 506/750-0046; jardbot@racsa.co.cr), located a couple hundred yards inland from the Black Sand Beach on a side road just north of El Pizote lodge. Hosts Peter and Lindy Kring have poured time and love into the creation of this meandering collection of native and imported tropical flora. There are medicinal, commercial, and just plain wild flowering plants, fruits, herbs, trees, and bushes. Visitors get to gorge on whatever is ripe at the moment. There is also a rigorous rain-forest loop trail leaving from the grounds. The gardens are generally open Friday through Monday from 10am to 4pm, but visits can sometimes be arranged for other days with prior notice. Entrance to the garden or loop trail is $3 per person, or $9 including the guided tour.

A LITTLE MIND & BODY REVITALIZATION   Check in with **Samasati** ⊛ (© **800/563-9643** in the U.S., or 506/224-1870 in Costa Rica; fax 506/224-5032; www.samasati.com), a lovely jungle yoga retreat with spectacular hillside views of the Caribbean sea and surrounding forests. Rates here run between $55 and $130 per person per day, all-inclusive, depending on occupancy, room type, and tour, massage and class packages. If you're staying elsewhere in Puerto Viejo or Cahuita, you can come up for yoga classes ($8), meditations ($5), or private massages ($45) with prior notice. Samasati is located a couple of kilometers before Puerto Viejo (near the turnoff for Bribri) and roughly another mile (1.6km) up into the jungle.

MANZANILLO & THE MANZANILLO-GANDOCA WILDLIFE REFUGE ⊛⊛

If you continue south on the coast road from Puerto Viejo, you'll come to a couple of even smaller villages. **Punta Uva** ⊛⊛ is 5 miles (8km) away, and **Manzanillo** ⊛⊛ is about 9¼ miles (15km) away. For a good day trip, you can catch the 7am bus from Puerto Viejo down to Manzanillo and then catch the 5:15pm bus back. (It's always wise to check with ATEC about current local bus schedules.) You could also hire a cab for around $5 to Punta Uva, or $8 to Manzanillo. Alternatively, it's about 2 hours each way on bicycle, with only two relatively small hills to contend with. However, since the road and most of the bikes rented in town are rather rugged, expect your wrists and rear end to take quite a beating. It's also possible to walk along the beach all the way from Puerto Viejo to Manzanillo, with just a couple of short, and well-worn, detours inland around rocky points.

Manzanillo is a tiny village with only a few basic cabinas and funky *sodas*. The most popular place to eat and hang out is **Restaurant Maxi** ⊛ (no phone), an open-air joint located on the second floor of an old wooden building facing the sea. This place gets packed on weekends, especially for lunch.

The **Manzanillo-Gandoca Wildlife Refuge** ⊛⊛ encompasses the small village and extends all the way to the Panamanian border. Manatees, crocodiles, and more than 350 species of birds live within the boundaries of the reserve. The reserve also includes the coral reef offshore—when the seas are calm, this is the best **snorkeling and diving** spot on this entire coast. Four species of **sea turtles** nest on one 5½-mile-long (8.9km) stretch of beach within the reserve, between March and July.

If you want to explore the refuge, you can easily find the single, well-maintained trail by walking along the beach just south of town until you have to wade across a small river. On the other side you'll pick up the trailhead. Otherwise, you can ask around the village for local guides or check out **Aquamor** (© **506/391-3417;** aquamor@racsa.co.cr), a kayak and dive operation located on the one main road in town. These folks rent kayaks for $5 per hour, and offer a variety of guided excursions for between $15 and $55 per person. Depending on tides and sea conditions, this is a great way to explore the mangroves and estuaries, visit several nearby beaches, and even snorkel or dive the nearby coral reef. A one-tank beach dive, with equipment and guide, costs $30 per person. They have a whole variety of tour and diving options, including PADI dive certification courses, hikes into the Talamanca Mountains, and trips to Bocas del Toro, Panama.

SHOPPING

Puerto Viejo attracts a lot of local and international bohemians, who seem to survive solely on the sale of handmade jewelry, painted ceramic trinkets (mainly pipes and cigarette-lighter holders), and imported Indonesian textiles. You'll find them at makeshift stands set up by the town's "little park" or *parquecito*, a few wooden benches in front of the sea between Soda Tamara and Stanford's.

In addition to the makeshift outdoor stands, **Boutique Tabu**, located near the Mepe bus stop, sells hand-painted T-shirts, batik beachwear, and coconut-shell jewelry. **Casa Sistaz** (© **506/750-0394**), located 200m inland from the bus stop, has a small collection of locally produced craftwork, including shell mobiles and mirrors with mosaic-inlaid frames. **The Jewelry Factory,** across the street from Cabinas Grant (© **506/750-0075**) sells a wide range of jewelry and gift items, as well as Costa Rican hammocks.

The **ATEC shop** is a great place to get reading materials relevant to the region. Here, you can usually pick up Paula Palmer's oral history, *What Happen: A Folk-History of Costa Rica's Talamanca Coast* (Publications in English, 1993). If you'd like to learn more about the culture of the local Bribri Indians, look for a copy of *Taking Care of Sibö's Gifts* by Paula Palmer, Juanita Sánchez, and Gloria Mayorga. ATEC itself publishes and sells *Coastal Talamanca, A Cultural and Ecological Guide,* a small booklet packed with information about this area.

ACCOMMODATIONS
IN PUERTO VIEJO

True budget hounds will find a host of basic cabinas in downtown Puerto Viejo in addition to the hotels listed below. Of these, **Hotel Pura Vida** (© **506/750-0002;** fax 506/750-0296) and **Cabinas Maritza** (© **506/750-0003;** fax 506/750-0313) are your best bets. For a more isolated option, try **Cabinas Black Sands** (© **506/750-0124;** fax 506/750-0188; bsands@racsa.co.cr), on the northern end of Black Beach.

Moderate

El Pizote   El Pizote is the largest and most modern hotel in Puerto Viejo proper, but that's not necessarily saying much, as none of the rooms here have televisions or telephones, and some even have shared bathrooms. The hotel is located a hundred yards or so inland from a long, quiet stretch of Black Sand beach, about 500 yards before you reach downtown proper. The four newer deluxe bungalows are modern concrete-block affairs, with a small kitchenette, two separate bedrooms, one small bathroom, air-conditioning, and a private porch. Although a bit older and slightly funkier, the standard bungalows have much more character. These raised wooden buildings have dark, stained wood walls, steep pitched roofs, ceiling fans, private porches, and larger step-down bathrooms. The most basic rooms are in a U-shaped wooden building. These rooms are cool, and come with two double beds, a ceiling fan, a shared wrap-around veranda, and shared bathroom facilities. Everything is set amidst lush gardens, assorted tropical fruit trees, and a few towering rain-forest trees. For activity, there are hiking trails in the adjacent forest and there's good bird watching here, too.

Just off the main rd., about 275m (300 yd.) before you enter downtown, Puerto Viejo, Limón (A.P. 1371-1000, San José). © **506/750-0088.** Fax 506/750-0226. 8 units, none with bathroom; 10 bungalows. $48 double; $60 double bungalow, $86 double deluxe bungalow. Rates include breakfast. AE, MC, V. **Amenities:** 1 restaurant (Costa Rican/international); 1 bar; swimming pool and adjacent kid's pool; volleyball court; laundry service. *In room:* No phone.

Inexpensive

Cabinas Jacaranda This basic backpackers' special has a few nice touches that set it apart from the others. The cement floors have recently been tiled, Japanese paper lanterns cover the lights, and mosquito nets hang over the beds. Guatemalan bedspreads add a dash of color and tropical flavor, as do the tables made from sliced tree trunks. If you're traveling in a group, you'll enjoy the space and atmosphere of the big room. If the hotel is full, the owners also rent a few nearby bungalows.

1½ blocks inland from Marco's Pizzeria, Puerto Viejo, Limón. ℂ and fax 506/750-0069. 10 units, 7 with private bathroom. $15 double without private bathroom, $20 double with private bathroom. MC, V. *In room:* No phone.

Casa Verde ✦ ✓*Value* This little hotel is located on a side street on the south side of town and is my favorite hotel right in Puerto Viejo, regardless of price. The older rooms, with shared bathrooms, are in an interesting building with a wide, covered breezeway between the rooms and the showers and toilets out back. The front and back porches of this building are hung with hammocks and surrounded by lush gardens. A quiet sense of tropical tranquillity pervades this place. The newer rooms are toward the back of the small complex and are a bit larger, with high ceilings, tile floors, private bathrooms, and a veranda. There's also a small separate bungalow with a kitchenette. Everything is well maintained, and even the shared bathrooms are kept immaculate. Recent additions here include a small gift shop, coffee shop, and small poison-dart frog garden. Even though it's an in-town choice, there's great bird watching all around the grounds here.

A.P. 1115, Puerto Limón. ℂ 506/750-0015. ℂ and fax 506/750-0047. cabinascasaverde@ hotmail.com. 14 units, 6 with private bathroom. $24 double without private bathroom, $36 double with private bathroom. AE, MC, V. *In room:* Mini-fridge; no phone.

BETWEEN PUERTO VIEJO & MANZANILLO

All the hotels listed below are located along the road south of Puerto Viejo heading toward Manzanillo. This is one of the most beautiful and isolated stretches of beach in Costa Rica. The single coastal road here has recently been paved as far south as Punta Uva, greatly improving access to this area; still, I recommend that you have a vehicle if you plan to stay at one of these hotels, since public transportation is sporadic.

In addition to the hotels listed below, budget travelers should check out **La Isla** (ℂ and fax **506/750-0188**), a simple hotel catering to surfers, located at the start of Playa Cocles.

Moderate

Almonds and Corals Tent Camp This isn't camping in any traditional sense, so don't expect to rough it. You'll find large raised platforms, big enough so that within the stretched-tarp roof and screened walls there's another large standing-room tent, providing double protection against rain and mosquitoes. This second tent takes up about half of the platform's screened-in floor space and still leaves room for a hammock, table, chairs, and a bathroom area with a cold-water shower and toilet. Inside the tent, you'll find either two single beds or one double bed, a small table, two oil lamps, and a small closet. The tents are in dense secondary forest, with nothing but screen and cloth for walls, so you'll feel very close to nature. There are wooden walkways connecting the tents to the main lodge and dining area. Perhaps the best part of the whole setup is the fact that Manzanillo Beach is just about 200 yards away through the jungle. Snorkel equipment, sea kayaks, and a variety of tours are also available.

Manzanillo, Limón (A.P. 681-2300, San José). © **506/272-2024** or 506/272-4175. Fax 506/272-2220. www.geoexpediciones.com. 23 tents. $60 per person. Rates are based on double occupancy, including breakfast, dinner, and taxes. Slightly lower rates in the off-season. AE, MC, V. **Amenities:** 1 restaurant (international); Jacuzzi; water-sports equipment; laundry service. *In room:* No phone.

Cariblue Bungalows ★ *Value*   This new bed-and-breakfast offers guests a lot of comfort and character for the price. The rooms are spread around the well-tended and lush grounds. My favorites are the raised stilt wood bungalows, with spacious bedrooms featuring either one king and one single bed, or two queens. The beds are covered with mosquito nets and there's a small veranda with a hammock. The nicest features here are the bathrooms with their intricate mosaic tile designs. The five newer rooms are in a couple of concrete-block buildings with high-pitched thatch roofs. They are clean and comfortable, but not quite as private, charming, or well-ventilated as the bungalows. There's also a two-bedroom house with a full kitchen, for families or for longer stays. Cariblue is located about 100 yards or so inland from the southern end of Playa Cocles.

Playa Cocles, Puerto Viejo, Limón. © **506/750-0035**, or © and fax 506/750-0057. www.cariblue.com. 5 units, 5 bungalows, 1 house. $55–$75 double; $150 house. Rates include breakfast buffet. AE, MC, V. **Amenities:** 1 restaurant (international/Italian); 1 bar/lounge; bike and boogie-board rental; laundry service. *In room:* No phone.

Casa Camarona   Casa Camarona is a new hotel and has the enviable distinction of being another of the handful of hotels in this area right on the beach—no road to cross, no path through the jungle, just a small section of shady gardens separates you from a quiet section of Playa Cocles and the Caribbean Sea. The rooms are in two separate two-story buildings. Definitely get a room on the second floor. Up here you'll find spacious rooms painted in pleasant pastels, with plenty of cross-ventilation and a wide shared veranda. Nine of the rooms have air-conditioning. I don't know who designed the first-floor rooms, but several of them have such low ceilings that it felt as if the walls were closing in on me. The hotel keeps some chaise longues on the beach under the shade of palm trees, and there's even a beach bar open during the day, so you barely have to leave that chaise to quench your thirst.

Playa Cocles, Puerto Viejo, Limón (mailing address: A.P. 2270-1002, Paseo de los Estudiantes, San José). © **506/283-6711** or 506/750-0151. Fax 506/222-6184. www.casacamarona.com. 20 units. $60–$75 double. Rates include continental breakfast. AE, MC, V. **Amenities:** 1 restaurant (seafood/international); 1 bar. *In room:* No phone.

Shawandha Lodge ★★ *Finds*   If you're looking for an isolated and romantic getaway, in a style best described as rustic luxury, this small collection of individual bungalows is a great choice. Set in a lush patch of forest about 200 yards or so inland from Playa Chiquita, Shawandha has the feel of a small village. Artistic flourishes abound. The thatch-roofed, raised bungalows feature painted exterior murals, high-pitched ceilings, varnished wood floors, and either one king or a mix of queen and single beds. The bathrooms are practically works of art, each with original, intricate mosaics of hand-cut tile highlighting a large, open shower. Every bungalow has its own spacious balcony, with both a hammock and a couch, where you can lie and look out on the lush, flowering gardens. The beach is easily accessed by a private path, and a host of activities and tours can be arranged.

There's a large open-air restaurant and lounge, where meals and drinks are served. The menu is an eclectic mix, featuring fresh fish and meats in a variety of French, Caribbean, and Polynesian sauces.

Puerto Viejo, Limón. © **506/750-0018.** Fax 506/750-0037. www.shawandha-lodge.com. 12 units. Dec 15–Apr 30 $92 double; May 1–Dec 14 $72 double. Rates include full breakfast. AE, MC, V. **Amenities:** 1 restaurant (international); laundry service. *In room:* No phone.

Villas del Caribe ✴   If you want to be right on the beach and have spacious, comfortable accommodations, there isn't a better choice in this area. Villas del Caribe offers two-story villas with full kitchens and a choice of one or two bedrooms. The living rooms have built-in sofa beds, and just outside there is a large terrace complete with barbecue grill. The kitchens are attractively designed, with blue-and-white–tile counters, and fully equipped. Bathrooms feature wooden-slat shower doors, potted plants on a platform by the window, louvered and screened walls that let in light and air, and more blue-tile counters. Upstairs, you'll find either a large single bedroom with a king-size bed or two smaller bedrooms (one with bunk beds). Either way, there's a balcony with a hammock and an ocean view.

The water, which is usually fairly calm, is only steps away through the coconut palms, and there's some coral just offshore that makes for good snorkeling. The hotel offers beach towels and beach chairs.

Puerto Viejo, Limón (A.P. 8080-1000, San José). © **506/750-0202** or 506/233-2200. Fax 506/750-0203. www.villascaribe.net. 12 units. $79 double; $89 triple; $99 quad. AE, MC, V. **Amenities:** 1 restaurant (Costa Rican/international); limited water-sports-equipment rental; tour desk; laundry service. *In room:* Kitchen; no phone.

Inexpensive

Cabinas Selvyn   The atmosphere here is friendly and funky. Rooms are located in two old wooden buildings behind the small open-air restaurant. There are no fans, so try for a second-floor room, which receives a bit of the sea breezes. All the rooms come with mosquito nets, but beyond that, the accommodations are Spartan. Nevertheless, the hotel is located about 100 meters down a dirt lane from one of the most isolated and beautiful beaches in Costa Rica, and the owner is a great cook and wonderful raconteur.

Punta Uva, Limón. No phone. 10 units, all with shared bathroom; 2 apts. $8–$12 double; $150–$200 per month for an apt. No credit cards. **Amenities:** 1 restaurant (Costa Rican). *In room:* No phone.

La Costa del Papito *Value*   This small collection of individual and duplex cabins offers some of the same feel and character as Shawandha and Cariblue, with fewer amenities and less luxury—but at lower rates. La Costa del Papito is located just across from Cocles beach, about 1 mile (1.6km) south of Puerto Viejo. The wooden bungalows, which are a little dark inside, come with one or two double beds, artfully tiled bathrooms, and an inviting private porch with a table and chairs and either a hammock or swing chair. Only breakfast, snacks, and drinks are served here, so you'll have to head into Puerto Viejo or farther on down the road for the rest of your meals.

Playa Cocles, Puerto Viejo, Limón. © and fax **506/750-0080.** http://greencoast.com/papito.htm. 6 units. $44–$50 double. AE, MC, V. *In room:* No phone.

Playa Chiquita Lodge   Set amid the shade of large old trees a few miles south of Puerto Viejo toward Punta Uva (watch for the sign), the lodge consists of unpainted wooden buildings set on stilts and connected by wooden walkways. There are wide verandas with built-in seating and rocking chairs. The basic, spacious rooms have recently been painted, which lightens things up, but it's still hard to read in bed at night. There is a short trail that leads down to a private little swimming beach with tide pools and beautiful turquoise water. Lately, this stretch of beach has become the site of a daily 4pm volleyball game. Throughout the day there are free bananas and coffee. The owners also rent out fully equipped houses for those interested in longer stays or more privacy and independence.

Puerto Viejo, Limón. ✆ **506/750-0408.** Fax 506/750-0062. www.playachiquita.com. 10 units. $39 double; $49 triple. Lower rates in the off-season. MC, V. **Amenities:** 1 restaurant (international). *In room:* No phone.

DINING
IN PUERTO VIEJO

To really sample the local cuisine, you need to look up a few local women. Ask around for **Miss Dolly** and see if she has anything cooking. Her specialties are bread (especially banana) and ginger biscuits, but she'll also fix a full Caribbean meal for you if you ask a day in advance and she has time. **Miss Daisy** also makes *pan bon* (a local sweet, dark bread), ginger cakes, patties (meat-filled turnovers), and coconut oil (for tanning). **Miss Sam, Miss Isma,** and **Miss Irma** all serve up sit-down meals in their modest little *sodas.* Just ask around for these women and someone will direct you to them.

Puerto Viejo has become a very popular destination for Italian immigrants, and it seems there's a pretty decent Italian restaurant everywhere you turn. In addition to the restaurant listed below, you can get very good Italian cuisine at both **Caramba** and **Marco's Pizzeria and Ristorante,** right in town.

My favorite restaurant in the area, **The Garden** (✆ 506/750-0069), located next to Cabinas Jacaranda, has been closed more often than not in recent years. As of press time, the restaurant was again open, but the owner plans to totally streamline the menu and begin showing nightly videos. Regardless of what form this place takes, it's worth your while to see if it's open during your stay.

Reservations are not needed at any of the restaurants in town.

Amimodo ★★ *Finds* NORTHERN ITALIAN   This is my favorite Italian restaurant in Puerto Viejo. The dining room occupies the open-air bottom floor of a traditional local raised stilt house. It's airy, and there's lots of whitewashed wood and gingerbread trim. On good days you can feel the sea breeze coming in off the ocean about 100 meters away. The sturdy wood tables have hand-painted trim patterns that match the painted chairs. Be sure to begin your meal with the *jamon de tiburon,* thin slices of home-smoked shark served with fresh baked bread and a light avocado dressing. I also recommend the homemade ravioli stuffed with lobster in a lobster-and-cognac–based red sauce, and the gnocchi, which melt in your mouth. If you've got room for dessert, opt for the chocolate salami. There's a small bar that sometimes fills with locals and a big-screen TV that broadcasts the most important soccer games and Italian television programs.

On the left-hand side of the main rd. heading south of Puerto Viejo, just after Cabinas Salsa Brava. ✆ **506/750-0257.** Main courses $4–15. AE, MC, V. Mon–Wed and Fri noon–3pm and 6–11pm; Sat–Sun noon–11pm.

That Rundown Feeling

Don't be discouraged by signs advertising "rundown" soup or stew. It's not what you think. Rundown (or "rondon") soup is a spicy coconut-milk stew made with anything the cook can run down. Be sure to try this authentic taste of the Caribbean.

The Place INTERNATIONAL   If you want a quick, casual meal, check out this humble collection of tables under an open A-frame roof, located on a side street just off the bus stop. The Place features a small menu with daily specials and excellent sandwiches. The menu is eclectic—it might feature anything from vegetarian nori rolls to curried chicken to the local "rondon" stew.

On a side st. ½ block inland from the bus stop. ☎ 506/750-0195. Main courses $2.50–$7. No credit cards. Fri–Wed 7am–10pm.

Salsa Brava ☞ SPANISH/MEDITERRANEAN   Fresh grilled seafood and meats are the specialty here, and everything is simply yet expertly prepared. There's usually a wide range of fresh-caught fish available, grilled either whole or in fillets, plus grilled calamari, shrimp, or filet mignon. Wash down whatever you choose with the homemade sangria. The dozen or so wooden tables are painted bright primary colors and are set on a gravel floor under an open-air thatched roof. Service is attentive and informal. Most nights, you'll find owner José Gutiérrez working the outdoor grill himself.

On the left-hand side of the main rd. heading south of Puerto Viejo, just after El Bambú. ☎ 506/750-0241. Main courses $7–$15. No credit cards. Tues–Sun 6–10pm.

Soda Tamara COSTA RICAN   This little Tico-style restaurant has long been popular with budget-conscious travelers and has an attractive setting for such an economical place. There's an open-air dining area, which is larger and more comfortable than the somewhat cramped indoor dining room. The painted picket fence in front gives the restaurant a homey feel. The menu features standard fish, chicken, and meat entrees, served with a hefty helping of Caribbean-style rice and beans. You can also get *patacones* (fried chips made out of plantains) and a wide selection of fresh-fruit juices. *Be forewarned:* Service can be slow. At the counter inside, you'll find homemade cocoa candies and unsweetened cocoa biscuits made by several women in town. They're definitely worth a try. Soda Tamara recently added a second-floor open-air bar that's open nightly from 6pm until the last straggler calls it quits.

On the main rd. through the village. ☎ 506/750-0148. Main courses $3.50–$8. AE, MC, V. Daily 7am–9pm.

BETWEEN PUERTO VIEJO & MANZANILLO

As the beaches stretching south of Puerto Viejo keep getting more and more popular, there has been a corresponding increase in the number of places to grab a meal. In addition to the restaurants listed above, **Cabinas Selvyn,** at Punta Uva, and **Elena Brown's Restaurant,** at Playa Chiquita (☎ 506/750-0265), are two very popular and dependable spots for local cuisine. **El Ranchito,** at Punta Uva (☎ 506/750-0218), is a great spot for lunch, especially if you're already on the beach at Punta Uva.

If you make it as far south as Manzanillo, **Restaurant Maxi** ☞ (no phone) is your best bet. This open-air spot is always packed, especially for lunch. A fresh-fish plate will cost you between $5 and $7; lobster, in season, will cost around $12. Whatever you order will come with rice and beans, patacones, and a small side of cabbage salad. For fancier fare, check out the restaurant at **Shawandha** (☎ 506/750-0018), and for Italian food, look for **El Duende Feliz** (☎ 506/750-0356), which has recently reopened on the roadside, between Playa Cocles and Playa Chiquita.

PUERTO VIEJO AFTER DARK

There are two main disco-bars in town. **Johnny's Place** ⊛ is near the Rural Guard station, about 100 meters or so north of the ATEC office. You'll find **Stanford's** overlooking the water out near Salsa Brava just as the main road heads south of town. Both have small dance floors with ground-shaking reggae, dub, and rap rhythms blaring. The action usually spills out from the dance floor at both joints on most nights. I like the atmosphere better at Johnny's, where they have tables and candles set out on the sand, near the water's edge.

Another place I like is **El Bambú** ⊛, just beyond Stanford's on the road toward Punta Uva. It's smaller and more intimate than either of the other bars, yet still packs them in and gets them dancing on the Monday or Friday reggae nights.

Tourists and locals alike take advantage of the pool table, board games, and DirecTV (usually showing sporting events) at **El Dorado,** in front of the ATEC office, as an alternative to the loud music and dance scenes of the other joints mentioned above. There's also an open-air bar on the second floor of **Soda Tamara,** which has become a casual and quiet place to gather after dark.

Appendix A:
Costa Rica in Depth

Costa Rica is, and has been for many years, a relative sea of tranquillity in a region that has been troubled by turmoil for centuries. For more than 100 years, it has enjoyed a stable democracy and a relatively high standard of living for Latin America. The literacy rate is high, as are medical standards and facilities. Perhaps most significant, at least for proud Costa Ricans, is that this country does not have an army. When former Costa Rican president Oscar Arias Sánchez was awarded the Nobel Peace Prize for negotiating a peace settlement in Central America in 1987, Costa Rica was able to claim credit for exporting a bit of its own political stability to the rest of the region.

1 The Natural Environment

Costa Rica occupies a central spot in the isthmus that joins North and South America. For millennia, this land bridge served as a migratory thoroughfare and mating ground for species native to the once-separate continents. It was also the meeting place of Mesoamerican and Andean pre-Columbian indigenous cultures.

The country comprises only 0.01% of the earth's landmass, yet is home to 5% of the planet's biodiversity. There are more than 10,000 identified species of plants, 850 species of birds, 800 species of butterflies, and 500 species of mammals, reptiles, and amphibians found here.

The key to this biological richness lies in the many distinct life zones and ecosystems that can be found in Costa Rica. It may all seem like one big mass of green to the untrained eye, but the differences are profound.

In any one spot in Costa Rica, temperatures remain relatively constant year-round. However, they vary dramatically according to altitude, from tropically hot and steamy along the coasts to below freezing at the highest elevations.

Costa Rica's **lowland rain forests** are true tropical jungles. Some are deluged with more than 200 inches of rainfall per year, and their climate is hot and humid. Trees grow tall and fast, fighting for sunlight in the upper reaches. In fact, life and foliage on the forest floor are surprisingly sparse. The action is typically 100 feet above, in the canopy, where long vines stream down, lianas climb up, and bromeliads grow on the branches and trunks of towering hardwood trees. You can find these lowland rain forests along the southern Pacific coast and Osa Peninsula, as well as along the Caribbean coast. **Corcovado, Cahuita,** and **Manuel Antonio** National Parks, as well as the **Manzanillo-Gandoca Wildlife Refuge** are fine examples of lowland rain forests.

At higher altitudes you'll find Costa Rica's famed **cloud forests.** Here the steady flow of moist air meets the mountains and creates a nearly constant mist. Epiphytes—resourceful plants that live cooperatively on the branches and trunks of other trees—grow abundantly in the cloud forests, where they must extract moisture and nutrients from the air. Since cloud forests are found in generally steep, mountainous terrain, the canopy here is lower and less uniform than in lowland rain forests, providing better chances for viewing elusive fauna.

Costa Rica's most spectacular cloud forest is the **Monteverde Biological Cloud Forest Preserve** in Guanacaste province (see chapter 6).

At the highest reaches, the cloud forests give way to **elfin forests** and *páramos.* More commonly associated with the South American Andes, a páramo is characterized by a variety of tundralike shrubs and grasses, with a scattering of twisted, windblown trees. Reptiles, rodents, and raptors are the most common residents here. **Mount Chirripó, Chirripó National Park,** and the **Cerro de la Muerte ("Mountain of Death")** are the principal areas of páramo in Costa Rica.

In a few protected areas of Guanacaste, you will still find examples of the otherwise vanishing **tropical dry forest.** During the long and pronounced dry season (late Nov through late Apr), no rain relieves the unabated heat. In an effort to conserve much-needed water, the trees drop their leaves but bloom in a riot of color: purple jacaranda, scarlet poró, and brilliant orange flame-of-the-forest are just a few examples. Then, during the rainy season, this deciduous forest is transformed into a lush and verdant landscape. Because the foliage is not so dense, the dry forests are excellent places to view a variety of wildlife species, especially howler monkeys and pizotes (*coatimundi*). Dry forests can be found in **Santa Rosa** and **Guanacaste** National Parks.

Along the coasts, primarily where river mouths meet the ocean, you will find extensive **mangrove forests and swamps.** Around these seemingly monotonous tangles of roots exists one of the most diverse and rich ecosystems in the country. All sorts of fish and crustaceans live in the brackish tidal waters. Caimans and crocodiles cruise the maze of rivers and unmarked canals, and hundreds of herons, ibises, egrets, and other marsh birds nest and feed along the silty banks. Mangrove swamps are often havens for water birds: cormorants, frigate birds, pelicans, and herons. The larger birds tend to nest up high in the canopy, while the smaller ones nestle in the underbrush. The **Gulf of Nicoya** is particularly popular among frigate birds and brown pelicans, and all manner of terns and seagulls.

Over the last decade or so, Costa Rica has taken great strides toward protecting its rich biodiversity. Thirty years ago, it was difficult to find a protected area anywhere, but now more than 11% of the country is protected within the national park system. Another 10% to 15% of the land enjoys moderately effective preservation as part of private and public reserves, Indian reserves, and wildlife refuges and corridors. Still, Costa Rica's precious tropical hardwoods continue to be harvested at an alarming rate, often illegally, while other primary forests are clear-cut for short-term agricultural gain. Many experts predict that Costa Rica's unprotected forests will be gone by the early part of this century.

This is also a land of high volcanic and seismic activity. There are three major **volcanic mountain ranges** in Costa Rica, and many of the volcanoes are still active, allowing visitors to experience the awe-inspiring sight of steaming fumaroles and intense lava flows during their stay. Two volcanoes near the capital—Poás and Irazú—are currently active although relatively quiet. The best places to see volcanic activity are farther north in **Rincón de la Vieja National Park** and at **Arenal Volcano.**

SEARCHING FOR WILDLIFE

Animals in the forests are predominantly nocturnal. When they are active in the daytime, they are usually elusive and on the watch for predators. Birds are easier to spot in clearings or secondary forests than they are in primary forests. Unless you have lots of experience in the tropics, your best hope for enjoying a walk through the jungle lies in employing a trained and knowledgeable guide. (By the way, if it's been raining a lot and the trails are muddy, a good pair of rubber boots comes in handy. These are usually provided by the lodges or at the sites where necessary.)

Here are a few helpful hints:

- **Listen.** Pay attention to rustling in the leaves; whether it's monkeys up above or pizotes on the ground, you're most likely to hear an animal before seeing one.
- **Keep quiet.** Noise will scare off animals and prevent you from hearing their movements and calls.
- **Don't try too hard.** Soften your focus and allow your peripheral vision to take over. This way you can catch glimpses of motion and then focus in on the prey.
- **Bring your own binoculars.** It's also a good idea to practice a little first, to get the hang of them. It would be a shame to be fiddling around and staring into space while everyone else in your group oohs and aahs over a quetzal.
- **Dress appropriately.** You'll have a hard time focusing your binoculars if you're busy swatting mosquitoes. Light, long-sleeved pants and shirts are your best bet. Comfortable hiking boots are a real boon, except where heavy rubber boots are necessary. Avoid loud colors; the better you blend in with your surroundings, the better your chances of spotting wildlife.
- **Be patient.** The jungle isn't on a schedule. However, your best shot at seeing forest fauna is in the very early-morning and late-afternoon hours.
- **Read up.** Familiarize yourself with what you're most likely to see. Most lodges and hotels have a copy of *Birds of Costa Rica* and other wildlife field guides, although it's always best to have your own.

2 Costa Rica Today

Costa Rica has a population of roughly 4 million, more than half of whom live in the Central Valley and are classified as urban. The people are ethnically the most homogeneous of Central America: Nearly 96% of the population is of Spanish or otherwise European descent, and it is not at all unusual to see blond Costa Ricans. This is largely because the indigenous population in place when the first Spaniards arrived was small and thereafter was reduced to even more of a minority by wars and disease. There are still some remnant indigenous populations, primarily on reservations around the country; the principal tribes include the Bribri, Cabécar, Boruca, and Guayamí. In addition, on the Caribbean coast, there is a substantial population of English-speaking black Creoles who came over from the Antilles to work on the railroad and in the banana plantations.

In general, Costa Ricans (who call themselves Ticos, a practice that stems from their tendency to add a diminutive, either "tico" or "ito," to the ends of words to connote familiarity or affection) are a friendly and outgoing people. In conversation and interaction with visitors, Ticos are very open and helpful.

In a region plagued by internal strife and civil wars, Costa Ricans are proud of their peaceful history, political stability, and relatively high level of development. This, however, can also translate into arrogance and prejudice toward immigrants from neighboring countries, particularly Nicaraguans, who make up a large percentage of the workforce on the banana and coffee plantations.

Roman Catholicism is the official religion of Costa Rica, although freedom to practice any religion is guaranteed by the country's Constitution. More than 90% of the population identifies itself as Roman Catholic, yet there are small but visible evangelical Christian, Protestant, and Jewish communities. By and large, Ticos are relatively religious. While many city dwellers lead quite secular lives, those in small villages and towns attend mass regularly.

Time has relative meaning to Ticos. While most tour companies and other establishments operate efficiently, in general, don't expect punctuality.

Modern Costa Rica is a nation of contrasts. On the one hand, it's the most technologically advanced and politically stable nation in Central America and has the largest middle class. Even the smallest towns have electricity, the water is mostly safe to drink, and the phone system is relatively good. On the other hand, Costa Rica finds itself in the midst of a huge economic transition. Several "Free Zones" and some high-tech investments have dramatically changed the face of Costa Rica's economy. Intel, which opened two side-by-side assembly plants in Costa Rica in 1997, currently accounts for over 35% of the country's exports—compared with traditional exports like coffee (4.5%) and bananas (9%). More importantly, while Intel and other international companies are used to trumpet a fast-growing gross domestic product, very little of the profits actually make their way into the Costa Rican economy.

Instead, the gap between rich and poor is widening. The government and banking institutions are regularly embroiled in scandal. In an attempt to come to terms with decades of trade deficits and pay back its debt, there has been a move toward economic austerity and privatization, causing the country's vast network of social services, as well as its health-care system and its educational institutions, to become overburdened and underfunded. This has led to public protests and demonstrations, increased unemployment, lower wages, and more expensive goods and services.

Finally, tourism has quickly grown to become the nation's true principal source of income, surpassing both cattle ranching and exports of coffee and bananas. In 1999, for the first time, one million tourists visited Costa Rica. Increasingly, Ticos whose fathers and grandfathers were farmers find themselves hotel owners, tour guides, and waiters. While most have adapted gracefully and regard the industry as a source of new jobs and opportunities for economic advancement, restaurant and hotel staff can seem gruff and uninterested at times, especially in rural areas. And, unfortunately, an increase in the number of visitors has led to an increase in crime, prostitution, and drug trafficking. Common sense and street savvy are required in San José and Limón.

3 History 101

EARLY HISTORY Little is known of Costa Rica's history before its colonization by Spanish settlers. The pre-Columbian Indians who made their home in this region of Central America never developed the large cities or advanced culture that flowered farther north in what would become Guatemala, Belize, and Mexico. However, from scattered excavations around the country, primarily in the

Dateline

- 13,000 B.C. Earliest record of human inhabitants in Costa Rica.
- 1,000 B.C. Olmec people from Mexico arrive in Costa Rica searching for rare blue jade.
- 1,000 B.C.–A.D. 1400 City of Guayabo is inhabited by as many as 10,000 people.
- 1502 Columbus lands in Costa Rica in September, at what is now Limón.

continues

northwest, ancient artifacts have been unearthed, indicating a strong sense of aesthetics. Beautiful gold and jade jewelry, intricately carved grinding stones, and artistically painted terra-cotta objects point toward a small but highly skilled population.

SPAIN SETTLES COSTA RICA

In 1502, on his fourth and last voyage to the New World, Christopher Columbus anchored just offshore from present-day Limón. Whether he actually gave the country its name is open to discussion, but it wasn't long before the inappropriate moniker took hold.

The earliest Spanish settlers found that, unlike the Indians farther north, the native population of Costa Rica was unwilling to submit to slavery. Despite their small numbers, scattered villages, and tribal differences, they fought back against the Spanish until they were overcome by superior firepower and European diseases. When the fighting was finished, the European settlers in Costa Rica found that there were very few Indians left to force into servitude. The settlers were thus forced to till their own lands, a situation unheard of in other parts of Central America. Few pioneers headed this way because they could settle in Guatemala, where there was a large native workforce. Costa Rica was nearly forgotten, as the Spanish crown looked elsewhere for riches to plunder and souls to convert.

It didn't take long for Costa Rica's few Spanish settlers to head for the hills, where they found rich volcanic soil and a climate that was less oppressive than in the lowlands. Cartago, the colony's first capital, was founded in 1563, but it was not until the 1700s that additional cities were established in this agriculturally rich region. In the late 18th century, the first coffee plants were introduced, and because these plants thrived in the highlands, Costa Rica began to develop its first cash crop.

- **1519–61** Spanish explore and colonize Costa Rica.
- **1563** City of Cartago is founded in the Central Valley.
- **1737** San José is founded.
- **Late 1700s** Coffee is introduced as a cash crop.
- **1821** On September 15, Costa Rica, with the rest of Central America, gains independence from Spain.
- **1823** San José is named the capital. The decision is disputed and isn't officially settled until 1835.
- **848** Costa Rica is proclaimed an independent republic.
- **1856** Battle of Santa Rosa: Costa Ricans defeat the United States, which backed pro-slavery advocate William Walker.
- **1870s** First banana plantations are established.
- **1889** First election is won by an opposition party, establishing democratic process in Costa Rica.
- **1890** Inauguration of the railroad connecting San José with the Caribbean coast.
- **1899** The United Fruit Company is founded by railroad builder Minor Keith.
- **1941** Costa Rica's social security and health system instituted by President Rafael Angel Calderón.
- **1948** After aborted revolution, Costa Rican army is abolished.
- **1949** Women are given the right to vote.
- **1956** Costa Rica's population tops one million.
- **1963** Cabo Blanco Reserve becomes Costa Rica's first national park.
- **1987** Pres Oscar Arias Sánchez is awarded the Nobel Peace Prize for orchestrating the Central American Peace Plan.
- **1994** Pres Rafael Angel Calderón hands over the reigns of government to José María Figueres, in a peaceful replay of their fathers' less amenable and democratic transfer of power in 1948.
- **1999** More than 1 million tourists visit Costa Rica for the first time in a single year.

Unfortunately, it was a long and difficult journey transporting the coffee to the Caribbean coast and then onward to Europe, where the demand for coffee was growing.

FROM INDEPENDENCE TO THE PRESENT   In 1821, Spain granted independence to its colonies in Central America. Costa Rica joined with its neighbors to form the Central American Federation, but in 1838 it withdrew to form a new nation and pursue its own interests. By the mid-1800s, coffee was the country's main export. Free land was given to anyone willing to plant coffee on it, and plantation owners soon grew wealthy and powerful, creating Costa Rica's first elite class. Coffee plantation owners were powerful enough to elect their own representatives to the presidency.

This was a stormy period in Costa Rican history. In 1856, the country was invaded by William Walker, a soldier of fortune from Tennessee who, with the backing of U.S. President James Buchanan, was attempting to fulfill his grandiose dreams of presiding over a slave state in Central America (before his invasion of Costa Rica, he had invaded Nicaragua and Baja California). The people of Costa Rica, led by their own president, Juan Rafael Mora, marched against Walker and chased him back to Nicaragua. Walker eventually surrendered to a U.S. warship in 1857, but in 1860 he attacked Honduras, claiming to be the president of that country. The Hondurans, who had had enough of Walker's shenanigans, promptly executed him.

Until 1890, coffee growers had to transport their coffee either by oxcart to the Pacific port of Puntarenas or by boat down the Río Sarapiquí to the Caribbean. In the 1870s, a progressive president proposed a railway from San José to the Caribbean coast to facilitate the transport of coffee to European markets. It took nearly 20 years for this plan to reach fruition, and more than 4,000 workers lost their lives constructing the railway, which passed through dense jungles and rugged mountains on its journey from the Central Valley to the coast. Partway through the project, as funds were dwindling, the second chief engineer, Minor Keith, proposed an idea that not only enhanced his fortunes but also changed the course of Central American history. Banana plantations would be developed along the railway right-of-way (land on either side of the tracks). The export of this crop would help to finance the railway, and in exchange Keith would get a 99-year lease on 800,000 acres of land with a 20-year tax deferment. The Costa Rican government gave its consent, and in 1878 the first bananas were shipped from the country. In 1899 Keith and a partner formed the United Fruit Company, a business that would eventually become the largest landholder in Central America and cause political disputes and wars throughout the region.

In 1889, Costa Rica held what is considered the first free election in Central American history. The opposition candidate won the election, and the control of the government passed from the hands of one political party to those of another without bloodshed or hostilities. Thus, Costa Rica established itself as the region's only true democracy. In 1948, this democratic process was challenged by Rafael Angel Calderón, who had served as the country's president from 1940 to 1944. After losing by a narrow margin, Calderón, who had the backing of the Communist labor unions and the Catholic Church, refused to concede the country's leadership to the rightfully elected president, Otillio Ulate, and a civil war ensued. Calderón was eventually defeated by José "Pepe" Figueres. In the wake of this crisis, a new constitution was drafted; among other changes, it abolished Costa Rica's army so that such a revolution could never happen again.

In 1994, history seemed to repeat itself—peacefully this time—when José María Figueres took the reins of government from the son of his father's adversary, Rafael Angel Calderón.

More than a century of nearly uninterrupted democracy has helped make Costa Rica the most stable country in Central America. This stability, adherence to the democratic process, and staunch position of neutrality in a region that has been torn by 200 years of nearly constant strife are a source of great pride to Costa Ricans, who like to think of their country as the "Switzerland of Central America."

4 Gallo Pinto, Ceviche & Frescos: Costa Rican Food & Drink

Costa Rican food is not especially memorable. Perhaps that's why there's so much international food available throughout the country. However, if you really want to save money, you'll find that Costa Rican, or *típico*, food is always the cheapest nourishment available. It's primarily served in *sodas*, Costa Rica's equivalent of diners.

MEALS & DINING CUSTOMS

Rice and beans are the basis of Costa Rican meals—all three of them. At breakfast, they're called *gallo pinto* and come with everything from eggs to steak to seafood. At lunch or dinner, rice and beans are an integral part of a *casado* (which translates as "married," and is the name for the local version of a blue-plate special). A casado usually consists of cabbage-and-tomato salad, fried plantains (a starchy, bananalike fruit), and a chicken, fish, or meat dish of some sort.

Dining hours in Costa Rica are flexible, but generally follow North American customs. Some downtown restaurants in San José are open 24 hours; however, expensive restaurants tend to be open for lunch between 11am and 3pm and for dinner between 6 and 11pm.

APPETIZERS Known as *bocas* in Costa Rica, appetizers are served with drinks in most bars. Often the bocas are free, but even if they aren't, they're very inexpensive. Popular bocas include *gallos* (tortillas piled with meat, chicken, cheese, or beans), *ceviche* (a marinated seafood salad), *tamales* (stuffed cornmeal patties wrapped and steamed inside banana leaves), *patacones* (fried green plantain chips), and fried *yuca* (yucca).

SANDWICHES & SNACKS Ticos love to snack, and there's a large variety of tasty little sandwiches and snacks available on the street, at snack bars, and in *sodas*. *Arreglados* are little meat-filled sandwiches, as are *tortas*, which are served on little rolls with a bit of salad tucked into them. Tacos, tamales, and *empanadas* (meat pies) also are quite common. *Gallos* (see above) are also popular snacks.

MEAT Costa Rica is beef country—one of the tropical nations that have converted much of their rain-forest land to pastures for raising beef cattle. Consequently, beef is cheap and plentiful, although it may be a bit tougher than it is back home. In general, steaks are cut and served thinner here than in the United States or Europe. One very typical local dish is called *olla de carne*, a bowl of beef broth with large chunks of meat, local tubers, and corn. Spit-roasted chicken is also very popular here and is surprisingly tender.

SEAFOOD Costa Rica has two coasts, and as you'd expect, there's plenty of seafood available everywhere in the country. *Corvina* (sea bass) is the most commonly served fish, and it's prepared innumerable ways, including as *ceviche*, a sort of marinated salad. (Be careful: In many cheaper restaurants, particularly in San José, shark meat is often sold as corvina.) You should also come across *pargo* (red snapper), *dorado* (mahi-mahi), and tuna on some menus, especially along the coasts. Although Costa Rica is a major exporter of shrimp and lobster, both are relatively expensive here—that's why most are exported, causing them to be in short supply at home.

VEGETABLES   On the whole, you'll find vegetables surprisingly lacking in the meals you're served in Costa Rica—usually nothing more than a little pile of shredded cabbage topped with a slice or two of tomato. For a much more satisfying and filling salad, order *palmito* (hearts of palm salad). The heart (actually the stalk or trunk of these small palms) is first boiled and then chopped into circular pieces and served with other fresh vegetables, with a salad dressing on top. If you want something more than this, you'll have to order a side dish such as *picadillo,* a stew or purée of vegetables with a bit of meat in it. Most people have a hard time thinking of *plátanos* (plantains) as vegetables, but these giant relatives of bananas require cooking before they can be eaten. Green plantains have a very starchy flavor and consistency, but become as sweet as candy as they ripen. Fried plátanos are one of my favorite dishes. *Yuca* (manioc root or yucca in English) is another starchy staple root vegetable in Costa Rica.

One more vegetable worth mentioning is the *pejibaye,* a form of palm fruit that looks like a miniature orange coconut. Boiled pejibayes are frequently sold from carts on the streets of San José. When cut in half, a pejibaye reveals a large seed surrounded by soft, fibrous flesh. You can eat it plain, but it's usually topped with a dollop of mayonnaise.

FRUITS   Costa Rica has a wealth of delicious tropical fruits. The most common are mangoes (the season begins in May), papayas, pineapples, melons, and bananas. Other fruits include the *marañon,* which is the fruit of the cashew tree and has orange or yellow glossy skin; the *granadilla* or *maracuyá* (passion fruit); the *mamón chino,* which Asian travelers will immediately recognize as the rambutan; and the *carambola* (star fruit).

DESSERTS   *Queque seco,* which literally translates as "dry cake," is the same as pound cake. *Tres leches* cake, on the other hand, is so moist you almost need to eat it with a spoon. Flan is a typical custard dessert. It often comes as either *flan de caramelo* (caramel) or *flan de coco* (coconut). There are many other sweets available, many of which are made with condensed milk and raw sugar. *Cajetas* are popular handmade candies, made from sugar and various mixes of evaporated, condensed, and powdered milk. They are sold in differing-sized bits and chunks at most *pulperias* and street-side food stands.

BEVERAGES

Frescos, refrescos, or *jugos naturales* are my favorite drinks in Costa Rica. They are usually made with fresh fruit and milk or water. Among the more common fruits used are mangoes, papayas, blackberries (*mora*), and pineapples (*piña*). You'll also come across *maracuyá* (passion fruit) and *carambola* (star fruit). Some of the more unusual frescos are *horchata* (made with rice flour and a lot of cinnamon) and *chan* (made with the seed of a plant found mostly in Guanacaste—definitely an acquired taste). The former is wonderful; the latter requires an open mind (it's reputed to be good for the digestive system). Order *un fresco con leche sin hielo* (a fresco with milk but without ice) if you are trying to avoid untreated water.

If you're a coffee drinker, you may be disappointed here. Most of the best coffee has traditionally been targeted for export, and Ticos tend to prefer theirs weak and sugary. The better hotels and restaurants are starting to cater to gringo and European tastes and are serving up better blends. If you want black coffee, ask for *café negro;* if you want it with milk, order *café con leche.*

If you want to try something different for your morning beverage, ask for *agua dulce,* a warm drink made from melted sugarcane and served with either milk or lemon, or straight.

WATER   Although water in most of Costa Rica is safe to drink, bottled water is readily available, and a good option if you're at all worried about an upset stomach. *Agua mineral,* or simply soda, is sparkling water in Costa Rica. If you like your water without bubbles, be sure to request *aqua mineral sin gas,* or *agua en botella.*

BEER, WINE & LIQUOR   The German presence in Costa Rica over the years has produced several fine beers, which are fairly inexpensive. Most Costa Rican beers are light pilsners. Licensed local versions of Heineken and Rock Ice are also available.

Imported wines are available at reasonable prices in the better restaurants throughout the country. You can usually save money by ordering a Chilean wine rather than a Californian or European one.

Costa Rica distills a wide variety of liquors, and you'll save money by ordering these rather than imported brands. The national liquor is *guaro,* a rather crude cane liquor that's often combined with a soft drink or tonic or mineral water. Both the Café Britt and Salicsa brands produce a couple of types of coffee-based liqueurs. Café Rica is similar to Kahlúa and quite good. You can also find delicious cream-style coffee liqueurs.

5 Recommended Books

Some of the books mentioned below may be difficult to track down in U.S. bookstores, but you'll find them all in abundance in Costa Rica. A good place to check for most of these titles is **Seventh Street Books,** on Calle 7 between Avenidas 1 and Central (© **506/256-8251**).

GENERAL   For a straightforward, albeit somewhat dry, historical overview there's *The History of Costa Rica,* by Ivan Molina and Steven Palmer (University of Costa Rica, 1998).

For a more readable look into Costa Rican society, check out the newly published *The Ticos: Culture and Social Change* ⊛, by Richard, Karen, and Mavis Biesanz (Lynne Rienner Publishers, 1999), an examination of the country's politics and culture, by the authors of the out-of-print *The Costa Ricans.*

To learn more about the life and culture of Costa Rica's Talamanca Coast, an area populated by Afro-Caribbean people whose forebears emigrated from Caribbean islands in the early 19th century, pick up a copy of *What Happen: A Folk-History of Costa Rica's Talamanca Coast* ⊛, by Paula Palmer (Publications in English, 1993). Or read Palmer, Sánchez, and Mayorga's *Taking Care of Sibö's Gifts: An Environmental Treatise from Costa Rica's Kéköldi Indigenous Reserve* (Editorama, 1991).

If you're looking for literature, *Costa Rica: A Traveler's Literary Companion* ⊛⊛, edited by Barbara Ras and with a foreword by Oscar Arias Sánchez (Whereabouts Press, 1994), is a collection of short stories by Costa Rican writers, organized by region of the country. If you're lucky, you might find and pick up a copy of *Stories of Tatamundo* (University of Costa Rica Press, 1998), *Years Like Brief Days* (Peter Owen, 1996) by Fabian Dobles, or *The Lonely Men's Island* by José León Sánchez (Escritores Unidos, 1997). Sánchez is Costa Rica's "Papillon," and the book details his death-defying escape from a prison island.

Young adults might enjoy the interesting biology and photographs of Adrian Forsyth's *How Monkeys Make Chocolate* ☙ (Owl Books, 1995), while David Norman's *Let's Help Costa Rica's Endangered Animals* (WWF, 1998) is a coloring book with short descriptive texts, aimed at younger children.

Finally, anyone interested in a possible longer-term stay in Costa Rica should look at *The New Golden Door to Retirement and Living in Costa Rica (10th edition)* by Christopher Howard (Editora de Turismo Nacional, S.A., 1999) and/or *Living Overseas Costa Rica (7th edition)* by Robert Johnson (Living Overseas Books, 2000).

COFFEE TABLE   *Costa Rica* by Ricardo Zuniga (Incafo, 1999) and *Todo/All Costa Rica* by Ricardo Vilchez Navamuel (Editorial Escudo de Oro, 1999) are two bilingual coffee-table books that highlight the people, architecture, and natural beauties of Costa Rica. Other good selections, which focus more on the flora and fauna, are *Costa Rica: The Forests of Eden* ☙, by Kevin Schafer (Rizzoli, 1996); *The Illustrated Geography of Costa Rica,* edited by Alonso Trejos (Trejos Hermanos, 1996); *Birds of the Rain Forest: Costa Rica,* by Carmen Hidalgo (Trejos Hermanos, 1996); *Portraits of the Rainforest,* by Adrian Forsyth, with photos by Michael and Patricia Fogden (Firefly Books, 1995); and *Costa Rica: Wildlife of the National Parks and Reserves* ☙, written and photographed by Michael and Patricia Fogden (Editorial Heliconia, 1997). The Fogdens are perhaps the most prominent wildlife photographers working in Costa Rica.

NATURAL HISTORY   Mario A. Boza's beautiful *Costa Rica National Parks* ☙ (INCAFO, 1998) has recently been reissued in an elegant coffee-table edition. *Costa Rica's National Parks and Preserves* by Joseph Franke (The Mountaineers, 1993) is similar but with fewer photos.

For an introduction to a wide range of Costa Rican fauna, there's *The Ecotraveller's Wildlife Guide: Costa Rica* ☙☙, by Les Beletsky (Academic Press, 1998), which packs a lot of useful information into a concise package. It's a great field guide for amateur naturalists and inquisitive tourists.

A Guide to the Birds of Costa Rica ☙☙, by F. Gary Stiles and Alexander Skutch (Cornell University Press, 1989), is an invaluable guide to identifying the many birds you'll see during your stay. It's often available for examination at nature lodges. Some serious bird watchers also like to have *The Guide to the Birds of Panama, with Costa Rica, Nicaragua and Honduras,* by Robert S. Ridgely and John A. Gwynne (Princeton University Press, 1992), in order to have two different illustrations for identifying some of those more subtle species variations. Bird watchers might also enjoy Dennis Rodgers's *Site Guides: Costa Rica & Panama* (Cinclus Publications, 1996), which details each country's bird-watching bounty by site and region.

Turtle enthusiasts should read pioneering turtle researcher Archie Carr's *The Sea Turtle* (University of Texas Press, 1984). *Lessons of the Rainforest,* edited by Suzanne Head and Robert Heinzman (Sierra, 1990), is a collection of essays by leading authorities in the fields of biology, ecology, history, law, and economics, who look at the issues surrounding tropical deforestation.

Other interesting natural-history books that will give you a look at the plants and animals of Costa Rica include *Sarapiquí Chronicle,* by Allen Young

(Smithsonian Institution Press, 1991); *Costa Rica Natural History,* by Daniel Janzen (University of Chicago Press, 1983); the two-volume collection of *Butterflies of Costa Rica,* by Philip DeVries (Princeton University Press, 1987 and 1997); *A Field Guide to the Mammals of Central America & Southeast Mexico,* by author and illustrator Fiona A. Reid (Oxford University Press, 1998); the new *A Guide to the Amphibians and Reptiles of Costa Rica* by Twan Leenders (Distruibuidores Zona Tropical: 2001); the classic *A Neotropical Companion* ⚘, by John C. Kricher (Princeton University Press, 1997), which was recently reissued in an expanded edition with color photos; *The Monkey's Bridge: Mysteries of Evolution in Central America,* by David Rains Wallace (Sierra Club Books, 1999); and my all-time favorite book on tropical biology, *Tropical Nature* ⚘⚘, by Adrian Forsyth and Ken Miyata (Simon & Schuster, 1984), a well-written and lively collection of tales and adventures by two neotropical biologists.

Appendix B: Glossary of Spanish Terms & Phrases

Grandiosa

1 Basic Spanish Phrases & Vocabulary

English	Spanish	Pronunciation
Hello	**Buenos días**	*bway*-noss *dee*-ahss
How are you?	**Como está usted?**	*koh*-moh ess-*tah* oo-*stead*?
Very well	**Muy bien**	mwee byen
Thank you	**Gracias**	*gra*-see-ahss
Good-bye	**Adiós**	ad-*dyohss*
Please	**Por favor**	pohr fah-*vohr*
Yes	**Sí**	see
No	**No**	noh
Excuse me	**Perdóneme**	pehr-*doh*-neh-may
Give me	**Deme**	*day*-may
Where is . . . ?	**Donde está . . . ?**	*dohn*-day ess-*tah* . . . ?
the station	**la estación**	la ess-*tah*-syohn
the bus stop	**la parada**	la pah-*rah*-da
a hotel	**un hotel**	oon oh-*tel*
a restaurant	**un restaurante**	oon res-tow-*rahn*-tay
the toilet	**el servicio**	el ser-*vee*-see-o
To the right	**A la derecha**	ah lah day-*ray*-chuh
To the left	**A la izquierda**	ah lah is-*kyayr*-duh
Straight ahead	**Adelante**	ah-day-*lahn*-tay
I would like . . .	**Quiero . . .**	*kyehr*-oh . . .
to eat	**comer**	ko-*mayr*
a room	**una habitación**	oo-nah ah-bee-tah-*syohn*
How much is it?	**Cuánto?**	*Kwahn*-toh?
The check	**La cuenta**	la *kwen*-tah
When?	**Cuándo?**	*Kwan*-doh?
Yesterday	**Ayer**	ah-*yayr*
Today	**Hoy**	oy
Tomorrow	**Mañana**	mahn-*yah*-nah
Breakfast	**Desayuno**	deh-sai-*yoo*-noh
Lunch	**Comida**	co-*mee*-dah
Dinner	**Cena**	*say*-nah

NUMBERS

1 **uno** (*ooh*-noh)	9 **nueve** (*nway*-bay)
2 **dos** (dohs)	10 **diez** (dee-ess)
3 **tres** (trayss)	11 **once** (*ohn*-say)
4 **cuatro** (*kwah*-troh)	12 **doce** (*doh*-say)
5 **cinco** (*seen*-koh)	13 **trece** (*tray*-say)
6 **seis** (sayss)	14 **catorce** (kah-*tor*-say)
7 **siete** (*syeh*-tay)	15 **quince** (*keen*-say)
8 **ocho** (*oh*-choh)	16 **dieciseis** (de-*ess*-ee-sayss)

17	**diecisiete** (de-*ess*-ee-*syeh*-tay)	60	**sesenta** (say-*sen*-tah)
18	**dieciocho** (dee-*ess*-ee-*oh*-choh)	70	**setenta** (say-*ten*-tah)
19	**diecinueve** (dee-*ess*-ee-*nway*-bay)	80	**ochenta** (oh-*chen*-tah)
20	**veinte** (*bayn*-tay)	90	**noventa** (noh-*ben*-tah)
30	**treinta** (*trayn*-tah)	100	**cien** (see-*en*)
40	**cuarenta** (kwah-*ren*-tah)	1,000	**mil** (meal)
50	**cincuenta** (seen-*kwen*-tah)		

350

2 Some Typically Tico Words & Phrases

Boca   Literally means "mouth," but also a term to describe a small appetizer served alongside a drink at many bars.

Chunche   Knicknack; thing—as in "whatchamacallit."

Con mucho gusto   With pleasure.

De hoy en ocho   In one week's time.

Diay   An untranslatable but common linguistic punctuation, often used to begin a sentence.

Macha, or machita   A blond woman.

Mae   Translates a lot like "man"; used by teenagers as constant verbal punctuation.

Maje   A lot like *mae* above, but with a slightly derogatory connotation.

Ponga la maría, por favor   This is how you ask taxi drivers to turn on the meter.

Pulpería   The Costa Rican version of the "corner store" or small market.

Pura vida   Literally, "pure life"; translates as "everything's great."

Si Dios quiere   God willing. You'll hear Ticos say this all the time.

Soda   A casual diner-style restaurant serving cheap Tico meals.

Tuanis   Means the same as *pura vida* above, but is used by a younger crowd.

Una teja   100 colones.

Un rojo   1,000 colones.

Un tucan   5,000 colones.

3 Menu Terms

FISH

almejas	clams	**langosta**	lobster
atún	tuna	**langostinos**	prawns
bacalao	cod	**lenguado**	sole
calamares	squid	**mejillones**	mussels
camarones	shrimp	**ostras**	oysters
cangrejo	crab	**pargo**	snapper
ceviche	marinated seafood salad	**pulpo**	octopus
corvina	sea bass	**tiburón**	shark
dorado	dolphin, or mahi-mahi	**trucha**	trout

MEATS

albóndigas	meatballs	**costillas**	ribs
bistec	beefsteak	**jamón**	ham
cerdo	pork	**lengua**	tongue
chicharrones	fried pork rinds	**mondongo**	tripe
chuleta	cutlet	**pato**	duck
conejo	rabbit	**pavo**	turkey
cordero	lamb	**pollo**	chicken

VEGETABLES

aceitunas   olives
alcachofa   artichoke
berenjena   eggplant
cebolla   onion
elote   corn on the cob
ensalada   salad
esparragos   asparagus
espinacas   spinach
hongos   mushrooms

palmito   heart of palm
papa   potato
pepino   cucumber
remolacha   beet
repollo   cabbage
tomate   tomato
vainica   string beans
yuca   yucca, or manioc
zanahoria   carrot

FRUITS

aguacate   avocado
banano   banana
carambola   star fruit
cerezas   cherries
ciruela   plum
fresa   strawberry
limón   lemon or lime
mango   mango
manzana   apple

melocotón   peach
mora   raspberry
naranja   orange
pera   pear
piña   pineapple
plátano   plantain
sandía   watermelon
toronja   grapefruit
uvas   grapes

BASICS

aceite   oil
ajo   garlic
arreglado   small meat sandwich
azúcar   sugar
bocas   appetizers
casado   plate of the day
frito   fried
gallo   corn tortilla topped with meat or chicken
gallo pinto   rice and beans
hielo   ice
mantequilla   butter
miel   honey

mostaza   mustard
natilla   sour cream
olla de carne   meat and vegetable soup
pan   bread
patacones   fried plantain chips
picadillo   chopped vegetable side dish
pimienta   pepper
queso   cheese
sal   salt
tamal   filled cornmeal pastry
tortilla   flat corn pancake

Index

Spyrogyra Butterfly Garden (San José), 117
Stone spheres (pre-Columbian), 287
Street addresses, 84
Students, services/discounts for, 37–38
Sun exposure, risks from, 33
Surfing
    best sites for, 10, 67–68
    Playa de Jacó, 246
    Playa Guinone, 180
    Playa Hermosa/Playa Panamá area, 153
    Playa Pavones, 307
    Playa Tamarindo, 170
    Puerto Jiménez area, 291
    recommended tour operators, 68
    Salsa Brava/Puerto Viejo, 333–334
Swamps, 344
Swimming. See also Beaches
    Lake Arenal, 220
    San José area, 121

Tabacón Hot Springs (nr. La Fortuna), 2, 5, 211
Tai chi classes, 66. See also Spas, resorts
Talacanca Mountains (central Pacific coast), 276
Tapanti National Wildlife Refuge, 61
Tárcoles River (central Pacific coast), 246
Taxes, 54
    in San José, 90
Taxi services, 54. See also specific cities and towns
    Jacó, 243
    Puerto Viejo, 332–333
    in San José, 86
    to/from San José airport, 80
Telegrams/telegraph services, 54
    in Jacó, 244
    in San José, 90
Telephones, 55
    in Jacó, 244
    in Puerto Viejo, 333
    in San José, 90–91
Television, 53
Temperatures, average, 30

Tempisque River bridge, 162
Tempisque River Ferry, 161–162, 167, 177
Tennis, in San José, 120
Terciopelo Cave (Barra Honda National Park), 185
Theater, in San José, 126
Theft, protecting against, 54
Tibás (nr. San José), soccer stadium, 121
Timeline, historical, 346–347
Time zones, 55, 91
Tipping, 55, 86
Tirimbina Biological Reserve (Puerto Viejo de Sarapiquí), 203
Toad Hall (Lake Arenal), 3, 221
Tobías Bolaños International Airport (Pavas), 41, 81
Tortuga Island (Caribbean coast), 239
Tortuguero National Park (Caribbean coast, nr. Límon), 76, 136, 200
    entry points, fees, 318
    touring, 316, 318–319
    traveling to/in, 314–317
    turtle watching, 317–318
Tortuguero Village (Caribbean coast), 5–6, 317, 319
    accommodations, 319–321
Tourism, role of in economy, 246
Tourist information, 25
    recommended reading, 351–352
    in San José, 81, 89
    websites, 20–21, 25
Tours, guided. See also Adventure travel/tours; Boat tours, cruises; Eco-tours, ecotravel
    for gay and lesbian travelers, 36
    Jacó, 246
    for people with disabilities, 35
    Playa Flamingo area, 163
    Playa Grande, 170–171
    Playa Pavones, 307

Playa Tamarindo, 168–169
    Puerto Viejo de Sarapiquí, 203
    Rincón de la Vieja National Park, 145
    San José area, 114, 131, 132–136
    for senior travelers, 36
    Tortuguero National Park, 317–318
    tour companies, 56–59
Towels, need to bring, 64
Traveler's checks, 29
Travelers with disabilities, services for, 35
Tropical diseases, risk of, 32–33
Tropical dry forests, 344
Tuna fishing, 65. See also Sportfishing
Turrialba (nr. San José), 137–138
Turtles. See Sea turtles, nesting sites; Wildlife watching

United Fruit Company, 299, 348
United States Embassy, 52
University of Costa Rica (San José), 119
Upala corn festival, 31

Vegetables
    availability, 350
    Spanish terms for, 356
Venado Caverns (Caño Negro National Wildlife Refuge), 212
Views, recommended, 19, 250, 263
Visitor information, 25
    recommended reading, 351–352
    in San José, 81, 89
    websites, 20–21, 25
Volcanoes, touring, 344
    Arenal volcano, 208
    San José area, 134–135

Walker, William, 348
Walking/walking tours, in San José, 86. See also Hiking trails, walking trails
Water, drinking, quality of, 55, 91, 351

FROMMER'S® COMPLETE TRAVEL GUIDES

Alaska
Amsterdam
Argentina & Chile
Arizona
Atlanta
Australia
Austria
Bahamas
Barcelona, Madrid & Seville
Beijing
Belgium, Holland &
 Luxembourg
Bermuda
Boston
British Columbia & the
 Canadian Rockies
Budapest & the Best of Hungary
California
Canada
Cancún, Cozumel & the
 Yucatán
Cape Cod, Nantucket &
 Martha's Vineyard
Caribbean
Caribbean Cruises & Ports
 of Call
Caribbean Ports of Call
Carolinas & Georgia
Chicago
China
Colorado
Costa Rica
Denmark
Denver, Boulder & Colorado
 Springs
England
Europe

European Cruises & Ports of Call
Florida
France
Germany
Greece
Greek Islands
Hawaii
Hong Kong
Honolulu, Waikiki & Oahu
Ireland
Israel
Italy
Jamaica
Japan
Las Vegas
London
Los Angeles
Maryland & Delaware
Maui
Mexico
Montana & Wyoming
Montréal & Québec City
Munich & the Bavarian Alps
Nashville & Memphis
Nepal
New England
New Mexico
New Orleans
New York City
New Zealand
Nova Scotia, New Brunswick &
 Prince Edward Island
Oregon
Paris
Philadelphia & the Amish
 Country
Portugal

Prague & the Best of the Czech
 Republic
Provence & the Riviera
Puerto Rico
Rome
San Antonio & Austin
San Diego
San Francisco
Santa Fe, Taos & Albuquerque
Scandinavia
Scotland
Seattle & Portland
Shanghai
Singapore & Malaysia
South Africa
Southeast Asia
South Florida
South Pacific
Spain
Sweden
Switzerland
Texas
Thailand
Tokyo
Toronto
Tuscany & Umbria
USA
Utah
Vancouver & Victoria
Vermont, New Hampshire
 & Maine
Vienna & the Danube Valley
Virgin Islands
Virginia
Walt Disney World & Orlando
Washington, D.C.
Washington State

FROMMER'S® DOLLAR-A-DAY GUIDES

Australia from $50 a Day
California from $70 a Day
Caribbean from $70 a Day
England from $70 a Day
Europe from $70 a Day

Florida from $70 a Day
Hawaii from $70 a Day
Ireland from $60 a Day
Italy from $70 a Day
London from $85 a Day

New York from $80 a Day
Paris from $80 a Day
San Francisco from $60 a Day
Washington, D.C.,
 from $70 a Day

FROMMER'S® PORTABLE GUIDES

Acapulco, Ixtapa &
 Zihuatanejo
Alaska Cruises & Ports
 of Call
Amsterdam
Australia's Great Barrier Reef
Bahamas
Baja & Los Cabos
Berlin
Boston
California Wine Country
Charleston & Savannah
Chicago

Dublin
Hawaii: The Big Island
Hong Kong
Houston
Las Vegas
London
Los Angeles
Maine Coast
Maui
Miami
New Orleans
New York City
Paris

Phoenix & Scottsdale
Portland
Puerto Rico
Puerto Vallarta, Manzanillo &
 Guadalajara
San Diego
San Francisco
Seattle
Sydney
Tampa & St. Petersburg
Vancouver
Venice
Washington, D.C.

FROMMER'S® NATIONAL PARK GUIDES

Family Vacations in the
 National Parks
Grand Canyon

National Parks of the American
 West
Rocky Mountain
Yellowstone & Grand Teton

Yosemite & Sequoia/
 Kings Canyon
Zion & Bryce Canyon

FROMMER'S® MEMORABLE WALKS

Chicago
London

New York
Paris

San Francisco
Washington, D.C.

FROMMER'S® GREAT OUTDOOR GUIDES

Arizona & New Mexico
New England

Northern California
Southern California & Baja

Southern New England
Vermont & New Hampshire

FROMMER'S® BORN TO SHOP GUIDES

Born to Shop: France
Born to Shop: Hong Kong,
   Shanghai & Beijing

Born to Shop: Italy
Born to Shop: London

Born to Shop: New York
Born to Shop: Paris

FROMMER'S® IRREVERENT GUIDES

Amsterdam
Boston
Chicago
Las Vegas
London

Los Angeles
Manhattan
New Orleans
Paris
San Francisco

Seattle & Portland
Vancouver
Walt Disney World
Washington, D.C.

FROMMER'S® BEST-LOVED DRIVING TOURS

America
Britain
California
Florida

France
Germany
Ireland
Italy

New England
Scotland
Spain
Western Europe

THE UNOFFICIAL GUIDES®

Bed & Breakfasts in California
Bed & Breakfasts in
   New England
Bed & Breakfasts in the
   Northwest
Bed & Breakfasts in Southeast
Beyond Disney
Branson, Missouri
California with Kids
Chicago
Cruises
Disneyland
Florida with Kids

Golf Vacations in the
   Eastern U.S.
The Great Smoky &
   Blue Ridge Mountains
Inside Disney
Hawaii
Las Vegas
London
Mid-Atlantic with Kids
Mini Las Vegas
Mini-Mickey
New England with Kids

New Orleans
New York City
Paris
San Francisco
Skiing in the West
Southeast with Kids
Walt Disney World
Walt Disney World for
   Grown-ups
Walt Disney World for Kids
Washington, D.C.
World's Best Diving Vacations

SPECIAL-INTEREST TITLES

Frommer's Britain's Best Bed & Breakfasts and
   Country Inns
Frommer's France's Best Bed & Breakfasts and
   Country Inns
Frommer's Italy's Best Bed & Breakfasts and
   Country Inns
Frommer's Caribbean Hideaways
Frommer's Adventure Guide to Australia &
   New Zealand
Frommer's Adventure Guide to Central America
Frommer's Adventure Guide to India & Pakistan
Frommer's Adventure Guide to South America
Frommer's Adventure Guide to Southeast Asia
Frommer's Adventure Guide to Southern Africa
Frommer's Gay & Lesbian Europe
Frommer's Exploring America by RV
Hanging Out in England

Hanging Out in Europe
Hanging Out in France
Hanging Out in Ireland
Hanging Out in Italy
Hanging Out in Spain
Israel Past & Present
Frommer's The Moon
Frommer's New York City with Kids
The New York Times' Guide to Unforgettable
   Weekends
Places Rated Almanac
Retirement Places Rated
Frommer's Road Atlas Britain
Frommer's Road Atlas Europe
Frommer's Washington, D.C., with Kids
Frommer's What the Airlines Never Tell You

Frommer's ®

Let Us Hear From You!

Dear Frommer's Reader,

You are our greatest resource in keeping our guides relevant, timely, and lively. We'd love to hear from you about your travel experiences—good or bad. Want to recommend a great restaurant or a hotel off the beaten path—or register a complaint? Any thoughts on how to improve the guide itself?

Please use this page to share your thoughts with me and mail it to the address below. Or if you like, send a FAX or e-mail me at frommersfeedback@hungryminds.com. And so that we can thank you—and keep you up on the latest developments in travel—we invite you to sign up for a free daily Frommer's e-mail travel update. Just write your e-mail address on the back of this page. Also, if you'd like to take a moment to answer a few questions about yourself to help us improve our guides, please complete the following quick survey. (We'll keep that information confidential.)

Thanks for your insights.

Yours sincerely,

Michael Spring

Michael Spring, *Publisher*

Name (Optional) _____

Address _____

_____

City _____ State _____ ZIP _____

Name of Frommer's Travel Guide _____

Comments _____

_____

_____

_____

_____

_____

_____

_____

Please tell us a little about yourself so that we can serve you and the Frommer's community better. We will keep this information confidential.

Age: ( )18-24; ( )25-39; ( )40-49; ( )50-55; ( )Over 55

Income: ( )Under $25,000; ( )$25,000-$50,000; ( )$50,000-$100,000; ( )Over $100,000

I am: ( )Single, never married; ( )Married, with children; ( )Married, without children; ( )Divorced; ( )Widowed

Number of people in my household: ( )1; ( )2; ( )3; ( )4; ( )5 or more

Number of people in my household under 18: ( )1; ( )2; ( )3; ( )4; ( )5 or more

I am ( )a student; ( )employed full-time; ( )employed part-time; ( )not employed at this time; ( )retired; ( )other

I took ( )0; ( )1; ( )2; ( )3; ( )4 or more leisure trips in the past 12 months

My last vacation was ( )a weekend; ( )1 week; ( )2 weeks; ( )3 or more weeks

My last vacation was to ( )the U.S.; ( )Canada; ( )Mexico; ( )Europe; ( )Asia; ( )South America; ( )Central America; ( )The Caribbean; ( )Africa; ( )Middle East; ( )Australia/New Zealand

( )I would; ( )would not buy a Frommer's Travel Guide for business travel

I access the Internet ( )at home; ( )at work; ( )both; ( )I do not use the Internet

I used the Internet to do research for my last trip. ( )Yes; ( )No

I used the Internet to book accommodations or air travel on my last trip. ( )Yes; ( )No

My favorite travel site is ( )frommers.com; ( )travelocity.com; ( )expedia.com;

other_____

I use Frommer's Travel Guides ( )always; ( )sometimes; ( )seldom

I usually buy ( )1; ( )2; ( )more than 2 guides when I travel

Other guides I use include _____

What's the most important thing we could do to improve Frommer's Travel Guides?

_2045 / liter_____ _clci @ 8pm_____

_.245_____

_Blanc Plancha_____

Yes, please send me a daily e-mail travel update. My e-mail address is

_____

Mail to: Michael Spring, Publisher and Vice President, Frommer's Travel Guides
909 Third Ave., New York, NY 10022   FAX: 212.884.5432